# CAPON'S
# MARKETING
# FRAMEWORK

*www.axcesscapon.com*

# CAPON'S MARKETING FRAMEWORK

**Noel Capon**

Graduate School of Business

Columbia University

New York, NY

*Library of Congress Cataloging-in-Publication Data*

Capon, Noel
   Capon's Marketing Framework / Noel Capon
      p.  cm.
   Includes index
   ISBN 978-0-9797344-6-5
     1. Capon's—Marketing.   I. Title: Capon's marketing framework.

2007930021

Editor: Lyn Maize
Copy Editors: Margaret Allyson, Christy Goldfinch
Permissions Editor: Sandra Lord
Designer: Anna Botelho
Cover Design: Bill Maize, Anna Botelho

Credits and acknowledgments are a continuation of the copyright page; they are on pages xxix, xxx, C1 and C2.

This book contains references to the products of SAP AG, Dietmar-Hopp-allee 16, 69190 Walldorf, Germany. The names of these products are registered and/or unregistered trademarks of SAP AG. SAP AG is neither the author nor the publisher of this book and is not responsible for its content.

## DEDICATION

To Marvela, Elmira,

Alaina, and Noel.

..............................................

## ABOUT THE AUTHOR

**NOEL CAPON** is the R. C. Kopf Professor of International Marketing and past Chair of the Marketing Division at the Graduate School of Business, Columbia University. Professor Capon's early education was in Britain: he holds B.Sc. and Ph.D. degrees from London University – University College. He also holds a Diploma in Business Administration from Manchester Business School, an MBA from Harvard Business School, and a Ph.D. from Columbia University — Columbia Business School.

Professor Capon joined the Columbia Business School faculty in 1979. Previously he was on the faculty of, and received tenure from, the University of California – Graduate School of Management, UCLA. He has taught and held faculty positions at Harvard Business School, in Australia — Monash University, England — Bradford Management Centre and Manchester Business School, France – INSEAD, Hong Kong — The Hong Kong University of Science and Technology (HKUST), the People's Republic of China — China European International Business School (CEIBS – Shanghai), and India — Indian School of Business (ISB – Hyderabad). Professor Capon currently holds the position of Distinguished Visiting Professor at Manchester Business School.

Professor Capon has published eleven books: *Corporate Strategic Planning, The Marketing of Financial Services: A Book of Cases, Planning the Development of Builders, Leaders and Managers of Twenty First Century Business, Why Some Firms Perform Better than Others: Towards a More Integrative Explanation, The Asian Marketing Case Book, Marketing Management in the 21st Century* (also in a Chinese edition), *Key Account Management and Planning, Total Integrated Marketing, Managing Global Accounts, The Marketing Mavens,* and *Managing Marketing in the 21st Century.* He is also editor for sections on Marketing, as well as Sales Management and Distribution, in the *AMA Management Handbook.*

Professor Capon has published more than 60 journal articles and edited book chapters. Journals that have published his work include *Academy of Management Research, Academy of Management Review, American Journal of Public Health, Annals of Operations Research, Cognition and Instruction, Columbia Journal of World Business, Communication Research, Congressional Record, Developmental Psychology, Harvard Business Review, Industrial Marketing Management, Journal of Advertising Research, Journal of Applied Developmental Psychology, Journal of Applied Psychology, Journal of Business Administration, Journal of Consumer Research, Journal of Financial Services Research, Journal of International Business Studies, Journal of International Forecasting, Journal of Management Studies, Journal of Marketing, Journal of Marketing Research, Journal of Strategic Marketing, Laboratory of Comparative Human Cognition, Management Decision, Management Science, Public Opinion Quarterly, Review of Marketing, Strategic Management Journal,* and *Transactions of the Faraday Society.*

In addition to teaching in Columbia Business School's full-time MBA and Executive MBA programs, Professor Capon is active in executive education. He has directed *Competitive Marketing Strategy, Strategic Account Management, Sales Management,* and *Strategic Pricing* programs. In addition, he directs and teaches executive seminars for leading business schools and corporations around the world. Professor Capon inaugurated Columbia Business School's highly successful executive-level *Marketing Management* program as a joint venture in Shanghai, PRC with CEIBS and the Global Account Manager Certification program with St. Gallen University in Switzerland.

## TABLE OF CONTENTS IN BRIEF

## TABLE OF CONTENTS IN DETAIL

# PREFACE

In this book you will learn about marketing's language, logic, strategy, and implementation. To get us off to a good start, we'll begin by providing you the positioning for this book.

## POSITIONING

The positioning statement has four elements:

- **Customer targets.** Marketing faculty who specify texts for graduate and senior undergraduate business students and the students who will learn to practice marketing in their courses.
- **Competitor targets.** All textbooks entitled *Marketing Management*, or some close approximation, seeking to serve graduate and senior undergraduate business students.
- **Value proposition.** This text will help faculty to enhance their students' grasp of marketing. Students will learn how to successfully address simple and complex marketing problems. They will be able to infuse the organizations in which they work with a customer-focused view of business. And they will pay a fraction of the price of competitor texts.
- **Reason to believe.** Professor Capon is among the world's most experienced marketing educators, from one of the world's leading business schools. The author has extensive experience educating students at all levels of business degree programs, as well as senior and mid-level executives in major corporations globally.

## PURPOSE

This book is about understanding how to develop market strategy and managing the marketing process. It is not a book that attempts to describe all there is to know about marketing, but focuses on what the prospective manager needs to know. This book differs from other senior undergraduate and introductory graduate-level marketing texts. We take a position on what we believe is a better or worse course of action for marketers. Marketing is an applied field, and we believe that textbook writers should provide guidance for good marketing practice.

Also, we focus on the manager, not just the marketer. For readers committed to a career in marketing (and we hope there are many), this book will form a solid foundation as you study marketing further and deeper. But the vast majority of you will not work in marketing departments, and will instead become senior executives, general managers, CFOs, and CEOs. We write for you also because an understanding and appreciation of marketing is central to virtually every important decision that managers make. Because this will be the only marketing course many of you will take, in a sense, this book provides what every general manager and senior executive must know about marketing.

Marketing activity lies at the core of leading and managing a business. It provides the focus for interfacing with customers. Marketing is also the source of insight about the market, customers, competitors, and complementers, and the business environment in general. Marketing is concerned with the firm's long-run relationships with customers as well as its short-run sales activity. Marketing must be a major organizational thrust, not just a responsibility assigned to a single functional department. For this reason, *Capon's Marketing Framework* emphasizes the role of marketing in creating value for customers — this leads to the creation of value for other firm stakeholders, including shareholders and employees.

## OUR CUSTOMERS: STUDENTS

To better understand how marketing fits into the broader challenge of leading and managing a corporation, we address marketing at the firm or business-unit level, as well as in the marketing function. We provide you with a set of concepts and ideas for approaching marketing decisions. We also provide you with a common language for thinking about marketing issues. You will learn to structure and analyze managerial problems in marketing. This book will prepare you to deal with the core marketing issues that future marketers, senior executives, general managers, and CEOs will have to face. We also help you think strategically about your firm's markets, products, and services and help you to:

- Develop frameworks for approaching simple and complex marketing problems.
- Be able to analyze markets, customers, competitors, your company, and complementers.
- Have the ability to assess market opportunities and develop market strategy.
- Be able to design implementation programs comprising product, price, place, promotion, and service — the 4Ps and an S, otherwise known as the marketing mix.
- Understand the importance of working across organizational boundaries to align all of the firm's capabilities.
- Assess the success of your marketing initiatives.
- Gain practical experience in addressing marketing issues in a variety of contexts — domestic and international, entrepreneurial startups and established corporations, industrial and consumer, products and services, and private and public and not-for-profit sectors.

As you work your way through this book, we expect you to develop a high tolerance for ambiguity — this is a quality of all successful senior executives, general managers, and CEOs. You will learn that there are no right or wrong answers to marketing problems, just some answers that are better than others. There are no simple — or even complex — formulae in which to plug a set of numbers and find the *right* answer. Rather, you must learn to approach complex and unstructured marketing problems in a creative and measured way. Throughout the book are questions that you can address with the material in the chapter. When appropriate, we urge you to use secondary sources, especially the Internet, to dig into these questions.

## OUR CUSTOMERS: MARKETING FACULTY

For professors of marketing, this book provides an opportunity to support your efforts in the classroom by presenting a contemporary perspective on how marketing works within the modern corporation. The book not only provides a firm basis in which to ground a first graduate-level or senior undergraduate marketing course, but will also challenge your students by including material and ideas not typically covered in marketing texts. Of course, we focus on how marketing should address customers' needs, but we also emphasize marketing's *bottom line* — shareholder value. By understanding and acting upon the principles and frameworks we develop in this book, students will avoid many of the pitfalls of competing in an increasingly complex, competitive, and global environment.

We believe that in order to learn how to think appropriately about marketing problems, students must develop skills in marketing problem-solving and analysis. We recommend that your course also use marketing cases and/or simulations in context with this text.[1] Rather than write or include lengthy cases in the body of the text, the Instructor's Manual and website provide numerous suggestions for cases and activities linked to the topics covered in the text. The website also shows ways to approach case analysis.

---

[1] We have had very good experience with Markstrat, *www.stratxsimulations.com.*

Some faculty like to use a fully-blown several-hundred-page marketing text; *Managing Marketing in the 21ˢᵗ Century* is the book for them. Others prefer a more concise textbook; that is the purpose of this book. Essentially, *Capon's Marketing Framework* is shortened version of *Managing Marketing in the 21ˢᵗ Century* that, nonetheless, provides a solid framework for marketing students.

## OUR DIFFERENTIAL ADVANTAGE

As we indicated in the foreword, many good marketing textbooks have been published over the years, but they can grow into comprehensive tomes or reference books. Further, they often contain excessive descriptive data and lots of pictures, as they move from edition to edition. We decided that we wanted to create a fresh look and feel for how marketing really works and also offer students and faculty many other compelling reasons to switch to *Capon's Marketing Framework*. We've highlighted a few of these benefits and values that we believe clearly differentiate this book from the others:

1. **More useful and less costly.** When you access *Capon's Marketing Framework*, you pay a fraction of the price of traditional marketing texts. There are three options: a printed book, a pdf file for downloading, and an electronic file to read online — for this option you *pay what you think it's worth*. Quite simply, students who use this book will also be able to afford lunch.

2. **Improving shareholder value.** Business is ever more complex, and we show students the important link between success in delivering value to customers and success in improving shareholder value. We make this relationship explicit and show how world-class marketing decision-making must always consider the impact on shareholders.

3. **Normative focus.** We take a position on what should/and should not be appropriate courses of action. We believe readers should know where we stand and what we believe. In Chapter 1 we identify a set of Marketing Imperatives and a set of Marketing Principles as guides for developing market strategy. The Marketing Imperatives form the basis for the book's macro-organization. In Chapter 9, we lay out core elements of a market strategy. We believe that a strategy that does not include these elements is incomplete.

4. **New ideas relevant to modern marketing environments.** We introduce several genuinely new ideas drawn from our research and writings, and we help students develop critical thinking and problem-solving skills to use them. We believe that a textbook should present established procedures, processes, and generalized norms. However, we also believe that limiting ourselves to such a narrow mandate would perform a disservice to our readers. Changes taking place in marketing are dramatic and rapid. They require good problem-solving and analytic skills, as well as sound understanding of principles and practice.

5. **Applying the marketing mix** — as the means of **implementing the firm's market strategy**. For far too long, marketing students have completed their introductory marketing courses believing that marketing equals the marketing mix — product, price, promotion, distribution, and service. We believe other critical questions must necessarily precede decisions about marketing mix elements. For example:

   • What is the essential role of marketing?

   • What is marketing's role in increasing shareholder value?

   • What is a market strategy, and how do you know if your market strategy is complete?

   • Why are brands important, and what are key issues for developing a branding strategy?

   Only after these and other questions have been resolved should the firm make marketing-mix decisions.

6. **Balance between B2C and B2B strategies** is critically important. In our discussion, sometimes customers are consumers; other times they are organizations. We favor neither one nor the other, but put significant effort into B2B marketing to address some of the more interesting developments in marketing practice today.

7. **Branding** is an increasingly important strategic issue for firms — we devote a full chapter to this topic. On the other hand, we choose to integrate into the text other topics that sometimes command full chapters — such as international marketing or marketing information systems. This integration is more reflective of *real-world practice*, and learning is greater when these topics are presented in context.

8. **Public and not-for-profit marketing.** In this book, we focus squarely on marketing challenges facing managers in for-profit businesses. We also believe this book will prove useful for those interested in not-for-profit and public-sector marketing. First, the vast majority of concepts we discuss are readily transferable to these sectors — the major difference concerns organizational objectives. In the for-profit sector, objectives are unambiguously concerned with profit and shareholder value — in the not-for-profit and public sectors, setting objectives is often a complex undertaking. Second, our experience shows that students who develop a firm grounding in for-profit marketing are better prepared for the challenges of not-for-profit and public-sector marketing.

## A PEDAGOGICAL FRAMEWORK FOR STUDYING AND LEARNING

We include several features in each chapter to enhance your learning experience. They are:

- **Learning objectives.** In each chapter, we highlight the learning you will gain from diligently studying the material in the chapter.
- **Opening case.** To bring the chapters to life, we open each chapter with a real-life example of an organization that helps focus the upcoming material.
- **Showcase examples.** Throughout the book, we showcase examples to illustrate specific elements in the chapter. We also weave examples into the body of the chapters.
- **Key ideas.** Key ideas are distributed throughout the book. They are highlighted in the margins for easy reference.
- **Marketing questions.** Within the chapters, we shall ask you questions about the material or a specific case example. Our aim is to engage you with the text and deepen your understanding.
- **Questions for study and discussion.** After the final chapter, we present a few questions that will help you reflect on the chapter material and gain deeper insight.
- **Glossary.** At the end of the book, we gather together and provide an explanation of a set of key terms by chapter. These are highlighted for easy reference.

Additional learning materials are on the website. These include:

- **Video clips.** A series of interviews with marketing experts address issues pertinent to the chapter.
- **Caselets.** Each chapter has one or more caselets that pose contemporary real marketing problems faced by companies.
- **Problem sets.** In chapters where it is appropriate we pose numerical problems and then show how to secure the right answer.

The book is pretty light on pictures, fluff, and entertainment value; after all, marketing is a serious business.

## ORGANIZATION OF THE BOOK

As laid out in the Table of Contents, *Capon's Marketing Framework* comprises three sections and 19 chapters:

**SECTION 1 — MARKETING AND THE FIRM.** This section has two chapters:

- Chapter 1, *Introduction to Managing Marketing*, provides an introduction to the book. The chapter makes the case for the critical importance of marketing in the modern corporation. We describe two key meanings of marketing — **marketing as a philosophy** and the **six marketing imperatives** that encompass the task of strategic marketing. We also discuss four principles that should form the basis for all marketing decision-making — they continue thematically throughout the book.

- Chapter 2, *The Value of Customers: Optimizing Shareholder Value* delves into the notion of customers as critical firm assets. We introduce the concept of customer lifetime value (LTV) and emphasize the importance of customer retention. We also show that, in addition to measuring product profitability, the firm should work to emulate those organizations that successfully measure customer profitability.

**SECTION 2 — FUNDAMENTAL INSIGHTS FOR STRATEGIC MARKETING.** The four chapters in this section focus on securing insight into the market, laying the foundation for developing market strategy.

- Chapter 3, *Market Insight*, focuses on understanding the market. We use a framework that embraces market structure, market and product evolution, industry forces, and environmental forces.

- Chapter 4, *Customer Insight*, focuses on customers — consumers and organizations. The chapter addresses three main questions: Who are the customers? What do the customers need? How do the customers buy?

- Chapter 5, *Insight about Competitors, Company, and Complementers* focuses on each of these three areas. We offer an extended section on competitors and present a five-step process — identify, describe, evaluate, project, and manage.

- Chapter 6, *Marketing Research*, focuses on marketing research methodologies to gain the insights relative to markets, customers, competitors, company, and complementers.

**SECTION 3 — MARKETING IMPERATIVES.** We organize the third and longest section of the book around the **Six Marketing Imperatives** that are the core of understanding the *to dos* of marketing: when and how to apply the four marketing principles.

### Marketing Imperative 1 — Determine and Recommend Which Markets to Address

- Chapter 7, *Determine and Recommend Which Markets to Address*. This chapter focuses on growth opportunities. We develop growth strategy frameworks, introduce the venture portfolio, explore criteria to evaluate growth opportunities, and identify implementation methods.

### Marketing Imperative 2 — Identify and Target Market Segments

- Chapter 8, *Market Segmentation and Targeting*. We cover two basic topics— methods of grouping customers into market segments, and targeting — the process of deciding which segments to address.

Both Imperatives 1 and 2 exemplify the *Principle of Selectivity and Concentration*.

### Marketing Imperative 3 — Set Strategic Direction

This imperative comprises three separate chapters and advances the concept of strategy as a fundamental integrating force.

- Chapter 9, *Market Strategy — The Integrator*. In this chapter, we present critical market strategy components in some depth and show how they play an integrating role in the marketing mix and the firm's other functional programs. This chapter, in particular, illustrates the application of the Principles of Differential Advantage, Customer Value, and Integration.

- Chapter 10, *Managing Through the Life Cycle*, uses the product life cycle to focus on the competitive aspects of strategy. We adopt a scenario approach to developing strategic options in different competitive and life-cycle situations.

- Chapter 11, *Managing Brands*. We address the management of brands and the increasingly important brand equity concept.

### Marketing Imperative 4 — Design the Marketing Offer

We take eight chapters to address Imperative 4. These chapters describe the marketing mix and when and how to manage each component in a way that reinforces the firm's market strategy.

- Chapter 12, *Managing the Product Line*, concerns managing product line composition. It leans heavily on strategic portfolio frameworks to complement traditional financial analysis methods. We address complementarity, product line breadth (including the trade-offs between product proliferation and simplification), extending product life, product quality, bundling, counterfeiting, secondary markets, product safety, and packaging and product disposal.

- Chapter 13, *Developing New Products*, discusses success factors for innovative companies, the relationship between marketing and innovation, and different ways to approach the innovation challenge. The chapter also describes the evolving new-product development process.

- Chapter 14, *Managing Price and Value*, focuses on pricing. Pricing has tremendous revenue and profit implications. In the chapter's two parts, we discuss developing pricing strategy and actually setting prices.

- Chapter 15, *Marketing Communications and Advertising*, presents an integrated communications framework for developing communications strategy. The chapter focuses on impersonal communication, specifically advertising, direct marketing, publicity and public relations, sales promotion, and the Internet.

- Chapter 16, *Directing and Managing the Field Sales Effort*, deals with personal selling efforts. We discuss contemporary challenges in managing the field sales effort, and use six tasks to develop elements of a sales strategy and organizational issues that the firm must address to implement the strategy.

- Chapter 17, *Distribution Decisions*. We focus on providing customers with products and services, when and where they want them. We discuss choosing and managing marketing-channel relationships, an area of substantial innovation.

- Chapter 18, *Managing Services, Customer Service, and Customer Relationship Management*. Services are important factors in all advanced economies. As product quality has improved across the board, customer service has become an increasingly important competitive weapon. We address these issues and provide a framework for customer relationship management.

Imperatives 3 and 4 draw heavily on the *Principles of Customer Value and Differential Advantage*.

**Marketing Imperatives 5 and 6 — Secure Support from Other Functions: Monitoring and Controlling Performance**

- Chapter 19, *Implementing the Marketing Offer: Monitoring & Controlling Firm Performance.* Here we return to the distinction between marketing as a philosophy and marketing as a function. We highlight successful externally oriented firms and develop a system for making the firm externally oriented and customer-focused. The chapter also discusses ways of ensuring the firm implements its planned marketing effort and achieves the desired results.

Both Imperatives 5 and 6 rest on the *Principle of Integration.*

## SUPPLEMENTAL MATERIAL FOR TEACHING AND LEARNING

*Capon's Marketing Framework* is a standalone book, but we also provide several additional materials to help instructors design their courses and to make the learning experience more meaningful for students. Instructors can access several of these materials in a protected area at *www.axcesscapon.com* or *www.mm21c.com.*

- **Instructors manual:** The manual employs a consistent format, chapter by chapter. Essentially, the manual summarizes the critical learning points in each chapter and provides approaches to answers to *Marketing Questions* that are in the body of the chapter. For the *Questions for Study and Discussion* at the end of the book, we offer answers or suggestions for managing a discussion, as appropriate.

- **Test item file:** Prepared by experienced test developer, Andrew Yap, this file contains well over 1,000 multiple choice and essay questions for use by instructors in setting tests and examinations. We have organized the file by chapter and linked each question to the relevant pages in the book.

- **PowerPoint files:** Each chapter comes with a set of teaching materials in the form of PowerPoint files. For each slide, we provide a *notes* page that suggests how that particular slide should be used for teaching. The slides are available for faculty on a restricted basis at *www.axcesscapon.com* and *www.mm21c.com.*

- **The Virgin Marketer:** This companion volume (see below) contains all of the material necessary to develop a marketing plan.

- **Case studies:** We provide two sets of materials. First, there is a list and short descriptions of many traditional marketing case studies. Second, we offer a large number of short case studies for FREE pdf download. In both cases, we organize the items by book chapter. We also include two approaches to studying marketing cases — a faculty perspective that we developed and an approach prepared by Mary Cunningham Agee, then a Harvard Business School student, to help fellow students.

- **Website:** As noted, all of these above materials are available at the book's website, *www.axcesscapon.com.* We also host an open chat room for students and a restricted-entry chat room for faculty. We hope that students and faculty will use these chat rooms to enhance their course experiences.

We also offer additional study aids that students may access in a student area at *www.axcesscapon.com.*

- **Student study guide:** The purpose of this publication is to help students in their marketing studies. The guide is structured in the same way as the textbook so that students can easily work back and forth between the two volumes.

- **Electronic flash cards:** Similar in concept to traditional flash cards, electronic flash cards are designed to improve students' marketing expertise.

- **Marketing videos:** Students may sign onto YouTube and go to the *noelcapon* channel. There are a series of videos by marketing experts to aid understanding of marketing.

## THE VIRGIN MARKETER

No matter how well-written the textbook, the only way to really learn marketing is by doing it. You simply have to take the ideas, concepts, and frameworks and put them into practice. *The Virgin Marketer* is a companion volume to *Capon's Marketing Framework* and *Managing Marketing in the 21ˢᵗ Century*. Each chapter contains a set of tried-and-true experiential exercises designed to help the user analyze a marketing situation, develop a market strategy, and design a series of implementation programs.

We recommend that you select a product or service as your *marketing case*. Your instructor may assign the case — perhaps a local firm or a startup product. Alternatively, you may select your own product or service. The ideal way to *learn by doing* is to complete each chapter of *The Virgin Marketer* right after you have completed a chapter of this book. Then you will use the ideas, concepts, and frameworks while they are fresh in your mind. If you work through your marketing case assiduously, you will finish the book with an operating marketing plan.

**Noel Capon**
R. C. Kopf Professor of International Marketing
Graduate School of Business
Columbia University, New York, New York.

## ABBREVIATIONS GLOSSARY

To improve readability we avoid spelling out the full names of organizations in examples. Rather, we use the shortened versions or mnemonics by which they are typically known.

### Corporations

| | |
|---|---|
| Advanced Micro Devices | AMD |
| American Express | AmEx |
| America Online | AOL |
| Barnes & Noble | B&N |
| Black & Decker | B&D |
| Boston Consulting Group | BCG |
| Bristol-Myers Squibb | BMS |
| British Airways | BA |
| Cisco Systems | Cisco |
| Electronic Data Systems | EDS |
| General Electric | GE |
| General Motors | GM |
| General Motors Acceptance Corporation | GMAC |
| GlaxoSmithKline | GSK |
| Hewlett Packard | HP |
| Home Box Office | HBO |
| Industrial Research Institute | IRI |
| International Business Machines | IBM |
| International Paper | IP |
| Johnson & Johnson | J&J |
| Lucent Technologies | Lucent |
| Procter & Gamble | P&G |
| Scandinavian Airlines System | SAS |
| Texas Instruments | TI |

### General Business Terms

| | |
|---|---|
| Fast moving consumer goods | FMCG |
| Chief executive officer | CEO |
| Chief financial officer | CFO |
| Chief marketing officer | CMO |
| Customer relationship management | CRM |
| Personal computer | PC |
| Research and development | R&D |
| Senior vice president | SVP |

### U.S. Government Departments

| | |
|---|---|
| Consumer Product Safety Commission | CPSC |
| Department of Justice | DOJ |
| Department of Justice – Antitrust Division | DOJ-ATD |
| Federal Drug Administration | FDA |
| Federal Trade Commission | FTC |
| Securities and Exchange Commission | SEC |

### International Organizations

| | |
|---|---|
| European Union | EU |
| United States | U.S. |
| World Trade Organization | WTO |

# SECTION I MARKETING AND THE FIRM

# CHAPTER I

# INTRODUCTION TO MANAGING MARKETING

## LEARNING OBJECTIVES

When you have completed this chapter, you will be able to:

- Define the term *marketing*.
- Explain the fundamental model of business.
- Articulate why marketing is so important for business organizations.
- Explain how success in attracting, retaining, and growing customers improves shareholder value.
- Articulate how marketing as a philosophy embraces an external orientation.
- Understand how an external orientation differs from various internal orientations.
- Be ready to act on the six marketing imperatives.
- Identify the four marketing principles.
- Understand the book's structure and additional features to enhance learning.

## OPENING CASE: STARBUCKS

*In 1982, Howard Schultz, then 28 years old, joined Seattle's specialty coffee emporium, Starbucks Coffee, Tea & Spice and persuaded the owners to transplant Italy's espresso bar concept to downtown Seattle. It was wildly successful. In 1987, together with local investors, Schultz purchased Starbucks and began a major store expansion. By 2006, Starbucks was the world's leading retailer, roaster, and brand of specialty coffee with 7,950 stores in the U.S. and over 11,000 globally. Starbucks purchases coffee direct from growers, roasts all its coffee, and distributes to its stores. All Starbucks' stores are wholly owned, except in foreign countries, where it has partnership and licensing agreements with local business people, and in licensed locations in the U.S., such as campus bookstores and airports. All people in company-owned stores work for Starbucks.*[1]

*For Schultz, Starbucks should be its customers' third place — after home and work. "As a customer, I walk into the store and I'm swept away for a minute, even if I get a coffee to go, because I'm part of this experience that makes me feel better. A missing part of our lives as consumers is that we don't feel valued. So we really take notice when someone touches us and says, 'I appreciate you, I respect you, and I can help you.' … We open five new stores a day, so we have to ensure that there's incredible consistency without having every location seem to be stamped out like a fast-food franchise. That is part of the genius of Starbucks."*

*Starbucks enhances customers' experience value by focusing on its employees —* partners. *Schultz observed: "The keys are the culture and values of our company that allow our people to feel the way they do about Starbucks, so that they genuinely want to convey the attributes, the characteristics, the aspirational qualities of what we offer the customer … .We've made a very large investment over the last 20 years in training.We've spent more money every year on training than we do on advertising." Early on, Starbucks did no advertising, preferring to let its clusters of stores fulfill the communications function. Schultz went on: "Starbucks has the lowest attrition of any retail restaurant in North America.We do a cultural, internal audit every year where we go to our people, and we ask them to evaluate our behavior and practices and their trust and confidence in management. And we share those scores with the company."*

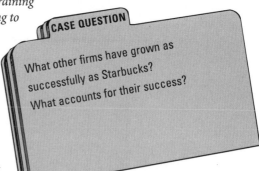

**CASE QUESTION**

What other firms have grown as successfully as Starbucks? What accounts for their success?

*Currently more than 40 million customers every month frequent Starbucks locations around the world. The most loyal customers visit Starbucks an average of 18 times a month. Starbucks' customer loyalty has brought significant financial success: In 2008, revenues were $10.4 billion; net profits were $316 million (down from a $673 million high in 2007).*

## WHAT DOES MARKETING MEAN TODAY?

Marketing plays a critical role in today's business environment, where maximizing **shareholder value** is an increasingly important goal. The essence of marketing focuses on how firms attract, retain, and enhance their relationships with customers. Success in delivering **customer value** leads directly to improving shareholder value and long-run prosperity for the business. In this book, we explore both the strategic aspects of marketing and the tactical decisions that marketers make every day. First, we investigate two quite different but related meanings of marketing.

**MARKETING AS A PHILOSOPHY** embraces the view that marketing is the guiding force or orientation for the entire organization. Firms with a marketing philosophy operate with an external orientation. Such firms focus their attention and resources *outside* the corporation — to acquire, retain, and enhance customer relationships — but take careful account of competitors and the broader environment in which they do business. By contrast, internally oriented companies focus on internal organizational issues like products, services, and processes. This book embraces the *marketing-as-philosophy* perspective. The author believes, and has seen in his own work, how powerful and effective a business can be when the entire organization is attuned to the external factors that affect it. Such agile firms not only sense critical environmental factors, but also adapt and change to address them.

**KEY IDEA**

➤ Marketing is a guiding philosophy for the firm as a whole.

This leads us to the second meaning of marketing. In addition to the philosophical perspective, you must also possess the tools and decision-making skills to get the job done, to be an effective marketer and bring success to your firm. We call these the marketing imperatives:

**MARKETING IMPERATIVES** describe the specifics of the marketing job. These are the *must dos* of marketing. In our experience, executives with marketing and product management titles generally implement six imperatives. They are:

**KEY IDEA**

➤ Marketing is a set of six imperatives — the *must dos* of marketing.

➤ Four marketing principles guide execution of the six imperatives.

- Imperative 1: Determine and recommend which markets to address.
- Imperative 2: Identify and target market segments.
- Imperative 3: Set strategic direction and positioning.
- Imperative 4: Design the marketing offer.
- Imperative 5: Secure support from other functions.
- Imperative 6: Monitor and control execution and performance.

As a broader framework when thinking about markets and market strategy, we shall also reference the **four principles of marketing**. These principles form the basis of marketing decision-making. They act as guidelines for implementing the six imperatives. The four principles are:

- Principle 1: Selectivity and Concentration
- Principle 2: Customer Value
- Principle 3: Differential Advantage
- Principle 4: Integration

This chapter's discussion of these issues sets the stage for the entire book.

## WHAT IS MARKETING?

William Rosenberg, the pioneering entrepreneur of Dunkin' Donuts (DD), had a very simple philosophy: "The boss is the customer." By implementing Rosenberg's philosophy, DD operates 7,000 outlets in 40 countries and sells 4 million donuts and 2.7 million cups of coffee daily.

Target has grown successfully for many years. By contrast, Target's competitor Kmart has struggled — in 2002, Kmart declared bankruptcy. Target understands and addresses customer needs in a compelling manner — Target has a cool brand, the right product mix, and excellent service. Target illustrates the essence of effective marketing.

People are often confused about marketing. It seems so intuitive. Can't anybody be a marketer? Real people at real companies told us that:

- "Marketing is just advertising."
- "Marketing is giving away tee-shirts, products, and concert tickets to potential clients."
- "Marketing's job is to support our sales force."
- "Marketing is what consumers do at the supermarket on a Saturday morning."

All these activities relate to the two broader meanings of marketing we just discussed — **marketing as a philosophy**, and **marketing as six imperatives**, but none really captures the true essence of marketing that we highlight in Figure 1.1.

**KEY IDEA**

➤ There are two sides to value. When the firm delivers high customer value, it attracts, retains, and grows customers. When the firm attracts, retains, and grows customers, it earns high value for shareholders.

Because of its focus on customers, marketing is the firm's fundamental activity. When marketing delivers *customer value* to satisfy customers' needs, the firm *attracts, retains, and grows customers*. If costs are in line, *profits* follow. Profits help the firm survive as an independent entity and secure the resources to grow. *Survival and growth* are the critical links between earning profits and enhancing *shareholder value* by increasing the stock price. Enhanced shareholder value makes funds available for renewed investment in the firm.

Marketing's role includes identifying opportunities, figuring out customers' needs, understanding the competition, developing appealing products and services, and communicating value to potential customers. When these tasks are done well, shareholder value increases. Well-known authors Michael Tracy and Fred Wiersema state that, "Creating shareholder wealth is not the purpose of the business. It is the reward for creating customer value."[2]

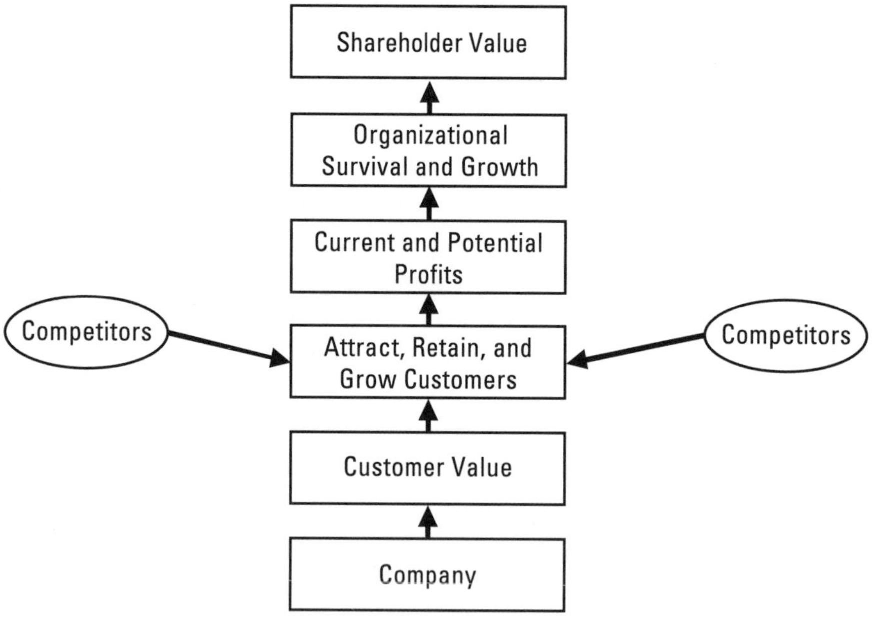

FIGURE 1.1

THE FUNDAMENTAL
BUSINESS MODEL

> *Marketing Question*
>
> Pluto Inc., an electronics firm, spends $100 million a year on R&D. If Pluto eliminated all R&D, management believes profits would increase by $80 million in the current year. What would happen to Pluto's stock price? Why?

Figure 1.1 also demonstrates the process for enhancing shareholder value. It works for a private company with few shareholders or a public firm with many. Growth and long-run profits are the means to that end. Increasing profits in the short run is easy: Just reduce research and development (R&D) spending, cut advertising, and fire half the sales force — but such a course may well lead to significant long-run problems. For forward-looking businesses seeking long-run profits, customers are the firm's core assets. Of course, *competitors* seek these same customers. The competitive battle to attract, retain, and grow customers is central to all business activity.

The critical weapon in the battle for customers is straightforward in concept, but may be complex and difficult in execution. Quite simply, the firm must deliver greater value to customers than its competitors deliver. Customers reward firms that deliver greater customer value by purchasing their products and services, today and tomorrow. This exchange is the basis of all markets. Customers prefer the value inherent in the firm's products and services to their own money or other resources. The firm prefers the customer's money or other resources to its own products/services.

In sum, when the firm delivers greater customer value than its competitors, it should earn profits, survive, grow, and make shareholders very happy. If customers perceive that competitors deliver greater value, ultimately the firm will perish. Just ask one of the more than 100,000 businesses that fail each year in the U.S. Don't just take my word for the power of this framework. Lou Gerstner led IBM's rejuvenation from its near-death experience in the early 1990s — in 1993, IBM lost over $8 billion. Gerstner stated, "Everything starts with the customer."[3]

The late Peter Drucker, the pre-eminent management theorist, is generally credited with developing the entire idea of customer orientation and modern marketing. Drucker stated, "If we want to know what a business is, we have to start with its purpose. There is only one valid definition of any business purpose: to create a customer. It is the customer who determines what a business is. For it is the customer, and he alone, who through being willing to pay for a good or service, converts economic resources into wealth, things into goods." Drucker went on to add, "What the business thinks it produces is not of first importance — especially not to the future of the business and its success. What the customer thinks he is buying, what he considers 'value' is decisive … . Because it is [the purpose of a business] to create a customer, [the] business enterprise has two — and only these two — basic functions: marketing and innovation."[4]

> **KEY IDEA**
>
> ➤ The firm's major task is to attract, retain, and grow customers by developing and delivering valued offers.
>
> ➤ The firm enhances shareholder value by successfully attracting, retaining, and growing customers.

**KEY IDEA**

➤ The firm has two basic functions — marketing and innovation.

**KEY IDEA**

➤ Marketing is critical for a firm's success in today's increasingly complex and fast-changing environment.

Today's customers are increasingly aware and knowledgeable about competitive offers and prices. The Internet is driving much of this transparency. Travelers can easily compare prices of airline trips using Expedia, Travelocity, Orbitz, and the airlines' own websites. Google is challenging Microsoft's dominant position by offering high levels of customer value over the Internet. In the future, intelligent agents may shop for us and make buying decisions. And in advanced societies, greater affluence provides consumers with greater numbers of choices. Consumers often choose between different types of products and services, like a new personal computer or a European vacation.

Marketing encompasses many activities the firm undertakes to attract, retain, and grow customers — of course, competitors are trying to do the same thing. If the firm is more successful than its competitors in creating customer value, it will make profits, survive and grow, and enhance shareholder value.

## MARKETING AND SHAREHOLDER VALUE

Electronic Accounting Systems (EAS) successfully sold payroll services to customers with 50 to 100 employees. Customers filled in payroll sheets, and EAS arranged pickup by courier. But EAS could not serve smaller customers profitably with this model. Tom Golisano, an EAS employee, founded Paychex to address the needs of smaller businesses. Paychex's system was priced lower than that of EAS — partly because customers simply phoned in payroll information. Paychex also provided a payroll tax return service. Golisano became a billionaire and created significant value for Paychex's other shareholders.

Progressive identified a relationship between a person's credit history and driving record, then used this insight to profitably insure customers rejected by mainstream insurers — mainly young drivers and those with poor driving records. Progressive is now fourth in market share; its success has considerably enhanced value for its shareholders.

**KEY IDEA**

➤ The shareholder-value perspective is increasingly widespread around the world.

The central focus on shareholder value is deeply rooted in many capitalist countries — particularly the U.S. The **shareholder-value perspective** defines management's job as maximizing returns for the firm's owners — its shareholders. When this perspective dominates, government regulations tend to favor the owners. Active shareholder opposition, and sometimes-unfriendly takeover bids, tend to occur when the firm underperforms in increasing shareholder value.

The firm also has other *stakeholders*, like management, labor, or the public at large. In some countries, these stakeholders are often more favored than shareholders. Regulation in these countries has generally favored managers and protected them from unwelcome attempts at mergers and takeovers. This stakeholder view is particularly popular in Asia, where many firms and politicians are ardent advocates of managerial power.

In recent years, developing global capital markets have favored the shareholder-value perspective. Conservative Japanese electronics giant Matsushita has share-repurchase plans, provides stock options for senior executives, and links managers' salaries to stock market performance. Even in the communist-run People's Republic of China (PRC), stock markets are now firmly established. The shareholder-value perspective is also having a significant impact on public companies in France, Italy, the Netherlands, and Germany. Restrictions on corporate acquisitions have diminished, and when new owners take control, significant corporate restructuring often occurs. Today, forward-thinking firms focus on augmenting value through partnerships and other types of relationships. Increased globalization will inevitably spread the shareholder-value perspective. Enhanced share ownership gives shareholders greater political power — both directly as individual investors and indirectly via third-party investment vehicles like mutual funds.

Traditionally, we find the firm's assets — cash, accounts receivable, inventory, land, plant and equipment — on its balance sheet. These assets are important for the firm but only if they contribute to attracting, retaining, and growing the firms' core assets — paying customers! Indeed, sometimes balance-sheet assets act as *strategic liabilities* by inhibiting the firm from addressing new opportunities. In the early 1990s, Barnes & Noble was the dominant U.S. bookseller using a bricks-and-mortar strategy. But as the Internet grew, B&N was slow to introduce an e-commerce strategy that embraced a new way to purchase books. In 1994, Jeff Bezos launched Amazon.com with no investment in bricks and mortar. Amazon is now successfully established as the premier online bookseller and has gone on to develop online businesses far beyond books. B&N eventually reacted and now has a decent online book business, but is a distant second to Amazon.

The firm increases shareholder value only if its incoming cash flows earn a return on investment at least equal to its **cost of capital** (the weighted average of the firm's cost of equity and cost of debt). When the firm fails to earn its cost of capital, it destroys shareholder value. Unfortunately, managers sometimes forget that the major source of the firm's cash flows comes from attracting, retaining, and growing customers.[5] Customers provide revenues and cash flow when they believe that the firm's products and services offer better value than competitive alternatives.

## MARKETING AS A PHILOSOPHY: EXTERNAL AND INTERNAL ORIENTATIONS

We learned that the firm enhances shareholder value by attracting, retaining, and growing customers. At a *philosophical* level, then, each employee has some responsibility and marketing is everybody's business. At a personal level, because customers are the firm's only revenue source, they also pay everyone's salary! To quote Drucker again, "Marketing is so basic that it cannot be considered a separate function (i.e., a separate skill or work) within the business … it is, first, a central dimension of the entire business. It is the whole business … seen from the customer's point of view. Concern and responsibility for marketing must, therefore, permeate all areas of the enterprise."[6] More recently, David Haines, brand czar of Vodafone, the world's largest cell phone firm, said, "Marketing is too important to be left to the marketers. It's the obligation of every single individual in the company, whether you're a phone operator, the CEO, or anyone else in the company."[7]

Marketing as a philosophy concerns the firm's entire *orientation*. A firm embracing marketing as a philosophy has an **external orientation**. Other firms focusing on internal business drivers have one of several **internal orientations**.

## THE EXTERNAL ORIENTATION

> Lou Gerstner described the IBM he inherited as CEO: "[IBM had a] … general disinterest in customer needs, accompanied by a preoccupation with internal politics … a bureaucratic infrastructure that defended turf instead of promoting collaboration, and a management class that presided rather than acted."[8] Gerstner described one of his key strategic decisions: "Drive all we did from the customer back, and turn IBM into a market-driven rather than an internally focused, process-driven enterprise"[9]

The externally oriented firm looks outward to the environment — Gerstner really understood this aspect of marketing. The externally oriented firm knows customers are central to its future. Marketing is the *point person*[10] — and marketing must gain insight into customers, competitors, and broader environmental variables. The externally oriented firm knows that its current products, services, and processes are the reasons for past and present success. The firm also knows that as its external environment changes, its products, services, and processes must also change. The

**KEY IDEA**

➤ Customers are the firm's core assets, yet they do not appear on the balance sheet.

➤ Some balance-sheet assets act as strategic liabilities.

**KEY IDEA**

➤ Customers are the major source of cash inflows.

*Marketing Question*

Can you identify some firms that work especially hard to enhance shareholder value by focusing on creating customer value? Specifically, what do they do?

**KEY IDEA**

➤ An externally oriented firm goes beyond a customer focus. It works hard to understand competitors, markets, and environmental forces in general.

externally oriented firm does not fear change — it knows that change is inevitable and that new opportunities are its *lifeblood*. The externally oriented firm invests in new capabilities and competencies to exploit opportunities and create and serve customers.[11]

In difficult economic times, when profits are under pressure, many firms cut spending and investment. The externally oriented firm invests. It may increase its marketing budget, acquire weaker rivals, and/or cut prices. In the early 21st-century recession, several firms invested in customers and markets and bypassed competitors that were more internally oriented[12]:

- Best Buy acquired the 91-store Future Shop chain and quadrupled its Canadian presence.
- Wal-Mart increased capital spending to $10 billion annually.
- Sara Lee increased advertising by 25 percent.
- Dell cut prices on its personal computers.
- Starbucks aggressively expanded internationally.
- Intel maintained R&D and production spending. Said Intel CEO Craig Barrett: "You never save your way out of a recession. The only way to get out of a recession stronger than when you went in is to have great new products."[13]

CEOs and top managers are generally responsible for establishing an external orientation as the overarching corporate thrust. Leaders of firms like Toyota, Amazon, Starbucks, and The Body Shop understand this; they really *get it*. Only a CEO like John Medlin, formerly with Wachovia Bank, can dismiss the *tyranny of the quarterly earnings statement* and say, "You've got to expect a down quarter from time to time."[14] Only a CEO like James Burke at Johnson & Johnson can make customer concerns central to the firm's decision-making. In the Tylenol cyanide-lacing crisis in 1982, J&J immediately withdrew Tylenol capsules until it developed fail-safe packaging. J&J's $250 million write-off demonstrated a long-term investment in customers, and Tylenol quickly returned to market leadership.

**KEY IDEA**

➤ The firm should view marketing expenditures as an investment, not as an expense.

Some of the world's most successful companies practice marketing as a philosophy. A key executive at global pharmaceutical giant Pfizer explains: "Our strong belief at Pfizer is that marketing is really an investment, not an expense. Our former CEO, Bill Steers, believed it was important to invest in R&D. He also believed it was equally important to invest in marketing. He said if you are best at both, there's no way you can be beat! … We parallel our R&D spending with a similar investment in research about markets and customers. What separates us from competitors is an assiduous pursuit of information, knowledge, and understanding of our customer."[15]

**TABLE 1.1**

**GENERAL CHARACTERISTICS OF INTERNAL AND EXTERNAL ORIENTATIONS**[34]

| Dimension | Internal | External |
|---|---|---|
| Focus | Products | Markets |
| Know-how | Inherent in patents, machinery | Inherent in people, processes |
| Process | Mass production | Mass customization |
| Priorities | Efficiency and productivity | Flexibility and responsiveness |
| Measurement | Profit, margin, volume | Customer value, satisfaction, retention |
| Customer perspective | Transactional | Relational |
| Organizational philosophy | Bureaucracy | Adhocracy |

## INTERNAL ORIENTATIONS

In a small and simply organized firm, the sole proprietor (SP) or owner conducts most activities. The SP seeks and serves customers, arranges financing, performs operational functions, and manages the payroll. At a visceral level, the SP knows that customers are critical assets and operates with an external orientation almost by instinct. Can you recall an occasion when your local garage, dry cleaner, hardware store, or other small business treated you personally as an important and valuable asset?

As firms grow, they seek efficiency through specialization and differentiation — operations, sales, product design, finance, legal, technology, and other functions each have specific responsibilities. Ideally, they work together to deliver customer value but, typically, they develop their own missions, objectives, systems and processes, and business philosophies. In addition, management systems that measure, motivate, and reward managers for securing departmental objectives often encourage nonproductive differentiation that history and internal political rivalries may exacerbate.

Frequently, internal functions act in mutually inconsistent ways. The sales department tries to increase sales, but operations, working to produce acceptable-quality products at low cost, reduces the number of product varieties. Marketing wants to spend more on advertising, but finance reduces budgets to meet financial targets. When firms operate in silos, or stovepipes, there is one common denominator — delivering customer value often takes a back seat. These firms follow an **internal orientation**. At an internally oriented firm, you often hear the statement, "That's the way we do things around here." Regardless of changes in customer needs, competitor actions, and/or the external environment in general, the firm continues on its current course. Frequently found internal orientations are:

- **Operations Orientation.** The firm with an **operations orientation** typically focuses on reducing unit costs. In principle, there is nothing wrong with cutting costs; after all, lower costs often lead to increased profits. But cost reduction that reduces customer value and leads to dissatisfied customers can be a serious problem.

- **Sales orientation.** Firms with a **sales orientation** focus on short-term sales volume. They place excessive effort in *getting customers to buy what the firm has to offer*, versus the externally oriented alternative of *getting the firm to offer what customers want to buy*.

- **Finance orientation.** The firm with a **finance orientation** focuses too heavily on short-term profits. It tends to avoid expenditures with long-term payoff and mortgage its future by indiscriminately cutting back on R&D, capital investment, marketing research, and/or advertising.

- **Technology orientation.** A firm with a **technology orientation** focuses on RD&E (research, development, and engineering) and pays little attention to customer value.

Matsushita demonstrated a technological orientation. Its engineers believed that lots of buttons and technical gadgets would add technical value to camcorders and increase market share. Unfortunately sales stagnated because customers wanted easy-to-use products and manuals in everyday language. See Table 1.1 for characteristics of firms with external and internal orientations.

## KEY IDEA

- ➤ Long-run success is difficult for internally oriented firms.
- ➤ Internal orientations often focus on operations, sales, finance, and/or technology.

### Marketing Question

Interview an executive. Identify examples where functional silos hurt performance — and where different functions worked well together.

## THE SIX MARKETING IMPERATIVES

The job of putting the marketing philosophy into practice normally falls to people who have marketing and/or product-management titles. These people tend to engage in many marketing activities, such as securing data on customers and competitors, developing advertising campaigns, designing direct-mail brochures, meeting with R&D on new products, devising Internet strategies, setting prices, and/or preparing persuasive messages for the sales force. Certainly all these activities can enhance the firm's market position, but deciding how to allocate their time and/or other resources requires answers to several questions:

- Which of these activities are critical?
- Do these activities represent the core elements of marketing?
- What critical tasks must the firm perform to truly accomplish its marketing agenda?
- In what order should the firm perform these tasks?

We now discuss the six marketing imperatives that capture the firm's *must dos*; they are the core elements of *Capon's Marketing Framework*. These imperatives are:

> **The Six Marketing Imperatives**
>
> - Imperative 1: Determine and recommend which markets to address.
> - Imperative 2: Identify and target market segments.
> - Imperative 3: Set strategic direction and positioning.
> - Imperative 4: Design the marketing offer.
> - Imperative 5: Secure support from other functions.
> - Imperative 6: Monitor and control execution and performance.

## MARKETING IMPERATIVE 1: DETERMINE AND RECOMMEND WHICH MARKETS TO ADDRESS

Simply put, the firm must choose those markets where it will compete. To help make this choice, the firm should ask: What businesses are we in? What businesses do we want to be in? Market-choice decisions are typically strategic for the firm, or at least for individual business units. Choosing markets is often more important than choosing technologies and/or products. Given the choice of owning a market or owning a factory, most senior executives would prefer owning a market.

The firm must continually make these market-choice decisions. Faster environmental changes open up new market opportunities, but may also lead the firm to exit current markets. Market-choice decisions can totally transform a corporation. Nokia exited its traditional paper-making, rubber-goods, and electric-cable markets as it evolved from a diversified conglomerate to global leadership in wireless communication.

The firm must decide where to invest — to compete, or not, in various markets. It must also decide how much to invest. In particular, the firm must answer critical questions about its business and market portfolio:

- In which new businesses and markets should the firm invest — people, time, dollars?
- From which businesses and markets should the firm withdraw?
- Which current businesses and markets should continue to receive investment?
- How much investment should these various businesses and markets receive?

Typically, marketing does not make these decisions. Top management has this responsibility, but marketing must provide good advice. For Imperative 1, marketing plays two key roles:

- **Identify opportunities.** Marketing is the only function with explicit responsibility to focus attention outside the firm. Marketing personnel should research the environment to identify potential opportunities and bring these to top management's attention. They should also collect and analyze data that bear on the entry decision. Marketing should also be intimately involved with the firm's current markets and businesses and advise on investment and exit decisions.

- **Advise on proposed strategic actions.** Many parts of the firm develop strategic initiatives. Finance may suggest acquisitions and divestitures, R&D may propose strategic alliances, and the sales force may champion a new distribution system. Marketing has the responsibility to insert itself into these decisions and provide advice to top management. If the firm does not fully explore the marketing ramifications of its decisions, disaster may ensue. For example, despite significant attention, most acquisitions do not generate value for the acquiring firm's shareholders. Both AOL's acquisition of TimeWarner and Quaker's acquisition of Snapple are widely believed to have failed. Perhaps the acquirers would have made superior decisions with better marketing advice!

**KEY IDEA**

➤ Marketing should identify market opportunities and advise top management on potential strategic actions.

## MARKETING IMPERATIVE 2: IDENTIFY AND TARGET MARKET SEGMENTS

In any **B2B** or **B2C** market, customers have a diverse set of needs. A single offer directed at the overall market may satisfy some customers, but typically many customers are dissatisfied. Marketing Imperative 2 states that marketing must identify **market segments** — groups of customers with similar needs that value similar benefits, with similar levels of priority.

When the firm does **market segmentation** well, the needs, benefits, and values that define one segment are quite different from the needs, benefits, and values that define other segments. After the firm has identified segments, it must decide which to target.

As a simple example, a tea provider seeking to serve the entire market might offer *warm* tea. A savvier provider might discover that one customer segment wants *hot* tea and that another segment wants *iced* tea. Further, one provider might have the skills and competences to target the *hot* tea segment; another might be similarly positioned with *iced* tea. The original provider will lose customers.

Note that there are two parts to Marketing Imperative 2: a *creative and analytic* part — identifying market segments; and a *decision-making* part — choosing which segments to target, based on the firm's ability to deliver value. Boeing purchased de Havilland Canada (DHC) to address the small, regional segment of the overall aircraft market with the Dash 8. In six years, Boeing lost nearly $1 billion and then sold DHC to Bombardier. Bombardier tripled the Dash 8's market share to 35 percent. Both Boeing and Bombardier did a good job of identifying the small, regional segment, but only Bombardier had the appropriate skills and resources to compete successfully. Boeing did not. This lesson is important — a market segment may be attractive to one firm but unattractive to another.

Market segmentation and targeting is arguably the most critical marketing imperative. Effective segmentation and targeting drive profits.

## MARKETING IMPERATIVE 3: SET STRATEGIC DIRECTION AND POSITIONING

> Gillette is the global leader in both the men's and women's shaving market. It continually introduces higher-value products in advanced countries. In the U.S., Gillette offers Trac II, Atra, and Sensor brands (with two blades), Mach3 and M3Power (battery operated) (with three blades), and Fusion and Fusion Power (with five blades). In less-developed countries, Gillette offers double-edge blades, twin- and four-blade shaving systems, and disposable razors.

In Marketing Imperative 3, the firm decides how to compete in the market segments it has targeted. For each target segment, marketing must formulate performance objectives. Performance objectives guide the firm's future strategic decisions in these segments. Second, the firm must decide on its positioning for each segment. It must identify target customers and target competitors — design a more persuasive value proposition than its competitors — and provide a reason for customers to believe the firm can deliver that value. Together with Marketing Imperative 2, positioning completes the STP triumvirate — **s**egmentation, **t**argeting, and **p**ositioning.

Further, individual market segments are at different developmental stages, and different stages require different approaches. As the Gillette example shows, the appropriate way to address a growing segment is typically quite different from a mature or declining segment. Finally, decisions about strategic direction also include questions of **branding** — how the firm wants its customers to view the corporate entity and its products. Top management increasingly views the firm's brands as major corporate assets, and decisions about branding are among its most important.

**KEY IDEA**

➤ Marketing must identify market segments — groups of customers with similar needs that value similar benefits, with similar priority levels.

**KEY IDEA**

➤ The firm should target those market segments that best use its strengths and exploit competitors' weaknesses.

Of course, the firm does not make these decisions only once. It faces an ever-evolving landscape — customers' needs evolve over time; competitors enter, exit, and adopt different competitive postures. The firm's products also evolve through growth, maturity, and into decline. The firm must continually assess its strategic direction and make the necessary course corrections.

## MARKETING IMPERATIVE 4: DESIGN THE MARKETING OFFER

Marketing Imperative 4 focuses on design of the **marketing offer**. The marketing offer is the total benefit package the firm provides its customers. Tools for designing the offer are the most well-known part of marketing. If you took a previous marketing course, the professor probably spent a lot of time talking about the **marketing mix** (aka the **4Ps**). The marketing mix elements comprise the basic building blocks of the firm's offer to the market. They are:

- **Product.** In general, the product embodies the major benefits the firm offers to satisfy customer needs — these benefits provide value to customers. If the firm offers greater value than its competitors, customers' purchases of the firm's products will increase. The term *product* typically embraces both physical products and services — like airline travel — and packaging.

- **Promotion.** Promotion embraces the various ways the firm communicates with customers — informing and persuading them to purchase its products. Promotion includes *impersonal communications*, like advertising and sales promotions, and *personal communications*, like the sales force. In addition to informing and persuading, communications may add customer value directly by providing imagery, status, and reassurance.

- **Distribution.** Distribution focuses on how and where the customer secures the product. To conform to the 4Ps framework, marketers sometimes refer to *distribution* as **place**.

- **Price.** Price is what the customer pays. The firm establishes its feasible price by the equivalent amount of value it offers through its product, promotion, distribution, and service.

- **Service.** The original 4Ps formulation did not include service. We treat service as a separate item — now 4Ps and an S. Services can be a key distinguishing aspect, one that is very important in persuading customers to buy. FedEx's core offering is overnight package delivery — but special handling, insurance, tracking, and other services are important competitive weapons.

If the firm offers significant benefits and high customer value from its product, service, location, and communications, it can set a high price. But if customer benefits and value are low, price must also be low. If the firm designs good marketing offers, customers will purchase its products. When the firm targets a market segment, it can combine any of the marketing elements — product, promotion, place, service, and price — in an infinite number of ways. Creativity, imagination, innovation, and capability are core ingredients.

## MARKETING IMPERATIVE 5: SECURE SUPPORT FROM OTHER FUNCTIONS

Marketing Imperatives 1, 2, 3, and 4 are strategic and directional. Imperatives 1 and 2 focus on *where* the firm will place resources; Imperatives 3 and 4 focus on *how* the firm will use its resources. Imperative 5 focuses on how the firm's functions work together to ensure it makes the *right* marketing offer. Marketing requires two very different types of support:

- **Support for design.** This support relates to technical, operational, and economic feasibility.
- **Support for implementation.** This support assumes the design is agreed upon and fixed.

**SUPPORT FOR DESIGN.** The firm's ability to deliver the marketing offer depends on its capabilities and resources. The *best* design for customers may require a product feature the firm cannot make. When the best design is not feasible, marketing must develop extraordinary strength to keep the firm focused on satisfying customer needs — and push it to evolve its capabilities.[16]

**SUPPORT FOR IMPLEMENTATION.** We often call this support *internal marketing*, or getting *buy-in*. In many firms, marketing designs the offer — but marketing has no authority to implement the design. Marketers must possess the leadership and interpersonal skills to encourage and stimulate cooperation across multiple functions. After all, *the chain is only as strong as its weakest link*. If a key function does not perform, other functions may waste their efforts.

## MARKETING IMPERATIVE 6: MONITOR AND CONTROL EXECUTION AND PERFORMANCE

Pfizer has a strong reputation for optimizing spending on the marketing mix. Pfizer continually tests different budgets for selling effort and advertising and promotion. Says a senior Pfizer executive, "We're measurement-intense. So 'metrics are us.' We believe in it. We measure everything. That is the root of our business."[17]

It's one thing to plan and implement, but figuring out the firm's performance is quite another. Marketing Imperative 6 focuses on monitoring and control — letting the firm know whether or not it is achieving its desired results. All things equal, if the firm is successful, it should keep on truckin'. If results are not on track, it must make changes. Essentially, marketing should continually secure answers to three questions and act accordingly:

- Are the firm's various functions and departments *implementing* the marketing offer?
- Is the firm's market and financial *performance* reaching planned objectives?
- Based on the current *environment*, are the firm's objectives, strategies, and implementation plans on track, or should it make changes?

**IMPLEMENTATION.** The firm may have many implementation problems — like lack of buy-in. But even with excellent buy-in, antiquated or inappropriate management systems may still create difficulties in implementing the offer.

**POOR PERFORMANCE.** If market and/or financial performance are under plan, marketing may require more data and further analysis. If environmental change is low, marketing should focus on course corrections — fine-tune the strategy or modify implementation plans.

**ENVIRONMENTAL CHANGE.** The firm bases its objectives, strategy, and implementation on the best insight into customer needs, competitive offers, and the external environment. A good strategy should accommodate evolutionary changes — more significant change may require new objectives and strategies.

## THE FOUR PRINCIPLES OF MARKETING

We just learned that the six imperatives are the *must dos* of marketing and are essential for conducting marketing's role. Marketing principles that have been developed over the years serve as guidelines for acting on these imperatives. These four fundamental principles are:

## THE PRINCIPLE OF SELECTIVITY AND CONCENTRATION

Providing advice on market selection and deciding which market segments to target are among marketing's primary responsibilities. The basic principle underlying these imperatives is the **Principle of Selectivity and Concentration.**

The two aspects comprising this principle are:

- **Selectivity.** Marketing must carefully choose targets for the firm's efforts.
- **Concentration.** The firm should concentrate its resources against those targets.

This principle is about choosing the firm's battles. It is dangerous to dissipate limited resources over too many alternatives by trying too much. No organization, no matter how large or how successful, has infinite resources. Each must make timely choices. The selectivity element comes into play when marketing recommends which markets to target — Imperative 1. The best-known manifestation is identifying and targeting market segments — Imperative 2.

## THE PRINCIPLE OF CUSTOMER VALUE

According to the **Principle of Customer Value**, the firm's marketplace success depends on providing value to customers. This principle is central to marketing's job. Customer insight should drive design and implementation of marketing offers. Customer value should drive the firm's product and investment decisions — and its performance evaluation. The firm develops, produces, and delivers products and services, but customers perceive value only in the benefits these products and services provide.

Customer value is a moving target. As the environment changes, customers accumulate experience and their needs change — the values they seek change also. World-class companies continuously invest in marketing research to probe deeply into customers' needs, priorities, expectations, and experiences. They feed these results into the product development process to produce greater value for customers.

Cisco Systems continues to be the market-share leader and a major force in high technology. Said an important Wall Street analyst, "They [Cisco] don't have the best technology, but they do have the best [customer] relationships."[18] Firms that take their eye off the customer ball can get into serious trouble. Sears and Kmart (U.S.), and Sainsbury's and Marks & Spencer (Great Britain), were once powerful and successful retailers. In recent years, they have all been in crisis.

## THE PRINCIPLE OF DIFFERENTIAL ADVANTAGE

The **Principle of Differential Advantage** is closely related to the Principle of Customer Value. Differential advantage is similar to having a *competitive advantage*, a *unique selling proposition (USP)*, or an *edge*. Differential advantage lies at the heart of every successful market strategy. The Principle of Differential Advantage asserts that the firm should offer customers something they value but cannot get elsewhere.

More formally, *a differential advantage is a net benefit or cluster of benefits, offered to a sizable group of customers, which they value and are willing to pay for but cannot get, or believe they cannot get, elsewhere.* To implement this principle, the firm must develop well-designed market offers based on the marketing-mix elements we discussed earlier. If the firm achieves a differential advantage, it should secure improved prices. This principle leads to several implications:

- **Competition.** The principle emphasizes competition. Offering customer value is not enough. To avoid competitive parity, the firm's offer must be better than competitors' offers. The firm must create and re-create its differential advantage to beat competitors.

- **Superiority of differential advantages.** Some differential advantages are better than others. A differential advantage based on product design or product availability may be more sustainable than a differential advantage based on communications. A differential advantage based on an organizational process like a parts delivery system or qualified technicians may be even more sustainable.[19]

- **Eroding differential advantages.** Competition will eventually erode away even what appears to be the most sustainable differential advantage. Maintaining differential advantage is marketing's most fundamental challenge. The search for differential advantage must be ongoing. Ideally, the firm should have a hidden differential advantage, ready to trump the competitor's ace!

- **Cannibalizing a differential advantage.** To stay ahead of competition, the firm must be willing to cannibalize its own offerings. Many firms will not pay this price, in part because political constituencies for current offerings are so strong.
- **Differential advantage and difference.** A *differential advantage* is not the same as a *difference.* To develop a market offer that is different from competitors may not be difficult. The critical issue is for the differences to create benefits that customers recognize, truly value, and are willing to pay for.

KEY IDEA

➤ To secure a differential advantage, customers must perceive greater value in the firm's offer than in competitors' offers.

## THE PRINCIPLE OF INTEGRATION

Integration is critical to Target's success. "Every one of us, in every functional group, from Stores to Merchandising, from Logistics to Support, identifies with the role as marketing. We're all attempting to build better relationships with our guest [Target's term for customer]. And every decision starts with the guest, so everyone becomes a marketer. We instill that attitude with evangelical passion and great consistency — the evangelizing starts at the top with our Chairman and CEO. Our core brand promise since 1962 has been, 'Expect more, pay less.' We live it — every single function of this company lives it. We search the globe for the best products to serve our guest needs and everyone in the store is hard-wired to meet guest expectations at all times."[20]

Successful integration — critical for all marketing efforts — has two dimensions:

- **At the customer.** The firm must carefully integrate and coordinate all design and execution elements it offers to customers. For example, poor advertising can ruin an excellent product, or delayed promotional materials can doom a product launch.
- **In the firm.** To achieve integration at the customer level, the firm must also integrate and coordinate all of its functional activities. This is often very difficult. Different functions or departments often squabble over priorities — and senior management may send ambiguous messages. All too often, individual departments focus on defending their *turf* at the expense of delivering customer value.

The firm with an external orientation is most likely to achieve integration because the shared value of serving customers promotes a common purpose. Those who design and implement the marketing offer agree on priorities and develop close and cooperative working relationships.

KEY IDEA

➤ The firm achieves integration by agreeing on priorities — those involved in designing and implementing the offer must develop close and cooperative working relationships.

## KEY MESSAGES

- Firms that deliver greater customer value than their competitors are more successful in attracting, retaining, and growing customers.
- Firms that successfully attract, retain, and grow customers earn profits. They are more likely to survive and grow and enhance shareholder value.
- Enhancing shareholder value is an increasingly important objective for companies.
- Value has two sides. When firms deliver high levels of customer value, they attract, retain, and grow customers. When firms attract, retain, and grow customers, they create value for shareholders.
- Marketing as a philosophy embraces an external orientation—this is a responsibility of all organizational members.
- The six marketing imperatives represent the *must dos* for the firm.
- The four principles of marketing provide the guiding framework within which the firm implements the six marketing imperatives.

# CHAPTER 2

# THE VALUE
# OF CUSTOMERS:
# OPTIMIZING
# SHAREHOLDER
# VALUE

## LEARNING OBJECTIVES

When you have completed this chapter, you will be able to:

- Identify the critical elements that define customer lifetime value.
- Calculate customer profitability and customer lifetime value.
- Recognize the importance of retaining the *right* customers.
- Relate delivering customer value to generating long-term customer loyalty.
- Explain the importance of measuring customer profitability.
- Develop justifications for firing current customers and/or rejecting potential customers.

## OPENING CASE: ROYAL BANK OF CANADA

*Toronto-based Royal Bank of Canada (RBC) serves over 14 million personal, business, and public-sector customers via offices in North America and 30 other countries. RBC is Canada's leading bank, with more than 1,400 offices and 4,000 banking machines. What sets RBC apart from competitors and many other firms is its focus on customer profitability. RBC's retail arm found that 17 percent of its customers accounted for 93 percent of its profits — an extreme version of the 80/20 rule at 93/17. RBC concentrates on this 17 percent and discourages, or even discards, its least profitable and loss-making customers.*

*As we learn from* Angel Customers & Demon Customers, *the excellent book by Larry Selden and Geoffrey Colvin, RBC calculates economic profit by customer.[1] Identifying revenue, product profit margins (spreads), and invested capital is easy. RBC tracks labor costs via activity-based costing. It monitors the costs to serve customers through its various channels; back office processing, call center responding, and other activities.*

*RBC's retail bank has nine customer segment managers and many product managers. Each segment and product manager has individual and primary responsibility for strategy, as well as profit and loss (P&L), for their segment or product. This matrix organization encourages collaboration, and it works because RBC's culture has always been customer-centric and consensus driven. Also, senior management has clearly signaled that managing for team success is an important criterion for career advancement.*

**RBC'S NEW APPROACH.** *RBC traditionally ran mortgage promotions in the spring home-buying season. These promotions emphasized RBC's rates. Competitor banks operated similarly. But Louise Mitchell, RBC's leader for the builders and borrowers segment, pursued a different approach — she targeted the life event of a first home purchase. Mitchell created and promoted a value proposition — mortgage, free financial review, $500 savings deposit, free online banking, and a no-fee Visa card — to serve the total needs of first-time home buyers. She believed that her customer segment could add significant value to RBC's shareholders:*

- *First-time home buyers have most of their financial lives ahead of them, with significant prospects for future growth. On average, first-time home buyers borrow larger amounts for longer terms than other buyers and are less sensitive to rates.*

*RBC could probably not have executed this promotion within its traditional product-centric organization. It required coordination among managers responsible for mortgages, savings accounts, financial advice, marketing, and others. As segment leader, Mitchell was a powerful catalyst. She stated that, by "looking through the customer lens," … the promotional ideas "jump right out at you."*

*The result? RBC's share of first-time versus new mortgages is 62 percent versus 50 percent — and most new customers chose the longest, most profitable (for RBC) terms. From 1994 to 2004, RBC's revenues jumped from $7.39 billion to $17.35 billion; profits escalated from $1.17 billion to $2.84 billion; year-end market value went from $8.9 billion to $40.9 billion; and P/E ratio increased from 8/9 to 14/9.*

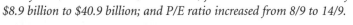

**CASE QUESTION**

What are the challenges in securing customer-focused data and implementing customer-focused strategies as RBC did?

**KEY IDEA**

➤ When the firm creates value for customers, it successfully attracts, retains, and grows those customers. By being attracted, retained, and grown, customers create value for the firm and its shareholders.

In Chapter 1, we discussed the critical role customers play for the firm's well-being. By attracting, retaining, and growing customers, the firm makes profits today and promises profits tomorrow. Profits allow the firm to survive and grow and to enhance shareholder value. Because of these relationships, customers are the firm's core assets. More precisely, customers are core assets because of two sides of the concept of value. When the firm creates value for customers,

**KEY IDEA**

➤ Customer lifetime value (LTV) is the link between delivering value to customers and creating value for shareholders.

it successfully attracts, retains, and grows those customers. By being attracted, retained, and grown, customers create value for the firm and its shareholders.[2] Because a retained customer returns to buy more products and services, a key firm goal is to deliver customer value and generate long-term customer loyalty.

This chapter moves beyond the concept of customers as assets to measuring the value that customers bring to the firm over time. The critical concept is **customer lifetime value (LTV)** — what the customer is worth to the firm. We define LTV as the discounted future stream of profits the customer generates over the life of its relationship. LTV is the crucial link between the value the firm delivers to its customers and the value that customers deliver to the firm's shareholders. Increasing LTV enhances shareholder value. We show how to use LTV to increase the value that customers bring to the firm and discuss approaches for current customers, as well as implications for acquiring new customers. We also identify the *right* customers and show that some customers are undesirable.

Specifically, we address two questions:

- How can we put a monetary value on the firm's current customers and on potential customers the firm might try to acquire? This is customer lifetime value (LTV).
- How can we use the LTV concept to help the firm enhance shareholder value?

## CUSTOMER LIFETIME VALUE (LTV)

**KEY IDEA**

➤ Customer lifetime value depends on just three factors — margin, retention rate, and discount rate.

When customers purchase the firm's products and services, it earns revenues; the firm also accrues costs. If sales revenues are greater than costs, the firm earns a profit. The profit earned from an individual customer during a single time period (year) is the profit margin — the annual value the customer brings to the firm.[3] Of course, both consumers (B2C) and partners, distributors, and resellers (B2B) often continue to purchase the firm's products for several years into the future. In each year, the firm receives sales revenues, accrues costs, and earns a profit margin. Customer lifetime value (LTV) takes into account the margin the firm earns in each of these years.

Some of the firm's customers this year will not be customers next year. Some customers may defect to competitors; others may stop buying the types of products the firm offers and leave the market. In calculating LTV, we must consider customer *defection* and customer *retention*. **Retention rate** is simply the number of customers at the end of the year, divided by the number of customers at the start of the year. If the firm starts the year with 100 customers and ends the year with 80 of these same customers, its retention rate is 80 percent. Retention is the inverse of defection or churn. In this example, the **defection rate** is 20 percent (100 percent minus 80 percent).[4] Understanding LTV allows the firm to better manage its customer base.

**CALCULATING CUSTOMER LIFETIME VALUE (LTV)** In each year, the firm earns a portion of its LTV. In the first year, it earns LTV (1):

$$\text{LTV (1)} = \mathbf{m} \times \mathbf{r}/(1 + \mathbf{d})$$

Restating this simple expression in words, in year 1, the firm earns:

- the *margin (m)* from year 1,
- multiplied by the *retention rate (r)* — the probability that a customer at the start of the year will still be a customer at the end of the year,
- *discounted* back to the start of the year, using the term **1/(1+d)**. The **discount rate, d**, is the firm's **cost of capital** — typically, the firm's chief financial officer (CFO) provides this.

To calculate a customer's total LTV, we add up the LTV contributions for each successive year.[5] This is complicated mathematically. We simplify the calculation by assuming that each variable, margin (m), discount rate (d), and retention rate (r), is constant year to year.

With these assumptions, LTV equals the margin (m) multiplied by a term we call the **margin multiple**.

The margin multiple = r/(1 + d − r), so that:

$$\text{LTV} = \mathbf{m} \times \mathbf{r}/(1 + \mathbf{d} - \mathbf{r})$$

Calculating the LTV is quite straightforward using this formula. Table 2.1 makes it easier by providing margin multiple values for different retention rates (r) and discount rates (d).

Suppose the firm earns an annual margin of $500,000, customer retention rate is 70 percent, and the firm's discount rate is 12 percent. From Table 2.1, the margin multiple is 1.67. Hence, **LTV = $500,000 × 1.67 = $835,000**. Of course, we lose some precision with these assumptions, but if they put us in the right ballpark, that is sufficient for most situations.

| Retention Rate (r) | Discount Rate (d) | | | |
|---|---|---|---|---|
| | 8% | 12% | 16% | 20% |
| 60% | 1.25 | 1.15 | 1.07 | 1.00 |
| 70% | 1.84 | 1.67 | 1.52 | 1.40 |
| 80% | 2.86 | 2.50 | 2.22 | 2.00 |
| 90% | 5.00 | 4.09 | 3.46 | 3.00 |
| 95% | 7.31 | 5.59 | 4.52 | 3.80 |

Note that, in general, improving the retention rate (r) has a greater impact on the margin multiple than reducing the discount rate (d):

a. When the retention rate (r) is 90 percent, reducing the discount rate (d) from 20 percent to 8 percent improves the margin multiple from 3.00 to 5.00 — 67 percent.

b. When the discount rate (d) is 12 percent, increasing the retention rate (r) from 60 percent to 90 percent increases the margin multiple from 1.15 to 4.09 — well over three times!

All things equal, the firm is better off increasing customer retention than reducing the discount rate (d) — its cost of capital — by financial engineering. Finance students, please note! Customer retention is a big deal. More on this later.

**TABLE 2.1**

**THE MARGIN MULTIPLE = r/(1+d−r)**

---

**Example: Lifetime Value of a FedEx Customer**

FedEx has identified a market segment — these data apply to FedEx's customers in that segment:

**Assumptions**

- Total FedEx letters shipped per month = 2,285
- Number of FedEx customers = 140
- FedEx margin per letter (m) = $8.25
- Discount rate (cost of capital) (d) = 12%
- Annual retention rate (r) = 90%

We assume that these numbers remain constant year to year.

**Customer lifetime value calculation:**

Number of FedEx letters per customer per annum = 2,285 × 12/140 = 195.8

FedEx margin per customer per annum = $8.25 × 195.8 = $1,616

Discount rate (d) = 12%

Retention rate (r) = 90%

From Table 2.1, the **margin multiple** = 4.09

**LTV** = FedEx margin per customer per annum × margin multiple = $1,616 × 4.09 = **$6,609**

Quite simply, the firm has three, and only three, ways to increase customer lifetime value:

- Increase the margin (m) the firm earns from its customers
- Increase the customer retention rate (r) (reduce the customer defection rate)
- Reduce the discount rate (d)

If we spend resources to increase customer retention, we reduce customer margin. Or the firm may increase customer margin by raising prices — but this may reduce retention rate. Nonetheless, we consider these approaches separately but rely on financial managers to address the discount rate.

## INCREASING THE MARGINS THE FIRM EARNS FROM CUSTOMERS

The firm has several options for increasing LTV by raising the margins from current customers:

- **Customer selection.** Well-selected current customers provide a base level of profit margin.
- **Customer satisfaction and loyalty.** Research shows that well-served customers increase their purchases over time. Hence, the firm's revenues and profit margins increase.
- **Customization.** Specially targeted offers to defined segments provide greater customer value.
- **Reduce operating costs.** As the firm learns to serve customers, it reduces operating costs and may reap scale economies with individual customers.
- **Raise prices.** If the firm has really satisfied its customers, it may be able to set higher prices.

In addition, satisfied customers may help the firm with other customers:

- **Referrals.** Satisfied customers provide referrals to potential customers. Lexus secures more new customers from referrals than any other source.
- **Signals.** Securing a high-profile customer may provide the firm with credibility among other potential customers.
- **Learning.** The firm learns by working closely with customers and becomes better able to attract new customers.
- **Network externalities.** In some markets, customers bring value to other customers. Television, some printed media, and websites are free, yet their customer traffic has value to advertisers. The more *sellers* eBay attracts, the more valuable is eBay's service to *buyers*. The more *buyers* eBay attracts, the more valuable it is to *sellers*.

Figure 2.1 shows profit margin trends in the U.S. credit card industry. The annual profit margin from customers increases with customer longevity. In the first year, the average credit card issuer loses $80. By the second year, the customer is profitable, earning the firm $40. Over time, the dollar profit margin per customer increases steadily.[6]

**KEY IDEA**

➤ The profit margin the firm earns from a customer tends to increase over time.

*Marketing Question*

Do you tend to increase your purchases from firms that treat you well? Have you told others about these experiences?

.....................
**FIGURE 2.1**

**PROFIT MARGIN IN THE U.S. CREDIT CARD INDUSTRY BY LENGTH OF CUSTOMER RELATIONSHIP**

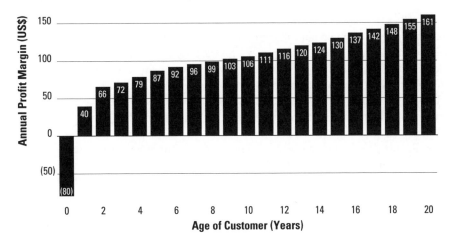

## INCREASE THE CUSTOMER RETENTION RATE — REDUCE THE CUSTOMER DEFECTION RATE

We just showed that an increase in margin (m) leads to an increase in customer LTV. Of course, margin is only relevant if the customer continues to be a customer! The firm continually loses customers and, of course, defection is greater at 80 percent retention rate than 90 percent. Regardless, first-year defection is greatest — the actual number of customers defecting decreases year by year. Assume the firm starts with 1,000 customers:

- 90% retention:   1st year – 1,000 customers
2nd year – 900 customers; lost – 100 customers
3rd year – 810 customers; lost – 90 customers
4th year – 729 customers; lost – 81 customers

- 80% retention:   1st year – 1,000 customers
2nd year – 800 customers; lost – 200 customers
3rd year – 640 customers; lost – 160 customers
4th year – 512 customers; lost – 128 customers

As we might expect from these data, customer retention rate has an important impact on customer LTV. Based on an empirical study, a 5 percent increase in customer retention rate enhances customer LTV by over 50 percent in several U.S. industries.[7]

## HOW CUSTOMER RETENTION WORKS

We just saw that customer retention rate is an important driver of customer LTV. We now show how small differences in customer retention lead, over time, to major differences in sales and market share. Figure 2.2 shows three hypothetical scenarios A, B, and C — each with two firms, Jane's Makeup Emporium and Joe's Beauty Aids, and two time periods, year 1 and year 2. Each scenario shows patterns of customer retention (defection) and customer acquisition. To keep things simple, we assume 1,000 customers in total and that Jane and Joe each start with 500. Our task is to figure out the number of customers that Jane and Joe eventually secure in each scenario, and the steady state market shares.

| | Scenario A<br>Year 2 | | | Scenario B<br>Year 2 | | | Scenario C<br>Year 2 | | | **FIGURE 2.2** |
|---|---|---|---|---|---|---|---|---|---|---|
| | Jane's | Joe's | | Jane's | Joe's | | Jane's | Joe's | | **LONG-RUN MARKET-SHARE SCENARIOS** |
| Jane's (Year 1) | 80% | 20% | Jane's (Year 1) | 90% | 10% | Jane's (Year 1) | 95% | 5% | | |
| Joe's | 20% | 80% | Joe's | 20% | 80% | Joe's | 20% | 80% | | |

**Scenario A.** In year 2, Jane retains 80 percent of her year-1 customers and acquires 20 percent of Joe's customers. Joe's pattern is identical. This scenario is trivial, but provides a useful baseline. Jane and Joe essentially swap equal numbers of customers back and forth. Jane's 80 percent retention yields her 400 customers — 500 x 80% = 400 — and she acquires 100 customers from Joe — 500 x 20% = 100. Jane ends up with 500 customers, the same as she had originally. Joe's situation is identical and each earns 50 percent long-run market share.

**Scenario B.** Jane does better. In year 2, she retains 90 percent of her year-1 customers — versus 80 percent in scenario A — but again, Jane acquires 20 percent of Joe's customers. Joe's retention pattern is identical to Scenario A — 80 percent — but he acquires only 10 percent of Jane's customers. Jane retains 450 of her original 500 customers — 500 x 90% = 450 — and acquires

### *Marketing Question*

Suppose a firm's revenue rate growth goal were 15 percent annually. Consider two situations: customer retention rate = 90 percent and customer retention rate = 95 percent. What would the firm's customer acquisition rate have to be in each case? What would be the implications for the firm?

100 customers from Joe — 500 x 20% = 100. Jane ends up with 550 customers — 450 + 100 = 550; Joe has 450 customers.

In year 3, Jane's starting customer base is higher — 550 versus 500 — so she retains 495 customers — 550 x 90% = 495. Joe's starting base is lower — 450 versus 500 — so Jane only acquires 90 customers — 450 x 20% = 90. But the combination of acquisition and retention increases Jane's customers from 550 to 585 — 495 + 90. Joe's customer base drops from 450 to 415. These numbers converge to a steady state where Jane and Joe have 670 and 330 customers — 67 percent and 33 percent market shares respectively.

**Scenario C.** Jane does even better. In year 2, she retains 95 percent of her year-1 customers and again acquires 20 percent of Joe's customers. Joe's retention pattern is the same as previously — 80 percent — but he acquires only 5 percent of Jane's customers. Using the same process as before, the steady-state customer numbers are 800 for Jane and 200 for Joe — 80 percent and 20 percent market shares respectively. (You may want to confirm this result for yourself.) See Table 2.2.

### TABLE 2.2

**STEADY-STATE MARKET SHARES**[8]

| Jane's Retention Rate | Jane | Joe |
|---|---|---|
| 80% | 50% | 50% |
| 90% | 67% | 33% |
| 95% | 80% | 20% |

To summarize:

- As retention rate increases, steady-state market share increases;
- The higher the retention rate, the greater the impact on market share for a given increase in retention rate. For example:
  - When Jane's retention rate is 80 percent, a 10 percent increase — to 90 percent — increases her market share by 17 points — from 50 percent to 67 percent; but,
  - When Jane's retention rate is 90 percent, a 5 percent increase — to 95 percent — increases her market share by 13 points — from 67 percent to 80 percent.

Of course, it may cost more to improve retention rate from 90 percent to 95 percent than from 80 percent to 90 percent!

This is a very simple exercise but it demonstrates an important truth — customer retention is a big deal! Relatively small differences in customer retention lead to large differences in long-run market shares.

**KEY IDEA**

➤ Small increases in customer retention can dramatically improve profitability and customer lifetime value.

## PROFIT MARGINS AND CUSTOMER RETENTION

Table 2.3 combines the credit card profit margin data from Figure 2.1 with customer retention data, assuming a 10 percent discount rate. We see the combined effect of the increase in profit margin over the length of the customer relationship, based on two different retention rates. Table 2.3 shows that:

- When the retention rate is 90 percent, total annual profit peaks at $53,460 (year 2), then declines annually. Ten-year discounted profits are **$208,824**.
- When the retention rate is 80 percent, annual profit also peaks in year 2, but at a much lower number — $42,240. Ten-year discounted profits are **$94,498**.

The 90 percent to 80 percent retention rate difference causes a **$114,326** ($208,824 – $94,498) difference in customer LTV.

### *Marketing Question*

Suppose a firm can sustain a customer acquisition rate of 15 percent and that its goal is to double its customer base. Consider two situations: customer retention rate = 90 percent and customer retention rate = 95 percent. In each case, when would the firm reach its goal?

| Age of Account | Annual Profit Margin per customer by Age of Account | 90% Retention Rate: Number of Customers Remaining | Total Annual Customer Profit Margin by Age of Account | Total Discounted Annual Customer Profit Margin by Age of Account | 80% Retention Rate: Number of Customers Remaining | Total Annual Customer Profit Margin by Age of Account | Total Discounted Annual Customer Profit Margin by Age of Account |
|---|---|---|---|---|---|---|---|
| 0 | –$80 | 1000 | –$80,000 | –$80,000 | 1000 | –$80,000 | –$80,000 |
| 1 | $40 | 900 | $36,000 | $32,727 | 800 | $32,000 | $29,091 |
| 2 | $66 | 810 | $53,460 | $44,182 | 640 | $42,240 | $34,910 |
| 3 | $72 | 729 | $52,488 | $39,435 | 512 | $36,864 | $27,696 |
| 4 | $79 | 656 | $51,824 | $35,396 | 410 | $32,390 | $22,123 |
| 5 | $87 | 590 | $51,330 | $31,872 | 328 | $28,536 | $17,719 |
| 6 | $92 | 531 | $48,852 | $27,576 | 262 | $24,104 | $13,606 |
| 7 | $96 | 478 | $45,888 | $23,548 | 210 | $20,160 | $10,345 |
| 8 | $99 | 430 | $42,570 | $19,859 | 168 | $16,632 | $ 7,759 |
| 9 | $103 | 387 | $39,861 | $18,595 | 134 | $13,802 | $ 6,439 |
| 10 | $106 | 348 | $36,888 | $15,644 | 107 | $11,342 | $ 4,810 |
| | | | Total LTV | $208,824 | | Total LTV | $94,498 |

**TABLE 2.3**

PROFITS IN THE CREDIT CARD INDUSTRY AT DIFFERENT CUSTOMER RETENTION RATES

*Marketing Question*

What is the source of customer LTV for: Capital One, Domino's Pizza, Potemkin automobile dealership, and Rolls-Royce aero engines?

## ACQUIRING NEW CUSTOMERS

So far, we used customer LTV to focus on the firm's current customers. We showed that increasing both customer margin and customer retention rate increases customer LTV. But what about the firm's potential future customers? How valuable are they? We can use the same approach to consider potential customers. The biggest difference is that, right now, the firm earns no revenue from these potential customers. To attract them, the firm has to incur an **acquisition cost (AC)**; this must be part of our LTV calculation. Using the same approach, we account for the costs to acquire these new customers:

$$\text{LTV} = m \times r/(1 + d - r) - \text{AC}$$

We now have a useful way to think about new customers. All things equal, the firm should acquire a customer if the first term in the LTV expression, $m \times r/(1 + d - r)$, is greater than the acquisition cost (AC). If the acquisition cost were greater, the firm would lose money by acquiring the customer.

KEY IDEA

➤ The firm should try to acquire customers if the expected customer lifetime value is greater than the acquisition cost.

## ENHANCING CUSTOMER LIFETIME VALUE

As discussed earlier, much of this book focuses on enhancing LTV from current customers and acquiring profitable new customers. From Chapter 7 on, we elaborate on the six marketing imperatives that encapsulate approaches for achieving these goals. Here, we identify a broad set of options for addressing current and potential customers.

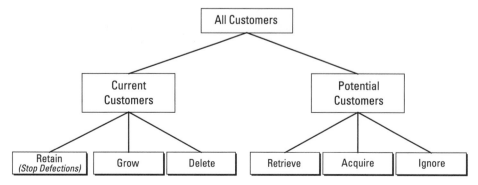

**FIGURE 2.3**

APPROACHES TO IMPROVING CUSTOMER LIFETIME VALUE

The first decision in the broad family of options concerns current customers and potential customers — Figure 2.3. When teaching marketing executives, I frequently ask them to divide their promotional expenses into two buckets: one for retaining current customers, one for attracting new customers. Almost without fail, the predominant focus is attracting new customers. Of course, the firm must attract new customers to grow: The issue is one of balance. Far too often, the firm takes its current customers for granted, spending far too little on customer retention! And retaining current customers is generally less costly than acquiring new customers. We do not suggest that current customers are more important than new customers. After all, new customers may have greater growth potential. But we do believe the firm should make its customer investment decisions deliberately.

## CURRENT CUSTOMERS

Figure 2.3 shows three firm options for current customers — increase retention, grow margins, and delete.

**INCREASE RETENTION.** The firm's customer base is like a leaky bucket; its holes should be plugged. By updating products and services to meet evolving customer needs and by taking other actions to bind customers more closely, the firm enhances customer satisfaction and reduces defections. Satisfied and delighted customers are more likely to continue buying than dissatisfied customers. A Gallup study showed that as Wachovia Bank's customer satisfaction scores improved from 5.5 to 6.5 (on a 1-to-7 scale) over a five-year period, annual customer defection declined from 20 percent to 11 percent. In the insurance and mutual fund industries, firms try to sell extra products to existing single-product customers; increased reliance on the firm's products and services creates **lock-in**. Some firms have implemented early warning systems to detect potential defection:

> OfficeMax has a *defection detector*. Said a senior executive: "We have automatic warning signs that apply to all major customers, and then for each one there are also special warning signs that we enter manually. Has the customer placed an order in the last 12 weeks? Are orders becoming less frequent? Has the buyer or purchasing manager changed? Has the content or size of the average order decreased? Has the sales rep changed? There may be eight warning signs for a customer, and if five of them go off, that's when our CEO gets on the plane and pays a call to see what's going on and make sure we don't lose a valuable account."[9]

Some firms budget **maintenance expenses** for extra services, offering current customers greater value. Maintenance expenses reduce the firm's margin from current customers, but are often more cost-effective than having customers defect. Maintenance expenses are not trivial, but the firm should consider placing extra resources into customer maintenance as a retention strategy.

**GROW MARGINS.** Satisfied customers are less likely to defect and they may also be willing to buy more. The firm may increase customer margins by **cross-selling**. Your cable company provides basic channels for a standard fee, but also offers *higher-value* channels like HBO and special sports events for extra fees. Amazon is a good dotcom example of increasing margins through cross-selling. Initially, Amazon offered books, then CDs, and now offers a vast array of different products, enabling and personalizing one-stop shopping.

**DELETE CUSTOMERS.** Generally, the firm tries to retain and grow current customers so as to increase the margins it earns from them. But some customers are not worth having. Most firms have unprofitable customers and should consider stopping serving them. We address customer deletion in the next section.

## POTENTIAL CUSTOMERS

Potential customers offer an excellent way for the firm to grow and sell more products and services. However, as we learned when we considered customer retention, not all customers are

**KEY IDEA**

➤ There are three approaches to improve LTV with current customers — improve customer retention, grow customer margins, and delete customers.

alike. Returning to Figure 2.3, we discuss three broad options for potential customers: retrieve, acquire, and ignore.

**RETRIEVE CUSTOMERS.** This is a special category because the firm often has more information about former customers than other potential customers. It should know what they purchased, what they spent, how they make decisions, why they left, and other data that can help the firm serve them again. If the firm understands why customers defect, **winbacks** can improve.

**ACQUIRE CUSTOMERS.** Retaining and growing current customers will take the firm only so far in securing growth and enhancing shareholder value. Most firms must also acquire profitable new customers. Sometimes the firm wants to acquire new customers with similar characteristics to its current customers — other times, it wants very different customers. In either case, the firm should be discriminating in only accepting customers who will be profitable and deliver LTV.

**IGNORE CUSTOMERS.** The firm must decide on desirable customer characteristics and make investments in potential customers that will bring value to the firm. By the same token, it should ignore customers that do not possess these favorable characteristics. Bottom line: The firm must be selective in making its new customer investments.

## BEING SELECTIVE ABOUT CUSTOMERS

Most customers bring value to the firm but some do not. In this section, we focus on customer profitability and suitability to be the firm's customer.

### ASSESSING CUSTOMER PROFITABILITY

Most firms understand and measure product profitability: revenues minus costs for an individual product. Indeed, product profit is typically a key metric for product managers. Most firms invest heavily in sophisticated accounting systems and data analysis tools that help managers answer such questions as:

- Are our current products profitable?
- Should we discontinue this old product and, if so, when?
- Should we introduce a new product?

By contrast, few firms can answer equivalent questions about individual customers. This problem is especially critical in multi-business firms, where profitability data typically resides in each business unit, quite separate from the others. The systems in one business unit may not easily interface with the systems in another. There is often no easy way to extract and integrate the relevant sales and profit data for individual customers across the business units.

The firm's inability to measure **customer profitability** is in sharp contrast to our earlier discussion of treating customers as assets and customer LTV. Product profitability is important, but products and their associated services are only a means to attract, retain, and grow customers. To paraphrase an old management saying: "If you can't measure it, you can't manage it!"

Firms use a variety of methods to gather and assess data relevant to customer activity and profitability. When they examine revenues, costs, and profits by customer, they often find an **80:20 rule**: 80 percent of revenues come from 20 percent of customers. Many firms have installed strategic (or key) account management systems to serve their most important customers.

The converse analogue is the **20:80 rule**; 20 percent of revenues come from 80 percent of customers. This rule raises two critical yet related questions:

- What does it cost the firm to serve these customers?
- Is it profitable to serve these customers? If not, what action should the firm take?

*Marketing Question*

Think of a particular local business. What approaches does it use to acquire customers? What alternative approaches could it implement?

KEY IDEA

➤ There are three approaches to improving customer LTV with potential customers — retrieve, acquire, and ignore customers.

KEY IDEA

➤ The firm should develop systems for measuring customer profitability.

Many firms find that the costs are very high and that many of these customers are unprofitable.

Please do not misunderstand. I am not suggesting that only small customers are unprofitable. Large customers may also be unprofitable. When small customers are unprofitable, usually the costs to serve are too high compared to the revenues they generate. Large customers can be an even bigger problem; they may require excessively expensive customization and service support. They may also use their bargaining power to extract very low prices and drive profit margins below sustainable levels. Furthermore, the firm should not make precipitous decisions to dump unprofitable customers. Today's small customers may become tomorrow's large customers! And an unprofitable large customer may carry a significant overhead allocation. If the firm eliminated the customer, it would reassign the overhead allocation and overall profits would drop.[10]

Once the firm understands its customers and their profitability, it can consider strategies for addressing unprofitable customers. However, in general, the more difficult problem is *identifying* the unprofitable customers. This becomes a key initiative for marketing. Figure 2.4 shows how a change in customer classification helped a financial services firm better isolate customer profitability. In particular, *heavy hitters* account for 55 percent of profits and *movers* actually lose money for the firm.

**FIGURE 2.4**

**CUSTOMER CLASSIFICATION BY A U.S. FINANCIAL SERVICES FIRM**

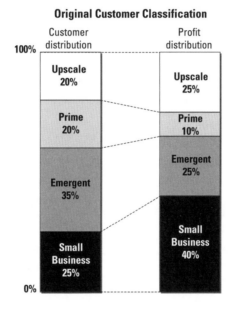

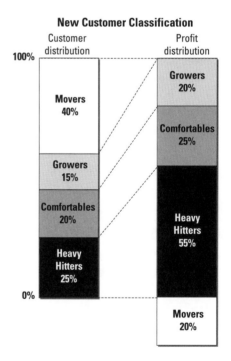

## CUSTOMER SUITABILITY

Unprofitable customers do not deliver value. But the firm might *fire* or cease doing business with a customer for several other reasons:

- **Instability.** Customers may be profitable, but too unstable. People-intensive service businesses like advertising or PR agencies often add employees to serve new customers. If those customers left, the necessary staff reductions could be very difficult.

- **Competition.** The customer is a current or potential competitor who could reverse-engineer the firm's product, then launch a similar product. Hi-tech firms often refuse to sell to competitors; they also stop customers from passing their products to competitors.

- **Non-payer.** This customer would be profitable if it paid, but it doesn't! Or it eventually pays, but the collection costs — money, human resources, aggravation — are too high.

*Marketing Question*

Which companies do you believe affirmatively seek to fire or reject customers? Are they successful in pursuing these activities? What firms inadvertently fire or reject customers?

- **Potential costs.** The future costs of doing business are too high. Selling to the customer might earn short-term profits, but future servicing costs could be prohibitive.

- **Foreclosing options.** The customer prohibits the firm from serving other customers. A P&G advertising agency is unlikely to work for Colgate or Unilever!

- **Impact on the firm's reputation.** A firm/customer relationship hurts the firm. Gucci does not sell products in Kmart! Or the customer may use the firm's product inappropriately.

- **Customization requirements.** Customization is a way to deliver extra value and generate customer loyalty; but the firm should customize only for the *right* customers. It should avoid customers whose value to the firm is less than the costs of customization.

- **Mismatched to the offer.** If the firm's offer is mismatched to customer needs, the customer may be dissatisfied. The firm may take a direct loss and/or suffer harmful word-of-mouth communications. *Boiler-room* practices in the securities industry often generate lawsuits against the firm and its salespeople. In a particularly serious mismatch, EDS (now part of HP) had great difficulty performing on an $8.8 billion computer modernization contract with the U.S. Navy, resulting in significant losses.

- **Impact on the offer.** In many service businesses, fellow customers are integral to the offer. Rowdy sports fans negatively affect the ambiance in expensive restaurants, and college admission departments screen out the *wrong* type of student. Specific customer profiles the firm should seek to avoid include *thieves*, like pickpockets and shoplifters who rob other customers or the firm; *belligerents*, like diners who display insufficient patience in waiting for their meals and verbally abuse waiters; *vandals*, who destroy equipment; and *rule breakers*, like unruly airline passengers who pose a physical danger and affect the service experience for fellow customers. They also raise the firm's costs.[11]

**KEY IDEA**

➤ Poor profitability is not the only reason to reject or fire customers.

---

*Marketing Question*

What economic value do you have to your educational institution? How might the institution enhance your value?

---

## KEY MESSAGES

- Customer lifetime value (LTV) is the critical link between delivering value to customers and creating value for shareholders.

- We can calculate customer LTV from customer margin (m), customer retention rate (r), and the firm's discount rate (d).

- Generally, increasing customer retention rate (r) has greater leverage on customer LTV than decreasing the firm's discount rate (d).

- The firm has three broad options for increasing the LTV of current customers — increase customer retention (decrease defection), grow customer margins, and delete customers.

- The firm has three broad options for earning LTV from potential customers — retrieve former customers, acquire new customers, and ignore unwelcome customers.

- The firm should strive to understand the reasons for customer retention and defection and act accordingly.

- Some portion of the firm's current customers is probably unprofitable — but a fraction of these customers may present future opportunities.

- In addition to poor profitability, there are several reasons to forgo a customer relationship.

- The firm's customer strategy should embrace retention, expansion, and acquisition.

- The firm should consider following the prescription from Charles Cawley, founder of credit card giant MBNA: **"Success is getting the right customers … and keeping them."**

# SECTION II FUNDAMENTAL INSIGHTS FOR STRATEGIC MARKETING

IN CHAPTER 1, WE INTRODUCED TWO CONCEPTS OF MARKETING that form the basis of this book — marketing as a **philosophy** and marketing as **six imperatives** — the *must-do* activities the firm must perform in marketing. Chapter 1 also showed the relationship between customer value and shareholder value. Chapter 2 focused on the value of customers to the firm and discussed various ways to maximize that value.

In this second section of the book — Chapter 3 through Chapter 6 — we focus on the data, knowledge, and insights the firm must secure to make effective marketing decisions. Data are facts about a particular topic, like a customer's demographic characteristics, and purchasing data. Knowledge is the meaning the firm gains from combining data, like in a customer profile. Insight results from further knowledge combinations that provide ideas for action, like linking a customer profile to an R&D project. The firm needs data and knowledge, but should also strive for insight.

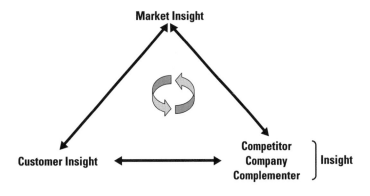

**INSIGHTS FOR STRATEGIC MARKETING**

To build a strong foundation, the firm must secure insight in several core areas — the market, customers, competitors, the company, and complementers — we call these the M4Cs.

- **Market.** Good market insight helps the firm decide what parts of the market to address. It must understand market demand, today's participants and the pressures they face, and how each may evolve over time.

- **Customers.** Customers have needs that the firm tries to satisfy through its market offers. The firm must have insight into these needs and into the processes customers use to make purchase decisions.

- **Competitors, company, and complementers.** Both the firm and its competitors seek to attract, retain, and grow similar customers. As it secures *competitive* insight, the firm also learns about its own *company* capabilities and how it can win in the market. We also discuss the firm's *complementers* — organizations that can help the firm achieve its objectives.

In the first chapter of this section, Chapter 3, we focus on market insight.

**KEY IDEA**

➤ The firm must secure insight in three broad areas: the market; customers; and competitors, the company, and complementers – the M4Cs.

# CHAPTER 3
# MARKET INSIGHT

## LEARNING OBJECTIVES

When you have completed this chapter, you will be able to:

- Analyze and understand market structure.
- Comprehend alternative ways of thinking about the products that firms offer to the market; in particular, distinguish among product class, product form, product line, and product item.
- Forecast the evolution of markets and products using a life-cycle framework.
- Summarize the industry forces that exert pressure on the firm.
- Recognize major environmental forces affecting the firm and the industry.

## OPENING CASE: NETFLIX

*In the past quarter-century, watching videos at home, typically on TV, has become a major socio-cultural trend. Sony introduced Betamax technology in the mid-1970s, but by the mid-1980s the market had turned sharply to VHS. (We describe the competition between Betamax and VHS later in the book.) Videotape recorders/players allowed consumers to record and play back TV programs and also play movies and other material they secured from retailers. Initially, many consumers rented videocassettes from local video stores but, in the 1990s, Blockbuster became the dominant national chain for cassette rentals, in part because its stores carried larger numbers of titles. Many small stores went out of business.*

*In the 1990s, in a further technological innovation, DVDs began to replace VHS tapes. To capitalize on this technological change and the growth of the Internet, California entrepreneur Reed Hastings founded Netflix, an online DVD-rental service, www.netflix.com.*

*Netflix subscribers log on to its website and create a list of movies they want to rent, selecting from 65,000 movies, TV programs, and other video material. Subscribers choose among several subscription plans that vary by numbers of movies rented per month. DVDs arrive by U.S. Mail in a distinctive red envelope. When a subscriber returns a movie in a prepaid envelope, Netflix sends another. There are no due dates, no late fees, and no shipping fees. Subscribers may rate each title, thus providing information and recommendations to others making their own rental decisions. Subscribers can even request movies that are not yet released on video. These choices simply go into the subscriber's list; Netflix sends them out when they become available. On any given day, 35,000 Netflix titles are in distribution: just 30 percent are new releases, versus 70 percent at Blockbuster.*

*To make its service work, Netflix has 55 warehouses in major metropolitan areas. Employees pick up envelopes containing returned DVDs from the post office early in the morning and take them to the warehouse, where they are opened and the DVDs sorted. By mid-afternoon, employees take envelopes filled with ordered DVDs back to the post office. Subscribers living within 50 miles of a warehouse typically receive delivery in one business day. By end 2008 Netflix had 9.4 million subscribers, up from 1.5 million in 2003. Netflix ships on average 1.4 million DVDs daily and has partnered with Wal-Mart to improve Wal-Mart's online video business. Netflix's 2008 revenues were $1.36 billion for net profits of $83 million.*

*Netflix faces competition from bricks-and-mortar video stores, notably Blockbuster. Blockbuster also offers online rentals, along with other new entrants, but Netflix's volume is well over three times their combined total. Netflix's user-friendly website allows subscribers to search by actor, critic and customer recommendation, decade, director, genre, new releases, studio, and title! Despite Netflix's success, concerns about video-on-demand technology have depressed its stock price. Netflix's Internet and U.S. Mail-based service is very convenient, but downloading movies may be even more so. To address this threat, Netflix acquires independent movies and is building its own download site.*

**CASE QUESTION**

What environmental changes enabled Netflix to successfully innovate in the home video market? How concerned should Netflix be about the emerging video-on-demand technology?

---

In 1994, Marc Andreessen and Jim Clark founded Netscape — the first commercial browser for the World Wide Web. They marketed Netscape as a purpose-specific tool for accessing the Web. Unfortunately for Netscape, Microsoft defined the market differently — as an integral part of the computer experience. Microsoft made web browsing a feature of its operating system, rather than a standalone tool. With superior technical and marketing resources, Microsoft quickly secured the leading position in browsers and relegated Netscape to second-tier status.

*Marketing Question*

What market information could have helped Netscape anticipate and address Microsoft's actions?

Defining the market is a tricky matter. If the firm defines the market too narrowly, it risks being blindsided by competitors, as was Netscape's experience. If the firm defines the market too broadly, it will not allocate its resources effectively to the *right* segments. The firm must also understand the market's evolutionary patterns and the forces that drive this process. Because most forces are external in nature, the firm that embraces an external orientation, with customers and competitors in mind, generally understands its markets better than firms with internal orientations.

Figure 3.1 shows the four aspects of **market insight** we cover in this chapter, each as important as the others. Each aspect provides a different window on the market. Together they help the firm anticipate market change and identify new opportunities:

- **Market structure.** We define the market. We show that effective market partitioning helps the firm identify opportunities and gain competitive advantage. We show how different product classes and product forms serve customer needs, and we explore factors affecting market size.

- **Market and product evolution.** Markets evolve over time. Sometimes evolutionary patterns are predictable, like the market for geriatric healthcare — easily knowable from age-distribution demographics. Other markets are unpredictable, like demand for home-rebuilding products in hurricane-prone areas. Products also evolve over time as customers' needs become more refined and competitors compete to serve them. Technological evolution can also drive market evolution. We use a life-cycle framework to show how markets and products evolve.

**KEY IDEA**

➤ Market insight comprises four separate aspects — market structure, market and product evolution, industry forces, and environmental forces.

- **Industry forces.** Industry forces include various competitive and supply-chain pressures. The *five-forces* we identify impinge directly on the firm.
- **Environmental forces.** These broad-scale environmental forces impact both the firm and other industry participants. We use the PESTLE framework — political, economic, socio-cultural, technological, legal/regulatory, and environmental (physical).

**FIGURE 3.1**

**CRITICAL BUILDING BLOCKS FOR SECURING MARKET INSIGHT**

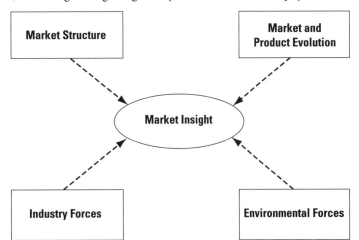

The firm must keep two things squarely in mind when it seeks insight in these four aspects:

- **State of nature.** The firm must understand the current market. For example: What competitors does the firm face today? How many baby boomers are in its target market?
- **Trends.** The firm must also identify trends. For example: What additional direct competitors will it face in two years' time? How will demographic changes affect the market?

Good market insight can put the firm ahead and provide significant competitive advantage. Post-September 11, 2001, Alcoa predicted significant demand for secure cockpit doors on passenger aircraft and won a commanding share of the retrofit market.

## MARKET STRUCTURE

We use three separate concepts to describe **market structure**: the market, products or services serving the market, and the firm's own products. We also discuss factors affecting market size.

### THE MARKET

**Markets** consist of customers — people and organizations — who require products and services to satisfy their needs. Basic customer needs such as food, clothing, and shelter are enduring; many offerings satisfy these needs. Other needs, like entertainment, are more transitory. Of course, to be in the market, customers must also possess sufficient purchasing power — and interest — to buy what suppliers are offering.

The concept of the *market* is slippery because we can identify it at different levels. The transportation market is the basic need to move people and things from point A to point B. In turn, the transportation market comprises several more narrowly defined markets: ground, air, and water transportation. Even more narrowly, we can define the automobile market and, more narrowly still, the market for particular types of automobiles such as sports cars and hybrids.

In defining a market, it's best to start broad, and then focus in as necessary. A broad approach ensures against **marketing myopia**,[1] the risk of defining a market too narrowly at the onset because of biases or insufficient data. Defining the market broadly provides greater scope in the firm's search for opportunities.[2]

**KEY IDEA**

➤ When firms secure good market insight, they do a better job of identifying opportunities and gaining competitive advantage.

*Marketing Question*

Select a product and industry with which you are familiar. Define the market at different levels. How much more broadly could you go and still maintain a focus?

**KEY IDEA**

➤ Markets consist of people and organizations that require goods and services to satisfy their needs and are able and willing to pay.

## PRODUCTS SERVING THE MARKET

Both the firm and its competitors provide products and services to the market. A useful categorization of product offerings is **product class**, **product form**, **product line**, and **product item**.[3] These distinctions help the firm identify opportunities and/or emerging competitors. A good example is P&G's early-2000s entry into the teeth-whitening market with Whitestrips. Consumer options included toothpaste, bleaches, gels, and professional dental procedures. Because P&G focused on customer needs for convenience, ease of use, safety, and economy, the firm quickly drove sales to $50 million annually with a new product form, in a seemingly mature market. (Note that we use the term *product* for anything a firm offers for sale, both physical products and services.)

- **Product class.** In any *market*, several *product classes* serve customer needs. For example, the product classes theater, live music, television, home video and DVDs, and theatrical movies each serve consumers' entertainment needs. Every product class provides distinct customer benefits. Several firms typically offer products in each product class.

- **Product form.** Several *product forms* comprise each *product class*. Comedy, science fiction, romance, action/adventure, and horror are each product forms in the theatrical movies product class. In general, products in a product form are more similar to each other than to products in other product forms; for example, comedy and science-fiction movies versus live theater. Hence, competition is typically more intense among product forms than among product classes. In each product form, several firms typically offer products.

Product classes and product forms provide a useful framework for thinking about markets, but things are not always straightforward. Competitive changes and technological evolution often blur the boundaries between product classes and product forms. In the entertainment space, Netflix changed movie-rental dynamics by introducing online ordering and home delivery. Several years ago, a consumer would have purchased cash management, life insurance, property and casualty insurance, and investments from different suppliers. Deregulation has led to a single *financial services* market, offering many consumers *one-stop* shopping. Similarly, engineering plastics now compete with metal in many applications. Previously, your automobile's oil pan and fuel tank were made of metal. Now, they are probably made of plastic.

## THE FIRM'S PRODUCTS

Product classes and product forms embrace products from all competitors. One firm may offer products in multiple product classes; another may specialize in just one or two product forms. IBM offers products and services in most, but not all, product forms in the information systems product class; Gateway offers only PCs. For an individual firm, we speak of a product line and a product item.

- **Product line.** A group of related products that a single firm offers.
- **Product item.** A subset of the product line. A product item is uniquely identified, like having a specific size and color.[4]

## FACTORS AFFECTING MARKET SIZE

Current and potential market sizes are important data for evaluating the firm's opportunities. The firm should know the number of current customers and potential customers and their purchasing power. It should approach these judgments by considering population size, population mix, geographic population shifts, income and income distribution, and age distribution.[5]

**POPULATION SIZE.** Today's world population is approaching 7 billion. Increasing by 200,000 people per day, by 2030, it will reach 8.2 billion. Population is unevenly distributed across

### KEY IDEA

➤ We can view any market as being made up of several different areas.

➤ The firm avoids marketing myopia by using a broad market definition.

### *Marketing Question*

Suppose you had been a senior marketing executive at Kodak in 1996; how would you have defined Kodak's market? How would you have changed this definition in 2009?

### KEY IDEA

➤ A useful way of categorizing products in a market is product class, product form, product line, and product item.

nations — from highs of 1.3 billion in China and 1.1 billion in India to lows of 12,000 in Tuvalu and 13,000 in Nauru.

Population growth rates differ markedly across countries. In many developed nations, annual growth rates are less than 1 percent, and some will likely turn negative in the next 15 years — these rates cannot sustain the population. Important drivers are social norms promoting education, work opportunities for women, and greater access to birth control. Conversely, in many less-developed countries, particularly in Latin America, population growth is well over 2 percent. Population control programs are successful in some countries, such as Bangladesh, and China has enforced a one-child policy. In some African countries, birth rates are high, but AIDS is taking a heavy toll.

**POPULATION MIX.** In many developed countries, immigration drives population-mix changes. Of the world's 175 million immigrants (foreign-born residents), the U.S. leads with 35 million. Other countries with large immigrant populations are Russia (13 million); Germany and Ukraine (each with 7 million); France, India, and Canada (each with 6 million); and Saudi Arabia (5 million). Most labor migration, legal and illegal, is from less-developed countries to more-developed countries. Frequently, provider and receiver countries are geographically close. Good examples are Mexico and the U.S., and Turkey and Germany. Reduced barriers in the European Union (EU) increase population shifts. And the long-standing pattern of Asian workers in mid-east countries continues apace.[6]

> Goya Foods, the largest Hispanic family-owned U.S. food firm (fourth-largest Hispanic firm overall), has sales over $800 million. In many grocery stores, Goya has its own shop within a shop. Goya offers a broad range of imported products including Spanish olive oil, seasonings like Mexican chiles, and Caribbean fruit juices.

*Marketing Question*

What industries and businesses are affected by population shifts?

**GEOGRAPHIC POPULATION SHIFTS.** Generally, as national income grows, people leave rural areas for urban areas. Then urban areas become overcrowded — São Paulo and Mexico City are good examples. In developed countries, a more recent trend is *exurban* growth — a return to rural communities. People's desires for less crowding, a slower life pace, and advances in information technology are enabling this trend. In contrast, some affluent empty-nester baby boomers are returning to regenerate city centers. Population shifts often follow the sun. In the U.S., the Northeast is losing population to the Southeast and Southwest. From 1990 to 2000, the U.S. population grew by 13.2 percent, but several states grew much faster — Nevada (66 percent), Arizona (40 percent), Colorado (31 percent), Utah (30 percent), Idaho (29 percent), and Georgia (26 percent).

**INCOME AND INCOME DISTRIBUTION.** For many years, the U.S. was the world's richest country in per capita income, but Switzerland, Japan, and Norway now surpass the U.S. Several countries are close behind but most are far less wealthy. In many poor countries, a small number of elites enjoy most of the national wealth.

Population, income, and income distribution influence the size of many markets. Economic development and demographic changes are shifting opportunities from traditional markets to emerging markets. Firms like ExxonMobil, Ciba Specialty Chemicals, and P&G continue to develop their global organizations to tap this potential.

**KEY IDEA**

➤ Critical variables affecting market size include population size, population mix, geographic population shifts, income and income distribution, and age distribution.

**AGE DISTRIBUTION.** Table 3.1 shows increasing median ages in both developed and developing countries. The major drivers are decreasing birth rates and family size and increasing life expectancy. These shifts have enormous implications for consumer marketers. In developed countries, retirement-age consumers are more active, have greater discretionary income, and are more sophisticated buyers — cruises and assisted-living facilities are growth markets. By contrast, countries with median ages in the mid-20s — like Mexico, Brazil, and Indonesia — offer opportunities for Coke, Pepsi, McDonald's, Kentucky Fried Chicken, and other marketers whose products appeal to a younger demographic.

| Country | Median age, 2000 | Projected Median Age, 2040 |
|---------|------------------|----------------------------|
| Australia | 35.2 | 43.3 |
| Japan | 41.3 | 54.2 |
| Spain | 37.4 | 52.3 |
| U.S. | 35.2 | 39.0 |
| Brazil | 25.4 | 38.8 |
| Indonesia | 24.6 | 37.4 |
| Mexico | 22.9 | 38.7 |
| Niger | 15.1 | 17.8 |

**TABLE 3.1**

**MEDIAN AGES IN SELECTED COUNTRIES**[7]

*Marketing Question*

How could an analysis of population, income, and income distribution help Pepsi-Cola defeat Coca-Cola in developing countries?

Other important market-size drivers include marriage, marrying age, divorce and remarriage, family size, births (in and out of wedlock), infant and adult mortality, and work force composition. These variables often help the firm make good market-size predictions. For example, birth rates and infant mortality influence demand for products like diapers and car seats.

## MARKET AND PRODUCT EVOLUTION

*Life cycles* are the most common means for describing the evolution of markets and products, product classes, product forms, product lines, and product items. Figure 3.2 shows a classic S-shaped curve depicting the sales trajectory. A good understanding of life-cycle phenomena helps the firm predict future market conditions and develop robust strategies. Typically, we partition life cycles into five phases or stages: introduction, early growth, late growth, maturity, and decline.

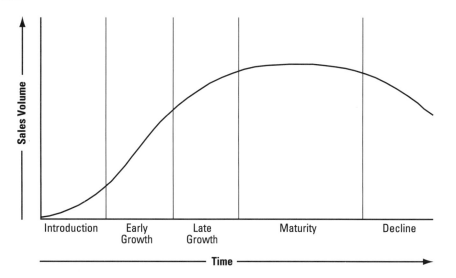

**FIGURE 3.2**

**THE CLASSIC LIFE CYCLE**

## THE FAMILY OF LIFE CYCLES

The several life cycles we discuss fall into a simple hierarchy based on longevity and demand. *Market life cycles* last the longest — in general, the firm has little impact on market life cycles. *Product-class* and *product-form* life cycles are each shorter than the market life cycle — understanding these two life cycles is helpful in developing market strategy.

**Product-line and product-item** life cycles are critical for product and brand managers as they provide important performance data. The firm's actions impact them greatly; they are shorter than other life cycles and come in many different shapes. But because they provide little insight into competitor activity, they are not very helpful for drawing strategic implications.

## PRODUCT-FORM LIFE CYCLES

The firm gains the greatest insight into market and product evolution by examining product forms. Although product classes compete with one another, competition both within and across product forms is typically more intense. For example, the various brands of laptop PCs compete fiercely with one another; but they also compete with desktop PCs. Although actual life-cycle curves often depart from the idealized shape in Figure 3.2, across product forms, life-cycle stages follow one from another in a remarkably consistent fashion. Hence, product-form life cycles can provide important strategic insights.

As Figure 3.2 shows, we typically categorize product-form life cycles into five stages:

- **Introduction.** Sales volume is initially low.
- **Early growth.** Sales volume grows at an increasing rate.
- **Late growth.** Sales volume grows, but at a decreasing rate.
- **Maturity.** Sales volume grows at about the same rate as GNP.
- **Decline.** Sales volume eventually declines.

**STAGE 1: INTRODUCTION.** Product introduction frequently follows many years of R&D and reflects the first market entry/or entries by leading firms. Honda launched the first gasoline/electric hybrid car in 1999, but modern-day research started in the mid-1970s! Uncertainty characterizes introduction. The firm explores such questions as: Will the product perform adequately? What is the best technology? What segments should we target? What is the optimal market strategy? Will customer demand be sufficient? What specific benefits do customers require? Which competitors will enter? When? What resources will be necessary? What are our chances of success? Products currently in introduction include implantable ID chips for humans and pets and RFID (radio frequency identification) chips for identifying products.

In the introduction stage, suppliers struggle to build profitable volume. Typically, the firm offers a single product design and prices may not cover total costs. Managers expect that unit costs will fall as sales increase over time and ultimately the firm will earn profits. Introduction requires significant educational effort. Firms use advertising and/or personal selling to show customers and distributors the product's value. But production problems, product failures, and/or an inability to expand capacity may cause delays.[8] Sometimes the first product version has low quality and performs poorly, yet it may possess the seeds of an important breakthrough. The Palm Pilot, BlackBerry, and other hand-held electronic devices are now widely popular, but their success built in part on the Apple Newton, the failed pioneer, launched in 1993, withdrawn in 1998. The introduction stage may last many years, but fierce competition, global demand for innovation, and customers' willingness to try new products are shortening this stage.

**STAGE 2: EARLY GROWTH.** Many products do not reach early growth, but the survivors' sales revenues grow at an increasing rate. Hybrid cars and cellular phones with built-in cameras are now in early growth — digital cameras are moving from early growth into late growth. Increasing sales revenues and high profit margins attract other suppliers. They often bring capacity, resources, and a loyal customer base that fuel market growth. As competitors struggle for market position, new distribution channels open up, and promotional effort remains high. Previously, advertising and promotion emphasized generating primary demand, like *use a cell phone*. Now the focus shifts to differentiation and selective demand based on features, functionality, and customer perceptions, like *use the new LG cell phone*. Firms secure production and marketing efficiencies, and price becomes a competitive weapon. In early growth, many firms increase sales volume and work at managing costs. One caution: While the firm's sales can increase, market share will decrease if competitors are growing faster!

**STAGE 3: LATE GROWTH.** By late growth, the uncertainties that dominated introduction are largely resolved. Sales continue to increase, but the growth rate slows. Strong competitors initiate tough actions to maintain their growth rates — they force weaker entrants to withdraw.

Laptop computers and personal digital assistants (PDAs) are now in late growth. Customers' experiences with the product lead to more specific customer needs and market segmentation opportunities. Firms differentiate their products by introducing and promoting design and packaging variations. The distribution infrastructure is usually well developed, but outlets are more selective about brands and product items. Price is a major competitive weapon, squeezing distributor margins. Purchase terms like credit, warranties, and service become more favorable to customers.

**STAGE 4: MATURITY.** Slow-growth or flat year-to-year sales characterize maturity. Most sales are to repeat and loyal users. Examples include most everyday products like detergents and kitchen appliances. Competitive situations vary widely so that the firm must secure deep market insight. We consider concentrated markets and fragmented markets:

- **Concentrated markets.** Economists use the term *oligopoly* to describe concentrated markets. The few major suppliers that together make most sales often coexist with some niche players. In concentrated markets, leading firms often enjoy entry barriers like economies of scale, brand preference, and/or distribution-channel dominance. Market positions that firms achieve by early maturity often survive for many years. Examples include IBM in mainframe computers, GE in steam turbine generators, and Gillette in shaving products.

  Many firms pursue product differentiation approaches, but competitors that quickly offer *me-too* products can cause problems. Increasingly, firms focus on value-added services, packaging, distribution, and branding and promotion. They streamline operations and distribution to reduce costs, and pricing is often competitive. Leaders get in trouble when they fail to innovate new products and processes and do not reduce costs.

- **Fragmented markets.** In fragmented markets, no supplier has a large market share. Fragmentation generally occurs because of some combination of low entry barriers, high exit barriers, regulation, diverse market needs, and high transportation costs. Examples include personal services like dentistry, education, and home plumbing and electrical contracting.

**STAGE 5: DECLINE.** Maturity may last many years, but eventually sales turn down. Products in decline include carbon paper, chemical-film cameras, and videotapes. Sometimes decline is slow — payphones; but it may also be precipitous — vinyl records. When decline is swift, overcapacity often leads to fierce price competition. Managing costs is a high priority — firms prune product lines and reduce inventory and marketing expenses. Strong firms may increase sales as weaker competitors exit. Firms often raise prices to cover costs as sales drop, but sales decline further, in a vicious cycle. Marketing efforts should target remaining customers. Firms with good cost management and a core of loyal price-insensitive buyers can be quite profitable.

Sometimes products in decline enjoy resurgence. In the 1990s, creative marketing led to growth in cigar smoking in the U.S. Improved technology has made yo-yo tricks easier; the product is now more attractive to young consumers and sales have increased.

The product-form life cycle is a useful framework, but two points are important:

- **Life-cycle shape.** A product's specific sales trajectory depends on several factors including underlying customer demand, product quality and consistency, and the overall commitment of resources by participating suppliers. In general, life cycles are shortening.[9]

- **Profit curves.** Profit curves do not mirror sales curves. On average, profit margins are greatest in early growth — they drop in late growth and maturity. Do not confuse profit margin with gross profit. Gross profit may be greater later in the cycle — lower profit margins, but higher volume.

**KEY IDEA**

➤ Markets and products generally evolve in a consistent manner over time.

➤ The life-cycle framework is useful for describing market and product evolution.

**KEY IDEA**

➤ Product-form life-cycle stages have consistent characteristics across products and services.

*Marketing Question*

Think about the firm and product you selected earlier (page 31). What factors help determine market size — population, income distribution, and/or age distribution? What other factors will help determine market size in three to five years?

## INDUSTRY FORCES

Figure 3.3 shows the **five-forces model** used by marketing professionals to identify the several industry forces that firms face: current direct competitors, new direct entrants, indirect competitors, suppliers, and buyers.[10] Some forces affect the firm, but others may impact the entire industry, like fuel prices for airlines. Strong industry forces may produce many unprofitable or marginally profitable players, as in the airline and worldwide paper industries. The firm must develop a good understanding of these forces and their implications.

**FIGURE 3.3**

INDUSTRY FORCES — THE FIVE-FORCES MODEL

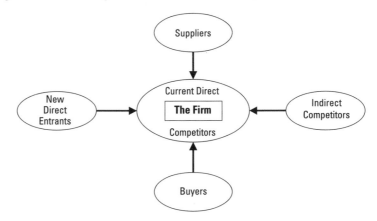

## CURRENT DIRECT COMPETITORS

A firm's **current direct competitors** offer customers similar benefits with similar products, technology, and/or business models. Current direct competitors are the competitive *status quo*, the traditional rivalry between established players. In the automobile industry, GM, Toyota, and Ford have been direct rivals for several decades; U.S. domestic banking rivals include Bank of America, Citicorp, and JPMorgan Chase; Sony, Matsushita, and Philips compete in consumer electronics; and Boeing and Airbus in large aircraft. Typically, managers in rival firms know their traditional competitors well. They observe their actions and performance, their successes and failures. They have good insight into competitors' strengths and weaknesses and likely strategic moves. And they may have worked for them! The marketing question shows an interesting challenge for Sprint concerning a direct competitor.

Current direct competitors may be traditional, or created through acquisitions and divestitures, mergers, and leveraged buyouts — continually changing the firm's landscape.

- **Traditional direct competitors** fight according to *established rules of the game*. In mature markets, one firm rarely gains advantage quickly; rather, an improved position typically results from long-run sustained effort. Establishing competitive advantage is difficult, and sometimes firms *cross the line* by working with competitors. In 1999, Hoffman-La Roche and BASF paid $725 million to settle U.S. Justice Department charges of collusion in maintaining high global prices for vitamins.

    Globalization and industry concentration affect direct competition in many markets. Consolidation leads to global oligopoly, where a few firms mostly share the market. In large aircraft, only Boeing and Airbus remain. In passenger tires, Bridgestone, Goodyear, and Michelin together enjoy over 70 percent market share.

- **Acquisitions and divestitures.** Suppose one of your competitors or an outside firm acquires a second competitor — an independent firm or a divestiture. Regardless, your competitor has changed. Its objectives, strategy, action programs, and available resources will most likely all be different.

- **Mergers.** In a merger, two entities combine as *equal* partners to create a stronger firm. By pooling strengths and mitigating weaknesses; the new entity is often a tougher competitor

*Marketing Question*

Suppose you were advising SABMiller, owner of the Miller beer brand. How would you react to InBev's acquisition of Anheuser-Busch?

with capabilities that outstrip either former firm. Mergers between Chase Manhattan and J.P. Morgan, then between JP Morgan Chase and Bank One, created JPMorgan Chase — a much tougher competitor for Citicorp and Bank of America. Of course, a merger may not succeed; many observers criticized Sears' merger with Kmart.

- **Leveraged buyouts (LBOs).** Sometimes firms rationalize their portfolios and *spin off* business units; typically, LBOs incur heavy debt as the price for independence. Lacking corporate resources, the now-independent unit may struggle. But it may also focus on debt reduction and become a more nimble and tough competitor. Firestone spun off its Accuride division — rims and wheels for truck manufacturers. Freed from Firestone's budget constraints, neglect, and low status, Accuride pre-emptively added production capacity, lowered prices, and offered better terms. In less than two years, Accuride doubled market share and increased profits 66 percent.[11]

**KEY IDEA**

➤ The firm's current direct competitors can change via acquisition, merger, and LBOs.

## NEW DIRECT ENTRANTS

**New direct entrants'** products and services are similar to the firm's — but previously they were not competitors. In the 1970s and 1980s, Nintendo and Sega dominated electronic games; Sony's PlayStation and Microsoft's Xbox were new direct entrants. Entry barriers significantly affect market entry by new firms but they may emerge from many sources:

**KEY IDEA**

➤ The firm faces many forces — current direct competitors, new direct entrants, indirect competitors, suppliers, and buyers — that can frustrate its ability to make profits and seize new opportunities.

- **Geographic expansion.** New direct entrants are often profitable, well-capitalized firms from a different geography. They have solid strengths and cost advantages but may lack market knowledge and customer relationships. They may use superior cost positions to support low price strategies and aggressively seek market share. Many Asian firms entered U.S. and European markets to devastating effect: Fuji in film and cameras; Sony, Panasonic, and Samsung in consumer electronics; Canon in high-speed copying; Toyota and Nissan in automobiles; and Samsung and LG in cell phones.

- **Start-Up entries.** A startup is unencumbered by the *status quo*; flexibility can make it a potent competitor. By contrast, the firm may have old facilities, technology, and processes, and/or an established organization and personnel set in their ways. Recent successful airline startups include Jet Blue in the U.S. and easyJet and Ryanair in Europe.

- **New sales and distribution channels.** Firms that develop new distribution channels can pose significant challenges to traditional players. Direct marketers L.L. Bean and Lands' End are tough competitors for department stores. Amazon competes with traditional distribution via the Internet. And pyramid sales forces like Amway in consumer goods and Primerica in life insurance are tough competitors.[12] Strong firms that add channels also heighten competition. Avon is more competitive with cosmetics firms by having added department store distribution to its traditional door-to-door Avon Ladies.

- **Strategic alliances.** Sometimes firms will not assume the risks and costs of new market entry. They may lack critical assets like capital, skills, technology, or market access. When two firms pool resources, the **strategic alliance** may be stronger than either firm separately. Many U.S. and European firms enter Asian markets with local partners. Of course, partnerships often fail — the partners' objectives may diverge, and/or a partner may not provide agreed-upon resources.

- **Networks.** A network is a group of firms and/or individuals that collaborate using their combined talents and resources. Networks are very flexible and change composition as requirements evolve.[13] *Capon's Marketing Framework* competes with traditional textbooks, but a network made it possible. Critical components were the author; reviewers; developmental, copy, and permissions editors; book, cover, and website designers; test-bank, caselet, and instructors' manual developers; video technicians; credit card processors; and for the printed version, a prepublication service provider, printer, fulfillment house, wholesaler, bricks and mortar and Internet retailers, and package delivery services.

*Marketing Question*

In the late 1990s and early 2000s, AT&T, MCI/Worldcom and Sprint PCS competed head to head in the U.S. cell phone industry. Then AT&T divested its network. When AT&T wanted to re-enter the cellular business, it needed a new network. AT&T wanted to lease space on its direct competitors' networks. As a Sprint marketing manager, how would you have reacted? AT&T was a long-time direct competitor. If you leased space, AT&T would have equivalent technology, but the leasing revenue would be substantial.

- **Firm employees.** In some industries, the firm's employees pose a significant competitive threat. If they have new business ideas or develop technologies the firm will not fund, they may leave to pursue them. Several former Fairchild Semiconductor employees founded Intel. Potential competition from employees is greatest when the firm's major asset is intellectual capital as in financial services, advertising, and consulting. In 1998, Credit Suisse First Boston hired Deutsche Bank's entire 132-person technology group. When *the firm's major assets arrive at 9 a.m. and leave at 5 p.m.*, retaining them is crucial.

## INDIRECT COMPETITORS

**Indirect competitors** offer customers similar *benefits* to the firm's, but *provide them in a significantly different way.* These *functional substitutes* often appear as different product forms or product classes. Xerox machines convey information — they compete with computers, fax machines, video conferencing, and the Internet. More broadly, cruise lines compete with automobile and clothing manufacturers — each seeks consumers' discretionary income. Movie theaters compete with cable TV, online and retail rental businesses, restaurants, sporting events, and other forms of entertainment.

Indirect competitors often attack from different industry sectors; incumbents sometimes ignore them. International Paper's (IP) market share in paper cups increased, but sales declined as plastic replaced paper. Sometimes regulations prohibit responding to indirect competitors. For years, U.S. commercial banks could not offer money-market and mutual funds to compete with Fidelity and Vanguard. Changes in the law removed this restriction.

## SUPPLIERS

Suppliers provide the firm's inputs. When the supplier is very important to the firm — like providing a critical product, a large percentage of its purchases, and/or a very attractive brand for the firm's customers — the potential for pressure increases. PC buyers value the Intel brand, and PC manufacturers feel pressure from Intel. Supplier pressure may lead to higher prices, but also to poor service, and/or poor delivery. Pressure is strongest when the supplier is a monopoly, like local telephone firms, government services, and railroads.

Of course, a supplier's most important job is to supply! Failure to honor its commitments can play havoc with the firm's operations. In the early 2000s, Nissan cut its steel supplier base from five to two — Nippon Steel and JFE. In December 2004, when they could not meet its needs, Nissan closed its plants and slashed automobile output by tens of thousands.

The most severe supplier threat is **forward integration** — the supplier becomes a direct competitor by conducting operations the firm currently performs.[14] Firms in less-developed countries are becoming outsourced manufacturers for U.S. and European firms; but they are also developing the skills for future forward integration. Indian diamond jewelry makers now sell branded products and compete with their former customers. Some firms work hard to inhibit such forward integration: One relabeled and repainted its suppliers' components to disguise their origin; another designed its products to be incompatible with its component suppliers.[15]

## BUYERS

Buyers purchase the firm's products. A firm with many small customers faces little buyer pressure, but a small number of large customers can exert tremendous pressure. Buyer pressure typically increases as its market share increases. The firm's margins can shrink when powerful customers demand price discounts and expensive extra services. De Beers sets the buying price for diamonds; suppliers can take it or leave it! Wal-Mart demands, and receives, many supplier concessions, and leading automobile firms secure large concessions from parts suppliers.

The most severe threat from buyers is **backward integration** — the buyer becomes a direct competitor by conducting operations the firm currently performs. Competition from backward-integrating buyers is especially difficult as they often enjoy better relationships with end customers. The fertilizer example illustrates the supplier's dilemma.

> A fertilizer distributor purchased bags of fertilizer from the manufacturer and resold them to farmers. The distributor believed it could increase profits by buying fertilizer in bulk and doing the bagging itself. It planned to erect a small bagging plant in its parking lot. The distributor asked the manufacturer to supply fertilizer in bulk rather than in bags. The supplier was unwilling to give up its margin on bagging and refused to supply. The distributor secured bulk fertilizer elsewhere and entered the bagging business anyway.

## ENVIRONMENTAL FORCES[16]

Environmental forces affect the firm and other industry participants. Figure 3.4 shows how these **PESTLE** forces — *political, economic, sociocultural, technological, legal/regulatory* and *environmental (physical)* — and industry forces relate to one another. Some PESTLE forces affect individual business units. Other PESTLE forces like the World Trade Organization (WTO) (political), exchange rate movements (economic), and the Internet (technological) impact the firm as a whole.

Forward-thinking firms seek out leading indicators of environmental trends, like the many firms developing *green* products that appeal to environmentally-concerned customers. Germany leads in environmental legislation and related political activism; California spawns many youth-oriented trends; African-American male teenagers are a leading fashion influence; and research at institutions like MIT and Cambridge, Columbia, and Stanford universities often leads the way in biotechnology, computers, medicine, and telecommunications.

 KEY IDEA

> ➤ The firm faces a broad set of environmental forces — political, economic, sociocultural, technological, legal/regulatory, and environmental (physical) — PESTLE.

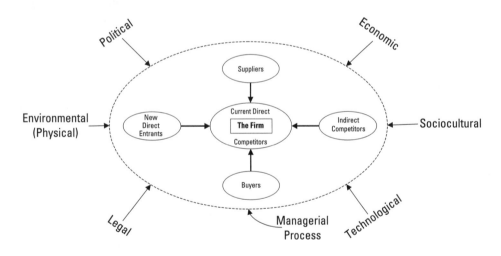

**FIGURE 3.4**

**THE PESTLE MODEL — ENVIRONMENTAL FORCES ACTING ON THE INDUSTRY**

## POLITICAL

Governments set the frameworks within which regulators develop the rules for business. Typically, governments intervene in economies to pursue political ends and enhance consumer welfare by creating a *level playing field*. In the late 20th century, many governments realized that regulations designed to protect consumers locked in competitive structures, restricted competitive entry, and stifled innovation, contrary to intended results.

Firms try to influence political actions by contributing to political campaigns and hiring lobbyists to influence legislation and the rule-making process. Sometimes trade associations undertake these actions.

## ECONOMIC

The country's economic well-being influences market demand. High inflation, high and rising interest rates, falling share prices, and a depreciating currency identify an unhealthy economy. But some measures can be ambiguous. High inflation rates are generally a negative indicator, but very low and negative inflation rates, like those in 1990s Japan, are also negative. High savings rates are generally positive, but rates that are too high lower consumption. Because *expectations* influence spending patterns, direction and rate of change are critical.

Per-capita GDP and disposable income are generally good indicators of market demand, but the firm must consider both distribution across the population and population size. Average incomes in India and China are low, but India's middle class exceeds 200 million people. Residents of Shanghai, Beijing, and other Chinese cities also have significant income.

## SOCIOCULTURAL

Culture is "... the distinctive customs, achievements, products, outlook, etc., of a society or group; the way of life of a society or group."[17] Culture is learned early in life, largely by influence from the family, schools, and religious institutions, and cultural norms are resistant to change. Generally, people do not notice culture in their everyday lives, but see cultural values by comparison with different cultures. What is normal in one culture may appear odd in another. Most cultures give gifts, but the meaning can differ widely. Chinese associate white, blue, and black gifts with funerals; sharp objects like knives, scissors, and letter-openers symbolize cutting off a friendship.

**CULTURAL GROUPS.** A cultural group may inhabit a nation-state, like Brazil and Iran; a geographic region within a nation, like the South or Midwest in the U.S.; a multinational region, like Latin America or Southeast Asia; or comprise a people, regardless of geographic location, like the Armenian, Jewish, and Kurdish diasporas.

A cultural group may comprise different subcultures, each reflecting group-culture and subcultural elements. Three important U.S. subcultures are Baby Boomers, Generation X, and Generation Y; each represents a different marketing opportunity.[18] Religious and social-issue groups may also play a critical role by pressuring firms to behave in what they view as appropriate ways; religious and family groups boycotted Ford for sponsoring gay rights parades.

**LOCALIZATION AND GLOBALIZATION.** An important contemporary cultural issue is the tension between localization and globalization. Enhanced travel, improved communications, the Internet, and globally available television and movies are ready lubricants. Indeed, Levi's jeans and Marlboro cigarettes benefited from scores of cowboy movies distributed around the world. But many individuals and groups resist globalization in general, and U.S. and Western influence in particular. Protesters routinely disrupt WTO meetings; the Iraq war spurred global boycotts of U.S. products, and U.S. consumers have boycotted French products.

## TECHNOLOGICAL

Since World War II, technological innovation has produced many products and services we now take for granted. A partial list includes color television, dry copiers, synthetic and optical fibers, cellular telephones, computers, integrated circuits, microwave ovens, passenger jet aircraft, communication satellites, ATMs, virtually all plastics, and antibiotic drugs. These innovations changed individual, household, and organizational life; re-structured industries; and drove economic growth.

Today, the pace of technological change continues to accelerate. In the 20 years from 1970 to 1990, six product classes in consumer electronics achieved mass acceptance — video recorders, video cameras, videogame consoles, CD players, answering machines, and cordless telephones.

*Marketing Question*

Nestlé Prepared Foods identified several trends: increasing time pressure on dual-income households, sharpening decline in culinary skills, growth of empty-nester households, increasing belief that good food equals good health, and growing concern with obesity. How would you advise Nestlé?

Since the mid-1990s, widely adopted products include personal digital assistants (PDAs), digital cameras, DVD players, MP3 players, and personal video recorders (PVRs). The Internet (see box on page 43) is changing the way entire industries compete and offering previously unimaginable customer benefits. eBay affects the way many people buy and sell products — half a million U.S. residents make their living selling products on eBay. In South Korea, 75 percent of households have access to broadband connectivity versus 20 percent in the U.S. Broadband speeds, at eight megabits per second, are *five times faster* than the U.S. and forecast to soon reach 100 megabits per second.

Some technological innovations are industry-specific; others affect the entire economy. Moore's law says that transistor density on computer chips and microprocessor speed double every 18 to 24 months; improving price/performance ratios are transforming industry and commerce. Access to computers will increase, and computing power will infuse many products. Automobiles, aircraft, surgical equipment, and elevators already use computer technology to operate more efficiently, predictably, and safely. Experts believe genetic engineering and nanotechnology will have similarly broad impact.

Technological change can be either sustaining or disruptive[19]:

- **Sustaining technologies** are often incremental. They improve performance for *current* products on dimensions that *existing* customers value. Included are *cordless* vacuum cleaners, *power* drills, and *mobile* telephones versus *plugged-in* products.

- **Disruptive technologies** bring new and very different value propositions. They change customer behavior by finding new applications and initially a few new-to-the-market customers. Included are PCs versus typewriters and digital music downloads to iPods and other devices versus store-bought CDs. Disruptive technologies spawn products that threaten and change entire industries. For existing customers, early product versions are typically inferior; like the first digital cameras — more expensive and complicated than chemical-film cameras. But as cost-benefit ratios improve, the disruptive technology surpasses the old technology. When disruptive technology becomes mainstream, it threatens old technology firms that do not adapt. Examples are digital cameras and discount brokerages that significantly affected market leaders Kodak and Merrill Lynch, respectively, and changed their industries.

Generally, current suppliers develop sustaining technologies to serve the needs of current customers; new entrants introduce disruptive technologies that initially satisfy new and different customers. In the disk-drive industry, current disk-drive suppliers pioneered 14-inch Winchester and 2.5-inch drives — sustaining innovations for mainframe and laptop computers, respectively. By contrast, 8.5-, 5.25-, 3.5-, and 1.8-inch drives were disruptive technologies. Initially, each innovation satisfied the needs of different customers — respectively, manufacturers of minicomputers, desktop PCs, laptops, and portable heart-monitoring devices.

## LEGAL/REGULATORY

The legal framework (LF) is the rules for business. It aims to protect societal interests, regulate market power, hinder collusion, and stop deceptive practices. LFs differ across countries, but generally govern mergers and acquisitions, capital movements, consumer protection, and employment conditions. The U.S. and Britain have well-developed systems based on statute and case law; the Napoleonic Code generally forms the foundation in continental Europe. By contrast, poorly developed systems of commercial law in Russia and China cause major problems for foreign firms. In China, product copying and illegal use of brand names is rampant, despite China having joined the WTO.

Individuals, firms, and governments use LFs to advance their interests. Individuals file lawsuits about poorly designed or manufactured products. Firms sue suppliers, customers, and competitors, and governments bring lawsuits. The U.S. Justice Department sued Microsoft for

**KEY IDEA**

➤ Technological innovation can be sustaining (improving performance of established products) or disruptive (offering new value propositions).

antitrust violations; then New York Attorney General Elliot Spitzer sued many financial service firms and their senior executives.

### The Internet

The Internet is a *killer app*.[20] Like movable type, the telephone, and the automobile, the Internet is changing the way society works and functions. The automobile changed the way people live, shop, work, and spend leisure time — the Internet is doing the same.

The Internet is an efficient distribution channel, interactive communications tool, marketplace, and information system. Firms are communicating with customers and suppliers in new ways; increasing interconnectedness, open standards, and new protocols will further ease information flow. The type and quantity of data the firm collects, stores, and distributes is also changing. Many retailers transmit cash register data direct to suppliers. The ratio of goods shipped to goods in inventory dropped from 1:2 in 1970 to 1:1.2 in the early 2000s, driving down inventory costs. Firms can also collect and manage data about current and potential customers, and take action in real time.

The Internet reduces transactions costs; Table 3.2 shows the dramatic impact on personal financial services. When insurance buyers and sellers meet on the Internet, they eliminate agents and brokers — and their fees. Internet purchases are common for financial instruments, airline travel, and hotel reservations.

**TABLE 3.2**

**AVERAGE COST PER TRANSACTION IN RETAIL BANKING**[21]

| Mode | Cost / Transaction |
|---|---|
| Branch teller | $2.50 |
| Telephone | $1.00 |
| ATM | $0.40 |
| Voice response | $0.24 |
| Internet | $0.10 |

Lead generation and advertising for small businesses is shifting from the Yellow Pages to real-time, adaptable, adjustable text ads spread across thousands of web pages. No longer must consumers' "fingers do the walking." Google Adwords and others ensure that contextually appropriate ads reach customers in online media.

Sellers reach more buyers on the Internet; buyers access more suppliers. eBay benefits from this *network effect*. As more sellers post products on eBay, eBay's buyers receive greater value. As more buyers purchase on eBay, eBay's sellers receive greater value!

B2B exchanges are popular. A firm like GE posts its requirements, and pre-approved suppliers bid in a *reverse auction*. (Note: In reverse auctions, prices go down, not up, as in traditional English auctions.) Some firms form B2B-exchange alliances with competitors to develop reverse auctions. In 1999, Ford, GM, and DaimlerChrysler formed the Covisint exchange (since sold).

Perhaps the Internet's greatest impact will be in industries where products can be digitized. Recorded music has seen significant turmoil, including widespread piracy — iTunes is bringing some stability. Movies and other videos may enter a turbulent phase as transmission capacity increases. Many Internet sites provide content — Google and Yahoo!, news, and interaction via chat rooms and bulletin boards, with suppliers, vendors, and customers.

Interactivity and accessibility of online content has upended the media industry. User-generated content and meta-data created by communities are watchwords for the next generation of Internet media firms. YouTube, Blogger, Wikipedia, and others have based their success on user-generated journals, videos, and other data. The firm's emerging role will be editor or gatekeeper, sorting out what's good and adapting as necessary.

## ENVIRONMENTAL (PHYSICAL)

Natural and man-made forces coexist in an uneasy equilibrium. Humans have little or no control over natural phenomena like tsunamis, earthquakes, asteroids hitting the earth, monsoons, hurricanes and tornadoes, and everyday weather patterns. By contrast, human action is driving rainforest and wetland destruction, global warming,[22] retreating coastlines, pollution, raw material shortages, and the shrinking ozone layer.

Firms face increasing pressure from governments, environmentalists, single-issue advocacy groups, and the public at large to assume greater environmental responsibility for their products, packaging, and production systems. Some firms are aggressively enacting *green* strategies. BP claims significant reductions in greenhouse gas emissions from its plants, and HP recycles 70,000 tons annually, about 10 percent of sales.

**KEY IDEA**

➤ Environmental forces are constantly in flux; they also interact with each other.

## INTERACTIONS AMONG PESTLE FORCES

Figure 3.5 shows each PESTLE force — political, economic, sociocultural, technological, legal, and environmental (physical) — interacting with its sister forces.

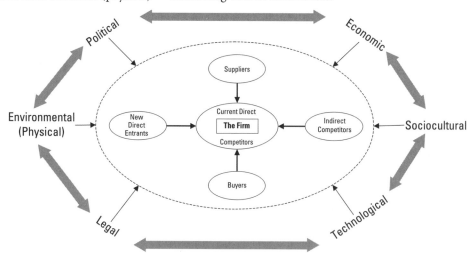

**FIGURE 3.5**

**THE AUGMENTED INDUSTRY ENVIRONMENT**

These inter-connected forces form the firm's environmental panorama. The Internet, a technological force, has major implications for sociocultural and political forces, especially in countries with little political freedom. In South Korea, huge government investment in broadband infrastructure, a political force, is spurring domestic innovation, a technological force. In Germany, recycling has vital economic, environmental (physical) and political dimensions. As environmental change and turbulence grow, environmental interconnectedness will increase.

### KEY MESSAGES

To gain market insight, the firm should focus on four broad areas: market structure, market and product evolution, industry forces, and environmental forces:

**Market Structure:**
- The *market* consists of customers that require goods and services to satisfy their needs.
- The firm should define the market at several levels.
- Product class and product form refer to products that all suppliers offer. Product class is a broader level of aggregation than product form.
- Firms offer product items to the market — a product line consists of multiple product items.
- Fundamental drivers of market size are population and purchasing power.

**Market and Product Evolution:**
- The life-cycle framework is a good way to think about market and product evolution.
- The length of life cycles is in the order: market > product class > product form.
- Life cycles have several stages: introduction, early growth, late growth, maturity, and decline — each with distinguishing characteristics.
- Profit-margin life cycles do not mirror sales life cycles.

**Industry Forces:**
- The *five-forces model* is a useful way of analyzing the pressures on the firm.
- The five forces are current direct competitors, new direct entrants, indirect competitors, suppliers, and buyers. Each force affects the firm in a different way.

**Environmental Forces:**
- Environmental forces have an impact on both the firm and other players in the industry.
- The environmental forces are *political, economic, sociocultural, technological, legal/regulatory,* and *environmental (physical)* — PESTLE.
- The PESTLE forces are in a continuous state of flux and are increasingly interconnected.

# CHAPTER 4

# CUSTOMER INSIGHT

## LEARNING OBJECTIVES

When you have completed this chapter, you will be able to:

- Identify customers; in particular, distinguish between macro and micro customers, and between direct and indirect customers.
- Define and describe customer insight.
- Recognize the data needed to assess and measure customer insight.
- Identify the various roles people play in the purchase-decision process.
- Use several frameworks to understand customer value.
- Analyze critical stages in the purchase-decision process.
- Highlight how customers choose among purchase alternatives.
- Understand the influences on consumer and organizational purchase decisions.
- Focus on the key factors influencing consumer and organizational purchase decisions.
- Classify the customer purchase process so as to help develop market strategies.

## OPENING CASE: IKEA

*IKEA is the world's most successful global retailer. All IKEA stores operate under a franchise from IKEA Systems B.V., which opened the first store in Almhult, Sweden, in 1958. IKEA's vision is "... to create a better everyday life for many people." IKEA is not just another furniture retailer; franchising supports its vision by easing market expansion. And IKEA provides its designers with customer insight for fashioning many different types of value.*

*In 2008, revenues for the 300 IKEA stores in more than 40 countries exceeded 31 billion euros. IKEA's target customer is the global middle class; it serves them by offering a broad range of affordable, IKEA-designed, contemporary home-furnishing products. IKEA has an immense product line; its products span 20 different categories including bathroom, beds and mattresses, bookcase and storage, pet products, lighting, TV and media solutions, tables and chairs, and work areas. In 2006, IKEA added edible products for its U.S. and Asian stores.*

*IKEA drives for low costs via a focus on design and function; high volumes push down costs and prices even further. To reduce transportation costs, IKEA ships in flat packs. Customers purchase in the store, pick up their goods at the warehouse, and drive them home. They do simple assembly with an IKEA-provided wrench and instructions. IKEA's mantra, "You do your part. We do our part. Together we save money," supports its low-price approach.*

*By close attention to customers' needs, IKEA has become an icon for home furnishings. In 2005, it distributed 160 million catalogs, printed in 24 languages, free to households in its stores' primary market areas in 32 countries around the world. Its stores had an astounding 454 million visitors.*

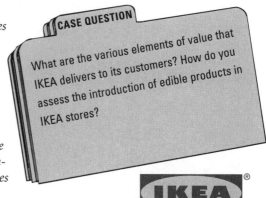

**CASE QUESTION**

What are the various elements of value that IKEA delivers to its customers? How do you assess the introduction of edible products in IKEA stores?

IKEA grounds its success in a vision of delivering great customer value. As we have emphasized, customers are the firm's core assets; they create value for the firm and its shareholders. The firm must design strategies to enhance the lifetime value (LTV) of current and potential customers. If it does a good job of attracting, retaining, and growing customers, it makes profits today and tomorrow, survives and grows, and enhances shareholder value. The starting point for the firm's challenges is developing good **customer insight**, based on a deep and unique understanding of customers. Securing that insight is the topic of this chapter.

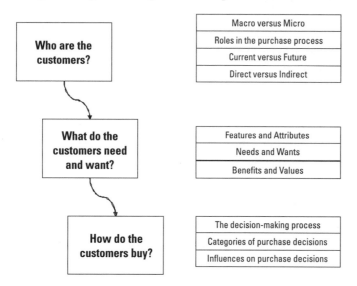

**FIGURE 4.1**

**CUSTOMER INSIGHT**

To deliver value to customers, the firm must answer the three questions in Figure 4.1:

- **Who are the customers?** So far, we have used the term *customer* fairly loosely. In this chapter, we sharpen focus by considering direct and indirect customers, and current and potential customers. The firm must also know who is involved in a particular purchase decision — and the various roles that individuals play in the **decision-making unit (DMU)**.

- **What do customers need and want?** Understanding customers' needs is critical for delivering benefits and values. Securing customer insight may require in-depth customer research and a deep understanding of customer value.

- **How do customers buy?** The firm must know how customers make purchases, the intricacies of the **decision-making process (DMP)**, and the factors that influence it. We consider consumer and organizational purchase decisions separately.

**KEY IDEA**

➤ Customer insight requires a deep and unique understanding of customers.

➤ Good customer insight requires answers to three questions: Who are the customers? What do they need and want? How do they buy?

## IDENTIFYING CUSTOMERS

Identifying customers is the crucial first step in securing **customer insight**. This is not a trivial matter. The most obvious response is: The customer pays for the goods and services. Right? This answer is often wrong and is almost always inadequate. Figure 4.2 shows that the firm must cast a wide net for customers. We prefer the following definition:

**A customer is any person or organization, in the channel of distribution or decision (excluding competitors), whose actions can affect the purchase of the firm's products and services.**

This definition is purposely broad because identifying customers is often like a detective's job. Many individuals may be involved in the decision to purchase the firm's products and services. The definition reflects the fact that:

- Both organizations, **macro level**, and individuals, **micro level**, are called customers.
- **Customers** play various roles in purchase decisions — influencers and decision-makers.
- The firm should consider both **today's customers** and **tomorrow's customers**.
- In addition to **direct customers** that pay for the firm's products and services, **indirect customers**, the customers of direct customers, frequently influence purchases.

**KEY IDEA**

➤ To secure customer insight, the firm must correctly identify customers.

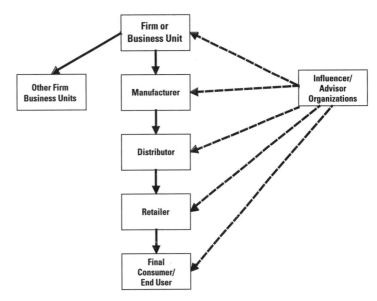

**FIGURE 4.2**

IDENTIFYING CUSTOMERS

**Marketing Question**

UPS makes offers to mailroom personnel; shipping, customer service, and logistics managers; CFOs; and CEOs. If you were developing a message for the CFO, what needs would you highlight? If you focused on the shipping manager, how might your message differ?

## MACRO-LEVEL CUSTOMERS AND MICRO-LEVEL CUSTOMERS

To gain customer insight, the firm must understand how its customers fit into the buying process. **Macro-level customers** are the organizational units, manufacturers, wholesalers, retailers, government entities, and families that purchase products and services. **Micro-level customers** are individuals within the macro-level customer that influence purchase or have decision-making authority. When micro-level customers jointly make a purchase decision, they act as a **decision-making unit (DMU)**.[1]

**KEY IDEA**

➤ Macro-level customers are organizations; micro-level customers are individuals.

**Marketing Question**

Who participates in your family's summer vacation decision?

## ROLES IN THE PURCHASE DECISION

Both macro-level and micro-level customers can play many different roles in a purchase decision. *Macro-level customers* like distributors and retailers *purchase* the firm's products; they also *sell, deliver, store,* and/or *service* them. Customers like governments, standards bodies, and consulting firms may *influence* other *macro-level customers* to buy the firm's products. Table 4.1 shows that *micro-level customers* play various purchasing-related roles in their organizations.

| Purchase Decision Roles | Organizational - B2B | Consumer – B2C |
|---|---|---|
| | Multinational firm seeks supplier for marketing training programs | Family is deciding whether to take a cruise for the family vacation |
| Decision-maker | CEO | Mother |
| Influencer | Senior line executives | Children |
| Spoiler | Two senior line executives with MBAs from Harvard and Wharton | Daughter's boyfriend — has summer job at a Caribbean resort |
| Champion | Senior executives committed to Columbia Business School | Second cousin (works for cruise line) |
| Specifier | Junior human resource (HR) personnel who develop the program | Grandmother (has some basic requirements that must be met) |
| Gatekeeper | Senior HR personnel | Live-in housekeeper |
| Buyer | Purchasing officer | Father |
| Information Provider | Bricker's — good source on executive education | Travel agent |
| User | Middle managers | Mother, father, children, grandparents |

**TABLE 4.1**

**ILLUSTRATION OF ROLES IN ORGANIZATIONAL AND CONSUMER PURCHASE DECISIONS**

Macro-level customers differ widely across B2C and B2B, but micro-level customer roles are similar:

- **Decision-maker.** Has the formal power to make the purchase decision.
- **Influencer.** The decision-maker values the influencer's opinion. In family purchases, the influencer may be a friend, colleague, spouse, child, or grandparent. Organizational influencers include operations, engineering, marketing, and/or general management. Two special types of influencer are spoilers and champions.
    - **Spoilers**, like disgruntled former employees or a firm's design engineer that try to prevent the purchase.
    - **Champions** are the opposite of spoilers. They promote the firm's interests, based on positive experiences with the supplier or personal relationships.
- **Specifier.** Exercises influence indirectly by providing expertise like setting specifications. Examples include an architect for a family house purchase or a firm's design engineer.
- **Gatekeeper.** Has the power to impede access to decision-makers and influencers. Secretaries, administrative assistants, and purchasing agents often play this role.
- **Buyer.** Has formal power to make the purchase, like company purchasing agents.
- **Information provider.** Provides the firm with important information about the customer.
- **User.** Has little direct role in the purchase decision, but often has veto power. Young children often have strong opinions about breakfast cereal, and the factory worker who says, "I'm not working with that red stuff," can be very influential.

## CURRENT CUSTOMERS AND FUTURE CUSTOMERS

**Today's customers** provide revenues and profits. As we discussed in Chapter 2, customer retention has enormous value for the firm. But it is not enough to focus on current customers; the firm must also identify potential customers. Some firms devote major efforts to identifying and creating **tomorrow's customers**. Alcoa works with universities to train students in metalworking design, and McKinsey happily places its consultants at senior positions in client firms.

## DIRECT CUSTOMERS AND INDIRECT CUSTOMERS

Typically, the firm's direct customers exchange money for its products and services. Indirect customers buy the firm's products from these direct customers or from other indirect cus-

---

*Marketing Question*

Think of when you were selling something — a product, an idea, or yourself for a job. Who played what roles in the decision? Hint: Don't underestimate gatekeepers, influencers, spoilers, or champions who may have worked in the background.

**KEY IDEA**

➤ Purchase decisions involve many customer roles: decision-maker, influencer, spoiler, champion, specifier, gatekeeper, buyer, information provider, and user.

**KEY IDEA**

➤ The firm must pay attention to both its current and potential customers.

*Marketing Question*

Banks are persistent in soliciting students for credit cards. Why? How could they be more effective?

### KEY IDEA

➤ Indirect customers may be more important than direct customers — they are often final users and ultimately drive product demand.

*Marketing Question*

What product did a firm target to you that did not satisfy your needs? What needs did the product not satisfy? Why do you think this occurred?

### KEY IDEA

➤ To attract, retain, and grow customers, the firm must:
  • Develop offers of value to satisfy customers' needs
  • Communicate the value of those offers to customers.

### KEY IDEA

➤ Customers have *recognized needs* and *latent needs*. Recognized needs may be *expressed* or *non-expressed*.

tomers. Sometimes direct customers are end users that buy and use the finished products. In other cases, they transform the firm's product before it reaches the indirect customer.

The direct-versus-indirect customer distinction is very important. The firm *may not know* its indirect customers, and so have little insight into the benefits and values they seek. Until **customer relationship management (CRM)** technology became widely available, FMCG firms like P&G typically could not identify their indirect customers — the consumers who purchased their products. Today, they learn about them via contests and promotions. Stouffer's encourages consumers to register at its website to learn about recipes and menu items. It engages potentially loyal customers and gains better insight into their needs.

To reinforce the importance of indirect customers, consider what a senior UPS executive told us: "As a company we are very focused, not just on our customers and what we do that helps them, but on what we do that helps their customer. We're always looking through our customer to their customer. We continually ask ourselves … how does our technology, our products/ services and opportunities transcend our customer's relationship with their customers. If they provide better customer service, and achieve lower costs, and really achieve their business vision, and help their customer be successful … we have a stronger relationship than if we just focus on our relationship with our customer."[2]

## CUSTOMER NEEDS, BENEFITS, AND VALUES

The firm attracts, retains, and grows customers by delivering unique value to satisfy their needs. **Customer value** equates to the value in the firm's offer less the customer's costs to secure it, including monetary, time, effort, and emotional costs. Two sorts of firm action are crucial:

- Make offers of value to satisfy customers' needs
- Communicate the value of those offers to customers.[3]

We saw in the opening case that IKEA both offers value and communicates value. If the firm offers value, but customers don't know about it, they will not purchase. If the firm communicates its offer extensively, but customers don't perceive value (like advertising the Hummer as gasoline prices rise sharply), they will not purchase. We discuss customer needs, how they affect product features and attributes, and the benefits and values that customers receive.

### RECOGNIZED NEEDS VERSUS LATENT NEEDS

An important insight is that sometimes customers understand their needs — **recognized needs** — and sometimes they don't — **latent needs**. Recognized needs may be expressed or non-expressed:

- **Expressed needs.** Customers often ask for advice on how to satisfy their needs.
- **Non-expressed needs.** Customers sometimes do not express their needs, like teenage girls contemplating condom purchases.

Customers are not consciously aware of *latent needs*. These needs may surface as technological innovation raises awareness and customers require benefits or values they could not previously express. A few years ago, few consumers could have articulated a need for cell phones. But widespread availability surfaced a latent need of wanting to stay in constant contact.

### FEATURES AND ATTRIBUTES VERSUS BENEFITS AND VALUES

Many firms define their products and services in terms of **features** and **attributes**. Think about television advertising touting *new and improved*. Now read very carefully. Customers *do not care* about *your* products and services — they are not interested in the features and attributes.

Customers *do care* about satisfying *their needs* and the *benefits and values* your products and services provide. You must communicate these clearly. Let us be very clear about these terms:

- **Features and attributes.** Design elements or functions the firm builds into its products and services — typically of great concern to design engineers.
- **Benefits.** Something the product or service delivers that satisfies a customer need.
- **Values.** Something the product or service provides that has broader scope than a benefit.

Most firms sell products and services that in turn provide benefits and values. Recently, some firms have begun selling benefits and values directly to customers. IBM's *on-demand computing* customers do not pay for hardware and software; they only pay for the computing power they use. Similarly, some airlines pay for airplane engines per hour of operating life.

## HIERARCHIES OF NEEDS, FEATURES, BENEFITS, AND VALUES

Psychologists have studied individual needs extensively. We explore a popular need framework developed by the psychologist Abraham Maslow. Marketers often use Maslow's ideas, and their extension into the feature/benefit/value ladder, to understand purchase behavior.

**MASLOW'S HIERARCHY OF NEEDS.** Maslow's classic framework identifies five major groups of needs: *physiological, safety and security, social, ego,* and *self-actualization,* ordered low to high.[4] Generally, we expect individuals to satisfy lower-level *physiological, safety and security* needs before higher-level needs like *ego* and *self-actualization.*

Products like groceries, clothing, and housing satisfy lower-level *physiological needs*; sports equipment and educational services satisfy higher-level *social, ego,* and *self-actualization* needs. But firms can design market offers for groceries, clothing, and housing (including products, advertising, distribution, and service) to also satisfy higher-level *social* and *ego* needs. Examples are organic food, designer fashions, and neighborhood location. Satisfying both *higher-level needs* and *lower-level needs* should provide greater customer loyalty than satisfying *lower-level needs* alone. A woman is more likely to buy hair shampoo she believes will make her attractive (*ego* need) than if it just cleans her hair. Table 4.2 applies Maslow's framework to two purchasing decisions.

> **KEY IDEA**
>
> ➤ Maslow's approach places a person's needs in an ordered hierarchy.

| Need \ Product | Folgers Coffee | Krispy Kreme Donuts |
|---|---|---|
| Self-Actualization (self-fulfillment) | Savoring | Be part of an emerging cultural phenomenon |
| Ego (prestige, success, self-respect) | Confidence, achievement | Be in vogue (especially among Gen-X'ers) |
| Social (love, affection, friendship, belonging) | Togetherness, freshness, taste | Eating donuts is a group experience that creates a sense of *togetherness* |
| Safety & Security (protection, order, security) | Easy on the stomach, no jitters | Safe, easy for kids to eat — and no mess |
| Physiological (food, drink, air, shelter, sex) | Satisfies thirst, keeps you alert, keeps you warm | Satisfies hunger and the sweet tooth |

> **TABLE 4.2**
>
> **USING MASLOW'S HIERARCHY OF NEEDS TO GAIN INSIGHT INTO TWO CONSUMER PURCHASES**

**LADDERING FEATURES, BENEFITS, AND VALUES.** Many marketers meld Maslow's hierarchical approach to individual needs with the feature/benefit/value distinction discussed previously to form a **feature/benefit/value ladder**. Figure 4.3 shows the ladder's three main characteristics:

- **Focuses attention on customer value.** Firms typically design features and attributes into their products and services. The feature/benefit/value ladder forces a translation into benefits and values. B&D's drills deliver many benefits and values.
- **Provides alternatives for communicating with customers.** The variety of benefits and values broadens the firm's options for communicating with customers. The best communications depend on factors like stage of market development and competitors' behavior. Potential B&D communications like *drill speed and bit hardness, makes holes easily,* and *supports do-it-yourself activity* are quite different from each other.

> **KEY IDEA**
>
> ➤ The feature/benefit/value ladder ensures that the firm focuses on providing value to customers, provides options for communication, and broadens the view of competition.

- **Broadens the view of competition.** When the firm focuses on features, its scope is direct competitors; a focus on customer benefits and values broadens this scope. With a features focus, B&D's competitors are electric drill manufacturers. Focusing on Benefit A — makes holes easily — introduces competitors like explosives, nails, lasers, water drills, and woodpeckers (!). Higher-level benefits broaden competitive scope even further.

**FIGURE 4.3**

FEATURE/BENEFIT/VALUE
LADDERS FOR BLACK &
DECKER ELECTRIC DRILLS
AND NIVEA SKIN CREAM

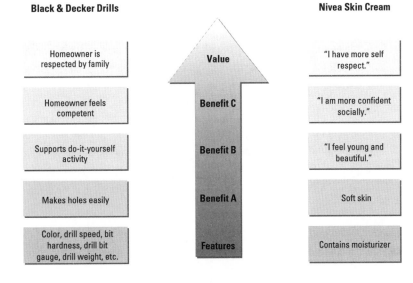

**KEY IDEA**

➤ The firm must deliver the *right* combination of functional, psychological, and economic benefits and values to those customers it wants to attract, retain, and grow.

In general, customers focus on the benefits and values the firm's products and services deliver. Resellers like distributors, retailers, and wholesalers are more interested in economic benefits like profit margins, net profit, and return on investment. Different customer types seek different benefits and values, so the firm should develop several feature/benefit/value ladders.

## FUNCTIONAL, PSYCHOLOGICAL, AND ECONOMIC BENEFITS AND VALUES

We just learned that customers base their purchase decisions on a need hierarchy. The firm must translate the features of its offer into a hierarchy of benefits and values that align with these needs. But we must go one step further to explore three types of benefits and values.

**FUNCTIONAL BENEFITS AND VALUES.** Firms design products and services to provide functional benefits and values that meet basic expectations. Food products satisfy hunger needs; disc brakes stop automobiles. Sometimes firms and customers discover functional benefits serendipitously (by accident). Pfizer developed *Viagra* to address heart disease but discovered it could treat erectile dysfunction. Avon's customers found that *Skin-So-Soft* effectively repelled mosquitoes.

**PSYCHOLOGICAL BENEFITS AND VALUES.** Psychological values typically satisfy status, affiliation, reassurance, risk, and security needs. Firms often offer psychological and functional benefits together. Fine-dining restaurants provide high-quality food and ambience (functional) and also prestige (psychological). An automobile may provide fast acceleration, efficiency, and comfort (functional), but also status (psychological). Generally, psychological values transcend functional benefits and appear higher up the feature/benefit/value ladder.[5]

**ECONOMIC BENEFITS AND VALUES.** Economic benefits and values concern financial aspects like price and credit terms. Price is often the primary purchase driver, especially in tough economies when customers trade off functional and psychological benefits to secure the lowest price. Wal-Mart, purchasing clubs, dollar stores, discount airlines, and generic drug producers provide economic benefits via lower prices. In B2B markets, price is often critical, but sometimes firms deliver cost-cutting economic benefits at *higher prices* by providing greater

**Marketing Question**

Think about one of your favorite products. What **functional** benefits does it provide? What **psychological** benefits does it provide? Be creative!

functional benefits. GE strengthens customer relationships by helping customers improve operational effectiveness.

**Economic value for the customer (EVC)** is the product's economic value represented as the maximum price a customer would pay. EVC is the price of the competitive product plus the added value from the firm's product. We show the EVC calculation for a polyester product used to make conveyor belts.[6]

---

### Illustration of Economic Value to the Customer (EVC)

Industrial-strength conveyor belts are made by covering a textile fabric core with rubber; textile fiber strength is crucial for conveyor belt life. Traditionally, *sevens*\* cotton yarn was the core; polyester yarn was a potential replacement. Critical data for calculating the value of polyester in conveyor belts are:

- Price of sevens cotton is 90 cents per lb.
- 750 denier polyester yarn is four times stronger than cotton.
- The extra cost of processing polyester yarn is 30 cents per lb.

EVC answers the question: What is the maximum price a conveyor belt manufacturer will pay for polyester fiber? (We assume that conveyor belt life does not change when polyester replaces cotton.) Since polyester is four times stronger than cotton, customers can use four pounds of cotton or one pound of polyester. See Figure 4.5:

- Cotton: sevens cotton yarn @ 90 cents per lb. — reference value
- Polyester equivalence: 1 lb. of 750 denier polyester yarn or 4 lbs. of sevens cotton = $3.60 — reference value plus positive differentiation value
- Extra cost to process polyester fiber = 30 cents per lb. — negative differentiation value
- Net polyester equivalence = $3.60 less $0.30 = $3.30 — total economic value[7]

In sum, based on the economic value analysis, customers should be indifferent between:

a. Sevens cotton @ 90 cents per lb. and
b. 750 denier polyester @ $3.30 per lb.

Hence, the maximum polyester price is $3.30 per lb. At any price above $3.30 per lb. conveyor belt manufacturers would be better off sticking with cotton.

\*Sevens cotton is the standard type of cotton yarn used in industrial applications.

---

Many EVC calculations are more complex than this simple illustration. Factors for inclusion are the customer's operating, maintenance, and financing costs, as well as revenue changes.

The firm's challenge is to deliver the *right* combination of functional, psychological, and economic benefits and values to those customers it wants to attract, retain, and grow.

........................................................

## CHARACTERISTICS OF BENEFITS AND VALUES

**WHEN THE CUSTOMER RECOGNIZES THE VALUE.** Sometimes customers have good data about the benefits and values a product will provide; at other times they are uncertain and cannot assess value until long after purchase. The categories of **search**, **use**, and **credence** benefits capture this uncertainty and can offer important insight.

- **Search benefits.** Lots of product and service data from the firm and/or independent sources like *Consumer Reports* before purchase. Customers may even inspect and try products, like test-driving a car.
- **Use benefits.** Relatively little data on customer value before purchase, as for many services. You won't know the value of an Eminem, McFly, or Rolling Stones performance until you've experienced it.

### KEY IDEA

➤ EVC is the maximum price customers will pay.

➤ The firm delivers economic value by reducing customers' costs and/or increasing their revenues.

### Marketing Question

Choose one product each that offers mainly *search*, *use*, and *credence* benefits and values. How would your communications to customers differ?

- **Credence benefits.** Customers cannot assess value until long after purchase. Examples include an investment's economic benefits and health benefits from some medical procedures.

**VALUE TODAY VERSUS VALUE TOMORROW.** Generally, customers purchase products and services for benefits and values they expect to receive directly. They may also purchase for expected future benefits and values. When a B2B customer purchases from a technology firm, a key factor may be benefits inherent in the supplier relationship like preferential access to *beta* (pre-release) versions of future technology. Dell buys most of its computer chips from Intel, rather than AMD, in part because Intel provides Dell with early insights into its new technologies.

**ACTUAL VALUE VERSUS POTENTIAL VALUE.** The critical value the firm offers may lie not in the product itself, but in the customer's ability to secure additional value, if and when needed. The AmEx Platinum Card's Concierge program locates hard-to-find items, delivers gifts, provides secretarial services in remote areas, and offers dining recommendations. Most cardholders rarely use these services, but their availability has high value.

**SCARCITY VALUE.** Some firms like fashion retailer Zara deliberately make small product volumes to provide scarcity value. Beanie Babies had limited production runs and ruthless retirements of prized stuffed animals; many Harley-Davidson models have long wait times.

**VALUE FOR WHOM.** In B2C marketing, consumers typically make purchases for themselves, a friend, colleague, family member, or a group like the family. In B2B marketing, the purchase may satisfy organizational or individual needs. To ensure the organization receives the value, firms like Wal-Mart go to great lengths to prohibit purchasing agents from receiving any individual benefits, like lunch, from suppliers.

**PRESENCE VALUE.** A firm can provide considerable value to a customer just by being a supplier, so long as its products are acceptable and its prices reasonable. When there is one strong and one weak supplier, the weak supplier's presence keeps the strong supplier *honest* and stops it from exercising monopoly power. For many years, Airbus played this role versus Boeing; AMD plays this role versus Intel.

## BEYOND CUSTOMER BENEFITS AND VALUES – CUSTOMER EXPERIENCES

In addition to explaining why customers buy, recent consumer behavior research focuses on consumption and needs for **experiences** — states, conditions, or events that consciously affect buying behavior. A single event can create many different experiences. A New York City ballet aficionado experiences a touring Bolshoi performance differently from someone seeing their first ballet. Also, the experience may have more value than the product. Consider coffee. McDonald's sells coffee for about 99 cents a cup. Starbucks' price is several dollars per cup but it also offers a personal and memorable experience.[8]

My Columbia colleague, Schmitt, identifies five modes of customer experiences:

- **Sense.** Creates sensory experiences through sight, sound, touch, taste, and smell.
- **Feel.** Appeals to inner feelings and emotions. Attempts to create affective experiences, ranging from mildly positive to strong emotions of joy and pride.
- **Think.** Appeals to the intellect. Creates problem-solving experiences that engage creatively.
- **Act.** Enriches by showing alternative ways of doing things, alternative lifestyles and interactions.
- **Relate.** Contains aspects of the first four experience modes, but reaches beyond the individual's personal, private feelings to something outside his/her private state.

This framework provides firms a methodical way of determining what customer experiences they want to associate with their products.

# CUSTOMERS' PURCHASE PROCESSES

The purchase **decision-making process (DMP)** ranges from the relatively simple, like buying a mid-morning snack, to the highly complex, like the U.S. government purchasing a new fighter jet. The DMP can be as quick as an impulse purchase or take months or years.[9] Marketers must understand the influence possibilities and how customers move through the process.

## PURCHASE-DECISION STAGES

Figure 4.4 shows the DMP as a robust purchase model in five stages. Each stage may involve multiple feedback loops both within and among stages. The customer may identify a need or problem early on and then elaborate on that need as he secures information and evaluates alternatives. The firm can use insight about customer needs, benefits, and values to map the DMP for individual and organizational purchasing decisions.

*Marketing Question*

Think about your favorite entertainment — a theater, restaurant, concert, or sports event. Which mode(s) — sense, feel, think, act, relate — best describe your experience? Did the provider consciously create this experience? How?

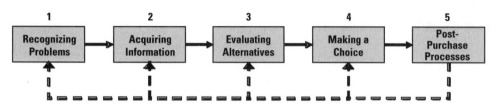

**FIGURE 4.4**

**THE PURCHASE DECISION PROCESS**

**RECOGNIZING PROBLEMS – STAGE 1.** Some customer needs are critical to system functioning: food and drink for individuals and raw materials and capital equipment for firms. Other needs are discretionary. The customer may recognize a need independently by being dissatisfied, or a potential supplier may point it out.

**ACQUIRING INFORMATION – STAGE 2.** After recognizing a problem, customers generally seek information to help identify:

- The *feature* set. Features/attributes that may satisfy the need.
- Criteria for evaluating satisfactory performance on the features/attributes.
- The *awareness* set. Alternatives that may satisfy the need.
- The degree to which each alternative meets the feature/attribute criteria.

Customers can acquire information *externally* and *internally*. External information: from *personal sources* like colleagues, family, friends, and salespeople and from *impersonal sources* like advertising, the press, or the Internet. The degree of external search relates to current knowledge, involvement in the purchase, and perceived risk. Internal information: the customer's own perceptual information store, which includes memory.

**EVALUATING ALTERNATIVES AND MAKING A CHOICE – STAGES 3 AND 4.** Customers evaluate alternatives based on information they acquire in Stage 2. Frequently, customers exclude several alternatives in the *awareness set* with little evaluation, by forming a short list, or *consideration set*, based on the purchase criteria. Customers' choices from the consideration set may be rational, or may deviate from rationality. By understanding the customer's evaluation process, the firm can influence the purchase decision in its favor. We examine a much-studied rational approach and others that deviate from rationality:

**A. Rational approach.** This approach implies that the customer:

- Identifies features/attributes that deliver the required benefits and values.
- Decides on the relative importance of those benefits and values.
- Forms a belief about how well the features/attributes of each alternative deliver those benefits and values.
- Chooses the highest value alternative by combining the beliefs and importances.

**KEY IDEA**

➤ The firm must learn the customer's decision-making process (DMP).

**KEY IDEA**

➤ The firm should try to understand customers' evaluation processes.

The firm can take several actions to improve the value it offers to customers:

- Improve performance on important attributes.
- Add new valued attributes, especially important ones.
- Show customers that it performs better than competitors on important attributes.
- Show that the attributes where it performs really well are highly important.

Some attributes may be baseline requirements, or *antes*; only alternatives scoring sufficiently well enter the consideration set. Airline safety records are often an *ante* for airline travel; customers do not trade off free drinks or frequent-flier miles for safety.

**B. Deviations from rationality.** Researchers in *behavioral decision theory* and *behavioral economics* have identified many purchase processes that do not seem *rational*. In both B2C and B2B, customers seem to base their choices on irrelevant factors.

Research shows several factors that affect deviations from rationality in purchasing decisions[10]:

- **The set of alternatives.** When the number of alternatives changes, purchase behavior can also change. In one experiment, customers chose between two microwave ovens: low-price — $109.99, medium price — $179.99: Forty-three percent chose the medium-price oven. Then customers chose among three ovens — the original two plus a high-price oven — $199.99. Customers chose the $179.99 oven 60 percent of the time.[11] How many drink choices do you have at McDonald's or Starbucks?

- **How customers evaluate the alternatives.** Many factors affect how people evaluate alternatives, even just focusing attention on an alternative. Suppose a waiter offers the diner yogurt and fruit salad, then says, "How much more or less attractive to you is yogurt?" The probability of choosing yogurt increases![12]

- **When customers evaluate the alternatives.** Time of purchase may be rational — we buy Coke and Pepsi when it is hot and we are thirsty. But researchers found that eBay prices for weekend purchases were 2 percent higher than during the week, for no rational reason.

**POST-PURCHASE PROCESSES – STAGE 5.** Customers typically engage in several post-purchase processes. These can affect future purchases — their own and those they influence[13]:

- **Use experience.** The customer may be satisfied or dissatisfied with the product or service.

- **Dissonance reduction.** If the product does not meet expectations, customers may reduce dissonance by changing their opinion of the product's performance. Most dissonance reduction occurs when the customer expends significant time and money to acquire the product.

- **Repurchase.** Repurchase drives customer lifetime value. All things equal, high customer satisfaction increases the chances that the customer will repurchase.

- **Communications with other customers and potential customers.** Word of mouth has always been an important post-purchase process; many firms hire people to stimulate it. The Internet has made customer-to-customer communication even more important. Anti-firm websites like *walmart-sucks.com* and *walmart-blows.com* can be a significant issue for firms.

- **Product and packaging disposal.** Environmental advocates are paying increasing attention to disposal. In many jurisdictions, customers must separate garbage into different categories. In France and Germany, firms have to recover packaging and used products! HP and Kodak encourage customers to return used printer cartridges and disposable cameras, respectively.

# INFLUENCES ON CONSUMER PURCHASE PROCESSES

We explore several influences on consumers' needs and their DMPs — Figure 4.5. Deep understanding of these influences can help the firm be proactive in developing its strategies.

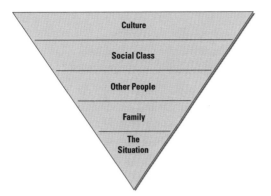

**FIGURE 4.5**

ENVIRONMENTAL
INFLUENCES ON
CONSUMERS'
PURCHASING
DECISIONS

**CULTURE**. Consumer purchasing behavior and product preferences are conditioned by cultural and subcultural norms (Chapter 3). In the West, the female head of household traditionally does the shopping; in rural Bangladesh, men do the shopping. Indonesians smoke more than 200 billion cigarettes annually, but only 10 percent are the standard "white" variety; 90 percent are *kreteks*, a clove cigarette incorporating cinnamon, licorice, coffee, pineapple, and chocolate, in addition to tobacco.[14] In the U.S., business-casual dress policies have affected fiber, garment, detergent, and washing machine manufacturers.

*Cosmopolitan*, the sex-oriented women's magazine, appears in almost 50 countries. Local versions consider cultural sensitivities and legal realities. Indian versions have no articles on sexual positions, sex is never explicitly mentioned in China, and Swedish society is so open that sex receives little attention. In Hong Kong, most models are local Asian celebrities, but in the PRC, most models are western.

Cemex, the Mexican cement producer, tapped into *tandas*, a traditional community savings scheme. In Cemex's *Patrimonio Hoy* program, groups of 70 persons contribute about 120 pesos per week for 70 weeks. Each week, the program selects a *winner* who receives sufficient materials to build an extra room onto his or her home. Cemex also provides technical building assistance. Cemex's cement consumption by do-it-yourself homebuilders tripled.[15]

The firm must be careful not to violate cultural and subcultural norms, especially abroad.[16] A U.S. technology firm was well placed to win a major contract in China. At a banquet given by the Chinese customer, the senior U.S. executive started eating before the host, a cultural no-no. A French firm won the contract, even though its technology was inferior. The Chinese just felt more *comfortable*.

**SOCIAL CLASS**. All societies have hierarchically ordered groupings or social classes. Wealth and income are key discriminators, but occupation, residential location, and education also matter. Sometimes individuals migrate across classes. Values and interests, and purchases like clothing and leisure activities, are often similar within a social class.

**OTHER PEOPLE**. Other people and groups influence consumers. Individuals have frequent face-to-face contact with **primary reference groups** — family members and organizational work groups. **Secondary reference groups** include club and church members and professional organizations. **Aspirational groups** are those a person would like to join for reasons like prestige. People with expertise are particularly influential if they belong to attractive reference groups. Soccer player David Beckham is influential with many teenagers; he has significant expertise and style and belongs to an aspirational reference group — professional soccer players.

**FAMILY**. The *nuclear family* (father, mother, children) and/or the *extended family* (grandparents, aunts, uncles, cousins, in-laws) may exert considerable influence. The relative influence of the nuclear family versus the extended family is culturally determined. Nuclear family influence predominates in the West, but extended family influence is very important in many Asian countries.

**THE SITUATION**. Consumers face situational influences daily — like how much, how presented, and how much time to process. *Purchase location aesthetics* are also important. People purchase

**KEY IDEA**

➤ By identifying sources of influence in the consumer decision-making process, firms formulate better market strategies.

real estate on vacation while enjoying free meals and other perks. U.S. college students purchase and consume more alcohol at football games, parties, and spring break than other times.

Important individual factors are economic resources, time availability, cognitive resources, comfort with technology, life-cycle stage, and lifestyle.

# INFLUENCES ON ORGANIZATIONAL PURCHASE PROCESSES

Organizational buying generally concerns larger sums of money than consumer purchases, is more protracted and complex, engages more people, and may involve company politics. Processes and/or rules often govern organizational purchasing or *procurement* and interfacing with suppliers.[17]

## INCREASED CORPORATE ATTENTION TO PROCUREMENT

For many firms, the *procurement spend/revenue ratio* has increased dramatically. Traditional *purchasing* is evolving from an unimportant managerial backwater into highly strategic *procurement*. Several factors are driving the increased purchasing ratio:

**REPLACING LABOR WITH CAPITAL.** Many firms have downsized and replaced labor with capital. Equipment, raw material, and supply expenses have increased, relative to labor costs.

**OUTSOURCING.** Outsourcing allows firms to increase productivity, functional expertise, and flexibility and to reduce fixed costs. Many major firms outsource their data centers and other business processes to firms like IBM, HP, and Accenture. Others outsource software development, human resource and accounting functions, and call centers to India.

**BRANDING.** Because of branding, many firms resell products made by others under their brand names. The author is writing this book on a Macintosh G4 Powerbook. Apple did not manufacture the carrying case or the power cord, but the complete package arrived ready to use.

## CHANGES IN THE PROCUREMENT PROCESS

As they seek to influence the DMP, suppliers should consider several changes in procurement:

**CENTRALIZATION.** Advances in telecommunications, computers, and the Internet provide corporate buyers with greater leverage. They can secure complete, accurate, and timely purchasing data on individual suppliers from the firm's decentralized units and track purchasing performance against benchmark databases.

**PROCUREMENT EXPERTISE.** Skilled procurement staffs introduce new strategies like **strategic sourcing** to reduce costs, improve quality, and increase efficiency. To become a *preferred supplier*, the firm must complete an extensive *Request for Information* (RFI). Only then can it respond to a detailed *Request for Proposal* (RFP). Long-standing relationships mean little as procurement personnel gain deep insight into suppliers' cost structures and aggressively negotiate for low prices.

**GLOBALIZATION.** The centralizing trend we just discussed is expanding globally as multinational firms broaden their supplier searches. They want global contracts and are increasingly ready to switch suppliers as price differentials appear and disappear.

**THE INTERNET.** Using *reverse auctions*, Internet-based B2B exchanges significantly affect the purchase of standard products. Buyers have better, and cheaper, access to information to drive out market inefficiencies and price differentials.

## REDUCING THE NUMBER OF SUPPLIERS

Traditional purchasing departments sent specifications to many potential suppliers and then chose on criteria like price and delivery. Streamlined supply-chain systems improve efficiency and effectiveness in converting raw materials to finished products. Hence, many firms are forging closer relationships with fewer suppliers.

## EVOLUTION IN BUYER-SELLER RELATIONSHIPS

Some firms are evolving their relationships with selected customers from vendor to quality supplier, and even to partner.

**VENDOR.** Customer and supplier operate at *arms-length* in this traditional adversarial relationship. Contracts are typically short-term with frequent re-bidding. Price is critical; buyers switch suppliers for small price differentials and/or better delivery. Salespeople meet with purchasing agents who restrict the information they provide suppliers to maintain negotiating positions.

**QUALITY SUPPLIER.** Both supplier and customer believe they receive value — like high quality final products — from a close long-term relationship. Each plans for continuous quality improvement. The supplier secures advantage by providing greater value than its competitors.

**PARTNER.** Both firms share or jointly develop future strategies, technologies, and resources. Each focuses on the entire value chain, and bases critical buying decisions on value versus price. Each firm is deeply involved in the other's product-development cycles. Routine and sensitive information flows freely, as the supplier solves important customer problems.

**KEY IDEA**

➤ Important considerations for the organizational purchase-decision process are increased corporate attention to procurement, changes in the procurement process, reducing the number of suppliers, and evolution in buyer-seller relationships.

---

## KEY MESSAGES

To attract, retain, and grow customers, the firm must gain deep customer insight by answering three critical questions:

**Who are the customers?** The firm should explore several issues in identifying customers:
- Macro-level customers — organizations, and micro-level customers — individuals.
- The many different roles that individuals play in the purchase process.
- Both today's customers and tomorrow's customers.
- Both direct customers that exchange money for the firm's products and services, and indirect customers that receive value from the firm's products and services through intermediaries.

**What do customers need and want?** The firm satisfies customers' needs by making offers of value. The firm should gain customer insight into:
- Recognized needs versus latent needs: recognized needs that customers express — expressed needs, and those they do not express — non-expressed needs.
- Who receives the value the firm delivers — the organization or an individual in the organization.
- Features and attributes the firm builds into the product; benefits and values the firm offers to customers.
- Hierarchies of needs, features, benefits, and values, including Maslow's Hierarchy of Needs, and the feature/benefit/value ladder.
- Different types of value, including functional, psychological, and economic.
- Elements that transcend customer benefits and values — customer experiences.

**How do customers buy?** The firm gains insight from the customer's purchase-decision process:
- The process comprises five stages — recognizing problems, acquiring information, evaluating alternatives, making a choice, and engaging in post-purchase processes.
- Customers may deviate from rationality in their purchase decisions.
- Environmental factors that influence consumer purchase decisions include culture, social class, other people, family, and the situation.
- Key factors influencing organizational purchase decisions are increased corporate attention to procurement, changes in the procurement process, reducing the number of suppliers, and evolution in buyer-seller relationships.

# CHAPTER 5

# INSIGHT ABOUT COMPETITORS, COMPANY, AND COMPLEMENTERS

## LEARNING OBJECTIVES

When you have completed this chapter you will be able to:

- Define *competitor* insight and articulate the importance of gaining insight about competitors.
- Identify the firm's current (today's) competitors and potential (tomorrow's) competitors.
- Identify the firm's direct and indirect competitors.
- Describe the firm's competitors by understanding their capabilities and difficulties.
- Evaluate competitors by identifying their strategic options.
- Assess the firm's competitive position.
- Project competitors' objectives and future actions.
- Manage competitors' behavior.
- Understand the various sources and types of complementarity.

## OPENING CASE: BOEING AND AIRBUS

*Boeing and Airbus — headquartered in Chicago and Toulouse, France, respectively — compete intensely in the large passenger jet aircraft market. Boeing launched modern jet-aircraft in 1958 and has 20,000 in service; Airbus started in 1972 and has 3,850 planes flying. Boeing was market leader for several decades, but recently Airbus has challenged its position. In 2003, for the first time, Airbus delivered more aircraft than Boeing; Airbus has also secured more aircraft orders. Although Airbus wins on annual plane sales, Boeing earns up to 55 percent of aircraft value because its 747 dominates the wide-body market.[1] Airbus' new A380 threatens Boeing's position in wide-body jets, but Boeing's 787 fuel-efficient* Dreamliner *is expected to compete strongly in shorter-haul markets. There is no love lost between Boeing and Airbus. Rival executives commonly denigrate each other's products, and the firms have a long-standing dispute over government subsidies.*

*Airbus was formed in the 1960s as a consortium of European aviation firms to compete with the U.S. In 2001, this loose alliance evolved into the European Aeronautic Defence and Space Company (EADS) when three Continental European firms merged. EADS (80 percent) and BAE Systems (formerly British Aerospace) (20 percent) owned the new Airbus. From the start, conflicts between its French and German shareholders troubled EADS. In 2006, British BAE Systems sold its 20 percent ownership and EADS CEO Noël Forgead and Airbus CEO Gustav Humbert resigned amid allegations of insider trading.*

*For the past several years, Boeing (2008 revenues $61 billion; 164,000 employees) has been integrating McDonnell Douglas (MD), acquired in 1997, into its operations. Boeing retired some MD aircraft, along with the Boeing 757, and now offers the following models:*

- *Boeing 737: twin-engine narrow-body, 85–215 passengers, short-medium range, 1966\**
- *Boeing 747: quad-engine large wide-body, 85–524 passengers, long haul, 1969\**
- *Boeing 767: twin-engine small narrow-body, 180–375 passengers, short-medium range, 1981\**
- *Boeing 777: twin-engine medium wide-body, 330–550 passengers, long haul, 1996\**

*Boeing's newest aircraft is the twin-engine medium wide-body 787 —* Dreamliner *— seating 210–330 passengers. Boeing claims the* Dreamliner *is 20 percent more fuel efficient than comparable planes. Fuel savings come from engine (GE and Rolls-Royce) and aerodynamic improvements, greater use of lighter-weight composites, and advanced systems. In early 2009, Boeing had 878 firm orders.*

*In early 2009, Airbus (2007 revenues € 25.2 billion, 56,000 employees) offered several passenger aircraft models:*

- *Airbus A320: twin-engine single aisle, seating 180 passengers, short-medium range, 1987\**
- *Airbus A318 (shortened A320): twin-engine twin aisle, seating 107 passengers, 2002\**
- *Airbus A319 (shortened A320): twin-engine single aisle, seating 145 passengers, 1995\**
- *Airbus A321 (stretched A320): twin-engine single aisle, seating 220 passengers, long haul, 1993\**
- *Airbus A330: twin-engine twin aisle, seating 253–440 passengers, 1992\**
- *Airbus A340: quad-engine twin aisle, seating 261–440 passengers, long haul, 1991\**

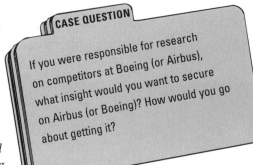

**CASE QUESTION**

If you were responsible for research on competitors at Boeing (or Airbus), what insight would you want to secure on Airbus (or Boeing)? How would you go about getting it?

*Airbus' newest aircraft is the A380, a quad-engine twin-aisle plane seating 555–840 passengers, the world's largest passenger aircraft. It also planned the A350, derived from the A330, a twin-engine twin-aisle plane seating 250–350 passengers designed to compete with Boeing's* Dreamliner*; its first flight is anticipated in 2011.*

---

\*first flight

In Chapter 5, we build on the five-forces model from Chapter 3 to discuss the firm's competitive challenges. We *identify* specific competitors and present a process for gaining competitor insight. **Competitive insight** is securing deep understanding of competitors to provide a unique strategic perspective. Specifically, we explore how to *describe* competitors — their strengths and weaknesses (capabilities and difficulties); how to *evaluate* competitors — their strategic options; how to *project* competitors' actions — figure out what they will do; and how to *manage* competitors — influence their behavior to benefit the firm. As the firm gains insight into competitors, it also gains insight into itself — **company insight**. We also explore complementers; these organizations can help the firm achieve its objectives — **complementer insight**.

# *Competitors*

## DEVELOPING COMPETITIVE INSIGHT

Competitive intensity is increasing across the board in virtually all industries. Any executive will tell you that increased competition is a global phenomenon. Competition is especially tough where: industries are deregulating, rapid changes are occurring in product and/or process technology, state-owned enterprises are privatizing, and governments are reducing or removing tariffs, quotas, and other competitive barriers. Competition is also challenging in industries where regulatory restrictions are increasing, like financial services and pharmaceuticals. The firm must work harder and smarter to attain in-depth competitive insight and build this into its strategic marketing decision-making. Only then will it develop differential advantage to attract, retain, and grow customers.

Research indicates that many firms put too little emphasis on gaining competitive insight. They may claim lack of time or resources, or simply be myopic, perhaps paralyzed by *groupthink*,[2] and not understand the competitive threat. Good competitor insight can reduce the uncertainty in your decision-making. The fundamental marketing job is to attract, retain, and grow customers, but other guys are trying to do the same thing! The firm should always know who their competitors are today and who they will be tomorrow: what they are doing now and what they may do in the future. In this chapter, we explore a framework for developing competitive insight and show its value for the firm.

Gaining sound competitive insight is not easy, but most major firms like IBM, Xerox, and Citibank put in significant effort. Challenges firms face in gaining competitive insight include:

- The firm will not commit resources necessary for gaining competitive insight.
- The firm claims that the cost of securing good competitive data is too high.
- The firm fails to go beyond a basic description of its competitors.
- The firm focuses on current competitors but ignores potential competitors.
- The firm bases its insight on out-of-date data from tired sources.
- An executive gains good insight, but cannot convince the firm to take action.

Figure 5.1 shows a five-step framework for gaining competitor insight. Steps 1 and 2, **identifying** and **describing** competitors, are critical but insufficient. Unfortunately, many firms stop right here. Identifying and describing are the foundation for *evaluating* (step 3), *projecting* (step 4), and *managing* (step 5) competitors. To gain superior competitor insight, the firm must excel in each area and be very clear about what it does and does not know.

**FIGURE 5.1**

**A FRAMEWORK FOR GAINING COMPETITIVE INSIGHT**

*Marketing Question*

Assume that you are responsible for the BlackBerry product line. What information would help you complete the competitive insight framework in Figure 5.1?

IDENTIFY — Step 1: Who are our competitors today? Who will they be tomorrow?

DESCRIBE — Step 2: What are our competitors' capabilities and difficulties?

EVALUATE — Step 3: What are our competitors' strategic options?

PROJECT — Step 4: What do we expect our competitors to do? In the short term? Medium term? Long term?

MANAGE — Step 5: How can we get our competitors to do what we want them to do?

## IDENTIFYING COMPETITORS

A **competitor** is any organization whose products and services provide similar or superior benefits and values to the same customers the firm seeks to attract, retain, and grow. Of course, by making purchases, customers decide who competes with whom. Today the firm faces **current competitors**; those it may face tomorrow are **potential competitors**. We argue for a broad view of competitors, just as, in Chapter 4, we argued for a broad view of customers. Many firms view competition too narrowly, focusing only on firms like themselves. For years, Hollywood did not realize that television was a competitor; paper cup manufacturers did not address competition from plastics firms. When it views competition too narrowly, the firm fails to identify many medium- and long-term threats. It must consider three key areas:

- The structure of competition
- Competitive dynamics
- The firm itself as a competitor

## THE STRUCTURE OF COMPETITION

Figure 5.2 reprises the *five-forces model* (from Chapter 3). Three of the five forces the firm faces are competition: *current direct competitors*, *new direct entrants*, and *indirect competitors*. The two other forces are *suppliers* and *buyers*. We learned earlier that extreme forms of supplier and buyer pressure are, respectively, *forward* and *backward integration*; by undertaking operations the firm currently conducts, they become *direct competitors*. We simplify the *five-forces* approach and develop two identifying dimensions that help evaluate competitors and gain deep insight.

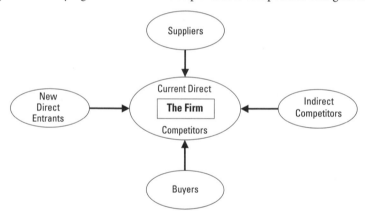

**DIRECT VERSUS INDIRECT COMPETITORS.** **Direct competitors** target similar customers by offering similar benefits and values with similar products, technology, and/or business models. **Indirect competitors** target the same customers with similar benefits and values, but have *different* products, technology, and/or business models.

**CURRENT VERSUS POTENTIAL COMPETITORS.** Today the firm faces **current competitors**; those it may face tomorrow are **potential competitors** — some may not even be around today.

The framework in Figure 5.3 uses both dimensions to identify four types of competitive threat. It helps the firm decide which threats are most serious and where it should deploy its resources:

- **Current direct competitors, cell A.** The competitive *status quo* — the traditional rivalry between established firms.
- **Current indirect competitors, cell B.** More difficult to identify than cell A competitors. They act differently and develop customer benefits and values differently.
- **Potential direct competitors, cell C.** Behave like those in Cell A, but may emerge from a different industry or geography.
- **Potential indirect competitors, cell D.** The most difficult competitors to identify. They do not compete today, and it is unclear when and where they will emerge.

**FIGURE 5.2**

**THE STRUCTURE OF COMPETITION**

**FIGURE 5.3**

**A FRAMEWORK
FOR IDENTIFYING
COMPETITIVE THREATS**

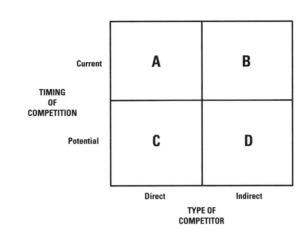

**FIGURE 5.3**

**A FRAMEWORK
FOR IDENTIFYING
COMPETITIVE THREATS**

*Marketing
Question*

Consider your most common mode of transportation — bicycle, automobile, train. Who are the **current direct** competitors? Who are **current indirect** competitors? Who are **potential** competitors — **direct and indirect**?

## COMPETITIVE DYNAMICS

We can extend Figure 5.3 to show how competition is likely to evolve. Dramatic changes may occur: New competitors may enter or local or regional competitors become national or multi-national. Figure 5.4 shows various paths competitors can take, and may help the firm forecast when one competitive threat may transition into another. We identify eight transitions:

- **Transition I.** from *potential direct* competitor (C) to *current* direct competitor (A)
- **Transition II.** from *potential indirect* competitor (D) to *current* indirect competitor (B)
- **Transition III.** from *potential direct* competitor (C) to *withdrawal* — no longer a threat
- **Transition IV.** from *potential indirect* competitor (D) to *withdrawal* — no longer a threat
- **Transition V.** from *current direct* competitor (A) to *withdrawal* — no longer a threat
- **Transition VI.** from *current indirect* competitor (B) to *withdrawal* — no longer a threat
- **Transition VII.** from *current direct* competitor (A) to *current indirect* competitor (B). The direct competitor has developed some new approach to satisfy customer needs.
- **Transition VIII.** from *current indirect* competitor (B) to *current direct competitor* (A). The indirect competitor has decided to compete on an *apples-to-apples* basis.

**FIGURE 5.4**

**A FRAMEWORK
FOR TRACKING
COMPETITIVE
THREATS**

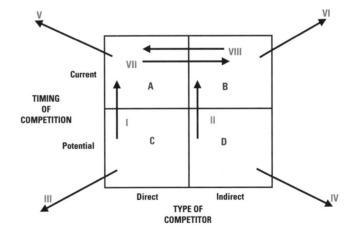

**KEY IDEA**

➤ Be aware of potential competition from within your own firm.

## THE FIRM AS A COMPETITOR

Our unstated assumption is that all competitors are other firms. But for product managers, the toughest competition may be internal. Different businesses always compete for resources like sales force time and financial, human resource, and systems budgets — but they may also compete for customers. The firm may encourage **intra-firm** competition, or it may occur by happenstance.

**DELIBERATELY INDUCED INTERNAL COMPETITION.** Motorola employees refer to its business units as *warring tribes*. Some firms foster Darwinian *internal* competition so as to improve effectiveness against *external* competition. They believe the resulting innovation more than compensates for resource duplication, especially if customers switch products and/or brands. P&G regularly mounts parallel product development efforts to develop better products and get to market faster.

**INTERNAL COMPETITION BY HAPPENSTANCE.** Internal competition often changes over time. Suppose the firm targets two market segments — segment A with product I, and segment B with product II. Over time, these segments may merge, and/or the firm's products and services evolve. Two originally independent approaches now become competitive.

In step 1 of the competitive insight framework, the firm probably identifies several external competitors. In steps 2 through 5, it should focus on the most serious competitive threats and develop deep competitive insight about them.

# DESCRIBING COMPETITORS

Describing competitors concerns four key areas:

- What *competitor data* should the firm collect?
- What *sources* of competitor data are available?
- What *processes* should the firm use for competitive data-gathering?
- What *frameworks* can the firm use to describe competitors?

Jackson and Walker are strategically important chemical subsidiaries of major U.S. multinationals operating in Asia/Pacific. Jackson has 60 percent market share and is highly profitable; Walker has 20 percent market share and is breaking even. Jackson learns that Walker's president is retiring. Information on the new president is: male; age, early 40s; chemical engineer by training; 20+ years with Walker's parent; joined Walker's parent after graduate school; known as a turnaround manager; has just successfully completed a smaller turnaround; known as a *margin-raiser*.

**Jackson's analysis and action:** Jackson decided that, within reason, it wanted Walker to be successful — a successful competitor would take predictable actions; an unsuccessful competitor could be a *wild card*. Jackson knew that Walker would not leave the market and also knew the new president's *margin-raiser* reputation.

Jackson raised prices modestly. Because of its 60 percent market share, it would significantly increase profits if Walker followed suit. When Walker's president arrived, he also raised prices. Walker became moderately profitable. Jackson invested some of its increased profits in additional services to strengthen its position.

Jackson based its action on good competitor insight. By learning about Walker's new president, it developed an innovative strategy that allowed it to *win*.

## COLLECTING COMPETITOR DATA

To describe competitors effectively, the firm must decide what it wants to know, based on the sort of decisions it has to make. We consider **level of data** and **type of data**.

**LEVEL OF DATA.** The firm should consider several organizational levels like corporate, business unit, market, and market segment. A competitive data profile on GE by a home appliance firm

## KEY IDEA

➤ When focusing on competitive data-gathering, the firm should be clear about the level and type of data it requires.

## KEY IDEA

➤ The firm can secure timely competitive information from many internal and external sources.

might include answers to several types of question. To illustrate:

- **Corporate.** How does GE allocate resources across its major businesses like financial services, entertainment, home appliances, and jet engines? What are its acquisition and divestiture plans? What effort is GE placing into innovation versus increasing efficiency?
- **Business unit.** How does GE allocate resources across its home appliance portfolio: refrigerators, dishwashers, washers and driers, and ranges?
- **Market.** What is GE's strategy in the refrigerator market? How does GE segment the market? Where is GE focusing its effort, by segment? What is GE's R&D in refrigerators? What is GE's capacity for making refrigerators? What is GE's capacity utilization?
- **Market segment.** For the segments where the firm competes with GE: What brand(s) does GE offer? How does GE position them? What models does GE produce? What are GE's prices? What are GE's credit terms? How do retailers display GE's products? What is GE's promotional emphasis: advertising, sales force, direct mail, etc.? What is GE's core message? How do target customers evaluate GE's offers? What is GE's segment profitability?

Responsibility for competitor data-gathering typically varies by level. At corporate and the business units, a competitive intelligence group often has direct access to industry analysts and consulting firms. Product and market managers are generally responsible for market and market-segment data. Responsible persons should develop their own data networks. Because the types of data vary by level, appropriate data-gathering approaches, analysis methods, and methodologies vary widely.

**TYPE OF DATA.** The firm should collect both quantitative and qualitative data. Quantitative data includes measures like profitability and market share: SEC filings often provide these data for public companies; business data services supply profiles for private firms. Qualitative data includes the expertise of competitors' managers and their anticipated strategic moves. The Internet offers many ways to obtain qualitative data. The data Jackson compiled on Walker's new president is in the qualitative category.

Competitive data-gathering should not focus solely on marketing issues. The firm needs information on competitors' products and services, operations, finance, costing systems, logistics, business philosophy (including willingness to innovate and take risks), and R&D. In his early days in the oil and gas industry, T. Boone Pickens learned about a rival's drilling activity by having a spotter watch the drilling floor with binoculars from half a mile away. By counting the number of joints connecting the 30-foot lengths of drill pipe, Pickens knew the depth of the competitor's wells.[3] Xerox purchases competitive products from dealers and carries out both customer value and manufacturing cost assessments. The firm should always be on the lookout for illegally acting competitors. Patent and trademark violations, predatory pricing, price fixing, and misleading advertising should all concern the firm.

## SOURCES OF COMPETITIVE DATA

The firm already has some competitive data internally; it needs a process to make these data available to the analyst. The firm must also seek competitor data externally. For both internal and external data, there are two approaches. **Secondary data** are available in published reports, filings, or on the Internet; the firm must collect, sort, and give them meaning, based on its questions about competitors. **Primary data** require a focused acquisition effort like customer interviews and surveys. For important data, the analyst should seek multiple sources, filter for reliability, and cross-validate. Table 5.1 lists data sources for different competitive issues.

| Generic Modes of Competition | Sample Internal Sources | Sample External Sources |
|---|---|---|
| Product line | • Sales, marketing, engineering personnel<br>• Industry studies | • Competitors' product catalogs<br>• Trade shows<br>• Trade associations, press, consultants<br>• Regulatory and patent filings |
| Features | • Sales, marketing, engineering personnel<br>• Internal analyses and trials | • Trade publication product reviews<br>• Competitors' literature, consultants<br>• Competitors' websites |
| Functionality | • Product comparison studies<br>• Reverse engineering | • Customers' reports<br>• Specialist trade reports/industry observers |
| Service | • Service personnel comparisons<br>• Comparative studies | • Customer, third-party assessments<br>• Mystery shopper reports |
| Availability | • Distribution and logistics personnel<br>• Sales force reports | • Customer satisfaction surveys<br>• Third-party (industry analysts) studies<br>• Distributor access |
| Image and reputation | • Marketing, sales, and advertising personnel<br>• Tracking studies | • Customer perceptions, third-party studies<br>• Competitors' advertising, promotion, and public relations |
| Selling and relationships | • Sales force reports<br>• Managerial assessments | • Interviews with customers and channel members |
| Price | • Marketing, sales, and service personnel<br>• Sales force reports | • Competitors' price lists<br>• Interviews with end customers |
| General information | • Senior firm executives | • The Internet, including<br>  • Competitors' websites<br>  • Rumor sites, e.g., www.gawker.com<br>  • Complaint sites, e.g., www.PayPalsucks.com<br>  • Blogs and forums<br>• Investment bankers/industry analysts |

**TABLE 5.1**

SAMPLE INTERNAL AND EXTERNAL DATA SOURCES[4]

## *Marketing Question*

Returning from an industry conference, the attractive young woman took her seat on the plane. The middle-aged man in the next seat glanced at her reading material, noting that they had both attended the same conference. He introduced himself as the marketing VP of a major pharmaceutical firm. She introduced herself as a product manager for its chief competitor. Trying to impress, the VP discussed, at length, his firm's marketing plans. The young woman listened attentively!

Did the young woman behave ethically? Would your answer change if she had not indicated her employment status? What do you think of the VP's behavior?

## INTERNAL PROCESSES FOR SECURING COMPETITIVE DATA

Many competitive data-gathering efforts fail because of a poor process — too complex, or short-term focused when a longer-term view is needed. Competitive data-gathering options differ by focus and required resources:

- **Competitive intelligence department.** This unit is responsible for collecting, analyzing, and distributing competitive information. The approach can be highly focused, but is expensive.

- **Competitive intelligence system.** The firm builds a culture where all employees are responsible for competitive intelligence. They come across competitive data daily; the critical step is to share them with a competitor intelligence group. Group members check, sort, and digest the data they receive, then send it to those who need it. This approach is less expensive than a competitive intelligence department, but is relatively unfocused.

- **Shadow system.** Individual executives or teams *shadow* specific competitors, either as a full- or part-time job. When shadowing is an extra responsibility, it can be an effective way of focusing attention on individual competitors, at relatively low cost.

- **Review of business lost and business gained.** When the firm wins or loses a sale it should find out why it won or lost. In well-managed firms, this process is standard operating procedure. Typically, customers are willing to share this information.

 KEY IDEA

➤ The firm should develop formal processes to secure timely and relevant competitive information.

- **Formal development of strategic plans.** When the firm has few major competitors, it can develop strategic plans as though it were the competitor. This highly-focused approach is usually only practical for one or two competitors. Boeing might use it (and the following) on Airbus, and AMD on Intel, and vice versa.
- **Gaming with multifunctional teams.** In these *war games*, executive teams play one of two roles: the firm or the competitor. Each team develops and presents its strategy and action plans; the *firm* and the *competitor* then develop counter-strategies and action plans. Conducted at one- or two-day offsite meetings, this process can generate important competitor insights.[5]

Students and executives are often concerned about the ethics and legality of competitor data-gathering. My position is clear: There are many ethical and legal approaches to securing competitor data; the firm should not use unethical or illegal methods like theft, bribery, covert recording, misrepresentation, knowingly jeopardizing someone's job, or placing *moles* at competitors. A widespread perception of industrial espionage by foreign governments led the U.S. Congress to pass the 1996 Economic Espionage Act making the theft or misappropriation of trade secrets a federal crime.

Some methods are not illegal but they may be unethical, like setting up job interviews to trawl for competitor data when no jobs are available. In 2006, HP hired agents to investigate information leaks from its board of directors. HP's chairman and other board members resigned because the agents secured information under false pretenses — a cautionary tale for those seeking competitive data.

Firms can secure good competitive data without bending any rules because most organizations are *leaky*. When the firm's competitive data-gathering efforts fail, the reason is usually insufficient resources and/or unfocused efforts. But, if competitors are leaky, your firm may also be leaky! Counter-intelligence is vital. The firm should take affirmative steps to protect its data:

- Classify information according to the degree of secrecy warranted.
- Train employees on the danger of loose tongues, especially when attending industry meetings and social events. Teach them to be good listeners — ears open and mouths shut!
- Execute employee **non-compete agreements** to prohibit former employees from working for competitors for a defined time period.
- Use **nondisclosure agreements (NDAs)** to prohibit revealing information to third parties. NDAs are standard for consultants and others working on a contract basis.

**KEY IDEA**

➤ The firm should not use unethical or illegal processes to collect competitor data.

➤ Leaky organizations help the firm secure competitive data.

➤ Good counter-intelligence procedures prevent proprietary data from leaking.

## FRAMEWORKS TO DESCRIBE COMPETITORS

The firm must organize competitive data into a useful framework. Good competitive insight can come via a *differential diagnosis* of the firm versus competitors. We use four basic building blocks: *competitor's organization, strengths and vulnerabilities, firm in the environment*, and *mind-set*. These analytic guidelines help the firm understand the competitor's *current strategy and performance*. The firm also gains insight into the competitor's future strategy.[6] It should adapt the framework for the level of competitive insight it seeks: corporate, business unit, market, or market segment.

### COMPETITOR'S ORGANIZATION. How the organization functions:

- **Infrastructure.** The line organization — basic responsibilities and reporting relationships.
- **Processes.** Accounting, information, control and reward systems, and processes.
- **Culture.** The behaviors, norms, beliefs, and values that together describe what the competitor stands for and how its members operate and behave.

*Marketing Question*

If you are a full-time student, select the firm you want to work for. If you are a part-time student, select your firm's major competitor. Use the Internet and other resources to complete the competitive analysis framework for the firm you chose.

**STRENGTHS AND VULNERABILITIES.**[7] Assets, capabilities, competences (and failings):

- **Assets.** Financial, physical, organizational, human, political, knowledge, and perceptual assets that embrace the competitor's brand equity and customer loyalty — proprietary and non-proprietary. The firm should also evaluate competitor liabilities, emotional commitments or *blind spots* that sometimes compromise hard-headed business decisions.

- **Capabilities and competencies.** Activities the competitor does well, including *local* expertise and broad-scale abilities, and areas where it does poorly. Specific abilities are: conceive and design, produce, market, finance, and manage. The competitor's approach to risk and its speed of action may also be a competence — or not!

**FIRM IN THE ENVIRONMENT.** Embraces relationships with other organizations:

- **Value chain.** Major work activities the competitor conducts and how they connect to external entities such as suppliers and customers. The firm asks four core questions:

  - Where does the competitor have a cost advantage?

  - Where is the competitor at a cost disadvantage?

  - Where does the competitor have a value advantage?

  - Where is the competitor at a value disadvantage?

- **Alliances and special relationships. Alliances** are formal economic relationships between the competitor and other entities (partners) — suppliers, customers, and distributors. **Special relationships** are informal and may embrace government agencies, political parties, and public interest groups — as well as suppliers and customers.

- **Networks.** Interconnected sets of alliances and relationships. Each fulfills a unique role. Rather than competing against a single competitor, the firm may compete against a network.

**MIND-SET.** How the competitor thinks and the bases for its decisions. What are its *assumptions*? What does the competitor take for granted, or as a *given*? Assumptions are the outcomes of analysts' judgments, inferred from competitive data.

**CURRENT STRATEGY AND PERFORMANCE.** How the competitor behaves and its results:

- **Market strategy.** The firm observes a competitor's actions and infers its market strategy.[8]

- **Other major resource commitments.** The competitor may build new factories, expand existing plants, and/or spend extensively on a particular type of R&D. The competitor may also display different levels of commitment to its various businesses.

- **Performance.** Most performance measures are financially based or market-oriented. Financial measures range from stock price performance to product-line profitability. Market measures include market share and customer satisfaction.

**KEY IDEA**

➤ The firm should use a rigorous framework to organize its data-gathering.

Won't the firm using this framework collect a tremendous amount of information, and won't it be overwhelming? Right! Describing competitors is not for the faint-hearted. When the task seems too great, remember that competitors are trying to attract, retain, and grow the same customers as you. If they are successful, they will survive and grow, and your firm will not. And you will be out of a job. The best way to appreciate this framework is to use it. We suggest you answer the Marketing Question on page 67.

## PULLING IT ALL TOGETHER

Sometimes the firm gains competitive insight directly from the data it collects. Other times it must integrate several data items. The firm can secure data on the competitor's product, advertising, service, distribution, and price — but it does not *see* what was behind these actions. The firm must make inferences from these data. Table 5.2 illustrates making inferences from *indicator* data.

**TABLE 5.2**

**DRAWING INFERENCES FROM DATA**[9]

| Indicators | Inferences |
|---|---|
| Hired new customer service manager | Competitor planning to upgrade service quality |
| Reorganized customer support and service (CSS) | Initial confirmation of service upgrade |
| CSS now reports to VP of marketing (versus sales) | Signals increased importance of service |
| Initiating new training programs for sales force | Enhancing service for all key customer segments |
| Emphasizes customer service in advertising | Service valuable to attract, retain, and grow customers |
| President comments: "Customers expect quality in services as well as in the product." | Service is becoming part of the competitor's mind-set — will be institutionalized |
| Customer to our salesperson: "ABC is now doing things for us they never did before." | Confirms competitor is institutionalizing and leveraging service |

**KEY IDEA**

➤ Organizations do not make decisions — people in organizations make decisions.

Finally, competitors *do not make* decisions: People working for competitors make decisions. The firm should identify competitors' decision-makers and influencers. The Jackson example (page 64) shows that career backgrounds, successes, and failures provide good competitor insight.

## EVALUATING COMPETITORS

The reason for evaluating competitors is to generate their strategic options. Knowing these options positions the firm to project competitors' actions. Identifying competitors (step 1) and describing competitors (step 2) are fine, but these are just the building blocks of competitive insight. The firm can only justify competitive intelligence efforts if they provide insight into competitors' future actions. Competitor assessment analysis helps answer three competitive evaluation questions:

- What options does the competitor have to be successful in the market?
- What would the competitor have to do to pursue each of these options?
- Is the competitor capable? (Does it have the resources to implement a particular option?)

### COMPETITIVE ASSESSMENT ANALYSIS

This powerful tool focuses on an individual competitor or group of similar competitors in a market or market segment and maps customer perspectives into corporate resources. Customers have needs that benefits and values can satisfy. The firm and its competitors must possess resources to deliver these benefits and values. The firm identifies where it has a *differential advantage* and where competitors have *differential advantages*. Recall from Chapter 1 that a *differential advantage is a net benefit or cluster of benefits, offered to a sizable group of customers, which they value and are willing to pay for but cannot get, or believe they cannot get, elsewhere.* Identifying differential advantage has five stages. Table 5.3 illustrates a market segment analysis.

**TABLE 5.3**

**ILLUSTRATION OF A COMPETITIVE ASSESSMENT ANALYSIS**

| Customer requirements: needs, benefits, values **A** | Importance Rank **B** | Necessary Capabilities / Resources **C** | | | | |
|---|---|---|---|---|---|---|
| | | Efficient Manufacturing System | Good Distribution System | Just-in-Time Delivery Systems | Well-Funded R&D | Access to Low-Cost Materials |
| Easy product availability | 1 | * YN | * YYY | | | |
| Low prices | 2 | * YN | | | | * YYN |
| Low inventories | 3 | | | * N | | |
| Access to cutting-edge technology | 4 | | | | * YYN | |
| *Etc.* | | | | | | |

- **Stage 1 – Identify customer requirements in terms of needs, benefits, and values.** Brainstorm or use marketing research.
- **Stage 2 – Importance order.** Reduce the items from Stage 1 to a manageable number, typically six to ten. Rank items in order of importance to customers — columns A and B.
- **Stage 3 – Necessary capabilities and resources.** Any firm would require these capabilities and resources to satisfy the customer requirements in column A; they map directly. To satisfy customers' most important item, *easy product availability*, requires a *good distribution system*. To offer *low prices* requires an *efficient manufacturing system*. Enter capabilities and resources in row C.
- **Stage 4 – Identify the matches.** Place an asterisk (*) in each matrix cell where a customer need/benefit or value — column A, intersects with a firm capability or resource — row C. Typically, the result is a sparse matrix; for any particular customer need/benefit or value, some capabilities and resources are irrelevant. For *easy product availability*, an *efficient manufacturing system* or *well-funded R&D* is not necessary. However, sometimes a capability or resource addresses more than one customer need/benefit or value.
- **Stage 5 – Examine the matches.** Ask up to three questions of each matrix cell with an asterisk. Asking a subsequent question depends on the answer to a previous question:
  a. **Relevance.** Does the firm have the capabilities or resources necessary to address the customer need/benefit or value? If yes, enter **Y**; if no, enter **N**, and stop.
  b. **Superiority.** For each cell where the firm entered **Y**. Are the firm's capabilities or resources superior to the competitor? If yes, enter **Y**; if no, enter **N**, and stop.
  c. **Sustainability.** For each cell where the firm entered **YY**. Would it be difficult for the competitor to match the firm's capabilities or resources? If yes, enter **Y**; if no, enter **N**.

The meaning of the entries is:

- **YYY.** The firm has a sustainable *differential advantage*. Its capabilities or resources match the customers' needs/benefits or values; they are superior to the competitor; it would be difficult for the competitor to catch up.
- **YYN.** The firm's capabilities or resources match the customers' needs/benefits or values; it has an advantage, but the competitor could match the firm relatively easily.
- **YN.** The firm's capabilities or resources match the customers' needs/benefits or values, but are no better than the competitor.
- **N.** The firm has a significant weakness or gap. The competitor completing a similar analysis would likely show a **YYY**; it would have a differential advantage.

The firm can explore the competitor's options by examining the cells in Table 5.3:

- **YYY** – *easy product availability/good distribution system*. The firm has a differential advantage in the customers' most important area. If the competitor is serious about this market segment, it would expend significant resources to improve its distribution system.
- **YYN** – *access to cutting-edge technology/well-funded R&D*. The firm is ahead of its competitor, but this is the customer's fourth most important requirement. The competitor may increase its R&D budget.
- **YN** – *low prices/efficient manufacturing system*. The firm and its competitor perform equally well in the customer's second most important area. The competitor may try to move ahead by improving its manufacturing.
- **N** – *low inventories/just-in-time delivery systems*. The competitor dominates. It will probably focus customer communications on *low inventories* to make sure it stays ahead.

Now that the firm views the market segment from its competitor's perspective, it can project which options the competitor will pursue. It should repeat the analysis for other market segments.

## KEY IDEA

➤ Competitive assessment analysis is a powerful tool for marketers. It maps customer requirements — needs, benefits, and values — into corporate capabilities/resources.

## PROJECTING THE ACTIONS OF COMPETITORS

The evaluation step generates a set of options for the competitor; the firm must assess which the competitor will choose. Will it continue its current strategy, or make a strategic change — short term, medium term, or long term? What specific change(s) will the competitor make? To start: what is the competitor trying to achieve? Specific questions include:

- What are the competitor's objectives in the market? Understanding objectives can help predict resource allocations.

- What market segments will the competitor address? How will it try to achieve its objectives — price leadership, operational excellence, product leadership, distribution strength, or what? What customer behavior is the competitor seeking to address?

- What is the competitor's staying power? Is it committed for the long run, or will it withdraw if the going gets tough? Sometimes withdrawal is not in the firm's best interest, as a divested unit may become a stronger and more difficult competitor.

**Scenarios** are a particularly effective way of evaluating the competitor's options.[10] They help the firm understand and predict competitor action. The scenario for a plausible option is a descriptive narrative of how the future may evolve; the firm should develop a scenario for each option. Based on various conditions and assumptions, the firm can compare and contrast the scenarios to gain insight into the competitor's possible actions. It projects the competitor's behavior by selecting the most probable action from the alternative scenarios. Three major types of scenarios are:

- **Emergent scenarios.** Start with the current strategy and consider what might emerge.
- **Unconstrained scenarios.** Based on open-ended *what-if* questions that suggest possible end states.
- **Constrained scenarios.** *What-if* scenarios that ask what the competitor might do under different market or industry conditions.

Effective scenarios have several important attributes:

- **Articulated plot and logic.** The *story* comprises a set of events and a logic an individual can follow.
- **Internally consistent logic.** The *story* hangs together.
- **Specific time frame.** The *story* specifies a time element for key events, actions, and results.
- **Decision/action-oriented.** The firm can derive and demonstrate implications for its current and future decisions.

As the firm builds scenarios, it must incorporate:

- **An end state.** An outcome at some specific future point.
- **A plot.** What the competitor must do to get to the end state.
- **Driving forces.** The conditions, trends, events, and circumstances that shape or drive the story described in a particular plot.
- **Logics.** The evidence and rationale for the end state and plot.

This description of scenarios and their attributes is fairly abstract, so we show an example. Our hypothetical firm is a yogurt manufacturer, Sunshine. Its major competitor, Moonglow, is contemplating a low-price market entry. We start by elaborating Moonglow's *projected strategy alternative* — low-price entry. This option, together with *supporting logics for Moonglow* and *supporting logics for Moonglow's environment*, allows us to *identify consequences for Moonglow*. These *consequences* lead directly to *implications for Sunshine*.

**MOONGLOW'S PROJECTED STRATEGY ALTERNATIVE.** Key elements in the strategy are to:

- Add a low-price product line aimed at customers for generic products.
- Use a different brand name.

**KEY IDEA**

➤ A good approach to projecting the competitor's future actions is to develop a set of robust scenarios that examine the competitor's strategic options.

- Maintain a high service level and use the same superior national distribution.
- Price similarly to low-end competitors and position against rivals' low-end products.
- Gain financial break-even in one year and 10 percent low-end market share in three years.

### SUPPORTING LOGICS FOR MOONGLOW.

- Moonglow must extend its product line to gain scope economies and pre-empt competition.
- Moonglow can acquire a supply of products from well-established vendors.
- Moonglow has demonstrated a capacity for building the required alliances.
- The entry fits Moonglow's apparent core assumptions that distinct market segments exist.
- The entry would leverage Moonglow's extensive marketing and sales capabilities.
- Moonglow's organizational culture — to be *the best in the industry* — supports the entry.

### SUPPORTING LOGICS FOR MOONGLOW'S ENVIRONMENT.

- Growth rates in Moonglow's segments will not support its announced revenue targets.
- Low-end segments have higher growth rates.
- The channels are demanding broad product coverage from suppliers.
- Successful competitors at the low end may be contemplating adding higher-end products.
- New vendors are specializing in providing products to branded competitors.
- The projected strategy could succeed if Moonglow can quickly establish a brand name, with a superior image, at a comparatively low price and with strong channel support.

### CONSEQUENCES FOR MOONGLOW. Moonglow will have to:

- Determine the product content.
- Develop the products.
- Organize its sales force.
- Acquire vendors.
- Establish its own manufacturing.
- Create marketing programs.
- Build trade relationships for the new product line.
- Moonglow could gain significant early market penetration.
- Moonglow will face significant issues on how best to differentiate its product, build brand name image, and leverage distribution channels.
- Moonglow will need to monitor each execution step.

### IMPLICATIONS FOR SUNSHINE. Moonglow's new market entry:

- Would pose a direct threat to Sunshine's current marketplace strategy.
- Would radically change the current marketplace assumptions.
- May eliminate potential sources of supply.
- May jeopardize potential alliance partners.
- Similar products would go after the same customers through the same channels.
- Sunshine's existing capabilities may be insufficient to sustain sales growth.
- Sunshine will need to introduce new options.
- Sunshine may need to introduce a new product line more quickly than planned.

Note how this scenario fulfills the conditions we outlined. It has an *articulated plot and logic*, an *internally consistent logic*, a *specific time frame*, and is *decision/action-oriented*. Of course, this is just one possible scenario that Sunshine might develop for Moonglow. To predict what Moonglow will actually do, Sunshine must develop a scenario for each of Moonglow's plausible options. Sunshine then selects, from the various scenarios, what it believes is Moonglow's most likely course of action.

**KEY IDEA**

➤ The firm projects the competitor's future actions by identifying the most likely scenario from the set of alternative scenarios.

## MANAGING COMPETITORS

Identifying the competitor's options and projecting its strategies put the firm in good position. But shaping, or managing, the competitor's actions is even better! Before trying to get competitors to behave in beneficial ways, the firm must answer two questions:

- What actions does the firm want its competitor(s) to take?
- What actions does the firm prefer that its competitor(s) not take?

In 2002, Dell tried to manage HP's actions. Despite an eight-year supply agreement with HP, Dell announced an alliance with Lexmark to sell Dell-branded printers. Four days later, HP broke the agreement. Observers believed that Dell was forcing price cuts in printers and toners, so that HP would be less able to support its money-losing PC business that competed with Dell.

### SIGNALING[11]

Sometimes firms send **signals** to competitors, hoping they will process the information and act accordingly. The firm should ensure its signals do not violate antitrust laws.

**PRE-EMPTIVE SIGNALS.** The firm sends *pre-emptive* signals so that competitors will make decisions favorable to the firm. For example, in mature industries, market share often approximates production-capacity share. To maintain market share, the firm maintains its capacity share by discouraging competitors from adding capacity and announcing its own capacity additions. In mid-2006, Daryl Ostrander, AMD's vice president of manufacturing, said, "We are fully positioned to service one-third of the market by 2008. We will manage, as we always do, these capacity additions. We aren't going to build too much, we aren't going to build too little."[12]

Other times, the firm must decide whether, and how, to *react* to a competitor. Many competitor moves do not require direct action, but if it does respond, the firm must make several related decisions:

- Where should it respond? Should it respond in the same market or in a different market?[13]
- How fast should it respond — immediately or wait to assess market reaction?
- How large should the response be? The firm could match or outdo the competitor.

This chapter forms a solid foundation for these decisions. Two types of response signal are:

**WARNING SIGNALS.** These signals tell competitors that if their actions reach certain thresholds, the firm will take serious steps to disadvantage them. It makes sure that competitors can predict its responses. A senior executive from a toothpaste market leader stated, "We believe there is a place in the market for a natural toothpaste. But if market share reached 3 percent, that could be a real problem! We would necessarily have to protect our market position!" The warning: "Don't increase your market share over 3 percent."

**TIT-FOR-TAT SIGNALS.** The firm designs these signals to bring competitors into line and stop them from making unilateral gains. It gets the competitor to behave by matching but not over-reacting to its actions.

## MISINFORMATION

**Misinformation** is a type of signal designed to mislead competitors. Relating to the capacity discussion above, capacity-increase announcements are relatively common in the chemical industry, but often the new capacity is never added! Misinformation may buy time for a developing strategy, but overuse can cause credibility problems.

**KEY IDEA**

➤ The firm may be able to *manage* its competitors by sending signals.

➤ The major signals available to the firm are pre-emptive, warning, and tit-for-tat. The firm may also send competitors misleading information.

# *The Company*

The firm does not need separate analytic frameworks for self-assessment. By developing good competitor insight, the firm secures good **company insight** as a by-product. Two approaches help the firm gain self-insight — *company description* and *company assessment analysis*.

## COMPANY DESCRIPTION

We used this framework for describing competitors — pages 67–68. The building blocks are *the firm's organization, strengths and vulnerabilities, firm in the environment* and *mind-set*. These four elements help in understanding how the firm settled on its *current strategy* and achieved its *performance*. To apply this framework, simply substitute *the firm* wherever *competitor* appears.

## COMPANY ASSESSMENT ANALYSIS

This analysis identifies where the firm *possesses* a differential advantage, and where it might place resources to *secure* a differential advantage. It is identical to the competitor assessment analysis, pages 69–70. We simply interpret the analysis from the firm's perspective, rather than from the competitor's. We take Table 5.3 as our starting point:

- **YYY** — *easy product availability/good distribution system.* The firm has a differential advantage in the customers' most important area. The firm should maintain its position by making deliberate investments to continually enhance its distribution system.
- **YYN** — *access to cutting-edge technology/well-funded R&D.* The firm is ahead of its competitor in the customer's fourth most important area. It should keep a close eye on the competitor and make the necessary investments to maintain its leadership position.
- **YN** — *low prices/efficient manufacturing system.* The firm has a significant vulnerability in the customer's second most important area. The firm and its competitor are equal, but effective investment would put the competitor ahead. The firm cannot afford this to happen.
- **N** — *low inventories/just-in-time delivery systems.* The competitor dominates; no doubt it emphasizes its good performance with customers. The firm may find it difficult to achieve parity, but this is the customers' third most important area.

These two approaches give the firm invaluable insight into its own position versus competitors. For *company description*, the firm must gather a significant amount of data. For *company assessment analysis*, it simply reinterprets the already-completed analysis from the firm's perspective.

# *Complementers*

A **complementer** is any organization whose actions affect the firm's sales;[14] of course, we exclude purchases. Both independent organizations and competitors can be complementers.[15]

## INDEPENDENT ORGANIZATIONS AS COMPLEMENTERS

The most obvious examples of complementary products are in economics texts: bread and butter, coffee and cream. More modern examples are laboratory equipment and chemicals; printers and toners; and hardware and software (computers and video games). Complementers can help each other generate sales, so they should develop mutually beneficial strategies.[16]

Another illustration is home laundry. Design changes in washers and driers have major implications for detergent manufacturers. Fabric designs have important implications for both appliance and detergent manufacturers. P&G and major appliance manufacturers work together

## KEY IDEA

➤ Independent organizations, including customers and suppliers, can be the firm's complementers.

to address new customer needs and to align innovations across the various industry sectors. Sometimes firms acquire very important complementers. GE is the global leader in medical imaging hardware; Amersham is a leading producer of complementary products, pharmaceutical agents that improve scanning images. In 2003, GE acquired Amersham for $9.5 billion.

**CUSTOMERS AS COMPLEMENTERS.** Customers act as complementers when they enhance the firm's offer. Comfort specializes in fraud detection systems based on statistical models.[17] Customers supply data to Comfort's data consortium. Comfort uses this data to improve its detection systems.

**SUPPLIERS AS COMPLEMENTERS.** Suppliers often complement the firm's actions to increase sales. Car makers expect suppliers to conduct R&D to improve automobile performance. McDonald's expects suppliers to contribute ideas and concepts to help grow McDonald's business — to be a *McPartner*, a supplier must do more than just deliver products!

## COMPETITORS AS COMPLEMENTERS

As a general rule, competitors are the firm's nemesis. They try to attract, retain, and grow the same customers as the firm. But competitors can also act as complementers, without getting into antitrust problems. We distinguish among strong, weak, and unwelcome complementarity.

**STRONG COMPLEMENTARITY: MARKETPLACE OR FRONT-OFFICE.** Sometimes competitors work together to better satisfy customer needs, like agreeing on technological standards. Verizon, SBC, and Bell South agreed on standards for ultra-fast fiber optic lines that reduced costs, sped introduction, and helped each firm compete with cable companies. Without this type of cooperation, customers are often uncertain about which technology will succeed and withhold purchases. As a result, the market develops more slowly.

A firm with new technology making a direct market entry essentially has two choices. It can go it alone, or offer its technology to competitors. If the firm acts alone, it has to shoulder the entire market development effort. When it decides on **marketplace cooperation**, the market develops faster, but the firm must accept a diminished position. This can be a difficult trade-off decision.

Apple chose to *go it alone* with Macintosh technology. Many observers believe that decision led to Apple's small market share in PCs; virtually all other firms settled on the DOS format championed by IBM and Microsoft. By contrast, Intel gave competitors AMD and Cyrix access to its MMX technology for graphics and video chips. For many years, Citibank successfully operated a proprietary ATM system, but when national and international networks like Cirrus, Maestro, and Star grew, Citibank eventually joined. At different times, Sony has used a *go-it-alone* approach and a *marketplace-cooperation* approach.

Sony was first to enter consumer videotape with Betamax. Sony failed, in part because JVC provided its VHS format to competitors. JVC's licensees helped expand acceptance, and Sony ultimately withdrew. More recently, Toshiba, Matsushita, Philips, and Sony avoided the multiple-standard problem by agreeing on a DVD format.

**STRONG COMPLEMENTARITY: BACK OFFICE.** Competitors may *compete* fiercely in the market, but their back offices *collaborate* extensively. **Back-office cooperation** in non-customer-facing activities aims to reduce costs and improve efficiency for all firms. Examples include:

- Retail brokerage houses work closely with competitors to clear trades.
- Italian tile manufacturers jointly purchase freight to reduce international shipping costs.
- General Mills, Columbo yogurt, and Land O'Lakes butter share delivery trucks.
- U.S. paper makers routinely swap products at list price to save freight costs.
- Major airlines collaborate in interline arrangements to move luggage among airlines.[18]

**WEAK COMPLEMENTARITY.** Marketplace and back-office complementarity generally require formal agreements. Other types of complementarity are weaker but may contribute positively:

- **Legitimacy.** Customers' purchases of one firm's products legitimize a competitor's products. Many U.S. farmers accept genetically modified seeds from industry leader Monsanto. Acceptance of Monsanto's products helps competitor DuPont to sell its products.

- **Cost reduction.** When several competitors have common suppliers, one competitor's actions may affect the others. Dell and HP compete in PCs, but if either's sales expand total volume, their joint purchases of computer chips increase. Chip suppliers achieve scale economies that reduce their costs — ultimately, chip prices decline for all PC producers.

- **Political action.** Competitors join trade associations to lobby governments for favorable decisions.

- **Greater customer value.** A firm's product may provide greater customer benefit when combined with a rival's product. Complementary drug regimens are an increasing trend — *drug cocktails*, often from different firms, dominate AIDS treatment. BMS initially introduced its blood-thinning product Plavix as a competitor to aspirin; today it positions Plavix as a complementer.

- **Increasing demand.** Competitors engage in joint advertising and other promotions so that all benefit. Shopping malls frequently draw consumers from large distances, and all stores gain.

- **Keep the firm sharp.** Tough competition keeps a firm on its toes. Some firms deliberately seek out tough competitors. One German engineering firm always launches new products in Japan.

**UNWELCOME COMPLEMENTARITY.** Sometimes firms do not want their products associated with other firms; these are unwelcome complementers. Automobile and aircraft manufacturers fight fiercely against unauthorized parts manufacturers; they believe these parts degrade their products. Callaway Golf is very successful with its oversized Big Bertha golf clubs. Spalding advertised that its Top-Flite/Club System C balls improved play with Big Bertha clubs. Callaway sued Spalding for trademark infringement, false advertising, and unfair competition; the case was settled out of court. Callaway later launched its line of Callaway Rule 35 premium golf balls!

**KEY IDEA**

➤ Competitors can complement the firm in the marketplace or in the back office. Competitors can also offer weak complementarity.

---

*Marketing Question*

What organizations are complementers for NBC (the U.S. television network)?

---

**KEY IDEA**

➤ A firm's complementary product activities may be unwelcome by its competitors.

---

........................................
## KEY MESSAGES

- The firm must gain deep insight about competitors that is both timely and relevant.

- To gain competitor insight, the firm should follow a structured process that asks several broad questions:
  - Who are our current competitors (today)? Potential competitors (tomorrow)?
  - Who are our direct competitors? Indirect competitors?
  - What are our competitors' capabilities and difficulties?
  - What are our competitors' strategic options?
  - What do we expect our competitors to do?
  - How can we get our competitors to do what we want them to do?

- Answering these questions is not a simple matter but, for each question, the firm can use several approaches to improve its competitor insight.

- The firm must know itself —company insight — but this is a simpler task.

- The firm must also understand its complementers, organizations that can help the firm increase its revenues.

- Both independent organizations and competitors can be complementers, each in different ways.

# CHAPTER 6
# MARKETING
# RESEARCH

## LEARNING OBJECTIVES

When you have completed this chapter, you will be able to:

- Translate your marketing problems and issues into actionable research questions.
- Think systematically about the marketing research process.
- Become familiar with the language and terminology of marketing research.
- Interact productively with specialist marketing researchers.
- Appreciate the advantages and disadvantages of several marketing research techniques.
- Use marketing research to obtain greater customer insight.
- Identify new marketing research techniques that may help you secure competitive advantage.
- Assess market and sales potential, and make market and sales forecasts.
- Become a sophisticated user (and client) of marketing research.
- Recognize the limitations and drawbacks of marketing research.[1]

## OPENING CASE: THOMSON FINANCIAL

*Thomson Financial (TF) provides information and decision analysis tools for the financial marketplace[2] and has evolved steadily since the 1990s through organic development and acquisition. TF has redefined its many offerings to keep pace with evolving market needs. TF focuses on helping organizations inform and build front-end customer strategy (FECS) by developing unique ways to gather, interpret, and disseminate customer insights. TF has a large customer base and many competitors; hence, insights gleaned from customers' experiences play a key role in differentiation and strategy development.*

*Warren Breakstone, TF's COO for global sales, marketing, and services, realized the importance of measuring customers' overall experience with all service touch-points — sales, account management, training, and help-desk support. He launched an annual global benchmarking satisfaction study, together with intermittent* check-ups *on clients who had recently used a training or help-desk service. Breakstone said, "The most important result was a deeper understanding of the drivers of customer satisfaction; that helped priority-setting and framed our resource allocation decisions. We began to understand the complex interplay between product satisfaction and customer services."*

*Breakstone said that customers might be very satisfied with a particular aspect of help-desk support. But that might not be a strong driver of customer satisfaction or increase the likelihood of referrals to others (an important customer-loyalty measure). Teasing out key customer-satisfaction drivers allowed TF to focus on actions that generated the greatest desired impact. TF found that one high-end customer subgroup greatly valued TF's financial-modeling consulting service. TF doubled its modeling investment, and its consulting services became more successful.*

*For Breakstone, gaining customer insight is more than simply executing quantitative benchmarking studies. "The key is to incorporate an understanding of how the data impacts ongoing decisions. Customer satisfaction measures have allowed us to challenge assumptions and make more fact-based decisions. We introduce more data into our discussions of what we should do differently going forward. We are dedicated to linking customer research to our day-to-day decisions." Breakstone said that many firms do not have this discipline; their research reports lie dormant, and their customer insights are never explored.*

*Kim Collins, SVP of marketing for TF's Corporate Services group, builds client insight via a structured series of monthly* pulse *surveys that measure customer satisfaction with its training and support functions. Collins said, "I believe that true* insight *is gleaned from comprehensive, detailed, and continual measurement of customer experiences with products and services at every touchpoint between us and our customers. Insight is the intelligence we gather when we stop to listen to clients. Only then do we begin to understand the impact, positive or negative, we're having on the customer's workflow."*

**CASE QUESTION**

What insights about marketing research can you draw from Thomson's experience?

*Collins' online surveys are briefer than the annual benchmarking studies — only five to ten questions — but they deliver important data for trend analysis. They also alert Corporate Services to potential problems with customers' experiences. TF's rapid response mitigates any dissatisfaction, but also lets customers know that TF is listening to their concerns and cares about their experiences. By involving cross-functional teams in the pulse initiative, customer insights infiltrate important functional areas.*

*Gaining customer insight is crucial for Thomson Financial. TF gains insight in the short-term and long-term, then applies this insight into its firm's decision-making processes.*

---

*I think one of the big dangers in today's marketing is that you get these big volumes of stuff, data, which mean nothing. In fact, I hate marketing research, but I love actionable customer insight. You have to work a bit harder. You have to apply your brain to really think through what questions you want to ask people. I think the issue is really thinking through what action you're going to take as a result of your study, rather than just producing a 150-page report that isn't actionable. What's important is research to take action, rather than research just to prove a point. We're not into that.*

—David Haines, Director of Global Branding, Vodafone[3]

Marketing research is any process of data collection, analysis, and interpretation the firm adopts to improve the quality of its marketing efforts. It may conduct marketing research on actual and potential customers, but also on customer influencers like legislators and regulators. Sometimes marketing research focuses on behavior. Other times its concern is with mental states like awareness, perceptions, attitudes, and intentions, at any and all stages in the customer experience. It also subsumes activities like gathering competitive intelligence, as we discussed in Chapter 5, and measuring marketing effectiveness. The related term *market research* has a narrower focus — specifically gathering data about current and potential markets.

It is not the purpose of this chapter to make you a marketing research expert. There are many books and courses to guide you if that is your goal. But we do believe that to be an astute marketer, you should become an *intelligent customer* of marketing research. You need to know where marketing research can be helpful and where it cannot. You must learn what sorts of questions to ask your marketing research suppliers and how to interpret their answers. We also spend time on a couple of very important topics for marketers: assessing market and sales potential and how to make sound marketing and sales forecasts.

## THE MARKETING RESEARCH PROCESS

Bristol-Myers Squibb's (BMS) marketing research mission is "to ensure the superior use of information and analysis to objectively identify opportunities, frame and validate strategic options, monitor results, provide insights, and build cumulative knowledge." BMS believes that superior customer understanding will provide critical insights for integrating into its decision-making processes. By championing industry-leading techniques, BMS' understanding and anticipation of the market provides critical insight into strategic issues. Insights from marketing research allow BMS to create leading programs, earn superior marketing and financial results, and develop and retain top business leaders. These lofty goals provide a window into the importance of timely and effective marketing research in developing a firm's future.

The purpose of marketing research is simply to help the firm make better marketing decisions. Figure 6.1 outlines a generalized **marketing research process** that follows a basic problem-solving approach. After all, without problems there would be no need for research. A critical element of success rests on the relationship between the manager and the researcher. Marketing research is a support function that helps the firm make decisions, but never forget: The manager is ultimately responsible for the decision and its outcomes. We know many cases where the manager, in effect, tossed the problem over the wall to marketing research with little guidance or direction and then expected an answer. This behavior is an abdication of managerial responsibility, often leading to dissatisfaction and frustration for all involved, not to actionable marketing research.

Responsibility for marketing research often extends beyond the marketing research department or a single manager or business unit. A senior executive at Target shared its approach with us: "We identify trends with a dedicated trend group that travels the world to find new trends in everything from apparel to home décor to food, and we use a tool called the trend curve to segment the life cycle of trends. This helps us determine when it will be hot, so we can get it into our stores at the right time for our guests. But we also involve the rest of the company. When anyone is traveling abroad, the expectation is that they will carve out time to go and understand what is happening in London, Berlin, Antwerp, Prague, Tokyo, or wherever they are. We want to know, what's emerging? What is the cool restaurant? What are the teenagers wearing? What are the young artists showing? We have an excellent trend department, but we also have people in every area of the company who have carved out the niche of being trend czars, because everyone has that role to play. We expect everyone to cultivate an eye."[4]

To ensure that marketing research is tightly aligned with marketing decision-making, the marketing research process must follow a consistent methodology. Key elements are in Figure 6.1.

## DEFINE THE BUSINESS ISSUE

As a manager, you have primary responsibility for defining the business issue. However, marketing researchers (either an internal department or an outsourced supplier) may encourage you to think more deeply about your concerns. Sometimes the *presenting* or immediate problem may actually be a symptom and not the real problem. You may believe that poor sales performance is due to lazy salespeople, but marketing research may suggest other potential causes like untrained first-line sales managers or an unsatisfactory product line. One methodology used in Total Quality Management, illustrated in Table 6.1, asks five "Whys?" as it seeks the root cause of an issue. Of course, you may believe you have sufficient data to solve the problem. If not, you should state your issue as clearly, completely, and simply as you can, then call in the marketing researchers to help you.

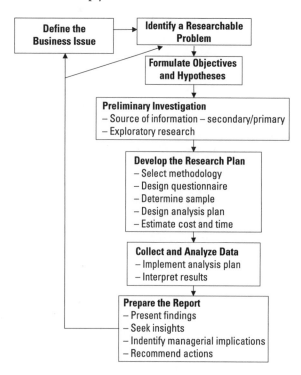

**FIGURE 6.1**

**THE MARKETING RESEARCH PROCESS**

| Round | Apparent Business Issue (Symptom) | Question (Cause) |
|-------|-----------------------------------|------------------|
| 1 | Our sales performance isn't up to par. | Why? |
| 2 | Salespeople aren't putting in enough effort. | Why? |
| 3 | It's hard to persuade customers to buy our products. | Why? |
| 4 | Our products don't really satisfy their needs. | Why? |
| 5 | Our product design process is deficient on customer insight. | Why? |

**TABLE 6.1**

**AN ILLUSTRATION OF DEFINING THE BUSINESS ISSUE**

## IDENTIFY A RESEARCHABLE PROBLEM

Marketing research may be unable to solve all your problems, but a good marketing researcher will help you frame the issues and problems so that research can be useful. (Sometimes managers expect too much, and exploratory research is necessary to frame the problem; an outside perspective from a consultant may also be useful.) Good marketing research can highlight the facts, point you in the right direction, and help you reduce uncertainty. But there is always a time cost of completing research, and if you wait for certainty, you will inevitably miss a window of opportunity. Collaborate with your researchers to define a researchable problem.

## FORMULATE OBJECTIVES AND HYPOTHESES

Together with the marketing researchers, you should agree upon the research objectives and hypotheses you will test. (You may revise these after exploratory research.) Objectives and hypotheses are usually related, but hypotheses are always more specific. For example, suppose your objective is to identify a market opportunity for a new product. Specific hypotheses may relate to positioning alternatives, price points, and brand name. You should be very clear about what insight you are looking for. Some examples are:

- **What:**
  - What do consumers think about our product and those from competitors?
  - What specifically do they think are the key benefits and values that we offer?
  - What benefits and values should we highlight in our communications?
- **Why:**
  - Why do some consumers switch among brands?
  - Why are some consumers fiercely brand loyal?
- **How and how much:**
  - How frequently do consumers purchase our product?
  - How do consumers prefer to buy?
  - How much do consumers purchase on each purchase occasion?
  - How much do consumers consume on each use occasion?
- **Who:**
  - Who makes the purchase decision for these products?
  - Who influences the purchase decision?
  - Who consumes these products?

Different research questions may require different methodologies like exploratory or causal research for *why* questions and qualitative research for *what*, *how*, and *who*.

## PRELIMINARY INVESTIGATION

Before conducting *primary* research directly with respondents, you should always check on available *secondary* data. Secondary data or existing sources may be inside the firm, but are often outside. (We'll talk more about distinctions between primary and secondary data later in the chapter.) Secondary data may provide partial, or even complete, answers to your research questions more quickly and less expensively than primary research. In other cases, you may start primary research by talking to colleagues. Job shifting within and between organizations means that someone may have previously addressed a problem like yours and can help you out. You may then conduct an exploratory qualitative study to secure insight. You may be able to narrow the scope of your enquiry by identifying gaps between the data you need to meet your research objectives and the data you already have. Typically, this information gap is the basis for larger-scale and more quantifiable research, where the costs really mount up. Skipping the preliminary stage can lead to heavy expenditures without commensurate insight.

## KEY IDEA

➤ The marketing research process contains several well-defined steps that the manager and the researcher should follow.

## DEVELOP THE RESEARCH PLAN

As the blueprint for your research, the more detailed research plan should include your data collection methodology (or methodologies), including developing data collection instruments like questionnaires, and a sampling plan identifying who will provide you with data. Quite simply, you want to make sure you get the right data from the right people at the right time. You should also specify the analytic methods you anticipate using. This can be intellectually challenging, but you should never collect data and then scratch your head wondering how to analyze it. Your research plan should also include time and cost estimates for management approval and negotiating contracts with any outside suppliers. Experienced firms apply a similar discipline to internal research projects and suppliers.

## COLLECT AND ANALYZE DATA

With a plan in place, you are now ready to begin your research. There are many ways to collect data, and you must make sure you use the *right* method, not just one that's easy. If you collect survey data, make sure your subjects are representative of the target population — don't just select them because they are easily available. You must also pay careful attention to response rates and implement procedures for dealing with non-responders; they may be systematically different from responders. You should always be concerned with data integrity and make sure it's collected honestly. No matter how carefully you plan your analysis, additional follow-up analyses may seem appropriate. But these add time and expense, and you will need to weigh their anticipated value versus the scope of your research plan.

Both manager and researcher should collaborate in interpreting the results. Marketing researchers should serve as experts on questionnaire design, sampling methods, analytic techniques, and interpreting statistically significant results. But managers are responsible for restricting researchers' interpretations to these types of issues, as they may lack insight into the problem context. Managers have ultimate decision-making responsibility and should not encourage researchers to make recommendations beyond their expertise. Correspondingly, the prudent researcher should always deflect such pressure.

## PREPARE THE REPORT

As a marketing manager, you will often review marketing research reports that others prepare. They will present the findings, but your goal and responsibility is always to seek insight. Many firms are rich in data and information, but lack knowledge and may have few insights. Take seriously David Haines' comments on page 78.

Accurate inferences drawn from raw data or processed information constitute knowledge. Many firms devote considerable effort to codifying knowledge and making it widely available (often with varying access); some firms even appoint *knowledge czars* (chief knowledge officers). Insight is different from knowledge. You develop insight by combining different knowledge elements, or using knowledge to create new meaning. Fred Smith's insight in the 1970s was that freight forwarders using passenger airlines could not provide reliable overnight package delivery; FedEx is an airline dedicated to packages. Steve Jobs and Steve Wozniak had insights that founded the PC industry. The insights of Jeff Bezos and Reed Hastings led to innovation and success with Amazon and Netflix respectively.

Make the assumptions in your research report transparent, clearly present the findings, and develop managerial implications. You may propose further research to clarify incompletely answered questions, but marketing research can only reduce uncertainty, never eliminate it entirely. A good report will propose alternative courses of action and make specific recommendations; after all, the goal of any research project should be some change in practice. Changes can range from minor course corrections to major innovations. If the report recommends no changes, at best you validated a current direction. At worst, you asked the wrong questions! Beware of research that is mere ritual, or managers who ignore results.

> ### Marketing Question
>
> Suppose that on the first day at your new job, your boss asks you to design a marketing research study to determine the reasons for customer loyalty. Outline the approach that you would present.

## CRITICAL DISTINCTIONS IN MARKETING RESEARCH

As a manager, you will be responsible for directing marketing researchers and the marketing research process. Here we make some critical distinctions that will help you as you devise your marketing research plans.

## KEY IDEA

➤ Secondary marketing research uses data relevant to your research needs that have already been collected for some other purpose. Primary market research requires you to collect new data.

## PRIMARY AND SECONDARY RESEARCH

The researcher should first consider the types of available secondary data and then fill in the information *gaps* with primary data collection.

**SECONDARY RESEARCH.** **Secondary research** uses secondary data — data that some person or organization collected for another purpose. There are three basic types of secondary data:

- **Public data.** Includes all information you can find about industry trends, customers, competitors, suppliers, and technologies. Sources include general business and industry-specific media and books, supplier white papers, trade show literature and presentations, trade associations, governments, published academic research, competitors' annual reports, competitor and public domain websites, other Internet sites (like dnb.com, Dialog.com, LexisNexis.com), and legal and government filings. Also included is semi-public data like syndicated research reports from firms like A.C. Nielsen and IRI and reports from industry and financial analysts. Locating data is often a challenge, but subscription databases and Internet search engines have made this job much easier.

- **Company data.** Comprises all of the routinely generated data from transactions with customers and suppliers and information from internal *enterprise* databases on costs, production, and capacity; customer lists; salesperson call reports; delivery, maintenance, and servicing reports; customer payment history; and previously completed marketing research reports. This category also includes data collected by the firm's customers, like bar code scanner data and RFID tracking data.

- **Technical analysis.** Includes objective, repeatable descriptions of products and services or production capacity collected by internal engineers or developers. Examples include benchmarking product design and reverse engineering competitors' products to estimate manufacturing costs and supply-chain processes.

**PRIMARY RESEARCH.** Typically, **primary research** is more expensive than secondary research. The firm usually collects primary data for a specific purpose, often to close gaps between data required to make decisions and data already available from secondary research. Primary data sources depend on the research problem but may include previous, current, and/or potential customers, including people in various roles in the purchase and consumption process; industry experts and trade association personnel; and distribution channel members like brokers, and distributors, wholesalers, and retailers. Sometimes the firm lowers primary data costs by joining a syndicate/consortium whose members seek data from similar respondents.

All primary research requires a stimulus. Frequently, this is a question the researcher wants answered. Sometimes the firm provides specific stimuli like advertising or positioning concepts, attribute lists or product profiles, advertising or sales messages, or competitive materials/products.

## Marketing Question

Suppose you need to know the sales for a product class or product form that interests you. What secondary sources will provide these data?

## QUALITATIVE AND QUANTITATIVE RESEARCH

The firm has two major approaches to marketing research — **qualitative** and **quantitative**:

**QUALITATIVE RESEARCH.** Qualitative research is not concerned with numbers. It is generally flexible and versatile, but is rarely conclusive and does not project to a larger population. Firms often conduct qualitative research to pursue interesting questions, uncover customer needs, identify buyer behavior, gain a better understanding of business issues and the *language* people use, develop ideas, and help define and prioritize research problems. Qualitative research can help assess how customers *feel* about products and suppliers. Small-scale exploratory primary qualitative research often precedes large-scale quantitative data collection.

A particular issue in qualitative research is the difference between self-reported response data and data on actual behavior. Both types can be valuable, but the researcher should always be skeptical about respondents' self-reports. Just because a respondent says "I did X" or "I will do

## KEY IDEA

➤ Qualitative marketing research is not concerned with numbers. Quantitative market research focuses on quantitative analysis.

X" does not mean the respondent actually did, or will do, X. Respondents may purposely mislead researchers, but mismatches between self-reports and actual behavior are often due to poor memory, bias, and unclear questions. Researchers should seek convergence; the Kimberly-Clark example is instructive:

> Focus groups provided Kimberly-Clark (KC) with little insight into why Huggies baby wipes were losing sales. It introduced a new observational technique, a camera mounted on a pair of glasses that consumers wore at home. In focus groups, mothers talked about changing babies on a diaper table. From the cameras, researchers saw that mothers changed babies on many surfaces, often in awkward positions, and struggled with containers requiring two hands. KC redesigned packages for wipes, shampoo, and lotions that could be easily dispensed with one hand.

**QUANTITATIVE RESEARCH.** Quantitative research uses numerical data and mathematical analyses, often from large representative samples. Marketing researchers employ quantitative research to test hypotheses formulated earlier in the research process. Some analyses are quite simple; others are highly complex. The researcher should ask three types of question when collecting and evaluating quantitative data:

- **Internal validity.** Do these data measure what I want to be measuring?
- **Reliability.** If I repeat the data collection, will I get the same results?
- **External validity.** Will the results I secure generalize to other populations?

Sometimes drawing the line between qualitative and quantitative research is difficult, as some forms of qualitative data are amenable to quantitative analysis. Researchers are always pursuing new forms of quantitative analysis, but qualitative data gathering is also evolving. Firms striving for increased customer insight are driving these innovations.

The 2x2 matrix in Figure 6.2 shows how primary and secondary research can be either qualitative or quantitative. Generally, quantitative approaches to primary research data yield more insight than qualitative approaches. But with secondary research, the firm can often gain significant insight from the large amounts of qualitative data that are often available.

|  | **Primary** | **Secondary** |
|---|---|---|
| **Qualitative** | Small-group discussions with customers about product alternatives | Review of advertising campaigns from various product suppliers |
| **Quantitative** | Large-scale sample survey of customers about product alternatives; test hypotheses by quantitative methods | Secure independent research reports on customers' views of product alternatives; conduct quantitative analyses |

**FIGURE 6.2**

**ILLUSTRATION OF RESEARCH TYPES**

# SECURING QUALITATIVE RESEARCH DATA

Now let's look at a few of the most popular primary data-gathering methods for securing insight into customers' needs and motivations.

## FOCUS GROUPS

**Focus groups** are one of the most popular qualitative data collection methodologies. Typically, focus groups comprise eight to 12 members (often paid for participation and selected for their

## KEY IDEA

➤ Focus groups, one-on-ones, and blogs and wikis are alternative means for collecting qualitative data directly from respondents. Projective techniques, observation, and ethnographic research are indirect qualitative data-gathering approaches.

interest, knowledge, and/or experience with the topic) moderated by a skilled facilitator. The facilitator asks carefully scripted probing questions, maintains good participant interaction, and tries to ensure that each member contributes. An advantage of focus groups is that one member's ideas can spark responses in another. Potential problems are having strong individuals dominate the discussion, less than honest responses, psychologically defensive behavior, and a conservative bias in favor of the known versus the unknown. Also, the necessity of a central location can limit participation and skew results if care is not taken with member selection. Managers and researchers often receive immediate feedback by watching focus group discussions through one-way glass. Typically, the researcher records the discussions and has them transcribed. *Virtual* focus groups (online or interactive conferencing systems) are newer alternatives. They reduce the problems of dominating participants and travel costs, but tend to limit the degree of participant interaction. Brainstorming (Chapter 13) is a variant of focus groups.

## ONE-ON-ONE INTERVIEWS

**One-on-one interviews** (OOOs) combine direct and indirect questions asked of individuals to probe their needs and underlying purchase motivations. Mostly, researchers conduct OOOs in person or on the telephone. OOOs avoid the group bias sometimes found in focus groups and can address more sensitive topics, but are generally more expensive and time-consuming. Although OOOs cannot build on ideas from others, dialog can be more open, and skilled interviewers can secure significant insight.

## BLOGS AND WIKIS

Blogs and wikis are two versions of online collaborative message boards, organized by individuals or firms, where people post complimentary or critical comments about products, brands, and/or firms. Vigilant analysis of dialogs on popular blogs and wikis can help the firm identify where performance is good, where it is poor, and what it might do differently. But because responders are generally anonymous, marketing researchers must weigh the validity of dialogs as a legitimate qualitative tool.

## PROJECTIVE TECHNIQUES

Researchers use projective techniques, aka motivation research, mainly to uncover latent customer needs. Developed by psychologists, these approaches have a long history in marketing and include:

- **Word associations.** The researcher supplies a stimulus word. The respondent offers the first word that comes to mind. Specific applications include image studies and branding research.
- **Role-playing.** The researcher asks respondents to pretend they are a brand's friend and write it a letter, or ask why a neighbor or work colleague may like or dislike a particular product. Role-playing and storytelling avoid arousing the respondent's subconscious defenses.
- **Storytelling.** The researcher shows the respondent a picture or provides a situation relevant to the research topic. The respondent makes up a story about one or more characters in the stimulus.
- **Imagery.** The researcher asks the respondent to draw a picture that shows her interacting with the product, and then asks her to interpret the picture.
- **Constructing a collage.** The researcher asks the respondent to collect pictures from newspapers and magazines that express his feeling about the topic.

## OBSERVATION

Yogi Berra said, "You can see a lot just by observing."[5] In this method, the researcher does not ask questions, but secures insights by watching and recording behavior (often by video) in naturalistic settings. He assesses the respondent's behavior, including emotional responses, body language, and person-to-person interactions, as well as the respondent's home environment. Observation is a reliable technique provided the researcher uses correct methods. Although difficult to code, observational data are objective, accurate, and unbiased by researcher intervention:

> Gerald Baliles, Governor of Virginia (1986 to 1990), said: "When I was in China a couple of years ago, I was struck by how often I encountered chicken feet in the soups, foods, and markets. When I got back, my people called the poultry industry to find out what they do with chicken feet. They were chopped off on the assembly lines and discarded. Today Virginia ships 40 tons a month of chicken feet to the Far East."

Observational data may be more accurate than other types of data. When PepsiCo surveyed owners/managers at 7,000 restaurants serving Pepsi, respondents said that price was the critical decision variable in choosing Coke or Pepsi. But a smaller observational study of 800 restaurant *switchers*, from Coke to Pepsi or vice versa, showed that four service variables were most highly correlated with switching behavior: poor delivery, unreliable equipment, emergency shipments, and poor equipment maintenance.[6]

## ETHNOGRAPHIC RESEARCH

Derived from anthropology, **ethnographic research** is an observational method where researchers spend *a day in the life (DILO) of their customers,*[7] corresponding to the anthropological process of *living with the tribe.* Observers gain insight into their subjects' culture and belief systems, uncover needs, and understand how customers integrate products into their daily lives. Tom Katzen, responsible for marketing Levi's jeans to teenagers, used to spend Saturday mornings with teenagers lining up for tickets at San Francisco's Fillmore Auditorium, observing the way they customized their blue jeans. Many firms employ *cool hunters* to observe people's behavior and clothing in their natural settings like inner-city basketball courts and fashionable nightclubs, and to hang out on social networking sites like Facebook and MySpace.

Before it designed the Lexus LS 400, a luxury car specifically for the U.S., Toyota's chief engineer and his team lived for several months in Southern California's upscale Laguna Hills. They visited many upscale metropolitan areas around the U.S., from Coral Gables near Miami, to north Lake Shore Drive in Chicago, to Westchester County, New York. They learned how luxury car owners drove, treated their cars, and dealt with valet parking. They figured out the role cars played in these people's lives and their product and service expectations. The Lexus was and remains an unqualified success.

> *Marketing Question*
>
> Go to your local supermarket and observe consumers' behavior in the cereal aisle. What can you learn? What hypotheses can you develop that you would like to test by quantitative methods?

## SECURING QUANTITATIVE RESEARCH DATA

There are several ways of securing data for quantitative analysis.

## SURVEYS

Sample **surveys** of the target population are the most common way to secure primary data for quantitative analysis. Selecting a sample that reflects the underlying population is critical. So is assessing the required sample size for estimating the parameter(s) of interest at the desired accuracy level. Both topics are beyond the scope of this chapter, but as a rule, there are critical trade-offs between cost, time, and flexibility. The firm can reduce its costs by joining a marketing research firm's omnibus survey, or it can sponsor its own research.

Questionnaire design is critical to survey success and should involve both the researcher and the manager. Development can be relatively unstructured and qualitative, but producing the final questionnaire requires much thought. The questionnaire should avoid biases from yea-saying (unreflective agreement), question order, and questions that are vague, difficult to answer, or easily misinterpreted. It should always be pretested. Good questionnaire design typically includes both open-ended and closed-ended questions. Table 6.2 identifies several standard approaches to asking questions.

**TABLE 6.2**

SELECTED STANDARD APPROACHES TO ASKING QUESTIONS

| Approach | Example | Comments |
|---|---|---|
| **Rank ordering** | Put a "1" against the brand you would be most likely to buy; "2" against the next most likely brand, etc., until you have ordered all brands:<br>    HP, Dell, Lenovo, Macintosh, VAIO | Researcher must rotate the order of the brands<br>Secures ordinal measures[8] |
| **Constant sum** | Allocate 100 points among these benefits so that the more important benefits get the most points. | Secures ratio measures |
| **Paired comparison** | Circle the brand in each pair that you would most likely buy:<br>    HP or Dell<br>    Dell or Macintosh<br>    Lenovo or VAIO | Comparisons limited by respondent fatigue[9]<br>Secures interval measures |
| **Likert-type scales** | Agree or disagree: VAIO computers are easy to maintain:<br><br>| 1<br>Strongly agree | 2<br>Agree | 3<br>Neutral | 4<br>Disagree | 5<br>Strongly disagree |<br>|---|---|---|---|---| | Be careful of positivity bias.<br>Use positively and negatively worded items<br>Use multiple items for reliability |
| **Semantic differential scales** | Rate (focal object) on these scales by circling the number that best reflects your opinion.<br>Dumb  1  2  3  4  5  6  7  8  9  10  Smart<br>Weak  1  2  3  4  5  6  7  8  9  10  Strong<br>Bad    1  2  3  4  5  6  7  8  9  10  Good<br>Soft   1  2  3  4  5  6  7  8  9  10  Hard<br>Easy   1  2  3  4  5  6  7  8  9  10  Difficult<br>Fast   1  2  3  4  5  6  7  8  9  10  Slow | Use 7–12 sets of bipolar adjectives<br>Factor-analyze to secure the underlying meaning[10] |

**KEY IDEA**

➤ When designing a process to collect survey data, the firm must make several important trade-offs, primarily between cost, time, and flexibility.

## PANELS

For many marketing research projects, survey data from different respondent samples is just fine. But sometimes the firm wants to follow up on individual responses. A **tracking study** (aka longitudinal study) requires forming a panel of individuals who agree to provide responses periodically over time. Maintaining a panel is challenging, but judicious replacement of panel members can keep a panel going almost indefinitely. Panel data allows the firm to *keep its pulse* on customers, conduct more sophisticated analysis, and better identify causal relationships. Because panel data tends to be expensive, firms like A.C. Nielsen and IRI offer syndicated services to form and manage panels. Not only do several user firms share the costs, the outside firm provides a sense of independence to the data. Online marketing research firms like Greenfield Online and Harris Interactive maintain large panels from which firms can select sub-populations for specific surveys.

Panels provide data with varying degrees of intrusiveness. Panelists may commit to write down their purchases, answer questionnaires periodically, or agree to a simple installation that monitors their TV watching. They may also use a supermarket value card that provides scanner data (next section) on their purchases. Combining self-reported panel data with actual use data can provide significant insights.

## OBJECTIVE SALES DATA

The firm's own sales reporting system can provide valuable quantitative data. Sales data to end-user customers can be more difficult to secure when products move through distribution channels. In supermarkets, the widespread use of barcodes and retail scanners makes it easy to collect and store sales data by sku (stock-keeping unit). IRI and A.C. Nielsen each secure scanner data from several thousand supermarkets in many urban markets, which they aggregate and sell to manufacturers. Collection and use of automatically collected sales data is likely to increase. For example, by monitoring vending machine sales remotely, a firm could better schedule deliveries, adjust the product mix, price dynamically, and make personalized offers for purchasing by cell phone. Internet firms collect sales data directly by individual and, together with search data from *cookies*, develop buyer profiles for making purchase recommendations. EZ Pass systems automatically measure your use of road services.

## EXPERIMENTS

**Experiments** allow researchers to definitively establish causal relationships like A → B. The researcher manipulates independent variables like advertising programs and price levels, and measures results, like awareness or product sales. Superior experimental designs include a control group that does not receive a manipulated variable treatment. Because many non-manipulated and unmeasured variables can affect results, researchers typically use random assignment for experimental and control groups. Experiments can range from limited-scale laboratory studies to large field experiments. The critical trade-off is between cost and the ability of researchers to draw conclusions.

Relatively few firms conduct experiments, and then mostly in the laboratory. FMCG firms often use field experiments for test marketing new products and assessing alternative promotional programs. Experiments are a serious business at Pfizer; it spends millions of dollars to test different promotional strategies and ways of allocating its selling effort. Amazon continuously tests different email messages.

What most firms fail to realize is that day-to-day business life can function as a **natural experiment**. Rather than manipulate independent variables, the firm can use the *natural* variability in its decisions to seek relationships with results. Costs of data storage and analysis are fast reducing, and some firms evolve their actions in real time. Leading firms are becoming learning organizations by treating their entire set of marketing actions as data in natural experiments.[11]

> *Marketing Question*
>
> How would you design an experiment to measure the impact of advertising spending and price on sales of your product? (Choose your own product.)

## ANALYZING QUANTITATIVE RESEARCH DATA

Quantitative research data are amenable to a broad variety of statistical analyses. If the underlying assumptions are valid, quantitative methods can have significant predictive power and be very helpful to the firm in making marketing decisions. This is a huge topic that we cannot address here, but many fine marketing research textbooks are available for interested students.

## MARKET AND SALES POTENTIALS, MARKET AND SALES FORECASTS

"It's tough to make predictions, especially about the future." — Yogi Berra[12]

Now you are armed with many options for designing and conducting research studies to provide you with greater insight into markets, customers, competitors, and complementers. These insights will enable you to build more powerful market strategies and implementation plans, as

> *Marketing Question*
>
> In 1999, Airbus predicted demand for its superjumbo A380 jet aircraft at 1,440 planes and forecast that 10 U.S. airlines would buy 281 of them. In spring 2007, with Airbus expected to deliver its first plane in October, it had orders for 156 aircraft from 14 airlines, yet none of these were U.S.-based. How do you explain the discrepancies?

you seek to deliver value to customers and secure differential advantage. We have not addressed yet the role of marketing research in predicting market size and the firm's sales. These predictions are critical for many reasons, ranging from identifying the attractiveness of a market opportunity to production planning and budgeting the firm's financial, human, and other resources.

Two related concepts — *potentials* and *forecasts* — are important for predicting market demand and the firm's own performance. Unfortunately, many managers are confused about these terms. Potentials and forecasts are quite different, but each has important quantitative aspects. *Potential* embraces having a *capability or future state*. **Market potential** is what the market could become; **sales potential** is what the firm's sales could become. By contrast, *forecast* concerns *expectations*. Forecast market size is the expected market sales in a given time period; sales forecast is the firm's expected sales. We now explore assessing both potentials and forecasts.

## DEFINING AND ASSESSING MARKET POTENTIAL

Market potential is the *maximum market-level sales* that the firm believes could occur in a future time period. Since all markets go through life cycles, the firm wants to have some idea of market sales at various growth stages and in maturity. Market potential is an upper bound to actual sales, based on a set of assumptions about future market conditions. Market potential is especially important when contemplating entry in a new market.

To assess market potential, the firm should estimate the number of likely customers and the amount they are likely to buy. Of course, the identity of likely customers may change as the market and product evolves, and their propensity to buy will change also. There are three steps:

- **Identify likely market segments.** Most markets comprise several segments. The firm must understand these segments, even though some may not purchase until later.
- **Estimate numbers of customers in each segment.** The firm estimates the number of customers that are likely to buy in the time period for which it seeks market potential.
- **Estimate the number of products to be purchased.** The firm estimates the numbers of products customers in each segment are likely to buy for the relevant time period.

Table 6.3 shows typical market potential calculations for a new consumer product, for three years, six years, and 10 years after launch. In this illustration, we assume three market segments.

**TABLE 6.3**

CALCULATIONS OF MARKET POTENTIAL

| Time Period | Market Segments | Total Number of Customers in Each Segment (millions) A | Percent Likely to Buy (%) B | Number of Customers Likely to Buy C = A x B (millions) | Number of Units that Those Purchasing Are Likely to Buy D | Segment Potential Calculation E = C x D (millions of units) | Market Potential (millions of units) Sum of the Es |
|---|---|---|---|---|---|---|---|
| 3 years after launch | Seg 1 | 10 | 50% | 5 | 5 | 25 | |
| | Seg 2 | 6 | 20% | 1.2 | 2 | 2.4 | **27.4** |
| | Seg 3 | 8 | 0% | 0 | 0 | 0 | |
| 6 years after launch | Seg 1 | 11 | 70% | 7.7 | 6 | 46.2 | |
| | Seg 2 | 6 | 40% | 2.4 | 4 | 9.6 | **58.6** |
| | Seg 3 | 7 | 10% | 0.7 | 4 | 2.8 | |
| 10 years after launch | Seg 1 | 12 | 70% | 8.4 | 7 | 58.8 | |
| | Seg 2 | 6 | 50% | 3.0 | 6 | 18 | **93** |
| | Seg 3 | 6 | 30% | 1.8 | 9 | 16.2 | |

There are several interesting points within this table:

- The firm believes the numbers of customers in each segment will change over time. Segment 1 increases, segment 2 stays the same, and segment 3 decreases.
- The percentage of customers likely to buy also changes. Segment 1 increases, then stays constant; segment 2 increases continuously; segment 3 is zero initially, then increases.
- For each segment, the firm predicts that only a fraction of customers will purchase.
- The amount purchased increases for each segment, quite dramatically for segment 3.
- For each time period, market potential is the sum of the individual segment potentials.

The firm can estimate *potential revenues* by multiplying *potential units* by the estimated price in each time period.

## DEFINING AND ASSESSING SALES POTENTIAL

Sales potential is the maximum sales the firm might achieve in a given time period. Of course, sales potential is conditioned on assumptions about the firm's likely efforts, market potential, and future market conditions, like the number and strength of competitors.

The firm can calculate sales potential directly from market potential by assessing its potential market share. The firm's potential share depends both on the resources it could commit to the market and the actions it believes competitors will take. If the firm contemplates increasing its resources over time (and/or believes that competitors will reduce their commitments), its estimated potential market share should also increase. Table 6.4 shows illustrative sales potential calculations based on the market potential estimates from Table 6.3.

| Time Period | Market Potential (millions of units) A | Firm's Potential Market Share (%) B | Sales Potential (millions of units) C = A x B |
|---|---|---|---|
| 3 years after launch | 27.4 | 10% | 2.74 |
| 6 years after launch | 58.6 | 20% | 11.72 |
| 10 years after launch | 93 | 30% | 27.9 |

**TABLE 6.4**

**CALCULATIONS OF SALES POTENTIAL**

## DEFINING AND FORECASTING MARKET SIZE

**Market forecasts** often focus on the short run, like the upcoming year, where the firm can assess market conditions with a fair degree of accuracy. To forecast market size, the firm can focus on the overall market or on individual segments that it later aggregates. Generally, a segmented approach provides better forecasts if data are available. The broad approaches to assessing market size are judgmental, time-based, and causal-factor. We look at several types of each.

**JUDGMENTAL METHODS.** These are the simplest methods for forecasting market size:

- **Executive judgment.** The responsible manager has deep familiarity with the product class, competitive offers, customer needs and satisfaction levels, and many environmental factors. She may make her own intuitive judgments.
- **Delphi method.** A valuable approach when several people have an opinion about the market. Each person makes a market forecast and specifies the rationale. Each person then receives all forecasts and rationales, and revises his or her forecast. Forecasts often converge after a couple of rounds, but the process can proceed for several rounds.

**TIME-BASED METHODS.** These methods use past sales to predict the future directly:

- **Judgmental extrapolation.** A special case of executive judgment using history to predict a percentage change from the previous year. The basis could be the most recent year-to-

year change, a simple average of the previous two (three, four, five) years' changes, or a weighted average of previous years' changes, with greater weight to more recent years.

- **Linear extrapolation.** Two-variable regression analysis estimates year-by-year change in sales. Forecast sales for next year are last year's sales plus an increment (or decrement) based on prior years' sales. The extrapolation increment is calculated mathematically, but the forecaster must decide how many prior years to use.

- **Moving average.** The manager uses sales data from previous years to calculate an average; this average is the forecast. For each successive year, the manager drops the earliest sales datum and adds in the most recent. Hence, sales from several years ago do not weigh too heavily in the forecast. Once again, the manager must judge how many years to include.

- **Exponential smoothing.** This method uses previous sales data in a slightly unusual way. Rather than forecasting based only on actual sales data from previous years, exponential smoothing uses both last year's actual sales and the last year's forecast sales. It calculates a smoothing parameter, "a," from previous sales data:

$$\text{Forecast sales}_{t+1} = a \times \text{actual sales}_t + (1 - a) \times \text{forecast sales}_t$$

The value of "a" depends on the relative weight for the prior year's actual sales versus the prior year's forecast sales; it ranges from zero to one. If historic sales were fairly constant, forecast sales weigh quite heavily, and "a" is on the low side. If sales change substantially year by year, as in a growth market, "a" may be close to 1.

Table 6.5 shows how to use these methods to forecast the global market size for laptop computers. The second column shows actual sales; columns to the right show market size forecasts using judgmental extrapolation, linear extrapolation, moving average, and exponential smoothing. In each case, the first forecasts are for 2000. Forecasts by judgmental extrapolation are based on the actual percentage change in sales for the most recent year. For the other methods, forecasts are based on the previous five years' sales. For example, the forecasts for 2000 are based on data for 1999, 1998, 1997, 1996, and 1995; forecasts for 2003 are based on 2002, 2001, 2000, 1999, and 1998. We can make several inferences about these data:

- Actual sales increase markedly in 2003 and subsequent years; the deviations are mostly greater for later years for all forecasting methods.

- Because actual sales growth is high in later years, simple judgmental extrapolation does best. The other methods are handicapped, to a greater or lesser extent, by their reliance on sales from earlier years. This is especially marked for the five-year moving average. (Moving-average forecasts with fewer years [not reported] do better.)

- For all years, the exponential smoothing forecast is the previous year's actual sales, because the smoothing constant, a = 1.

**TABLE 6.5**

**PREDICTING GLOBAL MARKET SIZES OF LAPTOP COMPUTERS (000S)**

| Year | Actual Sales | Judgmental Extrapolation | | Linear Extrapolation | | Moving Average | | Exponential Smoothing | |
|---|---|---|---|---|---|---|---|---|---|
| | | Forecast sales | Deviation from actual sales | Forecast sales | Deviation from actual sales | Forecast sales | Deviation from actual sales | Forecast sales | Deviation from actual sales |
| 1995 | 8,791 | — | — | — | — | — | — | — | — |
| 1996 | 11,148 | — | — | — | — | — | — | — | — |
| 1997 | 14,043 | — | — | — | — | — | — | — | — |
| 1998 | 15,482 | — | — | — | — | — | — | — | — |
| 1999 | 19,858 | — | — | — | — | — | — | — | — |
| 2000 | 26,352 | 25,470 | (882) | 21,805 | (4,547) | 13,864 | (12,488) | 19,858 | (6,494) |
| 2001 | 27,968 | 34,970 | 7,002 | 28,224 | 256 | 17,377 | (10,591) | 26,352 | (1,616) |
| 2002 | 30,799 | 29,683 | (1,116) | 32,357 | 1558 | 20,741 | (10,058) | 27,968 | (2,831) |
| 2003 | 39,365 | 33,917 | (5,448) | 35,715 | (3,650) | 24,092 | (15,273) | 30,799 | (8,566) |
| 2004 | 48,926 | 50,313 | 1,387 | 41,907 | (7,019) | 28,868 | (20,058) | 39,365 | (9,561) |
| 2005 | 65,271 | 60,809 | (4,462) | 51,646 | (13,625) | 34,682 | (30,589) | 48,926 | (16,345) |
| 2006 | 82,314 | 87,076 | 4,762 | 70,286 | (12,028) | 42,466 | (39,848) | 65,271 | (17,043) |

**CAUSAL-FACTOR METHODS.** The most common causal-factor method for predicting market size is **multiple regression analysis.**[13] The researcher selects several independent (predictor) variables that he believes could be related to market size, the dependent (criterion) variable. He uses historical data to determine the relationships, if any, between these predictor variables and market size. He then uses these relationships to predict future sales.

## DEFINING AND MAKING THE SALES FORECAST

The sales forecast is the firm's expected sales in a future time period, often for the upcoming year. The sales forecast is central to many processes for running the firm's day-by-day operations. Of course, many factors can cause the firm's actual sales to be quite different from a forecast. The following dialog reinforces the importance of sales forecasting and is part of a real conversation when the author gave an in-house seminar at a major U.S. computer firm. One participant asked several questions about sales forecasting, leading to this exchange:

> *Author:* "How come you're so interested in sales forecasting?"
>
> *Participant:* "Well, I have a sales forecasting department, and since you were here, I thought I might learn something."
>
> *Author:* "That's fine, but tell me, what's your position in the firm?"
>
> *Participant:* "I'm the production director."
>
> *Author:* "Oh! That's a little unusual. I'd have thought the sales forecasting department might have been in marketing, or in sales."
>
> *Participant:* "Sure, they have one too. But we can't believe a word they say, so we have to have our own."

Many firms use three broad approaches to sales forecasting: *top-down*, *bottom-up*, and *synthetic*.

**TOP-DOWN SALES FORECASTING.** Top-down sales forecasts follow directly from analyses of market potential, market-size (or individual market segments) forecasts, and the firm's market share estimates, typically contained in the marketing plan. Calculations are relatively simple, but the marketer must understand market subtleties and nuances:

> Sales forecast = forecast market size × forecast market share

**BOTTOM-UP SALES FORECASTING.** Bottom-up forecasts embrace the granularity (and reality) of sales by customer that is absent in top-down forecasts. Salespeople can personally discuss customer requirements. The firm aggregates forecasts from individual salespeople to develop an overall sales forecast. (In some firms, the sales forecast derives from a sales pipeline system — Chapter 16.) The downside of this approach is that salespeople may *low ball* their estimates if the firm uses bottom-up sales forecasts to set sales quotas that affect take-home pay.

**SYNTHETIC SALES FORECASTS.** Synthetic sales forecasts combine the best features of top-down and bottom-up forecasting. The top-down forecast comes from the marketing planning process; the sales department independently prepares a bottom-up forecast. If these numbers are similar, the task is over. In most cases, the top-down sales forecast is higher, and sales managers and individual salespeople must re-examine the forecasts customer by customer to see where increases are possible. These reworked forecasts are the building blocks for a revised bottom-up sales forecast. Simultaneously, marketing reworks the top-down forecast. Hopefully, the revised forecasts are in agreement. If not, a senior manager typically decides the forecast by executive decision, and sales management apportions increases to individual salespeople.

## KEY IDEA

➤ Many firms develop synthetic sales forecasts, using a combination of top-down and bottom-up approaches.

We have covered a lot of ground in this chapter, but in many ways we have only scratched the surface of marketing research. We hope your key take-away is that marketing research can be very helpful in securing insight the firm requires to successfully execute the six marketing imperatives. But you should also realize that marketing research is no panacea. The manager and researcher must make many decisions before investing in a particular study. We gave you a glimpse of some of the available options.

## KEY MESSAGES

- Marketing research results should be actionable.

- Good marketing research can give the firm a competitive advantage.

- Marketing researchers should provide analysis and insight; managers make decisions.

- Marketing research studies should follow a rigorous process.

- Marketing researchers make critical distinctions between primary and secondary research, and qualitative and quantitative research.

- Both qualitative and quantitative research use several methodologies. Qualitative research is becoming more popular.

- The various techniques for collecting survey data have advantages and disadvantages.

- Many methods can assess market and sales potentials, and make market and sales forecasts.

# CHAPTER 7

# DETERMINE AND RECOMMEND WHICH MARKETS TO ADDRESS

## LEARNING OBJECTIVES

When you have completed this chapter, you will be able to:

- Understand marketing's role in identifying new opportunities and being sure the firm makes its strategic decisions with marketing input.
- Determine the fundamental elements that make up a strategy for growth.
- Use the elements of a strategy for growth to assemble a venture portfolio.
- Develop criteria for evaluating individual growth opportunities.
- Assess alternative ways to implement a strategy for growth.

## OPENING CASE: FLEXCAR AND ZIPCAR

*Established nationwide firms in the car-rental business include Advantage, Alamo, Avis, Dollar, Enterprise, Hertz, National, and Thrifty. Hertz, Avis, and National compete on location and service, especially in airports. Advantage, Alamo, Dollar, and Thrifty compete on price. Enterprise became the leading car-rental firm overall by offering replacement cars for owners whose cars were being repaired. Surely the car-rental market is saturated with supply? Not according to Flexcar and Zipcar, who identified a new opportunity in car-sharing.*

*Car-sharing started in Germany in the 1980s, but Flexcar and Zipcar were first in the U.S. Car-rental firms offer minimum one-day rentals to customers who have good driving and credit records and meet age requirements. By contrast, Flexcar and Zipcar were founded as membership organizations — customers pay a membership fee, $35 to $50 annually, and rent by the hour. Cities with car-sharing service include Atlanta, Baltimore, Boston, Chicago, Gainesville, Los Angeles, New York,*

*Philadelphia, Pittsburgh, Portland (Oregon), San Diego, San Francisco, Seattle, and Washington D.C. In late 2006, combined membership in Flexcar and Zipcar was approaching 100,000. In late 2007, Flexcar and Zipcar merged under the Zipcar name.*

*Essentially, Zipcar members share cars, each of which has a "home" location in a pay garage, on a street, or in another designated location. Members can book hybrids, sedans, pickup trucks, SUVs, minivans, and sports cars online or by phone. They open the car with an access card (like a credit card), return the car to the same location, and check out with the card. Fees are around $10 per hour including gas and insurance, but the firm also offers monthly arrangements for specified hours (like 6 p.m. to midnight, Monday to Friday) and daily commuting. Zipcar operates with a small staff, monitoring its cars via wireless and computer technologies. Cities hoping to ease congestion even provide free or subsidized parking.*

*City dwellers use Zipcars in the evenings and on weekends; important customer groups for daily use are small business and government. Portland has a car-sharing program with Zipcar for its motor pool fleet; it aims to reduce annual operating, maintenance, and fuel costs by 25 percent and cut capital outlays. Starbucks has a business membership, mainly for hybrids.*

**CASE QUESTION**

Do you think Zipcar will be successful? Why or why not? If you were Hertz, Enterprise, or Alamo, what action would you take?

*Zipcar also partners with university parking and transportation departments to offer car-sharing to students, faculty, and staff. Because many students are in the 18–20 age group and ineligible for car rentals, Zipcar launched an under–21 program that offers them special deals.*

---

We have learned to develop *insights* into the M4Cs — markets, customers, competitors, company, and complementers. Now we shift direction to make *decisions* and focus on the six marketing imperatives. Marketing's first, and arguably most important, imperative is to influence the firm's decisions regarding which markets to address. **Market-choice decisions** are typically strategic for the firm or business unit as a whole. CEOs or general managers usually decide which opportunities are the most attractive, but marketing plays a critical role.

Marketing should identify opportunities by systematically screening many alternatives. The firm may identify opportunities in its core business or in adjacencies close to the core.[1] In consumer truck rental, U-Haul was barely breaking even with an older truck fleet, higher maintenance costs, and lower prices than competition. But when No. 2 Ryder exited, U-Haul prospered by tapping a *profit pool* for accessories — boxes, insurance, trailer rental, and storage space.[2] Other opportunities may be in less-related areas like the *white spaces* containing unsatisfied customer needs. Flexcar and Zipcar entered a *white space* in automobile rental. Other examples are Cirque du Soleil, a new entertainment experience that is neither a traditional circus nor theater; Starbucks; Viagra; and NetJets, offering partial ownership of corporate jets.[3]

Marketing should play a key role in designing the venture portfolio and developing screening criteria for individual opportunities. It should also help make the business case for the firm's investments. It should assess market potential, validate market size and growth, evaluate likely competitive challenges, and examine how individual opportunities align with the firm's strategic initiatives. Marketing may also be an internal entrepreneur, mobilizing resources for developing opportunities — market development, R&D, strategic alliances, and acquisitions. Of course, some opportunities may be unprofitable in the short run but offer significant long-run potential.

Proposals for new opportunities may originate throughout the firm. R&D develops new technologies and/or product ideas it believes have market viability. Sales and engineering may propose strategic alliances or buying, selling, or licensing technology. When these opportunities have marketing implications, marketing should be part of the discussion. The firm should make go/no-go decisions with the best available marketing insights — including voice-of-the-

### *Marketing Question*

Can you identify examples of firms that been successful by entering *white spaces*?

customer input. Unfortunately, in many firms, finance drives acquisition and divestiture decisions with little or no marketing input.

Figure 7.1 presents a systematic four-stage approach to developing, selecting, and implementing growth opportunities:

1. **Strategy for growth**: Provides guidance and analysis in generating investment opportunities.
2. **Venture portfolio**: The set of opportunities in which the firm decides to invest.
3. **Screening criteria**: Used to evaluate and select individual opportunities.
4. **Implementation**: Specific actions that the firm takes to achieve its objectives.

## FIGURE 7.1

**A COMPREHENSIVE APPROACH FOR SECURING HIGHER GROWTH**

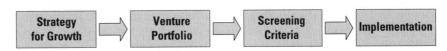

## A STRATEGY FOR GROWTH

### KEY IDEA

➤ A strategy for growth has four components: vision, mission, growth path, and timing of entry.

Some pizza restaurant chains are highly profitable, but IBM does not make pizzas. Advanced cell phones are fast growing and profitable, but Wal-Mart does not produce them. Downloading music from the Web is fast growing, but Carnival Cruise Lines does not offer this service. Each opportunity seems attractive, but these firms did not invest. Why not?

The reason is simple. Each firm has a **strategy for growth**; their strategies did not surface these options. A strategy for growth uses a set of frameworks to help the firm evaluate its current businesses, decide which businesses *to be in*, and which businesses *not to be in*. Figure 7.2 shows that firms can generate attractive growth opportunities using four components: **vision, mission, growth path**, and **timing of entry**.

## FIGURE 7.2

**COMPONENTS OF A STRATEGY FOR GROWTH**

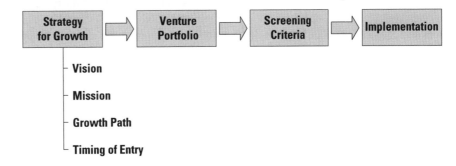

## VISION

**Vision** is a description of the firm's ideal future state — an impressionistic picture of what the future should be.[4] The **corporate** vision concerns the firm as a whole; the **business-unit** vision focuses on an individual business unit. Good vision statements set a broad direction — they should inspire employees for the long run. A good vision statement is not too broad, nor is it too specific or easily achievable.[5]

**Vision Statements**

Ford Motor Company – circa 1920s – "A car in every garage"

Microsoft – 1980s and 1990s – "A personal computer on every desk"

Microsoft – 2000s – "To enable people and businesses throughout the world to realize their full potential"

Ford's vision — "A car in every garage." led it to design the Model T, develop the production-line system, and continually reduce prices. Its market share in the U.S. automobile market grew to over 50 percent by the mid-1920s. Microsoft had one vision for much of the 1980s and 1990s — "A personal computer on every desk." When this vision was outmoded, it created a new, broader vision — "To enable people and businesses throughout the world to realize their full potential."

Marketing should make sure that the vision is outward-looking. Without marketing input, it may be too inwardly focused on what the firm does well. Of course, the firm's actions must support its vision — simply stating a goal doesn't mean you will achieve it. One CEO publicly announced his firm's vision — "to become our customers' most preferred supplier across all purchasing categories." This raised customers' expectations far beyond the firm's ability to deliver, ultimately creating customer dissatisfaction. British Airways' (BA) CEO made a similar mistake, publicly committing to "excellent customer service." He then single-mindedly pursued cost-cutting and outsourcing that alienated BA's staff. The ensuing strike stranded tens of thousands of very unhappy customers.

Developing a vision is one thing; having the firm's employees actively embrace the vision is another. When senior executives and consultants construct the firm's vision in isolation, employee buy-in may be minimal. When the firm involves its employees, it takes longer to develop a vision. But broad participation and input lead to better vision statements. At Aramark, the large Philadelphia-based services firm, more than 8,500 employees participated directly in developing the new vision.

## MISSION

The firm creates a vision to provide a lofty aspirational view of its overall direction. The **mission** guides the firm's search for market opportunities more directly.[6] A well-developed mission keeps the firm focused in a limited arena where success is likely. Mission avoids dispersing the firm's energy and resources in multiple directions. An ideal mission codifies opportunity areas where the firm does well or aspires to do well. A firm with several business units should develop missions at both the corporate and business-unit levels; the corporate mission should encompass individual business-unit missions.

**ARTICULATING THE MISSION.** The mission states what the firm or business unit *will do*; by what it omits, the mission also states what the firm *will not do*! In articulating its mission, the firm should consider three internal resource dimensions (IR) and two externally focused (EF):

- **IR — Core ingredient or natural resource.** The firm maximizes value from a core ingredient or natural resource. A firm with the mission *We are a forest products company* could make and sell products based on many technologies to many markets, so long as the products were made from wood.

- **IR — Technology.** The firm focuses on a core technology. The mission *We are an electronics firm* directs the search for opportunities to electronics. The firm could use any raw material and sell products into any market, so long as the core technology was electronics.

- **IR — Product or service.** This firm's mission concerns the value a product or service offers. The mission *We are an automobile firm* directs the firm to make cars that might use various fuels — alcohol, diesel, ethanol, gasoline, hydrogen, or natural gas based on several technologies — electro-mechanical, fuel cell, gas-turbine, internal-combustion, hybrid, or steam.

- **EF — Market or market segment.** A firm with this mission could make many products, from many raw materials, using many technologies. FMCG firms like P&G and Unilever focus on the family market but offer many household and personal-care products.

## KEY IDEA

➤ Vision is the description of an ideal future state for a firm or business unit. Vision sets a broad direction for the firm. When developed with employee participation, it can inspire the entire organization for the long run.

## *Marketing Question*

How do you evaluate the following vision statements? Are they too broad? Are they too narrow? Are they inspiring?

- Merck – "We are in the business of preserving and improving human life."
- IBM (1990s) – "To lead big companies into the brave new networked world, IBM will devise their technology strategies, build and run their systems, and ultimately become the architect and repository for corporate computing, tying together not just companies, but entire industries."

**Marketing Question**

Based on your knowledge and/or research on the Internet, write a one-sentence mission statement for AXA, Citigroup, Comcast, Disney, ExxonMobil, Ford, GE, Hitachi, IP, Morgan Stanley, Novartis, Siemens, Toyota, Verizon, and/or Xerox.

- **EF — Customer needs.** This mission directs the firm to serve customers having a specific set of needs, with any product, using any technology. The mission *Serving individuals' transportation needs* could embrace making bicycles, automobiles, trucks, helicopters, or airplanes.[7] Otis Elevator bases its mission on transportation — *to provide any customer a means of moving people and things up, down, and sideways over short distances with higher reliability than any similar enterprise in the world.*

The firm and/or its business units can choose among these dimensions to develop missions, or they may combine dimensions. Courtyard by Marriott's mission — *To provide economy and quality-minded frequent business travelers with a premier lodging facility, which is consistently perceived as clean, comfortable, well maintained, and attractive, staffed by friendly, attentive, and efficient people* — combines product or service and market or market segment.

To reiterate, every mission states what the firm or business unit *will do* — externally focused missions also specify *for whom*. But by what it omits, a well-crafted mission also states what the firm or business unit *will not do*!

**EVOLVING THE MISSION.** Typically, successful firms evolve their missions. If growth opportunities are scarce with its current mission, or if a target of opportunity appears, the firm should consider *broadening* the mission. Cannondale expanded its mission from high-end bicycles to embrace dirt bikes and all-terrain vehicles. Apple expanded its mission from personal computers to embrace digital music and introduced the iPod and iTunes.

Some firms *narrow* their missions by dropping products and/or divesting business units; they *return to the core business*, *stick to the knitting*, or *re-focus*. Precipitating factors include resources stretched too thin, poor financial performance, new or evolving competition, and/or a looming takeover threat. Capital-market pressures may play an important role in divestitures, even for relatively well-focused firms. Industry analysts were not kind when HP acquired Compaq; many believed HP should focus on printers and peripherals and divest PCs and other products. This scrutiny eventually led to a CEO change.

Some firms, like Guinness — the Irish brewer — successfully *narrow* their product scopes but *expand* their geographic scopes. Others, like Westinghouse (morphed into CBS) and American Can (became Primerica and is now part of Citibank), totally change their missions.

**KEY IDEA**

➤ The firm's mission should guide its search for opportunity.

➤ The five approaches to developing mission are: core ingredient or natural resource, technology, product or service, market or market segment, or customer needs.

➤ The firm's mission can use a single approach or combine approaches.

➤ The firm should pro-actively revise its mission.

## GROWTH PATH

Mission provides a broad approach to identifying potential opportunities; **growth path** is more focused. Growth path is specifically concerned with the trade-off between expected financial return and risk. The firm should consider three factors:

- Revenue and profit potential of its opportunities, relative to the required investment
- Core competencies — from its portfolio of businesses, technologies, products, and markets
- Its assessment of risk

The firm's competencies and expected financial returns and risks from the opportunities it pursues coexist in a dynamic relationship. By investing in one opportunity, the firm may develop new competencies. These enhanced competencies may, in turn, make previously unattractive opportunities attractive. Expected financial returns and risks also change.

The growth path matrix uses two dimensions to analyze opportunities: *market* and *product or technology* — Figure 7.3. We trisect each dimension — *existing, related,* and *new* — to develop nine matrix cells, A through I. Each cell represents a different type of opportunity. For ease of exposition, we combine individual cells to develop four broad approaches to growth: **market penetration, product growth, market growth,** and **product and market diversification.**

| | Existing | Related | New |
|---|---|---|---|
| **New** | **Market Growth 2:** Market Expansion (G) | **Business Expansion:** Concentric Products (H) | **Conglomeration** (I) |
| **Related** | **Market Growth 1:** Market Extension (D) | **Business Extension** (E) | **Business Expansion:** Concentric Markets (F) |
| **Existing** | **Market Penetration** (A) | **Product Growth 1:** Product Extension (B) | **Product Growth 2:** Product Expansion (C) |

**Market** (vertical axis)

**Product or Technology** (horizontal axis: Existing, Related, New)

**FIGURE 7.3**

**THE GROWTH-PATH MATRIX**

**MARKET PENETRATION (CELL A).** Most firms spend major resources pursuing market-penetration strategies. The firm focuses significant effort on existing (or slightly modified) products in existing markets. The firm bases its growth on core competencies — it has minimal *knowledge* risk. Of course, it may face significant risk from competitors.

**PRODUCT GROWTH (CELLS B AND C).** The firm brings new products to existing markets. A ski resort that adds ice-skating, downhill sledding, snowmobiling, and tubing pursues a product-growth strategy. *Product growth 1 (product extension — cell B)* and *product growth 2 (product expansion — cell C)* differ in the degree of product newness. Product extensions relate to current products; product expansions are unrelated and hence more risky. For a bank skilled in making corporate loans, lock-box services are a product extension. Complex derivative products, requiring significant new technical expertise, would be a product expansion.

**MARKET GROWTH (CELLS D AND G).** The firm sells existing products to new markets via market development. *Market growth 1 (market extension — cell D)* and *market growth 2 (market expansion — cell G)* differ in the degree of market newness. For our bank skilled in corporate loans, loans to public and/or nonprofit enterprises is a market extension. Making loans to individual consumers would be a market expansion. In general, market expansions are more risky than market extensions. Geographic expansion is a popular market growth option.

**PRODUCT AND MARKET DIVERSIFICATION (CELLS E, F, H, AND I).** A critical characteristic of *market penetration*, *product growth*, and *market growth* is that at least one growth dimension is *existing*. For product and market diversification, both *market and product or technology* change to either *related* or *new*. Opportunities are more risky, and the business as a whole shifts.

*Business extension (cell E)* requires moderate change for both *market* and *product or technology*. Nike made a product extension when it added athletic apparel to its core footwear line. By contrast, adding sporty street apparel was a business extension — *related* product to *related* market. *Business expansion* requires new products and related markets (*concentric markets — cell F*), or new markets and related products (*concentric products — cell H*). Risk is greatest in *conglomeration (cell I)* — new products and new markets. Conglomeration by internal development is generally more risky than by acquisition, but many conglomerate acquisitions also fail. Quaker purchased Snapple from Triarc for $1.7 billion but made significant errors in distribution and promotion. Three years later, Triarc repurchased Snapple for $300 million. Another conglomeration failure:

> Under CEO Jean Paul Messier, a French water utility company renamed itself Vivendi and began acquiring entertainment, media, and communications firms. Vivendi purchased the Seagram Company to secure Universal Studios and bought USA Networks' entertainment assets — it also began divesting the water companies. In 2002, Vivendi faced bankruptcy; the board fired Messier and started selling assets. By 2004, Vivendi had sold most entertainment and water assets and now focuses on telecommunications.

*Marketing Question*

Pick a country other than your own. Which firms from that country earn revenues from countries in more than three continents? What other forms of diversification have these firms taken on?

**CHOOSING THE *RIGHT* GROWTH PATH.** To identify and separate worthwhile opportunities from the others typically requires significant market research and analysis. The firm should identify the scope of the opportunity, competition, and assess its ability to deliver the necessary customer value. More generally, the firm should evaluate its ability to be successful in various growth paths. For example, it may perform well with *market growth* but poorly with *product and market diversification*. If so, it should probably favor *market-growth* opportunities and set a higher bar for *product and market diversifications*.

As a starting point for developing decision rules about new opportunities, the firm should conduct a retrospective growth-path analysis. For example, it could go back, say, five years and classify each opportunity it pursued into one of the nine cells, and then assess its success or failure. The firm may discover some areas where it generally performs well and others where it performs poorly.

## TIMING OF ENTRY

Along with identifying the *right* growth path, when to seize an opportunity — **timing of entry** — is also crucial. In Chapter 3, we discussed five product life-cycle stages — *introduction, early growth, late growth, maturity, and decline*. Early stages have high uncertainty in both products and markets, but this decreases as the life cycle evolves. Correspondingly, competitive pressures typically increase. Figure 7.4 explores links between the first four life-cycle stages and specific strategic options for the timing of market entry — **pioneer, follow-the-leader, segmenter,** and **me-too**.[8]

**FIGURE 7.4**

**TIMING OF MARKET ENTRY**

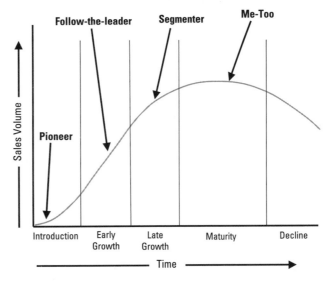

**PIONEER. Pioneer** firms blaze trails and create new markets by consistent and extensive R&D spending. They accept risk and understand that failure often accompanies success. Pioneers possess the R&D skills and internal processes to consistently develop new products and services, and the marketing capabilities to open up new markets. Pioneers have sufficient resources to support heavy R&D expenditures and fund market development. Sometimes their market-entry costs exceed R&D spending. Firms that commonly pioneer new products include DuPont, Intel, 3M, Sony, major pharmaceutical firms (like Pfizer, Novartis, and GSK), and biotech firms. Of course, pioneers are not always successful, even when they bring products to market. Apple pioneered personal digital assistants (PDA) with the Newton, but Palm became market leader.

**FOLLOW-THE-LEADER. Follow-the-leader** firms enter rapidly growing markets on the heels of pioneers. Pioneers make large research investments to develop innovative new products and services; follow-the-leader firms focus on development. Called the used-apple policy, the *follower* lets the pioneer take the first bite. If the apple is fine, they go ahead; if not, they pass.[9]

Follow-the-leader firms are happy for pioneers to invest heavily in R&D and market development — they follow quickly with developmental R&D. Market insight is critical; followers should enter soon after a successful pioneer. A successful follow-the-leader strategy must have:

- A vision of serving a mass market
- Good competitive intelligence to begin developing its products as soon as possible
- Good developmental engineers to leverage and enhance the pioneer's successful research
- Proactive patent lawyers to identify weak spots in the pioneer's patents
- Financial strength and commitment to outspend the pioneer
- The ability to differentiate their offers by delivering superior customer value.
- The will and persistence to succeed[10]

Many industry leaders like FedEx (air package delivery), Gillette (razors), Kodak (chemical film), Intel (microprocessors), Microsoft (operating system software and browsers), Pampers (disposable diapers), and Xerox (copiers) entered their markets as follow-the-leader firms.[11] In 2007, Nissan introduced its first hybrid car, a decade after Toyota.

**SEGMENTER. Segmenters** enter established markets in late growth by adding value for specific segments. Segmenter strategies can be very effective in maturing markets. As customers gain knowledge and experience, their preferences typically become more specific. Using insightful marketing research, segmenters identify the unique needs of a specific customer group or groups and offer them specially designed products and services.

Segmenters' skill sets and competencies differ markedly from pioneers and follow-the-leader firms. Technological expertise and innovation are no longer the driving forces. Segmenters require market research skills to identify unsatisfied market needs, but also the flexibility to address narrow market niches. Segmenters often address several segments simultaneously, at low cost — perhaps using modular-design strategies or platform engineering processes, combined with flexible operating systems.

Medical device maker Medtronics used successful segmentation and platform engineering to capture market share in cardiac pacemakers and implantable defibrillators.[12] Airbus and Boeing use modular design to produce their commercial aircraft families — Boeing produced the 707, 727, 737, and 757 aircraft on the same fuselage platform to outpace Airbus. The automobile industry is a heavy user of these design and engineering approaches.

**ME-TOO. Me-too-ers** enter mature markets with limited product lines. They base their low-price/low-cost strategies on value engineering, efficient high-volume production (often in low-cost countries), low overhead, aggressive procurement, and great attention to detail. Me-too-ers are often leaders in process innovation and have very focused marketing. They spend little on R&D, and their products are similar to well-known products. They can wreak havoc in segmented markets where firms compete with value-added offers. Dell pursues this approach: it minimizes inventory, continually reduces costs, and only makes PCs after receiving an order. Many Chinese firms are also me-too-ers.

**CHOOSING THE *RIGHT* TIMING OF ENTRY STRATEGY.** Similarly to its growth-path decisions, the firm should identify which *timing-of-entry* strategy best fits its capabilities. It should match this strategy to market opportunities. Of course, as markets evolve, the firm must also evolve its capabilities.

# THE VENTURE PORTFOLIO

We learned that the components of a strategy for growth are *vision*, *mission*, *growth path*, and *timing of entry*. Together, these elements form a set of lenses the firm can use to approach markets and identify, generate, and decide to invest (or not) in growth opportunities. Each entry strategy demands quite different capabilities for success. Maintaining contrasting growth strategies in a single business unit is very difficult. No full-service airline has operated a successful low-cost carrier! Discount broker Schwab stumbled badly when trying to serve both discount clients and high net worth clients through its U.S. Trust acquisition.

Furthermore, just as each individual growth opportunity has a characteristic expected financial return and risk, so the entire set of growth opportunities — its **venture portfolio** — also has an expected financial return and risk. When the firm decides to invest in a new opportunity, it alters the expected financial return and risk for the entire portfolio. Hence the firm must not only evaluate individual growth opportunities, but also define and clarify the characteristics of its proposed venture portfolio. A key issue is the overall degree of risk the firm will assume.[13]

**FIGURE 7.5**

**COMPONENTS OF THE VENTURE PORTFOLIO**

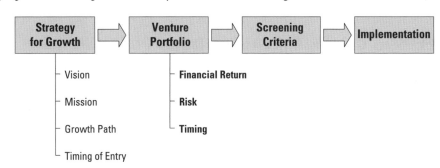

Among its opportunities the firm may identify several types of risk:

- **Demand risk.** Fundamental for every cell in the growth-path matrix: Is there an opportunity? Is there market demand?

- **Product/technology risk and market risk.** Generally, opportunities that are farther from the *market-penetration* cell of the growth-path matrix are more risky. The firm lacks experience with either the product/technology or the market. Product and market diversification is the most risky growth path — opportunities are very different from the firm's experience. Also, early life-cycle entries such as *pioneer* and *follow-the-leader* are more risky than the later *segmenter* and *me-too* strategies. Critical questions are: Will the technology work? Is there a viable market? Does (will) our product satisfy customer needs?

- **Competitor risk.** In general, the lower the product/technology and market risk, the tougher the competition; hence, competitor risk is typically high for market penetration. In contrast, for *pioneers*, current competition may be minimal.

Other risks the firm should evaluate for each opportunity are:

- **Firm risk.** Does the firm have the competencies, the resources, and the will to succeed?

- **Political risk.** How stable is the local government? Will it (or its successor) take actions to make the market less attractive?

- **Physical environment risk.** Are natural disasters likely to affect the business?

- **Financial risk.** Is the opportunity sufficiently sustainable to justify the investment?

**ASSEMBLING THE VENTURE PORTFOLIO.** The firm should use its strategy for growth — **vision, mission, growth path, and timing of entry** — to generate opportunities. Because opportunities differ in degree and type of risk, the firm should set different profitability cut-offs. In general, more risky opportunities should offer higher potential returns than less risky opportunities.[14] From its opportunity set, the firm must select individual opportunities to enter its venture portfolio. As discussed, the critical defining characteristics of an individual opportunity are financial return and risk. The timing of profit flows is also important. Depending on the firm's circumstances, a moderate medium-run return may be more attractive than a higher long-term return. Three characteristics define opportunities in the venture portfolio:

- Expected financial return

**KEY IDEA**

➤ A venture portfolio is the set of growth opportunities the firm addresses.

➤ The strategy for growth helps the firm develop its venture portfolio.

➤ The defining characteristics of the venture portfolio are expected financial return, timing of contribution to profits, and risk.

- Degree of risk
- Timing of the contribution to profits

The particular portfolio design the firm chooses will depend on factors like current and expected profitability, cash availability for investment, and appetite for risk. A firm with good cash flow but few high-performing units may decide to heavy up on longer-term, higher-risk options. A firm with little cash may focus more on low- or moderate-risk opportunities. In general, conservatively managed firms invest in low-risk opportunities and want their investments to pay off quickly. Aggressive firms accept greater risks for potentially higher returns and are prepared to wait longer for their opportunities to become profitable.

## SCREENING CRITERIA: EVALUATING OPPORTUNITIES

We showed how the growth strategy identifies various types of growth opportunity and helps the firm construct a venture portfolio. But which specific opportunities should the firm pursue? Figure 7.6 shows four screening criteria — **objectives**, **compatibility (or fit)**, **core competence**, and **synergy** — to help the firm evaluate its opportunities and decide where to invest.

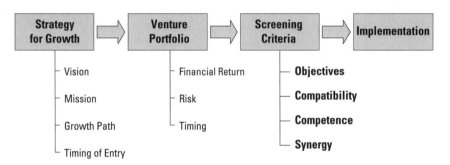

**FIGURE 7.6**

**SCREENING CRITERIA**

## OBJECTIVES

An investment opportunity must satisfy the firm's objectives. Revenue and profit growth are critical for creating shareholder value, but unmitigated growth can be a real problem. The firm must temper its desire for growth with concern for risk, stability, and flexibility.

**REVENUE AND PROFIT GROWTH.** To assess revenue and profit potential, the firm should consider several non-financial and financial measures. Typical items are market potential, current market size and expected growth rates, forces driving market growth, number and strength of competitors, and market-share forecasts. These market factors influence revenue and cost forecasts for calculating standard profit-related measures like timing of cash flows, payback, return-on-investment (ROI), profit margin, net present value, and internal rate of return.[15]

Sometimes firms reject new opportunities because forecast performance is inferior to the historical performance with some existing product. This comparison is incorrect. The firm should compare *forecast* market share, revenues, and profits from the new opportunity versus *forecast* market share, revenues, and profits without it. Despite its lead in expensive laser printers, HP introduced inexpensive inkjet printers (with lower margins) to avoid losing market share.

**RISK.** The firm must weigh forecast revenue and profit against the risk and required investment. It should consider the opportunity's return-risk profile and the impact that each opportunity has on the venture portfolio. Generally, potential return and risk are correlated, but some opportunities offer good returns at low risk.

KEY IDEA

➤ In setting objectives, the firm should strike a balance between revenue and profit growth, risk, stability, and flexibility.

**STABILITY.** A related criterion is *stability*. Suppose the firm must choose between two opportunities: A — high expected growth, significant variability; B — lower expected growth, low variability. The firm may prefer the lower growth option. Schneider Electric Mexico focuses on markets it can serve through existing distributors. It believes these revenues are more stable than revenues from large electricity generation projects requiring major investments.

**FLEXIBILITY.** All firms face increasing environmental change and complexity. No matter how good the firm's forecasting, it can be blindsided by unexpected events. *Insurance policies* give the firm flexibility to deal with changed circumstances. Examples are:

- **Research and development (R&D).** The firm hedges its bets by investing in competing fields. For example, car companies invest in hybrid, electric, and fuel cell technologies.
- **Venture capital.** The firm provides venture capital to startup companies, but retains options to increase ownership later. Cisco is a leader in this approach.
- **Partial ownership.** Major drug companies frequently take this approach with biotechnology firms. BMS purchased shares in cancer-drug developer, ImClone.
- **Joint technology agreements.** Oil companies often form partnerships for oil-drilling platforms and their operations, like Texaco and Shell in the Gulf of Mexico.
- **Acquisition.** Intel, Microsoft, and Cisco acquire firms with positions in adjacent markets.

Originally a textile power-loom producer, Toyota morphed into automobiles. Today its investments include prefabricated houses, resort development, helicopter operations and surveying, airport management, advertising agency, consulting, horticulture, golf course operations, and a professional soccer team. Some, but not all, have synergies with its automobile business.

## KEY IDEA

➤ The three important dimensions of compatibility (or fit) are: product-market fit, product-company fit, and company-market fit.

## COMPATIBILITY (OR FIT)

Can the firm be successful in the opportunity? Are its products, resources, culture, and insight sufficient for success?

**PRODUCT-MARKET FIT.** Is the product appropriate for the market? Or, restated: Does the product satisfy customer needs in target market segments better than competitors? Firms most often assess *product-market fit* through ongoing market research and market-testing. Timing is particularly important in assessing product-market fit as the firm and its environment evolve.

**PRODUCT-COMPANY FIT.** Compatibility extends to the firm. Does it possess the financial, human, and other skills and resources to enter the market? Can it successfully upgrade and market the product as the market evolves? Sometimes a firm has great product-market fit but lacks the distribution strength to reach customers. Independent inventors often have this problem — they may have a great product, but poor *product-company fit*.

**COMPANY-MARKET FIT.** Can the firm compete effectively in the market? Does it have sufficient customer insight, reputation, and the ability to defeat competitors? The firm may have good product-market fit and good product-company fit — yet reject an opportunity because of poor *company-market fit*. Geographic expansion offers many examples. Suppose a foreign market is attractive for the firm's product — good product-market fit — and the firm is skilled at producing, promoting, and distributing the product in its home market — good company-product fit. But if the firm has little experience in the foreign market — poor company-market fit — it may decide not to enter.

### Marketing Question

Can you identify three examples of successful product-market fit? Can you identify three examples of failed product-market fit? What are the risks of unsuccessful product-market fit?

## CORE COMPETENCE

Core competences are skills, knowledge, and other capabilities the firm possesses.[16] The **core-competence** criterion is quite straightforward: Does the firm *bring anything to the party*? Can the firm *take anything from the party*? Or more formally: Does this opportunity leverage the firm's core competencies or allow it to develop new ones?

Generally, the firm is better off pursuing opportunities that play to its core competencies. It can more easily gain a differential advantage, like Coca-Cola introducing a new sports drink or Toyota launching a new automobile. But core competence is not the only criteria for investing — the opportunity must satisfy other criteria. Further, an opportunity may be attractive *even if the firm has little competence* — if it can *secure* competence by its investment. Intel abandoned its core competence in memory chips, but gained competence in microprocessor technology and manufacturing. When Jeff Bezos left New York for Seattle in his second-hand car, he had little competence for building Amazon, but it became the leading online retailer.

## SYNERGY

Synergy explores how an opportunity relates to the firm's existing capabilities or resources.[17] *Positive synergy* reflects the notion that 2+2 can be greater than 4! The firm can pursue an opportunity on a standalone basis or use existing resources. Synergy kicks in when the firm uses existing resources. If it sells a new product through existing distributors, like P&G or Unilever when they add new products for supermarkets, it gains distribution synergy. If it makes the product in existing facilities, it gains manufacturing synergy. The firm should not decline an opportunity for lack of positive synergy — but positive synergy can enhance its returns.

When 2+2 is less than 4, *negative synergy* is at work; pursuing a new opportunity may erode revenues and profits from existing products. In the 1990s, allergy-relief prescription drug Claritin was a major profit-maker for Schering Plough (SP). In 2001, SP launched an over-the-counter version to reach the larger market for non-prescription allergy relief medicines. By 2002, Claritin sales dropped 43 percent ($3.16 billion to $1.8 billion).

## IMPLEMENTING GROWTH STRATEGIES

Figure 7.7 shows several options for implementing the firm's growth strategy and building its venture portfolio.[18]

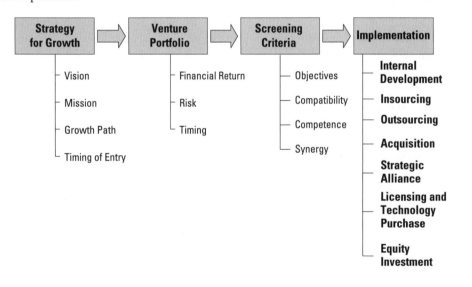

**FIGURE 7.7**

**IMPLEMENTING GROWTH STRATEGIES**

## INTERNAL DEVELOPMENT

Many firms put significant effort into **internal development** of new products and services. This is appropriate in all cells of the growth-path matrix and at all life-cycle stages. Some evidence suggests a strong positive correlation between R&D spending and corporate profitability.[19] Internal development is not just for technologists and engineers; marketing can play a major role in directing their efforts by infusing *market insight, customer insight, and competitor insight* at all developmental stages.

Advantages of internal development over alternative growth modes are:

- **Control.** The firm has control over the entire development process. It purchases or leases required resources and makes all decisions about suppliers and distributors.
- **Cost.** Internal development is typically less expensive than securing new products by acquisition and other means.

Disadvantages of internal development are:

- **Resource access.** Some resources may be unavailable, or too expensive to develop/acquire.
- **Expertise.** The firm must do a good job of directing the R&D effort, or the resulting products may require commercialization skills the firm does not possess.
- **Time.** Market windows are increasingly short, and internal development takes time.

## INSOURCING

With **insourcing**, the firm captures more added value in the supply chain by undertaking additional activities in developing, producing and marketing.  It can expand upstream by conducting suppliers' activities — *backward integration,* or downstream by conducting customers' activities — *forward integration.* Activities closely related to the firm's core competencies are prime insourcing candidates and may help it develop new core competencies.

Historically, Coca-Cola focused on syrup manufacturing and brand-building. During the 1990s, CEO Roberto Goizeuta increased Coke's shareholder value significantly by acquiring its bottlers. Because it could better manage relationships with supermarket chains, Coke fundamentally re-engineered its logistics and directly captured value from grocery, fountain, and vending distribution channels.

In 1993, Merck insourced pharmaceutical distribution by acquiring Medco, the largest U.S. drug-benefits manager. Unfortunately for Merck, Merck-Medco (MM) was a lightning rod for criticism and customer accusations that Medco favored Merck's products over competitors' lower-priced drugs. In 2003, Merck dissolved MM.

## OUTSOURCING

**Outsourcing** is the opposite of insourcing — the firm engages other firms to undertake activities it previously conducted in-house. The firm can better focus its resources on delivering increased customer value and secure differential advantage. Firms outsource a wide range of activities from managing information systems and technology infrastructure to business processes — discrete processes like accounts payable, benefits management and payroll, and some parts of procurement.

An aspect of outsourcing we hear much about is *offshoring* — contracting with a non-U.S-based firm to handle some elements. A common area is customer service operations. We're sure many readers have called a help desk or credit department and spoken with someone from India, Malaysia, or China. Cost reduction typically drives offshoring, but having a partner in a different time zone can also provide scalable, flexible staffing. Of course, quality control is important, especially when customer care is involved.

## ACQUISITION

We learned earlier that the firm can use **acquisitions** — individual business units or entire firms — to gain competencies that help provide customer value and secure differential advantage. Generally, growth by acquisition has a speed advantage — the firm gains immediate access to new products and new markets. It also gains the organizational infrastructure — operational capabilities, human resources, and organizational processes — that supports them. Firms that grow extensively by acquisition include Cisco, GE, Microsoft, and J&J. Former IBM CEO Lou Gerstner said:

> *IBM made 90 acquisitions during my tenure. The most successful were those that fit neatly into an organic growth plan. IBM's purchase of Informix is a great example. We were neck-and-neck with Oracle in the database business, and Informix, another database company, had lost its momentum and market leadership. We didn't need to buy Informix to get into the database business or to shore up a weak position. However, we did acquire a set of customers more quickly and more efficiently than we could have following a go-it-alone strategy.*[20]

But acquisitions are no panacea. Acquiring successful firms or business units can be expensive — it can also be difficult to marry the cultures of acquired and acquiring firms. The important question is whether or not acquisitions always add value. Value creation depends on the specific acquisition, but we can usefully distinguish between two very different acquisition types:

**MAJOR ACQUISITIONS.** These multi-million-dollar acquisitions often make the headlines: like Alcan's acquisition of Pechiney, the French aluminum firm; AOL's purchase of Time Warner; and Boston Scientific's bidding war with J&J for Guidant. But bigger is not always better, and many business leaders and scholars have spoken out against these types of acquisitions. They assert that CEO hubris often drives $100 million-plus acquisitions.[21] Academic studies suggest that 70 percent of acquisitions are dilutive for the acquiring firm's shareholders, and that *in the heat of the chase* acquirers typically overpay.[22]

**SMALL *FILL-IN* ACQUISITIONS.** The firm makes these acquisitions to complement an existing strategy. The IBM experience under CEO Lou Gerstner exemplifies this type of acquisition. Research suggests that modest acquisitions are the most successful[23]: Small acquisitions are easier to implement, and acquirers may get better deals with less risk. A firm making many small acquisitions gains experience and does a better job of identifying candidates, managing bids, and integrating the acquired entities. Cisco, IBM, and Affiliated Computer Services (ACS) are good examples of firms that make many small acquisitions.

## STRATEGIC ALLIANCE

Generally, **strategic alliances** address poor product-company fit and/or poor company-market fit without the capital investment and risks inherent in acquisitions. A good alliance partner complements the firm's strengths and/or compensates for its weaknesses. The combined entity is stronger than either firm acting alone. Prototypical alliances are between small, innovative firms and well-established firms with strong marketing, good customer reputations, and deep pockets.

Strategic alliances can be an attractive way to secure needed resources and reduce the firm's investment and risk. But like acquisitions, strategic alliances are no panacea; many fail due to lack of planning and/or managerial attention, incompatible organizational cultures, insufficient resources, and changed objectives by one or more partners.[24] What appears attractive in theory can be difficult to execute in practice.

**KEY IDEA**

➤ Options for implementing a growth strategy include internal development, insourcing, outsourcing, acquisition, strategic alliance, licensing and technology purchase, and equity investment.

*Marketing Question*

A startup biotech firm has a single R&D project that promises to produce a product that will significantly reduce the incidence of skin cancer. How would you advise this firm to proceed in drug development and marketing?

## LICENSING AND TECHNOLOGY PURCHASE

**Licensing and technology purchase** are alternative ways to access technology developed by others. In licensing agreements, the original firm owns the technology. Typically, licensing agreements specify a minimum royalty payment (fixed payment regardless of use) and an earned royalty rate based on volume (units/dollars) or profits. A technology purchase is typically for a fixed price. Either way, the acquiring firm avoids the risks and expenses of R&D, but may pay a high price to secure a successful new technology. Forest Laboratories licenses, develops, and sells drugs developed by small pharmaceutical firms.

## EQUITY INVESTMENT

Many firms augment internal development efforts by making equity investments — taking partial ownership — in startups. Sometimes they form or *incubate* startups by spinning off their own successful product development efforts. Typically, the firm retains the ability to increase its equity position later. As an example, Xerox Technology Ventures generated an internal rate of return of over 50 percent in the 1990s.

## KEY MESSAGES

Marketing's first imperative is to determine and recommend which markets to address. A marketing perspective should infuse the firm's critical strategic decisions — marketing's responsibility is to make sure this happens by focusing on two separate elements:

- Identifying potential opportunities.
- Making sure that marketing provides input for other strategic actions the firm is contemplating.

A systematic approach to developing, selecting, and implementing opportunities has four elements:

- **Strategy for growth** – a set of frameworks that help the firm decide which businesses to be in and which not to be in.
  - Vision – description of an ideal future state for the firm or business unit.
  - Mission – statement that directly guides the firm's search for opportunity.
  - Growth path – a focused approach to identifying opportunities, trades off return and risk.
  - Timing of entry – market-entry options related to stage of the product life cycle.

- **Venture portfolio** – the set of opportunities where the firm decides to invest. Key issues are:
  - Expected financial return.
  - Risk – including the risk of generated opportunities, and the firm's appetite for risk.
  - Timing of the contribution to profit.

- **Screening criteria** – a method for evaluating individual opportunities. Key considerations are:
  - Objectives – including growth, risk, stability, and flexibility.
  - Compatibility (or fit) – product-market fit, product-company fit, and company-market fit.
  - Core competence – using special capabilities to achieve differential advantage over competition.
  - Synergy – $2 + 2 = 5$.

- **Implementation** – specific actions to implement the firm's growth strategy are:
  - Internal development – new products and services developed through the firm's efforts.
  - Insourcing – capturing greater added value — either upstream or downstream.
  - Outsourcing – engaging other firms to conduct needed activities so the firm can focus on delivering greater customer value.
  - Acquisition – purchasing an entire firm or business unit.
  - Strategic alliance – an agreement with a partner firm to jointly exploit an opportunity.
  - Licensing and technology purchase – different ways to access technology developed by others.
  - Equity investment – taking ownership positions in startups.

# CHAPTER 8

# MARKET SEGMENTATION AND TARGETING

## LEARNING OBJECTIVES

When you have completed this chapter, you will be able to:

- Select a market segmentation scheme that deepens the firm's understanding of its opportunities.
- Deconstruct a market into readily distinguishable groups of customers.
- Understand the unique needs and preferences common to customers in each market segment.
- Assess identifying characteristics of each market segment.
- Recognize the differences between market segments and customer segments.
- Address several complex issues in developing and engaging market segments.
- Decide which segments to target for marketing effort.
- Develop criteria for effective segmentation and positioning.

## OPENING CASE: MARRIOTT HOTELS, RESORTS, AND SUITES

*In 1985, Marriott Hotels, Resorts and Suites was a domestic (U.S.) mid- to large-size hotel chain, managing 67,034 rooms at 160 properties. Marriott decided to enhance travelers' value by segmenting the market and then targeting selected segments, each with a different brand. Then as now, Marriott was the flagship brand. Each new brand would support Marriott's overall brand identity — a commitment to superior customer service — and train employees to have a passion for service. Employees would:*

- *Do whatever it takes to take care of customers.*
- *Pay extraordinary attention to detail.*

- *Take pride in their physical surroundings.*
- *Use their creativity to find new ways to meet the needs of customers.*

*Marriott believed all customers require a base service level. It also believed that customers differ in their willingness to pay for different levels of comfort and luxury. Management also knew that many customers stay a few nights in a hotel — but a growing number, like business people on assignment, need accommodations for several weeks. Recognizing the varying needs of hotel customers, Marriott was the first major hotel chain to base its strategy on market segmentation. Marriott grew new brands organically, but implemented its strategy in part by acquisition.*

*Marriott's flagship brand continues to target customers needing fine restaurants, meeting rooms, athletic facilities, and other upscale amenities. But Marriott added several additional brands — each addressing target segments. These include:*

- **Courtyard by Marriott:** *Business travelers wanting a moderately priced hotel providing some amenities, like an exercise room and a restaurant for breakfast.*
- **Fairfield Inn:** *Customers wanting an inexpensively priced, high quality hotel they can access by car, on or near the U.S. main interstate highway system.*
- **Residence Inn:** *Customers who require an extended-stay hotel for reasons like job relocation, job assignment, and government contracting.*
- **TownePlace Suites:** *Similar to Residence Inn, but for customers who want a lower price.*
- **SpringHill Suites:** *Customers seeking an all-suites hotel; willing to pay an upper-moderate price.*
- **Renaissance Hotels and Resorts:** *Customers wanting upscale amenities, internationally.*
- **The Ritz-Carlton:** *Customers looking for the ultimate in luxury hotels in urban centers.*

*Each Marriott brand has a distinct personality and style. Marriott works hard to communicate the essence and strength of each brand so that target customers know what to expect. There is some customer crossover, but each brand focuses on a defined market segment. Internal competition is small.*

*Marriott has achieved extraordinary results from its segmentation and targeting strategy. The Courtyard by Marriott brand now manages more rooms than the entire firm managed in 1985. Total number of rooms managed has increased sevenfold.*

**CASE QUESTION**

How do you assess Marriott's approach to segmenting the hotel market? Can you think of alternative approaches that might present marketing opportunities?

Market segmentation is a fundamental marketing concept. Simply stated, customers in a market either have different needs, or similar needs with different priorities. Either way, the firm's job is to place customers in groups so that each group is relatively homogeneous in its needs profile.

A specifically designed market offer will satisfy a customer group that has a homogeneous need profile. A second group of customers, with a different need profile, will require a different market offer. We call these groups *market segments*. To identify and develop effective market offers, the firm must understand these need profiles. The firm seeking to serve a large market like snack foods will require several market offers, at least one per market segment to meet varying customer preferences. Typically, a single offer, like potato chips, will fail to satisfy the many diverse customers who purchase snack foods.

Because customers have different need profiles, marketers must undertake three separate, but related, strategic tasks:

1. Figure out the best way to group customers and form market segments. The raw material is market insight, customer insight, and competitor insight, topics we covered in Chapters 3, 4, and 5. In the market segmentation process, in part using approaches we discussed in Chapter 6, the firm refines these insights.

2. Decide which market segments to target for effort. Resources are always scarce, and all firms must make targeting decisions. Rarely can a firm address all market segments.

Note an important distinction between these tasks. *Identifying* market segments is creative and analytic. *Targeting* market segments requires a strategic decision — the firm decides to apply resources to some market segments and to ignore others. Identifying, and then targeting, the *right* market segments are crucial tasks for strategic marketing.

3. For each target segment, develop a market segment strategy including a specific approach, or positioning. Positioning is central, but, as we see in Chapter 9, there is more to market segment strategy than just positioning. The firm's market strategy combines several market segment strategies.

After developing its market segment strategy and positioning, the firm must decide how to implement the strategy and design the marketing offer. We devote the remainder of the book to this topic.

# THE MARKET SEGMENTATION PROCESS

Most of National Car Rental's customers are corporate executives — most of Alamo's customers are leisure travelers. When the parent company emerged from bankruptcy, it combined the Alamo and National operations — airport counters, buses, rental agents, and automobiles. Dual Alamo/National logos were ubiquitous. Customers had difficulty distinguishing between the brands. Complaints doubled, especially from National's customers — they paid 10 to 20 percent more than Alamo's customers.

**Market segmentation** is a conceptual and analytic process critical for developing and implementing an effective market strategy. In the market segmentation process, the firm groups together actual and potential customers in a market into various **market segments**. The firm then chooses which of these market segments to **target** for effort. It must *position* itself in each target segment (segmentation, targeting, positioning [STP]) and develop a *market segment strategy*. When the segment strategy is set, the firm designs a suitable offer.

Figure 8.1 describes the process of designing and implementing market offers for each target market segment. A well-executed process provides the firm with:

- Better insight into the market, customers, competitors, the company, and complementers — in particular, customer needs.
- A clearer focus on market strategy. It targets specific customers, designs better offers, produces superior products, and better aligns its communication programs to reach these customers.
- Opportunities for customization to target segments.
- Higher levels of customer satisfaction and loyalty.
- More efficient resource allocation, superior differential advantage, and higher profitability.

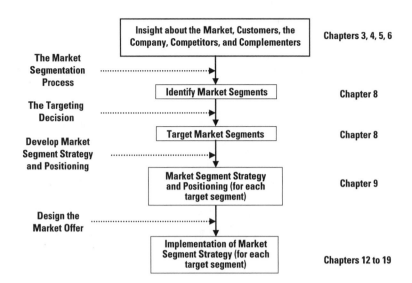

**FIGURE 8.1**

**SEGMENTATION,
TARGETING, AND
POSITIONING**

The fundamental premise underlying market segmentation is that, in any broadly defined market, customer need profiles are heterogeneous (different). Customers have different needs and/or different priorities of needs. They seek different benefits and values based on these differing need profiles. The segmentation task is to divide the market into several discrete groups of customers, each with relatively homogeneous (similar) need profiles. These customer need profiles differ from segment to segment, so an individual customer falls into one, but only one segment.[1] Alamo/National's parent (previous boxed insert) does not seem to understand that it is targeting two quite different market segments.

Market segmentation is often a compromise. At one extreme, the firm could develop one strategy, one positioning, and one offer for the entire market — often termed mass marketing. This one-size-fits-all approach is the most efficient, lowest-cost way to address a broad market. But, typically, customer need profiles are heterogeneous, so many would be unsatisfied. At the other extreme, the firm could develop a unique or specialized offer for each customer. This type of personalization or customization ensures a good match between customer needs and the firm's market offer. But firms rarely earn sufficient revenues to offset the development and implementation costs. Market segmentation operates between these extremes. The firm identifies homogeneous groups of customers — market segments — with similar need profiles, targets one or more segments, and develops specific offers to satisfy the needs of customers in those segments.

## LEVELS OF SEGMENTATION

Segmentation forms smaller, more discrete groups out of a whole. The firm chooses a broad market to address, Marketing Imperative 1, and then identifies several **market segments** within this broad market. Within any single market segment, the firm may segment further, forming sub-segments as it zeros in on target customers. Some practitioners define the first-level grouping as market segmentation, and the finer-grained, second-level segmentation as customer segmentation, forming **customer segments**.

We reinforce this idea with a simple example that we introduced in Chapter 1. Suppose half of the students in your class prefer *hot tea*, and half prefer *iced tea*. Figure 8.2 (left) shows a tea supplier that does not understand this segmentation and offers a single product — *warm tea*. Without alternatives, students wanting tea will purchase *warm tea*. They may desire *hot tea* or *iced tea* but at least *warm tea* is tea!

Suppose a new supplier understands the segmentation. If it offers *hot tea*, the *hot-tea* students will switch from *warm tea*. If a third supplier enters with *iced tea*, the *iced-tea* students will also

**KEY IDEA**

➤ Market segmentation is a conceptual and analytic process — it is critical for developing and implementing an effective market strategy.

switch. The *warm-tea* supplier quickly loses customers because its competitors are more insightful about market segmentation.

How should the original supplier respond? The *hot-tea* and *iced-tea* suppliers focus on different segments, and are doing just fine. One response is to segment at an even deeper level. Some students may like *sweetened tea*; others may like *unsweetened* tea. Figure 8.2 (right) shows how to deconstruct the market into four segments — *hot sweetened tea, hot unsweetened tea, iced sweetened tea*, and *iced unsweetened tea*. A focus on one or more of these segments would better satisfy customers' needs.

**FIGURE 8.2**

THE BENEFITS OF
FINER-GRAINED
SEGMENTATION:
A TEA MARKET
EXAMPLE

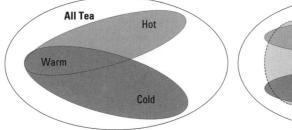
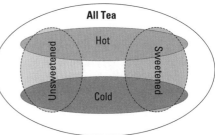

*Marketing
Question*

What firms demonstrate the *warm-tea syndrome* — they address their markets generally, even though customer groups have different need profiles?

## DEVELOPING MARKET SEGMENTS

The firm can approach the market segmentation process from two directions: **customer needs** first or **candidate descriptor variables** first. It can also use *qualitative* or *quantitative* approaches.

**CUSTOMER NEEDS FIRST.** The firm searches for differing customer need profiles; it uses them to form customer groups. Customers within each group have relatively homogeneous need profiles, but the various groups have different, heterogeneous, need profiles. The firm must select descriptor variables that identify these groups by distinguishing characteristics.

AT&T's data system organization identified three market segments based on the complexity of customers' communications needs:

- Tier 1 segment — needs satisfied by common *off-the-shelf* products.
- Tier 2 segment — needs satisfied by *off-the-shelf* products plus some options.
- Tier 3 segment — requires tailored solutions.

In the AT&T example, the three segments seem to make good sense — each segment has needs that differ from the other segments. AT&T's challenge is to identify customer characteristics in each of these segments. For example, Tier 1: What characteristics define customers that want *off-the-shelf* products? Are these small companies or large companies? Do they compete in specific industries? Are they located in specific geographic areas?

**CANDIDATE DESCRIPTOR VARIABLES FIRST.** The firm uses candidate descriptor variables to construct customer groups. It looks for homogeneous (similar) need profiles within each group, and heterogeneous (different) need profiles across groups. If the firm cannot find *good* need profiles, or similarity within groups and differences across groups, it tries again with different descriptors.

Popular categories of segmentation variables are geography and demographics. MTV frequently uses country or geography when tailoring offers to its customers. It operates 38 separate nationally focused channels like MTV Romania and MTV Indonesia. In the Philippines, local hamburger chain Jollibee (69 percent market share) outsells McDonald's (16 percent) by using national origin and demographics to better meet Filipinos' needs. Jollibee now has stores in Asia and California, targeting customers of Filipino descent.

In addition to geographic and demographic variables, many firms use behavioral and socio-psychological variables. Figure 8.3 shows a pharmaceutical firm's attempt to segment the physician market using two variables. Each variable has two levels: *approach to treatment* is either aggressive or conservative; *type of data* relies on scientific evidence or on clinical experience. The firm formed four segments: *risk taker, hard headed, pathfinder,* and *tortoise.* It was easy to identify a few physicians who characterized each segment. It was more difficult to specify distinguishing geographic and/or demographic characteristics for classifying many physicians.

The main difficulty with candidate descriptors is that customers within each group may not have distinct need profiles. Then the descriptor variables do not produce segments at all. The next step is to repeat the process with another segmentation variable or variables. The physician example shows that behavioral and/or socio-psychological variables may be more effective than geographic and demographic variables in forming *good* groups, or market segments. But assigning customers to market segments may be difficult. Generally, approaches to developing market segments that start with customer needs are preferable.

**KEY IDEA**

➤ Four categories of candidate descriptor variables or segmentation variables can define market segments: geographic, demographic, behavioral, and socio-psychological.

**Approach to Treatment**

|  | Aggressive | Conservative |
|---|---|---|
| Relies on scientific evidence | *Risk Taker* | *Hard Headed* |
| Relies on clinical experience | *Path Finder* | *Tortoise* |

Type of Data

**FIGURE 8.3**

EXAMPLE OF TWO-VARIABLES SEGMENTATION OF PHYSICIANS

## METHODOLOGICAL APPROACHES TO FORMING SEGMENTS

The many methodological approaches fall into two main categories.

**QUALITATIVE.** The segmentation task is highly judgmental, requiring significant conceptual skill. The firm's raw material is creative insight derived from existing and potential customers, typically gained from field marketing research and/or customer relationship management systems.

**QUANTITATIVE.** Large-scale market segmentation studies use extensive survey data secured from customers and sophisticated multivariate statistical techniques. Cluster analysis, a specific technique designed to form groups, might have the following steps:

- Develop many statements (variables) about customer needs.
- Develop a set of questions (variables) that identify customers.
- Administer statements and questions to a random sample of current and potential customers.
- Analyze customer need responses by cluster analysis. Choose the number of segments that form the *best* groupings of customer needs.
- Examine each customer cluster, or segment, for its identifying characteristics.

Mobil used a similar process to segment the gasoline market.[2]

*Marketing Question*

How would you segment the market for dog food based on two different approaches?
1. Descriptors of dogs.
2. The need profiles of dog owners.
Which approach is easier? Which approach provides greater insight into the dog food market?

*Marketing Question*

Identify the segment(s) that Porsche addresses with its cars. How does this segment(s) differ from the segment in which you would place yourself?

Before the Exxon merger, Mobil's profits were under severe pressure — gasoline prices were low, and Mobil was not the low-cost producer. Mobil conducted a large-scale segmentation study and identified the five segments of gasoline buyers shown in Table 8.1.

These five segments satisfied the criteria for *good* segments. Mobil decided to target three segments — Road Warriors, True Blues, and Generation F3. IT took the following actions:

- Upgrade convenience stores so they would become *destination* convenience stores.

- Speed up refueling by introducing the Mobil Speed Pass, based on new technology.

- Introduce widespread customer-service training for its employees.

- Develop a direct marketing program to recognize and encourage customer loyalty.

Through market segmentation, Mobil improved market share and profits in a highly competitive mature market. When Exxon and Mobil merged, ExxonMobil adopted Mobil's pioneering approach.

### TABLE 8.1

**MARKET SEGMENTS OF GASOLINE BUYERS**

| Segment | Size (% of all buyers) | Description |
|---|---|---|
| Road Warriors | 16 | Generally higher-income, middle-aged men; drive 25,000 to 50,000 miles per year; buy premium gas with a credit card; purchase sandwiches and drinks from the convenience store, sometimes use the car wash. |
| True Blues | 16 | Usually men and women with moderate to high incomes; brand loyal and sometimes gas station loyal; frequently buy premium gasoline and pay cash. |
| Generation F3 — Food, Fuel, Fast | 27 | Upwardly mobile men and women; half under 25; constantly on the go; drive a lot and snack heavily from the convenience store. |
| Homebodies | 21 | Usually housewives shuttling children around during the day; use whatever gasoline station is in town or along their travel routes. |
| Price Shoppers | 20 | Generally neither loyal to a brand nor a gas station; rarely buy premium; frequently on tight budgets; historically Mobil's target customers. |

The fundamental segmentation task is to link customers' need profiles to appropriate *descriptor* or *segmentation* variables. If segmentation is done well, each segment has a well-defined need profile and is easily described by segmentation variables. Frequently, the firm makes several successive attempts to segment a market. Each attempt uses customer need profiles and candidate descriptor variables; they converge somewhere in the middle.

## KEY IDEA

➤ In any market, customers have different need profiles.

➤ The market segmentation process identifies groups of customers. When segmentation is done well, customers within a segment have similar need profiles. Customers in different segments have different need profiles.

## MARKET SEGMENTS

We just discussed the market segmentation process for developing segments, but was this successful? **Good segments** are those the firm could target for marketing effort with a reasonable chance of success. So far, we have focused on two important segmentation criteria:

- **Differentiated:** Customers in different segments have different need profiles. Accordingly, they should respond differently to market offers.

- **Identifiable:** The firm can identify customers by using segmentation variables and hence reach them with its market offers.

*Good* market segments should satisfy four additional criteria:

- **Stable:** Customers will stay in the segment for a reasonable period of time.

- **Measurable:** The firm can measure important characteristics like size and growth.

- **Appropriate size:** Different firms like different size segments. Generally, large firms want large segments to justify their efforts and costs. By contrast, small firms like small segments so they avoid large and powerful competitors.
- **Accessible:** The firm can reach the segment via communications and distribution channels using an appropriate and cost-effective strategy.

Marketers must remember that market segments are not *real*, *correct* or *incorrect*, or *unchanging*. Customers do not have market segment membership stamped on their foreheads! Market segments derive from appropriate data collection and analysis, and creative insight. They *do* help firms to develop compelling offers for markets they choose to address.

## KEY QUESTIONS ABOUT MARKET SEGMENTS

In our research and consulting, managers often raise questions regarding their approaches to market segments and the market segmentation process. Here are the most common.

**HOW MANY MARKET SEGMENTS ARE ENOUGH?** How should the firm make the trade-off between enhancing customer satisfaction by defining large numbers of segments and the cost efficiency associated with few segments? Wal-Mart faces this problem. It has achieved great success with its low-cost, low-price business model. Now it is trying to address segments of local needs without incurring significant cost penalties.[4] The core options are:

- **Large number of segments.** As the firm develops more segments, the similarity of customer need profiles within each segment increases. Hence the firm can gain high customer satisfaction by targeting specialized groups. But, there are few economies of scale and product development and marketing costs are high. Also, managing large numbers of segments is a difficult process requiring significant resources.
- **Small number of segments.** When the firm develops few segments, customer needs are less granular and more diffuse. The firm necessarily targets fewer segments, and on average customer satisfaction is lower. But costs are lower, and the firm's management problems are less complex.

Firms experienced in market segmentation typically opt for a relatively small number of segments, often between five and eight. They may develop more discrete segments during the segmentation process, but then include a rationalizing step to a smaller number. (As noted earlier, firms may also identify finer-grained customer segments within their market segments.)

In some industries, firms segment at a fine-grained level, targeting several fine-grained segments with a **modularity** approach. Modularity speaks to product design, using individual components in multiple products to serve multiple segments. We noted in Chapter 3 that Boeing and Airbus each use modular design, parts standardization, and advanced information technology in airplane manufacture. The Boeing 727, 737, and 757 serve different customer needs, yet some fuselage sections are identical, all inherited from the 707.

Technological advances are increasing design and production flexibility. Computer-aided design (CAD) speeds development, and computer-aided manufacturing (CAM) reduces set-up times. CAD/CAM innovations make product variations less expensive and allow for customer personalization without the typical cost of making *one-offs*. Amazon.com is an excellent example of using information technology to personalize the user experience and reduce the cost of variety. It uses recommendation systems, based on historic purchasing patterns, to advise customers of products to meet their preferences and remind them of birthdays and other events that may trigger purchases.

**CAN AN INDIVIDUAL CUSTOMER BE A MARKET SEGMENT?** Firms that address B2B markets, or sell consumer goods through large retail chains, often focus their efforts on individual customers, known as **segments-of-one**. The firm treats an individual strategic (or key) account as a market segment in its own right.

---

*Marketing Question*

In summer 2000, the magazine *Mirabella* ceased publication. *The New York Times* noted that *Mirabella* was aimed at "women who are no longer 24 years old, who care passionately about literary criticism and serious articles about, say, contemporary philosophers — and equally as passionately about where to buy those just adorable hot-pink leather pants."[3] Where did *Mirabella* fail in its segment criteria?

---

**Criteria for *Good* Segments**

- **Differentiated**
- **Identifiable**
- **Stable**
- **Measurable**
- **Appropriate size**
- **Accessible**

---

**KEY IDEA**

➤ The best approach for forming market segments is to group customers based on their need profiles. The firm should then use descriptor or segmentation variables to identify the different segments.

Historically, in B2C markets, individual artisans like custom tailors offered personally designed *bespoke* products to individuals, typically at high prices. Today, firms can integrate personally designed products with flexible mass production techniques — **mass customization** — and gain two advantages.[5] First, more precisely tailored products enhance customer satisfaction and loyalty. Second, the firm reduces finished-goods inventory throughout its production and distribution system.

Panasonic's retailers measure consumers for bicycles, just as tailors measure consumers for suits. The retailer transmits measurements to the factory, and custom-made bicycles are available in a few days. Similarly, Levi Strauss and Lands' End offer custom-made pants through Internet-based systems. Optical retailers like LensCrafters deliver individually fashioned spectacles in a few hours. At Callaway's *performance centers*, golfers receive computer analyses of their golf swing — they can place orders for clubs cut to a certain length and bent to a specific angle. And Renault's goal is to build and deliver cars within 15 days of receiving a customer order.

Many Internet firms personalize products using *choiceboard* models.[6] Dell's customers design their own PCs. Mattel's customers can design their own Barbie dolls. And Hallmark stores dates for birthdays and other anniversaries — e-mail reminders arrive in time to send a Hallmark card.

**DO MARKET SEGMENTS EVOLVE OVER TIME?** We emphasized that market segmentation is critical to developing market strategy. If two firms are equally accomplished in designing market offers, the firm with better market segmentation will win. Its offers will be more precisely tailored to customer needs than its competitors' offers.

But customers' need profiles are constantly evolving, so the firm's segmentation must also evolve, based on good customer, competitor, and market insight. When markets are young, early entrants often gain success by providing basic functional benefits. Then, as the product life cycle evolves, competitors enter and basic functional benefits become the *cost of entry*. The firm achieves differential advantage by identifying customers with finer-grained needs and delivering them appropriate benefits and values.

Cell phones are a good example. Early in the product life cycle, the most important benefit was phone portability. Later, that benefit became less important in customer decision-making. The need profiles of some market segments focused on additional functional benefits like text messaging and taking pictures. Other segments focused on design and fashion statements.

**HOW DO CUSTOMER LIFE CYCLES AFFECT MARKET SEGMENTS?** In general, it is less expensive to promote and sell products to current customers than to new customers. Firms increasingly recognize the lifetime value of current customers and continually refocus their efforts to increase long-term customer loyalty. B2B customers may go on forever, but individual human consumers follow a predictable life cycle. The B2C firm has two polar options:

- **Retain consumers as they age.** The firm evolves its offer to match consumers' changing need profiles and reaps the benefits of customer loyalty. But eventually, consumers stop buying. GM and Daimler-Chrysler abandoned Oldsmobile and Plymouth, respectively. *Reader's Digest* is a dramatic example. The median age of U.S. subscribers is over 70 years. Literally, its customers are dying!

- **Focus on a fixed age group.** The firm targets an age-defined segment, continually adding new consumers as current customers age and no longer want its products. Magazines often favor this approach — *Teen People, Time for Kids, Sports Illustrated for Kids*, and *Seventeen*.

**IS THERE A DIFFERENCE BETWEEN A *SEGMENT* OF CUSTOMERS AND A *GROUP* OF CUSTOMERS?** We take a hard line on the definition of segments. Within a segment, customers have similar need profiles; these profiles differ from those of customers in other segments. Groups are different; they can be formed in many ways: by degree of use, propensity to buy innovative products, and customer loyalty. Groups may be very important for understanding buyer behavior, but they may not be segments.

**KEY IDEA**

➤ B2B firms often treat major customers as individual market segments. In B2C markets, many firms are practicing mass customization.

**KEY IDEA**

➤ The firm must continually evolve its segmentation, as customers' need profiles evolve.

To illustrate, many firms group customers by level of use — heavy, medium, and light users. This grouping is often very useful for allocating marketing effort; generally, firms place more effort on heavy users than on light users. But the heavy user group is **not** a segment; customers may be heavy users for very different reasons. For example, there are at least two segments of frequent car rental customers: traveling business people who want cars during the week and city dwellers who want to leave town on the weekends. Each segment has different needs and attends to different communication approaches. McDonald's has a heavy-user group, but those customers fall in separate segments: families with young children and single males in blue-collar jobs. In general, the firm should develop groups **before** segments.

**CAN WE DEVELOP SEGMENTS BASED ON JUST OUR OWN CURRENT CUSTOMERS?** Most firms segment the entire market, both current and potential customers. But when it has many current customers, the firm may use customer relationship management (CRM) approaches (Chapter 18) to place purchase transactions in a **data warehouse**. It can then use **data mining** techniques to identify groups based on purchasing patterns and tailor offers to individual customers based on those patterns.[7]

Tesco, the British supermarket, is a good example of data mining in action. In 1995, Tesco launched a loyalty card that paid a 1 percent quarterly rebate based on customers' cumulative purchases. Tesco now has 14 million card users; nine million consumers use their cards weekly. Tesco analyzes data from over 500 million shopping baskets annually and places its customers into 37,000 groups. Tesco tailors rewards and incentives to consumers in these groups via 36 million personalized mailings each year.[8]

# TARGETING MARKET SEGMENTS

The firm never has sufficient resources and/or abilities to address all segments in a market, so it must decide where to target its efforts. Some segments receive greater effort and resources; some segments receive little or no effort. By effective targeting, the firm can better serve customer needs and minimize direct competition. In its targeting decision, the firm must be conscious of the Principle of Selectivity and Concentration discussed in Chapter 1.

- Marketing must carefully choose targets for the firm's efforts.
- The firm should concentrate its resources against those targets.

The Principle of Selectivity and Concentration governs both Marketing Imperative 1 and Marketing Imperative 2, but there is a difference. For Marketing Imperative 1, **Determine and Recommend Which Markets to Address**, marketing's role is *advisory*, helping the firm to decide. For Marketing Imperative 2, **Identify and Target Market Segments**, marketing has a *decision-making* role. When the firm has chosen its markets, marketing has the explicit responsibility to identify target segments.

Whole Foods (WF) is a good example of successful segmentation and targeting in the competitive supermarket industry. WF targets the health-conscious segment with supermarket-style natural food stores, offering one-stop shopping and educational materials on its environmental practices. WF grew from a single store in 1980 to a $8 billion, 270-store chain with 54,000 employees by 2009. Average sales per square foot are close to twice those for regular supermarkets.

International document and package delivery firm DHL used successive approaches to targeting. Initially, it formed three segments based on customer needs:

- **Ad hoc** — small irregular shippers or occasional buyers
- **Regular** — high-volume shippers that do not need supply-chain solutions
- **Advantage** — shippers that need and want a supply-chain solution

The *advantage* segment offered DHL high revenue and profit potential and good partnership candidates. DHL also targeted this segment because its expertise could provide supply-chain solutions. It also selected 10 industry segments where it could offer industry specific knowledge and solutions. Finally, DHL selected specific firms in those industries for selling effort.

The multifactor matrix can help the firm decide which segments to target.

## TARGETING MARKET SEGMENTS: THE MULTIFACTOR MATRIX (STRATEGIC POSITION ANALYSIS)

The **multifactor matrix** or *strategic position analysis* is an analytic approach that helps the firm decide which market segments to address. For each candidate segment, the firm must answer two questions:

- How attractive is this segment?
- Does the firm have the business strengths to win in this segment?

**MARKET SEGMENT ATTRACTIVENESS.** The firm should identify useful factors for evaluating many segments. Sometimes it considers corporate-level attractiveness factors; other times, it focuses on an individual business unit. A business with growth and market share objectives would likely have different attractiveness factors than a business whose objectives focused on cash flow.

For each attractiveness factor, the firm should also consider *direction*. For example, many analysts use market segment size. A large firm may prefer large-size segments; a smaller firm may prefer small segments. Michael Steinbeis, CEO of Steinbeis Holding, the global leader in battery labels, says: "We want to be big in small markets. We may even pull out if a market becomes too large and, due to our size and resources, we can only be a small player."[9] Also, many firms view excessive government regulation as a negative factor. But for a firm with experience in dealing with regulatory bureaucracies, extensive regulation may be positive — regulation may act as an entry barrier for potential competitors. Table 8.2 lays out a five-step process to score market segment attractiveness.

### KEY IDEA

➤ For each segment it targets, the firm should develop a unique offer precisely tailored to the need profile of customers in that segment.

### KEY IDEA

➤ In deciding which segments to target, the firm should ask two questions:

- How attractive is this segment?
- Does the firm have the business strengths to win in this segment?

**TABLE 8.2**

**SCORING THE ATTRACTIVENESS OF A MARKET SEGMENT**

| Step Number | Step | Description |
|---|---|---|
| 1 | Identify factors | The firm seeks several factors (typically five to eight) according to the statement: "Given our history, objectives, culture, management style, successes, and failures, we like to be in market segments that offer ..." |
| 2 | Weight factors | Weight each factor by allocating 100 points based on its importance to the firm. Factor weights sum to 100. |
| 3 | Rate market segments | Rate each market segment according to how well it performs on each factor (1 = poor; 10 = excellent). |
| 4 | Develop factor scores | For each segment, form individual factor scores by multiplying the results of step 2 and step 3 for each factor. Factor score = Weighting × Rating. |
| 5 | Develop the market segment attractiveness score | Sum the individual factor scores. |

The firm completes Steps 1 and 2 once. These results are constant for all segments the firm is evaluating for which it has similar objectives. At Step 3, the analysis shifts to individual market segments. At Step 5, the firm develops a market segment attractiveness score — from 100 to 1,000. More attractive segments earn higher scores. Table 8.3 shows how Robinson, a plastics manufacturer, evaluated the plastic accessories segment. The segment scored 595 in attractiveness.

| Factor | Robinson's Weighting | Plastic Accessories Segment Rating (1 to 10 scale) | Factor Score (weighting × rating) |
|---|---|---|---|
| High market growth | 20 | 7 | 140 |
| Large potential size | 20 | 5 | 100 |
| Little regulation | 10 | 8 | 80 |
| Weak competition | 15 | 4 | 60 |
| Easy customer access | 15 | 9 | 135 |
| Ability to build new strengths | 10 | 6 | 60 |
| Use excess resources | 10 | 2 | 20 |
| Total | 100 | | **595** |

**TABLE 8.3**

**ANALYZING THE ATTRACTIVENESS OF A MARKET SEGMENT FOR PLASTIC ACCESSORIES**

**BUSINESS STRENGTHS.** Required business strengths are specific to each market segment being evaluated. First, the firm must identify those strengths that *any* competitor would require to be successful. Second, it must assess the firm's possession of those strengths. Table 8.4 lays out a five-step process to score the firm's business strengths for a market segment.

| Step Number | Step | Description |
|---|---|---|
| 1 | Identify factors | For each segment, the firm selects several factors (typically five to eight) according to the statement: "To be successful in this market segment, any competitor must possess the following strengths ..." |
| 2 | Weight factors | Weight each factor by allocating 100 points based on its importance for being successful in the segment. Factor weights sum to 100. |
| 3 | Rate the firm | Rate the firm according to its possession of these strengths (1 = poor; 10 = excellent) |
| 4 | Develop factor scores | For each factor, form individual factor scores by multiplying the results of step 2 and step 3 for each factor. Factor score = Weighting × Rating. |
| 5 | Develop the business strengths score | Sum the individual factor scores. |

**TABLE 8.4**

**SCORING THE FIRM'S BUSINESS STRENGTHS**

Steps 1 and 2 focus on the necessary strengths for being successful in the market segment. At Step 3, the analysis shifts to evaluating the degree to which the firm possesses these strengths. At Step 5, the firm develops a business strengths score — from 100 to 1,000. Higher scores demonstrate greater strengths for competing in the segment. Table 8.5 shows how Robinson assessed its strengths in the plastic accessories segment. It scored 645 on business strengths.

| Factor | Plastic Accessories Segment Weighting | Robinson's Rating (1 to 10 scale) | Factor Score (weighting × rating) |
|---|---|---|---|
| Good R&D | 25 | 7 | 175 |
| Well-trained sales force | 15 | 9 | 135 |
| Low-cost operations | 10 | 4 | 40 |
| High-quality service | 15 | 6 | 90 |
| Deep pockets | 10 | 9 | 90 |
| In-place distribution | 20 | 5 | 100 |
| Fast-moving organization | 5 | 3 | 15 |
| Total | 100 | | **645** |

**TABLE 8.5**

**ANALYZING ROBINSON'S BUSINESS STRENGTHS IN THE PLASTIC ACCESSORIES SEGMENT**

This analysis is a one-time snapshot; both the firm and its markets evolve. The attractiveness factors, their importance weightings, and/or the assessment of individual segments will change. Similarly, business strength factors, their importance weightings, and the firm's assessment will also change. Hence, this analysis is not a *one-time deal*; the firm should update periodically.

*Marketing Question*

Review the Robinson example in Table 8.5. How could Robinson secure a better business strengths score?

**WHICH MARKET SEGMENTS TO TARGET?** Figure 8.4 shows the **market segment attractiveness** versus **business strengths** matrix. We trisect each axis — high, medium, low — and label the nine cells, A through I. The firm should consider targeting cells in the top right corner — B, C, F, but avoid the bottom left corner — D, G, H. The diagonal cells — A, E, I — are more questionable; each has positive and negative features.

Our Robinson analysis produced two index numbers for the plastics accessories segment — 595 for **market segment attractiveness**, 645 for **business strengths** — the "X" point in Figure 8.4. The "X" position is not immutably fixed; we must assess whether Robinson can shift from cell E to cells B, C, or F. Robinson has two movement options:

- **Horizontal:** Robinson can shift the segment from X to Y, by improving important business strengths — like in-place distribution.
- **Vertical:** Moving from Y to Z is more subtle. Robinson requires a modified segmentation approach to identify a more attractive market segment.

**FIGURE 8.4**

**ROBINSON'S ASSESSMENT OF THE PLASTIC ACCESSORIES MARKET SEGMENT**

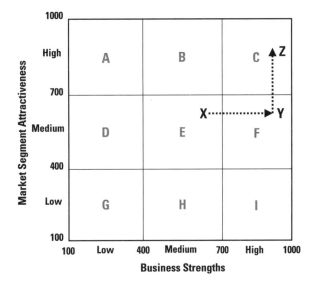

**KEY IDEA**

➤ A firm can improve its market segment position by investing in those business strengths that determine success.

➤ A firm may identify more attractive market segments by refining its segmentation approach.

## TARGETING MARKET SEGMENTS AND COMPANY SIZE

Large firms generally have greater resources than small firms, so a large firm that segments and targets well is difficult to beat. We already showed how hotel-industry leader Marriott targets several market segments with various brands. Marriott's performance is exemplary in its industry. Whirlpool is another large firm that targets multiple segments — in both developed and less-developed countries. In the latter, it targets low-income customers with its Ideale washing machine and makes minor design changes to appeal to local tastes. In Brazil, the appliance is white, has a transparent acrylic lid, and sits on four legs. In China, it is light blue and gray, has a foldable top, and a heavy-duty cycle — *grease removal*. In India, the Ideale is green, blue, and white; is on casters for easy rolling; and has a delicate *sari* cycle.

**KEY IDEA**

➤ Large firms and small firms each have advantages in targeting market segments. Mis-steps can cause each to lose a strong position.

Market segmentation and targeting can even the odds for smaller firms. Many large firms cannot achieve a specialized focus on market segments. Internal constituencies may disagree about segment targets, and decision-making is often protracted. Large firms may also spread themselves too thin over many segments, so that smaller, more-focused competitors can gain advantage. Startup Dell essentially defeated computer giant IBM in PCs. AirTran, Jet Blue, and Southwest Airlines are putting pressure on the majors like United and Delta, and easyJet and Ryanair are winning in Europe.

Sometimes smaller firms win when larger firms ignore, reduce service to, or withdraw from less attractive (for them) market segments. In passenger aircraft, Bombardier Aerospace (Canada) and Embraer (Brazil) profitably produce *short-hop* planes designed to travel between main hubs and smaller regional airports. They avoid stiff competition from the builders of larger planes — Boeing and Airbus.

With fewer resources, smaller firms enjoy focus advantages of targeting few segments and building strong customer relationships, almost by default. They don't *choose* to target fewer segments, they just don't have the resources to target more segments. But successful small firms must understand that their success is due to focus. When a small firm does not know why it is successful, it may expand into segments where resource-rich competitors are stronger. See the *www.Positively-You.com* example:

Launched in April 1998, virtual bookstore *www.Positively-You.com* focused on self-help and motivational books and was profitable in six months! *New York Times* columnist Thomas Friedman wrote a highly complimentary op-ed piece about the firm, and website traffic increased dramatically. Positively-You expanded to compete more directly with Amazon.com — the result was a disaster and within one year the store was out of business. Said owner Lyle Bowlin, "We were doing well as a small niche player, but when we decided to go after Amazon, we lost our way."[10]

Smaller firms face three other problems:

- **Demand shortage.** The small firm targets a few market segments. If demand drops, other segments cannot cushion the impact. An industry-wide recession can wreak havoc with a specialized firm — many dotcom and high-tech businesses failed in the early 2000s.
- **Too successful.** The small firm is *too* successful and attracts the attention of major players. Startup Guiltless Gourmet (GG) grew its line of baked low-fat tortilla chips into a $23 million enterprise. When snacks giant Frito-Lay entered, GG's revenues fell precipitously.
- **High costs.** A narrow focus may lead to high costs that the firm cannot offset by high prices.

### *Marketing Question*

Think of a small firm that failed. What role did segmentation and targeting play in its failure? Which of the pitfalls contributed to its failure? What could the firm have done better to understand the limitations of its strategy?

## KEY MESSAGES

- Market segmentation is fundamental to developing a market strategy. The firm has three separate, but related, strategic-level tasks:
  - Conduct a market segmentation process to identify market segments.
  - Decide which of the identified market segments to target for effort.
  - Develop a market segment strategy and positioning for each target segment.
  We discussed items 1 and 2 in this chapter; we take up item 3 in Chapter 9.
- Segmentation is a process for deconstructing the market into common groups of customers.
- All customers in a market segment have a similar, homogeneous need profile; customers in other market segments have different need profiles.
- The firm can approach the segmentation process in two different ways, by:
  - Identifying groups of customers that differ in their need profiles.
  - Using candidate descriptor (or segmentation) variables to form groups and then seeing if these groups differ in their need profiles.
- Useful segments must satisfy six separate criteria: differentiated, identifiable, stable, measurable, appropriate size, and accessible.
- The segmentation process is a creative and analytic exercise requiring good customer insight. By contrast, targeting requires the firm to make decisions.
- The *multifactor matrix* is a useful approach for making targeting decisions.

# CHAPTER 9

# MARKET STRATEGY— THE INTEGRATOR

## LEARNING OBJECTIVES

When you have completed this chapter, you will be able to:

- Articulate the purpose and functions of market and market-segment strategies.
- Provide direction to the firm.
- Know how to achieve differential advantage.
- Guide the effective allocation of scarce resources.
- Achieve cross-functional integration.
- Lay out the elements of a market-segment strategy.
- Develop and manage market strategies targeted at multiple segments.
- Identify effective and ineffective market and market-segment strategies.

## OPENING CASE: MAYO CLINIC

*Mayo Clinic is the best known and most powerful health care brand in the world. Since the late 1880s, it has delivered superb medical care to patients, provided value to many constituencies, and wielded differential advantage over competitors. Mayo Clinic's history continues to define its differential advantage over other direct health care providers, even in an age when every major hospital and medical institution has professional marketing and public relations staffs.*

*From the outset, Mayo Clinic's market strategy has had two core operating principles. First: "The best interest of the patient is the only interest to be considered." Second: "Two heads are better than one, and three are even better." Focused on these principles, Mayo Clinic now has 48,000 employees serving more than 500,000 patients a year from the U.S. and around the world — at three clinic and hospital operations in Rochester, Minnesota; Jacksonville, Florida; and Scottsdale and Phoenix, Arizona. Mayo also maintains offices in Canada, Mexico, and the United Arab Emirates (UAE) to facilitate appointments, and provide hotel and visa assistance.*

*Mayo Clinic's brand awareness is extraordinary. Kent Seltman, chair of Mayo's marketing division, said, "Our research shows that in the U.S. we register over 1.8 billion consumer impressions a year — 90 percent of the population is aware of Mayo Clinic, 33 percent know someone who has been a Mayo patient, and 18 percent would make us their first choice for a serious health need if there were no financial barriers. Patients from all 50 U.S. states as well as from 150 countries typically visit each of our three clinics every year."[1]*

*Part of Mayo Clinic's success results from its alignment of mission and organization. All caregivers serve as consultants to one another and function as members of multiple-patient care teams. Further, all physicians, nurses, custodians, secretaries — all employees — receive salary checks from the same account, signed by the same person. Mayo Clinic's collaborative model extends to its patients' referring physicians.*

*Mayo Clinic receives extensive public relations coverage when celebrities like entertainers, professional athletes, and government and business leaders visit for care. In small U.S. towns, word of mouth about someone's good experience at Mayo Clinic often leads to a feature story in the local paper or on local TV or radio news. These stories are frequently picked up by regional and national news services.*

*At a time of managed care and restricted provider lists, Mayo Clinic's tiny share of a huge market makes it attractive to many insurers. Research shows the greatest benefit from the Mayo brand is peace of mind — knowing it's there if you need it. Midwest U.S. consumers, in particular, find great value in insurance products that include Mayo Clinic.*

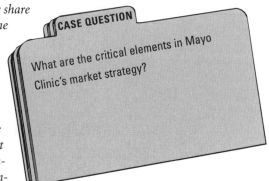

CASE QUESTION

What are the critical elements in Mayo Clinic's market strategy?

*Mayo Clinic grounds its market strategy in the customer value it delivers and the differential advantage it secures. Although a non-profit organization, Mayo Clinic's enormous financial success funds its leading-edge research and hospital facilities, its medical school, its high staff-per-patient ratio, and its roster of world-class physicians and researchers. All these constituents count on customers' willingness to pay and to face the inconvenience of traveling to a Mayo Clinic for treatment.*

In Chapter 7, we discussed Imperative 1, Determine and Recommend Which Markets to Address. In Chapter 8, Imperative 2: Identify and Target Market Segments, we addressed two separate, but related, strategic-level tasks. First, we learned how to conduct the *market segmentation process* and identify *market segments*. Second, we showed how the firm should decide which segments to *target* for marketing effort.

Chapter 9 is the first of three chapters that discuss separate aspects of Imperative 3: Set Strategic Direction and Positioning. Here we focus on developing **market strategy**, arguably one of marketing's most important roles and responsibilities. As we learned in earlier chapters, the market strategy goal is very simple — *to attract, retain, and grow customers, in the face of competitors trying to do the same thing*. The market strategy declares what the firm *will do* and what it *will not do*. Externally, a well-developed strategy reflects the common theme and emphasis of the firm's approach to the market. Internally, it coordinates the actions of many departments and people. An effective market strategy is crucial for success.[2]

The firm partitions its markets into several market segments; then decides which to target. If its segmentation is effective, customers in each segment have similar, homogeneous need profiles. But across segments, these profiles are different, heterogeneous. The extent and type of competition also varies by segment. Because of these differences, the firm must develop a separate strategy for each target segment; positioning is the heart of the *market-segment* strategy. The *market strategy* comprises one or more *market-segment* strategies.

**KEY IDEA**

➤ The goal of market and market-segment strategies is very simple — *to attract, retain, and grow customers in the face of competitors trying to do the same thing.*

# THE PURPOSE OF MARKET AND MARKET-SEGMENT STRATEGIES

Imagine an NFL team going through the football season without a strategy. What are its chances of reaching the Super Bowl? Very slim — luck only goes so far. The team would lack direction and focus and be unable to leverage its strengths. It would not deploy its players effectively, and they would not coordinate with one another. In short, the team would not develop a competitive advantage against its opponents. ***The same is true in business. To be successful, a firm must have a clear market strategy to "win" in the marketplace.***

## KEY IDEA

➤ The market strategy requires decisions about results, resources, and actions.

➤ Well-developed market and market-segment strategies fulfill four purposes for the firm — *provide strategic direction in the market,* state how to *secure differential advantage, guide the effective allocation of scarce resources,* and *achieve cross-functional coordination.*

*Strategy* is one of the most abused, misunderstood terms in business, yet important in any manager's vocabulary. The market strategy builds on market, customer, competitor, company, and complementer insight. It is the firm's game plan for the market, pointing the way to the firm's actions. The market strategy specifies what the firm is trying to achieve, which segments it will target for effort, and how it will position itself in those market segments. The firm must make three types of decisions:

- **Results.** What the firm wants to achieve from addressing the market.
- **Resources.** Broadly, how the firm will deploy its resources to achieve these results.
- **Actions.** Which actions the firm intends to take to be successful.

Well-developed market and market-segment strategies fulfill several purposes for the firm. They provide strategic direction in the market, show how to secure differential advantage, guide the effective allocation of scarce resources, and achieve cross-functional integration.

## PROVIDING STRATEGIC DIRECTION IN THE MARKET

Market and market-segment strategies provide strategic direction on how to attract, retain, and grow customers, in the face of competitors trying to do the same thing. Over time, we expect markets, customer needs, and competitive challenges to evolve and become more complex. The market strategy must guide the firm in the changing environment. Achieving this purpose is more difficult, yet more essential, the greater the complexity and change the firm faces.

## Marketing Question

What is *your* career strategy? Now you are in school. What will you do when you graduate? Describe your objectives, the segment of the job market you intend to enter, and your strategy for managing your career and achieving your goals.

## SECURING DIFFERENTIAL ADVANTAGE

Well-developed market and market-segment strategies must clarify why customers should buy from the firm rather than from its competitors. They also identify how the firm will gain a differential advantage. Recall from earlier chapters that a *differential advantage is a net benefit or cluster of benefits, offered to a sizable group of customers, which they value and are willing to pay for, but cannot get, or believe they cannot get, elsewhere.* Table 9.1 describes the criteria used to evaluate *good* market and market-segment strategies. The firm should reject any market strategy that cannot withstand probable competitor responses.[3] It should also develop contingency plans, or *what if* responses, to possible actions competitors may take. Contingency planning prepares the firm for action, leads to strategies that secure differential advantage, and helps it act pre-emptively — before competitors.

**TABLE 9.1**

**SECURING DIFFERENTIAL ADVANTAGE**

| Criteria | Strategy Description |
|---|---|
| **Cannot do** | The firm takes actions competitors cannot duplicate — typically, they lack a key resource or competence. |
| **Will not do** | The firm's competitors could match the strategy, but are unlikely to do so. The firm needs significant competitive insight to make this judgment. |
| **Will be relatively disadvantaged if they do** | The firm believes the competitor will duplicate its strategic moves — but believes the firm will receive a disproportionate benefit. |
| **Will be benefited by** | The firm believes its actions will be advantageous both to itself and its competitors. |

## GUIDING THE EFFECTIVE ALLOCATION OF SCARCE RESOURCES

All firms have limited resources like capital, plant capacity, technological capabilities, and sales force time. These limitations apply at each organizational level and functional area. Faced with these constraints, the firm must allocate resources to secure differential advantage. It must make two types of allocations. *Externally*, it allocates resources among target market segments, selecting the resources for securing differential advantage in each segment. *Internally*, it allocates resources among activities like product development, advertising, and selling.

## ACHIEVING CROSS-FUNCTIONAL INTEGRATION

Achieving coordination across different parts of the business is critical, but often elusive. The market strategy must coordinate the actions of various organizational functions, so they all pull together and secure differential advantage. Without effective integration, significant internal conflict can arise.

Market-strategy owners must develop support throughout the firm. The various functions likely have different opinions on the market strategy — the sales department wants to increase sales, the operations department to reduce costs. Actions that seem reasonable from a functional perspective may be inappropriate when market considerations are paramount. Well-managed contention is healthy, for it surfaces different perspectives on key issues. But managers from all functions must focus on external issues and take a holistic view on how the firm can win.

# ELEMENTS OF THE MARKET-SEGMENT STRATEGY

We have illustrated that a market is best viewed as a set of market segments. To be successful, the firm should target specific segments with strategies that create differential advantage over competitors. Firms tend to do well when they focus on one or more segments, rather than on the market as a whole. Hertz, Alamo, and Enterprise are major players in the car-rental market, but each focuses on a specific segment. Hertz targets business travelers with speed and convenience, Alamo targets vacation travelers with low-price rentals, and Enterprise offers local convenience to drivers whose cars are being repaired.

Because of market segment differences, the basic market-strategy unit is the market-segment strategy. If the firm targets several segments, its market strategy combines several interrelated market-segment strategies. Figure 9.1 shows the four pillars of a market-segment strategy:

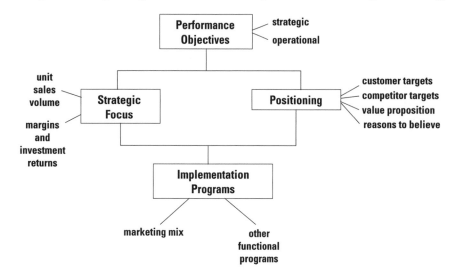

## KEY IDEA

➤ Effective market and market-segment strategies show how the firm will secure a differential advantage.

## KEY IDEA

➤ An effective market strategy helps the firm allocate its resources. Externally, the firm allocates resources to target market segments, and selects specific resources to secure differential advantage. Internally, the firm allocates resources across internal activities.

## FIGURE 9.1

**ELEMENTS OF THE MARKET-SEGMENT STRATEGY**

## KEY IDEA

➤ Inter-functional conflict is endemic. Formulating the market strategy should resolve this conflict and achieve cross-functional coordination.

**Marketing Question**

Suppose you were the marketing VP for a global medical-device supplier. How would you approach developing market strategy? Would you have each region supply you with their individual strategies (bottom-up)? Or would you start by developing a broader global strategy, then have each country and/or region incorporate their local market strategies (top-down)? Which approach would be more effective?

**Marketing Question**

Your firm is launching a new product. You anticipate high short-run market growth and six months competitive lead-time. How will these factors affect your marketing, sales, operations, R&D, human resources, and finance decisions?

**FIGURE 9.2**

**EVOLUTION OF STRATEGIC OBJECTIVES**

 **KEY IDEA**

➤ Priorities for strategic objectives evolve during product life-cycle stages.

**Marketing Question**

In rural areas of less-developed countries, the farmer uses a yoke on his team of oxen. Is the *yoke* a good metaphor for the market strategy?

*Performance objectives, strategic focus,* and *positioning* are conceptual devices requiring creativity. Product and brand managers, or marketing and business directors, typically develop these elements based on market, customer, competitor, company, and complementer insight. *Implementation programs* are more tangible. The firm secures integrated implementation by clearly articulating and gaining commitment to performance objectives, strategic focus, and positioning.

## PERFORMANCE OBJECTIVES

Before the firm figures out what it will do, it must know where it's headed. **Performance objectives** articulate the firm's market segment goals. They state clearly and simply what the firm is trying to achieve, broken down into two components: strategic objectives and operational objectives.

### STRATEGIC OBJECTIVES

**Strategic objectives** establish the type of results the firm intends to achieve; they are qualitative and directional. Strategic objectives are not concerned with numbers, but declare, in general terms, how the firm will measure its success. Many people confuse strategic objectives with mission statements (see Chapter 7). The difference is clear: The mission states where the firm will seek market opportunities; strategic objectives state the required types of results.

The three broad categories of strategic objectives are growth and market share, profitability, and cash flow. Each is attractive, but they often conflict. For example, many firms set growth and market share as key strategic objectives, but then have to spend on fixed assets, working capital, and marketing expenses. This negatively affects short-term cash flow and profitability.[4]

What is the best approach? Because these categories of strategic objectives conflict, the firm must make trade-offs. It must set explicit priorities — primary and secondary — for various stages of the market or product life cycle. It must resist the tendency to demand increased growth, market share, profit, *and* cash flow, all at the same time. The conditions for achieving on all dimensions simultaneously are very rare.

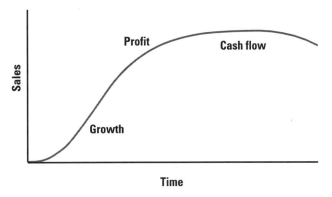

Figure 9.2 is a classic illustration of how strategic objectives evolve in a life-cycle framework. In the introduction and early growth stages, firms often set priorities on growth and/or market share. These often shift to profit in late growth and for much of the maturity stage. Late in the maturity stage, especially if decline is imminent, cash flow predominates; hence the term *cash cow*. These guidelines are not cast-iron prescriptions for selecting primary strategic objectives, but simply reflect many firms' behavior.

## OPERATIONAL OBJECTIVES

Strategic objectives are qualitative, establishing the general direction the firm wants to take; **operational objectives** are quantitative. They provide the numbers to attach to the strategic objectives. What types of numbers? Operational objectives answer the following questions: How much is required, and when? They should specify how much growth, market share, profit, or cash flow the firm should earn during a specific time frame.

The firm uses operational objectives to evaluate performance. They should be **SMART** — **s**pecific, **m**easurable, **a**chievable, **r**ealistic, and **t**imely. Operational objectives should also be challenging, but not out of reach and demotivating. During the market-segment strategy development process, the firm should establish and continually revisit short-term and long-term operational objectives in the context of budgetary implications.

## SETTING PERFORMANCE OBJECTIVES

Sometimes managers do not distinguish between strategic and operational objectives. Far too often, they state objectives in terms of profits, "Our profit target for 20XY is $45 million." In principle, setting a $45 million target is not wrong, but the problem is in not asking (yet alone answering) two basic questions. *How will achieving this profit objective affect the firm's overall objectives?* and *How shall we get there?*

Improving short-term profits is not that difficult. Just cut spending on new products, advertising, sales promotion, and salaries; raise prices; and tighten credit terms. The firm will quickly increase profits, but in time lose market share and profitability. To avoid such results, it must articulate the trade-offs among alternative strategic objectives and secure agreement from all functional areas. Only then should the firm insert numbers to form the operational objectives.

Generally, strategic and operational objectives should not change during the operating period. But if the assumptions underlying market forecasts or environmental factors change substantially, then the forecasts and performance objectives should change also.

## STRATEGIC FOCUS

Once the firm has established performance objectives for its market-segment strategy, it must decide where to allocate resources. The **strategic focus** does exactly that. Review Figure 9.1 before reading further. Figure 9.3 illustrates the firm's options using a **means/ends tree** to outline, assess, and choose among the various alternatives for improving profits and return on investment (ROI).[5] The tree has two main branches. Branch A focuses on increasing unit sales volume; branch B focuses on improving margins and investment returns. The firm must select among the branches and sub-branches to create a focus that best helps achieve its strategic and operational performance objectives.

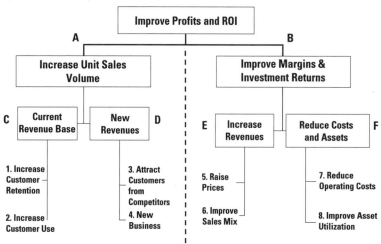

**KEY IDEA**

➤ The firm must make trade-offs among the three categories of strategic objectives: growth and market share, profitability, and cash flow.

**KEY IDEA**

➤ Managers should explicitly discuss the trade-offs and expectations among strategic objectives before setting operational objectives.

**FIGURE 9.3**

**STRATEGIC FOCUS – A TREE OF ALTERNATIVES**

**KEY IDEA**

➤ Operational objectives provide the numbers to attach to the strategic objectives; they specify how much is needed and by when.

*Marketing Question*

How does Amazon use purchase patterns to increase sales to existing customers?

## INCREASE UNIT SALES VOLUME (BRANCH A)

Figure 9.3 shows that branch A has two sub-branches, C and D, to increase unit sales volume. Sub-branch C offers two alternatives to enhance current revenues — *increasing customer retention* and *increasing customer use*. Sub-branch D secures new revenues by *attracting customers from competitors* and *securing new business* by identifying potential opportunities.

### Examples of Increasing Unit Sales Volume (keyed to Figure 9.3)

**C1. Increase customer retention**

In late 2004, interest rates were at historic lows. GM announced that consumers who financed a new GM automobile would receive identical financing for a second new car if they purchased within the financing period.

**C2. Increase customer use**

Verizon cross-sells long distance, Internet access, and DirecTV services. Similarly, cable TV firms sell telephone service and Internet access. Sometimes these firms make bundled offers.

**D3. Attract customers from competitors**

DirecTV explicitly targets the customers of cable TV firms; natural gas retailers target heating oil customers.

**D4. Secure new business**

Drug companies make *ask-your-physician* appeals. They target *non-users* to generate interest, leading to trial. Examples include Plavix — blood thinner, Viagra — erectile dysfunction, and Wellbutrin — anxiety disorder.

*Marketing Question*

Your firm wants to gain customers from competitors. How will you approach *win back*? How will this differ from gaining new customers?

## IMPROVE MARGINS AND INVESTMENT RETURNS (BRANCH B)

Figure 9.3 shows that branch B has two sub-branches, E and F, for improving margins and investment returns. Sub-branch E increases the firm's revenues by *raising prices* or *improving the sales mix* — selling more of its higher-profit products and less of its lower-profit products. Sub-branch F *reduces operating costs* (selling, marketing, operations) and *uses assets more effectively*, like reducing accounts receivable and inventory.

### Examples of Improving Margins and Investment Returns (keyed to Figure 9.3)

**E5. Raise prices**

Firms with monopoly-like positions often use this approach. Examples include cable TV firms and their suppliers like ESPN and Disney. Other examples are seasonal products like amusement parks and airline travel.

**E6. Improve the sales mix**

Many B2B firms add services or offer additional features. They try to persuade customers to trade up to more expensive offers that have higher profit margins.

**F7. Reduce operating costs**

In the 1990s, many firms reduced costs by firing workers, re-engineering processes, and outsourcing internal operations. In the early 2000s, many firms cut back on advertising, along with promotional and selling expenses.

**F8. Improve asset utilization**

Dell's make-to-order manufacturing system minimizes its inventory investment. Also, Dell often receives payment before making the product. The result is negative working capital for Dell.

## INCREASE UNIT SALES VOLUME OR IMPROVE MARGINS AND INVESTMENT RETURNS?

The big question is: How should the firm trade off the alternatives in Branch A with the alternatives in Branch B? After all, many are in conflict. Targeting a competitor's customers may be a viable option for increasing unit sales, but it won't be successful if the firm simultaneously cuts advertising and selling expenses!

The answer is straightforward. The firm's choice of alternative(s) should closely parallel its primary strategic objective. If this is growth, the firm should focus on alternatives from Branch A. If the firm wants to increase cash flow, it should select alternatives from Branch B. If it is improving profits, the firm should mix and match — select some alternatives from Branch A and others from Branch B. One thing is clear: The firm cannot pursue too many alternatives simultaneously without losing focus.

## POSITIONING

For many marketers and marketing faculty, **positioning** is the heart of the market-segment strategy (Figure 9.1, page 128). The firm seeks to create a unique and favorable image for the firm's product in customers' minds. Clarity is key; confusion is the enemy of positioning.

We must emphasize the distinction between *targeting* a market segment and *positioning* in a market segment. In Chapter 8, we discussed targeting market segments. In this chapter, we assume the firm has made the targeting decision. Now we are focusing on developing a strategy to compete successfully in the target segment. Positioning requires the firm to make four key decisions *within* the segment:

- Select customer targets.
- Frame competitor targets.
- Design the value proposition.
- Articulate the reasons to believe.

We discuss these decisions sequentially, but they are highly interrelated. Typically, the firm goes back and forth making these decisions until they form a coherent whole. Figure 9.4 illustrates the considerations in selecting customer targets, framing competitor targets, and designing the value proposition.

**KEY IDEA**

➤ The positioning decision has four core elements:
- Select customer targets
- Frame competitor targets.
- Design the value proposition.
- Articulate the reasons to believe.

**FIGURE 9.4**

**THE ELEMENTS OF POSITIONING**

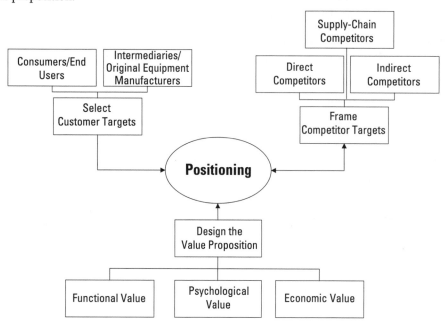

## SELECTING CUSTOMER TARGETS

**Customer targets** are where the firm places the bulk of its marketing effort. If you don't target the right customers, your chances of success will be slim. Three issues are important when targeting customers:

- Choosing the distribution system.
- Targeting levels within the distribution system.
- Targeting specific individuals or types of individual.

**CHOOSING THE DISTRIBUTION SYSTEM.** There are several ways for the firm's products or services to reach end-user customers.[6] Some are direct; others are indirect and may comprise third-party organizations. Examples include:

- A component manufacturer sells its products to finished-goods manufacturers.
- A component manufacturer sells its products to sub-assembly manufacturers; in turn, they sell their products to finished-goods manufacturers.
- Products produced by finished-goods manufacturers pass through distributors, wholesalers, and/or retailers before reaching end-user customers.

Many industries have well-established channel systems whereby products travel *downstream* from level to level, ultimately to reach end-user customers. The firm may also develop innovative channels to gain differential advantage. Today, many firms are successful by targeting consumers directly via the Internet, and avoiding distributors, wholesalers, and retailers (and their margins). Michael Dell believed that customer buying patterns would change as the PC market matured. Dell targets end users by direct marketing and the Internet and became the PC global market share leader; it also earned strong positions in servers and printers.

**TARGETING LEVELS WITHIN THE DISTRIBUTION SYSTEM.** With limited resources, the firm must decide which levels to target for effort. The broad options are *push* and *pull*; we discuss them in more detail in Chapter 15:

- **Push strategy:** The firm places most marketing effort *upstream* on direct customers, like manufacturers and distributors. A firm selling finished consumer products focuses on retailers; a raw material or component manufacturer focuses on finished-goods suppliers. The firm expects these customers (and/or their customers) to promote its products to end users.
- **Pull strategy:** The firm places most marketing effort *downstream* on indirect customers — consumers or end users. An FMCG firm focuses on consumers. A raw material or component manufacturer focuses on end-user customers. The *intel inside* advertising campaign is a good example.

Typically, the firm cannot apply equal effort at all potential customer targets. It must designate primary targets for most effort and secondary targets for less effort. The Mattel example shows the importance of customer targets:

Mattel introduced *Barbie* at the 1959 Toy Fair — retail buyers' response was negative. Essentially, they said to Ruth Handler, Mattel founder and Barbie's originator: "Little girls want baby dolls; they want to pretend to be mommies." Motivational researcher Ernest Dichter advised Handler to launch Barbie with TV advertising. When girls saw TV ads for Barbie, they — and their mothers — stampeded the stores.[7] By targeting the final consumer, Mattel achieved global market leadership in the toy industry.

**TARGETING SPECIFIC INDIVIDUALS OR TYPES OF INDIVIDUALS.** Once the firm has selected the distribution level, it must decide which specific influencers and/or decision-makers to target. Typically it wants to change or reinforce their behavior and/or mental states like knowledge, attitudes, and intentions to purchase. Recall that organizations do not make decisions — people in organizations make decisions! For a firm targeting households, possible individual targets are husband, wife, children, grandparents, uncles, and aunts. In China, because of the one-child policy, toy firms often target grandparents — they dote on their grandchildren. In the U.S., firms target children directly. Tweens, children between eight and 12 years old, are an increasingly important consumer segment.

B2B firms also make individual-level targeting decisions. A well-known floor-covering firm markets heavily to retailers, but focuses on retail salespeople — it provides spiffs (cash incentives). A firm selling raw materials to manufacturers can target operations managers, design engineers, marketing and sales, purchasing agents, and/or general managers.

**KEY IDEA**

➤ The firm competes for customer targets — decision-makers or influencers.

Creativity is important in the customer targeting decision. The firm should consider:

- **Reachability.** Target customers should be easy to reach — but gaining access may be difficult. In B2B, procurement personnel often block access to individual customers like designers, engineers, and senior executives.
- **Influentials.** Customer targets need not be decision-makers, but they should influence the buying decision. Neglecting important influentials can be fatal.
- **Personally benefits but does not pay.** The ideal customer target has significant influence, personally benefits from the purchase, but does not pay. Examples include:
  - Children influencing parental decisions.
  - Doctors writing prescriptions.
  - Business travelers whose firms pay for airline and hotel services.
  - Politicians and regulators serving their constituents — they spend taxpayers' money.
- **Obvious targets.** Obvious customer targets may be easy to identify and reach but can be ineffective, simply because they are obvious — perhaps they are also competitors' targets! Deep customer insight, creativity, and a contrarian position can pay great dividends.[8] FedEx's early success came from targeting professionals and their secretaries rather than shipping managers, the traditional decision-makers.

## FRAMING COMPETITOR TARGETS

The firm decides which competitors to compete against. **Competitor targets** can be current and/or potential competitors, direct and/or indirect competitors, and/or supply-chain competitors. The choice of competitor target depends on the firm's strength in the market segment.

The firm can place competitors in one of two categories — competitors to avoid and competitors the firm is quite happy, and chooses, to face. This partition helps the firm design its value proposition. Competitive targeting shapes customers' perceptions of the firm's offer and helps it to refine its claims. Note 7-Up's positioning alternatives in Table 9.2.

**KEY IDEA**

➤ The firm's competitive target can be current or potential, direct or indirect, or in the supply chain. Sometimes the targeted competitor is not immediately obvious.

| Claim | Type | Market Opportunities | Customer Implications |
|---|---|---|---|
| "7-Up tastes better than Sprite" | Comparison with direct competitor | One lemon-lime soda substitutes for another | Compare us |
| "7-Up, the best-tasting lemon-lime soda" | Product form superiority | The whole lemon-lime product form | The best choice when drinking lemon-lime |
| "7-Up, the uncola" | Out of product form | The cola product form | The alternative to cola. "We're different" |
| "7-Up, the real thing, the only one," etc. | Implied or claimed uniqueness | All beverages? | There's no other drink quite like it |

**TABLE 9.2**

**FRAMING COMPETITOR TARGETS**

**SUBTLETY IN COMPETITOR TARGETING.** The most effective competitor targeting may not be obvious. Who benefits from designating major accounting firms as the Big 3? — Number 3! The Big 3's competitor target is number 4. Visa advertises that many restaurants globally accept its card, but relatively few accept AmEx. Visa wants customers to believe that AmEx is a direct competitor as a way of improving its position against MasterCard, its real competitor target.

## DESIGNING THE VALUE PROPOSITION

A well-designed **value proposition** provides a convincing answer to a deceptively simple question: "Why should target customers prefer the firm's offer to those of competitors?" *Positioning is the heart of the strategy* — the *value proposition* is the heart of positioning. (Figure 9.1, page 128)

The firm bases its value proposition on functional, psychological, and economic value and related benefits it delivers to customers. The value proposition defines how the firm gains customers and beats competitors. Other terms are *key buying incentive, differentiated core benefit, core strategy,* and *unique selling proposition,* but *value proposition* best captures the critical concept.

---

**Examples of Clear and Effective Value Propositions**

- Federal Express delivers on time — *when it absolutely, positively has to get there overnight*
- Apple's Macintosh computers — *it just works*
- Telephone calls made with Sprint are very clear — *you can hear a pin drop*
- iPod — Take your music with you
- iTunes — Largest legal digital music library — it's easy to use
- HSBC — Global reach, local understanding
- Wal-Mart — Always low prices — *Always*
- UPS — we can do your logistics ... we get your stuff where it needs to go
- Dunkin' Donuts — It's worth the trip

---

The firm should base its value proposition on the principles of customer value and differential advantage we discussed in Chapter 1:

- Focus on satisfying important customer needs,
- Attempt to meet these needs better than competitors and, where possible
- Offer values and benefits that are difficult for competitors to imitate.

In particular, the value proposition should follow the BUSCH system; it should be **b**elievable, **u**nique, **s**ustainable, **c**ompelling, and **h**onest.[9] It plays two separate but related roles: externally as the firm's major competitive weapon for attracting, retaining, and growing customers; internally for defining the firm's implementation task.

⚷ KEY IDEA

➤ The value proposition is the firm's major competitive weapon for gaining its target customers; it also defines the firm's implementation focus.

➤ The firm must develop a value proposition for each target customer type.

## ARTICULATING THE REASONS TO BELIEVE

Declaring the firm's intentions in the *value proposition* is one thing; convincing target customers it will deliver on its promises is quite another. The **reasons-to-believe** statement is an essential component of positioning as it supports the firm's value proposition with compelling facts to make its claims believable — like scientific evidence, independent testing data, testimonials, the firm's proven competencies and/or prior performance, and/or factual information on product attributes. Examples of possible *reasons-to-believe* statements include:

- Cisco. Cisco has technical expertise in routers and many successful installations worldwide.
- P&G – detergents. P&G's long experience in detergents and a huge commitment to R&D.
- Citibank. Citibank's vast network of branches around the world.
- CommerceOne – a convenience bank. Opening hours — 7 a.m. to 7 p.m., 7 days a week.
- J&J – Tylenol. Clinical evidence of superior pain relief.

## DEVELOPING POSITIONING STATEMENTS

*"Positioning is not what you do to a product — positioning is what you do to the mind of the prospect."*[10]

The capstone of the positioning process is a compelling positioning statement: Positioning is vital for guiding and coordinating the firm's marketing efforts. But developing the positioning statement is complex, difficult, and time-consuming. Many individuals may be involved. A senior Unilever marketing executive alleged that it often takes longer to develop product positioning than to develop the product! When P&G introduced its teeth whitener, *Whitestrips*, it held off on expensive TV ads and store testing. Rather, it undertook a six-month online advertising and sales campaign while it assessed consumer interest, using that data to refine its positioning.

The positioning statement has a clear structure that must distinguish the firm's offer from competitors' offers.[11] It should:

| | |
|---|---|
| **Convince** | [customer target] |
| **In the context of other alternatives** | [competitor target] |
| **That they will receive these benefits** | [value proposition] |
| **Because we have these capabilities/features** | [reasons to believe] |

Table 9.3 shows a positioning statement for Cemex, the Mexican cement producer.

| Task | Focus | Positioning Item |
|---|---|---|
| Convince | Builders and contractors | Customer Target |
| In the context of other alternatives | Traditional cement producers | Competitor Targets |
| That they will receive these benefits | Consistent delivery within 30 minutes of Cemex receiving an order — versus the three-hour standard | Value Proposition |
| Because we have these capabilities | A global positioning satellite system on each truck. Computer software that combines truck positions with plant output and customer orders to calculate optimal destinations. The ability to redirect trucks en route. | Reasons to Believe |

Positioning statements should be **d**istinct, **c**ompelling, **a**uthentic, **p**ersuasive, and **s**ustainable (DCAPS). Creativity can be crucial. Guinness Stout traditionally served a limited market of older men and women. In the early 2000s, Guinness repositioned its product as a friendly beverage for younger consumers. It also leveraged its brand heritage by offering the *Guinness* experience at more than 2,000 Irish pubs worldwide. Sales increased dramatically.

Positioning is especially important for new products. Unilever and P&G *get it*, but many firms waste millions of dollars in ineffective advertising campaigns because of poorly developed positioning. Positioning statements are not advertising messages, but DCAPS positioning provides excellent guidance for creative personnel at advertising agencies.

## IMPLEMENTATION PROGRAMS

Strategic focus and positioning specify the firm's approach to achieve its performance objectives. **Implementation programs** (Figure 9.1, page 128) describe specific actions the firm must take to execute its approach. Any good market or market-segment strategy must seriously address both the marketing mix and other functional programs.

**TABLE 9.3**

**EXAMPLE OF A POSITIONING STATEMENT FOR CEMEX**[12]

 **KEY IDEA**

➤ "Positioning is not what you do to a product: Positioning is what you do to the mind of the prospect."

## KEY IDEA

➤ The marketing mix and other functional programs implement the market strategy.

## TABLE 9.4

**MARKETING MIX FOR STEUBENWARE IN THE GIFT SEGMENT**

## *Marketing Question*

What is the BlackBerry's value proposition? What is its marketing mix? Do the marketing mix elements support the value proposition and one another?

## KEY IDEA

➤ Marketing mix programs should support the value proposition, and all elements should support one another.

## KEY IDEA

➤ The firm's functional areas must support the market strategy.

## IMPLEMENTING THE MARKETING MIX

Chapters 12 through 19 focus on implementing the marketing mix. For now, we show how each element in the marketing mix must support the value proposition, and must also support the other elements. Table 9.4 shows how the Steubenware marketing mix elements support one another for high-quality glass crystal in the gift segment. We assume that the value proposition revolves around psychological value, assurance that recipients will love Steubenware gifts for their high quality, scarcity, and image.

| Marketing Mix Element | Steubenware |
|---|---|
| Product | Extremely high quality — Steuben destroys products with imperfections |
| Advertising | High-quality shelter magazines like *Good Housekeeping* |
| Sales promotion | Brochure material and display racks are high quality |
| Selling strategy | Focuses on product quality |
| Distribution | Few retail outlets, but high quality — specialty and upscale department stores |
| Service | High-quality pre- and post-sale service |
| Price | High price — reflecting high image |

## ALIGNING CROSS-FUNCTIONAL SUPPORT

Even though marketing may *own* the marketing strategy, today's competition is so intense that the entire firm must work together as a competitive weapon by aligning all functional areas to support the value proposition. A leading U.S. business periodical faced a difficult crisis when competition challenged its 50-year market dominance. The firm pulled together a cross-functional team of advertising, sales, operations, finance, marketing, editorial, publishing, fulfillment, and circulation executives to develop and implement a new market strategy. This approach successfully reinforced the periodical's leadership position and produced its best-ever financial result!

If one or more functional areas cannot provide support, the firm must revisit its value proposition. This analysis is critical. Going forward without full support commits the cardinal marketing sin — making promises to customers the firm cannot fulfill. Customers do not care which individual or department is at fault. They expect and want the benefits and values the firm promised. They rightly believe the firm should fix the problem.

## MANAGING MULTI-SEGMENT STRATEGIES

In this chapter, we showed how to construct a strategy for addressing a target market segment — performance objectives, strategic focus, positioning, and implementation programs. But the firm often targets several segments simultaneously; then it must develop several market-segment strategies. Each segment strategy requires its own performance objectives, strategic focus, positioning, and implementation programs. The firm must make sure that each segment strategy is distinct. Pottery Barn Kids' positioning is distinct from Pottery Barn — but Pottery Barn is not well distinguished from its down-market chain, West Elm. When the firm targets multiple segments, it should ask three related implementation questions:

- **Independence.** Are the individual segment strategies and implementation programs unrelated?

- **Positive synergies.** Could the firm enjoy positive synergies from implementation programs for additional segments? Are there cost efficiencies from using the same sales force, distribution channels, and/or sharing brand equity?

- **Negative synergies.** Will the firm suffer negative synergy by targeting an additional segment? New products may confuse the sales force. Extending a brand may confuse customers. Almaden is a strong brand of popularly priced wine, but a $100 bottle of Almaden would probably not do well!

The firm's individual market-segment strategies and implementation plans must together form a coherent market strategy. Because of increasing complexity in customer need profiles, multiple-segment issues are especially intriguing and challenging.

**KEY IDEA**

➤ Together, individual market-segment strategies must form a coherent market strategy. The segment strategies must be distinct, yet the firm should seek out positive synergies in implementation programs.

---

## KEY MESSAGES

A market strategy has four key purposes:

- Providing strategic direction in the market.
- Securing differential advantage.
- Guiding the effective allocation of scarce resources.
- Achieving cross-functional coordination.

The market-segment strategy has four key elements; each element has several constituent parts:

- **Performance objectives**: The results the firm hopes to achieve:
  - **Strategic objectives** — qualitative and directional. Strategic objectives typically fall into one of three categories: growth and market share, profitability, and cash flow.
  - **Operational objectives** — quantitative and time-bound. Provide the numbers—how much and by when.
- **Strategic focus**: The broad direction of the strategy. Has two main branches—*increase unit sales volume* and *improve margins and investment returns*.
- **Positioning**: How target customers should view the firm's offer. Positioning requires four key decisions:
  - **Select customer targets** — decide on the distribution system, the level to target, and the specific individual or types of individual.
  - **Frame competitor targets** — the competitors that the firm decides to go up against.
  - **Design the value proposition** — the basic reason that target customers will prefer the firm's offer to competitors' offers.
  - **Articulate the reasons to believe** — the supporting evidence to back up the firm's claims.
- **Implementation programs**: What the firm must do to execute the strategy. There are two types:
  - **Marketing mix**: The firm must integrate product, promotion, distribution, service, and price around the value proposition.
  - **Supporting functional programs**: The firm must integrate the functional areas that must work together to deliver the value proposition.

If the firm targets multiple market segments, each segment strategy must be distinct. The firm should seek positive synergy among its implementation programs.

# CHAPTER 10

# MANAGING THROUGH THE LIFE CYCLE

*There are risks and costs to a program of action. But they*
*are far less than the long-range risks and costs of inaction.*

— John F. Kennedy

## LEARNING OBJECTIVES

When you have completed this chapter, you will be able to:

- Appreciate the critical importance of pre-emption in developing competitive strategy.
- Use the product life-cycle framework to generate several plausible scenarios.
- Identify and assess the business characteristics and strategic considerations for each scenario.
- Generate several strategic options for each scenario.
- Recognize effective life-cycle strategies.

## OPENING CASE: RYANAIR

*Ryanair upset the life cycle for European air travel when it entered the Ireland-England market in 1985 with flights from Waterford (in southeast Ireland) to London's Gatwick Airport. In 1986, it challenged government-owned British Airways' and Aer Lingus' duopoly on the Dublin-London route with flights to London's Luton Airport.*

*Ryanair's initial £99 roundtrip price was less than half the £209 duopoly price. In response, British Airways and Aer Lingus slashed prices, but in 1986, Ryanair carried 82,000 passengers. Observers believed Ryanair's traffic came from three sources: British Airways' and Aer Lingus' passengers; new air-travel passengers from among the 750,000 annually who made the nine-hour trip by rail and ferry for fares as low as £55; and passengers who previously didn't travel because of high airline prices and/or the inconvenience of rail and ferry.*

*In 1987, Ryanair expanded its route network to 15 destinations in Britain and Ireland, offering business-class travel and frequent-flyer services. By 1990, it had more planes and a few new routes from Dublin to continental Europe. But intense price competition and new capacity from British Airways and Aer Lingus led to significant accumulated losses. Ryanair was forced to restructure and switched to a very different business model.*

*Ryanair used Southwest Airlines as its model to become Europe's first low-fare airline. It offered high-frequency schedules and aimed at being the low-fare carrier on every route. It scrapped business-class travel and the frequent-flyer club, shifting to a single class of service and using a single type of aircraft configured with the maximum number of seats.*

NEW AIRPORT SECURITY PROCEDURES

PUT FUN BACK INTO FLYING

*To support its low-price strategy, Ryanair obsessively cut costs. It eliminated free drinks and meals; high-capacity utilization pushed down overhead costs. Ryanair negotiated lower landing fees and in some cases persuaded municipalities to mitigate its costs because of the employment opportunities it would bring. Ryanair revamped its route structure so that the typical flight was an hour or less and organized its hubs to reduce maintenance costs and turn-around times.*

*By 2005, Ryanair was Europe's largest airline, carrying almost 31 million passengers, the vast majority via online booking. To celebrate its 20th birthday, and continuing its practice of airline-seat sales, Ryanair offered 100,000 seats at 99 pence. Ryanair estimated that by 2012 it would be flying 225 Boeing 737-800s, allowing it to carry 70 million passengers annually.*

**CASE QUESTION**

The Ireland-Britain market seemed to be in maturity when Ryanair entered. Ryanair's actions shifted the life cycle into a period of dynamic growth. How do you explain this transformation? What other examples of this phenomenon can you identify?

---

Chapter 10 is the second of three chapters to discuss separate facets of Imperative 3: Set Strategic Direction and Positioning. In Chapter 9, we showed how to develop strategy for market segments and a market. In this chapter, we expand on the life-cycle framework we introduced in Chapter 3. There we saw how life cycles analysis can help the firm generate useful insights about competitors; in Chapter 7, we used lifecycles to discuss timing-of-entry strategies. In this chapter, we use the life-cycle framework again, but to help the firm make more effective decisions in competitive environments.

By anticipating competitors' actions — and sometimes their timing — the firm can develop **pre-emptive** strategies. A pre-emptive strategy means acting before your competitors, perhaps targeting an emerging segment or introducing a new product. The Ryanair case is a good example of pre-emptive action. Acting pre-emptively often involves risks, and failure may be visible and costly. But there are also costs for not acting, particularly for established players. These costs are the forgone opportunities, the market share gains and increased profits the firm did not earn. **Opportunity costs** are insidious. They do not appear on the firm's income statement, but they may be more significant than costs that do.

Consider Apple and the iPod — many observers counseled caution. They said to Apple: "You are a computer company; you have no experience in digital music. Napster has closed, and downloading music via the Internet faces immense uncertainty. Sony owns portable music players with the Walkman; this is their turf, and they will fight you fiercely." Many would have heeded these arguments, but not Steve Jobs. The iPod launch was an enormous success and even helped Apple sell more Macintosh computers. Think of the opportunity costs Apple would have incurred by not launching the iPod.

**KEY IDEA**

➤ Firms failing to act pre-emptively may face significant opportunity costs.

By not acting, the firm opens up potential entry windows for competitors. Firms often hesitate because *going out on a limb* is visible and risky. Neither Aer Lingus nor British Airways acted effectively in the face of Ryanair's disruptive change in air travel. Market-leading firms should view pre-emption as an insurance policy — when change is swift, the costs of inaction escalate rapidly. Firms that will not pay *insurance premiums* should prepare for market share losses.

The life-cycle framework offers a good way to design insurance policies. Understanding how life cycles and competitive strategies evolve is valuable for forecasting and anticipating likely scenarios. With these scenarios, the firm is better equipped to generate good competitive strategic options.

## DEVELOPING COMPETITIVE STRATEGIC OPTIONS

**Marketing Question**

Try to identify firms and their products that correspond to the nine scenarios in Figure 10.1.

The firm generates **strategic options** by developing scenarios that let it anticipate competitors' future actions. The main building block is the classic life cycle of introduction, early growth, late growth, maturity, and decline, typically at the product form level. The **life-cycle approach** is very powerful because market conditions tend to be similar at the same life-cycle stage across many products and technologies. Hence, each of our scenarios has a limited number of strategic options. These options are valuable input for formulating the firm's strategy, but creativity is always important. The firm should avoid becoming too predictable, even when it has a leading market position. In this chapter, we discuss how to generate strategic options from nine scenarios based on the classic product life-cycle stages — Figure 10.1.

**FIGURE 10.1**

**LIFE-CYCLE SCENARIOS**

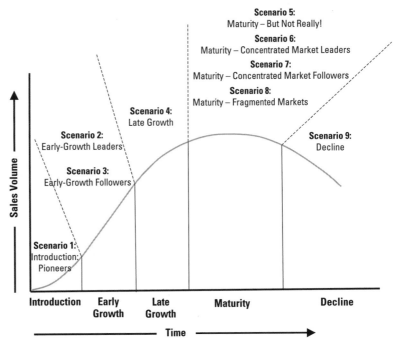

**KEY IDEA**

➤ Scenarios help the firm generate competitive strategic options.

➤ The main building block for these scenarios is product life-cycle stage.

➤ Successful strategies should have a strong creative element.

➤ Life cycles are shortening for many products.

Although the scenarios and strategic options we discuss are valid for many product life cycles, we must recognize that life cycles are shortening. This has several implications:

- When life cycles were longer, firms could enter a market, fail, redevelop their products, and re-enter with a chance of success. Today, re-entry windows are closing.

- Shortening life cycles reduce the time — in early growth — to earn the highest unit margins.

- Good strategic thinking early in the life cycle is more important than ever.

- Faster cycles require proactive management of strategy over the life cycle; evolutionary approaches may be too slow.

Each factor makes identifying scenarios and developing strategic options more difficult. But we designed this chapter specifically to improve your ability to formulate good competitive strategies using the life-cycle framework.

## BUILDING PRODUCT LIFE-CYCLE SCENARIOS

Let's walk through the nine product life-cycle-based scenarios identified in Figure 10.1. Each scenario description begins with a brief introduction; then we focus on creating and analyzing alternative objectives and strategies.[1] But we must be very clear about one thing: We cannot tell you what strategy to follow for a given scenario, because your best strategy depends in part on your competitors' actions. Instead, we give you some strategic options to think about.

### SCENARIO 1: THE INTRODUCTION STAGE: PIONEERS[2]

> Gillette spent $1 billion on developing and initially marketing its Mach3 razor. First-year marketing spending was $300 million for a simultaneous launch in 19 countries. Gillette's corporate profits dropped in the launch year due to Mach3's startup expenses.

Most products do not generate profits in the introduction stage. Pioneering firms typically incur significant R&D and market launch expenditures; they must also invest in plant, equipment, and systems before launch. Marketing expenses are high, and revenues may not cover the firm's ongoing operating costs, much less its fixed costs. Early on, cash flows are often negative. Kevin Plank, the entrepreneur who developed *Under Armour* garments, lived in his grandmother's basement for several years before earning profits from his launch of new athletic wear.

Some firms are better able to sustain new product losses and negative cash flows than others. Large firms typically subsidize new product launches with cash earned from more established products at later life-cycle stages, as part of a long-term product strategy. In this way, Tide laundry detergent funds many new ventures for P&G.

Small firms typically have fewer resources and often need outside financing. In the very early stages, wealthy individuals — aka **angel investors** — often provide startup funding for new ventures. Later, **venture capitalists** may provide financial backing when the venture starts to show promise. If the firm's value proposition is sufficiently compelling, the firm can raise funds from an initial public offering of stock — an **IPO**. Internet firms like Amazon, eBay, Healthion, Priceline, and Yahoo! all got off the ground with venture capital and/or IPOs.

There are few **pioneer** firms in the introduction stage, often only one. The pioneer's strategic objective is to lay the foundation for achieving market leadership and profitability, at least in the short and medium run. It must develop an appropriate strategy as the life cycle moves toward early growth. The pioneer must demonstrate value to target customers and reduce any market uncertainty that the product is just a *short-term wonder* — it may even work with competitors to agree on technological standards. The pioneer must also build a marketing organization and distribution infrastructure.

A critical pioneering task is to keep ahead of competitors by slowing their progress. Now some years after introduction, Apple's pioneering iPod has achieved iconic status and held its competitors to small market share. Its iTunes breakthrough in commercial music downloading and extending Macintosh compatibility to all PCs were critical factors in cementing its position. Sometimes partnerships and alliances can buttress the firm's position.

A particularly effective way of slowing or forestalling competitive entry is to create, or exploit, **entry barriers** — *government-imposed, product-specific,* and *firm-driven.*[3]

**KEY IDEA**

➤ Pioneers must be prepared to tap multiple sources to fund losses early in the life cycle.

**GOVERNMENT-IMPOSED BARRIERS.** Patents are the most common government-imposed barriers that firms can exploit. They provide owners with legal monopolies for several years. Firms can petition the courts to enforce these patent monopolies via patent infringement suits, effectively creating long-term barriers for competitors. Even the filing of patents that are not ultimately approved can act as a short-term barrier. Pharmaceutical companies are especially frequent users of patent barriers. Other government impediments include trade barriers, preferential tax treatment, and outright subsidies. Sometimes the pioneer benefits from a barrier or barrier structure already in place; other times, it may lobby the government for a specific benefit. Sun Microsystems, Netscape Communications, and Novell have all encouraged the U.S. government to take action against Microsoft, slowing its entry into various markets.

**PRODUCT-SPECIFIC BARRIERS.** Product-specific barriers relate directly to the product and include access to capital, raw materials, human resources, and a minimum scale of operations. Sometimes these barriers come with the nature of the product and the firm can exploit them; other times, the firm can actively raise barriers. Of course, innovations in technology or processes cause product-specific barriers to diminish over time. In previous decades, consumers sent film rolls to a central laboratory for processing. Then storefront mini-labs made the process much more convenient. Today, consumers print their own images from digital cameras.

**FIRM-DRIVEN BARRIERS.** The firm can build a *low-cost* barrier via a strategy we call **penetration pricing**. It may also develop and exploit **first-mover advantages**[4]:

- **Low-cost barriers and penetration pricing.** When the firm executes a penetration strategy, it plans on low profit margins for a substantial time period, aka *buying* market share. This strategy is risky and requires substantial resources as the firm continually reduces costs and prices, builds needed capacity, and grows quickly. If successful, low prices built on low costs and experience curve advantages are a significant entry barrier. Figure 10.2 shows the relationship between price and unit cost for a penetration pricing strategy.

---

**Barriers to Competitive Entry**

- Government-imposed barriers
- Product-specific barriers
- Firm-driven barriers

---

**FIGURE 10.2**

**PRICE AND UNIT COST TRAJECTORIES FOR PENETRATION PRICING AND SKIM PRICING**

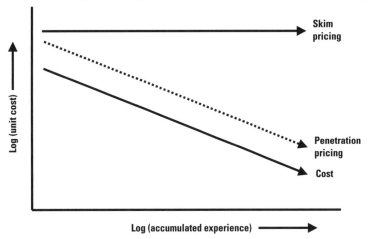

The most advantageous conditions for penetration pricing are price-sensitive markets with few government or product-specific entry barriers. The classic example was Henry Ford's goal to put a Model T in every American garage. Ford invented the assembly line, dramatically lowering production costs; reduced prices continuously; and by the mid-1920s, exceeded 50 percent market share.

---

**The Experience Curve**

The cost curve in Figure 10.2 is a classic **Experience Curve** (EC) — as the firm's accumulated volume (experience) in making, promoting, and distributing a product increases, costs decline in a predictable manner. The EC is a straight-line relationship when we plot log (unit cost) against log (accumulated experience). Cost reductions result from tough decisions that take advantage of organizational learning, economies of scale, advances in process technology, product redesign, and enlightened cost management. The EC has an important influence on many marketing decisions, especially pricing.

Penetration pricing is particularly attractive if customer-switching costs are high and the after-market for complementary products is significant. Firms selling durable goods and consumables — razors and razor blades, printers and toner — frequently price their durables low and their consumables high. Penetration pricing works only if demand for the basic product remains strong; it fails when customers demand variation.

- **First-mover advantage.** The pioneer may earn advantages because it was first. Many firms achieved long-run success from first-mover strategies they sustained by improving products and/or developing new applications.

If the pioneer's products are high-quality, it may earn a leading reputation among consumers and distributors. Early market entry also gives the pioneer superior market knowledge. But it must judiciously nourish these advantages, or a fast follower will surpass it. One key for sustaining first-mover advantage is to build a strong brand, establishing it as the *standard* against which customers judge subsequent entries.[5]

Whereas a successful penetration strategy delivers continued price reductions, a firm with first-mover advantages may maintain high prices — **price skimming**. As Figure 10.3 shows, price skimming keeps prices high, even as the firm reduces costs and earns high profits.[6] Price skimming works if government and/or product-specific entry barriers are high, customer willingness to try is strong, and customers are relatively price-insensitive. The pharmaceutical industry is a good example; patents protect firms from competition, and their products deliver significant health benefits. Price-skimming strategies fail when entry barriers are low and/or customers are price-sensitive. They also fail if the firm ignores customer needs and potential competition.

Generally, new competitors enter to erode first-mover advantages — as product life cycles shorten, advantages erode more quickly. Firms executing price-skimming strategies must be able to shift direction when their advantages disappear.

Pioneers face an environment full of risk. We discussed several strategic options that can lay the foundation for achieving market leadership and profitability.

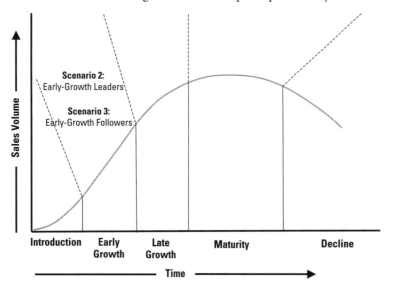

**KEY IDEA**

➤ A pioneer can sustain first-mover advantages by producing high-quality products. The firm earns a leading reputation and sets the stage for creating a strong brand.

*Marketing Question*

The iPod and iTunes have gained a large share of the digital music and music download business. What barriers did Apple erect for potential followers?

**FIGURE 10.3**

**EARLY GROWTH STAGE SCENARIOS**

## SCENARIO 2: EARLY-GROWTH LEADERS

Early growth scenarios are in Figure 10.3. Customers have accepted the product form, and market demand is growing rapidly. Generally, the market leader has a strong position. It has worked out its market-entry problems, and unit costs should be under control. As Figure 10.2 shows, unit costs should reduce as volume builds and the EC takes effect. The firm should be profitable, but cash flows may be negative as it invests in the market and adds new capacity.

**KEY IDEA**

➤ By the early-growth stage, customers accept the product, and the market leader should be profitable.

The leader has four strategic options — two each based on *continuing* and *surrendering* leadership:

- Continue to be leader — enhance position
- Continue to be leader — maintain position
- Surrender leadership — retreat to a market segment or segments
- Surrender leadership — exit the market

**KEY IDEA**

➤ Early-growth leaders should make affirmative decisions to continue to be leaders or surrender leadership.

**CONTINUE TO BE LEADER BY ENHANCING YOUR POSITION.** The firm leverages its success to seek outright market dominance. It grows and broadens the market by continuously investing in R&D to produce new products, extensive advertising, and personal selling. It increases production capacity ahead of market demand and aggressively reduces costs. As competition enters, the firm's communications shift from market development to emphasizing its superiority over competitors. Regarding the U.S. cell phone market, a senior marketing executive at Nokia told us, "While Motorola and Ericsson were still selling American consumers on switching to digital, we were already selling the superior features and performance of Nokia digital phones to separate customer segments."[7] Leaders may also block competitors by entering new emerging market segments, new geographic areas, and new distribution channels.

**CONTINUE TO BE LEADER BY MAINTAINING YOUR POSITION.** The firm may prefer a more conservative approach and try to maintain its market position. It may enjoy monopoly-like status and be concerned about potential political, legal, and regulatory difficulties, like Microsoft has faced. Alternatively, customers may demand additional sources of supply, and/or strong competitors may enter, making it clear they intend to stay. Sometimes technological standards are an issue. Multiple standards cause uncertainty, prospective customers postpone purchase, and the market develops more slowly. The firm may elect to work with competitors on a single standard, rather than go it alone. The early consumer video market, HDTV, and wireless technology markets are all good examples. Apple's early refusal to license its Macintosh operating system in the early 1990s undoubtedly stimulated Microsoft to develop its own graphical-user interface with Windows.

To maintain position, the firm needs good up-to-date competitive intelligence and must carefully select customer and competitor targets. It must have a clear strategy, sufficient resolve to stick to the strategy despite temporary hiccups, and thoughtful contingency or scenario planning. Historically, U.S. firms in the automobile, steel, and aluminum industries pursued this objective to mitigate antitrust action and possible break-up.

Whether the firm undertakes to *enhance* or *maintain* its market position, the broad thrust is the same: ride its leadership position through the life cycle to maturity. Along the way, the firm shifts focus from selling to first-time users to selling new offerings or derivative products to repeat users and acquiring competitors' customers. To achieve success, the firm must broaden and refresh its product line, add services, and build its brand by enhancing its communications. Amazon is a textbook example of this strategy. It began by selling books, and then added recorded music, electronics, and many other product category *stores*, where it personalizes customers' online shopping experiences. Unfortunately, some leaders become complacent; blinded by their early success, they may even treat customers arrogantly. As customers' needs evolve and they become comfortable with the product, followers may be more adept at listening to them.

**SURRENDER LEADERSHIP AND RETREAT TO A MARKET SEGMENT OR SEGMENTS.** Unlike market-share loss from competitive pressure, the firm makes a deliberate choice to surrender leadership. It may lack resources for developing the market and/or funding an ongoing stream of new products. Or a financially stronger competitor sets a market-leadership goal, and the firm knows it cannot win a head-to-head battle. It decides to target one or more market segments as a specialized competitor, believing that *discretion is the better part of valor*.

Sometimes, the follower initiates a penetration strategy by building economies of scale and cutting prices. The firm must identify less-price-sensitive segments where it can add value and overcome its cost disadvantage. It must have good market research capabilities to identify segments and the organizational flexibility to address them. Computer firms like Apple, HP, and IBM have all felt this sort of pressure at various times.

**SURRENDER LEADERSHIP BY EXITING THE MARKET.** Leaving a market after being the pioneering leader may seem defeatist, but it may be prudent. Throughout the life cycle, the firm should always assess the value of its market position, based on the projected discounted profit stream. If this value is less than the sale value of the business today, the firm should consider selling, especially if the product is not central to its mission. As customer needs and market dynamics evolve, the firm should continually evaluate the value of its offer and, if appropriate, identify an effective exit strategy.

The firm's product may be strategically significant for a potential acquirer, fit well with its products, and hence be of immense value. The acquirer may also have the resources to invest and drive product growth, like eBay's 2005 purchase of Skype Technologies' Internet telephony business. Biotech and other technology firms often face the *sell* decision by inventing products they are ill-equipped to commercialize. Successful innovators are often better off selling to firms with strong marketing expertise. Colgate's liquid soap and P&G's Crest SpinBrush were both secured from small firms that elected to sell.

## SCENARIO 3: EARLY-GROWTH FOLLOWERS

Some firms prefer to be **followers**, entering markets in the early-growth stage. By pursuing a *wait-and-see* strategy, they can better assess market potential. They leverage their past successes and learn from the leader's mistakes. But early on, the follower trails the market leader. It has lower volume, higher unit costs, and less experience than the leader. Unless the leader is price skimming, followers are often unprofitable, and cash flow is probably also negative.

**KEY IDEA**

➤ Generally, followers in growth markets are unprofitable and have negative cash flows.

➤ The follower's goal is to learn from others and minimize cost and risk.

Followers in early growth have strategic options similar, but not identical, to the leader. Because they start from inferior positions, choosing among them has a different tenor. The options are:

- Seek market leadership.
- Settle for second place.
- Focus on gaining leadership in a particular market segment or segments.
- Exit the market.

**SEEK MARKET LEADERSHIP.** The follower can pursue leadership by *imitating* or *leapfrogging* the market leader. In each case, it needs good competitive intelligence and entry as soon as possible:

- **Imitation.** Imitation means what it says. The follower copies the leader but executes more effectively. Successful imitators spend heavily to play *catch-up* on product development and outspend the leader in promotion. If possible, the follower leverages an existing marketing or distribution infrastructure and clearly highlights its differentiated value. The follower should not confuse imitation with a price-cutting strategy. Early in the PC life cycle, suppliers offered many designs that earned price premiums, but price competition accelerated as the industry standardized. In browsers, follower Microsoft eclipsed Netscape with a well-executed imitation strategy, but low price was not a factor.

- **Leapfrog.** The follower improves on the leader. It offers enhanced value by developing innovative and superior products, and/or it enters emerging market segments before the leader. Generally, the leapfrogger avoids head-to-head price competition. It may spend more heavily on R&D than the leader, while marketing spending is also high. In video games, Nintendo and Sega leapfrogged first-mover Atari's original videogame with 16-bit machines. In the mid-1990s, Sony Playstation leapfrogged both Nintendo and Sega by offering 3-D graphics and enhanced digital soundtracks. Playstation 3 and Microsoft's Xbox target a different segment — late teens and early 20-somethings — than Nintendo's young teenager target. But Nintendo leapfrogged both Sony and Microsoft by introducing the Wii.

**KEY IDEA**

➤ *Imitation* means copying the leader but being more effective in execution.

➤ *Leapfrogging* goes one better than the leader by developing innovative and superior products and/or targeting emerging market segments.

Effective leapfroggers often do an excellent job of anticipating customers' emerging needs. They spot segment opportunities before leaders, quickly offering new values and securing differential advantage. The most successful followers *change the rules*.[8]

For either *imitation* or *leapfrog*, followers must make long-run commitments. Because they have to play catch-up, resource requirements can be enormous. Of course, some pioneers make it easy for followers by neither improving their products, nor investing sufficiently in promotion and distribution, and keeping their prices high.

**SETTLE FOR SECOND PLACE.** A follower needs substantial resources to become market leader, so settling for second place may be a reasonable and profitable option. GE's former CEO, Jack Welch, famously mandated that GE be either number-*one* or -*two* in each of its markets. Several situations argue for this alternative. Perhaps the leader is content with its current share and does not seek an increase. Customers may demand a second supply source, multiple competitors may simplify product standards, and/or the political/legal/regulatory environment may be favorable.

**FOCUS ON A PARTICULAR MARKET SEGMENT OR SEGMENTS.** This option may be attractive if the follower has fewer resources than the leader and other followers, and if the segment (or segments) is attractive. When their drugs go off patent, pharmaceutical firms often withdraw marketing support, but add services for a narrow physician segment. In Britain, BMS earns sales and profits from Taxol, its anti-cancer drug, long after the patent expired. It provides kits to prepare the drug for patients and replaces these free of charge if patients miss their appointments.

**EXIT THE MARKET.** If the sale value of the business is greater than the projected discounted stream of profits, the firm should consider exiting the market. Because the product is in early growth, its value may be high to a potential acquirer eager to enter a particular market or market segment.

## SCENARIO 4: THE LATE-GROWTH STAGE

Figure: Late growth stage scenarios. Sales Volume (vertical axis) vs. Time (horizontal axis). Scenario 4: Late Growth. Stages: Introduction, Early Growth, Late Growth, Maturity, Decline.

The late-growth scenario is in Figure 10.4. By the late-growth stage, the value to the firm from early market leadership, or being a fast follower, is minimal. Although the customer benefits and values that drove purchase in introduction and early growth are still important, they may not enter the customer's choice decision. More likely, they have become *qualifiers* or *antes*, rather than *determining factors*. The firm must focus on identifying and offering customers' determining benefits and values. Early in the passenger air travel market, safety was critical for customers. Today, most travelers believe that major airlines, flying similar planes, are equally safe:

Safety is an *ante*. Determining benefits and values are items like frequent-flyer miles, time convenience, the availability of a direct flight, and the quality of on-board food (joke!).

The firm requires considerable market research skills to conduct market segmentation, decide which segment(s) to target, be able to satisfy customer needs in the target segment(s), and monitor evolving segments for new opportunities. Successful firms address target segments with *rifle shot marketing*, and then build defensible positions against competitors. Even small segments may offer good profit potential. We see many successful local and regional retail stores despite competition from national chains. Think about who has come and gone in your own town: What examples can you identify? Whole Foods successfully targets a market segment prepared to pay more for higher quality groceries.

The critical success issue for both leaders and followers boils down to commitment. There are really two broad strategic options — target many segments or settle for a more limited position by targeting just a few. The firm's decision should be based on clear insight about the markets and segments and a rigorous assessment of its ability to serve them successfully.

## KEY IDEA

➤ In late growth, the firm must decide whether to target many segments or just a few.

**Scenario 5:**
Maturity – But Not Really!

**Scenario 6:**
Maturity – Concentrated Market Leaders

**Scenario 7:**
Maturity – Concentrated Market Followers

**Scenario 8:**
Maturity – Fragmented Markets

Sales Volume

Introduction | Early Growth | Late Growth | Maturity | Decline

Time

## FIGURE 10.5

**MATURITY STAGE SCENARIOS**

## SCENARIO 5: GROWTH IN A MATURE MARKET

Maturity scenarios are in Figure 10.5. Before the firm examines strategic options in the maturity stage, it must affirm that the life cycle really is in *maturity*. Perhaps there are possibilities for future market growth. To make the point succinctly, some authors assert, "There is no such thing as a mature business, there are only mature managers!"[9] When assessing if the product is in maturity, the firm must analyze the barriers that would impede further growth:

- **Technological barriers.** Innovation may obliterate the product's underlying technological barriers to growth. AT&T's transistor technology rejuvenated radios. Improved microprocessors made PCs portable and much cheaper — the $100 computer is now in sight. In-line skates revived the almost-dead roller-skating industry.

- **Economic barriers.** Economic barriers are often linked to technology. When its Roundup herbicide came off patent in the Philippines, Monsanto cut prices to compete with cheaper generics. It discovered it had vastly underestimated price elasticity;[10] sales grew dramatically when many farmers could afford Roundup.

### Marketing Question

Assume you work for Ford or General Motors. What barriers to growth exist in the automobile market? Are these different for foreign manufacturers?

- **Behavioral barriers.** Requiring significant behavioral change by customers is often a barrier. *Techies* were early users of PCs and their difficult-to-use operating systems like CPM and MS-DOS. The mass market developed only when Apple, and then Microsoft, launched *easy-to-use* intuitive options. Customer behavior changes can also rejuvenate markets. Bicycles were old-fashioned by the late 1970s, but sales increased dramatically a decade later when exercisers used them.
- **Government-imposed barriers.** When the government removes regulations, competitors often enter, and growth explodes. When the U.S. government opened bandwidths to commercial use, wireless-based products expanded rapidly. And deregulation of air transportation spawned rapid growth in the airfreight and passenger markets.

If the market is not *really* mature, in general the firm's key strategic objective should be growth. The most serious barrier to growth may be lack of creativity. Creatively generating and analyzing opportunities and approaching seemingly mature markets can spur growth in several ways.

**INCREASE CUSTOMERS' USE OF THE PRODUCT.** The firm may be able to increase product use via reminder and reinforcement communications; promoting different use applications, occasions, or locations; providing incentives and bundling opportunities; and reducing undesirable consequences of frequency. Specific techniques include:

### KEY IDEA

➤ Creative ways to drive growth in the maturity stage:
- Increase customers' use of the product
- Improve the product or service
- Improve physical distribution
- Reduce price
- Reposition the brand
- Enter new markets

- **Increase the quantity per use occasion.** Options include increasing packaging size, like a 20- versus a 12-ounce Pepsi; and/or designing the packaging for dispensing ease, like adding a larger-sized opening for Tabasco hot sauce.
- **Make the product easier to use.** Consumers do not have to clean or disinfect disposable contact lenses. Pharmaceutical firms often redesign injectable drugs as tablets, time-release capsules, and long-lived patches to ease patient burdens and encourage use.
- **Design the product to expire.** Incorporate devices to indicate product discard dates and encourage repurchase like *best-if-used-by* dates for beer and soft drinks.
- **Change the model.** The fashion industry makes seasonal clothing styles; software companies continually introduce new and improved versions.
- **Improve packaging for better ease of use.** Examples include single-serving cereals, easy-to-pour condiments, and storage-friendly bulk items like Coke and Pepsi 12-paks for refrigerators.
- **Develop new uses for the product.** Arm & Hammer developed many new uses for baking soda, including removing refrigerator smells and sink odors, treating swimming pools, eliminating underarm perspiration, and sanitizing laundry.

**IMPROVE THE PRODUCT OR SERVICE.** Firms should expect sales to slow if their products do not satisfy customers' needs. The remedy is simple: *Improve the offering!* Sometimes even apparently minor changes can increase sales significantly. Clorox introduced a lemon-fresh version of Pine-Sol household floor and wall cleaner — sales grew by 25 percent. It added a squirt of floral scent or a twist of lemon to Clorox bleach and gained 1 percent market share.

Because product quality has improved significantly in many industries, and gaining product-based advantage is difficult, many firms use services to rejuvenate their brands. IBM based its recovery on providing services with its hardware and software products to ensure high customer satisfaction. You've seen the commercials. Today, IBM operates information technology systems and platforms for thousands of major firms like DuPont, Kodak, and Xerox.[11]

**IMPROVE PHYSICAL DISTRIBUTION.** Sophisticated package delivery and tracking systems have helped grow electronic commerce. Off the Alaskan coast, Bill Webber e-mails pictures of caught salmon to chefs, packs chosen items in insulated bubble-wrap liners for shipping boxes, then ships by FedEx. The premium-priced fish arrives at restaurants 48 hours from being taken out of the water.

### KEY IDEA

➤ Markets that seem mature may have growth potential waiting to be unlocked via creative approaches.

**REDUCE PRICE.** The opening case shows how Ryanair transformed a seemingly mature airline market into growth with a low-price strategy. Southwest Airlines previously had similar success in the U.S. The author is working to transform the marketing textbook market.

**REPOSITION THE BRAND.** The firm offers the same product but with new benefits and values for new customers. In a classic example, Honda repositioned motorcycles from a product bought by *longhaired guys* and the people chasing them (the cops) to a leisure pursuit for the whole family.

**ENTER NEW MARKETS.** Many firms define new markets by geography — in particular, emerging markets like the BRIC countries — Brazil, Russia, India, and China. Compared to the West, these countries have millions of low-income customers. To supply them with sufficiently low-priced products, firms must modify their traditional practices.

## SCENARIO 6: LEADERS IN CONCENTRATED MATURE MARKETS

Generally, **concentrated markets** support a few substantial competitors whose aggregate market share often exceeds 60 percent. Several small players may target market niches. If the market leader is also the low-cost leader, profit margins should be high. Investment should be relatively low, because growth is low, and the leader should earn high profits and generate strong positive cash flow.

The market leader has two strategic options:

- Maintain leadership over the long run
- Harvest the business.[12]

**MAINTAIN LEADERSHIP OVER THE LONG RUN.** The core decision for maintaining market leadership is choosing the *right* investment level. Generally, this should be cautious investment. With the *right* investment level, in the *right* areas, the firm can reap profits for many years. *Over-investment* to gain market share from entrenched competitors can often waste resources. Pressures for overinvestment are:

- Failure to consider alternative opportunities
- Internally focused funding criteria that underfunds new ventures
- Political power of entrenched product champions

Increasing short-run profits is not difficult; the trick is finding the right investment level to sustain profits so the product has a future. Reasons for underinvestment are:

- Limited view of the competition
- Misunderstanding the challenger's strategy
- Fear of cannibalizing higher profit products
- Inertia

Of course, complacency and arrogance can accentuate any or all of these mistakes, and past success can blind the firm to evolving marketplace realities.

Generally, the firm can maintain leadership via incremental product improvements. It should also invest in marketing activities to build and sustain brand equity and demonstrate the firm's superiority over competitors. When a clinical trial showed that Lipitor, a cholesterol-lowering drug, reduced heart attack risk by 16 percent, Pfizer widely advertised the result. Lipitor achieved over 40 percent market share.

The firm should develop more efficient product designs and invest in process technology for more efficient operations. Process technology change can severely affect market leaders that do not adapt. Large, traditional integrated steel firms like U.S. Steel and Bethlehem Steel suffered greatly from competition by Nucor and others with electric arc mini-mills. The firm should also consider *variating* fixed costs — reducing fixed costs and increasing variable costs. Then, if sales slip, costs also reduce. It should tightly manage working capital by reducing accounts receivable and inventory and lengthening accounts payable.

**KEY IDEA**

➤ Market leaders in mature, concentrated markets should have low costs, decent profits, and positive cash flows.

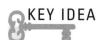

New product innovation can be a particular concern for market leaders. Products based on new technology can destroy a firm's leadership position — traditional chemical film to digital cameras. An external orientation is the best protection against this sort of market erosion. Distribution can also be challenging. Early in the life cycle, the firm may have developed a distribution system to reach end-user customers. But as some end users grow in size and expertise, they demand direct distribution to get lower prices by cutting out distributors' margins.

**HARVEST THE BUSINESS.** The firm is market leader, but a **harvest** strategy for short-term cash flow may be more important than maintaining sales and market share. Reasons include:

- New technology makes the product obsolete.
- Government regulations impose restrictions.
- Change in the firm's strategy.
- Investment requirements become too high.
- Desire to avoid specific competitors.

Once the firm decides to harvest, the critical question is *fast* or *slow*? For fast harvesting, the firm divests the product and gets immediate cash. For slow harvesting, it should focus on three issues:

- Cut costs by simpifying the product line and reducing support.
- Minimize investment in the product.
- Raise prices.

The more aggressive the firm's actions, the more quickly it will exit the market.

## SCENARIO 7: FOLLOWERS IN CONCENTRATED MATURE MARKETS

Followers have smaller market shares than the leader; they probably also have higher costs, lower profits, and are weaker financially. But leaders can lose position by poor decisions, so followers may attain leadership by inspired management. Airbus caught up with Boeing in large jet aircraft and for a few years surpassed it. Southwest Airlines is now the leading domestic U.S. airline. Most firms have products that fit this scenario; hence it is particularly important. Broadly speaking, the follower has three basic strategic options, each with several sub-options.

**IMPROVE MARKET POSITION BY GROWING SALES.** Careful and creative market segmentation, kenneling, and direct attack are three primary alternatives to grow and, perhaps, ultimately dethrone the market leader:

- **Market segmentation.** Options for segmentation typically appear in early growth and become numerous in late growth. Creative segmentation is the dominant option for counteracting the market leader's advantages.

  Firms often identify and target market segments by adding benefits to satisfy customers' ever more fine-grained needs, often at higher prices. In maturity, there is often one segment that just wants basic product benefits, *getting back to basics* — at a low price.

- **Kenneling. Kenneling** is a metaphor for bringing several *dog* (seemingly worthless) products together. A follower may acquire several unprofitable (or marginally profitable) low market share products, and then do a *roll-up* into a single offering. By rationalizing operations, distribution, and/or marketing, the follower can become a strong competitor. This is a common approach in commercial banking.

- **Direct attack.** If the leader has been lazy, underinvested, set prices too high, and/or served customers poorly, direct attack may be the follower's best strategy. Good market intelligence helps find the leader's weak spots, so the follower can invest to exploit them.

  In industries as diverse as credit cards and pharmaceuticals, market leaders have lost share to new entrants offering better products and/or lower prices. From late 2004 to early 2009, Firefox registered 500 million downloads; it earned 20 percent global market share of web browsers, mostly taken Internet Explorer. This free browser offers greater virus security and greater speed in moving from one website to another.

**KEEP ON TRUCKIN'.** This adage describes an approach to maintain or rationalize a firm's current position. The two alternatives are:

- **Maintain current position.** Holding market share roughly constant over the long run can be viable if the firm has a profitable market position and strengths in one or more segments.
- **Rationalize current position.** If profits are marginal or negative, rationalizing operations may be the way to go. The firm should examine all aspects of manufacturing, distribution, and sales with *a fine-tooth comb* and make the tough cost-cutting decisions.

**EXIT.** Followers should choose *exit* if profitability is unlikely or the product's future is doubtful, perhaps due to negative brand perception or slowing market demand. It can divest or liquidate:

- **Divest.** By finding a buyer for which the product is a good fit, the firm can secure cash quickly.
- **Liquidate.** If there is no buyer for the business, the only reasonable action may be liquidation — closing down and selling the assets.

## SCENARIO 8: FRAGMENTED MATURE MARKETS

**Fragmented markets** have many players, but no one firm is dominant. Hence the leader/follower distinction has little relevance. An important objective is increasing market share. The firm has two strategic options for restructuring or repositioning its offers: acquisition and standardization of branding.

**ACQUISITION.** Acquisition is similar to kenneling, page 151; it can be very successful when geography drives fragmentation. A global firm like AXA, the French insurance giant, acquired many local companies to secure greater global market share.

**STANDARDIZATION AND BRANDING.** In fragmented industries, many players typically offer a wide range of products and services. Standardization is a way to reduce variation and improve consistency across various suppliers; it assures customers that each provider associated with the brand supplies the same customer value.

Sometimes firms use *franchising* to attract many small independently-owned players (see Chapter 17). These firms maintain their independence but take advantage of the franchisor's brand and other services. Examples include Century 21 — real estate and Holiday Inn — hospitality.

## SCENARIO 9: MARKETS IN DECLINE

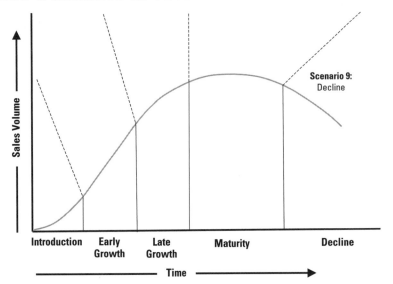

**KEY IDEA**

➤ In mature fragmented markets, no firm has a large market share.

**FIGURE 10.6**

**DECLINE STAGE SCENARIOS**

The decline scenario is in Figure 10.6. "So now you've graduated; we're delighted that you've joined us. We're going to throw you in the deep end. You will be in charge of our Deced product where sales have been declining for the past few years." How would you like this assignment? Most readers would not be happy, yet firms can make good profits from declining products. Table 10.1 shows the results of one study: 8 percent of businesses had losses and 13 percent made no profits. But 78 percent were profitable and almost 40 percent earned over 35 percent ROI.[13]

| | | | | | | | Total |
|---|---|---|---|---|---|---|---|
| Percent of Businesses | 8% | 13% | 38% | 25% | 5% | 9% | 100% |
| Return on Investment (ROI) | −10% | 0% | 15% | 35% | 55% | 60% | |

We learned earlier that the pioneer has little competition early in the life cycle. But as the market grows, competitors typically enter. At the end of the life cycle, in the decline stage, the reverse occurs — new entry is unlikely and competitors exit. Good examples of declining products are videotape recorders, many canned foods, public telephones, full-service travel agents, and *sake* in Japan. We assess declining products in two dimensions: market hospitality and the firm's business strengths.

A declining market is **inhospitable** if:

- Decline is rapid and/or uncertain.
- The market is commodity-based, versus having several price-insensitive segments.
- There are viable and credible competitors.
- Competitors have high fixed costs and are very sensitive to sales declines.
- Competitors are evenly balanced and view the market as strategically important.
- Customer switching costs are low.

The characteristics of **hospitable** markets are the opposite of these, but declining markets are *especially* inhospitable if, in addition:

- Competitors' exit barriers are high — for example, they cannot easily redeploy assets.
- The government or the community pressures, or subsidizes, some firms to remain.
- Bankruptcy laws allow failing competitors to return with lower costs, like U.S. airlines.
- Competitors are emotionally committed to the product.
- The product is part of a vertically integrated supply system.

Firms with good *business strengths* in declining markets should have low costs, good raw material contracts, and/or be able to keep productive assets running without major investment. If, in addition, the market is hospitable, pursuing leadership may be a viable option. The firm should publicly recognize the decline — but also demonstrate its commitment. It should market aggressively by adding new products, increasing advertising and promotion, and/or cutting prices. Newspapers are a good example. The firm should consider reducing production capacity like several U.S. domestic airlines. It may also encourage competitors to exit by offering long-term supply contracts for their customers and/or private-label manufacturing; buying competitors or their assets may be an option.

Generally, when the firm has poor business strengths it should harvest or divest. It should also exit from inhospitable markets unless it can dominate one or more price-insensitive segments.

*Marketing Question*

Many service businesses like doctors, dentists, plumbers, electricians, and general contractors are very local. Pick one of these services or another of your choice. How would you increase market share for one of the players?

**KEY IDEA**

➤ Firms can make considerable profits in declining markets.

*Marketing Question*

Suppose you were a full-service travel agent. What actions would you take to ensure your survival?

**KEY IDEA**

➤ In a declining market, the firm's options depend on market hospitality and its business strengths.

---

........................................
## KEY MESSAGES

Pre-emption is an important dimension of strategy-making; acting before competitors can put the firm in good competitive position. Using the product life-cycle framework, we developed nine scenarios for developing a pre-emptive strategy:

- Introduction
- Early-Growth Leaders
- Early-Growth Followers
- Late Growth
- Maturity – But Not Really
- Maturity – Concentrated Market Leaders
- Maturity – Concentrated Market Followers
- Maturity – Fragmented Markets
- Decline

These scenarios can help the firm think through its strategy by anticipating, and striving to influence change. For each scenario, we developed a family of strategic options. Notwithstanding the value of identifying these options, we believe the best competitive strategies are often contrarian. When the firm surprises its competitors, it can gain significantly.

# CHAPTER 11

# MANAGING
# BRANDS

*If this business were to be split up, I would be glad to take
the brands, trademarks, and goodwill, and you could have
all the bricks and mortar and I would fare better than you.*[1]

— John Stuart, former Chairman of Quaker

## LEARNING OBJECTIVES

When you have completed this chapter, you will be able to:

- Understand the nature of brands and the values they provide for buyers and sellers.
- Comprehend the changing role of brands and branding.
- Distinguish between customer brand equity and firm brand equity.
- Measure the monetary value of customer brand equity and firm brand equity.
- Build and sustain a strong brand.
- Construct brand architecture for the firm.
- Make decisions about multi-branding versus umbrella branding, global branding, brand broadening, and brand migration.
- Address branding issues for strategic alliances, and revitalize struggling brands.

---

## OPENING CASE: SAP

*In 2000, Germany-based SAP was the world's largest enterprise systems software firm and third-largest independent software supplier overall.[2] SAP had 12,500 customers and 25,000 software installations in more than 50 countries, mainly with large global firms. SAP's culture was technologically driven; it based its success on innovative product development. Marketing and branding*

*were not significant. Marketing was decentralized at the national level, and multiple advertising agencies produced local campaigns. SAP's branding tagline changed frequently and included "We Can Change Your Business Perspective" (1997), "A Better Return on Information," (1997-1998), "The City of 'e'" (1999), "The Time of New Management," (2000), and "You Can, It Does." (2000). SAP had one global Internet site, 30 local country sites, and many subsidiary sites — without a common theme. Overall, SAP had a weak and unclear brand identity. By 2000, SAP's CEO, Hasso Plattner, concluded that SAP's messaging, for the overall firm and individual products, was sprawling, inconsistent, and confusing.*

*Plattner broke several taboos by hiring Martin Homlish from Sony Electronics as SAP's new Global Chief Marketing Officer — outside SAP, outside the software industry, and outside Germany. Homlish's challenge at SAP was to transform marketing and reposition the SAP brand to have broader, sustainable appeal. Said Homlish, "I saw SAP as a marketer's dream ... great products, a strong history of innovation, and a loyal customer base. All we had to do was transform marketing." He faced three core challenges: communicate the brand consistently, align the organization, and create a brand flexible enough to support challenging business objectives in a dynamic industry.*

*Homlish was particularly concerned about the rapid swings in SAP's messaging. He wanted a brand identity that could evolve over time. Meeting with customers, Homlish said, "I found a common theme. SAP was considered a mission-critical part of almost every great company on the planet." SAP's brand identity became: SAP turns businesses into best-run businesses. The tagline to convey the new identity was, "The Best-Run Businesses Run SAP."*

*Homlish redesigned SAP's brand architecture to make SAP the masterbrand; product brands like mySAP CRM were sub-brands. SAP aligned national websites with the global site. Changes to the global site then triggered changes to local sites using state-of-the-art web content management (WCM) applications. SAP placed all global advertising with a single agency, Ogilvy & Mather. SAP reinforced its new brand identity with simple headlines that complemented the tagline: "Lufthansa runs SAP" and "Adidas runs SAP." Large posters in airports around the world helped globalize the SAP brand.*

*SAP Global Marketing developed a series of tools to align regional marketing. Homlish installed a branding culture by involving local field offices as co-developers of global messaging. He addressed Kick-Off meetings to field organizations in the North America and Europe, Middle East, and Africa (EMEA) regions. SAP Global Marketing created country champions to roll out each campaign and gain internal support. Said Homlish, "When I arrived at SAP and would ask questions about our company and our products, I would get a lot of jargon ... SAP-anese — it confused me and our customers." SAP Global Marketing distributed pocket-sized brand cards worldwide to all employees. The cards stated the core positioning, attributes, and personality of the brand. SAP Global Marketing also selected brand ambassadors to champion the brand locally.*

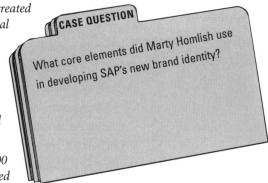

**CASE QUESTION**

What core elements did Marty Homlish use in developing SAP's new brand identity?

*According to BusinessWeek's (BW) annual brand rankings, from 2000 to 2008, SAP's brand value doubled to $12 billion. In 2008, BW ranked SAP at number 31, above established brands like Ford, Morgan Stanley, Volkswagen, and Xerox.*

This is the third of three chapters that discuss separate facets of Imperative 3: Set Strategic Direction and Positioning. Chapter 9 focused on developing strategy for a market segment; in Chapter 10, we used the life-cycle framework to develop scenarios for generating competitive strategic options. Here we focus on branding and managing brands. As with the previous chapters, deep insight into markets, customers, competitors, company, and complementers is critical for making good branding decisions.

Not so long ago, branding was a relatively low-level tactical issue. Today, the value of many firms' brands far outstrips the book value of their tangible assets. Accountants and financiers are re-examining the nature of brands, as they rethink basic assumptions about the value of the firm. Certainly, the brand has value to the firm, but the brand also has value to customers. Branding has shifted from the relatively minor role of naming products and services to become a critical driver of contemporary marketing practice. Branding is a major decision area for both senior managers and marketing executives alike.

**WHERE WOULD WE BE WITHOUT THEM?[3]**

## WHAT IS A BRAND?

Brands and products are different. A leading marketer once said, "A product is something that is made in a factory; a brand is something that is bought by a customer. A competitor can copy a product; a brand is unique. A product can be quickly outdated; a successful brand is timeless."[4]

Throughout history, sellers have branded their goods and services. Medieval goldsmiths and silversmiths branded their products. The branding iron was an essential tool for U.S. ranchers; if a rancher had a reputation for high-quality cattle, his brand secured higher prices at market. The traditional definition follows logically: A brand is a "name, term, sign, symbol or design (or letter, number, or character), or a combination of them intended to identify the goods and services of one seller or group of sellers and to differentiate them from the competition."[5] Brands have become a part of everyday life for firms and consumers — their names, symbols, logos, trademarks, package designs, and spokespersons are on everything we drive, drink, wear, and eat.

The brand name is most often used as a *signifier*, but other signifiers can be as (or more) important. Target stores are associated with the color red and UPS with brown; the *Financial Times* and fiberglass insulation from Dow Corning (U.S.) and ACI (Australia) are pink. Other well-known signifiers are the Coca-Cola and Absolut bottles, the Volkswagen *Beetle*, the Nike Swoosh, the Gerber baby, the Pillsbury doughboy, and the Merrill Lynch bull.

Today, brands have meaning far beyond these outward manifestations. By offering customers value via its brands, the firm secures value for its shareholders. The brand has become a symbol around which the firm and its customers construct a relationship. We define a **brand** as: *A collection of perceptions and associations that customers hold about a product, a service, or a company. This collection embodies values that create meaning for customers that represent a promise of the experience customers expect when they have contact with the brand.*[6] Important implications are:

- The primary meaning of any brand is carried in customers' minds. Rather than being owned by the firm, great brands are really owned by customers.

- The brand makes an implicit or explicit promise of a customer experience.[7] This promise provides customers with value over and above the basic product or service. By providing extra value to customers, the firm earns value for its shareholders.

- Figure 11.1 shows that the term *brand* applies widely to an individual product, a product line, or a group of product lines:

  - **Individual product.** An individual product such as Cayenne (Porsche), Corvette (Chevrolet), or RX-8 (Mazda).

- **Product line.** A group of closely related products serving a similar function. The Ragu **family** or **masterbrand** embraces several types of sauces — Cheese, Chunky Garden Style, Light, Old World Style, Pizza, and Robust Blend Hearty.
- **Group of product lines.** A group of product lines fulfilling many different functions. These **monolithic brands** are often *corporate brands* — Carrefour, CitiGroup, GE, IBM, Marks & Spencer, Nike, and Yamaha.

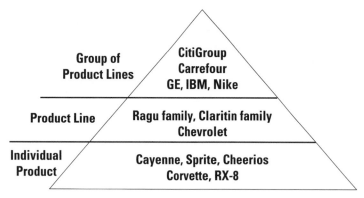

**FIGURE 11.1**

**LEVELS OF BRANDING**

Over time, brands can shift their meaning. In the U.S., Honda's original association was motorcycles — today, Honda's associations include automobiles and lawnmowers. Sometimes firms use multiple brands, like Toyota Corolla or the American Express Personal Card. The firm earns value from the monolithic brand, Toyota and American Express, and additional value from the individual product brand. Some other features of brands are:

- **Anything can be branded** — a product, service, country, or even yourselves!
- **Brands often provide psychological value** like safety and security — ADT, Volvo.
- **Customers often form communities** to demonstrate their commitments to brands — Harley-Davidson riders, Macintosh users.[8]
- **Brands can become synonymous with the product class, or generic** — U.S. examples include Aspirin, Band-Aid, Google, and Kleenex; in Britain, Biro and Hoover.
- **Customers' judgments and expectations about brands drive purchase decisions** — the firm tries to influence customers but they make their own judgments and form expectations.

For each brand, the firm must choose a **brand identity** — the associations it wants people to hold about its brand, like personal, lifestyle, or type of customer. It must also decide how, if at all, its various brand identities should relate to each other. We make an important distinction between **brand identity** — the firm's desired associations, and **brand image** — customers' actual associations about the brand. The firm should audit brand image on a regular basis.

## BRAND ASSOCIATIONS

The firm should strive to secure **brand associations** that reinforce its desired brand identity and bring brand image and brand identity into congruence. Brand associations are thoughts the customer generates when faced with a stimulus like brand name, logo, spokesperson, or message. They typically relate to products, the firm, or **brand personality**. Table 11.1 shows how brand personality captures the idea of enduring and distinct human or emotional characteristics associated with a brand.

Effective brand associations are:

- **Strong** — Personally relevant for customers and presented consistently over time.
- **Favorable** — Desired by customers and successfully delivered by the brand.
- **Unique** — Perceived by customers as unique, different from other brands.

*Marketing Question*

Find a working friend or relative, and give the Brand Coffee Machine Test. Stand at the coffee machine and ask, "What does your product or company brand stand for?" Then press the "fill" button or lever. If the person cannot give a good answer by the time your cup fills, the brand fails. The organization cannot expect customers to understand the brand's meaning if employees do not.[9]

**TABLE 11.1**

**BRAND PERSONALITY**[10]

| Dimensions | Descriptors | Examples |
|---|---|---|
| Sincerity | **Down-to-earth** — family-oriented, small-town, conventional, blue-collar, all-American<br>**Honest** — sincere, real, ethical, thoughtful, caring<br>**Wholesome** — original, genuine, ageless, classic, old-fashioned<br>**Cheerful** — sentimental, friendly, warm, happy | Hallmark cards, Skippy peanut butter |
| Excitement | **Daring** — trendy, exciting, off-beat, flashy, provocative<br>**Spirited** — cool, young, lively, outgoing, adventurous<br>**Imaginative** — unique, humorous, surprising, artistic, fun<br>**Up-to-date** — independent, contemporary, innovative, aggressive | MTV, Mountain Dew |
| Competence | **Reliable** — hardworking, secure, efficient, trustworthy, careful, credible<br>**Intelligent** — technical, corporate, serious<br>**Successful** — leader, confident, influential | *The Wall Street Journal* |
| Sophistication | **Upper class** — glamorous, good-looking, pretentious, sophisticated<br>**Charming** — feminine, smooth, sexy, gentle | Chanel, Dior |
| Ruggedness | **Outdoors** — masculine, Western, active, athletic<br>**Tough** — rugged, strong, no-nonsense | L.L. Bean |

*Marketing Question*

Select a brand. How did you learn about it? Write down all your associations. For each brand association, assess the extent to which it is *strong* versus *weak*, *favorable* versus *unfavorable*, and *unique* versus *common*.

 KEY IDEA

➤ The brand is a symbol around which the firm and its customers can construct a relationship.

Generally, the firm uses implementation tools like communications, product design, and quality to achieve congruence between brand identity and brand image. Sometimes brand associations, positive and negative, are outside the firm's control. Many people associate Levi's (jeans) and Marlboro (cigarettes) with U.S. cowboy movies; these associations have been very positive around the world. But widespread opposition to U.S. policies, like the Iraq war, has affected some brands negatively. To address negative associations, McDonald's focuses on local ownership, local suppliers, distinct store designs, and unique menu items — such as the *McArabia*, a chicken sandwich on Arabian-style bread. Some brands, like Virgin, move away from their origins and become quite abstract:

**Virgin — Evolution of a Brand**

The original brand associations for Virgin were tied to publishing rock and roll records. Expansion into record stores broadened Virgin's brand associations. But Virgin sold its record business and expanded into many product classes, like Virgin Atlantic (airlines), Virgin Books, Virgin Bridal Shops, Virgin Cars (retail distribution), Virgin Direct (financial services), Virgin Electronics, Virgin Limousines, Virgin Megastores (retail distribution), Virgin Mobile (cellular phone service), Virgin Sound and Vision (educational computer software), Virgin Vacations, and Radio Free Virgin. Most recently, Virgin has announced its entry into space travel.

The Virgin brand is now uncoupled from its origins, yet still articulates its origins' abstract values. Virgin bases its brand identity on a higher-order sense of fun-loving, hip, irreverent, anti-establishment *underdogness*. Its ongoing battles with British Airways and CEO Sir Richard Branson's personal activities — including attempts at around-the-world balloon flights — strongly support its brand identity. Some observers criticize Virgin's extensions as random and capricious. Branson's response is quite direct: "Branding is everything. I think it's also wise to diversify; this enables you to have a contingency plan when the economy is going through a rough patch."[11]

## BRANDING IS NOT JUST FOR CONSUMERS ...

Many people assume that branding is just for consumers. Not so![12] Branding is very important in B2B markets, especially for firms with many customers as in the SAP opening case. Branding is important in such diverse industries as banking, consulting, shipping, computing, office equipment, and capital goods, and critical for brands like Brother, Canon, DuPont, FedEx, IBM, Intel, Microsoft, Office Depot, Oracle, Sun, TNT, and Xerox — Figure 11.2.

**CATERPILLAR®**

**FIGURE 11.2**

**BRANDING IS
NOT JUST FOR
CONSUMERS!**

B2B and B2C branding language is different. B2B firms talk about customer trust, confidence, and building relationships versus brand images or associations. B2B firms want customers to view them as risk-free, trustworthy, and experienced suppliers, preferably with solid track records and stellar market reputations. Branding is particularly important as buying decisions in many industries shift from technologists to less technically-oriented employees. Oftentimes, branding is more important than the technology — a well-managed brand outlasts many technology changes.

## ... AND IS NOT JUST ABOUT ADVERTISING

Another common misunderstanding is that branding should focus only on consumers or end-user customers and that advertising is the only approach. Not so! Reaching a broad audience for its communications is as important for corporate brands as it is for many product brands. Communications targets surpass current and potential customers and include:

- Employees
- Prospective employees
- Suppliers
- Intermediaries
- Alliance partners
- Owners/shareholders
- Bondholders
- Investment analysts
- Regulators
- Other government bodies
- The media

In addition to advertising, the firm can reinforce its brand identity via other forms of communications like brochures, direct mail, promotions, publicity and public relations, web-sites, stationery, telephone interactions, its products, packaging, physical facilities, and managerial actions and speeches. The CEO can have a major impact on a firm's brand by becoming the *face* of the company; Lou Gerstner — IBM, Steve Jobs — Apple, Mark Cuban — Dallas Mavericks, and Warren Buffett — Berkshire Hathaway are good examples.

The firm's employees are an important branding audience. Eli Lilly, the pharmaceuticals giant, Verizon, a major telecommunications firm, and many others conduct extensive branding programs to ensure that employees internalize their firms' brand identities. They measure how employees perceive their brands, regularly and periodically. Internal branding is especially important for business services and consulting firms, and B2C firms like retailers, where employees regularly interface with customers. The firm should also conduct branding audits of other constituencies like suppliers and affiliates.

## BRAND EQUITY AND THE VALUE OF BRANDS

By effectively developing and implementing market strategy, the firm creates value for its brands. It can also use brand value to develop and implement market strategy. Excellent branding operates as a virtuous circle, continually employing and enhancing the firm's equity in its brands.

**Brand equity** captures the idea that brands deliver value, over and above actual products and services. The most widely accepted definition of brand equity is "a set of brand assets and liabilities linked to a brand, its name, and symbol that add to or subtract from the value provided by a product or service to a firm and/or that firm's customers."[13] This definition implies that brand value accrues to both the *firm* and its *customers*. It follows that there are two types of brand equity: **customer brand equity (CBE)** — the value customers receive, and **firm brand equity (FBE)** — the value that firms receive.

## CUSTOMER BRAND EQUITY

The brand gives customers two types of value: **pre-purchase equity** and **post-purchase equity**.

**PRE-PURCHASE EQUITY** reduces search costs and purchase risks because of what customers believe before purchase. In overnight package delivery, many business customers believe that FedEx offers great *functional* value — the package arrives on time. In the airline business, many consumers believe that Southwest Airlines, Jet Blue, easyJet, and Ryanair offer superior *economic* value. And many believe the American Express Platinum card, Air Jordan or Shox sneakers, and products from Dior, Versace, and Armani provide *psychological* values like status and prestige. The classic example of pre-purchase CBE is: "You never get fired for buying IBM."

**POST-PURCHASE EQUITY** enhances the customer's consumption experience. After purchase, brands offer *functional* value — doing the job they were designed to do, and *economic* value like low cost of ownership. They also offer *psychological* value, like feelings of security from insurance, and the assurance of continued *functional* value. Post-purchase customer value can have long-lasting effects, especially if ownership and use are transparent and communicated to others.

Sometimes high CBE focuses on a specific product class. Tide *detergent* typically engenders positive customer values, but consumers would probably view Tide *toothpaste* or Tide *cookies* negatively. Other brands extend value across several product classes, such as corporate brands like *Virgin*, or the way movie studios derive revenues from accessory products as with *Star Wars* and *Indiana Jones*. CBE, either pre- or post-purchase, is generally greater when:

- Customers are inexperienced or unfamiliar with the product class.
- Product quality from some suppliers is variable.
- Comparing alternative products is difficult.
- The product is socially visible.
- Customers do not realize value until some time after purchase.
- There is mental flexibility in portraying the brand.

## FIRM BRAND EQUITY

FBE results from customers' responses to the firm's actions and is directly linked to CBE. High brand awareness, positive attitudes, high perceived quality, positive word-of-mouth, intention to purchase, purchase, brand loyalty, positive brand image and associations, and satisfaction all enhance FBE. CBE and FBE reflect the trust between the brand and its customers. A former chairman of Sony opined: "Our biggest asset is four letters, S-o-n-y. It's not so much our buildings or our engineers or our factories, but our name."[14] AmEx has a similar philosophy:

As head of American Express' charge-card business, Lou Gerstner placed a high premium on customer brand equity. Shelly Lazarus, CEO of Ogilvy & Mather Worldwide, said: "I learned a big lesson from Lou. Once you've set a strategy, you never ever violate it. Nobody ever got a free card, a discounted card, or bundled pricing. Lou would say, 'This is a violation of the brand, and we're not doing it.'"[15]

High FBE levels have many positives. Firms with high FBE:
- Earn higher prices and better margins.
- More easily introduce similarly branded items in different product classes and markets.
- Encourage existing customers to purchase in different product classes by cross-selling.
- Generate leverage in their distribution channels by securing more and better shelf space with more favorable transaction terms.
- Raise entry barriers for competitors.
- Exploit licensing opportunities.

Generally, CBE and FBE build up slowly but new brands sometimes gain strength relatively quickly, like eBay, Google, Leapfrog, Red Bull, Under Armour, and Yahoo! However, CBE — and hence FBE — are fragile and can dissipate quickly if the firm mis-steps. Many firms unwittingly cause brand equity declines by product proliferation, price-cutting, discounts and promotions, using inferior components, squeezing suppliers or channel partners, and simple neglect.[16] In the early 2000s, Tommy Hilfiger's sales went from red hot to stalled. Observers attributed the *cool* sportswear's problems to brand value dilution caused by product proliferation and out-of-control distribution. At one point, more than 10,000 department stores and discount outlets offered Tommy Hilfiger merchandise.

Managerial mishaps can also wreak havoc with FBE, like Merck's recall of its anti-inflammatory drug *Vioxx*, *Dow Corning*'s breast-implant recall, and *Firestone*'s tire failures on the *Ford Explorer*. Brand equity is fragile, but some brands have great resilience. In the mid-1980s, J&J withdrew Tylenol capsules in the face of a cyanide-poisoning scare; sales plummeted to zero. J&J's timely and caring response led to a quick Tylenol rebound when it introduced more secure packaging that changed the consumer products industry and restarted distribution and promotion. Planning for damage control and crisis management are increasingly important.

# MONETIZING BRAND EQUITY

We just explored the value the brand brings to customers — customer brand equity (CBE), and to the firm — firm brand equity (FBE). Now we focus on the monetary value of brands.

## CUSTOMER BRAND EQUITY

A customer receives value from a *branded* product, and also from a generic product. The difference represents CBE. The **dollarmetric** method assesses the monetary value of CBE. The firm asks a customer how much extra she would pay for the branded product versus an unbranded product. This extra amount is CBE's monetary value. Actually, this figure is *potential* CBE — the customer receives brand equity only after purchase. If the price is higher than she is willing to pay, there is no CBE. The firm can also assess the *marginal* CBE of one brand versus another: How much extra will the customer pay for her favored brand?

Sometimes customers prefer a generic product to the branded product; then CBE's monetary value is negative. In the late 1990s, Encyclopedia Britannica (EB) refused Microsoft's offer to digitize its encyclopedia. Microsoft developed Encarta; within 18 months, it became the best-selling encyclopedia. EB went back to Microsoft, but Microsoft's research showed that EB had negative brand equity. EB would have to *pay* Microsoft to put its name on the Microsoft product!

## FIRM BRAND EQUITY

We assess FBE's monetary value at the firm level. FBE relates to the brand's current and future ability to attract paying customers and increase shareholder value.[17] Valuation components are:

- **Revenue.** The price difference between the branded product and an identical generic product, multiplied by the branded product's forecast sales volume, less

- **Cost.** The costs of supporting the brand.

FBE's monetary value is the sum of the year-by-year differences between revenues and costs, discounted to the present.[18] However, this straightforward approach for financial analysts has two inherent problems:

- An unbranded equivalent to the branded product may not exist.

## KEY IDEA

➤ Brand equity reflects the trust established between the brand owner and its customers.

## *Marketing Question*

Martha Stewart, the business — TV show, books, and magazines — has a long-term relationship with Kmart. Martha Stewart, the person, served a five-month prison term for felony convictions of lying and obstruction of justice. Martha Stewart, the brand, suffered. Assume the date is January 1, 2005 — Martha Stewart will be released from jail in March. As her strategic brand consultant, what advice would you offer? What advice would you offer Kmart?

## KEY IDEA

➤ Brand equity generally builds up slowly over time.

➤ A brand can quickly lose value if not managed properly.

- It ignores the potential for brand broadening (leveraging), using the brand to enter a new product form or product class. Brand value is not constrained by current products, product lines, or current customers. Many brands have customer-attracting properties, over and above the product or set of products to which they are currently attached. In the mid-1990s, the brand *Pan Am*, unattached to any aircraft or airline company, sold for several million dollars.

**MARKET VALUE METHOD.** The market provides the best FBE measure; this works well for publicly traded corporate brands. FBE equals market value less book value and non-brand intangibles like patents, know-how, and human resources. In 1989, Ford purchased Jaguar for $2.5 billion — its book value was $0.4 billion. Observers viewed the $2.1 billion difference as Jaguar's brand equity. When market value does not exist, as for most product brands, the firm must use internal methods.

**INTERNAL METHODS.** Two internal methods for assessing FBE are:

- **Replacement cost** is the anticipated brand-replacement cost *times* the probability of success.[19]
- **Cash flow methods** are intuitively more appealing, but the problem is estimating future cash flows. Branding consultant Interbrand uses a proprietary method to estimate firm brand equity based on future cash flows.

Calculating the *marginal* FBE of one brand over another is probably easier than calculating an absolute value. Starting in 1989, New United Motor Manufacturing Inc. (NUMMI), a Toyota/ GM joint venture, manufactured two virtually identical cars, the Corolla (Toyota) and the Geo Prism (GM). Corolla had a premium price and depreciated more slowly. Figure 11.3 shows Corolla's 120,000 (200,000 – 80,000) unit volume benefit and $400 ($11,100 – $10,700) price benefit.

### FIGURE 11.3

**THE MONETARY VALUE OF FIRM BRAND EQUITY — AUTOMOBILE EXAMPLE**

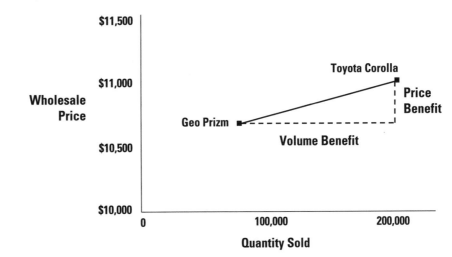

## BUILDING AND SUSTAINING A STRONG BRAND

An important goal of developing and implementing a market strategy is to build and sustain a strong brand. Strong brands induce positive responses from customers. In turn, these positive responses enhance brand strength and are a powerful influence on the firm's market strategy.

### BUILDING A STRONG BRAND

We emphasized that strong brands have value to both the firm and its customers. The firm builds a strong brand by making good decisions in the branding process — Figure 11.4.

**FIGURE 11.4**

**BUILDING A
STRONG BRAND**[20]

**BRAND IDENTITY.** Brand identity, including personality and the brand promise, is what the firm wants the brand to mean. Said Eli Lilly CEO Sidney Taurel, "Our brand is our identity. It is who we are in the eyes of our customers ... shareholders, prospective employees, suppliers, and the communities where we operate."[21]

Other considerations about brand identity are how customers should recognize the brand, including brand name and visual appearance. Choosing a brand name may involve extensive research with considerations of legal availability, length, memorability, pronounceability, and associations. The firm should be especially careful if it plans to use the brand in different countries with different language systems. Visual appearance requires careful choice of colors, shapes, materials, styles and themes, and related visuals for advertising and packaging.

**BRAND AWARENESS.** Typically, it takes significant investment to achieve **brand awareness** in target customers. If the brand is the first entrant into a new product form, the pioneer must educate potential customers about the product form, as well as about the brand. Gojo educated consumers and retailers about its new type of hand-washing liquid, Purell. Launching a new corporate brand is also very costly. Lucent spent $50 million to create corporate brand awareness. But a brand may stay in memory for many years like Datsun, Esso, and Master Charge in the U.S., even after retirement by the brand owner.

**BRAND ASSOCIATIONS AND BRAND IMAGE.** Brand associations are the meanings the brand has for customers — *brand image* is the overall meaning. The firm seeks congruence between brand image and brand identity. *Brand identity* is the blueprint for many marketing decisions. Executing on brand identity is critical to customers forming the desired associations and brand image. Brand identity defines the limits on product quality, price, distribution, service, and promotion. Brand equity always suffers when brand identity and brand image are mismatched. Suppose the basis of a product's brand identity was high prestige — yet customers formed brand image from poor advertising, product quality, and service; low price; and downscale distribution. Customer response would most likely be negative, and firm brand equity would suffer.

**BRAND QUALITY AND VALUE PERCEPTIONS.** Consistency in communications and customers' brand experiences are crucial for developing positive brand quality and value perceptions. Achieving consistency is always difficult, but organizational practices can make it impossible.

To explain: Many firms frequently rotate brand managers. New brand managers wanting to make their mark on a product or product line reformulate the brand identity. Each reformulation sacrifices consistency, brand quality, and customers' value perceptions. Because of brands' growing importance, responsibility is moving higher in firms, and the traditional brand manager's role is diminishing. The firm should also be wary of advertising agencies, identity and design firms, communications specialists, and consultants. By striving for creativity, they may sacrifice consistency and confuse customers. It's no accident that market leader L'Oreal has maintained the same tagline — "Because you're worth it" — for over a quarter-century.

Many global 100 firms have *brand police* or a *brand czar* to oversee branding consistency. They make sure that the brand name, logos and symbols, and all messaging — including advertising,

brochures, and websites — retain consistency. They provide specific guidance on words and graphics, font size, colors, stationery, vehicles, uniforms, and signs, and they ensure conformity to consistent standards. We saw this consistency in the SAP opening case.

**BRAND LOYALTY.** Consistency in brand quality and value perceptions is important for building **brand loyalty**. Vertical marketers like Starbucks (coffee) and Ben & Jerry's (ice cream) know the importance of consistency. They build brand coherence through their personnel and the design and decor of their retail facilities. By contrast, most car firms have difficulty providing brand-enhancing experiences in their dealerships. A serious problem for hotel management firms like Hilton, Sheraton, and Holiday Inn is *off-message* execution by individual franchised hotels; inconsistency in the customer experience affects loyalty to the entire chain.

Specifically, the firm earns high brand loyalty by:

- Selecting the *right* brand identity for target customers and consistently executing that identity.
- Ensuring that firm employees and third-party organizations, like advertising agencies, are motivated to deliver on the brand identity.
- Measuring customer satisfaction with the brand on an ongoing basis and making the necessary course corrections. (See the following section on Sustaining a Strong Brand.)

**BRAND BROADENING.** Repeat purchase, customer loyalty, and favorable word-of-mouth should follow successful brand identity development and execution. The firm may broaden (leverage) the brand to other products (see later in this chapter).

## SUSTAINING A STRONG BRAND

The key to sustaining a strong brand is continual assessment of *brand health*. Many firms measure brand managers on short-term profit, revenues, or market share. This is rather like examining the firm's income statement, but neglecting its balance sheet. FBE is really the brand's balance sheet. **Brand health checks** use metrics indicating changes in brand equity.

The firm can assess brand health using a *balanced-scorecard* approach. Table 11.2 shows four types of measures for a balanced scorecard and the sort of data required:

**TABLE 11.2**

REPRESENTATIVE SELECTION OF BRAND HEALTH CHECK MEASURES

| Type of Measure | Measure | Description of Measure |
|---|---|---|
| **Purchasing and Sales** | Market share | Brand sales versus total market sales (units and/or dollars) |
| | Market breadth | Number and type of customers purchasing the brand |
| | Market depth | Extent of repeat purchase |
| **Perceptual** | Awareness | Degree of awareness of the brand |
| | Uniqueness | Extent of differentiation from competition |
| | Quality | Perception of brand quality (from blind tests) |
| | Brand image | Brand associations, congruence with brand identity |
| | Value | Extent to which the brand provides good value for money |
| **Marketing Support** | Advertising | Market share/advertising share |
| | | Advertising/total marketing spend |
| | Distribution | Extent of distribution coverage in target outlets |
| | | For retail goods, quality of display, especially key accounts |
| | Relative price | Price compared to competitive brands |
| **Profitability** | Profit | Gross margin earned from the brand |
| | | Economic value added (EVA) of the brand |

- **Purchasing and sales data** secured from the firm's accounting and CRM systems and industry-focused research suppliers.
- **Perceptual data** secured from survey research.

- **Marketing support** data secured from the firm's accounting and business intelligence systems and industry-focused suppliers.
- **Profitability** secured from the firm's accounting system.

Brand health checks are not a one-time event. They should occur regularly — quarterly or bi-annually. The firm should compare current brand health to historic trends and benchmark competing brands.[22] Results from brand health checks should lead to appropriate changes in market strategy and execution.

# MANAGING BRAND ARCHITECTURE

Many firms maintain multiple brands — a brand portfolio — each having its own brand identity. The LVMH (French-global leader in luxury goods) corporate brand offers *Louis Vuitton* tan and brown monogrammed bags for several hundred dollars, *Murakami* bags at $1,000, and *Suhali* goatskin bags averaging $2,000. The firm's **brand architecture**, the organizing structure for its multiple brands, is an important decision area for the firm.

Because the firm's brands have a major impact on shareholder value, branding decisions should have high priority. The firm should carefully consider what to brand, brand identities, and the associations to support them. It should carefully plan brand deletions and additions — both internally developed and secured from other firms. The firm must also consider interrelationships among the corporate brand, product category brands, and individual product brands. The firms' brand portfolio should change over time. Anheuser-Busch evolved its portfolio as customers switched to different beers, from lower- to higher-end, and from fuller to lighter.

## MULTI-BRANDING VERSUS UMBRELLA BRANDING

In **multi-branding** — aka *House of Brands* strategy — the firm uses multiple brand names for its various products.[23] It seeks customer loyalty to these individual brands, but not necessarily to the parent-company brand. Do you know the corporate owner of Henry Weinhard, Icehouse, Leinenkugel, Miller, Milwaukee's Best, and Mickey's and Olde English 800 malt liquors? (SABMiller, from South Africa, owns all of these brands.)

By contrast, a firm using **umbrella branding** emphasizes a monolithic brand for several products. Consumers know Yamaha for electronic musical instruments (keyboards and guitars), traditional instruments (pianos), home audio products, computer peripherals, motorcycles, and even Grand Prix engines.

## GLOBAL BRANDING

Increasingly, global firms make branding decisions at corporate headquarters, rather than in individual countries.[24] Samsung's branding responsibility was previously diffused among dozens of overseas agencies, but a single global agency now directs its $600 million advertising budget. Arguments for **global branding** are:

- **Increased global media reach and lower costs.** Television — like Star TV (Asia), CNN, ESPN, and BBC World News — and the Internet reach multinational audiences. The firm can achieve scale economies in advertising, perhaps by dubbing in different languages.
- **Growth.** Some foreign markets, particularly less-developed countries, are growing faster than many domestic markets. The firm may be able to leverage brand equity to new markets.
- **Global appeal.** Some brands like Marlboro, Rolls-Royce, and BMW have global appeal due to international exposure over many years.

➤ Increasingly, global firms make branding decisions at head-quarters, rather than in individual countries.

➤ *Think global, act local!* guides many firms.

➤ Multinational firms should consider a brand portfolio that includes global, regional, and national brands. Over time, the geographic scope of some brands may narrow, and other brands may broaden.

- **Cross-border travel.** Increased travel is driving demand as consumers seek out their favorite brands while traveling.
- **Homogeneity of customer tastes.** Global media and global product availability are shaping consumers' tastes for global brands, and many B2B firms are introducing global standardization for parts and raw material purchases.
- **Aspirational values.** Only global brands can deliver aspirational values for certain products like cosmetics and associate themselves with global events like the Olympic Games and World Cup.
- **Competitive advantage.** Global brands often signify quality and innovation.[25]
- **Human capital.** A global brand can help recruit and retain better people worldwide.[26]
- **Best practice.** Global branding eases best practice transfer across geographies.
- **Brand identity.** A global brand promotes a consistent brand identity.

The major argument against pursuing a global branding strategy concerns segmentation and positioning. A global brand is less able to present a *local* appearance and tap into specific needs of geographic segments, especially when national markets develop differently. Anti-globalization forces can be a special challenge; Coca-Cola, McDonald's, and Nike have all been targets. Also, a single set of brand associations may not be appropriate for all countries.

Global branding does not imply that the firm's implementation programs must also be global. Differing national tastes often lead to product design variations; MTV is a global brand with local and regional adaptations. Pricing must reflect what local customers can pay, and the firm's distribution and promotion must be based on local available options. Citibank salespeople sold credit cards door-to-door in several Asian countries; this practice would be unthinkable in developed economies. *Think global, act local (glocal)* guides many firms. Petit Bateau (PB) is a good example:

PB makes and sells high-quality clothing for babies and children. PB has a consistent brand image around the world for comfort and quality. Its designs and fabrics are fairly standard, and all products bear PB's trademark blue-and-yellow logo. PB's national websites, posters, and hangtags are identical except for text translations. Yet in the U.S., young women in their 20s and 30s wear PB's tee-shirts. PB adjusts prices upward and dedicates the front half of its stores to *Les Grands* (for adults); posters depict young women wearing PB products.[27]

Even global branding firms have regional, multi-country, and/or national brands. Coca-Cola offers 400 brands in 200 countries. Four Coke brands are global — Coca-Cola, Diet Coke/Coke Light, Sprite, and Fanta. Many soft drink brands — fruit juice, bottled water, and sports drinks — are only available in specific regions, sometimes in a single country — Table 11.3.

**TABLE 11.3**

**SELECTED COCA-COLA SOFT DRINK BRANDS BY REGION**

| Americas | | Europe, Middle East, Africa | | Asia/Pacific |
|---|---|---|---|---|
| Cherry Coke | Fresca | Cherry Coke | Tab | Lift |
| Kinley | Mello Yellow | Kinley | Tab X-tra | Ambasa |
| Kuat | Minute Maid | Urge | Mezzo Mix | Kin Cider |
| Tai | Mr. Pibb | Lilt | Sensun | Mello |
| Barq's | Surge | Schizan | | Krest |
| Nordic Ginger Ale | Citra | | | Sarsi |
| Delaware Punch | Quatro | | | Lemon & Paeroa |

Figure 11.5 shows the Nestlé branding tree; Nestlé has 10 worldwide corporate brands, 45 worldwide strategic brands, 140 regional strategic brands, and 7,500 local brands.[28] Nestlé evolves its brand portfolio — it redefined Chambourcy and Findus from worldwide strategic brands to regional strategic brands and used the German brand Maggi to expand prepared foods into Eastern Europe.

**Nestle branding tree** ——————————————————— **Examples**

- 7,500 Local brands
- Responsibility of local markets

- Texicana
- Brigadeiro
- Rocky
- Solis

- 140 Regional strategic brands
- Responsibility of strategic business unit and regional management

- Mackintosh
- Vittel
- Contadina
- Stouffer's
- Herta
- Alpo
- Findus

- Worldwide strategic brands
- Responsibility of general management at strategic business unit level

- Kitkat
- Polo
- Cerelac
- Bacii
- Mighty Dog
- Smarties
- After Eight
- Coffee-Mate

- 10 Worldwide corporate brands

- Nestlé
- Carnation
- Buitoni
- Maggi
- Perrier

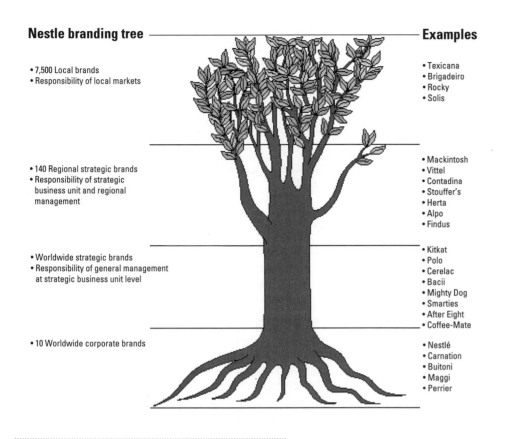

**FIGURE 11.5**

**THE NESTLÉ BRANDING TREE**[29]

## BRAND BROADENING (LEVERAGING)

**Brand broadening (leveraging)** occurs when the firm undertakes a brand extension — like Harley-Davidson restaurants and Kodak batteries. The firm uses an existing brand to address a new opportunity, typically in a different product form or product class. Brand leveraging reduces brand-launch costs and/or increases profits for a small investment.[30] A new product with a leveraged brand gains automatic brand awareness. Before leveraging, the firm must address two important areas: potential opportunities and obstacles, and branding issues.

**OPPORTUNITIES AND OBSTACLES.** Before considering a leveraging strategy, the firm must address the following sorts of questions:

- Is there sufficient potential demand?
- How strong is competition?
- Can the market be accessed through current distribution channels?
- Is the firm capable of making sufficient product quantities?
- Does the firm have access to the required production inputs?
- Does the firm possess other competencies necessary to be successful?

**BRANDING ISSUES.** These concern customers' brand associations and relationships between the current and new product form (class):

- Do customers perceive a fit between the original product form (class) and the new product form (class) in terms of product features and concepts?
- What are customers' brand image and associations for the core product? Will these associations *transfer* to the new product?
- What is the reverse relationship? How will customers' associations for the new product *back transfer* to the brand image and associations for the core product?
- How does the corporate brand, and/or monolithic brands, relate to these associations?

### KEY IDEA

➤ Firms that leverage brands secure automatic brand awareness for the new product. They avoid new brand introduction costs and may increase profits for little additional investment.

➤ For an extension to be viable, the brand must have strong positive associations. The difference between these brand associations and the product extension should not be incongruous.

### Marketing Question

Using well-known brands, suggest some brand extensions. Why will these succeed? Suggest brand extensions you think would not succeed. Why?

Once the firm has addressed opportunities, obstacles, and branding issues, there are two baseline conditions for a brand extension to be viable:

- The brand must have strong positive associations.
- Brand associations and the product extension should not be incongruous. How do you rate the likely success for *Tide* candies? *Mercedes-Benz* orange juice? or *Victoria's Secret* soup?

Brand extensions tend to fail when:

- Associations between the brand and product extension are not obvious.
- The brand has a unique image and associations that do not transfer.
- The new product class has a dominant competitor.
- The positioning is confusing or inconsistent.
- The quality of the new product does not match customer expectations about the brand.

Perhaps a more serious issue is brand dilution. The brand extension fails and firm brand equity reduces. The original product's sales decline and your brand is in trouble.[31]

## BRAND MIGRATION

We noted earlier that firms with multiple brands often retire some of them. Perhaps the target market/segment has declined, competition may be severe, and/or brand identity may no longer fit with evolving customer needs. Sometimes it's too expensive to support a brand, and/or a brand may have lost value because of managerial neglect, a lost internal battle for resources, and/or harvesting for profits and cash. Other times, the firm may decide to refocus its efforts on fewer, stronger brands via **brand migration** and/or seek economies of scale in its marketing efforts. Federated Department Stores retired Abraham & Strauss, L.S. Ayers, Bon Marché, Bullocks, Burdines, Famous-Barr, Filene's, Foley's, Goldsmith's, Hecht's, Jordan Marsh, Kaufmann's, Lazarus, I. Magnin, Marshall Field's, Meier & Frank, Rich's, Robinsons-May, Stern's, Strawbridge's, and The Jones Store — all rebranded as Macy's.

Sometimes the firm secures brands via acquisition and then retires them. Citicorp retired Salomon Smith Barney and Schroeder; Morgan Stanley retired Dean Witter. Also, the firm may be contractually obligated to stop using the brand. B&D acquired GE's small appliance (housewares) business but could use the GE brand for only five years. In these cases, the challenge is to retain the brand equity being retired by transferring or migrating to another brand.

Vodafone, the world's largest provider of cell phone service, previously comprised many strong domestic providers. It migrated them to a global brand, Vodafone (Vo - voice, da - data, fone - phone). "Vodafone uses a dual branding strategy designed to give all constituents, employees, customers, and trade-partners a period of time so people can intellectually *get it*. In Germany we did *D2/Vodafone*, then *Vodafone/D2*, and then we just dropped the *D2* to become *Vodafone*."[32]

**KEY IDEA**

➤ The firm can conserve brand equity by effective brand migration.

## STRATEGIC ALLIANCES

**Strategic alliances** can extend the firm's brand into new market segments. Alliances can range from informal or contractual working relationships to new entities structured as legal joint ventures. Most alliances focus on competency — one firm's strengths compensate for the other firm's weaknesses, and vice versa. Strategic alliances have important **co-branding** implications when the co-branding partner can transfer positive customer attitudes. Co-branding between customers and suppliers is increasingly common; many PC manufacturers co-brand with Intel.

When firms co-brand with themselves, they must ensure that brand associations are appropriate for the product and target segment. In Asia, Holiday Inn closely associates its parent brand with Crowne Plaza hotels; Crowne Plaza is then an **endorsed brand**. By contrast, in the U.S., Crowne Plaza is a **standalone brand**; Holiday Inn associations negatively affect Crowne Plaza's brand image.

**KEY IDEA**

➤ The firm can enhance brand equity by effective strategic alliances.

## AGING BRANDS

Some brands have a loyal core of customers and survive for many years. But these are exceptions. The marketing landscape is littered with the corpses of once-valuable and famous brands. As markets evolve, weakly positioned brands may not be economically viable. In Chapter 10, we saw that one option for improving sales in mature markets was *repositioning the brand*.

**Brand revitalization** is the key objective for *repositioning*. Key options are:

- **Target new market segments.** Colgate-Palmolive, Avon, and *Reader's Digest* each increased sales by targeting new geographic segments outside the U.S. Sears found its core customers were *not* male hardware buyers, but 25-to-50-year-old women with children. Sears successfully repositioned by refocusing its promotion and expanding clothing and cosmetics.

- **Change brand associations.** Successful examples are Honda's repositioning of motorcycling from *long-haired guys and the people chasing them — the police*, to *a family activity* — "you meet the nicest people on a Honda." The Labor government changed associations with Britain from backward-looking and tradition-based, to future-oriented youthfulness, excitement, and opportunity.

- **Alter the competitive target.** Bacardi successfully repositioned its light rum to compete against vodka and scotch, rather than other rums.

The firm can avoid the necessity for revitalization by continually innovating, adding new products, and keeping the brand vital and relevant.

## KEY IDEA

➤ Three ways to reposition a brand are: address new market segments, change brand associations, and alter the brand's competitive target.

➤ Continuous innovation pre-empts the need to revitalize a brand.

### *Marketing Question*

Founded during the California Gold Rush, Levi Strauss became an American icon. In 1996, Levi's sales were $7.1 billion, mostly in mid-market outlets like J.C. Penney and Sears. In 2003, Levi's sales were $4 billion — and most manufacturing was offshore. What advice would you give Levi's top management?

## KEY MESSAGES

- The nature of brands has changed from signifiers of goods and services to symbols for constructing relationships between firms and customers.

- Relationships between the brand and customers can significantly enhance shareholder value.

- The firm can brand individual products, product lines, and groups of products.

- The firm should choose a brand identity and supporting associations for each brand.

- Brand image is the associations customers hold about the brand. The firm should strive to achieve congruence between brand image and brand identity.

- Some important items about brands and branding are:
  - Branding is important in both B2C and B2B.
  - Branding is much more than advertising.
  - Customers are only one of several audiences for brand messages.
  - For product brands, we cannot assume that the brand owner is also the manufacturer.

- Customer brand equity (CBE) and firm brand equity (FBE) are two distinct constructs. Each can be monetized, but there is no necessary relationship between the monetary value of customer brand equity and firm brand equity.

- To build a strong brand, the firm must execute a process through which it: establishes brand identity, creates brand awareness, forms brand associations and brand image, develops consistent brand quality and value perceptions, builds brand loyalty and, possibly, leverages brand strength.

- To sustain a strong brand, the firm should regularly measure brand health and act on the results.

- To secure the best results from its branding efforts, the firm should make serious decisions about various facets of its brand architecture.

# CHAPTER 12
# MANAGING THE PRODUCT LINE

## LEARNING OBJECTIVES

When you have completed this chapter, you will be able to:

- Understand the importance of managing the product line as a portfolio of products.
- Apply alternative approaches to managing the product portfolio.
- Manage key interrelationships among products.
- Address the pressures for product proliferation and product-line simplification.
- Manage both diverse and complementary product lines.
- Deal with important product issues like extending product life, evolving the product line, product quality, bundling, counterfeiting, and secondary market products.
- Anticipate concerns about product safety and packaging and product disposal.

## OPENING CASE: SWIFFER

*P&G introduced the original Swiffer Sweeper (SS) in 1999. The SS was not just a new product; it was the first in a new product class — a line of products for cleaning surfaces. The Swiffer product line now comprises several individual cleaning products for a variety of surfaces. The Swiffer design includes both* hardware *and* disposables. *The hardware is a pole and attachment that grips the disposable, mostly either a dry or wet cloth. The choice of disposable depends on the surface needing cleaning; regardless, the consumer discards it after cleaning. P&G provides refills in various quantities. For example, dry cloths for the Swiffer Sweeper come in 16-, 32-, and 64-item quantities. P&G offers wet cloths in quantities of 12, 24, and 48; there are also two scented versions: Open-Window Fresh Scent and Fresh Citrus Scent. Some products are available as starter kits.*

*Swiffer comprises the following products:* Swiffer Sweeper, Swiffer Sweep+Vac, Swiffer Dusters, Swiffer Max, Swiffer WetJet, *and* Swiffer Carpet Flick. *Although each product has differently designed hardware and disposables, P&G's business model is similar. The hardware has a low price and generates little profit; P&G makes its money on the disposables. The premium-priced Swiffer* *line is part of P&G's over $33 billion Household Care business, making up almost 50 percent of its revenues. With its Gillette acquisition, P&G now has 22 billion-dollar brands. Swiffer is one of 16 brands with revenue between $500 million and $1 billion and the potential to become a billion-dollar brand.*

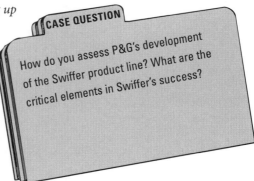

CASE QUESTION

How do you assess P&G's development of the Swiffer product line? What are the critical elements in Swiffer's success?

Products and services are central to the firm's marketing mix. Since decisions about products and services cross functional lines, they have a broader impact on the firm's operations than other variables like promotion, distribution, customer service, and pricing. Firms also have limited resources, and face difficult issues in allocating these resources across their product portfolios. Optimal product-line breadth is a critical issue; product proliferation and product-line simplification can each have dramatic effects on shareholder returns. Introducing new products (Chapter 13) is critical. Product safety issues can embroil the firm in legal and ethical problems, and increased societal expectations regarding health (like fast food and obesity) and environmental concerns (like pesticides and packaging and product disposal) highlight the importance of product decisions.

## THE PRODUCT PORTFOLIO CONCEPT

The firm's **product portfolio** is a collection of products.[1] Large firms offer thousands of products, often grouped by business unit. Corporate leaders allocate resources among business units. Business-unit heads make resource allocations among products based on their assessments of potential growth and profitability.[2]

The firm does *not* optimize overall profits by attempting to maximize short-run profits from each individual product. Instead, the firm should use a **portfolio approach** to product management so it can balance its objectives and resource allocations across all products. For example, when the firm launches a new product, it must invest in plant and equipment, R&D, and promotion to meet growth objectives. Newer products consume cash; profits are typically less important than securing market position. Later, as growth slows and investment requirements diminish, established products become more profitable and generate cash. The firm uses this cash to develop and support younger products, and the cycle continues. Or, as with Swiffer, the firm may set prices low for one product so it can make profits on another.

The firm and shareholder interests are at risk when the **product portfolio** is **imbalanced**. An imbalance occurs when the firm funds too many new products and creates problems with cash flow or other resources. An imbalance also occurs when the firm has too many old products; good short-term financial results may actually mask a failure to invest sufficiently in the future. Having the right balance of successful new products and profitable established products is important for enhancing shareholder value.

The key to a successful product strategy is setting objectives and allocating resources based on each product's role in the portfolio. Some products should have growth objectives; other prod-

### KEY IDEA

➤ The firm's products have important resource-related interrelationships.

➤ The firm does not optimize its overall profits by maximizing profits from individual products. It must consider the entire product line.

ucts are managed to maximize profits or cash flow. The challenge is allocating the right financial and human resources for each product so as to achieve the firm's objectives. Of course, internally, the firm's products compete for scarce resources. In this chapter, we show you portfolio analysis methods used by many firms to allocate resources. But first we describe some traditional financial analysis methods for making resource decisions.

## FINANCIAL ANALYSIS METHODS

Superior financial performance is critical for delivering increased shareholder value. Hence, a **financial analysis perspective** for assessing a product's potential financial return is both important and proper. There are several approaches[3]:

- **Return on investment (ROI).** ROI calculations project future accounting data. They compare the product's forecast rate of return with a target (or **hurdle**) rate. If the forecast rate exceeds the target rate and resources are available, the firm invests in the product.[4]

- **Payback.** Payback is the forecast time to pay back the investment. In general, shorter paybacks are better than longer paybacks. Payback's problem is ignoring profits earned after the payback period.

Neither **ROI** nor **payback** distinguishes among time periods; for example, financial flows in year 1 and year 5 are treated similarly. Because of this defect, most firms use approaches that account for the time value of money:

- **Net present value (NPV)** and **Internal rate of return (IRR)**. NPV and IRR are the most common financial analysis methods for assessing investment opportunities. Discount factors account for the time value of money; they use actual cash flows rather than financial and cost accounting data. They assess cash inflows, like sales revenues, when earned and cash outflows, like costs and investments, when paid out.[5]

  - **NPV** uses a predetermined discount factor, typically the firm's cost of capital. The firm calculates the NPVs for various opportunities, then ranks them by dollar value.

  - For **IRR**, the firm calculates the discount rate that equalizes the cash inflows and cash outflows. It typically ranks those opportunities whose IRR exceeds the hurdle rate.

More recently, firms are using **economic profit** or **economic value added (EVA)**. EVA is the firm's annual profit less an explicit charge for capital.[6] We summarize these approaches:

**KEY IDEA**

➤ Financial analysis methods rely on forecasts — these can be highly uncertain. Financial analysis does not consider strategic issues.

➤ Too much reliance on financial analysis can lead to misallocation of resources across products.

➤ Financial analysis methods ignore marketing considerations.

---

**Financial Analysis Approaches**

1. **Forecast Return on Investment (%) (ROI)** — Sales Revenues less Costs/Investment = Profits/Investment (based on forecast accounting data).

2. **Payback (years, months)** — time to pay back the initial investment.

3. **Net Present Value (NPV)** — the dollar value of an opportunity. Discounts all cash outflows and inflows by a predetermined factor, typically the firm's cost of capital.

4. **Internal Rate of Return (IRR)** — the discount rate that equalizes cash inflows and cash outflows.

5. **Economic Profit** — the opportunity's annual profit less an explicit charge for capital.

---

Today, many firms modify or augment financial analysis by examining the assumptions underlying financial projections, and forcing managers to think more deeply about them. Typically, precise answers are not possible, but the process leads to a more externally oriented approach for allocating resources, like portfolio analysis.

## PORTFOLIO ANALYSIS

**Portfolio analysis (PA)** is central to many firms' strategic planning processes. PA is best viewed as an *additional* tool for allocating resources, not as an *alternative* to FA. PA is a systematic, organized, and easily communicable way of assembling, assessing, and integrating important information about products and markets. PA helps the firm set strategic direction, establish investment priorities, and allocate resources.[7] The firm can use portfolio analysis to evaluate both products and businesses.

PA has dramatically affected many firms' resource allocation processes because it includes factors that traditional financial analysis ignores. Table 12.1 illustrates several differences between FA and PA.[8] Using FA and PA together leads to better investment decisions than either approach alone.

| Variable | Financial Analysis | Portfolio Analysis |
|---|---|---|
| Investment Decision Focus | Technologies/Facilities | Products/Markets/Customers/ Applications |
| General Approach | Financial- and budget-oriented | Market- and competitive-oriented |
| Key Concerns | Derived profit and cash flow numbers | Market and competitive factors underlying the financial numbers |
| Typical Measures | ROI, payback, NPV, IRR, EVA | Market — size, growth, and potential competitive strength |
| Tools | Capital budgeting | Growth-Share and Multifactor matrices |

Two important PA methods are the growth-share matrix and the multifactor matrix.

**THE GROWTH-SHARE MATRIX.** The Boston Consulting Group (BCG) developed the original PA. As the name implies, its dimensions are *forecast long-run market growth* and *relative market share.*[9] Figure 12.1 shows each dimension bisected to produce a four-cell classification. Matrix entries represent products (or businesses). Typically, each circle's size is proportional to sales revenues or invested assets.

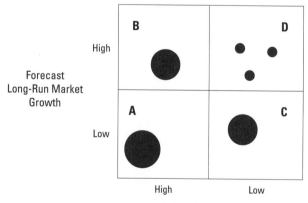

The growth-share matrix places heavy emphasis on the financial characteristics of products in each cell. High-share products are typically more profitable than low-share products. Growth products typically require significant investment in fixed assets, working capital, and market development. Figure 12.2 describes conventional labels and classic strategic recommendations for products in each cell.

## KEY IDEA

➤ Portfolio analysis is a systematic, organized, and easily communicated way of assembling, assessing, and integrating important information about product opportunities.

**TABLE 12.1**

**FINANCIAL AND PORTFOLIO ANALYSIS — INVESTMENT DECISIONS AND STRATEGIC DIRECTIONS**

## KEY IDEA

➤ Portfolio analysis addresses many problems with financial analysis.

**FIGURE 12.1**

**AN ILLUSTRATIVE GROWTH-SHARE MATRIX**

### *Marketing Question*

Suppose you were GE's marketing manager for refrigerators. How would you address assumptions underlying your financial analysis, like target market share, technological change, likely future competitive structure, competitor strategies, and the role of government?

## FIGURE 12.2

**PRODUCT CHARACTERISTICS IN THE GROWTH-SHARE MATRIX**

### KEY IDEA

➤ Long-run market growth and RMS define the growth-share matrix.

➤ The growth-share matrix can be overused and misinterpreted.

### KEY IDEA

➤ Portfolio analysis is best viewed as an additional tool for setting investment priorities — not as an alternative to financial analysis.

### Marketing Question

Identify all of Disney's businesses — like amusement parks, movies, retail stores, and character licensing — and place them in a growth-share matrix. (You may have to guess a bit.) Which businesses are Cash Cows? Dogs? Stars? Problem Children? How do you think Disney should allocate its resources? What additional factors should Disney consider in examining new wholly owned or alliance opportunities?

### Cash Cows. Low Market Growth/High Market Share (Cell A)

Classic characteristics of cash cows are:

- Low costs. From experience curve effects — Chapter 10.
- Premium prices. As market leader, cash cows may command premium prices.
- Low reinvestment. Low-growth, mature products require relatively little investment.

Cash cows should be highly profitable and are often the firm's primary internal source of cash. Examples are Microsoft Office, IBM's mainframes, and P&G's Tide detergent. If the firm successfully holds market share, it can *milk* a cash cow and generate cash for many years. Environmental changes like regulatory shifts, patent expiration, innovative competitors, or new technology can threaten a cash cow by changing demand patterns. Then the firm may *harvest* the product to increase short-term cash flow, by raising prices, reducing or eliminating services, and/or cutting promotional support.

Firms with cash cows can make two types of errors. First, they *over-milk* their cash cows, and the cash *dries up*. Starved of investment, the product trails in technology and loses its cost leadership and market position.[10] U.S. and European car and steel firms are good examples of this phenomenon. In a second scenario, the firm might over-invest, reducing its financial return, and leaving little cash for other opportunities.

### Stars. High Market Growth, High Market Share (Cell B)

Stars are relatively rare, as few products enjoy dominant positions in high-growth markets. Stars are often profitable in accounting terms, but they use up cash because their growth requires substantial investment. In the early 2000s, Under Armour gear, sports undergarments designed to pull perspiration from the body, worn by many NFL players, was a good example. Despite the firm's best efforts, market growth eventually slows. If the firm invests appropriately and retains good market share, profits and cash flow improve, and the star transforms into a *cash cow*. The major error firms make with stars is to cut back investment too early. The star loses its dominance and transforms into a *dog* in cell C.

### Dogs. Low Market Growth, Low Market Share (Cell C)

*Dogs* is a pejorative term for products with these unfavorable characteristics:

- High costs relative to the leader, as they do not enjoy the same economy-of-scale or experience curve (Chapter 10) advantages.
- Non-premium prices that may be lower than the market leader's prices.

Dogs are often unprofitable or earn only low profits. Better-positioned dogs often generate positive cash flows but may still be a drag on the firm's resources. Dogs are the most numerous of all products in any economy. Examples include Lenovo's personal computers and U.S. Airways. Firms with dogs should consider:

- Developing new segmentation approaches that strengthen their positions.
- Refreshing these products with additional value from new features.
- Maximizing short-run cash flows by liquidating or divesting. IBM sold its barely profitable PC business to Lenovo.
- Implement a *kennel* strategy (Chapter 10) by acquiring similar products to achieve viable scale.

### Problem Children, Question Marks, Lottery Tickets, and Wildcats. High Market Growth, Low Market Share (Cell D)

Problem children combine the uncertainties of high-growth markets with non-dominant market shares. Examples include Rio, iRiver, RCA, and Digitalway MP3 players; each has less than 10 percent market share versus well over 50 percent for Apple's iPod. If a problem child grows with the market, it will consume substantial investment capital. This may be a risky investment, as growth does not guarantee future profits. Growing with the market will move the problem child product from cell D to cell C. Hence the decision for problem children is often *double or quit*!

- *Double*. Large strategic investments can move the product to market leadership. Sony successfully overtook Nintendo in video games with high spending in product development and promotion. By contrast, Philips' CD-Interactive (CDI), a user-friendly interactive CD system launched when CD-ROM was in its infancy, was quickly overtaken. A less risky approach seeks dominance in a defensible market segment(s).
- *Quit*. Exit, immediately or gradually. The product may command a good price from an aggressive follower. Small biotech firms often sell their new drugs to the majors.

The firm should consider the generalized recommendations from Figure 12.2 carefully, because they are widely advocated and applied. The best way to view the growth-share matrix is as a device for raising and discussing *what-if* or contingency questions.

**THE MULTIFACTOR MATRIX.** The growth-share matrix spawned other portfolio approaches, some public and some proprietary. The most popular is the **multifactor matrix**, aka the GE/McKinsey screen.[11] This matrix redefines the growth-share axes. *Long-run market growth* becomes *market attractiveness; relative market share* becomes *business strengths.* The user identifies several factors to measure each dimension.

Figure 12.3 illustrates the multifactor matrix.[12] The firm has no products in the most attractive cell, C, but has some small entries in two other attractive cells, B and F; it should probably invest in these products. The large entries in cells A and E are questionable; the firm should examine them carefully. Finally, it should make tough decisions about the poorly positioned large product in cell G — retain or remove?

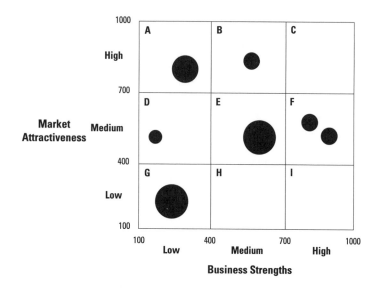

**THE GROWTH-SHARE AND MULTIFACTOR MATRICES.** Each method helps the firm make resource allocations, in part by its visual displays.

The *growth-share matrix* has only two criteria: market growth rate and RMS. Once managers agree on defining the market, the firm can measure these objectively. Reasonable people may disagree about market growth forecasts, but RMS is relatively simple to measure. Hence, managers have limited ability to manipulate entries for their favorite products. But two criteria can also be a weakness; forecast market growth rate and RMS may not capture all the relevant issues. By contrast, the *multifactor matrix* addresses the realism issue by using several criteria, and so embraces many factors that the growth-share matrix omits. But reasonable managers can disagree about the criteria, and their weightings and ratings are often highly subjective. Hence, political and organizational power issues can enter the analysis.

# OTHER IMPORTANT PRODUCT INTERRELATIONSHIPS

Products compete for resources, but may also be interrelated in other strategic ways.

## INTERRELATIONSHIPS AT THE CUSTOMER

Some products are directly complementary, like razors and razor blades, cameras and film, printers and toner, satellite dishes and program content, and hardware and disposables — as

**FIGURE 12.3**

**AN ILLUSTRATIVE MULTIFACTOR MATRIX**

**KEY IDEA**

➤ The firm can use the multifactor matrix (Chapter 8) for resource allocations among products.

➤ The growth-share and multifactor matrices have advantages and disadvantages that impact the viability of strategic recommendations that they generate.

with Swiffer. When two products have this relationship, the firm can be successful by placing either or both in its portfolio. If the firm offers both products, such as HP offering both printers and toner, pricing becomes particularly crucial.

**POSITIVE COMPLEMENTARITY.** In many markets, customers who buy one type of product are more likely to buy a related product — **positive complementarity**. Michelin sells passenger tires and the *Michelin Guide* book. The *Michelin Guide* encourages car travel; when travel increases, tire wear is greater and sales rise. Positive attributes associated with the *Michelin Guide* carry over to Michelin tires, and vice versa. Verizon knows that traditional local wire-based telephone service is declining, so it offers customers long-distance, DSL, and wireless services. Satisfied customers for Apple's iPod are favorably disposed to buy Macintosh computers. Sometimes a complementary product is closely related to an initial purchase. Positive complementarity occurs when customers trade up to higher-quality, higher-profit products. GM's historic strategy traded customers up from Chevrolet to Pontiac, Buick, Oldsmobile, and Cadillac.

**NEGATIVE COMPLEMENTARITY.** Customer dissatisfaction with one product can negatively affect sales of another. Before passage of the Sarbanes-Oxley Act, investment banks knew that critical equity research reports negatively affected their ability to sell investment banking services. Professional services and accounting firms knew that company audits exposing financial problems might cut off lucrative consulting contracts. Arthur Andersen failed to acknowledge and address Enron's irregular accounting because it feared such **negative complementarity**.

## INTERRELATIONSHIPS AT THE FIRM

Sometimes the firm's products have important internal interrelationships with each other.

**STRATEGIC ROLES.** Different products may have separate yet mutually reinforcing strategic roles. The Swatch Group (TSG) markets watch brands in three price-class ranges:

- A: Swatch, Flik Flak, Endura, and Lanco — prices up to 100 Swiss francs (SF).
- B: Tissot, Certina, Mido, Pierre Balmain, Hamilton, and Calvin Klein — prices reach 1,000 SFs.
- C: Omega, Longines, Rado, and Blancpain — prices up to and exceeding 1 million SFs.

Each class targets a different market segment and has a different strategic role. TSG earns most profit from C-class products and less from Class B. A-class products are profitable, but act as **firewalls**. They stop competitors offering low-price watches and later competing with B- and C-class products.[14]

**MULTIPLE BUSINESS UNITS.** Products from different business units may also have interrelationship issues. The firm has three options:

- **Develop separate missions.** Products from different business units have different missions. The firm does not *squander* resources by having multiple business units address a single opportunity.
- **Intra-firm competition.** In a Darwinian approach, products from different business units pursue overlapping missions. As long as one business unit seizes the opportunity, the firm accepts efficiency losses in product development and promotion.
- **Intra-firm collaboration.** The firm develops processes for separate business units to work together. At J&J, corporate account managers brought together products from several units to form a single offering for operating theaters: from Ethicon, sutures and topical products to stop bleeding; from Ethicon Endo Surgery, cutters, staplers, and electro-surgery devices; from Codman, surgical instruments and shunts to relieve pressure on the brain; from Dupuy, orthopedic implants; and from Cordis, peripheral stents.

# OTHER PRODUCT ISSUES

Now we discuss product proliferation, product line simplification, and other product-related issues.

## PRODUCT BREADTH: PROLIFERATION VERSUS SIMPLICATION

Firms often face conflicting pressure for product line size — some for *broadening* and some for *narrowing*. The firm must trade off these conflicting pressures.

**PRODUCT PROLIFERATION.** Variety in customers' needs often drives **product proliferation** as firms add products to fill product-line gaps. Time Inc. traditionally published magazines that were, for the times, male-oriented, like *Time*, *Sports Illustrated*, *Money*, and *Fortune*. In the 1980s, *Time* sought growth by targeting new audiences like women, children, teenagers, and minorities. *Time* broadened its product line to include *Entertainment Weekly*, *In Style*, *People*, *People en Español*, *Teen People*, *Parenting*, *Sports Illustrated for Kids*, *Sunset*, *Baby Talk*, and *Martha Stewart Living*.

Sometimes firms tap different customer needs by offering different features or variations. Common differentiators of these versions are[15]:

- **Time availability.** Package delivery firms like FedEx and UPS offer next-day delivery before 10 a.m., after 10 a.m., and delivery the following day. Publishers offer hardcover books; they sell paperback copies later. Hollywood launches movies in theaters, then releases them later on DVD or as Internet downloads.
- **Product performance.** Some firms, like plastics producers, make high-quality products for high prices and *degraded* products for price-sensitive customers. Production economics makes this approach more viable than manufacturing a lower-value version directly.
- **Access and functionality.** Some firms offer differing versions of information or media products for different audiences based on: user interface — simple for casual users, complex for serious users; speed of operation — slow for casual users, fast for professional users; and varied access to features or functionality.

In consumer products, firms seeking market dominance offer multiple products to maximize display space. They also offer **firewall products** to defend profitable products and deter competitive entry. P&G maintains market leadership in laundry detergents by offering seven brands, embracing 42 versions and 112 stock-keeping units. When product proliferation is excessive, costs spiral out of control and the firm loses market position. Motorola lost global leadership in cell phones — market share dropped from 26 percent in 1996 to 14 percent in 2001, in part because of its large product line. Fifteen teams of 20 people each supported 128 separate phone types, often with little parts commonality.

The difference between product proliferation and market segmentation confuses many students. *Product proliferation* refers to product variety; *market segmentation* explores differences in customer needs. In general, product variations do not target different market segments. They just offer variety. Customers for cereals, fasteners, jams and jellies, salad dressings, and spices demand a wide choice assortment. Conversely, a single product can generate separate offers for individual segments by varying brand name, price, distribution, and packaging.

**SIMPLIFYING THE PRODUCT LINE.** The late Peter Drucker famously posed the question, "If you weren't already in your business, would you enter it today?" If the answer is no, the firm must answer a second question: "What are you going to do about it?" One answer is to slim down the brand and product portfolio. In the early 2000s, Unilever cut its brands from 1,600 to 400 global and regional brands — approximately 90 percent of its $27 billion revenues. It then sold, reduced support for, and/or consolidated its remaining national and local brands into stronger core brands. Firms typically streamline their product lines due to pressure from increased competi-

tion and/or distribution-channel consolidation, where growth in store brands and rising buyer power pressure sellers for lower prices.

The firm may reap significant benefits from simplifying its product line, but it should make product deletion decisions carefully. Suppose the firm eliminates a high-volume *loss-making* product. It then discovers to its horror that this product was carrying a large share of overhead. The remaining products must assume this overhead, their costs increase, and overall profits fall!

## PRODUCT-RELATED ISSUES

**EXTENDING PRODUCT LIFE.** Firms often try to extend the product's life. We show the typical practice of pharmaceutical firms when their patents expire. Firms in other industries apply variations of these approaches:

- Get FDA approval for other *indications* — disease states.
- Develop new dosage formulations.
- Combine the drug with another drug that has a complementary effect.
- Switch the drug from prescription to over-the-counter.
- Devise a different method of drug delivery — like patch versus pill.
- Add additional services to support customers.
- Persuade more physicians to prescribe the product and educate pharmacists.

**EVOLVING THE PRODUCT LINE.** The firm must address three key issues:

- **Improving the product mix.** Firms can increase profits by introducing higher-margin products, possibly by replacing lower-margin products. Gillette pursued this strategy for many years with successively more expensive razor systems. The automobile industry offers similar examples like Toyota and Nissan entering the U.S. market with low-price cars and then moving upmarket, eventually introducing the Lexus and Infiniti, respectively.

- **Product cannibalization.** Firms often introduce lower margin products that **cannibalize** sales of higher-margin products to stave off a competitive threat. When contemplating cannibalization, the firm should consider three important issues:

  - **Fear of lower profits.** When the firm introduces a new lower-profit product, customers may switch from the original high-profit product to the new entry, reducing overall profits as the two entries compete with each other. Internal pressures often build up against a new entry and can immobilize the firm.

  - **Balancing effects.** A new product entry may cannibalize existing products and cause an immediate drop in profits. But the firm should enjoy incremental value from improved market share and/or brand presence.

  - **How to decide.** Many firms make product entry decisions by comparing their most recent history with forecast results after introducing the new product. This is incorrect. The firm should always compare forecast profits *with* the new product to forecast profits *without* the new product. In many markets, some customers want low-priced products. If they cannot buy from the firm, they will buy from competitors. The firm is generally better off accepting limited cannibalization, and selling lower profit products, than losing sales to competitors.

- **Product replacement.** When the firm secures differential advantage with a better product, competitors often imitate and reduce price. The best approach is to replace the older product with an innovative successor. Ideally, the firm introduces a higher-value replacement shortly before the competitor's launch. Successful pre-emption seriously affects the competitor and weakens its resolve to compete against the incumbent. Good competitive intelligence and appropriate timing is critical for managing the replacement cycle.

**PRODUCT QUALITY.** Product quality is very important to customers and necessary for any serious competitor. *BusinessWeek* showed that the share price of Baldridge winners, the well-known U.S. quality award, consistently outperformed the S&P 500 index by a factor of 3:1.

**BUNDLING.** The firm can sell its products as single **unbundled** items or can combine one product with another product or products and/or services as a *packaged solution,* or **bundled** offer. Firms often bundle attractive products with less-attractive products to increase overall sales and profits. Performing arts organizations sell series subscriptions of popular and less-popular events. B2B firms often bundle their products with technical or professional services support. In **mixed bundling**, the firm sells products both unbundled and bundled.

**COUNTERFEITING.** Illegal copying and brand piracy are increasingly prevalent. The best protection is vigilance regarding trademarks, copyright, and design patents. The firm should work with local law enforcement, but problems multiply when counterfeiters operate internationally.[16]

**SECONDARY MARKET PRODUCTS.** Owners of durable goods like automobiles often resell in the **secondary market**, where prices can significantly affect the original manufacturer. For customers purchasing new cars, the forecast resale price is often an important matter; car companies often certify previously-owned vehicles in an effort to keep prices high.

**PRODUCT SAFETY.** In many jurisdictions, regulatory bodies like the FDA and CPSC (U.S.) enforce laws protecting consumers from product hazards. Regardless, producers have a special responsibility to ensure their products do not harm customers. How the firm executes a safety campaign can also be a differentiating factor.

**PACKAGING AND PRODUCT DISPOSAL.** Sometimes packaging has an important communications function, but its main job is guaranteeing product integrity in storage and distribution. Social and governmental pressure has led firms to consider environmentally friendly product and package disposal. To address disposal, cost concerns, and the potential impact on brand image, many firms make new products with parts from discarded products. Good examples include auto parts, toner cartridges, car batteries, and computers. *Remanufacturing* is a $53 billion industry — firms can achieve 40 to 65 percent cost savings and also please customers.

## KEY MESSAGES

Managing the firm's product line is a major challenge. The firm must make decisions in four areas:

- **The product portfolio.**
  - The firm should construct a balanced portfolio where some products generate growth and market share, some products earn profits, and some deliver cash flow.
  - The firm's key challenge is allocating resources across the portfolio. Financial analysis methods have advantages and disadvantages. The firm should supplement financial analysis with portfolio analysis, using the growth-share or multifactor matrix.

- **Other product interrelationships.** The firm's products may be interrelated at the customer — the firm should seek positive complementarity and avoid negative complementarity. Products may also be interrelated at the firm, where each plays a different strategic role.

- **Product-line breadth: proliferation versus simplification.** The firm faces conflicting pressures for product proliferation and product simplification. Variety in customer needs drives proliferation, and many firms offer similar versions of the same product. The reader should not confuse product proliferation with market segmentation — the firm requires multiple offers to target multiple segments, but these offers may have the same product. Industry consolidation often drives simplification, but the firm should make product deletion decisions carefully, using well-thought-through criteria.

- **Other product-line issues.** The firm may need to address many other product management issues, including extending product life; evolving the product mix; and addressing product quality, bundling, counterfeiting, secondary market products, product safety, and packaging and product disposal.

# CHAPTER 13

# DEVELOPING NEW PRODUCTS

## LEARNING OBJECTIVES

When you have completed this chapter, you will be able to:

- Distinguish among different types of innovation to develop and market new products.
- Identify success factors used by innovative companies.
- Understand and explain the relationship between marketing and innovation.
- Contrast the different ways firms approach the innovation challenge.
- Learn how innovative firms develop successful new products.
- Understand the marketing significance of being an innovative firm.
- Implement the stage-gate, new product development process.
- Understand the types of adopters and the factors driving successful new product adoption.

---

## OPENING CASE: THOMSON FINANCIAL — BOARDLINK

*Thomson Financial (TF) provides information and decision tools for the financial marketplace. In 2005, it successfully launched BoardLink, a product that facilitates information flow between firms and their boards of directors.[1]*

*The process that led to BoardLink began in 2003. Greg Radner, marketing head at CCBN, a company acquired by Thomson, was responsible for identifying CCBN's next generation of products. Radner leveraged CCBN's traditional customer touch points like sales and service calls to understand the challenges clients were facing. These informal customer discussions identified a common pain point — providing board members with information they needed for board meetings in a timely manner.*

*Radner and CCBN's sales and support teams conducted in-depth informal customer discussions. They generated solution ideas and tested them with potential customers. Radner's new-product development team took detailed notes of every customer conversation and shared these data with every team member. Radner asserted the core underpinning of his new-product development effort was securing a deep understanding of customers' needs.*

*Business school graduate Jeron Paul joined Radner and CCBN's clients in developing the concept. Concept development quickly morphed into concept validation as potential customers became excited at the prospect of solving a significant problem. BoardLink also generated significant internal excitement because of the potential for organic growth.*

*Radner quickly built a 15-person product development team spanning technology, sales, quality assurance, and product developers in the U.S. and Bangalore, India. Radner and Paul also worked with market research professionals from Client Insight LLC (CI), a market research firm specializing in financial markets. CI implemented a three-phase marketing research plan that included: (1) a real-time concept test with a small sample of board members in several industries; (2) a more quantitative concept test with a large sample of potential customers; and, once the prototype was developed, (3) a usability study to understand potential users' ability to execute common tasks. Throughout development, Radner ensured that each team member heard every voice of potential customers as they gave feedback and interacted with the evolving prototype. Hence, internal pushback to design and user interface changes was minimal.*

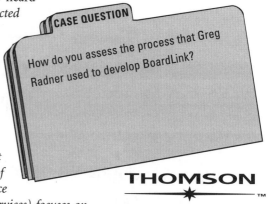

CASE QUESTION

How do you assess the process that Greg Radner used to develop BoardLink?

*TF successfully launched BoardLink in fall 2005. By early 2006, BoardLink was the solution of choice for board members in 12 organizations. Between 75 percent and 85 percent of the 100+ board members who signed up to access BoardLink were regular users.*

*Radner said that BoardLink's success was due to two key factors: First, the strong focus on product usability throughout the development process ensured that customers could easily make BoardLink part of their workflow. Second, Thomson launched BoardLink at a price customers expected to pay. TCES (Thomson Corporate Executive Services) focuses on product improvement. Said Radner, "Our customers are telling us what our next thing will be, and we're listening."*

**THOMSON BOARDLINK™**

---

Today, many firms are dissecting and improving internal processes and culture to increase their innovation capabilities. New technologies and development processes improve new product success rates and help firms reduce time to market. Both business and academia now pay great attention to managing innovation and developing new products as a critical way to achieve competitive advantage.

**KEY IDEA**

➤ Successful new products enhance shareholder value.

## WHERE AND HOW INNOVATION OCCURS

The late Peter Drucker asserted that marketing was one of the firm's two basic functions, but that:

> *... Marketing alone does not make a business enterprise. The second function of a business, therefore, is innovation. In the organization of the business enterprise, innovation can no more be considered a separate function than marketing. It is not confined to engineering or research, but extends across all parts of the business. Innovation can be defined as the task of endowing human and material resources with new and greater wealth-producing capacity.*[2]

In this chapter, we focus on new product innovation and its impact on developing and managing the firm's products. In general, successful **innovation** provides better, cheaper, and/or faster benefits and values to customers. In Chapter 3, we introduced the idea of *sustaining* and *disruptive* technologies. Sustaining technologies can spawn innovations that improve established products on performance dimensions valued by major customers. Innovations driven by disruptive technologies offer new and very different value propositions. Initially, these innovations may under-perform existing products or processes, but a few fringe customers recognize value.

**KEY IDEA**

➤ Innovation embraces new products, but also processes and technologies.

➤ Sustaining innovations improve products and processes on existing performance dimensions. Disruptive innovations offer different value propositions.

## KEY IDEA

➤ Leading firms often invest in sustaining versus disruptive innovations.

## KEY IDEA

➤ The firm should serve current, especially loyal, customers — it must also *create* new customers.

Later, as cost-benefit ratios improve, they surpass the old technology, and broaden their appeal. Researchers believe that leading firms often miss disruptive innovations because they are committed to an existing way of doing business via a *cultural lock-in*.[3]

Serving current customers is fine in the short run, but creating new customers is essential for the long run. Many firms focus on current customers by investing in **sustaining innovations**, but ignore **disruptive innovations** where entrenched interests may place roadblocks. Because *sustaining* and *disruptive* innovations are so different, when firms pursue both, they should do so in separate organizational units.[4]

## WHAT FOSTERS PRODUCT INNOVATION

We all know that new product success is critical for the many firms that introduce thousands of new products every year. Many leading FMCG firms earn over 20 percent of revenues each year from recently introduced products. Over 50 percent of HP's revenues are from products introduced in the previous two years.

**TABLE 13.1**

ESTIMATED PERCENTAGE OF 2001 SALES REVENUES FROM PRODUCTS INTRODUCED FROM 1995 TO 2001

| Firm | % Revenues from New Products | Firm | % Revenues from New Products |
|---|---|---|---|
| General Mills | 33% | Kimberly-Clark | 21% |
| P&G | 32% | Gillette | 21% |
| Kellogg | 25% | Kraft | 20% |
| J&J | 24% | ConAgra | 16% |
| Unilever | 22% | Pepsi | 15% |
| Clorox | 22% | Campbell Soup | 11% |

Source: Information Resources Inc., 2004

Not all firms are good at developing innovative new products. In a Columbia Business School study, less than one-third of a *Fortune* 500 sample were product innovators, but these firms earned the best returns on capital. What are common factors? Research identified the three most important factors:

- **Market selection.** High-growth markets stimulate innovation.
- **R&D.** Significant and consistent R&D spending, especially strategically applied versus fundamental.
- **Organization.** Established formal structures and cultures that foster R&D efforts; supportive cultures.

*Marketing Question*

Your CEO has asked why General Mills and P&G are successful innovators. What will you tell her? Use your competitive insight skills.

## THE CUSTOMER'S ROLE IN SUCCESSFUL PRODUCT INNOVATION

The opening case shows that current and potential customers can play important roles in new product innovation. In a two-way communication flow, firms learn from customers but customers also learn from innovations[5]:

- **Customer-to-innovation information flows.** Involves traditional market research from focus groups and surveys — Chapter 6. Includes the firm's informal knowledge about customers and observations of their behavior.[6]
- **Innovation-to-customer information flows.** Innovation changes customers' perceptions, expectations, preferences, and behavior. For example, customers learned to use the Internet — they now search for products and services online and purchase conveniently with a few simple keystrokes.

## KEY IDEA

➤ The customer-innovation relationship involves a two-way communication flow.

Two-way communication flows occur in every market. Some firms focus more heavily on innovation; others focus more on customers' needs. We identify four types of **firm approaches to innovation**:

- **Low customer focus, low innovation focus — Isolates.** Focus internally — little concern with innovation and little customer communication.[7] Market research is rare.
- **High customer focus, low innovation focus — Followers.** Customers heavily influence innovation. Customer-focused marketing research sets parameters for product design.
- **Low customer focus, high innovation focus — Shapers.** Focus on innovation, rather than customers — successful innovations *shape* the market. Potential customers may not be aware of their needs — they appreciate the benefits only when the product is available.
- **High customer focus, high innovation focus — Interactors.** The product innovation team has a true dialogue with customers — customer input is significant.

Interactors are most likely to be successful innovators: They invest significantly in new technology, but also monitor evolving customer needs. Shapers and Followers can also be innovators, but in different ways. Shapers do not fully understand customer needs, but are at the technological cutting edge. Followers have deep customer knowledge but may lack creativity to develop new technology. Followers and Isolates perform adequately, but in turbulent times, Shapers and Interactors are more likely to prosper.[8]

# NEW PRODUCT DEVELOPMENT

Approaches to innovation and new product development are deeply embedded in the firm's culture. If innovation performance is unsatisfactory, the firm's culture may have to change.

Firms believing that new product success is vital often set aggressive product development targets. 3M is a good example; recently, 30 percent of its targeted annual revenues were derived from products launched in the previous four years. Some firms benchmark product development processes, trying to identify global best practices, and make appropriate changes in their own processes. Other firms speed up development by re-engineering existing systems and processes. Finally, some firms encourage broad employee experimentation and allow unapproved *skunkwork* projects. 3M was a leader in this area, and newer firms like Google encourage employees to spend up to 20 percent of work time on their own ideas.[9]

One widespread problem is that R&D employees are sometimes indifferent to the potential marketability of their discoveries. The firm can address this issue by using market-oriented criteria in the development process. At BASF, scientists write marketing plans for the products they expect to develop. At GE, a bellwether example of innovation, scientists regularly meet with marketing and business-unit executives to ensure their projects are linked to the businesses. At Philips, research is no longer funded solely at the corporate level; product divisions pay two-thirds of the budgets for research projects.

We identify four approaches to new product development:

- **Basic technology research.** Typically aimed at disruptive innovations like DNA mapping, finding new chemical entities for pharmaceuticals, and electrical super-conductivity.
- **Applied technology research.** Uses basic technology to develop new products. Pharmaceutical research adopts new chemical entities to treat specific medical conditions.
- **Market-focused development.** Focuses on marketable products, often by improving ease of use or developing complementary products.
- **Market tinkering.** Makes minor modifications to its current products, like a new dessert flavor or a different scent for a floor cleaner.

*Marketing Question*

How does Microsoft demonstrate customer focus? What was its last internally developed innovation? Is Microsoft is an Isolate, Follower, Shaper, or Interactor?

*Marketing Question*

What are the opportunities of being a Shaper or Interactor firm?

KEY IDEA

➤ Firms can be Isolates, Followers, Shapers, or Interactors, based on their innovation focus and customer focus.

*Marketing Question*

Using the four approaches to new product development, how would you classify Apple's iPod, a new MP3 player from Sony, the BlackBerry, Coke Zero, Starbucks Frappuccino, *The Apprentice, The Apprentice: Martha Stewart*? Why?

KEY IDEA

➤ Four product development approaches are basic technology research, applied technology research, market-focused development, and market tinkering.

When approaching new product development, marketers should observe the following principles: manage risk appropriately, do not underestimate the value of market knowledge, conduct problem-focused research, treat data cautiously, and determine if the firm has the right competencies.

## THE STAGE-GATE PROCESS FOR NEW PRODUCT DEVELOPMENT

The **stage-gate process** is a systematic way of condensing a large number of ideas into a small number of products that the firm can successfully launch. Figure 13.1 shows a *gate* after each *stage* where the firm must make a go/no-go decision.

**FIGURE 13.1**

**THE STAGE-GATE NEW PRODUCT DEVELOPMENT PROCESS**

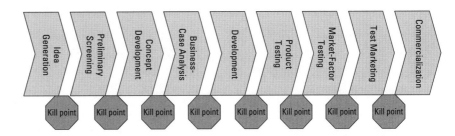

Table 13.2 indicates the type of criteria firms typically use to move products through the various gates or stages. Resource commitments increase dramatically as a project moves from idea to new product launch or commercialization. Dismissing an idea is inexpensive, but the costs of a failed launch are substantial. Each *gate* is a place to stop, a **kill point**. The firm should clearly specify criteria for each *gate*; only projects that meet the criteria pass though the *gate* and enter the following *stage*. Since each new stage typically involves greater risk and investment, the firm's projects should not pass a kill point lightly.

**TABLE 13.2**

**TYPES OF CRITERIA FOR MOVING FROM ONE STAGE TO ANOTHER IN THE STAGE-GATE PROCESS**

| Stage In The Process | Typical Criteria |
|---|---|
| Idea generation | Provides incremental customer value; makes sense as a potential product |
| Preliminary screening | Technologically feasible; likely market need; fits with firm strategy |
| Concept development | Well-defined product concept; continues to meet previous criteria |
| Business-case analysis | Fits with firm strategy; coherent business plan; forecasts meet market and financial goals |
| Development | Product fulfills concept definition |
| Product testing | Product performs as laid out in the business-case analysis |
| Market-factor testing | Customer attitudes and purchasing as anticipated in business-case analysis |
| Test marketing | Positive customer response; product secures anticipated revenues, market position, and profitability |
| Commercialization | Product secures anticipated revenues, market position, and profitability |

**KEY IDEA**

➤ The firm should develop clear criteria for a project to pass through each gate.

## IDEA GENERATION

The firm requires a large quantity of high-quality ideas to create a new product development portfolio as the basis for long-term growth. Customers are often a good source of new product ideas, but the firm should use any possible idea source; see the Hyatt example. It should document the most promising ideas, and then assess them. Typically, the firm discards many ideas quickly, but they may help generate related ideas with more potential.

In 1957, Jay Pritzker waited for a flight from Los Angeles International Airport. He noticed that Fat Eddie's coffee shop, in Hyatt Von Dehn's hotel, was unusually busy and that the hotel had no vacancies. Pritzker bet that executives would want to stay in quality hotels near large airports. He wrote out a $2.2 million offer on a napkin. In 2006, Global Hyatt Corporation had 213 hotels and resorts and annual revenues over $4 billion.

**NUMBER OF IDEAS.** If the firm generates only a few marginal-quality ideas, it will have few new product successes. Successful firms eliminate many ideas during the development process. Hence, they must identify a sufficient quantity of ideas to find the one idea that will produce a successful product. In many studies, the average ratio of new product ideas to successful products is about 100:1 — in agricultural chemicals it is 10,000:1.

**SCOPE OF SEARCH.** A focused search within the firm's mission typically generates better ideas than an unfocused search.[10] As the mission evolves, so should the firm's scope of search.

Most ski resorts focus resources on their ski hills. But skiers and snowboarders spend only 20 percent of their time on the hill, the rest in restaurants, après-ski bars, and shops. Vail Resorts (Colorado) understands; it manages six hotels, 72 restaurants, 40 shops, and more than 13,000 condominiums.

**NEW IDEA SOURCES.** The firm should secure ideas from many sources — inside the firm but also outside sources. The firm must resist the *not-invented-here* (NIH) syndrome that denigrates outside ideas, in part by embracing a *reapplied-with-pride* (RWP) approach:

➤ The stage-gate process is a systematic method for new product development. The stages are idea generation, preliminary screening, concept development, business-case analysis, development, product testing, market-factor testing, test marketing, and commercialization.

➤ The cost of failure increases at each stage.

- **Internal generation.** R&D is often a major idea source. Success rates depend on factors like budget, type of people hired, and their motivations. Kellogg's Institute for Food and Nutrition Research invests heavily in food laboratories and restaurant-quality kitchens. Researchers, from 22 countries, are very diverse in their education and training. They are also very productive; in one month they generated 65 new product concepts and 94 new packaging ideas. Manufacturing and operations also generate new product ideas, and many firms conduct employee competitions. Some firms even offer employees or franchisees financial incentives to pursue their own ideas.

- **From customers.** Many key innovations start with customers. Sometimes firm employees spend time with customers to observe their likes, dislikes, and difficulties with current products. Kraft used insight from customer focus groups to launch new variations of Oreo cookies. Other firms, like Staples, conduct idea competitions; one contest generated 8,300 ideas.[11] 3M is well known for its systematic approach to idea generation. It identifies **lead users** — individuals and organizations who think up, and may even prototype, products before producers. 3M secures inventions from lead users, completes development, and markets the products.[12]

- **Independent inventors. Independent inventors** can be a vital source of ideas. Inventors and outside firms now provide 35 percent of P&G's new product ideas. Examples of products developed by independent inventors include Cuisinart, Dental Implants, Kitty Litter, Matchbox Toys, the SuperSoaker water gun, and Velcro. Of course, independent inventors founded Apple, Nike, and many other major firms.

- **Regulations.** Regulations often cause market inefficiencies that stimulate ideas to build businesses. Leased lines, satellites, voice over the Internet, and automated callback systems all helped circumvent local monopolies for international telephone calls.

- **Serendipity.** New product ideas sometimes arise unexpectedly. Pfizer was testing sildenafil citrate to treat angina, when it discovered the unexpected side effect of treating erectile dysfunction. Pfizer developed the highly successful Viagra.

- **Idea libraries.** Ideas have their own right time. The environment changes; ideas with no value at time A may have great value at time B. Initially, AT&T's video telephone failed, but reappeared many years later as video conferencing. Firms should develop **idea libraries** and search them periodically and systematically.

➤ The firm should tap multiple sources for new ideas.

➤ "The best way to get a good idea is to get *a lot* of ideas."

**NEW IDEA PROCESSES.** The two main approaches for generating new product ideas are **structured thinking** and **unstructured thinking**:

**Structured Thinking for Generating New Product Ideas**[13]

- **Attribute listing.** Write down all product attributes: For a ballpoint pen, these include casing material and color, ink quality and color, point width, weight, and price. Construct a table with attributes as column heads. Identify attribute variations, focusing on ways to improve.
- **Morphological analysis.** Builds on attribute listing. Combine the items in each column to develop new and interesting new product ideas.

**Unstructured Thinking for Generating New Product Ideas**

- **Brainstorming**. Focus on a problem and seek radical solutions. Brainstorming helps participants break out of everyday patterns and find new ways to look for solutions. Ideas should be as broad and odd as possible. Discussion or evaluation is prohibited until the idea flow is exhausted, because judgment and analysis stunt idea generation. Individual brainstorming tends to produce a wider range of ideas, but group brainstorming tends to be more effective because of the experience and creativity of all members.
- **Random input**. Used to regenerate brainstorming sessions. The facilitator selects a random noun from book titles or a prepared word list or a random picture, to help generate ideas. In the ballpoint pen example, random words might be cars, trees, factories, or carpets.
- **Provocation**. Uses a stupid untrue statement to shock participants from established patterns. A *provocation* in the ballpoint pen example might be "Ballpoint pens cannot write."
- ***Six Thinking Hats***. Each of six different-colored real or imaginary *hats* represents a different nature of thought. *Green hat* means focus on creative ideas. *Red hat* means focus on emotions by expressing feelings about an idea or process.[14]
- **Mind mapping**. Write the problem in the center of a page and draw a circle around it. Write associations with the problem in circles elsewhere on the page and draw links to the problem. Each *association* is the focus for another linked set of associations. Seek a solution by examining local clusters of associations.

## PRELIMINARY SCREENING

The goal of **preliminary screening** is to create a balanced portfolio of successfully screened new product ideas. For most firms, a balanced portfolio includes low-return/low-risk and high-return/high-risk ideas, and revenue generation in both the short and long run. Screening decisions for high-risk, high-return, long-time-to-revenue ideas are quite difficult. Figure 13.2 shows a well-balanced portfolio.

**FIGURE 13.2**

**RISK AND RETURN IN NEW PRODUCT IDEAS — A WELL-BALANCED PORTFOLIO**

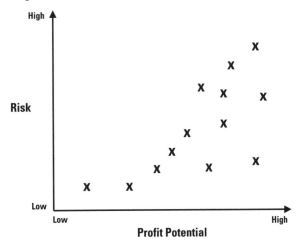

Typically, preliminary screening involves knowledgeable marketing and/or technical personnel, customers, and even suppliers. The exact mix depends on the idea, but customers may not be helpful in screening *new-to-the-world* products. Preliminary screening is the first stage for eliminating new product ideas.

Because return and risk profiles differ markedly among ideas, the firm should use several sets of criteria. For example, criteria for new-product-line ideas should differ from existing-product-revision ideas. A useful way to assess new ideas is with the *spider web* diagram. Each 10-point scale spoke in Figure 13.3 represents a screening criterion; poor scores are near the center, good scores near the periphery. The firm has assessed an idea on eight criteria; it scores relatively well on several criteria, but poorly on two.

**KEY IDEA**

➤ Preliminary screening aims to form a balanced portfolio of new product ideas.

➤ Different types of new product idea require different screening criteria.

**FIGURE 13.3**

**ASSESSING NEW PRODUCT IDEAS**

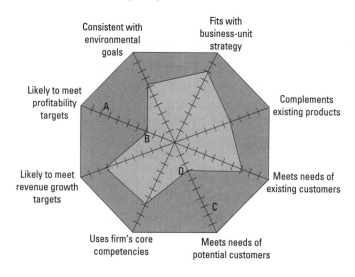

## CONCEPT DEFINITION

The **product concept**, or **concept definition**, describes the product idea. Good concepts detail deliverable customer benefits. FMCG firms take pains to express new product ideas as robust product concepts. The process is highly iterative. Some examples (status) are:

- Breath fresheners for dogs (a successful new product)
- Diet baby foods (not under development)
- A global positioning satellite (GPS) locator for children (launched and doing well)

Criteria for approval should be similar to preliminary screening. Understanding customer needs, particularly unmet needs, is very helpful in crafting and testing concept definitions.

Product concepts must appeal to customers and guide development teams. Firms get in trouble when concepts drift during development. Pontiac's concept for the Aztek was a small, youth-oriented sport utility. But to launch the car quickly and economically, Pontiac used GM's mini-van frame; the Aztec's appearance received mixed reviews, and its $22,000 to $27,000 price was too high for the youth market. It sold poorly.

**KEY IDEA**

➤ The product concept should appeal to customers and guide development.

## BUSINESS-CASE ANALYSIS

**Business-case analysis** sits between *concept approval* and *development*. It assesses the concept's financial viability and considers the various risk factors. Projects must meet minimum financial targets to move forward. The heart of business-case analysis is a draft marketing plan; the firm lays out its market strategy, given successful development. The firm must think through market segmentation, choose target segments, and decide on a value proposition for securing differential advantage.

**KEY IDEA**

➤ Business-case analysis assesses the financial viability of a product concept.

➤ The most difficult step in business-case analysis is forecasting sales revenues.

## Marketing Question

Talk to an executive about her firm's new product development process. How does it compare with the process described in this chapter? Where is it better? Worse?

Four considerations underlie forecast financial performance:

- **Sales revenues.** These forecasts can be highly uncertain.
- **Cost of goods sold (COGS).** All ongoing costs to make and sell the product. **Gross profit** is sales revenues less COGS. In the launch phase, the firm may incur losses.
- **Investment costs.** Include all costs to develop the product, plus fixed investment for factories and equipment. The firm incurs many of these costs before it earns any revenues.
- **Discounting.** The firm must discount all cash flows to the present.

## DEVELOPMENT

A successful business-case analysis sets the stage for **development**. Development typically occurs deep in the firm. Design and engineering focus initially on the product's design and functional performance, but other groups must also be involved. Input from manufacturing and service helps ensure the product can be made and serviced efficiently.[15] Development also benefits from customer involvement.

Development by multifunctional teams, including *voice of the customer*, helps avoid time-consuming, back-and-forth interactions that slow linear, sequential processes. Achieving consensus may be difficult, but teams often produce better products. A potential problem in using teams is loss of specialist expertise if members become organizationally disconnected from their specialties. The firm can mitigate these problems by requiring clear written reports, intensive problem-solving meetings, good direct supervision, and standard work procedures.[16]

In spring 2003, Motorola charged engineer Ron Jellico to create the thinnest phone ever. His engineering team, eventually growing to 20, met daily at 4 p.m. for one-hour meetings that often lasted until 7 p.m. The team flouted Motorola's development rules by keeping the project secret, even from close colleagues, and using materials and processes never tried before. Motivated by a design team, engineers made breakthroughs like putting the antenna in the mouthpiece and the battery alongside the circuit board instead of beneath it. Originally planned as a niche product, the RAZR sold more than 20 million units in 2005 and more phones than Apple sold iPods in 2006.

**PRODUCT DESIGN.** As product quality improves, design becomes increasingly important for customer satisfaction. During development, as the firm makes performance trade-offs among product attributes, it must keep the value proposition squarely in mind. It must also address any negative side effects, possibly with creative design approaches.

### Product Design at Sony

A senior Sony Electronics executive said: "The most exciting thing about Sony to me is when you're in a line-up review and they're showing you product and you get this 28-year-old product planner and this 30-year-old designer and they walk into a room and they pull back a piece of cloth and they show you a product that you've been working together on for a year and you go 'Oh my God, it's perfect.' And when you get into those moments, you know, it's about the passion that Sony has for great products. This is a passionate organization that really believes in creating the best possible product that you can create. But the core strength of this company is passionate designers and product planners and the senior marketing managers that just absolutely love what they're doing.

"There's this one designer in Tokyo. He's in his 30s now, but when you see this guy! He's going to walk into the room and you're going to think, 'Oh my God, a street person has escaped and he's loose in the building.' And his pants are four sizes too big and his clothes just hang on and he looks like he hasn't slept in a week ... You will know his product before he comes in the room ... Because most products you'll look at and you'll say, 'OK, with that tape recorder I could give you 20 comments on how to improve the design on that tape recorder.' But when he pulls back the drape, you're not going to have anything to say. On this one occasion I was in Tokyo and he showed us a CD player, and the stuff was perfect. It was just perfect. That line of CD players sold six million units in the U.S. alone. And we didn't have to touch it. So that's the strength of Sony, people like that ... somebody with passion designed that thing."[17]

Development is typically the most time-consuming stage in making new products. Faster development helps gain first-mover advantage and enhances revenue opportunities. Continuous development on a 24/7 cycle is one option. At Bechtel and other firms, development teams in London, the U.S., and Japan take over from each other as the day ends/begins. Toyota uses competitive teams that work in parallel toward the same goal.

## PRODUCT TESTING

Ultimately, the firm tests its new product for functional, aesthetic, ergonomic, and use characteristics. There is no single test or type of test. Rather, development follows a series of *develop → test → develop* feedback loops until the product is ready for market-factor testing.

The two major types of test are **in-company alpha tests** and **customer beta tests**.

- **In-company alpha tests.** Most new products have many in-company alpha tests where firm employees provide critical feedback. Several alpha tests may run simultaneously, and sometimes a successful test leads to further development.

- **Customer beta tests.** Beta tests typically follow successful alpha testing, but firms sometimes conduct beta tests on product features before they finish development. Firms may also conduct several beta tests as development is concluding. Beta tests give customers an early look at developing and soon-to-be-introduced new products.

  The firm should move speedily through testing, but inadequate testing can cause big problems. Daimler-Benz (DB) had to stop shipping its first subcompact, Mercedes A-Class, for three months. In a moose-avoidance test, a Swedish journalist tipped the car in a sharp turn at 38 mph. DB invested $1.5 billion in the car and $171 million to solve the problem.

## MARKET-FACTOR TESTING

The product is only one part of a marketing offer. First-rate products can fail if the firm poorly designs and/or implements other marketing-mix elements. Conversely, marginal products can be successful if other marketing-mix elements are superior. The firm should evaluate implementation plan elements, like advertising and distribution, by **market-factor testing**. Generally, this type of testing is done after development, but sometimes it occurs in parallel. The firm can test using simulated environments, like in a mock-up store display, or virtually on the Internet.

## TEST MARKETING

**Test marketing** simulates actual market conditions. Typically, the firm selects two or more geographic areas with similar market and customer profiles, considering issues like seasonality. It implements the full market launch program in one or more test markets. The other test market(s) acts as a control, to isolate product launch results. For any test market, measurement is crucial and includes:

- **Input measures.** Include advertising, training, and sales effort.
- **Intermediate measures.** Include customer awareness and interest.
- **Output measures.** Include sales, profits, and customer satisfaction.

FMCG firms collect point-of-sales data from supermarket scanners. Consumer panels and/or independent surveys provide intermediate measures and customer satisfaction.

Test marketing has its pros and cons.

- **Pros** — Saves launch costs, fine-tunes launch, may provide unexpected insight.
- **Cons** — Expense and time, competitors' actions interfere with results, alerts competitors.

## KEY IDEA

➤ Many firms make very large investments in product development.
➤ Multi-functional teams and customer involvement aid the development process.
➤ Design is an increasingly important part of the development process.

## KEY IDEA

➤ The firm should conduct in-company alpha tests throughout development. It should conduct customer beta tests in the latter phases.
➤ Failure to test products sufficiently can have serious marketing and financial consequences.

## KEY IDEA

➤ Market-factor testing includes simulated environments and virtual testing.
➤ Product testing is insufficient — the firm should test the entire marketing offer.

## Marketing Question

Have you ever been part of a test market in your local grocery store or retail outlet? Did you try the product? Did the firm launch it successfully, or was it killed?

**KEY IDEA**

➤ In deciding on test marketing, the firm should be aware of several pros and cons.

**KEY IDEA**

➤ Commercialization is often where firms make their biggest bets.

**KEY IDEA**

➤ There are several types of new product adopters.

➤ The interplay of several factors determines the speed of new product adoption.

## COMMERCIALIZATION

Successful completion of the stage-gate process paves the way for launch and **commercialization**. The firm assigns resources to build a plant and expend marketing effort. The firm's launch strategy must consider issues like forecast sales, time to build the plant, production and inventory requirements, competitive lead time, competitive response, patent or trade secret protection, and available resources.

All marketing-mix elements are important for launch, but especially communication. B2C firms often use celebrity spokespersons and advertising to promote their new products. They also use *product placement*, working with producers so that actors use their products in movies and TV shows. B2B firms focus on good distribution and customer support programs, including getting key opinion leaders to use their new products.

Traditionally, firms launched new products in domestic markets and then later in foreign markets. Today, many firms launch in multiple national markets simultaneously, especially information products where copying is a problem.

No one likes commercialization failure, but the best companies learn from their mistakes. Corning failed with a DNA chip designed to print all 28,000 human genes onto slides for research, but identified the drug-discovery market and now sells Epic for testing potential drugs. British Airways' flat beds upstaged Virgin's new reclined sleeper seats, but Virgin used its learning to develop a *leapfrog* innovation, the *upper-class suite*, that helped improve its business-class market share.

## PRODUCT ADOPTION

The goal of commercialization is for customers to adopt the firm's product. But not all customers adopt at the same time. As part of its product planning, the firm should anticipate five **adoption categories**[18]:

- **Innovators** (2.5 percent).[19] The first group to adopt the innovation, but only a small part of the population. Typically, other customers do not emulate these *venturesome* risk-takers.
- **Early adopters** (13.5 percent). Follow the innovators. They are more *respected* in their communities and are opinion leaders for others.
- **Early majority** (34 percent). Make decisions *deliberately*, based in part on the experience of early adopters. They are in the first half of adopters but are not leaders.
- **Late majority** (34 percent). A *skeptical* group that adopts only when half the population has adopted.
- **Laggards** (16 percent percent). These *traditionalists* are suspicious of change and adopt when most customers have adopted and use is widespread.

Identifying potential customers by adopting category for a new product innovation is a critical marketing challenge. In B2C, early adopters tend to be better educated, younger, and socio-economically advantaged. Avon maintains a database on innovators and early adopters for cosmetics and targets them for new product launches. But innovators and early adopters for one product may be early or late majority for another. A product innovation must **cross the chasm** from early adopters to the early majority and the mainstream market to be successful — Figure 13.4.[20] Many new products fail to cross the chasm; for others, it takes a long time.

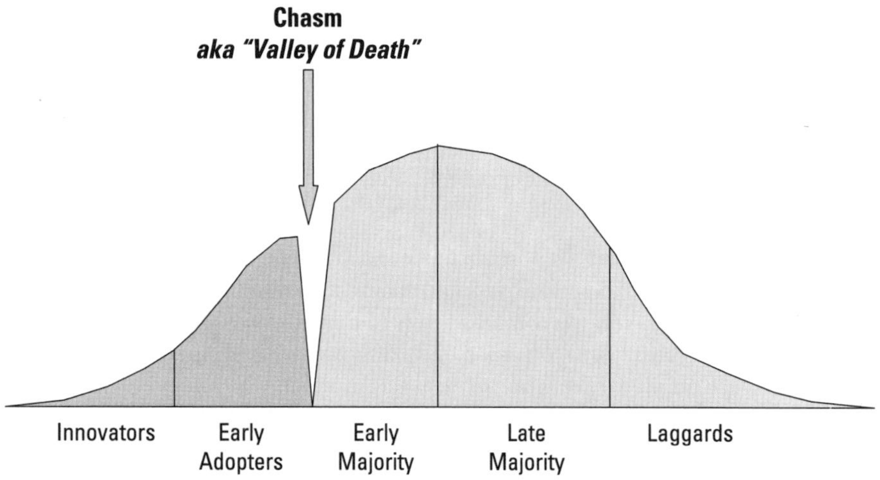

FIGURE 13.4

THE ADOPTION
CURVE AND CHASM

The **ACCORD** acronym summarizes several factors that affect speed of adoption and commercial success. Consider the successful introduction of EZ Pass on toll roads and bridges. The EZ Pass device attaches to a vehicle's windshield. An electronic signal at the tollbooth recognizes the device, allows passage, and deducts payment from an account linked to a credit card. The account automatically replenishes when the balance falls to a pre-set level:

- **Advantage.** Saves time at tollbooth; automatic bill payment more convenient than cash.
- **Compatibility.** Driver's behavior largely unchanged; starting the credit-card account is trivial.
- **Complexity.** Learning minimal; driver attaches the device; drives through the tollbooth.
- **Observability** (Communicability). Benefits easy to understand and communicate.
- **Risk.** Little risk to trying the EZ Pass system — no upfront payment.
- **Divisibility** (Reversibility). Driver can easily switch back to cash.

## *Marketing Question*

The Segway is a battery-driven personal-transportation vehicle developed by Dean Kamen. Launched in 2002, the Segway has been less successful than its inventor predicted. What barriers to adoption did the Segway face? Could Segway have done a better job in addressing these barriers?

## *Marketing Question*

What products can you identify that never *crossed the chasm*? What products took a long time to cross the chasm?

---

## KEY MESSAGES

- Successful new products are a major factor in creating shareholder wealth.
- Innovations can be either sustaining or disruptive.
- The most important factors for innovation success are market selection, R&D spending, and organization.
- In terms of innovation, firms are either: isolates, followers, shapers, or interactors.
- Four approaches to new product development are: basic technology research, applied technology research, market-focused development, and market tinkering.
- The stage-gate process is a systematic approach to new product development. Key stages are:
  - Idea generation
  - Preliminary screening
  - Concept definition
  - Business-case analysis
  - Development
  - Product testing
  - Market-factor testing
  - Test marketing
  - Commercialization
- The cost of failure increases as a project moves through the new product development process. Hence, each gate should be a kill point.
- New product success depends on *crossing the chasm* from early adopters to early majority.
- The speed of adoption for a successful project depends on the ACCORD factors. (Do you know what they are?)

# CHAPTER 14

# MANAGING PRICE AND VALUE

## LEARNING OBJECTIVES

When you have completed this chapter, you will be able to:

- Discriminate between pricing strategy and pricing tactics.
- Recognize the key role of price in capturing customer value.
- Analyze the role of costs in pricing decisions.
- Incorporate competitor objectives and strategies in determining your prices.
- Relate strategic objectives to your pricing decisions.
- Use the pricing toolkit and price waterfall concept for price setting.
- Manage and monitor pricing tactics.
- Integrate pricing with other elements of marketing implementation.

## OPENING CASE: SOUTHWEST AIRLINES

*Southwest Airlines (SWA) is the U.S.' largest domestic airline. But in 1973, it was a puny upstart battling Braniff, then the major Texas airline. That SWA survived a harrowing period was due in no small part to some astute pricing decisions by then CEO Lamar Muse.*[1]

*SWA was formed in the mid-1960s to fly among three major Texas cities — Dallas, Houston, and San Antonio. Flight distances ranged from 190 to 250 miles; flight times were about 45 minutes. Because SWA's proposed routes were all within Texas, the Texas Railroad Commission, rather than the Civil Aeronautics Board (CAB), was its regulator.*

*Braniff's and Texas International Airlines' (TI) fares from Dallas were $27 to Houston and $28 to San Antonio. SWA entered at $20 on both routes. Braniff and TI immediately met those prices. In November 1971, SWA added San Antonio-to-Houston, also $20, and shifted some flights from*

*Houston Intercontinental airport (HI) to the close-in Hobby airport (HH). In late 1992, SWA abandoned HI.*

*During the next few months, SWA made several pricing moves and held numerous publicity stunts including onboard parties and decorating aircraft cabins. In November 1971, it experimented with $10 on weekend evening flights; in May 1972, it extended the $10 fare to all flights after 9 p.m. Load factors were higher than for full-fare flights. In July, facing a deteriorating financial condition, SWA raised its basic fare to $26, increased leg room, and provided free drinks. In one week, TI matched SWA's fares; Braniff followed two days later and increased onboard service. Now flying into Hobby (as well as HI), Braniff started its $10 evening fare at 7:30 p.m.*

*By July 1972, SWA's market share was 40 percent on the important Dallas-to-Houston route. Braniff's share dropped from 75 to 48 percent and TI's from 25 to 11 percent. But Braniff's passenger load was roughly the same as before SWA's entry. In October 1972, SWA replaced its $10 fares with $13 fares after 8 p.m. on weekdays and all weekend, supported with heavy advertising; traffic increased. SWA was now profitable on Dallas-to-Houston, but was unprofitable on Dallas-to-San Antonio where Braniff had four times as many flights. On January 22, 1973, SWA announced a "60-Day-Half-Price Sale" from Dallas to San Antonio. Passenger loads increased threefold almost immediately and reached an 85 percent load factor. On February 1, Braniff responded with a 60-day half-price-"Get-Acquainted"-sale — $13 — for all Dallas-HH (but not HI) flights.*

**SOUTHWEST**

*Muse said he believed the public should realize that SWA's highly reliable hourly service was worth $26, and that it should be disgusted at Braniff's action. SWA ran double-truck advertisements in Dallas and Houston newspapers with a picture of Muse, a statement — "Nobody's Goin' to Shoot Southwest Airlines Out of the Sky for a Lousy $13," and all the reasons the public should not let that happen. It also printed 50,000 brochures with even stronger language. SWA gave these to all passengers, and off-duty hostesses handed them out at lunch hour in downtown Dallas and Houston.*

*SWA also offered a premium. It told passengers that the flight was worth $26; it would like them to pay $26. But if they felt they had to fly Braniff because of the $13 price, Southwest would also take them for $13. Those who paid the full fare received a gift — a fifth of Chivas Regal or Crown Royal, or a nice leather ice bucket. These items cost SWA around $7 to $8, but each had a retail value of around $13. Businessmen, in particular, put $26 on their expense reports and took a fifth of Chivas Regal home! On April 1, Braniff ended its "Get-Acquainted" sale; SWA also went back to $26. February 1973 was SWA's best month, and in March it made its first profit. SWA has not looked back.*

> **CASE QUESTION**
>
> How do you assess Southwest Airlines' pricing actions? How do you assess Braniff's pricing actions?

Pricing is critical for earning profits and creating shareholder value. It is also pivotal for introducing new products, entering new markets, repositioning, and changing the firm's objectives and/or strategy. Figure 14.1 shows how price decisions have a greater profit impact than other profit levers because:

- Price affects profit margin since margin equals price *less* cost.
- Price affects unit volume via the demand curve.
- Because price affects volume, it also affects costs via economies of scale.
- Price often affects customers' quality and value perceptions.

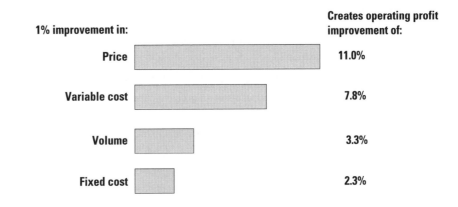

KEY IDEA

➤ Price has a larger
impact on profits than
any other lever. Price
affects margins, unit
volumes, costs, and
often customers' quality
and value perceptions.

KEY IDEA

➤ In setting prices, the
firm should consider
perceived customer
value, costs, com-
petition, and strategic
objectives. Excessive
focus on a single
element leads to
suboptimal pricing
decisions.

KEY IDEA

➤ What seems to be a
pricing problem may
be a perceived value
problem.

KEY IDEA

➤ The firm creates value
for customers primarily
via non-price elements
in its offer — the
marketing mix.

➤ Many factors affect the
value that customers
perceive in the firm's
offer.

# *Developing Pricing Strategy*

**Pricing strategy** is the firm's overall approach to setting price. Four critical considerations should enter into pricing decisions: *perceived customer value, costs, competition,* and *strategic objectives.* Too much emphasis on one single element leads to suboptimal pricing decisions, like the destructive, downward pricing spiral that can follow from an excessive focus on competitors. Skilled pricing executives assess all factors before developing pricing strategy.

## PERCEIVED CUSTOMER VALUE

When increased competition brings more options, customers invariably seek lower prices. As they turn elsewhere, the firm may believe it has a pricing problem. More likely, it has a **perceived value** problem — it is delivering insufficient value, or has not established a good relationship between price and value. As a first step in our strategic pricing analysis, we focus on three value-related issues: creating, measuring, and capturing value. Then we turn to a closely associated issue — price sensitivity.

### CREATING VALUE

We learned in earlier chapters that the firm's value proposition is central to its market strategy. The firm creates value for customers primarily through the non-price elements in its marketing mix — product, promotion, distribution, and services can each add value.

Price may also create value by contributing to brand image. Products like Rolls-Royce, Bentley, and Ferrari automobiles; Rolex; and Apple's iPod are all perceived as quality brands. Factors outside the firm's control also affect the value that customers perceive in its offer. On a hot day, you may value a can of Coke at $3 if that is your only option, but if you could also get Pepsi and 7-Up, Coke's value would be less. When making pricing decisions, the firm must consider several factors:

- **Perceived substitutes.** What competitive offers and prices do customers consider? Can the firm influence customers' price expectations with its positioning decisions?
- **Unique value.** How do customers weigh the attributes and benefits that influence their decisions? Do the firm's attributes and benefits distinguish it from competitors?
- **Switching costs.** What costs or investments would customers incur if they switched suppliers? Are they locked in to current suppliers? For how long? Could the firm encourage switching?

- **Competitive comparison.** Can customers easily and fairly compare alternatives? Can they compare without purchasing? Are experts required? Do customers know how to use the firm's and competitors' products? Are prices directly comparable, or are calculations needed to understand differences?

- **Price/Quality.** Is there a positive price/quality relationship for the product?

- **Expenditures.** How significant are the absolute purchase expenditures? What percentage of annual spending, income, or wealth does the purchase represent?

- **Terms.** Are financing options available and clearly communicated?

- **Non-monetary costs.** What effort, time, and/or risk is needed to make the purchase?

- **End benefit.** What end benefit or value does the product help deliver? How price sensitive are end-user customers? What percent of the end benefit's price does the firm's product represent? Can the firm reposition its product to deliver an end benefit to price-insensitive customers?

- **Shared cost.** Do customers pay the full cost? If not, what portion do they pay?

- **Fairness.** How does the current price compare to customers' experiences with similar products? What do they expect to pay? Is the price justified?

- **Inventory.** Do buyers hold inventory? Do they expect current prices to be temporary?

- **Education.** Do firms compete fiercely on price, so educating customers to focus on price?

## MEASURING VALUE

Measuring the value customers perceive in the firm's offer is critical. If you don't know customers' value perceptions, you'll never make good pricing decisions. Some measurement approaches are:

**DIRECT VALUE ASSESSMENT.** The firm simply asks customers what they would pay for various products. It must be concerned about a downward response bias, but carefully phrased questions can provide helpful data. In launching the original Ford Mustang, Lee Iacocca asked customers to estimate its price. Estimates were much higher than Ford's planned price, so Iacocca knew it would be a winner. The Mustang was the U.S.' best-selling new car ever.

**DOLLARMETRIC METHOD.** For each pair of options, customers say which they prefer and how much extra they would pay. Summing positive and negative differences reveals the relative value of the options. Table 14.1 shows the responses for four products: A, B, C, and D.

**⚷ KEY IDEA**

➤ Measuring value delivery to customers is difficult but critical.

| Options Compared | Preferred Option | Extra Price for Preferred Option |
|------------------|------------------|----------------------------------|
| A and B | B | $10 |
| A and C | C | $13 |
| A and D | A | $5 |
| B and C | C | $3 |
| B and D | B | $8 |
| C and D | C | $12 |

**TABLE 14.1**

ILLUSTRATIVE DATA FROM THE DOLLARMETRIC METHOD

We calculate the customer's relative value for these products as follows:

- The *extra price* is positive for the preferred option, negative for the non-preferred option.
- Each option has three comparisons. Sum these *extra prices* for each option.
- Divide the sums of *extra prices* by three to calculate the average *extra price*.

  The average extra prices customers are prepared to pay for the four options are:

  $$A = -10 - 13 + 5 = -18/3 = -\textbf{6} \qquad B = 10 - 3 + 8 = 15/3 = +\textbf{5}$$
  $$C = +13 + 3 + 12 = 28/3 = +\textbf{9.3} \qquad D = -5 - 8 - 12 = -25/3 = -\textbf{8.3}$$

- Use the least valued option as a base, and add the average *extra price* for each option to the average *extra price* for the base. The figure is what the customer would pay over the base.

  D is the least valued option. The *extra prices* for the other options are:

  $$A = -6 + 8.3 = \$2.3 \qquad B = 5 + 8.3 = \$13.3 \qquad C = 9.3 + 8.3 = \$17.6$$

**PERCEIVED VALUE ANALYSIS.** Table 14.2 identifies five steps for measuring an offer's perceived value. The firm secures data directly from customers, but sometimes experienced managers provide *best-guess* data that can be validated later by marketing research.

**TABLE 14.2**

**MEASURING THE PERCEIVED VALUE OF AN OFFER**

| Step Number | Step | Description |
|---|---|---|
| 1 | Identify required benefits and values | Identify the key benefits and values customers require — typically 5 to 8 — but exclude price. |
| 2 | Weight benefits and values | Weight each benefit or value by allocating 100 points based on its importance to customers. Weights sum to 100. |
| 3 | Rate each offer from the various suppliers | Rate each offer based on how well customers believe it delivers the required benefit or value (1 = poor; 10 = excellent). |
| 4 | Develop benefit/value scores | For each offer, form individual benefit/value scores by multiplying the results of step 2 and step 3 for each benefit or value. Benefit/Value score = Weighting x Rating. |
| 5 | Develop the perceived value scores | For each offer, sum the individual benefit/value scores. |

Table 14.3 is a numerical illustration: A, B, and C represent three different suppliers of easy chairs. Perceived value measures for each option are in bold. (We note the actual prices but these do not enter the calculations.) The results and interpretation are:

- **Perceived Value.** Supplier B — 820 offers the greatest perceived value, followed by A — 665, and C — 580.
- **Price.** Supplier A has the highest price at $500, followed by B — $450, and C — $300.

Supplier C has the lowest perceived value and the lowest price, but A and B are misordered. Supplier B has the greatest perceived value — 820 versus 665 for supplier A. But supplier A's price is higher — $500 versus $450. Since supplier B provides greater value for a lower price, it should be gaining market share.

*Marketing Question*

The Chevy *Volt* is GM's new plug-in electric car. How would you measure its customer value?

**TABLE 14.3**

**ILLUSTRATION OF PERCEIVED VALUE ANALYSIS FOR SUPPLIERS OF EASY CHAIRS**

| Benefits Required | Relative Importance Weighting | Supplier A Price = $500 | | Supplier B Price = $450 | | Supplier C Price = $300 | |
|---|---|---|---|---|---|---|---|
| | | Rating (1–10) | Total | Rating (1–10) | Total | Rating (1–10) | Total |
| Chair design | 20 | 5 | 100 | 7 | 140 | 6 | 120 |
| Comfort | 30 | 6 | 180 | 8 | 240 | 4 | 120 |
| Fabric quality | 15 | 10 | 150 | 9 | 135 | 8 | 120 |
| Fabric design | 15 | 5 | 75 | 7 | 105 | 4 | 60 |
| Ease of purchase | 20 | 8 | 160 | 10 | 200 | 8 | 160 |
| **Grand Total** | **100** | | **665** | | **820** | | **580** |

**ECONOMIC ANALYSIS — ECONOMIC VALUE FOR THE CUSTOMER (EVC).** Many B2B firms use EVC — the maximum price customers will pay — to calculate the economic value of new products. EVC analysis depends critically on competitive products that customers consider. EVC helps the firm clarify its options: Should it add more value for a higher price or less value for a lower price? — See Chapter 4, p. 52 for an EVC calculation.

**PRICE EXPERIMENT.** The firm offers the test product at different prices in different market areas, like geographic locations. Sales levels at different prices reflect customer value.

## CAPTURING VALUE

The firm incurs many costs to develop an offer; it creates value if these costs are less than the value customers perceive. Figure 14.2 shows how price apportions the created value: The firm retains some value; customers receive some value. High prices imply that the firm retains most value; low prices imply that it transfers most value to customers.

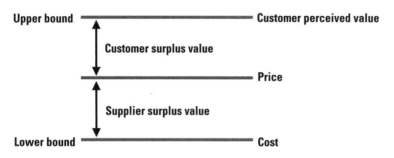

Most firms develop new products, then set prices based on costs or some value estimate using a method like we just discussed. By contrast, Avon starts with the value it wants a new product to deliver to customers, then sets the target price. It translates this price into cost parameters that enable it to meet profit targets. Engineering and manufacturing must then design a product that delivers customer value within the cost parameters.[3]

## CUSTOMER PRICE SENSITIVITY

Sometimes, reducing price a little (increasing customer value a little) leads to a major increase in the amount customers purchase. Other times, it takes a large price reduction (a major increase in value) for them to buy more. (Equivalent effects hold for price increases.) Sometimes customers are **price sensitive**; other times they are **price insensitive**. Classical microeconomics focuses on price sensitivity at the market level; we also discuss individual price sensitivity.

**MARKET-LEVEL PRICE SENSITIVITY.** Figure 14.3 shows that elastic and inelastic **demand curves** are critical to creating a valid pricing strategy:

- **Price elasticity.** Includes products like many grocery items. When price goes down a little, volume increases significantly; when price goes up a little, volume decreases significantly.
- **Price inelasticity.** Includes products like heart pacemakers, electricity, and critical raw materials. Volume does not change much, even with significant price changes.[4]

A final related item: Pundits often advise marketers to set prices at what *the market will bear*. This advice is useless because all markets *bear* many prices. Each price produces a different volume. The firm should decide what volume it wants to sell, then set the appropriate price. Understanding the value it delivers to customers and price sensitivity helps them do just that.

## COSTS

Costs are important for setting prices. After all, they represent one-half of the profit equation: Profit = sales revenues minus costs. In practice, many firms use costs in setting prices, but do so inappropriately. Because it's important that you understand these issues, we start with them. Then we show how the firm *should* use costs in pricing.

### THE INAPPROPRIATE ROLE FOR COSTS: COST-PLUS PRICING

**Cost-plus pricing** is a pricing methodology used by most firms, harkening back to our earlier discussion of an *internal* orientation. Despite its popularity, it is the wrong way to set prices.[5] Cost-plus pricing proceeds simply by identifying the product's costs, then adding a pre-determined profit margin (mark-up). Table 14.4 shows how this works.

| | | |
|---|---|---|
| Variable costs | | $400,000 |
| Direct fixed costs | $200,000 | |
| Indirect fixed costs | $100,000 | |
| Total fixed costs | | $300,000 |
| Total costs | | $700,000 |
| Standard mark-up: 15% of costs | | $105,000 |
| **Price** | | **$805,000** |

The advantages of cost-plus pricing that lead to its widespread popularity are:

- **Profitability.** All sales seem profitable as price must, by definition, be above cost.
- **Simplicity.** If the firm knows its costs, pricing is simple. Anyone can do the math.
- **Defensibility.** It is legally acceptable and is often required for government contracts.

Despite its popularity, cost-plus pricing has three main disadvantages:

**PROFIT LIMITATIONS.** Because of the internal focus, customer value has no role in price-setting:

- **Prices are too low.** Customers value the offer at more than the cost-plus price — say $900,000 in the Table 14.4 example. The firm forgoes $95,000 profit ($900,000 – $805,000).
- **Prices are too high.** Customers value the offer at less than the cost-plus price — say $750,000. Customers will not purchase and the firm forgoes $50,000 profit ($750,000 – $700,000) on the lost sale.

In both cases, the firm sets prices incorrectly because it has not bothered to assess customer value. Cost-plus pricing leads to over-pricing in price-sensitive markets and under-pricing in price-insensitive markets. Also, by using cost-plus pricing, the firm is vulnerable to competitors. The competitor can forecast the firm's prices by estimating its costs; this is valuable information.

**ARBITRARY COST MEASUREMENT.** Firms frequently classify costs as fixed and variable:

- **Variable costs.** Vary directly with the volume of sales and production. Variable costs usually include raw materials, direct labor, and sales commissions.
- **Fixed costs.** Do not vary with the volume of sales or production, over a reasonable range. Fixed costs include overhead and allocated items like rent, salaries, depreciation, and SG&A.[6]

As noted earlier, the cost-plus price is the firm's costs plus a predetermined margin, where:

Cost per unit = *variable* cost per unit plus *fixed* cost per unit

**TABLE 14.4**

ILLUSTRATION OF COST-PLUS PRICING FOR AN ITEM OF CAPITAL EQUIPMENT

KEY IDEA

➤ In cost-plus pricing, the firm identifies its costs and adds a profit margin.

➤ Cost-plus pricing does not consider customer value.

KEY IDEA

➤ Disadvantages of cost-plus pricing are profit limitations, arbitrary cost measurement, and mismatch with market realities.

➤ Firms often determine fixed costs per unit arbitrarily by assuming some level of sales or production.

Calculating the firm's variable cost per unit is straightforward. But fixed cost per unit is a problem because, logically, it is unknown before the fact. To calculate fixed cost per unit, we need to know the number of units, but these depend on the price. And that's what we're trying to to figure out! (In practice many firms arbitrarily assume some sales level.)

**MISMATCH WITH MARKET REALITIES.** When demand falls, logic suggests the firm should lower prices. Pure cost-plus pricing does not allow this. As sales fall, and the firm spreads its fixed costs over lower volumes, fixed costs per unit increase — and so must price! When demand surges, logic suggests the firm should raise prices. But it spreads fixed costs over larger volumes, and fixed costs per unit decrease. And so must price! Variable mark-ups based on demand can partially solve this problem.

## THE APPROPRIATE ROLES FOR COSTS

Cost-plus pricing is the lazy way to set prices. But we should not underestimate the role costs play in price-setting. Costs are important in three critical areas:

**BIRTH CONTROL.** Costs are particularly important for new product introduction. Typically, a new product must meet or exceed financial criteria like the firm's hurdle rate to receive go-ahead approval.[7] The firm bases cash flow estimates on target prices, volumes, and costs. The relevant costs are **fully loaded costs**, meaning that they include all incremental costs related to the new product, *including* incremental overhead.

**DEATH CONTROL.** Costs are also important when the firm is considering dropping a product. The relevant cost is the **marginal cost** — the cost to make and sell one additional unit. Marginal cost includes all variable costs plus some incremental fixed costs,[8] but *excludes* all allocated overhead. The marginal cost is the **floor price**; only in rare circumstances should the firm set prices below the floor price.

**PROFIT PLANNING.** Birth and death control are special cases; the major role for costs is profit planning. The firm explores various possible price points and estimates unit volumes and unit costs. It uses these data to forecast sales revenues and profits.

**KEY IDEA**

➤ Costs have an important price-setting role for birth control, death control, and profit planning.

## THE RELATIONSHIP BETWEEN CUSTOMER VALUE AND COSTS

The real purpose of price is not to recover costs, but to capture value in the customer's mind. Of course, the firm incurs costs to deliver value to customers but, in general, customers *do not care* about the firm's costs. They care only about the value they receive.[9] Hence, costs should bear little relationship to price, but they should almost always be less. As Figure 14.4 shows, the actual relationship between customer value and costs has important implications for the firm:

- **High customer value/low cost.** Nirvana! The firm should seek similar opportunities.
- **High customer value/high cost.** The firm should add more value and/or reduce costs.
- **Low customer value/high cost.** The firm should withdraw; it is probably unprofitable.
- **Low customer value/low cost.** The firm must make tough judgments; stay or go.

**KEY IDEA**

➤ Customers *do not care* about the firm's costs; they care only about the value they receive.

➤ The real purpose of price is *not* to recover costs but to capture value in the customer's mind.

**FIGURE 14.4**

**THE RELATIONSHIP BETWEEN CUSTOMER VALUE AND THE FIRM'S COSTS**

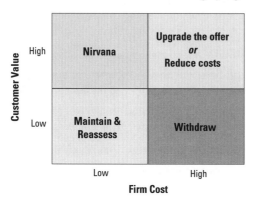

## COMPETITION

The firm should always consider competitive implications. Basing the firm's price on the competitors' price is legal and ensures price parity, but there are distinct disadvantages to focusing too heavily on the competitor's pricing strategy:

- *Price parity* with competitors devalues features and benefits and tends to *commoditize* products. It leads customers to focus their buying decisions on price.
- An *excessive price focus* may lead to losses for everyone, both the firm and its competitors.

Generally, the firm should not focus on beating the competitor's *price*. Rather, it should beat the competitor's *offer* — product, service, and other marketing-mix elements. The firm should make offers with greater value per unit price than the competitor. *Offer* superiority is crucial, not *price* superiority. Of course, price plays a critical balancing role.

**KEY IDEA**

➤ In high fixed cost/ low variable cost oligopolies, firms often cut prices to gain extra volume. Prices can spiral downward and profits vanish.

### HOW WILL COMPETITORS RESPOND TO THE FIRM'S PRICE CHANGES?

When making price changes, the firm should always consider competitors' likely responses. Although pricing tactics can be quite complicated, basically competitors have only three pricing options: raise, hold constant, or lower. Whether or not the firm's price moves are successful depends on these responses.

Assessing likely competitor response is always important. But in oligopolies, when there are few major competitors and fixed costs are high and variable costs are low, like airlines and many other highly capital-intensive industries, it is vital. When several competitors have poor profits, sometimes one firm cuts price to gain volume; others follow, and prices spiral downward. Sometimes firms launch *trial balloons*, strategic pre-announced price intentions to gauge likely competitor response. Warnings and other signals may pre-empt competitive moves but can raise antitrust issues. Successful and unsuccessful price leadership examples are:

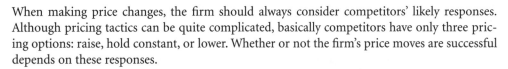

**Oligopoly Pricing**

**Successful price leadership**. In late 1999, Coca-Cola raised its concentrate price by 7 percent, twice the usual rate. Two weeks later, PepsiCo announced a similar increase.

**Unsuccessful price leadership**. In the early 1990s, American Airlines (AA) attempted to change the pricing structure in the domestic U.S. airline industry. Delta, United, Continental, Northwest, USAir, and American West quickly followed AA's lead. But TWA undercut AA's prices by 10 to 20 percent, and the attempt failed.

**Successful price leadership**. British Aluminum Company (BACO) competed fiercely against Alcoa and Alcan in the low-growth, barely profitable, British aluminum oligopoly. BACO divided the market into three areas: BACO's long-term contract customers — *ours*; competitors' long-term contract customers — *theirs*; and switchers — *up-for-grabs*. BACO resolved not to lose any *our* business on price. If it did lose some, BACO *punished* the competitor by pricing low at one of *theirs*. BACO effectively executed this *tit-for-tat* strategy; Alcoa and Alcan *got the message*.[10]

### HOW SHOULD THE FIRM RESPOND TO COMPETITORS' PRICE REDUCTIONS?

The firm's response to competitors' price reductions depends on its market position. Generally, strong firms should match price cuts only after exhausting other options. But weak firms with minimal sustainable differential advantage may have to respond right away. In general, only the low-cost producer wins when price-cutting is rampant; how it uses its cost advantage determines other competitors' fates.

Firms with dominant market shares often face severe price competition from small competitors and/or new entrants. These competitors may believe that the leader:

- has not carefully managed its costs, and that its own costs are lower.
- does not know individual product costs because of difficulties in allocating overhead.
- will not retaliate directly because it would sacrifice profits on its much larger volume.

Unless demand is *price elastic*, the firm should minimize direct price-cutting responses.[11] The nature of the competitive price reductions governs the firm's price and non-price options.

*Price options* include price retaliation in a different segment, selective price cuts, introducing a lower priced *fighting* brand, and — ultimately — cutting prices across the board. *Non-price* options include signalling to competitors, investing in fixed cost expenditures to reinforce the firm's position, clarifying and reinforcing the price/quality relationship, changing the basis of competition (for example, by bundling), and reducing customers' bargaining power by making pricing opaque. If these actions fail, the firm may have to partially or totally withdraw.

**KEY IDEA**

➤ Rampant price-cutting is disastrous for all but the low-cost producer.

**KEY IDEA**

➤ The firm should link pricing strategy to its strategic objectives.

## STRATEGIC OBJECTIVES

Choosing strategic objectives is a major component of developing market strategy. The three major options are growth in volume and market share, maximizing profits, or maximizing cash flow. Generally, each strategic objective relates to a particular pricing strategy:

**MAXIMIZE GROWTH IN VOLUME AND/OR MARKET SHARE.** The firm must offer high customer value — a value-to-price (V/P) ratio superior to competitors. Conditions for a high V/P strategy are:

- A price-elastic market
- Good ability to cut costs in the future
- Sufficient capacity to fulfill increases in demand
- Deep pockets to absorb initially low profit margins
- A desire to deter competitors

**KEY IDEA**

➤ The firm's major options for strategic objectives are: maximize growth in volume and/or market share, maximize profits, or maximize cash flow.

Dell's leadership drive in PCs and P&G's aggressive price strategy in disposable diapers follow this **penetration-pricing** approach.

**MAXIMIZE PROFITABILITY.** When the firm's major objective is maximizing profits, it provides less value to customers and retains more for itself. Firms using this **skim-pricing** approach include those whose products have patent protection, like pharmaceuticals, and pioneering high technology products — like DVD players and HDTV.

---

**Skim Pricing and Penetration Pricing**

Here we review *penetration pricing* and *skim pricing*, introduced in Chapter 10. These pricing strategies correspond to different strategic objectives: maximizing growth and/or market share, and maximizing profits, respectively.

**Penetration pricing.** The firm provides significant customer value by setting prices close to costs. Volume increases, unit costs fall, the firm reduces price, and volume increases... in a virtuous spiral. The firm forgoes high profits today in favor of achieving high volumes and ultimately earning profits from high unit volumes, but low profit margins.

**Skim pricing.** The firm retains value for itself by pricing high. It earns high profit margins, but provides less value to its relatively few customers. It reduces prices periodically — sequential skimming — to attract increasing numbers of customers.

---

**MAXIMIZE CASH FLOW.** If the firm plans a market withdrawal, maximizing cash flow is often a good short-term strategic objective. In Chapter 12, we discussed *harvesting* products as the approach to short-term cash-flow maximization.

# *Setting Prices*

## USING PERCEIVED CUSTOMER VALUE, COSTS, COMPETITION, AND STRATEGIC OBJECTIVES

As the firm sets prices, it should start with perceived customer value, consider costs, then factor in competitors and its strategic objectives.

### SETTING PRICE FOR A NEW PRODUCT

We illustrate the approach by considering Ace; this firm is setting price for a new manufacturing furnace. Ace believes its furnace offers superior value versus its competitor, Beta. Table 14.5 shows some data collected by Ace. Customers' startup costs and post-purchase costs are the same for both Ace and Beta. To frame the *right* approach to setting price, we first show the cost-plus and competitive-equivalence approaches, and then introduce the correct method:

**TABLE 14.5**

**DATA FOR PRICE-SETTING COLLECTED BY ACE FURNACE**

| Beta | Furnace price | $260,000 |
|------|---------------|----------|
| Ace | Economic value to the customer (EVC) | $360,000 |
| Ace | Direct out-of-pocket cost: variable and fixed | $100,000 |
| Ace | Fully loaded cost, including overhead allocations | $160,000 |

**COST-PLUS PRICING.** Since the pricing decision concerns a new product, Ace must consider the fully loaded cost — $160,000. Commonly used mark-ups in this industry are 75 percent and 50 percent. Price options are:

75 percent mark-up: Price = $160,000 × 1.75 = **$280,000**

50 percent mark-up: Price = $160,000 × 1.5  = **$240,000**

Note that at 75 percent mark-up, Ace's price exceeds Beta's — $280,000 versus $260,000. At 50 percent mark-up, Ace's price is less than Beta's — $240,000 versus $260,000. We do not know which is best.

**COMPETITIVE EQUIVALENCE PRICING.** Strict competitive equivalence suggests a $260,000 price. But Ace offers considerable extra value. If Ace sets price at $260,000, it should sell lots of furnaces. But does a $260,000 price represent appropriate value-sharing between Ace and its customers? Does this approach take into consideration Beta's response?

**THE *RIGHT* WAY TO SET PRICE.** Figure 14.5 diagrams the recommended three-step approach:

- **Step 1: Determine the maximum price.** The maximum price is the EVC from Ace's furnace — $360,000.[12] At $360,000, rational customers should be indifferent between furnaces from Ace and Beta. (Of course, customers may believe Ace's furnace poses a greater risk because the new product has no track record — we ignore this factor in the illustration.)
- **Step 2: Determine the minimum price.** The minimum price is Ace's fully loaded cost — $160,000. Ace earns profit contribution at any price above direct out-of-pocket cost — $100,000, but this is an incorrect figure for the minimum price of a new product.
- **Step 3: Set the price based on Ace's strategic objectives and Beta's likely competitive response.** From steps 1 and 2, Ace's price should be between $360,000 and $160,000 — the crucial question is where. Ace should consider its strategic objectives and its forecast of Beta's likely response — these variables are probably correlated. Possible strategic objectives are:
  - **Toehold.** Ace wants a market presence but has little other ambition. Perhaps it identified a small high-price segment. It sets price around $320,000. Sales will be low, but profit margins will be high. Beta is unlikely to respond.

- **Short-term profit.** Ace has greater ambition than in the toehold option, so its price is closer to Beta's $260,000. Because Ace offers greater customer value, it may set the price between $260,000 and, say, $300,000. Ace will probably take some volume from Beta — the closer Ace's price to $260,000, the more likely Beta will reduce price. Prices significantly above $260,000 signal Beta that Ace wishes to avoid price competition.

- **Market share.** Ace is ready to battle Beta for market share. At $260,000 and below, Ace offers customers significant value. Between $220,000 and $240,000, Ace may sell many furnaces with good profit margins. But these prices will encourage a strong response from Beta. Ace must plan how to address Beta's likely actions.

When setting price, Ace should also consider customers' *potential lifetime value.* It should ask and answer several questions. Is this a one-time purchase, or will customers purchase more furnaces? Can Ace sell furnace parts and accessories and/or multi-year service contracts? Can Ace sell complementary products and services? Will customers recommend Ace to others?

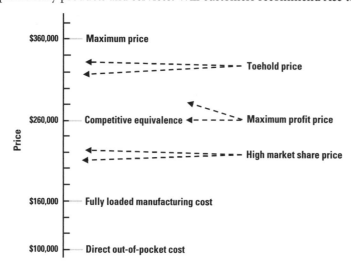

**FIGURE 14.5**

**PRICING ANALYSIS FOR A NEW ITEM OF CAPITAL EQUIPMENT**

## CHANGING THE PRICE OF AN EXISTING PRODUCT

There are many reasons to change price. Sometimes competitive pressures are critical, but other pressures may be internal. Financial managers may want to increase profit margins by raising prices. The sales force may lobby for price decreases to gain increased volume. Critical questions for the firm are:

- Can the firm *increase price* without losing significant volume? How much volume will it lose? Will the incremental profit margin offset the lost volume?

- If the firm *decreases price*, will it gain significant volume? How much volume will it gain? Will the extra volume make up for the reduced profit margin?

Figure 14.6 shows a recommended five-step process for considering price changes.

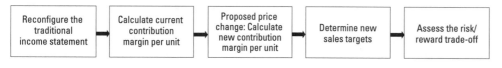

**FIGURE 14.6**

**A PROCESS FOR DETERMINING PRICE CHANGES**

**Step 1: Reconfigure the traditional income statement.** We partition costs into two categories: variable costs and fixed costs[13] — Table 14.6.

**TABLE 14.6**

**EXAMPLE OF PRODUCT INCOME STATEMENT ($000s)**

| | |
|---|---|
| Sales revenues (SR) (40 million lbs. @ 50 cents/lb. selling price [SP]) | $20,000 |
| Variable costs (VC) | $12,000 |
| Contribution margin (CM) | $ 8,000 |
| Fixed costs (FC) | $ 6,600 |
| Net profit before taxes (NP) | $ 1,400 |

**Step 2: Calculate current contribution margin per unit.** Contribution margin (CM) is an important concept. CM must cover fixed costs; any remainder is profit. CM equals sales revenues (SR) less variable costs (VC). (Hence, variable costs do not enter future calculations using CM.) Table 14.7 shows that **contribution margin per unit (CMU)** is simply CM on a per-unit basis — similarly for **variable cost per unit (VCU)**:

**TABLE 14.7**

**CALCULATION OF CURRENT CONTRIBUTION MARGIN PER UNIT (CMU)**

| | Total Revenue | Unit Sales (000s)* | Per Unit Basis | |
|---|---|---|---|---|
| Sales revenue (SR) *less* | $20 million | 40,000 | Price per unit (SP) | 50 cents |
| Variable costs (VC) *equals* | $12 million | 40,000 | Variable cost per unit (VCU) | 30 cents |
| Contribution margin (CM) | $ 8 million | 40,000 | Contribution margin per unit (CMU) | 20 cents |

\* In lbs.

**Contribution margin rate (CMR)** is closely related to CMU. CMR is the fraction (percentage) of sales revenues available for fixed costs and profit. CMR equals CMU divided by the selling price (SP).

$$CMR \equiv CMU/SP$$
$$CMR = 20¢/50¢ = 0.4 = 40\%$$

**Step 3: Proposed Price Change: Calculate new contribution margin per unit.** Suppose the firm is considering two options: Raise price by 5 cents, and lower price by 5 cents. VCU does not change. But:

- **Decrease price.** A price cut from 50 cents to 45 cents *decreases* CMU:

$$SP \equiv VCU + CMU \qquad \text{so that:}$$

    45 cents ≡ 30 cents/lb + 15 cents/lb.
    Hence, new CMU = **15 cents**

- **Increase price.** A price increase from 50 cents to 55 cents *increases* CMU:

    55 cents ≡ 30 cents + 25 cents
    Hence, new CMU = **25 cents**

**KEY IDEA**

➤ CMU and CMR are critical concepts in price-setting. They allow the firm to calculate breakeven sales volumes for various pricing options.

**Step 4: Determine new sales targets.** Determine the necessary sales volumes at the proposed prices to make the same profit — $1.4 million — as at the old 50-cent price. These are minimum requirements.

- **Decrease price.** Unit sales volume for $1.4 million profit when price = 45 cents:

    Target sales volume (lbs.)    = (Fixed costs + profit objective)/CMU
                                  = ($6.6 million + $1.4 million)/15 cents
                                  = $8 million/15 cents
                                  = **53.3 million lbs.**

    Target sales revenue ($)      = 53.3 million lbs. × 45 cents
                                  = **$24 million**

- **Increase price.** Unit sales volume for $1.4 million profit when price = 55 cents:

    Target sales volume (units)   = (Fixed costs + profit objective)/CMU
                                  = ($6.6 million + $1.4 million)/25 cents
                                  = $8 million/25 cents
                                  = **32 million lbs.**

    Target sales revenue ($)      = 32 million lbs. × 55 cents
                                  = **$17.6 million**

We summarize these results in Table 14.8.

| Price | CMU | Target Volume | Sales Volume Percentage change | Target Revenues |
|-------|-----|---------------|-------------------------------|-----------------|
| 50 cents | 20 cents | 40 million lbs. | — | $20 million |
| 45 cents | 15 cents | 53.3 million lbs. | + 32.5% | $24 million |
| 55 cents | 25 cents | 32 million lbs. | − 20% | $17.6 million |

**TABLE 14.8**

**SUMMARY OF PRICING CALCULATIONS**

**Step 5: Assess the risk/reward trade-off.** The results from Step 4 *do not make* the pricing decision. The firm must assess the likelihood it can meet and exceed the new volume targets: 53.3 million lbs. @ 45 cents/lb., or 32 million lbs. @ 55 cents/lb. The answer depends, in part, on the competitive response. Considering all factors, the firm must decide if it will change price and take the chance of meeting or exceeding its volume targets.

**A SHORT-CUT APPROACH.** Breakeven volumes depend heavily on the firm's cost structure. We capture cost structure with CMR = CMU/SP. There were three CMRs in the prior illustration:

SP = 50 cents per lb., CMR = 20 cents/50 cents = 40.0%

SP = 45 cents per lb., CMR = 15 cents/45 cents = 33.3%

SP = 55 cents per lb., CMR = 25 cents/55 cents = 45.6%

Table 14.9 is a generalized chart showing CMR on the horizontal axis, and *percentage price change* on the vertical axis. Let's consider two situations: low CMR and high CMR:

- **Low CMR.** Variable costs are high; fixed costs are low. Table 14.9 shows that if CMR = 10% and the firm cuts price by 5%, it would have to double sales to maintain profits — 100 to 200.

- **High CMR.** Fixed costs are high; variable costs are low. If CMR = 40% and the firm cuts price by 5%, it would need a 14% sales increase to maintain profits — 100 to 114.

| Percentage Change in Price | Current Contribution Margin Rate (CMR) | | | | | | | |
|---|---|---|---|---|---|---|---|---|
| | 10% | 15% | 20% | 25% | 30% | 35% | 40% | 45% |
| +25 | 29 | 38 | 45 | 50 | 55 | 58 | 61 | 64 |
| +20 | 33 | 43 | 50 | 56 | 60 | 64 | 67 | 69 |
| +15 | 40 | 50 | 57 | 63 | 69 | 70 | 73 | 75 |
| +10 | 50 | 60 | 67 | 72 | 75 | 78 | 80 | 82 |
| +5 | 67 | 75 | 80 | 83 | 86 | 88 | 89 | 90 |
| 0 | 100 | 100 | 100 | 100 | 100 | 100 | 100 | 100 |
| -5 | 200 | 150 | 133 | 125 | 120 | 117 | 114 | 113 |
| -10 | | 300 | 200 | 187 | 150 | 140 | 133 | 129 |
| -15 | | | 400 | 260 | 200 | 175 | 160 | 150 |
| -20 | | | | 500 | 300 | 233 | 200 | 180 |
| -25 | | | | | 600 | 350 | 267 | 225 |

**TABLE 14.9**

**PERCENTAGE OF CURRENT UNIT VOLUME REQUIRED TO MAINTAIN CONSTANT PROFITS FOR VARIOUS PRICE CHANGES AT DIFFERENT CONTRIBUTION MARGIN RATES**

**IMPLICATIONS.** The CMR is critical to setting prices. Generally, if CMR is high, the firm should identify price-sensitive segments where small price reductions lead to significant volume increases. Major airlines use this approach; each carrier has myriad prices for each flight.[14] For software, variable costs are typically very low and CMRs are very high. By contrast, if CMR is low, the firm should focus on increasing profit margins by reducing variable costs and raising prices.

*Marketing Question*

The sales force is pressuring you to cut prices, so they can increase sales. Finance pushes for price increases to raise margins. How would you respond?

## *Marketing Question*

Identify six specific pricing tools you have observed. Why do you think they were used?

# TACTICAL PRICING

**Tactical pricing** is the ongoing stream of pricing decisions the firm makes on a daily basis. Generally, robust strategic pricing drives good tactical pricing, but tactical pricing has a major impact on firm performance. A common misconception is that a product has a single price; in fact, single prices are rare.

## THE PRICING TOOLKIT

Sometimes the firm wants a price change to be highly visible to customers and competitors; other times, it wants to keep it secret. Firms often set highly visible list prices (or rate cards), but then use the list price as the basis for discounts and rebates; actual prices may be 20 or 30 percent off list. The firm can base discounts on many factors like quantity, firm/customer relationship, inventory, selling effort, timing, and matching competitors.

Other less visible ways to change prices include allowances — for advertising, selling effort, trade-ins, and returns. Credit availability and terms (time to pay and interest rates) can be potent tools, especially during inflation. Freight or shipping charges are important price-changing mechanisms. In a CIF (cost, insurance, freight) price, the supplier pays; in a FOB (free on board) price, the customer pays.[15] The firm can change price by modifying the customer's inventory; in JIT (just-in-time) systems, the firm holds inventory near the customer's plant and cuts the customer's inventory holding costs.

Leasing versus purchasing offers customers the ability to reduce their capital employed; and product guarantees and warranties reduce prices by protecting customers from repair costs. The firm should recognize that **toolkit** elements are differentially important across customers. For an equivalent price reduction, one customer may prefer a larger discount, another may want an advertising allowance. In B2B, the reward system for purchasing staff may be important. Some customers incentivize staff based on price reductions off the invoice price. A cash discount applied when the firm receives the order may be very attractive! Sometimes firms, and customers, prefer barter and buy-backs to money transactions.

**Barter**

- British Aerospace earned $20 billion revenues from Saudi Arabia for Tornado fighters, Hawk trainers, and backup services. Most payments were in oil.
- During Argentina's early 2000s deep recession, consumers acquired food and clothing, psychological counseling, and dental work, all by barter.
- In Siberia's Altai territory, over 50 percent of economic transactions are bartered; some large firms transact 90 percent of their business by barter.
- A Polish organization contracted with Norton to erect a turn-key grinding wheel factory. Part of Norton's payment was a buyback of products made in the plant.[16]

## KEY IDEA

➤ Single product prices are rare in the real world.

➤ Pricing actions vary between highly visible and opaque.

Finally, a firm can modify prices by shifting between **unbundling** — pricing items separately like an a la carte restaurant meal, and **bundling** — each offer has a single price, much like a prix fixe meal. **Mixed bundling** combines bundled and unbundled prices (Chapter 12).

## THE POCKET PRICE AND PRICE WATERFALL

Sometimes firms use toolkit items appropriately, but many have poor systems for tracking their use. List price and invoice price are transparent, but other pricing elements are often buried in myriad financial accounts. Early payment discounts are in an interest expense account; cooperative advertising allowances are in promotion and advertising accounts.[17] Hence, these firms do not know their **pocket prices** — the money they actually receive (in their pockets). When they do the analysis, they are surprised to find broad variability with little rationale. Small unprofitable customers may receive large volume discounts, but larger profitable customers do not. The most aggressive, clever, or persistent customers get the best price, aka the *squeaky wheel* syndrome. They work the supplier's management systems for extra discounts; the firm's salespeople often cooperate:

> Knowing Oracle's concern with end-of-quarter results, customers waited for salespeople to offer larger discounts. Oracle booked most sales at the end of the quarter. To address the problem, Oracle started rejecting last-minute deals with large discounts.

The **price waterfall** in Figure 14.7 illustrates how pricing toolkit elements cumulate to produce the pocket price. Customers earn 27.6 percent from four separate discounts to make the invoice price 72.4 percent of the standard list price. They earn 15.3 percent from seven other toolkit items to make the pocket price 57.1 percent of list price.

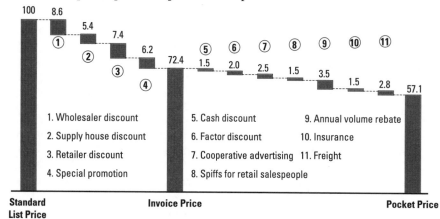

1. Wholesaler discount
2. Supply house discount
3. Retailer discount
4. Special promotion
5. Cash discount
6. Factor discount
7. Cooperative advertising
8. Spiffs for retail salespeople
9. Annual volume rebate
10. Insurance
11. Freight

Standard List Price    Invoice Price    Pocket Price

**FIGURE 14.7**

HYPOTHETICAL PRICE WATERFALL FOR A CONSUMER DURABLES MANUFACTURER AVERAGED OVER ALL ACCOUNTS. AVERAGE DISCOUNT FROM STANDARD LIST PRICE, (PERCENT)

To optimize its pricing, the firm must understand the pocket price for each customer and the way these prices developed. This task may not be easy; the firm may have to modify its accounting systems. One firm took several initiatives to address its price-waterfall problems:

- Acted aggressively to bring over-discounted customers into line with other customers.
- Delivered specific benefits to profitable customers to increase their volumes.
- Brought price-setting under control by improving the accounting system.
- Tightened up on discounts and based sales force compensation on the pocket price.

## KEY ISSUES IN SETTING PRICES

Despite the various tactics and tools available for price-setting, one important issue should be very clear. The degree of discretion open to the firm depends on its perceived customer value and costs. Firms like Microsoft and P&G that offer high customer value at low costs have the most flexibility. In this section, we discuss designing pricing approaches, setting the actual price, and special topics associated with price-setting.

**DESIGNING PRICING APPROACHES.** The firm can choose among several pricing methods:

- **Price discrimination and variable pricing.** The firm could set a single price for all customers, but profits are higher if it sets different prices for different customers or segments. The firm can amplify this effect by designing multiple offers with different values: AmEx offers several personal credit cards — green, gold, platinum, and black — at successively higher prices. The core benefit is identical, but extra services differentiate the offers.

  But there are benefits to price inflexibility. When salespeople have no price discretion, aggressive customers cannot negotiate price discounts. Also, a single price is simpler to understand and account for, and provides a perception of fairness that multiple prices do not.

KEY IDEA

➤ The firm needs good systems to track elements in the pricing toolkit.

➤ The pricing toolkit produces the pocket price via the price waterfall.

➤ Pricing toolkit elements are differentially important to customers.

"It is not because of the few thousand francs which would have to be spent to put a roof over the third-class carriages or to upholster the third-class seats that some company or other has open carriages with wooden benches ... What the company is trying to do is to prevent the passengers who can pay the first-class fare from traveling third-class: it hits the poor, not because it wants to hurt them, but to frighten the rich ... And it is again for the same reason that companies, having proved almost cruel to the third-class passengers and mean to the second-class one, become lavish in dealing with first-class passengers. Having refused the poor what is necessary, they give the rich what is superfluous."[18]

*Marketing Question*

Compare and contrast pricing in 19th-century French railroads with 21st-century passenger air travel.

- **Dynamic pricing.** Some firms employ this special case of price discrimination where demand varies over time. Some prices change *predictably*, like cities setting road and bridge tolls higher during rush hours or on weekdays. Electric utilities, movie theaters, and telecommunications firms price by time of day, hotels by day and season. Airlines use dynamic pricing continuously via **yield management** systems, algorithms that adjust fares based on demand and available seat capacity.

- **Variable-rate versus flat-rate pricing.** Firms selling services price by use — **variable-rate** pricing — or by time period — **flat-rate** pricing. Variable prices may earn greater revenues, but fixed prices are easier to administer. In the past, ski hills priced by chair lift ride; today, most charge by flat rate — per day, week, or season. Commuter rail travelers and season ticket holders for sporting and cultural events pay a single price per season; others pay by the trip or event. Some firms set both flat fees and use fees, like cellular phone providers.

- **Customer-driven pricing.** Mostly, sellers set a price, and buyers can accept it or not. In customer-driven pricing, the customer names the price; the firm can accept it or not. At Priceline.com, customers *name their own price* for plane tickets, hotel reservations, mortgages, and cars. If the product is available, they must complete the purchase. Customer-driven pricing has potential in services, where products cannot be inventoried.

*Marketing Question*

Next time you fly, ask fellow travelers their prices, and compare. What is the basis for the price differences? Be prepared for them to be disgruntled!

- **Auction pricing.** A form of customer-driven pricing where customers compete with other potential buyers to purchase a product. In an English auction, prices start low, and potential buyers bid up the price. Auctioneers seek the buyer willing to pay the highest price. In Vickery auction (sealed-bid) the winning bidder pays the price of the second-highest bids; Google uses Vickery auctions for online advertising. In a Dutch auction, prices start high and reduce until a buyer bids.

**SETTING THE ACTUAL PRICE.** Several issues are important when setting the actual price:

- **Promotional pricing versus steady pricing.** In many cases, sales are sensitive to short-term price promotions. Firms often execute price promotions by comparing the sale price with the regular (or reference) price. In **loss-leader pricing**, retailers deliberately take losses on some products to build customer traffic for others. Despite sales increases, promotions can have long-term negative effects:

  - **Time-shifting.** Customers buy for inventory to avoid paying the full price later.

  - **Poor forecasting.** Demand exceeds forecast and customers are upset. Hong Kong Disneyland's one-day discounted tickets were not valid on *special days* like Chinese New Year. Chinese New Year was four days in Hong Kong, but longer on the mainland. When Chinese New Year was over in Hong Kong but still continued on the mainland, mainlanders flooded into Hong Kong, and Disneyland had to close its gates.

  - **Diversion.** Retailers and/or distributors may *divert* the product to non-competing outlets, often in different geographic areas.

  - **Brand image.** The promotion has a negative effect especially for upscale brands.

  - **Hidden costs.** Frequent price promotions can be difficult and costly to administer. Some firms have abandoned promotional pricing altogether.

- **Fees and surcharges.** Many firms use **fees and surcharges** to increase their pocket prices, especially in difficult times. Banks charge for bounced checks and ATM use; airlines charge for airport security, landing, change of flight, checked bags, and fuel. Revenues and profits increase, but overly aggressive fees may lead customers to go elsewhere:

- **Psychological pricing.** For many customers, the psychological distance from $9.95 to $10.00 is greater than from $10.00 to $10.05; hence, firms set prices to end with 95 cents.[19]

> As hotel occupancy declined in 2001, many hotels added fees for housekeeping; *amenities* like tennis courts, putting greens, the pool; unordered newspapers; parking; and unopened water bottles. Guest reaction was negative, and many hotels dropped the fees.

- **Pricing bases.** Most industries have accepted bases for setting prices, but some are changing. Major advertisers are paying advertising agencies by *results* rather than by *percentage of billings*, and *Capon's Marketing Framework* is available online to students who *pay what they think it's worth* at the end of the semester.

## PRICING MANAGEMENT AND PRICING POLICY

Now you have learned about both strategic considerations and tactics and tools in pricing, you probably have several questions: How should the firm actually set prices? Who should be responsible, managers closest to the products or a centralized team? Generally, centralized pricing provides greater control. Decentralized pricing offers greater market sensitivity and may lead to short-term profit maximization, but may have long-run negative effects like[20]:

- **Information sharing.** Customers talk to each other about prices; those paying higher prices exert pressure on the firm to reduce them.

- **Limited perspective.** A local decision-maker like a salesperson is unlikely to consider the long-run impact on the firm's customer base of a price reduction to one customer.

- **Negotiation.** Customers learn to place end-of-period orders when suppliers are anxious about revenues and are prepared to reduce prices. They also learn to play off multiple vendors against one another.

For these reasons, many firms develop pricing policies through a governance process that addresses long-run strategic questions like pricing new products, as well as short-term tactical decisions. They set guidelines for addressing multi-person buying decisions like those involving purchasing agents (who tend to focus only on price), and engineers, operations, and marketing personnel who have other concerns.

Some experts argue that price-setting is a strategic capability, comparable to new product development and advertising.[21] Most firms have significant capabilities for creating customer value; they have less expertise in measuring and capturing value. Far too often, managers with pricing responsibility do not understand price-volume-profit trade-offs. They lack good analytic skills and rely instead on gut instinct, hearsay, responding to competitors, and rules of thumb.

The "Marketing University" at pharmaceuticals giant Roche builds pricing knowledge and teaches three areas of pricing capability:

- **Human capital.** Broad pricing knowledge at the decision-makers' command.

- **Systems capital.** Supports price decisions by: providing product and customer profitability; tracking competitors' prices and discounts; managing price changes; quickly responding to requests for price quotations; assembling accurate information on customers'

## KEY IDEA

➤ The firm should develop pricing policies at high levels in the firm.

➤ Price-setting can be a strategic capability.

purchase history including actual prices paid; tracking the firm's prices, discounts, and reasons for different customers' discounts; and testing different prices.

- **Social capital.** The ability to negotiate agreements on prices among the firm's decision-makers.

Firms with these capabilities make better pricing decisions.

## LEGAL AND ETHICAL ISSUES IN PRICING

**KEY IDEA**

➤ Many governments scrutinize prices for illegal activity.

Most firms engage professionals to advise on the legal implications of pricing decisions; we can only scratch the surface. Marketers should have a working knowledge of three broad topics: anticompetitive pricing, fairness in consumer pricing, and dumping.[22]

**ANTICOMPETITIVE PRICING.** Includes price conspiracies, predatory pricing, and discriminatory pricing:

- **Price conspiracies.** Price conspiracies occur when a firm and its competitors overtly collude to fix prices or make implicit agreements to price in parallel or exchange price information. These actions generally lead to higher prices and harm customers. A high-level U.S. businessman, secretly recorded by an FBI whistleblower, summed up the price-fixing philosophy: "Our competitors are our friends; our customers are the enemies!" Two senior executives at Archer Daniels Midland, a giant U.S. agribusiness company, earned long jail terms for price collusion.[23]

- **Predatory pricing.** Dominant firms sometimes engage in **predatory pricing** to protect market share from competitive threats. They temporarily price very low to thwart the threat, often using profits from one product to cross-subsidize another. The U.S. defines predatory pricing as pricing below average variable costs, with the intention of putting the competitor out of business.

- **Discriminatory pricing.** Under the U.S. Robinson-Patman Act, firms cannot sell identical products to different customers at different prices when the effect is to lessen competition or create a monopoly. Defenses against Robinson-Patman are cost-justification for price differences and meeting a competitive threat.

**FAIRNESS IN CONSUMER PRICING.** Key fairness issues for consumers are deceptive pricing and **bait and switch:**

- **Deceptive pricing.** False prices or prices that might confuse or mislead customers are deceptive. To illustrate: If the firm advertises a product, price = $X, but the product cannot function without other critical elements, the $X price is deceptive. (That's why many products carry the disclaimer "batteries not included.") Difficult-to-understand prices and price information in *fine print* can also be deceptive.

- **Bait and switch.** Retailers advertise a low price product but have only limited availability. The *bait* sells quickly, then retailers offer most customers a higher price product, the *switch*.

**DUMPING.** Some firms **dump** products in foreign markets at "less than fair market value," below home market prices, and often below average costs. Dumping prices are often higher than variable costs, so the firm earns a positive contribution margin. This practice may be illegal in the receiving country if it causes or threatens material harm to a domestic industry.

## KEY MESSAGES

- Pricing is a big deal. Pricing decisions have a major impact on profitability.

- Four critical considerations should enter the firm's pricing decisions: perceived customer value, costs, competition, and strategic objectives.

  - **Perceived customer value**. The firm must make key decisions about creating, measuring, and capturing value. It must understand customer price sensitivity.

  - **Costs**. Many firms use cost inappropriately by implementing cost-plus approaches to setting price. Costs have three proper roles: birth control, death control, and profit planning.

  - **Competition.** Critical issues for the firm are predicting how competitors will respond to its price changes, and deciding how to respond to competitors' price reductions. The firm can take a variety of price and non-price actions.

  - **Strategic objectives**. The firm should link its strategic objectives — growth in volume and/or market share, maximizing profits, or maximizing cash flow — to its pricing actions.

- To set price for a new product, the firm should start with perceived customer value, consider costs, then factor in competitors and its strategic objectives.

- When contemplating changing price for an existing product, the firm should use a contribution margin approach to assess volumes needed to meet various profit targets.

- The firm has many pricing toolkit elements available for setting the actual price.

- Undisciplined use of pricing toolkit elements leads to price waterfall problems. Appropriate systems and pricing discipline can address these problems.

- The firm should consider many issues in designing pricing approaches and setting actual prices.

- The ability to set prices well requires the firm to invest in human, systems, and social capital.

- The firm should be aware that price-setting is fraught with legal and ethical issues.

# CHAPTER 15

# MARKETING COMMUNICATIONS AND ADVERTISING

## LEARNING OBJECTIVES

When you have completed this chapter, you will be able to:

- Understand the communications challenges and opportunities that firms face.
- Articulate the causes of miscommunication problems.
- Enumerate the various communications tools that the firm can use.
- Integrate communications tools into a communications strategy.
- Distinguish between *push*, *pull*, and combination *push/pull* communications strategies.
- Understand the key issues in setting communications objectives.
- Articulate how advertising works.
- Define and measure advertising objectives.
- Design an advertising campaign.
- Know when to use each of the firm's major non-personal communication options — advertising, direct marketing, publicity and public relations, sales promotion, and the Internet.
- Evaluate the non-personal communications mix.

## OPENING CASE: MASTERCARD INTERNATIONAL

*In 1997, MasterCard (MC), a credit card company owned by its member banks, was in trouble. Market share had declined for ten straight years, and competitive pressures from Visa, Discover, and AmEx were intensifying. Although MC enjoyed the same retail acceptance as Visa, its top-of-mind awareness was ten percentage points inferior. MC was also losing the support of member banks, both domestic and international, and in the U.S. its share of direct-mail solicitations trailed Visa significantly.*

*MC conducted an extensive advertising agency review and selected McCann-Erickson (ME). ME concluded that this once-dominant brand had lost emotional relevance with consumers. It had also lost credibility with critical member banks; they were claiming brand ownership and MC was losing power. Worse, the MC brand had different campaigns in almost every international market and was being outspent by Visa and AmEx.*

*ME's research in the U.S. and key international markets indicated that consumers viewed MC as a stodgy, functional, everyday brand, with little relevance for consumer aspirations. By contrast, AmEx was professional, worldly, and responsible, and Visa was sociable, stylish, and on-the-go. MC was unassuming, unpretentious, and practical. ME saw its task as shifting MasterCard from an emotionally neutral generic card to a card that consumers felt good about using.*

*ME's analysis of secondary data revealed a shift from the materialistic and outer-directed consumer culture of the 1980s and early 1990s. Success symbols like wearing designer clothes, shopping at prestigious stores, staying at luxury hotels, owning expensive cars, and using a prestigious credit card had been replaced. The new success symbols were being in control of, and satisfied with, one's life, having a good home and family, and being able to afford what was really important. The vast majority of consumers believed that an unpaid credit card balance was "necessary and justified." ME dubbed this emerging mindset as* good revolving *and set out to target* good revolvers, *by helping them to lead* rich lives. *Its selling idea was that MasterCard is* The Better Way To Pay For Everything That Matters.*

*Armed with this insight and direction, the three-person creative team of Joyce King Thomas, Jeroen Bours, and Jonathan Cranin brainstormed extensively for a month. The tag line, "Some things money can't buy" came to Cranin in the shower. A couple of weeks later, over Sunday morning coffee and bagels, Thomas and Bours conceived the first advertisement — set at a baseball game featuring some ordinary transactions. In the ad, voice-over actor Billy Crudup intoned, "Two tickets, $28; hot dogs, popcorn and soda, $18; autographed baseball, $45; real conversation with 11-year-old-son, priceless ... there are some things money can't buy. For everything else, there's MasterCard."*

*Since its inception in October 1997, ME has crafted more than 300 TV commercials, in 50 languages, shown in 108 countries. Globally, its work for MasterCard is the largest singular campaign ever and has won well over one hundred creative awards. Most important, the* Priceless *campaign has delivered impressive results for MasterCard. From 1997 onwards, MasterCard's gross dollar volume increased by well over 250 percent, banks issued 980 million cards, brand awareness rose significantly, and the gap with Visa narrowed.*

**CASE QUESTION**

How do you account for MasterCard's success? What other advertising campaigns do you consider memorable? Why?

---

We've all heard the popular saying, "If we build a better mousetrap, customers will come." Rubbish! Customers will not come unless they know about the mousetrap; that's the purpose of communication. To be successful, the firm must communicate the benefits and value of its offer to target customers. Also, good communication by itself has value in its impact on customers. Many communications tools and techniques are available for the firm — personal selling, advertising, direct marketing, packaging, publicity, public relations, sales promotion, trade shows, product placement, websites, e-mail, quasi-personal communication, and viral marketing — aka managed word-of-mouth. This vast array is both a blessing and a curse for marketing professionals. As a blessing, firms now have many alternatives for sending messages to their communications targets. The curse is the difficulty, in time and cost, of coordinating multiple messages to multiple targets, to produce a coherent, consistent, and integrated whole.

The term **integrated marketing communications** captures the idea of coordinating all communications messages with the *right* communication tools and techniques to the *right* audiences, at the *right* times. In this chapter, we review communications strategies and tactics for reaching target audiences and achieving the firm's objectives.

After introducing integrated communications in general, we explore the advertising process, strategies and methodologies. We also address marketing communications tools like direct marketing, publicity and public relations (P&PR), and sales promotion, and explore how the Internet is affecting marketing communications strategies.

## COMMUNICATIONS: PROCESS AND TOOLS

P&G used demographic and psychographic research to identify *chatters* — consumers who effectively influence others about new products. It launched its Physique brand of hair-care products by targeting *chatters* with direct-to-consumer samples. P&G's website encouraged visitors to tell a friend — it generated one million referrals in six months.

### THE COMMUNICATIONS PROCESS

Before we get into the marketing aspects of integrated communication, let's revisit the principles of communication. Figure 15.1 shows the basis for any **communication process**. The *sender* sends a *message* to a *receiver*. In turn, the *receiver* receives that message. The dotted line shows that, in some communication processes, the *receiver* also communicates with the *sender*.

The ideal situation occurs when the receiver receives the message that the sender intended to send. If this does not occur, there is **miscommunication** — not a good outcome for the firm. There are three main causes of miscommunication:

- **Encoding.** Typically, someone in the firm decides on the intended message, but this message is not sent. Perhaps the advertising agency misinterprets the product's positioning and does not craft an appropriate message. Or salespersons' training is ineffective, and they don't communicate the *right* message.

- **Distortion.** The communication is distorted while being sent, and the receiver does not receive the sent message. Consumers receive similar print and TV advertisements differently, and they may receive a TV ad running on *Comedy Central* differently from an identical message on *60 Minutes*. Or the salesperson's accent may affect the message the customer receives.

- **Decoding.** Communications targets have selective attention, selective perception, and/or selective retention, perhaps related to perception, memory, or belief systems. Hence, the message is misperceived and/or misunderstood.

A critical challenge for marketers is understanding and minimizing these causes of miscommunication.

### KEY IDEA

➤ In the communications process, senders send information, and receivers receive information.

➤ Miscommunication arises from problems in encoding, distortion, and decoding.

**FIGURE 15.1**

THE COMMUNICATIONS PROCESS

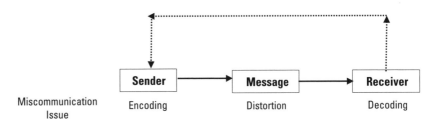

### COMMUNICATIONS TOOLS

Communications tools are the ways marketers communicate with target audiences. Two traditional categories are **personal communication** and **non-personal communication**. We add two extra categories: **quasi-personal communication**, like the Internet, and **word-of-mouth communication (WOM)** that occurs between customers and potential customers.

**PERSONAL COMMUNICATION.** Interpersonal (often face-to-face) communications occur between individuals or groups. In a marketing context, most **personal communication** is between salespeople and other firm representatives like technical- and customer-service personnel, interacting with customers individually or as team members. In many firms, **telemarketers** supplement and/or replace field salespeople. The firm scripts some personal communications, but most is spontaneous, evolving during the interaction.

**NON-PERSONAL COMMUNICATION.** Much communication that marketers use occurs without interpersonal contact between sender and receiver, particularly in B2C marketing.[1] The firm has greater control over message content in non-personal communication:

- **Advertising.** The firm pays for communications directed at a mass audience. Advertising embraces different modes and types of media. *Visual-static media* — printed matter — includes billboards, brochures, magazines, newspapers, point-of-purchase displays, signage, and trade journals. *Visual-dynamic media* includes television, movies, and online advertising. *Audio* includes radio and newer communications types like podcasts.[2]

- **Direct marketing.** Includes all paid and sponsored communications directed at individuals. Most direct marketing is printed mail, but more modern versions include audio/video tapes, DVD, CD-ROM, e-mail, and fax.

- **Packaging.** The value of the package extends beyond containing the product. It can also be a communications vehicle, delivering information and visual appeal.

- **Publicity.** Publicity is usually defined as communication for which the firm does not pay directly. Typically, the firm provides or *places* information like a story, press release, photograph, or video with a third-party transmitter. The transmitter, like a news organization, magazine, or industry analyst, incorporates the material in its own communications.

- **Public relations (PR).** PR embraces publicity but is broader, including other ways of managing the firm's image to gain favorable responses. It might include sponsoring events, giving speeches, participating in community activities, donating money to charity, and other public-facing activities.

- **Sales promotion.** These communications provide extra value to customers and are often created to induce immediate sales. Consumer promotions include coupons, contests, games, rebates, premiums, samples, and point-of-purchase materials. Special forms of sales promotions are:

  - **Trade shows.** In many industries, suppliers or vendors display and demonstrate their products to large numbers of current and potential customers, at one time, in one convenient location. In turn, customers can communicate with large numbers of suppliers offering similar products and services.

  - **Product placement.** The firm places its products in movies and TV shows. Placement can be real or virtual via electronic insertion of signs, logos, and products.

- **The Internet.** We see promotional information electronically through banners and pop-ups on websites, blogs, and other methods. These differ from other non-personal communications inasmuch as customers often initiate or self-select the information they receive. Primitive or Web 1.0 websites are mere *brochureware*, but more sophisticated sites engage recipients, morphing into *quasi-personal communication*.

**QUASI-PERSONAL COMMUNICATION.** Interaction and feedback without human involvement, usually via artificial intelligence, is quasi-personal communication (QPC). Customers can talk to computer servers via voice recognition software. QPC is developing rapidly on the Internet, where firms and customers communicate on a one-on-one basis.[3]

**KEY IDEA**

➤ Personal communication is *face-to-face* with individuals or groups.

**KEY IDEA**

➤ Non-personal communication occurs without interpersonal contact between sender and receiver.

---

*Marketing Question*

When you last contemplated getting a cellular phone: How did potential suppliers communicate with you? What personal communication methods did they use? What non-personal methods? Was any quasi-personal method involved? Did any supplier encourage WOM? Which communication method(s) were credible and engaging? Which methods had the greatest impact on your cell-phone selection and cellular service? Did the communication methods change during your buying process?

---

**KEY IDEA**

➤ Quasi-personal communications embrace interaction and feedback without human involvement.

➤ Word-of-mouth communication occurs among customers and potential customers.

**WORD-OF-MOUTH (WOM) COMMUNICATION.** Communication among customers and potential customers about a firm or product can be positive or negative for the firm, depending on customers' experiences. Because customers have no commercial interest, they often have higher credibility than paid communicators. Typically, firms have little control over **WOM**, but increasingly, they orchestrate **buzz-marketing**, **guerilla-marketing**, or **viral-marketing** campaigns to encourage positive word-of-mouth. A new phenomenon is *social networking* or online communities of practice. Here, like-minded customers or advocates can share information and opinions about the firm and its products. Many firms now hire agents to locate websites hosting word-of-mouth about their products or services.

## DEVELOPING THE COMMUNICATIONS STRATEGY

Table 15.1 depicts critical questions for the firm when developing its communications strategy.

**TABLE 15.1**

**CRITICAL QUESTIONS FOR DEVELOPING A COMMUNICATIONS STRATEGY**

| Basic Questions | Subsidiary Questions |
|---|---|
| 1. Who are our communications targets? | Specifically, with what entities shall we communicate? |
| 2. What are our communications objectives? | How do communications objectives and messages vary by communications target? What is the unique message for each target? |
| 3. What communications tools shall we use? | What combination of personal, non-personal, quasi-personal, and WOM communications shall we use? |
| 4. What communications budget shall we set? | How shall we apportion the communications budget among the different communications tools? |
| 5. When is the *right* time to communicate? | What is the appropriate timing for the various targeted messages, considering seasonality and other factors? |

### IDENTIFYING COMMUNICATIONS TARGETS

The firm has two major types of communications targets: *directly related* to the firm's offers and *not directly related* to such offers. Some targets are decision-makers; others are influencers.

**DIRECTLY RELATED COMMUNICATIONS TARGETS.** The firm should be most concerned with reaching customers specified in its positioning statement, including current and potential customers, direct and indirect customers, and third-party specifiers and advisors. Broadly speaking, communications strategies for these audiences fall into one of two types: **push** or **pull**.

- **Push strategy.** Communications focus on *direct* customers. The firm expects direct customers to communicate with indirect customers further down the channel.
- **Pull strategy.** Communications focus on *indirect* customers further down the channel. The firm might place its effort on final consumers or end-user customers. Its goal is to persuade these customers to purchase finished goods and encourage the firm's direct customers to buy its products. Successful persuasion generates *pull* and drives the firm's sales.

Most firms use *either* push or pull strategies, but large firms often use a combination. FMCG firms like P&G and Unilever rely heavily on *pull*-based advertising directed at consumers. But they also place major *push* efforts at retailers. Figure 15.2 shows a general approach and an illustration for Intel.

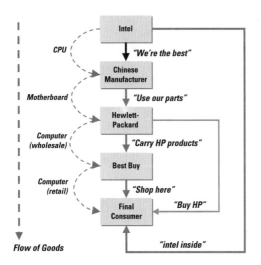

**FIGURE 15.2**

**EXAMPLE OF PUSH AND PULL STRATEGIES WORKING TOGETHER**

Regulations influence communications targets in some industries. Historically, the FDA banned direct-to-consumer prescription-drug advertising. It has relaxed this prohibition in recent years (many countries still ban the practice), and pull strategies now encourage patients to "ask your doctor." The firm may also attempt to *signal* competitors — Chapter 5.

Marketing may also have various internal communications targets. A critical marketing job is ensuring that salespeople use the *right* communications when addressing customers. Marketing may also communicate with the entire employee base to make sure that all employees consistently understand the firm's strategy and brand identity.

**NOT DIRECTLY RELATED COMMUNICATIONS TARGETS.** Many firms have communications targets *not directly related* to their products. Capital markets are a special case; firms or their agents (like investment banks) target investors to secure debt and equity financing. Although these communications targets are *not directly related* to the firm's products, they can have a serious impact on customers. For example, help-wanted advertisements for highly trained personnel may persuade customers the firm is a technology leader and its products are worth buying.

### DECIDING ON COMMUNICATIONS OBJECTIVES

Typically, the firm's long-run marketing communications objectives are to increase sales units and revenues. But achieving other objectives, like communications clarity and comprehending the firm's value proposition, may be short-run requirements. Major considerations are the type of target and the firm's market strategy.

**COMMUNICATIONS TARGET.** Table 15.2 shows possible communications objectives for different customer types.

| Type of Customer | Communication Objectives for Customers |
|---|---|
| Component manufacturer | – Learn how to assemble the firm's subcomponent into the customer's component |
| | – Purchase subcomponent for use in component |
| | – Inventory sufficient component quantities to satisfy finished-goods manufacturer |
| Third-party advisor | – Provide targeted information so that advisor recommends the firm's subcomponents to the component manufacturer |
| Finished-goods producer | – Agree to purchase component for finished product |
| | – Agree to use subcomponent brand on finished product |
| Retailer | – Agree to budget co-op advertising funds for finished product |
| Consumer | – Purchase the finished product |

**KEY IDEA**

➤ Most firms use either push or pull strategies — large firms often use combination push/pull strategies.

**KEY IDEA**

➤ Firms have many communications targets other than customers.

**TABLE 15.2**

**ILLUSTRATIVE COMMUNICATION OBJECTIVES FOR A SUBCOMPONENT MANUFACTURER**

**Marketing Question**

Using the Table 15.2 frame-work, identify target cus-tomers and short- and long-term communications objectives for a firm that makes global position satellite (GPS) systems for pleasure boats.

**Marketing Question**

Identify a firm (or firms) that relies heavily on a *pull* strategy. Is it successful? If so, why? If not, why not?

**Marketing Question**

What are the benefits and challenges of using a *pull* strategy?

Communications objectives for customers differ radically from objectives for competitors and complementers. Objectives for customers typically relate to incentives to purchase. For competitors and complementers, the firm may try to influence their actions so that its offerings and brand are more favorably positioned within a market.

**THE FIRM'S MARKET STRATEGY.** In the positioning statement in the market segment strategy, the firm identifies customer targets; we learned how to do this in Chapter 9. Because these customer targets are also its communications targets, the firm must align its communications objectives with the growth alternatives defined in the *strategic focus*:

- Increase customer retention (reduce defection)
- Increase customer use and satisfaction
- Attract new customers from competitors
- Grow new business, attract new users to the product category

Communications objectives also depend on the age and type of the firm's business and market conditions. In new markets, the firm must necessarily focus on identifying, qualifying, communicating, and selling to *non-users*. Conversely, if the firm is well-placed in a mature market, its objectives will probably focus more on retaining *current customers*.

## SELECTING COMMUNICATIONS TOOLS

Communications objectives drive the firm's choice of communication tools. Suppose the objective is to build awareness for a new product among a broad consumer group. Common sense tells us that advertising is probably more effective than sending salespeople door-to-door. But if the objective is selling sophisticated capital goods to large industrial companies, personal selling would likely be more productive. Table 15.3 helps firms match communication tools to communications objectives and targets. In the illustration, a wholesaler is trying to distribute and sell a new product. It decides to:

- *Identify* potential retailers via direct mail.
- *Qualify* retailers by telemarketing.
- *Sell* to qualified retailers via personal selling.
- *Provide* ongoing sales and service via a sales and service team.

The table also shows that the wholesaler chooses *not* to use advertising, publicity and public relations, trade shows, the Internet, or individual service personnel. The wholesaler should develop a similar chart for each customer target.

**TABLE 15.3**

**MATCHING COMMUNICATIONS TARGETS, OBJECTIVES, AND TOOLS**

| Communication Tools | Communications Targets and Objectives | | | |
| --- | --- | --- | --- | --- |
| | Identify potential retailers | Qualify potential retailers | Sell qualified retailers | Sell and service retailers |
| Advertising | | | | |
| Direct mail | **** | | | |
| Publicity and public relations | | | | |
| Sales promotion/ Trade shows | | | | |
| Internet | | | | |
| Telemarketing | | **** | | |
| Personal selling | | | **** | |
| Individual service | | | | |
| Sales and service teams | | | | **** |

**KEY IDEA**

➤ Communications objectives and timelines drive the choice of communication tools.

Budgeting and timing of the firm's communications efforts are critical for determining the most effective communications strategy. Both are directly related to the selected communication tools.

## INTEGRATING COMMUNICATIONS EFFORTS

By now, you should understand the communications process, be familiar with communications tools, and know the key questions for developing a communications strategy. The firm's core challenge is to develop an effective **integrated marketing communications** program to maximize the impact of its strategy and reach its goals. The firm should strive for four types of integration:

A. Integrate communications for all targets in a single market segment.

B. Integrate communications with other marketing implementation variables like product, price, distribution, and service.

C. Integrate communications for all targets in several market segments.

D. Integrate communications for all targets — market segment, market, business, and corporate.

The reader should keep these various types of integration in mind as we explore the specifics of the various communications tools available for non-personal integrated marketing campaigns.

## ADVERTISING FOUNDATIONS

The firm has many ways of reaching its audiences with nonpersonal communications. No matter which communications approaches the firm chooses, it must set objectives, select the specific tool(s), execute the program, and measure the results. Advertising is the most visible, consuming the largest percentage of the marketing budget for many FMCG firms. Advertising, in traditional media outlets or online, is also becoming increasingly important for a growing number of B2B firms.

At its essence, advertising is a service. When you pay attention to an advertising message, you receive the functional value of information and sometimes even find it entertaining. Many of us look forward to the Super Bowl ads. You may also receive psychological and economic value from ads, but you rarely ever pay for them! From the customer's point of view, TV advertising (and TV) is free, and advertising subsidizes your cost for newspapers and magazines..

How does this system work? Mostly, you (as a customer) receive advertising messages together with some content you desire, like a newspaper or magazine story or TV show. The advertiser pays the media company to *bundle* its advertising with this content, but it receives nothing *directly* in return. The advertiser receives its value *indirectly*, from the attention of your eyes and ears and, hopefully, your switched-on brain.

Customers receive value from highly subsidized or free content; advertisers receive value from customers' attention to their messages. These customers have immense value to advertisers. Google's high market valuation is based on the sheer number of people who visit its website and then click through to the advertiser's website.

In many industries, particularly FMCG, advertising is a central vehicle for implementing market and communications strategies. Table 15.4 shows critical questions for developing an **advertising strategy** and the relevant links to market and communications strategies. Similar questions help develop strategy for other non-personal communications.

**TABLE 15.4**

**ELEMENTS OF
AN ADVERTISING
STRATEGY**

| Element | Question | Link to Market and Communications Strategies |
|---|---|---|
| Target audience | Whom are we trying to influence? | Target segments from the market strategy |
| Advertising objectives | What are we trying to achieve? | Directly related to strategic and operational objectives in the market strategy |
| Messaging | What content should the target audience receive? | Related to the value proposition in the market strategy |
| Execution | How shall we communicate the message? | The most effective way to target customers |
| Media selection and timing | Where and when shall we place our advertising? | Select media to reach target customers at the appropriate time |
| Advertising budget | How much shall we spend on advertising? | Advertising budget is one element of the entire communications budget. |
| Program evaluation | How shall we test our advertising and measure its effectiveness? | Choose from a variety of measurement methodologies. |

**KEY IDEA**

➤ Advertising is critical for both market and communications strategies.

Firms should consider advertising as an *investment*. Today's advertising should achieve short-term results, but may also have long-run impact. It may contribute to building the brand, and lead to future customer purchases. Unfortunately, advertising spending is an expense on the firm's income statement and counts against this year's revenues. Hence, many firms under-fund advertising.

## THE ADVERTISING PROGRAM

*Marketing
Question*

Apply a hierarchy-of-effects model to your purchase of a HDTV set.

### TARGET AUDIENCE: WHOM ARE WE TRYING TO INFLUENCE?

As we learned earlier, a key element in formulating the market strategy is deciding which segments to target. For each target segment, the positioning statement identifies customer targets with whom the firm wishes to communicate. As discussed earlier, for a *push* strategy, the firm focuses on direct customers; for a *pull* strategy, it focuses on indirect customers. The firm must also decide whether to reach influencers, decision-makers, and/or other entities in the purchase decision process. Because advertising dollars are scarce, the firm must carefully select its target audience before making advertising budget allocations.

---

**How Advertising *Works***

Advertising effectiveness is studied more than almost any other marketing topic.[4] **Hierarchy-of-effects** models are central to understanding how advertising works. Figure 15.3 shows two models: one for high-involvement products, the other for low-involvement products.[5] The firm's ultimate goal is typically to reinforce the brand and encourage *repeat purchase*. Note particularly the intermediate steps between *awareness* and *repeat purchase* in each model.[6]

**FIGURE 15.3**

**HIERARCHY-OF-EFFECTS
ADVERTISING MODELS**

**High Involvement**

Awareness
↓
Knowledge
↓
Liking
↓
Trial
↓
Repeat purchase

**Low Involvement**

Awareness
↓
Trial
↓
Liking
↓
Repeat purchase

**High involvement.** The customer believes that the purchase, like a new automobile, involves financial and/or psychosocial risks. The customer engages in a staged learning process:

- **Awareness.** Learning that the product is available for purchase
- **Knowledge.** Understanding the product's features, benefits, and values
- **Liking or preference.** Developing favorable or positive feelings about the product
- **Trial.** Testing the product before purchase and use
- **Repeat purchase.** Purchasing the product again. Advertising can reinforce positive feelings that lead to repeat purchase.

**Low involvement.** Customers see little risk and require little pre-purchase knowledge — FMCG categories such as soda or cereal. Because risk is low, the hierarchical process is quite different. Advertising's role is to create high *awareness* and motivate customers to *trial*. If customers like the product, they repurchase.

🔑 KEY IDEA

➤ Hierarchy-of-effects models for high involvement and low involvement products are central to understanding how advertising works.

## ADVERTISING OBJECTIVES: WHAT ARE WE TRYING TO ACHIEVE?

Once the firm has validated advertising as the appropriate communications vehicle, it should formulate **advertising objectives**. There are two considerations:

- **Output objectives** are what the firm ultimately wants to achieve, like sales, repeat purchase, market share, and brand loyalty.
- **Intermediate objectives** relate to hierarchy-of-effects models and include awareness, knowledge, liking or preference, trial, and emotional commitment (to a brand). For a new product launch, the firm may initially focus on *awareness* as the crucial advertising objective. The importance of other intermediate objectives depends on the particular hierarchy-of-effects model governing product purchase.

🔑 KEY IDEA

➤ There are two types of advertising objectives — output and intermediate.

➤ Output objectives are what the firm ultimately wants to achieve. Intermediate objectives relate to hierarchy-of-effects models and include awareness, knowledge, liking or preference, and trial.

## MESSAGING: WHAT CONTENT SHOULD THE TARGET AUDIENCE RECEIVE?

The firm's advertising message derives directly from the positioning statement in the market strategy discussed earlier.

| | |
|---|---|
| **Convince** | [customer target] |
| **In the context of other alternatives** | [competitor targets] |
| **That they will receive these benefits** | [value proposition] |
| **Because we have these capabilities/features** | [reason to believe] |

The firm's advertising message should follow directly from the positioning statement, with special emphasis on the value proposition. It should focus upon core benefits and values and reflect unique claims where the firm has a differential advantage. Clear positioning statements provide excellent guidance for creative personnel in advertising agencies to develop effective messages. By contrast, poor positioning statements provided by marketers often lead to unsatisfactory and/or confusing messages. The messaging must also reflect the amount of time the audience might be exposed to advertisements.

Firms active in multi-country markets must decide whether, and to what extent, they should *standardize* messages globally or *localize* them for national or regional markets. If the firm standardizes, it should still seek local input to avoid potential translation problems like the "Got Milk?" advertising campaign in Mexico (Spanish translation: "Are you lactating?").

*Marketing Question*

Can you think of advertising messages or slogans that would not work globally?

## EXECUTION: HOW SHALL WE COMMUNICATE THE MESSAGE?

Execution focuses on the method or style firms use to turn their core messages into effective advertising. This is a daunting and challenging task. Our Columbia colleague, branding guru Schmitt, explains: "Creative output [is] the most visible part of advertising. Although judging creative output may be easy, the creative process is an enigma, more art than science, mysterious and unexplainable. The essence of creativity seems to be a willingness to alternate between divergent and convergent thinking, between brainstorming and analytic reasoning, between pushing the limits and being reasonable and practical. [The result, ideally,] culminates in an illumination — the Big Idea."[7]

Figure 15.4 shows typical Absolut ads, beginning with a two-word headline, or *tag line*, starting with Absolut, then adding carefully chosen words to reinforce its imagery, like Absolut Perfection, Absolut Appeal, Absolut Original, in the context of the bottle's image. Absolut's campaign, featuring several hundred executions on a single theme, won many awards for its elegance, simplicity, and effectiveness.

**FIGURE 15.4**

**EXAMPLES OF ABSOLUT ADVERTISEMENTS**

Advertising executions come in two major forms — **rational** and **emotional** approaches.

**RATIONAL APPEALS.** Advertising approaches appealing to people's sense of logic. Five main styles are:

- **Demonstration.** Shows the product in use and focuses on its performance. Many B2B communications use *demonstration ads*; they are also common in sales force materials.

- **Comparative.** Makes a direct comparison to competitive products. Small market share firms often compare their products to the leader, so as to enter the customer's consideration set, like "We try harder" (Avis) and the "Pepsi Challenge."[8]

- **One-sided and Two-sided.** *One-sided advertising* focuses only on the product's positive attributes; *two-sided advertising* presents both positive and negative messages.

- **Refutational.** A special case of two-sided advertising that explicitly mentions competitors' claims, but then directly refutes them.

- **Primacy or recency.** Research shows that items at the beginning of a message, **primacy**, and at the end, *recency*, are more effective than those in the middle.[9] When the audience is less interested in a product, or has an unfavorable prior impression, primacy advertising is generally more effective in gaining attention or minimizing objections. When the audience is initially favorable, and disinterest or objections need not be overcome, recency advertising generally reinforces a favorable product impression.

**EMOTIONAL APPEALS.** Advertising approaches appealing to emotions. Four main styles are:

- **Humor-based.** Humor is widespread in advertising but should be used carefully. It helps create awareness, sets a positive tone, and enhances memory, but if improperly crafted may distract from the core message. The result: The audience remembers the ad, but not the product. Worse, the audience may *mis-index*; it links the humor with a competitive product. Further downsides are that humor comes in many shapes and sizes and can be tedious if not varied; also, humor for one person may be unfunny to another.

- **Fear-based.** Fear appeals create anxiety; behaving as the advertising suggests removes the anxiety. *Physical danger* is common for insurance advertising, *social disapproval* for personal hygiene products, *monetary loss* for security products and credit cards, and *female insecurities* for cosmetic creams.

- **Celebrity endorsement.** Advertisers often use well-known people to endorse products, especially on TV. A good celebrity/product match creates product awareness and credibility. But celebrity endorsement is not a *slam dunk*. To be effective, the audience must attend to the product, not just to the celebrity! A celebrity can lose credibility if he or she endorses too many products. Also, negative publicity for the celebrity can affect the product.

- **Storytelling.** Storytelling can be a very effective way of appealing to people's emotions. MasterCard's *Priceless* campaign and Nike's *Just Do It* are based on storytelling.

In practice, many firms blend these pure-form approaches. Moreover, they must understand the language and word meanings for target customers, especially when venturing abroad. A British firm whose product is great for "knocking you up" might be surprised at its reception in the U.S.!

## MEDIA SELECTION AND TIMING: WHERE AND WHEN SHALL WE PLACE OUR ADVERTISING?

In 2008, global advertising spending was $643 billion; U.S. spending was $271 billion.[10] Figure 15.5 shows U.S. spending by major media class. Media choices are expanding; Internet advertising is growing fastest.

**KEY IDEA**

➤ Rational-style advertising includes demonstration, comparative, one- and two-sided appeals, refutational, and primacy or recency.

➤ Emotional-style advertising includes humor, fear, celebrity endorsement, and storytelling.

*Marketing Question*

Go to the GoDaddy website and view its advertisements. Do you think they are funny? Why or why not? Bring your favorite humorous advertisement to class.

*Marketing Question*

Identify an advertisement using a fear appeal. What is the objective and the advertiser's anticipated outcome? Do you think the ad works?

## FIGURE 15.5

**U.S. ADVERTISING SPENDING BY MAJOR MEDIA CLASS 2008[11]**
($Billions)

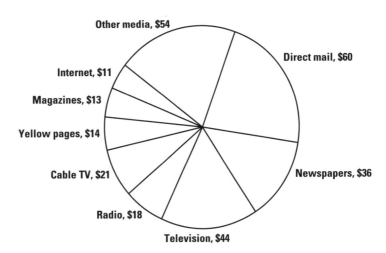

Other media, $54
Direct mail, $60
Internet, $11
Magazines, $13
Yellow pages, $14
Newspapers, $36
Cable TV, $21
Radio, $18
Television, $44

### KEY IDEA

➤ In setting media objectives, the firm must consider reach, frequency, and gross rating points.

To select the appropriate media, the firm must answer five related questions:

- **Media objectives.** What do we want to accomplish with our media strategy?
- **Type of media.** Which media classes shall we use — print, broadcast, outdoor?
- **Specific media.** Which media vehicles shall we use — *Vanity Fair*, *Survivor*, bus stops?
- **Timing.** When will our advertising appear?
- **Media schedule.** Specifically, where and when shall we place our ads?

### MEDIA OBJECTIVES: WHAT DO WE WANT TO ACCOMPLISH WITH OUR MEDIA STRATEGY?

Key concerns are **reach**, **frequency**, and **impact**:

- **Reach.** Number of targeted individuals exposed to the advertising at least once.
- **Frequency.** Average number of times a targeted individual is exposed to the advertising.
- **Reach and frequency.** We use reach and frequency to calculate **gross rating points (GRPs)**.

**Gross rating points (GRPs) = Reach × Frequency**

Advertisers often want high frequency for complex messages, messages in competition with others, and/or messages for new products. Generally, advertisers trade off reach and frequency. GRP objectives are popular, but can cause a problem. For example, to secure 250 GRPs:

- 100 percent of the audience receives, on average, 2.5 exposures.
- 10 percent of the audience receives, on average, 25 exposures.

Many advertisers require a minimum number of exposures; hence, they set GRP objectives, subject to a minimum required frequency. The firm must also be concerned with excessive frequency and diminishing returns. Media objectives should relate directly to the advertising objectives.

---

### Illustration of Media Objectives

- *Reach* 50 percent of the target audience five times in the next six months — *frequency*.
- Deliver 250 *GRPs* — 50% (reach) x 5 (frequency) = 250, subject to a minimum 70 percent *reach*.

### Illustration of Advertising Objectives (AO) and Media Objectives (MO)

**AO**: Increase repeat purchase of Munchee candy bars from 30 to 50 percent among 10- to 16-year-old boys by end of June.

**MO**: Deliver 1,500 GRPs, subject to a minimum 60 percent reach.

When the firm uses several media classes, duplication is important. Suppose it chooses two media, like radio and TV. There are two relevant measures:

- **Duplicated reach:** Receive a message from *both* radio and TV.
- **Unduplicated reach:** Receive just one message, *either* from radio or TV, but not both.

Sometimes the firm wants to maximize *duplicated reach* by exposure to several media classes. Alternatively, it may want to maximize *unduplicated reach* regardless of media class.

- **Impact.** Impact is directly related to creativity in generating advertisements — indeed, many *creatives* view the media department's job as boring and routine. But mass media has fragmented, and consumers' media habits are more varied, so the media task is increasingly challenging. In the early 1980s, it took less than 10 advertising spots on network TV to reach 70 percent of women aged 25 to 54. Today, it takes more than 100 spots.

> Häagen-Dazs successfully launched super-premium ice cream in Britain, using only black-and-white newspaper ads, for just £375,000. This controversial copy gained significant publicity and the creatives won a major advertising award.

**TYPE OF MEDIA. WHICH MEDIA CLASSES SHALL WE USE?** A **media class** is a group of closely related media. Media classes differ from one another on dimensions like time availability and intrusiveness. A common category system is:

- **Print** — like newspapers and magazines. Read at leisure — are relatively non-intrusive.
- **Broadcast** — like television and radio. Exist for short time periods — are much more intrusive.[12]
- **Online** — like e-mail and web alerts. Delivered in real time. Read at leisure — more intrusive than print.
- **Outdoor** — like billboards and in-store. Have a long presence — are relatively non-intrusive.

Table 15.5 shows advantages and disadvantages of selected classes.[13]

| Media Class | Advantages | Disadvantages |
|---|---|---|
| Newspapers | High coverage<br>Low cost<br>Short lead time for placing ads<br>Ads can be placed in interest sections<br>Timely (current ads)<br>Reader controls exposure<br>Can be used for coupons | Short life<br>Clutter<br>Low attention-getting capabilities<br>Poor reproduction quality<br>Selective reader exposure |
| Magazines | Segmentation potential<br>Quality reproduction<br>High information content<br>Longevity<br>Multiple readers (high pass-along) | Long lead time for placing advertising<br>Visual only<br>Lack of design flexibility |
| Direct mail | High selectivity<br>Reader controls exposure<br>High information content<br>Opportunities for repeat exposures | High cost per contact<br>Poor image (junk mail)<br>High level of in-store clutter |
| Television | Mass coverage<br>High reach<br>Impact of sight, sound, and motion<br>High prestige<br>Low cost per exposure<br>Attention-getting<br>Favorable image | Low selectivity<br>Short message life<br>High absolute cost<br>High production costs<br>Clutter |

**TABLE 15.5**

**ADVANTAGES AND DISADVANTAGES OF SELECTED MEDIA CLASSES**

*Marketing Question*

We deliberately omitted the online media class from Table 15.5. How do you assess its advantages and disadvantages?

**TABLE 15.5**

**(CONTINUED)**

| Media Class | Advantages | Disadvantages |
|---|---|---|
| Radio | Local coverage<br>Low cost<br>High frequency<br>Flexible<br>Low production costs<br>Well-segmented audiences | Audio only<br>Clutter<br>Low attention-getting<br>Fleeting message |
| Outdoor | Location specific<br>High repetition<br>Easily noticed | Short exposure time requires short ad<br>Poor environmental image<br>Local restrictions |
| In-store | Location specific<br>Customers ready to buy<br>Many options — special displays, packaging, TV | Difficult to measure impact |

*Marketing Question*

You are launching an Internet security system for large and small businesses. Identify your communications targets. Identify media classes. Why these?

Figure 15.5 (page 225) shows the most-used media classes are direct mail, newspapers, and television, but others may also be attractive. Some firms use unusual placements for outdoor advertising. Siemens used special tabletops in 8,000 French cafés to advertise a new cell phone. In Beijing, groups of 15 teenagers, wearing identical Ai Jia (love home) neon-yellow warm-up jackets and matching baseball caps, ride bicycles in formation along set street routes.

**SPECIFIC MEDIA: WHICH MEDIA VEHICLES SHALL WE USE?** A **media vehicle** is a specific entity in a media class. The *newspaper* media class includes *The New York Times*, *The Boston Globe*, and *The San Francisco Examiner*. The *magazine* media class includes *Time*, *Vanity Fair*, and *Good Housekeeping*. The *television* media class includes *60 Minutes*, *American Idol*, and *As the World Turns*. How do you select which vehicle is right for your product or service? Critical issues in choosing media vehicles are audience type, audience size, cost, and nature of the vehicle (in particular whether the advertisement is complementary, like a serious ad on a TV news show).

*Marketing Question*

Can you identify examples of unusual advertising placements?

**TIMING: WHEN WILL OUR ADVERTISING APPEAR?** The four main timing patterns are:

- **Concentration.** Commit all expenditures at one time.
- **Continuous.** A regular periodic advertising pattern.
- **Flighting.** Repeated high advertising levels followed by low (or no) advertising.
- **Pulsing.** Combined continuous and flighting advertising. Pulsing can occur within a media vehicle, within a media class, or across multiple media vehicles and classes.

Generally, advertising experts believe **continuous advertising** is most effective for products purchased throughout the year. **Flighting** and **pulsing** are more effective when demand is variable, like seasonal products — cruises and air travel.

**THE MEDIA SCHEDULE.** In selecting its media schedule — where and when to place its ads — the firm tries to optimize media objectives like reach, frequency, and GRPs subject to a budget constraint. Securing the best media buy in one media class is a complex task. Designing a campaign for multiple media classes is even more difficult. Major advertisers use computer models, modified by managerial judgment, to develop optimally effective **media schedules**.

**KEY IDEA**

➤ The advertising message must appear in the right place at the right time.

➤ Major timing options are continuous, flighting, and pulsing.

## ADVERTISING BUDGET: HOW MUCH SHALL WE SPEND ON ADVERTISING?

The **advertising response function (ARF)** relates advertising spending to advertising objectives like sales (as discussed above). The ARF is crucial for setting the **advertising budget**, but unfortunately, its exact shape is uncertain. The firm faces two questions in deciding its advertising budget:

- What shape is the ARF? Figure 15.6 shows two alternative ARFs, A and B. Each has some intuitive appeal and research support.[14] Spending implications are different for low and moderate spending.

- Where is the firm currently operating? If the firm was at I on ARF **A**, it would probably increase spending; if it were at II, it would probably hold or reduce spending. This would be similar for ARF **B**.

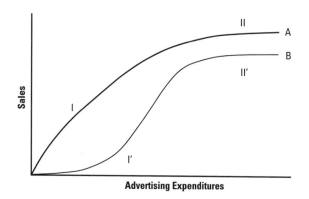

**FIGURE 15.6**

**ALTERNATIVE ADVERTISING RESPONSE FUNCTIONS**

If the firm can answer these questions, budgeting is simply a matter of marginal analysis: set the budget where marginal revenue equals marginal cost. Managers estimate sales, or other advertising objectives, at various advertising levels; the models estimate ARFs in different media vehicles and calculate the optimal spending level and media allocations.

The **objective and task** method is a *bottom-up* approach that focuses on advertising objectives; for example, *achieving 80 percent awareness* by a specified time, then identifies the necessary tasks. The firm uses historical and/or experimental data to estimate the budget for each task, then adds up the total cost. Because linking advertising spending to advertising objectives is difficult, this method is not broadly popular. But as pressures grow to justify marketing and advertising expenditures, more firms will use the objective and task approach, if only to get *ballpark* estimates.

Firms sometimes use *top-down* methods to calibrate budgets they develop by *objective and task.* These include **percentage of sales (A/S)**, where *sales* is current sales, anticipated next-year sales, or some combination of the two, and **competitive parity**, where the firm bases its advertising on competitors' actions by using competitors' spending as a benchmark.

## PROGRAM EVALUATION: HOW SHALL WE TEST OUR ADVERTISING AND MEASURE ITS EFFECTIVENESS?

Now we have answered the advertising questions of who, what, how, where, when, and how much to spend, we must evaluate the advertising relative to objectives. The firm can test individual advertisements and different levels and types of spending and/or evaluate the entire advertising program.

**TESTING INDIVIDUAL ADVERTISEMENTS AND SPENDING LEVELS.** The firm tests ads with target customers, individually or in groups; in a laboratory or experimental field setting. Typical effectiveness measures are **recognition, unaided recall** (without prompting), **aided recall** (with prompting), and purchase (for field studies). The firm also tests alternative spending patterns using experimental design procedures. It sets its advertising objectives then selects appropriate advertising effectiveness measures.

**EVALUATING THE ENTIRE ADVERTISING PROGRAM.** Over and above testing individual ads and spending levels, the firm may wish to evaluate an entire advertising program so it can make needed adjustments. **Tracking studies** measure customer responses over time, using either a customer panel or randomly selected respondents. If the firm's objectives mirror the high-involvement, hierarchy-of-effects model — awareness → liking → trial → repeat purchase — it should base its advertising objectives on these stages. In tracking studies, the results from one period help set objectives for the following period.

**KEY IDEA**

➤ Evaluating advertising effectiveness is a complex task. The firm must choose among various types of tests and measures.

*Marketing Question*

Suppose your school, college, or university is going to advertise to increase student applications. Develop a creative brief for developing a campaign idea.

## THE ADVERTISING AGENCY SYSTEM

Most major U.S. advertisers outsource advertising programs to **advertising agencies**, but some firms like The Prudential conduct advertising activities in-house. By outsourcing, firms have better access to creative talent and greater flexibility. They can demand refreshed creative teams and switch agencies on short notice. The firm usually works with three groups in an agency:

- *Account or relationship managers* are the key agency interface and help craft the strategy.
- The *creative department* develops the advertising message and executions.
- The *media department* prepares the media schedule and provides supporting data.

The agency's core job is to translate the firm's market strategy into an advertising message and execute on that message. Firm and agency personnel should jointly develop a **creative brief**, simply a *contract* between the firm and agency, particularly with the *creatives*. Each messaging initiative should have a creative brief — for advertising, but also for visual aids like displays and sales force materials.

### Core Elements of the Creative Brief

**Marketing objective.** What the firm wants to achieve — output and intermediate.

**Assignment.** The type of campaign including media type, timing, and approval process.

**Customer insight.** Informs the creative process — critical insight into target market; identifies rational and emotional factors that drive product use.

**Competitive insight.** Informs the creative process — includes barriers to achieving the firm's objectives.

**Target audience.** Whom the firm wishes to influence — customer types and segments — includes demographics, psychographics, and current products.

**Key benefit.** The most important benefit or value the firm wishes to emphasize.

**Reason to believe.** Why the target customer should believe the firm's claims.

**Brand identity.** How the firm wants the target audience to feel about its product. Should be important to the audience, deliverable by the firm, and unique to the brand.

**Mandates.** Elements outside the advertiser's control — must or must not be included — like corporate and/or legal requirements the advertising must meet.

**Measurement.** How the firm will know if the campaign has been successful.

## DIRECT MARKETING

Direct marketing is a fast-growing communications tool embracing many ways of requesting a direct response from customers. Today, direct marketing includes traditional print and broadcast advertising, packaging, package inserts, warranty cards, take-ones, and newer digital options like fax, e-mail, and the Internet.[15] Firms like L.L. Bean, Lands' End, and Lillian Vernon develop and refine demographic and product preference databases on customers to fine-tune product development, product assortments, and communications programs. Low bulk postal rates, online shopping, and widespread credit card use are helping to grow direct marketing. Other factors are:

- **Technology.** Using technological advances in computers and telecommunications, firms can develop, manage, and mine customer databases.
- **Demographics and lifestyles.** The growth of dual-income families facing increasing time pressures, especially in developed countries, has reduced available shopping time. Direct marketing is attractive because consumers can shop without leaving home.
- **Product quality.** The generalized increase in product quality has reduced customers' risks when buying products remotely.

**KEY IDEA**

➤ Direct marketing offers advantages over mass advertising: flexibility, action-oriented customer response, better measurement, predictability, better customer knowledge, ability to tailor the offer, and ability to identify prospects.

- **Professionalism.** Direct marketing firms are more professional and sophisticated, especially in segmenting, targeting, and communicating.
- **Delivery systems.** Package delivery firms like FedEx, UPS, and DHL increasingly offer greater varieties of services.
- **The Internet.** The Internet allows for far greater personalization/customization and immediacy than other direct marketing methods.

Direct marketing can be more expensive than advertising on a CPM basis, but offers several advantages:

- **Flexibility.** The firm can develop some direct marketing campaigns, like e-mail, much more quickly than mass advertising.
- **Action-oriented customer response.** Advertising programs typically work via an effects hierarchy; purchase often occurs after awareness, knowledge, and liking. By contrast, direct marketing is more action-oriented and typically requests purchase.
- **Better measurement.** The firm can test program elements like message, price, incentives, and/or type of direct marketing to assess their impact on sales and adjust accordingly.
- **Predictability.** Because it is closely related to sales, predictions for new direct marketing programs can be fairly accurate. Budgeting for direct marketing is simpler than for advertising.
- **Better customer knowledge.** Many direct marketing firms have extensive information on customers. However, they must be sensitive to privacy concerns and act appropriately.
- **Ability to tailor the offer.** Direct marketers know the products their customers purchase; hence, they can tailor messages and offers to individuals.
- **Ability to identify prospects.** By relating customer profiles to purchase patterns, direct marketers can identify high-quality prospects.

## PUBLICITY AND PUBLIC RELATIONS

**Publicity and public relations (P&PR)** are closely related; publicity is really a subset of public relations. **Publicity** focuses on securing neutral or favorable short-term press coverage. **Public relations (PR)** is broader in scope and more multifaceted. PR embraces corporate reputation, crisis management, government relations (lobbying), internal relations, press relations, product publicity, and shareholder relations. P&PR generally relies on an intermediary to transmit messages, hopefully positive, to a target audience. It has the advantage that the intermediary may be viewed as impartial, and the firm doesn't pay for media space and time!

Many firms focus their communications efforts on P&PR. Pharmaceutical firms use news releases so patients will ask their physicians about products. Mutual fund giant Vanguard does little advertising, but gets favorable press for its low expense ratios. College Saving Bank launched its CollegeSure CD by focusing its initial communication efforts on news releases and press conferences. Within one month, more than 300 news stories were written or broadcast. Articles and editorials appeared in all major U.S. newspapers; weekly news magazines like *Time*, *Newsweek*, and *U.S. News and World Report*; major business magazines; and local newspapers.[16]

Firms can also use P&PR and advertising synergistically. Victoria's Secret (VS) spends several million dollars advertising its annual fashion show; the extensive publicity sends millions of visitors to the VS website. For difficult situations in the public eye, P&PR can be negative or positive. In 1999, 200 Coke drinkers suffered nausea, headaches, and diarrhea, and several children were hospitalized. Observers criticized Coke for "forget[ing] the cardinal rule of crisis management — to act fast, tell the whole truth, and look as if you have nothing to hide." *The Economist* concluded that "Coca-Cola has made a big mess of what should have been a small public-relations problem."[17] By contrast, J&J received considerable praise for handling the mid-1980s Tylenol poisoning scare by temporarily withdrawing Tylenol tablets and then relaunching in tamper-free packaging. J&J's actions and its related P&PR campaign put senior executives,

**KEY IDEA**

➤ Publicity and Public Relations relies on an intermediary, typically the press, to transmit a message to a target audience.

including the CEO, on many U.S. talk shows; they explained J&J's actions and its commitment to customers. J&J turned a major debacle into a major coup.

P&PR has several drawbacks. The firm cannot select the audience, except as it selects intermediaries like journalists, editors, and media personalities. Also, it loses control over the message; the intermediary may ignore, shorten, or modify it. And it may portray the firm inconsistently, or even negatively.

## SALES PROMOTION

**SALES PROMOTION (SP)** is a complex blend of communications techniques providing extra value to customers, most often for trial to stimulate immediate sales. Sometimes SP has longer-run objectives like increasing awareness. The three main SP types are:

- **Consumer promotion** — Manufacturer to Consumer
- **Trade promotion** — Manufacturer to Retailer
- **Retail promotion** — Retailer to Consumer

*Consumer and retail promotions* include cash refunds, contests, coupons, deals, games, rebates, point-of-purchase displays, premiums, prizes, samples, and sports sponsorships. *Trade promotions* include advertising and merchandising allowances, contests, deals and prizes, trade shows, special price deals, and *spiffs*.[18] Firms are continually creating new SP techniques. Like other communications methods, the firm must be clear about its objectives before selecting an SP device.

Generally, SP is not a good standalone approach. The firm should tightly integrate SP with other communications strategies to support or enforce the brand or message. Firms often advertise several sales promotions simultaneously, but these should all support, or be supported by, the firm's advertising and/or personal selling efforts. Rarely is SP the central element in the firm's communications strategy, but it can be a large portion of the budget.

The firm should stay focused on the long-term impact of SPs, particularly those that give short-term price reductions. If the product is regularly discounted, competitive escalation may occur; also, customers will accumulate inventory and never pay the *regular* higher price.[19] Volume fluctuations from frequent price changes may also lead to mismatched production schedules and inventory build-up; hence, costs increase. Also, multiple SP programs are costly to manage.

## THE INTERNET

The Internet has spawned many ways for firms to communicate with customers. Here are three of the most common approaches: online advertising, websites, and blogs.

### ONLINE ADVERTISING

As a communications tool, the Internet offers many ways for marketers to communicate with customers, each with its own characteristics. The Interactive Advertising Bureau notes four broad areas: search, display advertising, classifieds, and e-mail (40 percent). New online video formats like YouTube or social networks like MySpace are emerging but are small right now.

**SEARCH.** Best exemplified by Google, search has two important facets for marketers: **paid search** and **search engine optimization**:

- **Paid search.** Advertisers pay to appear next to and be associated with search results based on keywords. An electronics retailer might pay to appear next to searches for HDTVs or digital cameras. The advertiser pays only when a searcher actually clicks on the ad next to the search results. Advertisers paying more are listed higher up the advertisement order.

- **Search engine optimization.** The goal for advertisers is to appear high up in the rankings for unpaid "natural" search results. To achieve this goal is a somewhat arcane process that ranges from understanding the mechanics of search engines and *optimizing* the firm's website to best attract them and selection of significant key words. Some firms use less aboveboard methods that attempt to *goose* the natural rankings.

**DISPLAY ADVERTISEMENTS.** Display advertising comprises banner ads on websites. Originally based on a magazine model, banner ads come in many standard sizes to make them easy to purchase, track, and measure. The basic banner ad has been standard for many years, but renewal occurs with new and creative sizing, like tall, skyscraper-like ads, and newer forms of rich media like interactive and flash motion.

**CLASSIFIEDS.** Online classifieds are typically text listings for specific types of products and services like jobs, real estate, automobiles, yellow pages, and auctions — that are often time-sensitive. The migration of these ads from offline to online has been swift and devastating to many newspapers. An important entry is Craigslist, a network of local community sites that allows free listing and commands a huge audience.

**E-MAIL.** E-mail communications are very popular for firms to maintain contact with customers. Retailers like Amazon regularly send e-mail communications to stimulate purchases and maintain relationships. Many community-oriented sites and content publishers send regular communications like e-mail news alerts to keep readers returning so as to maintain the user base for advertising. A specific problem is unsolicited e-mail communications, or spam, that continually clog up all of our e-mail boxes.

## WEBSITES

At a minimum, websites are a form of mass communications, or brochureware. A website can also enable sales promotion by offering free samples, discounts, and competitions. But the web's true potential is in its ability to generate quasi-personal communication (QPC). QPC creates a dialog with customers by generating product awareness, explaining and demonstrating products, and providing product information. When creatively designed, customers self-generate their communications, and customers with like interests can form online communities.

**KEY IDEA**

➤ Only quasi-personal communication taps the web's true potential.

> Nestlé builds highly targeted consumer communities for its products. Nespresso is a 250,000-person club whose members "treasure quality coffee as part of the simple moments of pleasure in everyday life." Club Buitoni was aimed at Italian culture lovers — they could click on favorite Italian recipes — made with Buitoni pasta and enter to win a trip to Buitoni's testing kitchens in Tuscany.

Firms can use websites to generate feedback on product performance. Some firms encourage customers to use the Internet for routine tasks like searching for product information, placing orders, and checking delivery status to free up salespeople's time to sell. Many merchants, like Amazon and Netflix, exist only on the Internet. The Internet also supports many tiny specialty merchants like Germany-based Wurzburger, selling sheet music for accordion players, and Wessex, the publisher of *Capon's Marketing Framework*.

The Internet will continue to transform marketing communications. In B2C markets, information traditionally flowed as one-to-many mass communication. Using the Internet, the firm can address consumers as individuals. Further, consumers can easily communicate with suppliers and other consumers. Many firms are finding it difficult to adapt to two-way interactive marketing. But for those willing to make the effort, new potentials lie ahead.

*Marketing Question*

Firms are increasingly trying to use blogs for their purposes. Search the Internet. Which company blog do you think is the most effective? Why? What are the benefits and limitations of blogs?

## BLOGS

Originally online diaries, **blogs** (from web logs) are a platform to offer highly opinionated comments; sometimes, bloggers allow readers to comment on their blogs. Some marketers see bloggers as important opinion leaders and try to capitalize on the blogging phenomenon. Technology firms often provide bloggers with advance versions of their products, hoping for favorable comments. Others have started their own blogs. *Brandweek* reported, "Nike, Dr Pepper, Mazda, SBC, and others have ... found blogging an easy, cheap way to appear hipper and keep customers engaged with the brand."[20] Microsoft lets 1,000 developers set up personal blogs to build customer and complementer relationships. But firm blogging can backfire if bloggers view it as the invasion by commercial interests into a non-commercial domain.

## KEY MESSAGES

The firm's communications program is a critical element for implementing its market strategy and achieving its objectives. To develop a successful program, the firm must **address** many external challenges from the environment and many internal challenges from with**in the** firm.

Problems in the communications process lead to miscommunication between senders and receivers:

- The encoding problem – the firm does not send the *intended* message
- The distortion problem – the communication process distorts the *sent* message
- The decoding problem – the receiver misperceives and/or misunderstand the *received* message

The firm's communications options fall into four categories:

- Personal communication
- Non-personal communication
- Quasi-personal communication
- Word-of-mouth communication

The firm's core challenge is to integrate the various elements of its communications strategy to form a coherent whole. The firm must strive for four types of integration:

A. Integrate communications tools for targets in a single market segment strategy.
B. Integrate communications with other marketing implementation variables.
C. Integrate communication tools for targets in several market segment strategies.
D. Integrate communication tools for all targets.

Advertising *works* via hierarchy-of-effects models incorporating awareness, knowledge, liking, trial, and repeat purchase as the major variables.

- High-involvement and low-involvement products have different hierarchies.
- A well-developed advertising strategy requires answers to seven critical questions:
  - **Target audience**. Whom are we trying to influence?
  - **Advertising objectives**. What are we trying to achieve?
  - **Messaging**. What content should the target audience receive?
  - **Execution**. How shall we communicate the message?
  - **Media selection and timing**. Where and when shall we place our advertising?
  - **Advertising budget**. How much shall we spend on advertising?
  - **Program evaluation**. How shall we test our advertising and measure its effectiveness?

- The core of the advertising message should reflect the positioning statement in the market segment strategy.

- Advertising messages can embrace many rational and emotional approaches.

- Key issues for media selection are reach, frequency, and impact.

- The firm should approach the marketing budget from a marginal analysis perspective and limit rule-of-thumb approaches.

- Direct marketing (DM), publicity and public relations (P&PR), and sales promotion (SP) are non-personal communications approaches that can supplement or replace advertising.

- The Internet is fast becoming an important communications medium having the special advantage of effecting quasi-personal communications.

# CHAPTER 16

# DIRECTING AND MANAGING THE FIELD SALES EFFORT

## LEARNING OBJECTIVES

When you have completed this chapter, you will be able to:

- Articulate the evolution in managing the field sales effort.
- Address the challenges of selling to customers of varied size and importance.
- Implement the six tasks of sales management.
- Integrate sales strategy with the overall market strategy.
- Develop sales strategies: Set sales objectives, determine and allocate selling effort, and design sales approaches.
- Design and staff the sales organization to implement the sales strategy.
- Manage critical organizational processes to support sales strategy implementation.
- Understand the value of developing customer relationships.

## OPENING CASE: HONEYWELL BUILDING SOLUTIONS

*Honeywell Building Solutions (HBS) provides building automation, security, and fire and life safety solutions and services to public- and private-sector facilities. It is also a global leader in the energy services industry, helping organizations conserve energy, optimize building operations, and leverage renewable energy sources. HBS has a storied many-decade history as a Honeywell business unit. Chances are that when you adjust your heat or air conditioning at home or in the office, you are using a Honeywell product.*

*HBS addresses three market segments for commercial buildings:*

- **Installation.** *Mostly for new buildings where the decision-making unit frequently includes owners, architects, and mechanical and electrical contractors.*

- **Service.** *Making sure that customer installations and equipment perform optimally.*
- **Energy.** *Retrofitting current buildings to improve energy efficiency. HBS acts as the project designer and general contactor, but most work is sub-contracted.*

*In 1999, Honeywell merged with AlliedSignal to form Honeywell International Inc. In 2000, United Technologies held merger talks with the new firm, but these broke down when GE attempted to buy Honeywell. The U.S. Justice Department approved the GE acquisition; but in 2001, the European Commission refused and Honeywell continued as an independent firm.*

*Following months of turmoil, notably in 2000 and 2001 when many GE employees populated HBS in preparation for the then impending GE acquisition, HBS did not perform well: Sales were declining at 20 percent annually. In an attempt to save the business, Honeywell's CEO Dave Cote appointed a new leadership team for HBS including a President and VPs of operations, marketing, and sales. Kevin Madden became new worldwide VP of sales. Cote gave the team 90 days to develop a turnaround plan, and to "get rid of their ancestors" — the cause of the poor performance.*

*Madden, a 20-year Honeywell veteran, described the situation when he arrived. "Not only were sales declining, internally a* victim *mentality was pervasive. Because of the turmoil, 35 to 40 percent of the intellectual capital had left and the business unit was in a tailspin. The entire organizational focus was on productivity and cost, and most sales were to current HBS customers; we were securing a minimal number of new customers. We had dismantled most of the sales teams that focused on the installations of our systems. HBS had outsourced this activity to transaction-oriented partners who had little interest in building deep relationships or delivering complete solutions. Quite frankly, customers had lost confidence in HBS to do an installation, and we no longer had any competitive advantage."*

*Madden said that energy and many installation projects were* make *businesses. Sales reps had to be proactive in getting in front of customers and writing specifications. But that was not happening, for several reasons:*

- *HBS had lost many of its good salespeople.*
- *Current salespeople were generalists; they sold in all three lines of business. Yet the nature of the challenges and the skills required tended to be quite different by market segment.*
- *The first-line sales leaders' **span of control** averaged 25-to-1. They were too preoccupied with administrative tasks, and gave little guidance and coaching to their salespeople.*

*Madden said that the turnaround plan focused on five key areas:*

- **Marketing and sales alignment.** *Marketing and sales became tightly integrated. The sales force not only agreed on all new marketing initiatives, but often stimulated new ideas.*
- **Customer coverage model.** *In 2001, the Americas region had 192 generalist salespeople. In early 2007, it had over 400 salespeople, many hired from competitors with the challenge to be part of the build, focused in individual market areas. Many new salespeople displaced outsourced partners as HBS returned to the installation marketplace.*
- **Sales planning.** *The five-stage sales process — HBS's playbook — was tightly linked:*
  - **First calls:** *The salesperson figures out the customer's decision-making unit, what needs to be done, and secures agreement to develop a list of requirements.*
  - **Requirements definition:** *The salesperson prepares the list of requirements — technical, financial, legal — and gets the customer to agree.*
  - **Commitment:** *The salesperson identifies HBS resources that meet the customer's requirements, and gets agreement from the customer.*
  - **Solutions development:** *The salesperson brings in Honeywell engineers to design the installation.*
  - **Final negotiation:** *The customer and HBS sign the contract.*

  *For all jobs over $750,000 HBS conducts an impact review with senior sales executives. The review team focuses on the customer's best competitive alternative and HBS' next move. At these reviews, the team may telephone the customer to check its understanding and probe* *additional ways to add value. HBS also rigorously qualifies all sales opportunities and only allocates expensive sales support manpower where it believes it can win. HBS rigorously debriefs all wins and losses.*

- **Roles and responsibilities.** *HBS reduced first-line sales managers' spans from 25-to-1, to an average of 10-to-1, to increase salesperson coaching.*
- **Performance management.** *HBS implemented a rigorous performance measurement system and pays for results. Base pay is comparable to competition, but HBS designs its incentive compensation and rewards to be among the most lucrative in the industry.*

*Madden said an important investment was in a sales force data system. The sales process also functions as a funnel and HBS knows, for example, that a certain number of agreements to prepare a list of requirements will lead to a certain number of contracts. HBS manages the funnel aggressively and salespeople must update their funnels continuously. If ten days have lapsed without a salesperson updating, Madden knows about it and sends that salesperson a letter.*

**CASE QUESTION**

To what extent are HBS' sales force initiatives generalizable to other sales forces?

*Since the new leadership team took over; sales have turned around; HBS is now a multi-billion-dollar business and a strong member of the Honeywell portfolio. HBS has beaten the industry's 4- to 5-percentage growth rate each year since 2002. From the 20 percent decline, sales growth rates have ranged from 6 percent to 30 percent during the last five years, almost doubling the business.*

**Honeywell**

In most firms, the sales force is the only group specifically charged with making sales and securing revenues. Field salespeople's efforts are the firm's critical persuasive component. Some sales forces are huge. Several U.S. life insurance firms employ more than 10,000 salespeople. Pfizer has 20,000 salespeople around the world; GE maintains 34,000 salespeople and 6,000 sales managers.

In B2B marketing, the direct sales force has always been critical, as salespeople typically introduce the firm's products and services to customers. By contrast, in B2C marketing, advertising is often the main communication channel to consumers, and the sales force has played a supporting role. But today, retail industry concentration in many countries has led a few large retailers or distributors securing significant power. Hence B2C field sales efforts are increasing, and some FMCG firms now spend more heavily on direct selling to wholesalers and retailers than on advertising to consumers; at P&G, more than 400 persons work exclusively with Wal-Mart. In this chapter we discuss the various elements for effectively directing and managing the field sales effort.

## MARKETING'S ROLE IN THE FIELD SALES EFFORT

This is a marketing framework book, so why do we include a chapter on directing and managing the field sales effort? Aren't there enough dedicated books on sales management? Of course! But throughout this chapter, we discuss the importance of aligning the firm's selling efforts with marketing and show how salespeople's actions can *make or break* the market strategy. A simple illustration of improving alignment is:

At SalesCo,[1] marketing's job was to develop sales force leads. Despite significant marketing effort, salespeople often did not follow up, and the leads languished in files. A new management team harvested 3,000 dormant leads and assigned a special group to work them. Although some leads were old, within six months 250 new customers were providing $5 million in new revenues.

If a nice metaphor for marketing is *architect* — designing the overall way the firm addresses the market — then our metaphor for sales is *builder*. In construction, the architect/builder interface should be seamless. So should the marketing/sales interface. In many firms and business units, separate VPs head up marketing and sales. Even though they are on the same team, they may have different backgrounds, philosophies, objectives, and approaches that can create different cultures within their groups and discord between them. For this reason, some externally focused firms pointedly create a combined position, VP of Sales and Marketing, to align these functions.

Whatever organizational structure the firm selects, senior management must shift the emphasis away from old-fashioned stereotypes: Marketing — "Salespeople don't understand the complexities involved in developing a market strategy"; Sales — "Marketing is full of *ivory-tower* types, removed from the market with limited understanding of customers' needs and unwilling to *get their hands dirty* fighting competitors." In today's increasingly competitive world, these perceptions just don't cut it. Marketing and sales must be on the same team, each performing its own critical functions.

**KEY IDEA**

➤ Effectively managing the sales/marketing interface is critical for achieving sales excellence.

We do not pretend this is easy. Marketing tends to have a long-run view, but sales must deliver short-term performance. Perceived compensation inequities can cause disconnects, and even the very nature of market and sales strategies can be a problem. Marketing typically develops market strategies for the firm's various products. We saw in Chapter 9 that each product-market strategy comprises several market-segment strategies, and a multi-product firm has several product-market strategies. The sales strategy must play an important integrative role; it focuses on selling multiple products to *all* target market segments. A badly coordinated or ill-formed sales strategy can lead to distracting competition among various product managers and detract from the firm's overall efforts and performance:

The sales force at a well-known FMCG firm was responsible for the entire product line. Brand managers competed for resources, including sales force time. Some brand managers even devised incentive schemes so that salespeople would place more effort on their products than on others.

To be truly effective in the marketplace, marketing and sales must work hand-in-hand to seamlessly implement the market strategy. When they coordinate poorly, the sales force fights competitors *with one hand tied behind its back*. Well-managed firms have processes that tightly coordinate their marketing and sales efforts. They develop market plans in good time, with significant sales force input, and the sales strategy process starts when the market plans are well developed, but not yet complete. Senior marketing and sales managers meet frequently to hammer out realistic and coordinated marketing and sales objectives and priorities, in a spirit of cooperation. Some firms even appoint sales/marketing coordinators whose job is to build senior marketing and sales manager relationships.

## CHANGES IN MANAGING THE FIELD SALES EFFORT

The traditional field sales force system is under increasing scrutiny. A U.S. study by Deloitte & Touche revealed that many firms are making changes: 69 percent expanded their sales forces, 58 percent simplified sales management hierarchies, 44 percent adjusted sales territories, 39 percent

created partnerships/alliances, 35 percent implemented new selling approaches via consultative (or relationship) selling, and 32 percent instituted sales force automation and technology.[2]

One factor driving change is a heightened awareness of firms' revenue distributions. We talked about the **80:20 rule** in Chapter 2. In many cases, 80 percent of a firm's revenues come from 20 percent of its customers; these customers are very important. But if only 20 percent of revenues come from 80 percent of customers (**20:80** rule), a critical question is: What does it cost the firm to serve all those customers that make small purchases? Typically, *a lot*! Across many industries, the average sales call cost is well over $200, a hefty price to pay for underperforming customers.[3] Many firms have used these insights to revolutionize their selling efforts. They decide which customers should receive face-to-face selling effort and which should not. Then they decide how to deal with these two groups.

## FACE-TO-FACE SELLING EFFORT

Today, firms are making serious decisions about the nature and level of resources they provide to different types of customers. They partition customers into several tiers based on current and potential revenues — like **Tier I** (platinum), **Tier II** (gold), and **Tier III** (bronze) — and allocate resources accordingly. Microsoft uses a three-tier system for its most important customers — 40 *global* accounts, 250 *strategic* accounts, and 1,000 *corporate* accounts.[4] Some firms' tiering is more complex, based on profits and potential revenues and more tiers. Whatever the basis, the firm has few Tier I customers, more Tier II customers, and many more Tier III and smaller customers. It addresses each tier differently in terms of selling effort, technical service, customer service, and other resources.[5] Of course, tiering is not the same as *segmentation* — based on customer needs (Chapter 8). Figure 16.1 shows segments overlaying **customer tiers**.

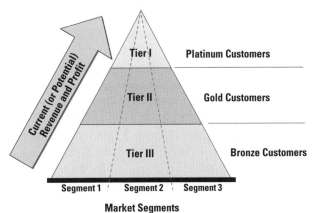

**HIGH-TIER CUSTOMERS.** Tier I customers provide the highest levels of sales and profits. They are considered **strategic or key accounts** due to the high percentage of revenues and profits they represent today and/or tomorrow. Losing a current strategic account or winning a new one is a significant event. For many years, Foot Locker was one of Nike's strategic accounts, but in 2003, disagreements led Foot Locker to slash Nike orders by 40 percent. To serve Tier I customers, many firms establish strategic account (SA) programs headed by senior executives. Sometimes firms form partnerships with their Tier I customers, who then have input into product development and other key decisions. These partnerships may even embrace shared risk/return agreements for targeted cost savings. High resource commitments mean that most firms have few Tier I customers. In 1990, two UPS salespeople managed 100 large accounts; in a shift to a strategic account management, by 2002, 25 to 30 personnel managed 265 accounts.

In most SA programs, **strategic account managers** (SAMs) are responsible for individual accounts. SAMs develop and execute plans to optimize the firm's business. They direct teams that may include local sales and customer service and personnel from brand management, finance, HR, logistics, market research, operations, product classes, and trade marketing.[6] SAMs work closely with their customers and may be responsible for millions of revenue dollars. Wal-Mart is a strategic account for many FMCG firms, and P&G and many others base team members in Bentonville, Arkansas, Wal-Mart's head office.

Increasingly, multinational firms are making their procurement decisions on a global basis. To better serve these customers, suppliers must adopt SA practices at a global level. As a senior 3M executive opined, "The fact that we are a multi-product, multi-business, multi-national company should not be the customer's problem." **Global account managers (GAMs)** develop plans for these multinational accounts and manage the global account teams that implement their strategies. IBM has about 150 global accounts, each with a GAM; for its top 40 customers, IBM's GAMs are senior executives. GAMs function similarly to domestic SAMs, but the job scope is much greater. They must develop significant understanding of the global business environment, have comprehensive knowledge of global supply chains, and be sensitive to local cultural differences.[7] Sometimes the top executive acts as the account manager or *point person* for the most critical accounts: Oracle's Larry Ellison for GE, Nestlé's U.S. head for Wal-Mart, and its French head for Carrefour. Another firm that *gets it* is Goldman Sachs, where former CEO Hank Paulson spent about a third of his time just visiting clients. And at Merck, IBM wrested an important contract away from Accenture when CEO Sam Palmisano came calling.

**LOWER-TIER CUSTOMERS.** Although typically not as valuable individually as high-tier customers, in total these accounts are very important for most firms. Together they provide significant revenues and profits; some may grow to become strategic accounts. Most of this chapter focuses on key sales force management issues for addressing these customers.

## NO FACE-TO-FACE SELLING EFFORT

Typically, when firms focus on the value of customers, they find face-to-face selling effort does not justify the revenues and profits that many customers deliver. Lower-cost ways to address these customers are:

- **New communications strategy.** Many firms have eliminated face-to-face interactions in favor of telesales and/or Internet approaches. Technological advances have made these systems quite user-friendly; some customers prefer them to intermittent salesperson visits. Combination systems can cue website visitors to call toll-free and talk to a telesalesperson.

- **Hand off to third parties.** In many industries, distributors, contract sales forces, or value-added resellers make sales for the firm. These third-party firms often have lower fixed costs; hence, a firm's unprofitable customers may be profitable for a distributor. Cisco once sold direct to end-user customers; today it sells mainly through channel partners.

- **Fire customers.** Sales and profit potential are so low that the firm stops selling to them.

Before taking any of these actions, the firm should consider several issues:

- A customer may object to losing its field salesperson and shift its business to a competitor.

- The firm shifts a customer to a distributor, and it grows. Later, the customer wants a direct relationship with the firm. Yet this would *cut out* the distributor that developed the customer. Firm/distributor relationships can get tricky.

- A customer misallocated to the *firing* category may later become a significant player.

Creative approaches to serving small customers can reduce costs and increase profits. In Scandinavia, Reebok withdrew an expensive sales force that called monthly on *mom-and-pop* shoe retailers. Instead, each retailer received a telesalesperson who initiated weekly contact and was always available to answer questions. Reebok reduced costs, and customer service improved.

## THE TASKS OF SALES FORCE MANAGEMENT

To mount an effective selling effort, sales managers must focus on six tasks. Three sales force management tasks address *developing* sales strategy; three deal with *implementing* sales strategy.

*Marketing Question*

Has a firm ever identified you as a low-priority customer? Did you ever phone a supplier, enter your customer number, then wait forever, listening to Musak? How can firms better engage low-priority customers?

**KEY IDEA**

➤ Tier I customers provide the highest levels of sales and profits.

➤ Strategic account managers are responsible for individual accounts.

➤ Global account managers are responsible for multinational customers that want to make global purchases.

The chapter discusses the tasks sequentially but shows how each task relates to the others. A new sales approach (task 3) may require new sales staffing (task 6). For further illustration, go to *www.sellingpower.com/video* for a series of short videos about selling.

## TASK 1: SET AND ACHIEVE SALES OBJECTIVES

Simply defined, **sales objectives** are the firm's desired results. Achieving sales objectives is the sales force's central task. The firm makes profits, survives, grows, and enhances shareholder value only by selling products and services to customers. Hence, achieving sales objectives takes precedence over all other activities like gathering information, collecting payments, delivering goods, providing service, and entertaining. Sales objectives turned into specific performance requirements are called **sales quotas**.

**DEFINING SALES OBJECTIVES.** The firm can choose among several sales force performance measures. Most firms set sales objectives in terms of volume measures like gross sales revenues (in current dollars) or gross unit volume. But focusing solely on volume can short-change profits, so some firms also set profitability objectives like profit contribution — gross profits less direct sales force costs. Well-set objectives specify *how much* and *by when* the sales force must meet its targets.

**KEY IDEA**

➤ Sales objectives are the firm's desired results. Achieving sales objectives is the sales force's central task. Sales objectives turned into specific performance requirements are called quotas.

---

**Illustration of Sales Objectives**

In 20xy, sales revenue objectives — $40 million.

In 20xy, gross profit contribution objectives — $14.5 million.

---

**KEY IDEA**

➤ Sales objectives integrate the firm's market strategy and sales strategy.

**RELATING SALES OBJECTIVES TO MARKETING OBJECTIVES.** We noted earlier that integrating market strategy with sales strategy is a difficult problem for many firms. One way to help this integration is to rigorously translate marketing objectives into sales objectives. Table 16.1 illustrates sales revenue objectives for a firm selling three products (I, II, III) to three market segments (A, B, C). We can view the objectives in several ways:

- Overall objectives — $40 million.
- Objectives by market segment: A — $10 million, B — $20 million, and C — $10 million.
- Objectives by product: I — $26 million, II — $5 million, and III — $9 million.
- Individual cells show objectives by product/market segment. The firm sets positive revenue objectives for IA, IB, IC, IIB, IIC, IIIA, and IIIB — but zero revenue objectives for IIA and IIIC.

Although each approach to the sales revenue objectives has value, only the product/market segment objectives integrate the market strategy and sales strategy perspectives.

**TABLE 16.1**

ILLUSTRATION OF SALES REVENUE OBJECTIVES BY PRODUCTS AND MARKET SEGMENTS ($ MILLIONS)

| | | Product | | | Totals |
|---|---|---|---|---|---|
| | | I | II | III | |
| Market Segment | A | $7 | $0 | $3 | **$10** |
| | B | $13 | $1 | $6 | **$20** |
| | C | $6 | $4 | $0 | **$10** |
| | Totals | **$26** | **$5** | **$9** | **$40** |

**BREAKING DOWN SALES OBJECTIVES.** Typically, the most common way the sales force deals with overall sales objectives is by breaking them down into **control units** like sales regions, sales districts, and individual sales territories. Top sales managers can then gain significant insight by comparing actual sales performance for the control unit with sales objectives to see if a particular region, district, or territory is performing well or poorly.

Firms also establish sales objectives in time units like quarterly — Table 16.2, monthly, and sometimes even weekly. **Calendarizing** allows the firm to monitor performance on a continuous basis and sets the stage for making course corrections if performance deviates negatively from the objectives.[8]

| Quarter 1 | Quarter 2 | Quarter 3 | Quarter 4 | Total |
|-----------|-----------|-----------|-----------|-------|
| $1,100 | $1,450 | $950 | $1,500 | **$5,000** |

**TABLE 16.2**

ILLUSTRATION OF SALES
REVENUE OBJECTIVES
BY QUARTER ($000s)

**ALTERNATIVE MEASURES OF SALES PERFORMANCE.** Although sales and profit-type objectives are the most popular, the firm can select from many other performance measures, depending on the nature of its business:

-   **Customer retention.** The proportion of customers from the start of the year remaining at the end of the year — the opposite of customer defection, or churn. (This measure speaks to customer lifetime value issues discussed in Chapter 2.)
-   **Market share.** This measure focuses on the firm's performance versus competitors.
-   **Price realization.** The extent to which the firm achieves planned price levels.
-   **Close rate.** The proportion of sales attempts that result in an actual sale.
-   **Customer satisfaction.** Specific metrics that focus on how customers feel about the firm.

## TASK 2: DETERMINE AND ALLOCATE SELLING EFFORT

We discussed how to set sales objectives; now we consider the best ways to determine and allocate **selling effort** by examining three interrelated decisions:

-   **Sales force size.** How much selling effort should the firm expend in total? In particular, how many salespeople should sell the firm's products?
-   **Sales force activities.** What activities should salespeople do? What proportion of their time should they spend in *selling* activities?
-   **Selling effort allocation.** How should salespeople allocate their selling time among the firm's products and segments?

**SALES FORCE SIZE.** For effective selling effort, the firm must have the *right* number of well-trained, motivated salespeople. Managing *headcount* is typically a crucial HR function, and sales managers often wage difficult internal battles to optimize the size of their sales teams. Figure 16.2 shows the underlying conceptual framework for deciding sales force size — the **sales response function**. When selling effort is low, the firm makes few sales. As selling effort increases, sales increase. Ultimately, sales *top out* at a maximum level, even if the firm adds extra salespeople. Conceptually, the firm should continue to hire until the marginal revenue from adding/ subtracting a salesperson equals that salesperson's marginal cost. Many sales managers find this function intuitively reasonable, but do not know where their sales force falls on the curve. Methods for approaching the sizing decision are experimental or analytic.

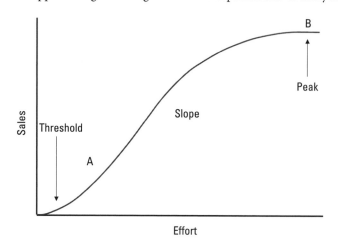

**FIGURE 16.2**

THE SALES
RESPONSE
FUNCTION

- **Experimental method.** Essentially, sales managers change sales force size and see what happens. From Figure 16.2, there are two broad hypotheses:
  - The sales force is too small, perhaps at A.
  - The sales force is too large, perhaps at B.

  Sales managers should decide what criteria would support or reject each hypothesis. Then they select one or more sales districts/regions for a trial and comparable districts/regions as controls. They increase or decrease sales force size for a predetermined period. If the experimental data supports hypothesis A, the firm should add salespeople; if the data support hypothesis B, the firm should maintain or reduce sales force size.

- **Analytic method.** The analytic approach has three steps:

  **1. Total number of selling hours required to achieve sales objectives.** Single-factor models and portfolio models are two broad approaches to assessing time required by type of customer:

  - **Single-factor models** typically classify customers by account type — A, B, C, D — like sales potential. Table 16.3 shows how to assess required selling hours per annum. Single-factor models are simple to use, but may not fully capture the complexity of selling to various customers. Portfolio models often do a better job.

**TABLE 16.3**

**ILLUSTRATION OF SINGLE-FACTOR MODEL FOR CALCULATING REQUIRED SELLING TIME**

| Account type, I | Sales potential II | Number of accounts, III | Selling time per account per annum, IV | Required selling time per annum, III x IV = V |
|---|---|---|---|---|
| A | >$2M | 100 accounts | 100 hours | 10,000 hours |
| B | $250K to $2M | 250 accounts | 50 hours | 12,500 hours |
| C | $10K to $250K | 800 accounts | 12 hours | 9,600 hours |
| D | <$10K | 3,000 accounts | 4 hours | 12,000 hours |
| Total | | | | 44,100 hours |

  - **Portfolio models** classify accounts on multiple dimensions. Figure 16.3 uses *account potential* and *account market share* and partitions each into low, medium, and high. The firm identifies the number of accounts in each cell, III, and the required selling time for those accounts, IV. The analysis proceeds as before.

**FIGURE 16.3**

**PORTFOLIO MODEL FOR DETERMINING REQUIRED SELLING TIME**

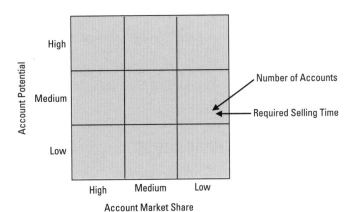

**2. Number of available selling hours per salesperson.** Salespeople conduct many activities (see next section). Sales managers must calculate the time available for selling.

**3. Required sales force size.** We continue the Table 16.3 illustration. From this point on, calculations for single-factor and portfolio models are identical:

  i. Total available salesperson time per annum (hours)
     = (365 days less 104 [weekends] less 30 [holidays/vacations])
     = 231 × 10 hours per day = **2,310 hours**

ii. Actual selling time per salesperson
= Total available salesperson time x 30% (assumed)
= 2,310 x 30% = **693 hours**

iii. Number of salespeople required
= Total number of selling hours required A/actual selling time per salesperson
= 44,100/693 = **64 salespeople**

In practice, this calculation provides a *ballpark* estimate for sales force size. The firm should expect some variation from the actual size, but significant variation demands action.

**SALES FORCE ACTIVITIES.** The sales force's main job is to make sales. But claims on salespeople's time include checking credit, checking inventories, collections, customer service, delivering products, education and training, gathering market intelligence, internal communications, meetings, qualifying sales leads, receiving payments, record-keeping, report writing, sales planning, and travel. In many firms, even the best salespeople spend less than 20 percent of their time, the equivalent of one day per week, face-to-face with customers trying to make sales.

Firms regularly deploy technology to improve salesperson effectiveness. Most salespeople now use cell phones, e-mail, laptop computers, BlackBerrys, standardized slide show presentations, voice mail, and websites. Other devices and applications enable advertising coordination, best practice and knowledge sharing, reseller training and virtual meetings, sales training, trade show participation, technical support, well-designed sales literature, and working models. Sales managers should develop guidelines specifying salespeople's time commitment to various activities.

In 2005, IBM faced a salesperson **face-time** problem. Senior managers wanted data from the field; salespeople wanted information, resources, advice, and decisions from their managers. Internal communications were sporadic and time-consuming. IBM developed guidelines for communications within the sales organization and requires that salespeople and sales managers at all levels adhere to them. Salesperson face time increased considerably.

**SELLING EFFORT ALLOCATION.** The firm's selling effort or selling time allocation should mirror the *structure* of its sales objectives. For sales objectives by product, it should allocate selling effort by product. For sales objectives by product and market segment, it should allocate selling effort by product and market segment. Sales objectives by old versus new products require a similar selling effort allocation.

Similarly to sales objectives, the firm should break down selling effort allocations by individual control units — sales regions, sales districts, and sales territories. Sales managers must make these selling effort allocations and ensure that salespeople stick to their guidelines. If managers do not lead, salespeople will set their own priorities. Their individual decisions will likely not optimize the firm's performance.

················································································

## TASK 3: DEVELOP SALES APPROACHES

The value proposition (Chapter 9) anchors the **sales approach** — the central message the salesperson delivers to customers. The firm should offer a different value proposition for each product/market segment. Hence, salespeople selling multiple products to multiple segments must have multiple sales approaches. Sales managers and product managers should help salespeople modify messages for specific customers and competitive threats. They should:

• Analyze the specific customer needs and competitive threats at the salesperson's accounts.

• Understand the various perspectives of the customers' decision-makers and influencers.

• Develop sales approaches that address critical customer needs, answer objections, and counter sales approaches from competitors.

**KEY IDEA**

➤ Salespeople conduct several activities. In many firms, they spend less than 20 percent of time face-to-face with customers trying to make sales.

*Marketing Question*

If you, a friend, or a colleague have worked in sales, what percentage of time was *face time* with customers? What other activities were part of the job? Were the time allocations good? Why, or why not? What were the challenges of increasing face time?

**KEY IDEA**

➤ Guidelines should specify how salespeople must allocate their time.

**KEY IDEA**

➤ The value proposition anchors the sales approach — the central message the salesperson delivers to customers.

**KEY IDEA**

➤ The firm should tailor the sales message to different customer targets and design a process to explain the firm's benefits.

The traditional sales approach has two major components:

- Tailoring the sales message for different customer targets, and
- Designing a process to explain the firm's values and benefits.

**TAILORING THE SALES MESSAGE FOR DIFFERENT CUSTOMER TARGETS.** Customer needs and competitive offers drive the sales approach. Sometimes customers are clear about their needs; other times, individual decision-makers and influencers have different perspectives. Salespeople must decide whom to target, and how to tailor their sales message for each person.[9] Procurement personnel are typically interested in price, engineers focus on product design, and manufacturing personnel are concerned about production efficiency. The salesperson must orchestrate the sales approach for each customer role.

> Enterprise is now the U.S.' largest car rental firm. Starting in 1964, Enterprise provided temporary replacement cars for drivers whose cars were being repaired. Key customer targets were garage mechanics. Salespeople made morning calls and always carried donuts. This sales approach got garage mechanics' attention very quickly!

In designing the sales approach, the firm should sharpen its competitive focus. In Table 16.4, firms I, II, and III are each trying to sell to a customer requiring four benefits, A, B, C, and D.

**TABLE 16.4**

**FORMULATING SALES APPROACHES**

| Customer Benefits | Relative Importance | Firm I | | Firm II | | Firm III | |
|---|---|---|---|---|---|---|---|
| | | Benefit | Rank | Benefit | Rank | Benefit | Rank |
| A | 1 | A | 1 | A | 2 | A | 3 |
| B | 2 | | | B | 1 | | |
| C | 3 | | | C | 1 | C | 2 |
| D | 4 | D | 2 | | | D | 1 |

**Developing the Sales Approach: Sharpening Competitive Focus**

- The customer seeks four benefits in importance order, Benefit A > B > C > D.
- The three firms each offer different sets of benefits.
- Each firm performs better on some benefits than on others:
  - Benefit A: All three firms offer — firm I > II > III
  - Benefit B: Only firm II offers
  - Benefit C: Firm II > III; firm I does not offer
  - Benefit D: Firm III > I; firm II does not offer
- **Firm I.** Should focus on the customer's most important benefit, A. Firm I dominates on this benefit but is vulnerable on the other benefits.
- **Firm II.** Dominates firm III on benefits A, B, and C and is inferior only on the least important benefit, D. Hence, firm II's major challenge is from firm I. Firm II's major problem is that firm I ranks best on the most important benefit, A. Further insight and possible sales approaches for firm II are:
  - The competitive ranking on benefit A is incorrect; actually, firm II > I. Firm II should persuade the customer that it offers the best A. Firm II then dominates its competitors on the three most important benefits, A, B, and C.
  - The customer's benefits are incorrectly ordered; actually, B > A > C > D. By persuading the customer of its error, firm II dominates on the now most important benefit, B, and also on benefit C.
  - The customer should base its decision on the benefit set. Firm II offers the superior set for the most important benefits, A, B, and C.
- **Firm III.** Has little hope of making the sale. Its best sales approaches focus on benefit D and the combination of A, C, and D. More importantly, why is firm III spending time with this customer when its benefits are so inferior?

No firm offers all of the desired benefits, so each is vulnerable to competition.

When Xerox launches a new product or product upgrade, it makes sure that salespeople have in-depth knowledge about competitive products. It provides easy-to-use charts and a professional video showing key strengths and weaknesses versus *face-off* products. Xerox's laboratories create courses for salespeople including hands-on experience with competitive products and techniques to combat competitive threats.

### Marketing Question

Based on Table 16.4 and the boxed insert, what market research and product development would you suggest for Firm I? Firm II? Firm III?

**DESIGNING A PROCESS TO EXPLAIN THE FIRM'S BENEFITS.** Selling is a process to facilitate customer buying. A completely standardized process is undesirable, but sales managers should guide salespeople via coaching, counseling, and well-designed training programs. Good sales managers break the selling task into discrete easy-to-learn steps:

- **Call objectives.** Know the desired results from each sales call and at each stage in the buying process. A pre-call planning process can support these initiatives.
- **Sales interviews tone.** Decide how strident or aggressive to be in different situations.
- **Need elicitation.** Develop procedures to elicit customers' needs.
- **Presenting product benefits.** Present product benefits in the context of customer needs.
- **Handling objections.** Anticipate the customer's objections and know how to address them. Objections differ from product to product and from customer to customer.
- **Communications timing and closing the deal.** Communicate in a strategic sequence. For example, do not elicit customer needs after presenting product benefits. Learn how to close a sale and when to ask for the order. Learn when to accept rejection and move to another customer and learn to better qualify prospects.

In Bose's retail stores, customers relax on a sofa and enjoy exquisite sound from a large TV and huge speakers. When the show is over, the salesperson executes *the reveal*. She removes the *fake* speakers to show baseball-sized Bose speakers.

## TASK 4: DESIGN THE SALES ORGANIZATION

Tasks 1, 2, and 3 address *developing* the sales strategy. Tasks 4, 5, and 6 focus on *implementing* the sales strategy. They ensure that the sales force delivers the planned levels and types of selling effort. Task 4 covers sales organization design; it should reflect strategic realities. If the product line is complex and heterogeneous, perhaps the firm should have separate sales forces. Three critical issues are:

- Should firm employees conduct the selling effort? Or should selling be outsourced?
- How should an employee-based sales force be organized? Or reorganized?
- How should the firm design its sales territories?

### KEY IDEA

➤ Selling is a system to facilitate customer buying.
➤ Coaching, counseling, and training can improve the selling process.

**SHOULD FIRM EMPLOYEES CONDUCT THE SELLING EFFORT? OR SHOULD IT BE OUTSOURCED?**
Today, many firms outsource functions like call centers, computer systems, financial processes, legal, production operations, and security. Should the firm outsource its selling effort? To answer this question, it should consider three issues:

- **Control.** Employee-based sales forces are more likely to follow managerial directions. Because agents, reps, and brokers earn commission, the firm often has little control over their efforts, particularly if they also sell other firms' products.
- **Cost.** Employee-based sales forces incur substantial fixed costs, like salespeople's salary, travel and entertainment, sales management, and other overhead, regardless of sales volume. In contrast, third-party sellers on commission are a variable cost; no sales, no costs!
- **Flexibility in modification.** To modify an employee-based sales force takes time and almost always involves HR. Third-party sellers typically work with short-term contracts and strict performance criteria.

### Marketing Question

Baby food firm Gerber fired 250 salespeople and sold to grocery store chains via food brokers. In the education market, Apple shifted from third-party sellers to an employee-based sales force. Why did these two organizations move in opposite directions? When is outsourcing the better decision?

In 2000, software firm Altiris' direct sales force costs were too high, so it fired the entire sales staff. Altiris partnered with Compaq, Dell, Microsoft, IBM, and others to sell its products. It customized partner relationships, like making communication materials partner-specific. Sales increased from $1 million in 1999 to $190 million in 2005.

Sometimes the balance favors employee-based selling; sometimes it favors outsourcing the selling function. There is no right or wrong answer. If the firm has insufficient salespeople for a new market entry, third-party sellers can take up the slack. Conversely, long lead times and/or high market share in mature markets with predictable sales favor employee-based selling.

**HOW SHOULD AN EMPLOYEE-BASED SALES FORCE BE ORGANIZED? OR REORGANIZED?**
Three interrelated design variables for sales force organizations are degree of centralization/decentralization, number of management levels, and managerial span of control.

Avon's sales organization has a group vice president of sales, three regional vice presidents, seven regional sales directors, 85 division sales managers, and 2,500 district sales managers. In some geographies, district sales managers have several hundred reps. Avon also aligns its sales force ethnically in terms of language and culture.

## KEY IDEA

➤ The employee-based or outsourced sales force decision involves control, cost, and flexibility trade-offs.

One of the most important design issues is specialization. Should the firm specialize its selling effort? And if so, how? Essentially, sales organizations can be unspecialized or specialized:

- **Unspecialized.** Two organization forms are generally considered unspecialized:
  - No geographic bounds on a salesperson's search for sales opportunities.
  - Territories organized by geography where salespeople sell all products, to all customers, for all applications.
- **Specialized.** Specialization can be by product, maintenance/new business, distribution channel member, market segment, and/or customer importance (strategic accounts). Generally, specialized selling effort leads to higher sales, but selling costs are higher.

## KEY IDEA

➤ The firm should implement sales force reorganizations very carefully.

Some firms combine different types of specialized organizations. Salespeople specialized by product are often effective in urban areas where travel times are low. In rural areas, customer density is low, travel times are high, and general sales forces often work better. Product specialists sometimes back up general sales forces. At Wachovia Bank, cash management, leasing, and commercial finance specialists support account managers. In a variant of the product-based organization, some pharmaceutical firms have used *mirroring* organizations in which multiple salespeople called on identical doctors with the same drugs.

As the firm's environment changes, so must its market and sales strategies. The sales organization must also evolve but effective implementation is critical. Poor implementation can have serious implications:

Incoming Xerox CEO Rick Thoman shifted Xerox's sales organization from a product and geographic focus to an industry focus. Thoman saw the salesperson's job as analyzing a firm's entire business and identifying the best way to manage complex flows of data, images, and graphics. He believed that salespeople's intellectual capital would generalize among firms in an industry. But Xerox changed to an industry organization before salespeople were trained, and did a poor job of switching accounts among salespeople. It *orphaned* previously well-served accounts. Many salespeople left rather than relocate. Competitors hired disgruntled Xerox salespeople, and Xerox fired Thoman.

Apple's shift to an employee-based sales force was also less than stellar:

Apple's CEO Steve Jobs said: "We were very straightforward and told these third-party salespeople that, 'Hey, in four months we're going to switch [the sales force organization] and you're going to be out of a job.' Obviously these folks did everything they could to sell as much as they could by June 30, when we let them go, and did absolutely nothing to build for sales in the July quarter. So when our folks got there, they found there was no pipeline work at all: They had to start from scratch. And, duh, this was during the *peak buying time for schools* [emphasis added]. It was just stupid on our part to do this then, and that was my decision. It was a train wreck, and it was totally my fault."[10]

**HOW SHOULD THE FIRM DESIGN ITS SALES TERRITORIES?** Within the structure imposed by its sales organization, the firm must design **sales territories** for each salesperson. The two key variables are **sales potential** (available sales); and **salesperson workload**, the time to complete the required activities. The four steps in designing sales territories are:

- **Initial design by sales potential.** The firm identifies geographically contiguous territories with roughly equal *sales potential*. Some trial territories are geographically larger than others. Equivalent potential territories for Xerox might be a few blocks of midtown Manhattan or several Western states.

- **Calculate workload.** Use sales effort allocation decisions (Task 2) to determine *workload*. In some territories, salespeople may have time left over, but in others there is insufficient time to complete the work.

- **Adjust for workload.** Make territory design adjustments to optimize sales potential and salesperson workload. Ensure that all salespeople can cover their territories effectively.

- **Continuous monitoring.** Sales managers must monitor salespeople and their territories and continually adjust, as some customers may grow faster or slower than expected, and new customers may emerge.

**KEY IDEA**

➤ Sales territories should have roughly equal sales potential and workloads.

ConstructCo's analysis showed that market share by territory ranged from 8 to 50 percent.[11] Also, many high-revenue salespeople had low territory shares. ConstructCo redesigned its sales territories to take advantage of its untapped potential and added salespeople. It turned a revenue decline into revenue growth.

## TASK 5: CREATE CRITICAL ORGANIZATIONAL PROCESSES

All sales organizations employ processes like sales planning, pipeline analysis and sales forecasting, evaluation methods, and reward systems to help implement the planned selling effort.

**SALES PLANNING.** The firm should actively engage salespeople in a detailed sales planning process. As discussed earlier, senior sales managers work with regional and district sales managers to decompose the firm's overall sales objectives into individual control units like sales regions, districts, and territories. They also decide on broad selling effort allocations by product and market segment. In bottom-up planning, salespeople analyze their territories and work with district sales managers to agree on territory objectives, and develop individual sales action plans. Sales managers must ensure the firm implements the planned selling effort at each control unit and achieves its sales objectives. Deviating from the sales strategy can cause significant problems.

**KEY IDEA**

➤ The firm should actively engage salespeople in the sales planning process.

A startup medical device firm, specialized in hemodialysis treatments,[12] decided to focus its selling effort on major teaching hospitals. The sales approach required salespeople to provide customers with high service levels to ensure proper use. But in implementation, salespeople made sales to a large number of hospitals. The product was widely misused, and the firm suffered serious credibility problems.

**PIPELINE ANALYSIS AND SALES FORECASTING.** The sales pipeline consists of stages in the selling process that customers traverse in moving from prospects (potential customers) to buyers. **Pipeline analysis** tracks the firm's success in moving customers through these stages and is important for both sales and marketing management. IBM's pipeline comprises:

- **Discover.** The salesperson believes the customer may be going to buy.

- **Identify.** A customer is interested in working with IBM.

- **Validate.** The customer states its need and buying vision. It allows IBM access to the project sponsors — customer personnel responsible for the purchase.

- **Qualify.** Project sponsors and the IBM team go forward with a preliminary solution.

**KEY IDEA**

➤ A pipeline system continually tracks success at different stages in the selling process. Rigorous pipeline analysis leads to better forecasts.

**Marketing Recap**

Talk to a salesperson about current and potential customers. Do IBM's six stages in the selling process — Discover, Identify, Validate, Qualify, Conditional Agreement, and Business Won — work for them? Don't forget to check if customers' expectations were met.

- **Conditional agreement.** Project sponsors conditionally approve IBM's proposed solution.
- **Business won.** The customer and the IBM team sign a contract.
- **Customer's expectations met.** The customer is satisfied as purchase and installation move forward — and IBM receives payment as scheduled.

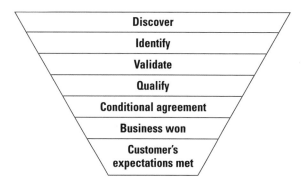

A pipeline system continually tracks success at different stages in the selling process. Rigorous pipeline analysis leads to better forecasts.

Sometimes salespeople resist entering pipeline data, but the firm must make this mandatory. Today, many firms use software applications to track and manage their pipelines. These applications have many tools for salespeople to conduct better analyses of customer data; they also provide sales managers with greater insight into sales force performance so they can make appropriate interventions. Table 16.5 illustrates typical pipeline data for a sales territory.

**TABLE 16.5**
**ILLUSTRATION OF PIPELINE ANALYSIS**

| | Total Sales Leads Discovered | Opportunities Indentified | Opportunities Validated | Opportunities Qualified | Conditional Agreements Made with Customer | Business Won |
|---|---|---|---|---|---|---|
| Territory total | $76 million | $28 million | $17 million | $13 million | $10 million | $8 million |
| Percentage of total pipeline leads | 100% | 37% | 22% | 17% | 13% | 11% |

In 2000, to meet *explosive customer demand*, Nortel Networks (NN) added 9,600 jobs and spent $1.9 billion to boost production. One year later, NN lost $19 billion in a single quarter and eliminated 10,000 jobs. Cisco vastly overestimated demand by basing its forecasts on orders. It did not realize that end users, worried about product shortages, placed orders with several distributors, not just Cisco. Cisco sales were less than expected, and inventory swelled.

**EVALUATION METHODS.** We address monitor-and-control processes in Chapter 19. For salespeople, the most critical measure is sales performance versus sales objectives. Sales managers should use several measures to evaluate selling effort — Table 16.6; a single measure can be misleading. Suppose a salesperson has high sales per existing account; this seems like great performance, so we assume that effort is high. Not so fast; he could also have few existing accounts so that overall territory sales are low. Sales managers at every level — district, regional, and national — should receive regular data on their direct reports and be able to access selective data deeper in the sales force as needed.

**TABLE 16.6**
**MEASURES FOR ASSESSING A SALESPERSON'S EFFORT**

| Measure | Value | Limitations |
|---|---|---|
| Calls per day | Identifies level of calling effort | Measures quantity of calls, not quality |
| Calls per account | Identifies level of calling effort | Measures quantity of calls, not quality |
| Calls per new account | Identifies where time is spent; link to sales strategy | Should be used together with calls per existing account |
| Calls per existing account | Identifies where time is spent; link to sales strategy | Should be used together with calls per new account |

**REWARD SYSTEMS. Reward systems** are powerful motivators for salespeople. To establish a truly motivating system, salespeople should answer "yes" to the following questions:

- Can I *achieve* my sales objectives?
- Do I *value* the rewards I will receive for meeting my sales objectives?
- Do I believe I will truly *receive* these rewards if I achieve my sales objectives?
- Is the reward system fair?

Sales reward systems can have several components:

- **Financial compensation.** The firm combines three financial rewards in various ways:
  - **Base salary.** Paid to the salesperson regardless of sales performance (in the short run).
  - **Sales commission.** Variable compensation based on sales or profits. In some industries, like life insurance, salespeople earn no base salary and work strictly on commission.
  - **Bonus:** Reward paid for achieving quota — typically a target sales or profit level.
- **Recognition.** This important reward is relatively inexpensive but can be a powerful motivator. Creative sales managers recognize salespeople for performance like highest revenues, best sales growth, most profitable sales, most new accounts, and/or most lost accounts retrieved. Many sales forces recognize high performers with membership in a President's club, often associated with an annual trip (with spouse) to an exciting destination.
- **Promotions and work assignments.** Promotions and more interesting and responsible job possibilities are highly motivating for some salespeople. Others may not value such advancement or change.

Generally, financial compensation is the most important motivator. The firm should decide the take-home target pay range for salespeople, then decide on the particular combination of salary, commission, and bonus for reaching the target range. The amount of incentive pay — commissions and bonus — should be proportionate to the role of selling effort in making sales. A U.S. trend is to put more salespeople's pay *at risk* by increasing the incentive portion. By developing a fair and consistent compensation plan, the firm drives the behavior it desires.

> Every six months, Siebel Systems collects satisfaction data on its various departments and individual salespeople from 400-500 of its 2,500 customers. These data drive bonuses and commissions. Salespeople do not receive full commissions until a year after a sale, and then only if their customer satisfaction scores are up to par.

## TASK 6: STAFF THE SALES ORGANIZATION

Salespeople are the sales force's most important resource. Sales managers must ensure the sales force is fully staffed and all territories filled, at all times. Far too often, sales managers do not plan for natural attrition, transfers, promotions, and/or dismissal, and are forced to scramble when a salesperson leaves. Sales managers should *inventory* salespeople and have their own *pipeline* of candidates ready to move to a territory when one opens up.

If the firm recruits salespeople internally, it can create a career path in related departments like sales support or customer service. These employees are committed to customers, know the firm's products, and are ready to transfer into the sales force as needed. If the firm recruits externally, sales managers should continually interview candidates, develop short lists, and be ready to hire when needed. There are several staffing trade-offs:

- **Time.** If a new hire must perform effectively and immediately, there may not be time for a broad search and significant training.
- **Tolerance for failure.** Hiring only the best salespeople may be critical. In other cases, a sink-or-swim philosophy can be more effective.
- **Hiring philosophy.** The firm may require salespeople *uncontaminated* by *bad habits* from previous selling experiences.

 **KEY IDEA**

➤ The firm's reward system should motivate salesperson behavior. Primary components are financial incentives, recognition, and promotions.

➤ The primary ways to pay salespeople are salary, commission, and bonus.

*Marketing Question*

Think about jobs you have had. How were you compensated? What types of incentives did the employer provide? What did you find demotivating?

*Marketing Question*

What are the challenges of consistently motivating a sales team? How would you address these challenges?

**KEY IDEA**

➤ The firm should develop rigorous systems for recruiting, selecting, training, retaining, and replacing salespeople.

- **Availability.** If experienced competent salespeople are not available, as in a new and growing industry, the firm must be ready to provide significant training.

The staffing process to hire and prepare effective salespeople involves several steps:

- **Recruiting.** Sizing and defining the pool from which the firm will select salespeople.
- **Selecting.** Identifying and using selection criteria to choose salespeople from the recruitment pool.
- **Training.** Ensuring salespeople have the knowledge, skills, and abilities (KSAs) to be effective.
- **Retaining.** Maintaining high-performing salespeople.
- **Replacing.** Weeding out and replacing poorly performing salespeople.

**SALES MANAGEMENT.** Securing effective salespeople is one thing; finding effective sales managers is quite another. First-line sales managers may have the most critical role in the entire sales force; they require very different knowledge, skills, and abilities (KSAs) than successful salespeople. Regrettably, many firms thoughtlessly promote their best salespeople to be sales managers. The firm may lose a great salesperson and gain a poor sales manager![13] The firm should implement a rigorous recruiting, selecting, and training process for sales managers by developing a clear set of job competencies. A particularly serious problem is the minimal training often given to new sales managers. At one leading life insurer, first-level sales managers often directed 50 or more salespeople. Said one newly appointed district manager, "The company brought us to New York for a two-day *dog-and-pony show.* That was it. Essentially no training for my new position."[14]

Sales managers must carry out the six tasks of sales management. Senior sales managers should also have the skills to interface with marketing and other firm functions. All sales managers must develop a sales culture, using values, heroes, rituals, and symbols, that shapes and reinforces appropriate salesperson behavior.

---

**KEY MESSAGES**

- The marketing and sales interface should be seamless.
- Increasingly, firms are separating customers into tiers and addressing each tier differently.
- Many firms are developing strategic account programs for their most valuable customers.
- Many firms are finding alternate ways of addressing their less valuable customers.
- For an effective selling operation, sales managers must successfully complete six tasks.
- The first three sales management tasks address developing sales strategy:
  - **Task 1.** Set and achieve sales objectives.
  - **Task 2.** Determine and allocate selling effort.
  - **Task 3.** Develop sales approaches.
- The second three tasks focus on implementing the sales strategy:
  - **Task 4.** Design the sales organization.
  - **Task 5.** Create critical organizational processes.
  - **Task 6.** Staff the sales organization.

# CHAPTER 17

# DISTRIBUTION DECISIONS

## LEARNING OBJECTIVES

When you have completed this chapter, you will be able to:

- Understand the nature and function of distribution systems.
- Develop and implement effective distribution strategies.
- Trade off alternative forms of direct and indirect distribution.
- Identify challenges and opportunities in ongoing management of distribution channels.
- Manage power and conflict in distribution systems.

## OPENING CASE: CISCO SYSTEMS

*Cisco Systems is the world's leading supplier of products to power the Internet. Fourteen percent of its $40 billion revenues goes though direct channels, 86 percent through 28,000 channel partners in 160 countries. Originally, Cisco sold direct to end-user customers, but in the late 1990s shifted its major efforts to three types of intermediaries:*

- **Tier 1 partners.** *Systems integrators including global players like EDS and Accenture, but also well-established local partners. Tier 1 partners integrate Cisco's products with technology products from other firms to provide end-user customers with complete solutions.*
- **Tier 2 resellers.** *Intermediaries that sell to smaller end-user customers than Tier 1 partners. Resellers' sales range from a few thousand to several million dollars; they secure Cisco's products from distributors. Distributors hold inventory and provide logistics value to Cisco. Cisco may have thousands of resellers in a particular geography, but only a few distributors.*
- **Service provider partners.** *Mainly telecommunications firms that supply Cisco equipment to their customers. These channel partners may also make customer-service agreements to relieve their customers of the management burden of operating the equipment.*

*Cisco's sales force works hand-in-hand with channel partners to serve large end-user customers. Salespeople develop end-user customer relationships and make joint sales calls with channel-partner salespeople. Channel partners are responsible for local relationships, developing business solutions, consultancy assistance, product delivery, after-sales support, and financing their customers' purchases. Cisco develops and monitors joint business plans with its channel partners; they provide significant value to Cisco.*

*Cisco classifies its channel partners as Premier, Silver, or Gold,[1] based on their investment in securing capabilities to provide value to end-user customers. Higher value levels earn greater recognition from customers and greater resources and support from Cisco. Introduced in 2000, this classification does not consider revenues, so some gold accounts are smaller than other premier accounts. In 2002, Cisco introduced an incentive system for three types of performance:*

- **VIP** — *Developing advanced technological expertise*
- **OIP** — *Seeking out new opportunities and/or new customers*
- **SIP** — *Developing new and innovative solutions*

*Cisco encourages channel partners to earn VIP, OIP, and SIP incentives; an individual partner may earn incentives in more than one category. In 2005, Cisco began an emerging-markets initiative. Previously, these countries were in a conventional regional geographic organization. For example, Saudi Arabia belonged to the Europe, Middle East, and Africa (EMEA) region and competed for resources with advanced western countries like France and Germany.*

*The new emerging-market organization contains channel partners from 140 countries, including Latin America, the Middle East and Africa, Central and Eastern Europe, and Russia. Cisco's tasks in these markets are:*

- *Develop enough channel partners to have good coverage. Cisco hired country managers and salespeople and identified partners in each country.*
- *Develop replicable channel-partner models for industry verticals for transfer across countries, like tourism, and oil and gas. These partners may be non-traditional, so Cisco partners with Schlumberger in oil and gas markets.*
- *Work with country-level policy makers to encourage investment in information technology infrastructure and spur economic growth.*

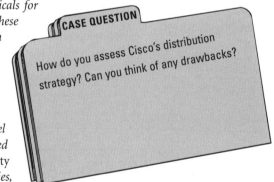

**CASE QUESTION**

How do you assess Cisco's distribution strategy? Can you think of any drawbacks?

*Ninety-six percent of emerging markets revenues go through channel partners (100 percent in many countries); annual growth rates exceed 40 percent. Cisco's challenge is to increase its channel partner capacity by adding channel partners, increasing existing partners' capabilities, or both.*

---

The firm's products reach customers via distribution channels. Distribution can be direct from supplier to customer, but may also be very complex, involving many intermediaries. Intermediaries fulfill many different functions and frequently enjoy mutually beneficial relationships with suppliers. But their goals rarely overlap completely, and distribution systems are riddled with conflict and power inequalities. FMCG firms like P&G, Colgate, and Gillette all compete for good shelf positions in supermarkets so as to earn higher profits. Conversely, chains like Wal-Mart, Albertsons, and Royal Ahold put store brands in the best positions and want suppliers to lower prices and pay fees for shelf space.

Power inequalities sometimes prevent firms from making distribution innovations. Yet no distribution system lasts forever, and new approaches that add value and reduce costs can unseat market leaders. Look at the video-rental market. Traditionally, consumers rented from retail outlets like Blockbuster or Hollywood Movies. Netflix's innovation allows consumers to order movies online. Blockbuster has countered, but both must now compete with cable and satellite providers that bring video-on-demand directly into the home.

---

### Two Views of Distribution — Broad and Narrow

Inputs like raw materials, sub-assemblies, and assemblies undergo changes in *state*, *physical location*, and/or *time* before a firm delivers a finished product to an end-user customer.[2] The **broad view of distribution** includes all of these changes. For example, consider the delivery of prefabricated steel beams for a new office tower to an Argentinean builder.

- **Raw materials**. Iron ore, coal, and limestone are mined in Australia and shipped to an integrated steel manufacturer in Korea.

- **Processing equipment**. Sourced in Germany for use in Korea.

- **Capital**. Bank loans to finance equipment purchasing and working capital for manufacturing based on bank deposits made by Korean citizens.

- **Steel beams**. Manufactured in Korea

- **Completed steel beams**. Shipped to a distributor in Argentina.

- **Finishing**. The Argentine distributor does minor finishing operations and delivers beams to the building site.

The major changes that these activities embrace include:

- **Change of state**. Iron ore, coal, and limestone into prefabricated steel beams.

- **Change of physical location**. Australian raw materials and German processing equipment shipped to Korea. Completed steel beams shipped to Argentina.

- **Change in time**. This process takes time to accomplish.[3]

Along with most marketers, we adopt a **narrow view of distribution**. We focus on changes in *physical location* and *time* of finished products. Other functions focus on *state* changes. For steel beams, procurement secures iron ore, coal, limestone, and capital equipment for the steel manufacturer; finance secures capital. Marketing addresses minor *state* changes like final processing and repackaging, as well as finishing by the distributor.

Most people understand that firms create value by making *state* changes. Firms also create value by making *physical location* changes and in the *timing* of those changes. The Korean manufacturer creates value by forming steel beams from iron ore, limestone, and coal. But the Argentinean builder receives no value if the beams are in Korea or on a cargo ship; they have value only at the building site. And unless they arrive on time, the entire construction project will stop. Delays may cost millions of dollars.

---

## DISTRIBUTION SYSTEMS AND THEIR EVOLUTION

Table 17.1 describes intermediaries that facilitate a supplier firm's goods and services reaching consumers and/or other end-user customers. A **distribution channel or network** comprises a subset of these entities; the functions they perform and their interrelationships are continually in flux. Changes in environmental forces, customer needs, and competitor actions exert pressure to evolve distribution channels. Leading indicators of impending changes include unhappy consumers, end-user customers, and/or suppliers; unexplored channels; new technology; market coverage gaps; deteriorating system economics; complacent intermediaries; poor logistics; and dated system interfaces.[4]

**TABLE 17.1**

**DEFINITIONS OF SELECTED DISTRIBUTION ENTITIES*[5]**

* Developed in part from the American Marketing Association Glossary of Terms

| DISTRIBUTION ENTITY | DESCRIPTION OF DISTRIBUTION ENTITY |
|---|---|
| Agents, brokers, manufacturers' representatives | These entities have similar functions. Generally, they sell products but do not take title or physically handle goods. They may work for the supplier, the customer, or be impartial between supplier and customer. |
| Banks and finance firms | Provide financing to customers to aid in purchasing products. |
| Distributors | Provide promotional support for suppliers, especially for selective or exclusive distribution (discussed later). Often a synonym for wholesaler. |
| Retailers | Display and sell products to consumers, typically from a fixed location. |
| Shipping companies | Transport products. |
| Warehouse operators | Receive and inventory products, arrange product pickup, often break bulk. |
| Wholesalers | Primarily buy, take title, store, and physically handle goods in large quantities. Usually break bulk — resell to retailers or industrial businesses. |

Ultimately, customers' needs drive distribution arrangements. Early in the life cycle, products are often unreliable and service needs are high; customers need help to make choices and support to use the new technology. These requirements diminish as customers become more self-sufficient. They may no longer require the benefits that intermediaries provide, and early market leaders' distribution strategies are increasingly outdated.

A distribution system's effectiveness can change over time, but the supplier firm often has difficulty making distribution changes. It can change prices overnight and, in the short run, develop new promotions or even make product and service changes. By contrast, the firm's distribution arrangements often stay unchanged, sometimes for decades, in part because of end-user customer loyalty to distributors. The average tenure of Caterpillar's 186 dealer relationships worldwide exceeds 50 years!

## DEVELOPING A DISTRIBUTION STRATEGY

To develop its distribution strategy, the firm must make several critical decisions:

- **Distribution functions.** What exactly must be done in the distribution channel?
- **Distribution channel: direct or indirect?** Should the firm deal directly with consumers and/or end-user customers? Or should it use intermediaries, and if so, which ones?
- **Distribution channel breadth.** How many intermediaries should there be at each distribution level? For example, how many wholesalers and/or retailers? Should there be exclusivity?
- **Criteria for selecting and evaluating intermediaries.** How should the firm decide whether a particular intermediary is appropriate for handling its products?

We focus largely on physical goods, but distribution is also important for services. Sometimes our concern is the manufacturer; sometimes another entity in the distribution system. For example, Whirlpool makes its kitchen appliances, but Nike outsources production to others.

## DISTRIBUTION FUNCTIONS

Distribution closes gaps in physical location and time between factory-finished products and consumers and end-user customers by completing many functions. Sometimes the supplier undertakes a particular function; other times intermediaries or end users do so. In a complex distribution channel, some functions, like physical movement, must be done several times.

Increasingly, channel members, especially retailers, try to enhance the customer buying experience. At Forum shops in Las Vegas, Atlantis rises and falls on the hour. The Mall of America (Minneapolis) attracts consumers to its 400 retail stores with Camp Snoopy, an indoor amusement park, and Underwater World, a walk-through aquarium. At Wizards stores (owned by toy manufacturer Hasbro) a game room occupies one-third of the retail space.

**KEY IDEA**

➤ A distribution channel comprises many enterprises, their interrelationships, and the functions they perform.

➤ A distribution system's effectiveness changes over time.

➤ Distribution arrangements are more difficult to change than other marketing implementation elements.

**Marketing Question**

Which distribution entities do a good job of providing quality assurance; risk coverage — insurance, warranties, and guarantees; impartiality — identifying alternatives and the buying experience? Why did you select them?

**KEY IDEA**

➤ Distribution closes gaps in *physical location* and *time* between finished products at the factory and consumers and end-user customers.

When distribution channel entities perform the required functions, the firm should align incentives so each is motivated to perform its functions well. Actions that improve the firm's sales and profits should also benefit channel members. Unfortunately, distribution channels often contain inefficiencies and misaligned objectives.

## DISTRIBUTION CHANNELS: DIRECT OR INDIRECT?

Figure 17.1 shows alternative channel designs for carrying out the various distribution functions:

- **Direct channels.** Suppliers manage most contact with consumers and end users.
- **Indirect channels.** Intermediaries like distributors, wholesalers, and retailers play a major role in transferring products to consumers and end users. Some indirect channels have a single intermediary; others have multiple intermediaries.

## FIGURE 17.1

REACHING CONSUMERS: DIRECT AND INDIRECT CHANNELS

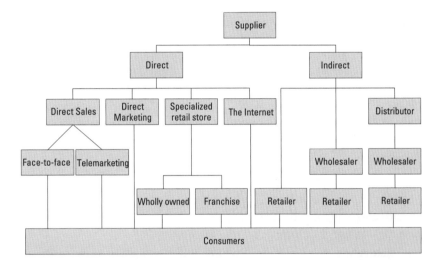

**REACHING CONSUMERS THROUGH DIRECT CHANNELS.** Direct distribution methods, combined with database marketing,[6] are alternatives to indirect distribution channels. In B2C, **direct distribution** has several forms:

- **Face-to-face direct sales.** Direct customer contact can give suppliers intimate insight into customers' needs. In advanced economies, the costs of direct selling and distribution are often too high for consumer goods, but Avon, Mary Kay, and Tupperware have been successful. In less-developed countries, lower incomes make personal selling more viable. When Citibank launched credit cards in India, face-to-face sales were quite successful.
- **Direct sales by telemarketing.** The firm contacts customers directly by telephone. Customers receive purchased products directly by package delivery from remote locations. Centralized telemarketing gives the firm greater message control and cost efficiencies in reaching target customers.
- **Direct marketing.** Direct marketing involves sending messages to targeted customer lists, usually by mail or e-mail. Purchasers respond directly and receive products by package delivery from remote locations.
- **The Internet.** The Internet, combined with package delivery services, is the fastest-growing inbound communications method. Customers initiate the buying process at the suppliers' website. Some firms integrate the Internet with telesales. When a Landsend.com visitor clicks on a *help* icon, a salesperson uses instant messaging to help navigate the site. The Internet reduces search costs and often *disintermediates* wholesalers and retailers.

- **Specialized retail distribution.** The supplier controls product display and customer experiences in retail outlets. Retail outlets are either wholly owned by the supplier — like Apple, Gap, Body Shop, and Starbucks — or **franchised** to a third party — like H&R Block (tax preparation) and 7-Eleven (convenience stores). Many fast-food brands like McDonald's, Kentucky Fried Chicken, and Taco Bell use franchising. Typically, the franchisor develops the business model and seeks entrepreneurs to invest their own capital. The franchisee agrees to implement the franchisor's strategy and pays an initiation fee and ongoing fees.

**REACHING CONSUMERS THROUGH INDIRECT CHANNELS.** Many B2C firms' products reach consumers via indirect **distribution**: wholesalers and retailers provide *physical location* and *time* value. By constructing product assortments from many suppliers, these indirect channels reduce customers' search costs and provide an entire shopping experience. They may also add brand value to suppliers' products, like Macy's (U.S.) or Harrods (Britain). Intermediaries may provide market access that would otherwise be very expensive, or impossible, for the firm to secure. Individuals and organizations in Amazon's Associates program send millions of customers to its website. Market access is particularly important when venturing abroad. Many products fail because firms do not understand local cultures, markets, and customers; local partners can be invaluable. Channel partners also reduce costs for supplier firms because of cost efficiencies:

- Agents, manufacturers' representatives, and brokers — selling economies.
- Package delivery and transportation companies — transportation economies.
- Independent warehouses — inventory economies.
- Banks and financial institutions — financing economies.
- Wholesalers and retailers — inventory, selling, and transportation economies.

**REACHING ORGANIZATIONAL CUSTOMERS.** B2B firms use both direct and indirect distribution to reach organizational customers:

- **Direct distribution.** Firms sell directly to end-user customers using on-the-road sales forces, telemarketing, direct marketing, and/or the Internet. (Few B2B firms operate retail stores.) They use various transportation methods to deliver products to customers.
- **Indirect distribution.** Some suppliers reach customers, especially small businesses, through retail stores like Office Depot and Staples for office supplies. Plumbing, electrical, and home building firms use The Home Depot and Lowe's. More generally, many firms reach customers via wholesalers and distributors.

Distribution speed is increasingly important as firms use **just-in-time** (**JIT**) inventory systems to increase operating efficiencies. Industrial distributors must provide customers with complex product assortments in a timely manner. Typically, some requirements are predictable but others are not. Holding sufficient inventory to satisfy both can be very expensive. Volvo uses an innovative approach:

> Volvo GM (VGM) Heavy Truck Corporation sells replacement parts via commercial truck dealers; it supplies dealers from regional warehouses. Parts inventories in Volvo's warehouses were rising, but, frequently, dealers could not secure parts they needed because of stockouts! VGM worked with FedEx Logistics to set up a warehouse in Memphis (FedEx's hub). When a dealer has an emergency, it calls a toll-free number. FedEx ships the required parts; it delivers to dealer offices, holds for airport pickup, or drops off at the required site. VGM closed three warehouses, reduced total inventory by 15 percent, and regained much business previously lost to stockouts.[7]

## DISTRIBUTION CHANNEL BREADTH

**Distribution channel breadth** is the number of channel members the firm uses at a particular level — like wholesalers or retailers. The firm can add or subtract distributors as appropriate.

**KEY IDEA**

➤ Advantages for wholly owned retail distribution are greater operational control and earning the entire retail margin; disadvantages are capital required for growth, and operating risk.

**KEY IDEA**

➤ Direct channels: Supplier firms manage the contact with consumers and end users. Indirect channels: intermediaries like distributors, wholesalers, and retailers play a major role in transferring products from suppliers to consumers and end users.

➤ Intermediaries offer value-added benefits that suppliers cannot. They provide product assortments, shopping experience, market access, and often reduce the costs of conducting various distribution functions.

KEY IDEA

➤ For B2B suppliers, conditions typically favor either direct or indirect distribution. In each case, there are several options.

The firm can also add/subtract different types of distributor. Adding a new type is important when customers have preferred outlets for purchasing products and services. In the Pacific Northwest, marine and forest-products distributors each address different types of customers and can relate to their specific problems and issues. Many firms use both types of distributor.

Adding new types of distribution can be both positive and negative. In 2001, Tupperware halted a 15-year slide by placing booths in shopping malls and selling over the Internet. In 2003, it added distribution in all of Target's stores, but customers lost a reason to go to Tupperware parties; also, salespeople were poorly trained at in-store demonstrations. Sales dropped 17 percent, profits by 47 percent. Tupperware's sales force shrunk by 25 percent, losing many of its "good, solid performers." Tupperware stopped distributing at Target, and profits doubled.

When the firm distributes through multiple channels, it must be concerned with channel crossing — customers secure product information from one channel, try the product at a second channel, and purchase from a third channel. The first two channels provide free service, but only the third earns revenues.[8] As Internet commerce grows, this is an increasing problem for traditional channels. The firm benefits from making the sale, but other channel partners receive no revenues for their services. In the long run, this practice may cause channel breakdown.

Firms have three broad channel-breadth options:

- **Intensive distribution.** When customers put in little search effort, the firm's products should be easily available. It maximizes the number and type of outlets where customers buy. Intensively distributed consumer products include convenience goods like soft drinks and cigarettes.
- **Exclusive distribution.** When customers are willing to search and travel, the firm should be very careful in outlet selection. If retailers provide brand equity and a positive shopping experience, a B2C firm may choose a few prestigious outlets.
- **Selective distribution.** Selective distribution is a sort of compromise between intensive and exclusive distribution. Too many outlets can lead to excessive competition, but too few outlets make the firm's products difficult to find. Sony and Samsung distribute their products selectively, making careful outlet decisions.

Distribution breadth raises three related exclusivity questions:

- Should the firm give **geographic exclusivity** to distributors?
- Should the firm give **product exclusivity** to distributors?
- Should the distributor give **exclusivity to the supplier**?

## CRITERIA FOR SELECTING AND EVALUATING INTERMEDIARIES

Both parties to a distribution arrangement win when the criteria for selecting channel partners are clear and unambiguous. The firm should clearly specify the functions and performance standards that its distributors should meet. Would-be distributors can then fairly assess their capabilities versus requirements and commit to meet the outcomes desired by both parties.

Both the firm and its distributors should recognize their obligations before entering into an agreement. To improve the chances of success, the supplier should ask several questions of potential distributors[9]:

- What is the distributor's credit and financial condition?
- What is the distributor's selling capability? What is its historic sales performance?
- Will the distributor forgo competitive products? Does it welcome the supplier's products?
- What is the distributor's general reputation among suppliers and customers?
- Does the distributor have adequate market coverage?
- How competent is the distributor's management?
- How does the distributor rate on aggressiveness, enthusiasm, and taking initiative?
- Is the distributor the appropriate size to do business with us?

KEY IDEA

➤ Suppliers should select distribution channel(s) that are appropriate for their target segment(s) and perform the required functions.
➤ Providing customer benefits and values, rather than traditional industry practice, should guide the supplier's distribution choices.

KEY IDEA

➤ Critical distribution strategy decisions include identifying the functions to be performed, deciding on direct versus indirect channels and distribution channel breadth, and setting criteria for intermediaries.

## PUTTING IT ALL TOGETHER: THE DISTRIBUTION STRATEGY

Figure 17.2 shows an eight-step method for developing distribution strategy.[10]

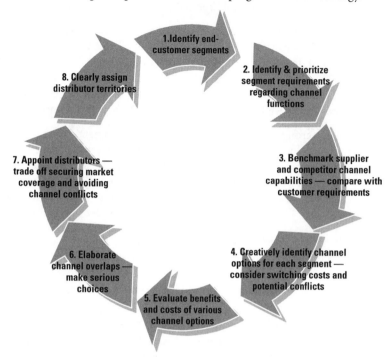

**FIGURE 17.2**

A STEP-BY-STEP
APPROACH TO
DEVELOPING AND
IMPLEMENTING
DISTRIBUTION
STRATEGY

# MANAGING DISTRIBUTION CHANNELS

Ensuring top performance from distributors day by day can be a significant challenge. We discuss intermediary compliance, power inequalities, conflict, and the emerging-partnership model.

## INTERMEDIARY COMPLIANCE

The supplier must ensure that channel intermediaries stick to their agreements and implement its market strategies.

If the firm compensates intermediaries with standardized commissions for all products and customers, it may encounter compliance problems. The firm can better direct its distributors if it varies commissions by product and customer type. It can also tie evaluation and compensation directly to contract requirements like maintaining inventory levels, providing customer service, and ensuring customer satisfaction. Table 17.2 shows a partial list of performance measures to evaluate distribution partners.

**KEY IDEA**

➤ A well-designed compensation system can help the supplier direct its distributors' efforts.

**TABLE 17.2**

CHANNEL MEMBER
PERFORMANCE
EVALUATION[11]

| Criterion | Frequently Used Operational Performance Measures | |
|---|---|---|
| Sales performance | Gross sales<br>Sales by product and market segment<br>Sales growth over time | Actual sales/sales quota<br>Market share<br>Price levels realized |
| Inventory maintenance | Average inventory maintained<br>Inventory/sales ratio | Inventory turnover<br>On-time delivery |
| Selling capabilities | Total number of salespeople<br>Salespeople assigned to the supplier's<br>products | Salespeople assigned by geography<br>Account managers assigned to strategic<br>customers |
| Information provision | Sales data by customer<br>Information on end-user needs | Information on inventories and returns |

The firm should continuously evaluate its intermediaries' performance. But it must remember that intermediary relationships are a two-way street. The distributor is also evaluating its supplier's performance. Are the supplier's products selling? Are consumers and/or end-user customers complaining about the supplier's products? Are the supplier's deliveries prompt? Is the supplier easy to do business with?

## POWER IN DISTRIBUTION SYSTEMS[12]

Power and conflict are endemic in distribution systems. **Power** is one channel member's ability to get another member to act as it wants. Typically, some channel members have more power than others; they also have different objectives. When a supplier is more powerful, it can impose demands. Microsoft sets many conditions for PC manufacturers. Similarly, powerful intermediaries may exert power based on their market positions. Wal-Mart pressures suppliers for low prices and demands adherence to its supply-chain guidelines. Over time, power tends to shift from one channel member to another.

Figure 17.3 shows entities in a distribution system. We explore the power relationships among manufacturers and brand owners, distributors and wholesalers, retailers, and end-user customers.

**FIGURE 17.3**

**POWER IN DISTRIBUTION SYSTEMS**

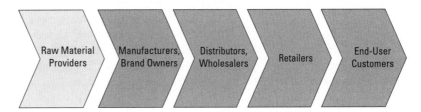

**MANUFACTURERS AND BRAND OWNERS.** In the early 20th century, manufacturers grew and increased their power over distributors and wholesalers. They researched customer needs, designed good products, and reduced costs and prices via mass production. Firms like Coca-Cola, PepsiCo, Kodak, Kellogg's, Budweiser, Gillette, Frito-Lay, Levi's, and Campbell's all used consumer advertising to build powerful brands and become *channel captains*. Not all brand-owners are manufacturers: Nike, Polo, and Calvin Klein outsource production but carefully manage distribution. Sometimes raw material/ingredient providers like NutraSweet (artificial sweetener) and Intel (chip maker) earn significant distribution power.

**DISTRIBUTORS AND WHOLESALERS.** In the late 19th century, full-line, full-service wholesalers like Alexander T. Stewart and H.B. Claffin, now long defunct, were *channel captains*. They dominated U.S. consumer goods distribution, linking distant manufacturers with retailers and consumers.[13] Economic changes and growth in manufacturer and retailer power have diminished these once-powerful intermediaries, but they still play a major role in many industries. As depicted in the movie *Blood Diamond*, De Beers buys nearly all of the world's raw diamonds and virtually sets diamond prices worldwide. **Value-added resellers (VARs)** are a new type of intermediary, building additional software modules on other firms' platforms, and modifying computer hardware for niche markets. **Systems integrators** like Accenture and EDS add value by installing and servicing software and hardware (IT integration services) from many vendors and making them work together.

Intermediaries often provide information value. Insurance brokers dominate business insurance by identifying and analyzing business risks and helping firms obtain coverage from insurers. Intermediaries also provide end-user customers with product choices and reduce the number of needed supplier relationships. Consider the time you would spend to buy groceries from individual specialists: milk from a farm, produce from various growers, and meat from a butcher. Dairies, grocers, and butchers were once valuable intermediaries, but now supermarkets provide their products in one convenient location.

**RETAILERS.** In many sectors, strong retail chains have evolved via industry concentration. In the U.S., *category killers* like Best Buy, Toys "R" Us, and The Home Depot virtually dictate industry direction. Tesco, ASDA, and Sainsbury's dominate British supermarkets; Wal-Mart, Royal Ahold, Kroger, and Safeway play a similar role in the U.S. But national warehouse clubs like Price Club, Costco, and Sam's Club place significant pressure on grocery suppliers. Retailing has trailed many industries in globalization, but Carrefour (France), Wal-Mart (U.S.), and Zara (Spain) now have significant global operations.

Major retailers like these are often price leaders. They use buying power and efficient logistics to drive down costs. They study customer needs and use powerful information technology to tailor their product assortments. They also force suppliers to make direct payments to secure shelf space, aka **slotting fees**.[14] In 2001, slotting fees for five major food companies — Campbell's, Kellogg's, Coca-Cola, PepsiCo, and Kraft — equaled 14 percent of sales at retailers that sold their products. Kraft spent $4.6 billion, PepsiCo $3.4 billion, and Coca-Cola $2.6 billion, just to get their products well placed on retailers' shelves. At Christmas, to enhance its own highly profitable battery sales, Wal-Mart *persuades* Kodak to stop supplying batteries with its cameras.

**END-USER CUSTOMERS.** In B2C markets, individual consumers seldom have significant power, but consumer groups can profoundly influence producers. European consumers boycotted genetically modified products like Roundup Ready corn, and local groups protesting McDonald's presence have vandalized its restaurants. In Germany, environmentally minded consumer coalitions encourage strict recycling laws. In B2B, mergers and acquisitions have left the remaining customers in several industries with significant power. The few global automobile firms and aircraft manufacturers Boeing and Airbus are good examples.

## CONFLICT IN DISTRIBUTION SYSTEMS

Because distribution channel members have multiple organizational relationships, there is high potential for conflict. **Operational conflicts** occur daily due to late shipments, invoice errors, unfulfilled promises, or unacceptable product quality. ESPN's distributors, the cable companies, continually complain about price increases but don't dare stop distributing ESPN. These conflicts are frustrating, annoying, and can disrupt the channel, so most channel members try to minimize them. But some firms, downstream customers or upstream suppliers, take actions to create **strategic conflicts** and gain advantage.

**STRATEGIC CONFLICTS INITIATED BY DOWNSTREAM CUSTOMERS.** We discuss four conflicts:

- **End-user customers grow and desire direct-to-supplier relationships.** Many suppliers start out using distributors to reach end-user (especially small business) customers. As these end users grow, they often want direct supplier relationships. They believe that distributors provide insufficient value for their margins, and the end users want lower prices.

- **Distributors become large and change the power balance.** In the U.S., small single-location retailers once characterized automobile retailing, and manufacturers like GM, Ford, and Chrysler were very powerful. But mega-dealers like Potemkin, AutoNation, and CarMax have emerged, with multiple locations selling huge volumes from several producers. Their growth has shifted the power balance from car manufacturers to car retailers.

- **Distributors commence production.** Sometimes innovative distributors disrupt channel relationships via backward integration — making products they formerly distributed. Nucor began as a steel distributor; dissatisfaction with suppliers led it to manufacture steel. It is now the U.S.'s most profitable steel producer.

- **New buying influences enter the distribution channel.** In some industries, independent buying groups amass buying power for their members. The Independent Grocers Association (IGA) and TruValue have long served small grocery and hardware stores respectively. In hospital supply, Novation and Premier purchase for many small and large hospitals.

**KEY IDEA**

➤ Distribution channel members have high conflict potential.

**STRATEGIC CONFLICTS INITIATED BY UPSTREAM SUPPLIERS.** We consider two conflicts:

- **To reach end-user customers more efficiently, the supplier goes direct.** Sometimes suppliers believe they can be more effective than distributors. They bypass distributors and sell directly to end-user customers; distributors typically resent these initiatives:

  Growth of the Internet for direct-to-end-user customer sales increases the likelihood of conflict with intermediaries. Schwab and E*Trade successfully provide on-line trading to individual investors. Progressive and QuickQuote allow insurance customers to compare prices and connect directly to their preferred suppliers. But potential distribution conflicts hampered the early efforts of Merrill Lynch and many insurance firms from doing likewise.

  Sometimes suppliers go direct in a limited way that minimizes conflict. Firms like Apple and Nike — NikeTown — have their own retail stores. Wholesalers and retailers believe NikeTown and Apple stores enhance these brands, so there is little conflict. Mattel sells a wide range of toys and apparel over the Internet, but avoids conflict by never undercutting its distributors' retail prices and not offering some popular items.

- **To better penetrate the market, the supplier adds new types of distributors.** Suppliers sometimes add new types of distributors to address new segments; current distributors are often unhappy with these initiatives. Hill's Science Diet pet food experimented with a store-within-a-store pet-shop concept in grocery channels, but lost support from pet shops and feed stores.[15]

**KEY IDEA**

➤ When suppliers attempt to improve their power positions, they should try to anticipate the actions of other distribution channel members.

## PLANNING FOR POWER CHANGES

In general, the firm is better off improving its power position. If it initiates strategic conflict, it must assess the likely impact on other channel members. A supplier should predict the impact on distributors and other downstream customers, and anticipate how they may respond. One channel member may initiate strategic conflict but nonetheless maintain relationships with the others. Major U.S. airlines eliminated travel-agent commissions and encouraged passengers to purchase on the web. But travel agents have few options and so continue to sell airline seats.

## THE PARTNERSHIP MODEL

When firms exercise power and generate strategic conflict, they assume a *zero-sum game*; if the firm *wins*, another channel member *loses*, and vice versa. But the **partnership model** can be a *positive-sum game*. By developing trust and working together, several channel members win; there are no losers.

**KEY IDEA**

➤ The partnership model is an increasingly popular alternative to the power/strategic conflict approach. Channel members jointly set goals and work together for greater efficiency and effectiveness.

P&G and Wal-Mart have adopted a highly effective distribution partnership. Wal-Mart captures point-of-sale data for P&G products at its stores and transmits these to P&G in real time using state-of-the-art information systems. By combining these data with seasonal purchasing trends, P&G improves its forecasts and gains manufacturing, purchasing, and packaging efficiencies; reduces inventory; and cuts costs. For example, P&G codes its products by store destinations and places them directly onto Wal-Mart trucks at warehouse interchange points. Full trucks leave frequently for store-to-store deliveries. The firms also use paperless systems for receiving goods and managing receivables and payables.[16]

By developing partnerships, channel members can establish joint strategic goals like cutting costs and reducing supply-chain inventory while limiting stockouts. Better forecasting allows retailers to offer more efficient product sets, do more effective promotions, and eliminate heavy discounts on unwanted merchandise. By working with retailers, suppliers can achieve lower production and distribution costs and better use promotional funds.

# LEGAL ISSUES IN DISTRIBUTION

Other than pricing, distribution issues are more subject to legal concerns than other marketing-mix variables. The legality of various distribution practices varies by industry and geography. What is illegal in the U.S. may be normal business practice elsewhere. Distribution is the focus of many **antitrust** lawsuits; violations occur when a firm with market power takes actions that reduce competition. Offended competitors often file these suits, but the federal government (U.S.) sometimes initiates legal action — typically, the FTC and DOJ-ATD. Critical issues are:

- **Price discrimination.** The Robinson-Patman Act prohibits suppliers from setting different prices for different buyers, where this would reduce competition.

- **Resale price maintenance (RPM).** Suppliers set retail prices for their products. For many years, **resale price maintenance** was illegal in the U.S., but a 2007 Supreme Court decision allowed for its reestablishment in many situations. Many other countries also allow RPM.

- **Tying agreements.** Strong suppliers try to force resellers to sell their entire product line. **Full-line forcing** is illegal if it reduces competition.

- **Exclusive territories.** In general, the courts look unfavorably on arrangements that give distributors exclusive territories when this reduces competition.

- **Selecting and terminating distributors.** Generally, suppliers are free to select and terminate distributors.

- **State and local laws.** Many local laws focus on distribution. Some states tightly regulate alcohol sales — especially type of outlet and opening hours. In some localities, *blue laws* prohibit certain types of store from opening on Sundays.

## KEY IDEA

➤ Distribution laws vary by industry and geography. What is illegal in the U.S. may be normal business practice in other countries.

➤ In the U.S., many antitrust lawsuits involve distribution issues.

## KEY MESSAGES

- A broad view of distribution embraces *changes in state, physical location*, and *time*. Marketing generally takes a narrow view — distribution includes *changes in physical location* and *time*.

- Distribution channels continuously evolve; the firm can gain competitive advantage by innovating its distribution arrangements.

- In developing distribution strategy, the supplier firm must make crucial decisions in four areas:
  - **Distribution functions.** What exactly must be done in the distribution channel?
  - **Distribution channels: direct or indirect?** Should the firm deal directly with consumers and/or end-user customers? Or should it use intermediaries? If so, which?
  - **Distribution channel breadth.** How many intermediaries at each distribution level? For example, how many wholesalers and/or retailers? Should there be exclusivity?
  - **Criteria for selecting and evaluating intermediaries.** How should the firm decide whether a particular intermediary is appropriate for handling its products?

- Implementing strategy through distributors can be very challenging. The supplier must clarify each channel member's responsibilities, understand potential distributor problems, and take steps to gain compliance.

- Typically some channel members have more power than others, but each has options to improve its position. Distributors/wholesalers, manufacturers/brand owners, retailers, and consumers or end-user customers may each be *channel captains*.

- Operating conflict is endemic, but sometimes firms initiate strategic conflict to improve their positions. Many firms are moving to partnership models where each member gains.

# CHAPTER 18

# MANAGING SERVICES, CUSTOMER SERVICE, AND CUSTOMER RELATIONSHIP MANAGEMENT

## LEARNING OBJECTIVES

When you have completed this chapter, you will be able to:

- Distinguish among products, services, and customer service.
- Understand why services are becoming increasingly important to firms and customers.
- Identify critical dimensions across which products differ from services.
- Discriminate among different types of services.
- Diagnose quality-related problems and opportunities in service delivery.
- Specify the dimensions of customer service.
- Establish a customer relationship management (CRM) program for delivering customer service.
- Appreciate the strategic role of customer service.

## OPENING CASE: CELEBRITY CRUISES

*Captained by its Master, Ioannis Papanikolaou, the 91,000-ton Celebrity Constellation is one of Celebrity Cruises' nine-vessel fleet. Celebrity, a subsidiary of Royal Caribbean Cruises Ltd., is positioned upscale of Holland America and Carnival Cruise lines. One of four ships in the Millennium class,* Celebrity Constellation *has a 940-person crew and can carry up to 2,450 passengers. It serves mainly U.S. guests in the Caribbean, the Americas, and Europe.*

Key officers are the Chief Engineer, Staff Captain, and Hotel Director. The Hotel Director is responsible for the entire guest experience, from embarkation to disembarkation. He described how Celebrity optimizes every guest's experience. "Celebrity has made sure that the ship's design and craftsmanship are first rate — from the guest staterooms to all public areas like the Celebrity Theater, San Marco restaurant, and the pools.

"Many guest options are continuously available. We have over a dozen restaurants, cafés, and bars. There's a show every night in the Celebrity Theater — our own Celebrity Singers and Dancers do four shows a week, but we also have comedians and a capella singers. There's a library, casino, Internet café, swimming pools, whirlpools, a shopping arcade, and a fully equipped gym and schedule of classes. On the day at sea from Aruba to San Juan, we have an art auction, bingo, karaoke, shuffleboard, bridge, ping-pong, and many other activities. Then there are special children's programs. We provide guests with many options — they can partake of them or not — and we change them from time to time, based on feedback.

"The crew is the most important factor in delivering the guest experience; we call them Celebrity Family Members (CFMs). We think of ourselves as a family and believe very strongly that happy employees lead to happy guests. We carefully select the entire staff. Agents in many countries around the world source CFMs from the many applications they receive. Celebrity Constellation has CFMs from 58 different countries. That makes for a more interesting guest experience.

"All CFMs are on contracts, ranging from eight months for waiters to four months for officers, with two months off. Fleet-wide, staff retention is 60 to 70 percent. Our on-board training and development manager puts a lot of effort into training, especially the first week of a contract to set clear expectations. There's a lot of management by walking around and a systematic staff-appraisal system. The CFMs work hard and for long hours — that's partly the reason for the two-month break between contracts. Each month we give the Shining Star award for outstanding service. We select five CFMs from a host of nominations — the winners earn cash and other prizes.

"If we provide a great guest experience, we get customer loyalty. On this cruise, about 800 of our 2,000 guests are repeaters from all Celebrity ships. On European cruises, the loyalty rate is often more than 50 percent. There are three levels to the Captain's Club customer loyalty program: Classic — 1 to 5 cruises, Select — 6 to 10 cruises, and Elite — 11+ cruises. Each level offers rewards like stateroom upgrades, interaction with the captain and senior officers, preferential treatment for embarkation and disembarkation, and restaurant seating. Guests can book future cruises on board, and we keep in touch after the cruise.

"We use a comprehensive formal system for guest evaluations, including CFMs' performance — both scaled and open-ended responses — at the end of each cruise. They go to the head office in Miami, and we get the results in a couple of days. These are very important — they are the raw material for appraising our crew and making changes in the guest experience."

*In 2008, Celebrity expanded its fleet by introducing* Celebrity Solstice, *the first ship in the new Solstice class. In 2009, it plans to add* Celebrity Equinox, *followed by* Celebrity Eclipse *in 2010.*

Celebrity ✕ Cruises®

Used with permission of Celebrity Cruises Inc.

**CASE QUESTION**

What special human resource issues relate to managing a cruise line? How do these differ for a passenger airline?

---

Some firms produce and sell *tangible* products like cars, computers, TVs, and kitchen equipment. We spent much of the book talking about these firms and their approach to markets. But many others produce and sell *intangible* services like transportation, beauty treatments, tax preparation, information technology services, and retail distribution. The product/service distinction is often fuzzy, as many products also have service components. Car companies like GM offer warranties, financing, and insurance. Sony provides delivery, installation, and extended warranties. Further, technology advances are allowing some products to morph into services as customers purchase the benefits and values the product delivers as a service, rather than the product itself. They lease, rather than buy, an automobile or hire IBM or EDS to support and manage their information systems, rather than buy the hardware and software directly.

Because they are intangible, services can pose a real managerial challenge. Yet well-designed and well-delivered services create customer satisfaction and loyalty, positive word of mouth, competitive advantage, and high profits. Customer service is a special type of service; we're sure you have direct experience from businesses you deal with. It's a key way for the firm to augment its **core product** or **core service** and differentiate itself from competitors. FedEx offers web-based package tracking for its package delivery service, and firms like Dell offer online and phone support for electronic products. Today, many firms provide value by personalizing customer service through customer relationship management (CRM) programs.

## PRODUCTS, SERVICES, AND CUSTOMER SERVICE

The distinction between products and services is one of marketing's great confusions. Some people use the term *product* to describe any core offering — including both *physical products* and *services*. We use this convenient shorthand in much of the book. In this chapter, we separate a tangible **physical product**, one that can be touched and perhaps kicked or sat upon, from a service. A **service** is *any act or performance that one party can offer another that is essentially intangible and does not result in the ownership of anything. Or, "anything that cannot be dropped on your foot!"*[1] Most services concern people — like education, medical treatment, restaurants, theater, and transportation; products — like car repair, house cleaning, real estate, and retail distribution; or information — like legal and financial services and marketing research.

**KEY IDEA**

➤ Customers buy *offers* or promises of benefits and values; the key element may be a product or a service.

Essentially, *customers do not want your products or services; they want the benefits and values your products and services provide!* Sometimes customers receive benefits and values from a physical product like a house, car, washing machine, clothing, or food. At other times, they receive benefits and values from a service like a haircut, travel, sporting event, Internet provider, or medical procedure. Products are morphing into services as more firms promote the benefits and values their products provide as services, rather than the products themselves. Rolls Royce's *TotalCare* program offers its jet engine product *per hour of flight* — a service.

**KEY IDEA**

➤ A service is: any act or performance that one party can offer another that is essentially intangible and does not result in the ownership of anything.

➤ Customer service enhances value inherent in the core product or service.

The firm can enhance the value of its offer by adding a **customer service** component, including warranties, delivery, repair, technical support, sales support, and information. Marketing's *4Ps* of product, price, promotion, and place have expanded to *4Ps plus an S*, to recognize customer service's critical role. GM offers the Saturn as a core physical product, but also provides customer service before, during, and after a purchase. These benefits differentiate Saturn from other auto brands. FedEx's core service is overnight package delivery, but it surrounds this offer with logistical advice and information, billing statements, package-tracking, documentation, pickup, supplies, and order-taking. Finally, a core service for one firm can be customer service for another. Delivery may be *customer service* for your local pizza parlor, but for a chain that only delivers pizza, delivery is its *core service*.

## GROWTH IN THE SERVICE SECTOR

The service sector of the economy has grown dramatically in recent years, making product, service, and customer-service distinctions increasingly important. Services are upward of 70 percent of total employment and GDP in developed countries.[2] Many service firms now populate the *Fortune* 500, and social enterprises like government and non-profit organizations (NGOs) almost exclusively offer services. Prime examples are education, health and human services, garbage collection, and policing. Rising incomes and age-related demographic shifts are driving the growth of services. Other important factors in the private sector are:

- **Outsourcing.** Many firms are narrowing their missions to focus on core competencies; hence, they **outsource** activities and processes previously performed internally, often securing better value-cost ratios. Examples include technology, financial transactions, HR functions like payroll and benefits, telephony, legal advice, security, call-center customer-service support, and even manufacturing. Outsourcing provides suppliers with service opportunities and profit margins that may be higher than for physical products. Unisys, EDS, and IBM design, install, and operate firms' computer and information systems; Xerox runs imaging centers; and firms like Accenture manage various transactional and transformational business processes.

- **Leveraging core competence.** Some firms find that in-house activities are valuable to other firms, so they repackage and sell them as services. Florida Light and Power, winner of Japan's prestigious Deming quality award, offers quality workshops; Xerox also consults on quality management. Disney offers executive programs in leadership and customer service. SAS trains flight crews from other airlines, maintains their planes, and helps Swedish firms prepare employees for relocation.[3]

- **Franchising. Franchising** is the backbone of the restaurant, hotel/motel, and tax preparation industries, with leading brands like McDonald's, Hilton, and H&R Block respectively. But businesses like window-cleaning, closet installation, commercial property restoration, and onsite computer repairs are also growing via franchising.

- **Customer behavior changes.** Customers' preference for purchasing is decreasing. Consumers want to avoid ownership responsibilities; firms want to remove investments from their balance sheets to increase return-on-investment (ROI). Correspondingly, financial services like credit, rental, and leasing have grown.

- **Deregulation.** Deregulation in industries like electricity, financial services, natural gas, telecommunications, and transportation has eased market entry, and entrants with innovative strategies have fueled growth.

- **Technology.** Technological advances allow firms to connect to their customers and deliver ongoing and complementary services.

- **Globalization.** Innovations in technology and communications are making products and services accessible to broader global markets. Firms doing business across the world use many service strategies to meet the diverse needs of their new customers.

# CHARACTERISTICS OF SERVICES

Physical products differ from services in several important ways:

## INTANGIBILITY

Services that *focus on people* generally require the customer's physical presence or interactivity. *Focus on products and information* generally does not. The location for certain services like factory maintenance, house-cleaning, and gardening is fixed. Other services can occur in various places: We may see a movie in a theater or at home and receive medical services at a hospital, doctor's office, or perhaps also at home.

Some services like restaurant meals or in-store product purchases are more tangible than others, but the core experience is still **intangible**. In general, intangibility makes customers' evaluation of services more subjective than for physical goods. Hence, tangible service elements often play an important role in forming expectations of, and evaluating, the service experience. Service tangibles include facilities, equipment, and personnel. Some firms provide additional tangibility via service guarantees.

---

*Marketing Question*

Next time you call a customer service department, ask where the rep you are speaking to is located (if the person can say). It may be South Dakota, but most likely it is somewhere south of Pudhi, where English-speaking skills are well developed. Today, India, Kenya, Malaysia, and Bangladesh all support call centers for major U.S. and European firms, but with lower wage costs. Ask a couple of reps how they like their jobs, and what their biggest challenges are. What are the implications for firms doing the outsourcing?

---

KEY IDEA

➤ Services represent over 70 percent of employment and GDP in developed countries.

➤ Factors driving services growth are rising incomes, age-related demographic shifts, outsourcing, leveraging core competence, franchising, customer behavior changes, deregulation, technology, and globalization.

**Marketing Question**

Think about the last time you purchased a computer. During the purchase, how important to you was the product? How important was the associated service?

**SERVICE FACILITIES.** Where the firm delivers the service comprises an:

- **Exterior.** Includes the location, outside view, and signage. Provides information about the interior where the firm provides the service; it either attracts customers to, or detracts customers from, the service.
- **Interior.** Has two dimensions:
  - **Offstage.** Out of customers' sight
  - **Onstage.** Where customers experience deeds, performances, or efforts.

**SERVICE EQUIPMENT.** Generally, a service requires physical products: A haircut needs scissors and a mirror, air travel needs an airplane. **Service equipment** quality often influences the service experience. Many passengers prefer airlines with new planes, like Singapore Airlines, to those with older fleets.

**SERVICE PERSONNEL.** Some work offstage, others work onstage. Airline mechanics and baggage handlers generally work offstage; ticket agents and flight attendants are onstage. The customer experience depends on how well all **service personnel** — offstage and onstage — perform their functions. Because appearance, demeanor, and manner of onstage personnel are often important, many service personnel wear uniforms. Bringing offstage personnel onstage can enhance the customer experience. David Letterman frequently brings his crew onstage on his late-night talk show. Airline pilots make frequent announcements and often converse with deplaning passengers.

Customers have many interactions with onstage service personnel. Jan Carlzon, former SAS president, coined the phrase **moment of truth** to emphasize their importance. At each *moment of truth*, customers can be satisfied or dissatisfied.[4] Customers make judgments about their own interactions and about the interactions of service personnel with other customers. Managing customer/service personnel interactions is a major challenge. Disney's elaborate training and management program carefully controls employees' response behavior so that each customer has a *magical* and consistent experience. Even more difficult is managing customer interactions with distributors' or franchisees' employees; yet consumer interactions with GM dealers, for example, strongly influence perceptions of GM.

**KEY IDEA**

➤ *Moments of truth* are opportunities for customer satisfaction or dissatisfaction.

A serious concern for some service firms is the relative strength of employee and firm relationships to customers. When the service person-to-customer relationship is strong, employees may resign and take customers with them. Because of close working relationships with customers, advertising agencies, beauty salons, and professional services firms have this problem. Better company communications can strengthen firm-customer bonds. The firm can also bind critical employees more closely by enlightened contractual provisions that make employees happy but also place barriers to working for competitors.

**SERVICE GUARANTEES.** Promises about the service experience provide tangible elements of value if the firm does not keep its promises. Good **service guarantees** are unconditional, painless to invoke, and easy and quick to collect.[5] Cort Furniture Rental guarantees on-time delivery and pickup, showroom-quality products, upgraded replacement if substitution is necessary, exchange of any item within two days, and a total refund if any problem cannot be fixed. The service agreement should be simple to understand and communicate and meaningfully related to the service it guarantees. Good guarantees work because customers have positive experiences with the guarantee. Also, employees improve service quality by working hard to avoid customers invoking the guarantee.

**Marketing Question**

Think about your purchase of cell phone service. Was there a service guarantee? Did the guarantee meet the noted criteria? Did the provider communicate the guarantee well? What could the provider have done better? Have you received a guarantee for any other purchase?

## INSEPARABILITY

Firms manufacture, ship, store, and sell physical goods. They deal with demand and supply fluctuations and imperfect forecasting via inventory. For services, provider and customer are inexorably linked — production and consumption are innately **inseparable**. Because firms cannot inventory services, demand forecasting is more critical. Crowded restaurants, long ski-lift lines, and standing-room only on public transportation all result from excess demand. To address supply/demand imbalances the firm must modify supply and/or demand.

**MODIFYING SUPPLY.** The firm can *increase* short-run services supply by stretching its capacity, like working longer hours, outsourcing, renting or sharing extra facilities and equipment, and adding full-time or part-time workers. The critical challenge is maintaining service quality; an upscale hair salon should not hire temporary stylists unless their skills meet the salon's standards. The firm can *decrease* supply by scheduling renovations, maintenance, and employee training.

**MODIFYING DEMAND.** The firm should analyze demand patterns, answering such questions as:

- Does service demand follow a regular, predictable cycle? If so, is the cycle length daily, weekly, monthly, or annual?
- What causes these fluctuations: work schedules, paydays, school vacations, or climate?
- Are there also random demand fluctuations like the weather, births, or crime?
- Can we disaggregate use patterns by market segments or profitability?

Based on the answers to these questions, the firm must decide which segments to target — then increase or decrease demand as necessary. To *increase* demand, it can improve its service offering, improve time and place convenience, communicate better with potential customers, and/or reduce price. To *decrease* demand, the firm can offer customer incentives to switch to lower demand periods or use *demarketing* techniques like cutting advertising and promotion, reducing service availability, and increasing price.[6]

## VARIABILITY

Lack of consistency in the service, **variability**, follows directly from human involvement in service delivery. Firms address variability in product manufacturing output by using quality tools. Generally, these are more difficult to use for services. Nonetheless, tools like **six sigma**, a data-driven methodology that eliminates defects in any process, are effective for service systems.

**FOCUS ON HUMAN CAPITAL.** Employee selection and training are important for improving employee performance and reducing service variability, especially at firms like Singapore Airlines and Virgin. Virgin puts employees ahead of customers, under the philosophy that "happy employees mean happy customers." It believes that poorly treated employees will not deliver high customer satisfaction. For manufactured products, variability is typically a negative; for services, it can be positive.

Service providers can enhance satisfaction by tailoring their actions to individual customers and responding to customer needs in real time. Reward systems should encourage employees *to go the extra mile* to serve customers, not penalize them for innovating or for breaking rules to provide a better customer experience. Ritz Carlton Hotels allow each employee a dollar amount to remedy customer service issues on the spot — no questions asked. Many firms identify and applaud company heroes who deliver exceptional service.

**SUBSTITUTION OF CAPITAL FOR LABOR.** The firm can remove human variability via automation like using dispensing machines for cash, drinks, sandwiches, or subway cards. Cost reduction often drives these innovations, but they reduce variability nonetheless. The downside is that machines can break down, and some customers prefer human contact. Some bank customers prefer human tellers to ATMs, and many people object to voice recognition in call centers; they prefer human interaction. Do you?

## PERISHABILITY

The **perishability** concept in services marketing is tightly linked to inseparability and the inability to inventory services. When a psychiatrist's patient misses an appointment, or a plane

**KEY IDEA**

➤ Customers often focus on tangible aspects of intangible services — service facilities, service equipment, service personnel, and service guarantees.

➤ Service guarantees should be unconditional, painless to invoke, and easy and quick to collect. They should also be simple to understand and communicate and meaningfully related to the service being guaranteed.

**KEY IDEA**

➤ For services, production and consumption are inseparable.

➤ Since the firm cannot inventory services, it must either increase or decrease supply and/or demand.

**KEY IDEA**

➤ Reducing variability is more difficult for services than for products.

**KEY IDEA**

➤ Service variability can be positive when human service providers tailor their behavior for individual customers.

➤ The firm can reduce human variability through automation.

has empty seats, the revenues from that service are lost forever. Service firms must balance the cost to serve additional customers with the lost revenues from unused capacity. Increasing demand is one approach. New York and London theaters sell full-price tickets at the theater and via ticket-ordering services, but also sell discounted tickets shortly before the performance at TKTS booths in theater districts.

## DIVISIBILITY

We view most products as single entities: an automobile as a single unit, not a collection of components like an engine, transmission, wheels, and seats. **Divisibility** is a key service characteristic; many core and surrounding services comprise a sequence of activities conducted over time. Consider, for example, the many activities required for your marketing course, from registration to posting the final grades.

## LACK OF ACQUISITION

People acquire and frequently own products, but not services. They experience the physical manifestation of services like a smoother-running car, a dashing haircut, or a department store purchase. But typically the service is, at best, a set of associations in memory. Yet a service experience can be highly salient, and related associations very influential. Positive associations drive repurchase and positive word of mouth. Negative associations lead customers to avoid the service provider and dissuade others.

## THE ROLE OF CUSTOMERS

Firms rarely refuse to sell products to customers because of the effect on other customers. But customers experience many services in group settings, so customer-customer interaction is a critical issue for many service firms. The drunken airline passenger, the sleeping student in a finance class, and the baseball fan behind home plate shouting out pitches — each affects other customers' experiences. The firm must not unthinkingly believe that *the customer is always right*. Some organizations have systems for rejecting customers — like nightclub bouncers, college admission departments, and restaurant maitre d's.

> *Marketing Question*
>
> Think about a recent positive service experience. Did you buy the service again? Did you tell friends, family, and colleagues? Did they buy the service? Think about a recent negative service experience. Did you buy the service again? Did you tell friends, family, and colleagues? Did they buy the service?

## SERVICE QUALITY

In general, high customer satisfaction drives repurchase and positive word of mouth, and enhances shareholder value.[7] The converse is also true. In the **SERVQUAL** model, Figure 18.1, customer satisfaction relates to service quality via **expectations disconfirmation**, **Gap 5** is the *difference* between perceived quality and expected quality[8]:

- **Customer satisfaction.** Perceived service is better than expected service.
- **Customer dissatisfaction.** Perceived service is worse than expected service:

> Computer manufacturer **A** promised service visits within four hours of a request. Firm **B** promised eight hours. **A** averaged five and a half hours — **B** averaged seven hours. **A**'s service performance was better, but **B**'s satisfaction ratings were higher!

The extent of **Gap 5** depends on four other gaps:

- **Gap 1.** The firm does not understand the customer's service expectations.
- **Gap 2.** Service quality specifications do not reflect the firm's beliefs about service expectations.

- **Gap 3.** Service delivery performance does not meet service specifications.
- **Gap 4.** External communications about service quality do not reflect service performance.

SERVQUAL identifies a dilemma. The firm may increase short-run sales by advertising high service quality, but if quality is lower than promised, customers will be dissatisfied. Yet, if the firm under-promises on service quality, sales may be low. Also, rising customer expectations make it increasingly difficult to deliver greater-than-expected service.

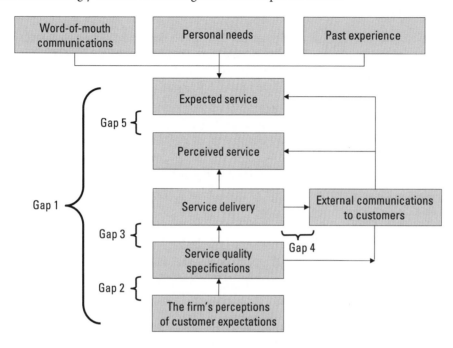

**FIGURE 18.1**

**THE SERVQUAL MODEL FOR DIAGNOSING SERVICE QUALITY**

## MEASURING AND MANAGING SERVICE QUALITY

In SERVQUAL, five key variables influence perceived service quality:

- **Tangibles.** Appearance of physical facilities, equipment, personnel, and communication materials
- **Reliability.** Ability to perform the promised service dependably and accurately
- **Responsiveness.** Willingness to help customers and provide prompt service
- **Assurance.** Knowledge, courtesy of employees, and ability to convey trust and confidence
- **Empathy.** Provision of caring, individualized attention to customers

The 22-item SERVQUAL scale, Table 18.1, measures these variables. Respondents provide service quality expectations data — $QE^9$ — and service perceptions data for providers — QP. A provider's total SERVQUAL score is made up of QP minus QE differences, summed over all 22 items. Subscale scores for responsiveness, reliability, assurance, empathy, and tangibles provide finer-grained data and offer action recommendations. Figure 18.2 plots hypothetical scores for one provider: *Reliability* and *empathy* are fine, but it may be overemphasizing *empathy*. It should focus on *assurance* — high expectations, but low perceived performance, and *tangibles*. The provider should also keep its eye on *responsiveness*.

 **KEY IDEA**

➤ Expectations disconfirmation is perceived quality less expected quality.

➤ SERVQUAL identifies five gaps for diagnosing service quality.

**KEY IDEA**

➤ Variables influencing perceived service quality include responsiveness, reliability, assurance, empathy, and tangibles.

➤ SERVQUAL's related subscale scores provide actionable items for improving service performance.

## TABLE 18.1

### THE SERVQUAL SCALE

| SERVQUAL Dimensions | SERVQUAL Expectations Item, QE | SERVQUAL Perception item, QP |
|---|---|---|
| Tangibles | 1. Excellent_____companies will have modern-looking equipment. | XYZ has modern-looking equipment. |
| | 2. The physical facilities at excellent _____ companies will be visually appealing. | XYZ's physical facilities are visually appealing. |
| | 3. Employees at excellent _____ companies will be neat-appearing. | XYZ's employees are neat-appearing. |
| | 4. Material associated with the service (such as pamphlets or statements) will be visually appealing in an excellent _____ company. | Material associated with the service (such as pamphlets or statements) are visually appealing at XYZ. |
| Reliability | 5. When excellent _____ companies promise to do something by a certain time, they will do so. | When XYZ promises to do something by a certain time, it does so. |
| | 6. When a customer has a problem, excellent _____ companies will show a sincere interest in solving it. | When you have a problem, XYZ shows a sincere interest in solving it. |
| | 7. Excellent _____ companies will perform the service right the first time. | XYZ performs the service right the first time. |
| | 8. Excellent _____ companies will provide their services at the time they promise to do so. | XYZ provides its services at the time it promises to do so, |
| | 9. Excellent _____ companies will insist on error-free records. | XYZ insists on error-free records. |
| Responsiveness | 10. Employees in excellent _____ companies will tell customers exactly when services will be performed. | Employees in XYZ tell you exactly when services will be performed. |
| | 11. Employees in excellent _____ companies will give prompt service to customers. | Employees in XYZ give you prompt service. |
| | 12. Employees in excellent _____ companies will always be willing to help customers. | Employees in XYZ are always willing to help you. |
| | 13. Employees in excellent _____ companies will never be too busy to respond to customers' requests. | Employees in XYZ are never too busy to respond to your requests. |
| Assurance | 14. The behavior of employees in excellent _____ companies will instill confidence in customers. | The behavior of employees in XYZ instills confidence in you. |
| | 15. Customers of excellent _____ companies will feel safe in their transactions. | You feel safe in your transactions with XYZ. |
| | 16. Employees in excellent _____ companies will be consistently courteous with customers. | Employees in XYZ are consistently courteous with you. |
| | 17. Employees in excellent _____ companies will have the knowledge to answer customers' questions. | Employees in XYZ have the knowledge to answer your questions. |
| Empathy | 18. Excellent _____ companies will give customers individual attention. | XYZ gives you individual attention. |
| | 19. Excellent _____ companies will have operating hours convenient to all their customers. | XYZ has operating hours convenient to all its customers. |
| | 20. Excellent _____ companies will have employees who give customers personal attention. | XYZ has employees who give you personal attention. |
| | 21. Excellent _____ companies will have the customer's best interests at heart. | XYZ has your best interests at heart. |
| | 22. The employees of excellent _____ companies will understand the specific needs of their customers. | Employees of XYZ understand your specific needs. |

a. All questions answered on a 1-to-7 scale: 1 = Strongly disagree, 7 = Strongly agree.
b. The blank line in the Expectations items is for the particular industry, sub-industry, or department being studied.
c. XYZ in the Perception items stands for the company being studied.

**FIGURE 18.2**

**CUSTOMER EXPECTATIONS AND PERFORMANCE PERCEPTION ON FIVE SERVICE VARIABLES**

*Trouble*

*Keep it up*

• Assurance

• Reliability

High

**Customers' Expectations of Performance on Service Variables**

• Tangibles    • Responsiveness

Low

• Empathy    *Too much effort*

*Be low key*

Low    High

**Customers' Perceptions of Firm Performance on Service Variables**

*Marketing Question*

Think about your favorite coffee shop. How do you perceive service quality? Evaluate responsiveness, reliability, assurance, empathy, and tangibles.

## SERVICE QUALITY ISSUES

There are several issues involved in improving service quality:

- **Service performance and information.** Customers want high service quality, but they also want to know when they will receive the service. London's Heathrow Express provides passengers with accurate estimates of train arrivals and departures, on the platform and on the train. In many cities, clocks advise motorists when traffic lights will change. And firms using queues set queue-time expectations.

- **Improving the service offer.** The firm enhances service quality by adding customer service. FMCG firms give retailers *plan-o-grams* for arranging shelf space. Private banks give money management seminars for children of high-net-worth clients. Extra service is particularly important in mature industries. Sometimes firms improve quality by removing services! Popular and profitable Southwest Airlines (SWA) uses secondary airfields, on-board ticketing, and non-assigned seats. It has no interline baggage transfer with other airlines, no meals, and no other services. By reducing its costs, SWA offers low fares, high-frequency flights, and on-time performance.

- **Customer co-production.** Some firms improve service quality via customer participation in service delivery. Examples are self-service restaurants and self-checkout supermarkets. FedEx customers used to track packages by phoning customer service reps; today they track packages via the Internet. Customers enjoy better service, and FedEx cuts costs. Nirvana! Some firms promote co-production via differential pricing like Internet airline prices that are often lower than phone bookings.

- **Maintaining the service environment.** Some services negatively affect the physical environment: dirty plates and glasses in restaurants and bars, dirty towels in health clubs, and hair on the barber's floor. Quickly restoring the environment improves service quality.

- **Service quality failures and service recovery.** Despite the firm's best efforts, service errors do occur. Service failures also happen when the firm's drive for efficiency leads to inflexible systems that cannot deal with idiosyncratic customer behavior.

The firm should minimize customer defections, deal swiftly with service failure, and aggressively manage service recovery. Done well, formerly unhappy customers become loyal, even advocates. Firms can address failure by upgrading products, services, and/or customer service. Overall, few aggrieved customers complain — they just defect. But complaints are often an opportunity to learn about customers' *pain points*.[10] Firms should make complaining easier but should follow up swiftly and aggressively.

**KEY IDEA**

➤ A drive for service efficiency can lead to inflexible systems — they cannot deal with idiosyncratic customer behavior.

**KEY IDEA**

➤ All firms experience service failures; how they address them is key.

➤ Few aggrieved customers complain — they just defect. Firms should make complaining easier, then follow up swiftly and aggressively.

Increasingly, customers complain in public, especially on the Internet. They post stories on bulletin boards or set up attack websites. United Airlines, AOL, McDonald's, The Gap, J.P. Morgan Chase, and Microsoft have all been targets. Some firms have complex web applications that search and alert executives to all postings; others employ web watchers to monitor complaints and answer questions. Sears tested a web answer line and received "a couple of hundred" questions per day. It abandoned the effort — too many questions to answer!

## CUSTOMER SERVICE

### A Glimpse of the Future

It's 6:30 p.m.; Joe is leaving his office. He remembers it's his turn to prepare dinner. He accesses the Pillsbury website; it recognizes Joe's address and queries the corporate database. Joe was here six days ago, and two weeks before that. Both times he wanted data on meals he could prepare with a minimum of fuss. Bet he's back for the same thing.

The computer accesses another database — it identifies popular meals with time-sensitive professional males (research-based). What's on the menu? — Garlic Pasta Chicken Salad? No! He had that last time — on a Saturday. Joe picked it the last three times. Something else in poultry? Ah! Fiesta Chicken. Quick, simple to prepare, spicy — Joe picks spicy meals every time he downloads a recipe. They're popular with males in his age range.

By the time Joe has finished clicking on "What's new in main dishes," an entire meal has been planned — including recipes, suggested side dishes, and even the wine. Joe looks at the Fiesta Chicken page and sees a lovely picture of the dish, recipe beside it.

Now, where is Joe located? Last time he requested data on stores carrying the Green Giant brand along Route 128 near the Mainfair intersection. A quick check of the MapInfo business-oriented geographic information system shows light industry populated by R&D startups. Joe is probably at work — he's going to pick up his dinner items on the way home. A map flashes on the screen, identifying stores where he can most easily pick up Green Giant products for Fiesta Chicken and Pillsbury baked goods for dessert![11]

*Marketing Question*

Joe's scenario with Pillsbury is feasible with today's technology. Do you regard it favorably or unfavorably? Why? Or why not?

We showed previously that core services differ from customer services. Core services like an airline trip or theater production are central to the offer; all other services are *customer service*. Customer service is any act, performance, or information that enhances the firm's core product or service. Customer service is critical for **customer relationship management (CRM)**, and can be as important as the core product. IBM did not dominate mainframes because of superior technology or lower prices; its differential advantage was customer service: "You never get fired for buying IBM."

GE Power Systems (GEPS) focused on improving customer service when electric utility deregulation spawned severe price pressure. GEPS reduced replacement time for old or damaged parts from 12 to six weeks and advised customers on doing business in Europe and Asia. GEPS provided maintenance staff for equipment upgrades and moved one-third of its engineers from new product development to new service development.

### TYPES OF CUSTOMER SERVICE

Figure 18.3 shows the **flower of customer service**, embracing eight dimensions for augmenting the core product or service.[12]

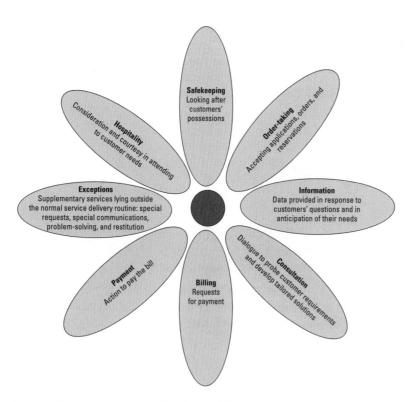

FIGURE 18.3

THE FLOWER OF
CUSTOMER SERVICE

## Marketing Question

Recall when you ordered something over the phone, like a product or airline reservation. Where did the provider do well — information, order-taking, safekeeping, hospitality, exceptions, payment, billing, or consultation? Where could it improve?

### KEY IDEA

➤ Customer service has eight *flower-of-service* dimensions.

We can also classify customer service by phase of the purchase process. Each phase has different customer requirements and different customer service activities[13]:

- **Pre-purchase.** Helps customers prepare for purchase. Includes help identifying needs and promotional activities that provide information about products and purchase locations.
- **During purchase.** Includes help with selection, customization agreements, financing, personal selling, product assortments, product trial, and quality assurance.

At The Musician's Planet, customers can try out a guitar and make a demo tape. At REI in Seattle, consumers can attempt a 64-foot climbing wall, examine a water pump in an indoor river, or test a Gore-Tex jacket in a rainstorm. Some clothing stores use advanced imaging technology to portray dresses with different styles and fabrics. Levi-Strauss' imaging machine takes precise customer measurements for custom jeans.

- **Post-purchase.** Most marketing activity occurs pre- and during purchase; most customer service occurs after purchase. Post-purchase service helps customers transport, receive, install, pay for, use, return and exchange, repair, service, and dispose of the product.[14] It addresses problems and complaints and includes remanufacturing, spare parts availability, technical service, toll-free service telephone numbers, training, warranties, and websites. The firm may provide some services (for some customers) free, but with astute segmentation and pricing, post-purchase services can be very profitable.[15] Post-purchase customer service can also act as an early-warning system for detecting quality problems; it can raise repurchase rates and cross-selling and increase customer retention.

## DELIVERING EXCEPTIONAL CUSTOMER SERVICE

Several considerations are important for delivering outstanding customer service:

**TOP MANAGEMENT SUPPORT AND INVOLVEMENT.** Top managers should over-communicate that serving customers is crucial — they should build a culture where all employees emphasize customer service. It's one thing to *talk the talk*, but top managers should also *walk the walk* by

### KEY IDEA

➤ Customer service can be more central than the core product or service.

**KEY IDEA**

➤ Customer service is different before, during, and after the purchase.

*getting their hands dirty* interacting with customers. In B2C firms, they might spend a day or so a month in customer service, like senior Toyota executives when introducing the Lexus. They should identify customer service *heroes* and publicly acknowledge their successes. In B2B firms, top managers should support strategic account managers by serving as *Partnership Executives* — Chapter 15. CEO Steve Ballmer is Microsoft's *Partnership Executive* for Wal-Mart.

**CUSTOMER SERVICE STRATEGY.** In developing its market strategy, the firm identifies customers' *product- or service-based needs*, then develops a value proposition to satisfy those needs — Chapter 9. In formulating a **customer service strategy**, the firm focuses on customers' *needs for customer service*. Customers with similar product- or service-based needs may have very different customer service needs, and vice versa.

**KEY IDEA**

➤ Customers requiring similar products and services may have differing needs for customer service, and vice versa.

Standard research techniques provide insight about customer service needs. Mystery shopping programs examine customers' experiences with the firm and its competitors. Generally, the firm should strive to surpass competitors' service levels. Setting customer expectations slightly below the firm's ability to deliver leads to positive expectations disconfirmations. Because customer service can be expensive to provide, some firms offer it at varying levels. All customers may receive a basic customer service backbone; additional service depends on the customer's importance to the firm.[16]

**HUMAN RESOURCE MANAGEMENT.** Human resource (HR) planning — especially for onstage personnel — is integral for delivering superior customer service.[17] Many *front-line* positions, particularly in retail, are low skill and low pay. The firm should develop good HR policies and apply them rigorously. Traditional recruitment, selection, training and development, appraisal, recognition, reward, and retention tools are important to ensure a good fit with the firm.

**KEY IDEA**

➤ Human capital planning requires special attention to recruitment, selection, training and development, appraisal, recognition, reward, and retention of customer service employees.

High costs are leading many firms to outsource customer service call-centers to countries like India and Kenya. Although well-educated and English-speaking, candidates typically need training in products and services and in learning to speak with U.S. accents. Costs often drive outsourcing decisions, but the firm must balance cost reductions with service quality. Understanding customers' service needs drives the knowledge, skills, and abilities (KSAs) that customer service personnel require. KSAs vary by specific customer service, but a general list includes competence, courtesy, credibility, responsiveness, and commitment.

**SERVICE INFRASTRUCTURE.** The firm must design the appropriate infrastructure, like technological and human resources, to support its customer service strategy. Some customer services, like repairs, depend heavily on people; others depend on technology, like web-based reservation systems. Paradoxically, some highly people-intensive service systems require the highest technology investments, like airline passenger and baggage check-in procedures.

Customer interfaces are crucial. Most customers want simple interfaces and a single customer service rep: They dislike being passed around. Firm employees often develop area knowledge, and specialization is often efficient — but this can reduce customer satisfaction. Many firms outsource customer service to third-party providers, but abdicating this responsibility can be a serious problem. The author purchased an HDTV and related accessories from BestBuy. The store experience was excellent, and an automated phone call provided installation information. But then the customer service experience fell apart: a half-hour on the telephone waiting to speak to a human — a third-party installer. And of course, I'm sharing this experience with *you*.

Many firms use technological solutions — often web-based — to reduce personnel costs. Well-designed systems — like airline reservations — guide customers seamlessly; they improve customer service and reduce costs. Poorly designed systems can be intensely annoying and highly dissatisfying.

Reporting relationships and customer service's interfaces with other functions are important infrastructure issues. Xerox's customers interfaced with its sales, service, and business operations. Commissioned salespeople strove to place machines, but were difficult to find when customers needed information or wanted to switch to better-suiting products. (The salespeople were searching for more commission opportunities.) Customer service had to clean up many problems created by the sales force. Xerox teamed up sales, service, and business operations to share responsibility in districts and regions, and harmonized reward systems.[18]

**MEASURING CUSTOMER SERVICE QUALITY.** *If you can't measure it, you can't manage it.* Customer satisfaction is a good measure, but across-the-board quality improvements have made it less useful. Customer defection rate is better.[19] Identifying defectors is easy when customers must terminate a relationship as for banking and phone services, but difficult when there is no individual customer record. Analyzing the causes of defection provides valuable information for improving service delivery. The firm should identify and regularly measure critical elements of customer service against performance standards. Differences between standards and performance should form the basis for modifying customer service. The firm should target reward programs based on these standards. But it should be careful not to rely exclusively on easy-to-collect *hard* measures, while ignoring difficult-to-collect *soft* or qualitative measures that capture the essence of customers' perceptions.

# CUSTOMER RELATIONSHIP MANAGEMENT

A customer relationship comprises the series of over-time interactions or *touch points* between the customer and the firm. **Customer relationship management (CRM)**, or relationship marketing, is a synthesis of marketing, quality management, and customer service that manages these *touch points*. More precisely, CRM is *the ongoing process of identifying and creating new value with individual customers and sharing these benefits over a lifetime of association with them.*[20] CRM helps the firm to *know* its customers better. In B2C, mom-and-pop stores often form personal relationships with customers; CRM helps large firms build relationships in a systematic way. Strong relationships should drive customer purchases over a long time period.

CRM's underlying rationale is customer lifetime value (LTV) — Chapter 2. Customers are the firm's most critical assets — forming *mutually beneficial relationships* is crucial. CRM systems are only really successful in firms with a true external orientation. Unfortunately, many firms invest millions of dollars in CRM programs but do not realize the promised benefits. Three issues are crucial for success:

- **Objectives.** The firm must be clear about its objectives. Without good direction, it cannot select from myriad CRM initiatives, and costs can easily spiral out of control.[21]

- **Customer benefits.** The CRM system must provide benefits and value to customers — from new core products and services, to high customer service levels — and the firm. Many firms focus on firm value, often by cutting costs, but give short shrift to customer value. The CRM system must drive *mutually* beneficial customer relationships.

- **Technology.** Many people think that computerized databases and information technology underpin CRM systems. Of course, technology, customer databases, and **data-mining** often play an important role, but CRM is not about technology. To repeat, CRM is about forming *mutually beneficial relationships* with customers.

## DEVELOPING A CRM SYSTEM

Customer databases for effective CRM systems must be relevant, structured, current, consistent, accurate, accessible, complete, and secure. According to one expert, "To implement CRM, a firm must have an integrated database available at every customer *touch point* and analyze that data well. ... [CRM] allows companies to automate the way they interact with their customers and to communicate with relevant, timely messages."[22] A large firm's database contains longitudinal (over-time) data on millions of customers. Adding state-of-the-art **data-mining** technology secures and manipulates these data to yield marketing insight. Capital One's expertise has

**KEY IDEA**

➤ Customer service infrastructure combines the technological and human resources necessary to deliver high-level customer service.

**KEY IDEA**

➤ Customer defection rate is a more valuable performance measure than customer satisfaction. The firm should identify and measure critical elements driving customer satisfaction.

**KEY IDEA**

➤ CRM is a synthesis of marketing, quality management, and customer service to form *mutually beneficial relationships* with customers.

➤ Technology has an important role in CRM, but CRM is not about technology.

shaken up the credit card industry, and Harrah's (casinos and hotels) has achieved marked success. Communications with customers are more personal, and the firm can mass-customize its offers. Direct marketer Fingerhut maintains 100 pages of data per customer, mostly about buying habits. Customer data is equally important for firms with few customers, like your local dry cleaner or garage — paper and pencil may be adequate technology.

The firm must identify each customer. In some service industries, customer databases *come with the territory*, like bank accounts, insurance policies, and telephone service. But these firms often collect and store data by account or policy number, rather than by customer. Hence, the best customers — those who buy multiple services — escape their attention.

Identifying customers that purchase from an intermediary like a retailer or distributor can be difficult. Indirect methods include mail inserts, factory warranties, customer-get-customer campaigns, syndicated questionnaires, customer value cards, third-party lifestyle databases, telephone *help* lines, websites, special events, and loyalty cards — supplemented by data from marketing information firms. Many firms spend highly to develop customer databases; the sorts of data include[23]:

- **Customer characteristics.** Demographic data independent of the firm: B2C — name, gender, age, and address. B2B — sales revenues, number of employees, age of organization, and industry.

- **Customer responses to firm decisions.** Marketing-mix variables like sales promotions, direct marketing offers, and price changes — includes perceptions and preferences from research.

- **Customer contact history.** B2C — phone calls for product information and customer service requests. B2B — deliveries, sales calls, and technical service calls.

- **Customer purchase history.** What was purchased — by SKU; when; by what method — cash or credit; and through what intermediary, if any; what price and what price discounts, if any; and how and when delivered. Data should include the firm's profit margin on each purchase.

- **Customer value to the firm.** Data for assessing customer lifetime value (LTV), like purchase history — Chapter 2.

The database should be sufficiently flexible to follow individuals and track life changes. In B2C, consumers move houses and cities and change jobs, marital status, names, and family size; their needs also change. In B2B, employees change jobs within firms, change firms, and have changing business and individual needs.

A well-developed customer database is valuable to the firm and others. Many firms earn large revenues by selling customer data to non-competitors. But the firm must carefully think through its privacy policy. Some firms like Amazon and UPS absolutely refuse to sell customer data. Said an Amazon spokesperson, "We don't want to create an enormous database that becomes a public relations risk or something that offends our customers. We believe that we have done well because of the trust customers have for Amazon and their belief that our privacy policies are taken very seriously. It's partly a moral point of view, but it's also a sensible business decision."[24]

## ASSESSING THE VALUE OF CUSTOMERS AND DESIGNING FIRM ACTIONS

The firm implementing CRM well acts with significantly greater focus. It estimates profitability and LTV by customer. It anticipates customers' key events and initiates action. A B2C firm might send consumers vacation ideas; a B2B firm might alert customers that ordering seasonal stock can add value. The more comprehensive the customer database, and the more creative the firm, the more valuable will be its initiatives. It can offer new products and services and

## KEY IDEA

➤ Superior customer databases are relevant, structured, current, consistent, accurate, accessible, complete, and secure.

➤ The customer database should distinguish among customers — on loyalty and value to the firm.

➤ Customer databases are more valuable when they also contain data about relationships with competitors.

give greater customer service to its more valuable and loyal customers. In making offers, the firm must be concerned about the **communications tipping point** — the level after which its communications create customer resentment. Amazon spends significant effort to identify its tipping point.

High-value, high-loyalty customers are very important, yet some firms offer better service to low-value customers. Express checkout lanes in supermarkets often reward customers who make few purchases. The Fairway supermarket on New York's Upper West Side strives to cut waiting time for all customers.

**Loyalty programs** are a central part of many CRM systems. Well-designed programs play a major role in retaining customers. All loyalty programs have a similar structure; customers earn rewards by purchasing goods and services. Some programs are simple, like J.C. Penney's *baker's dozen*: "Buy 12 panties, earn the 13ᵗʰ free." Other programs, like airline frequent flier and hotel and credit card loyalty, involve complex, multi-tiered incentives.

*Marketing Question*

Log on to *www.colloquy.com*. You have to register, but it's free. Which loyalty programs are especially good deals for customers? Why?

*Marketing Question*

Many students have low incomes. But your educational investment may lead to high future income. Which firms understand that and actively seek your business with an eye to your future, and how do they do so? Which firms seem oblivious?

**KEY IDEA**

➤ The firm should examine its privacy policy for the impact on customer relationships.

**KEY MESSAGES**

- Sometimes the firm's core offering is a service — sometimes a physical product.
- Sometimes customer service complements a core product, sometimes it complements a core service.
- Some products are transitioning to services as customers seek the benefits that physical products deliver, rather than the products themselves.
- Several characteristics distinguish services — core and customer — from physical products. Each has important marketing implications:
  - intangibility
  - inseparability
  - variability
  - perishability
  - divisibility
  - lack of acquisition
  - role of customers.
- SERVQUAL is an important diagnostic for understanding and improving services.
- In general, high service quality leads to greater customer satisfaction, but increased competition and overall quality increases are weakening the relationship between customer satisfaction and loyalty.
- The firm can deliver customer service pre-, during, and post-purchase.
- Well-designed and well-delivered customer service can reap significant benefits from repurchase and positive word of mouth.
- The firm can augment and better target high-value customer service via a well-designed CRM system.
- Understanding customer value to the firm and customer loyalty allows the delivery of the *right* service levels to the *right* customers.

# CHAPTER 19

# IMPLEMENTING THE MARKETING OFFER: MONITORING & CONTROLLING PERFORMANCE

## LEARNING OBJECTIVES

When you have completed this chapter, you will be able to:

- Know how several externally oriented firms became successful via functional excellence.
- Recognize the challenges of creating an externally oriented firm.
- Deploy an organizational development model to facilitate becoming externally oriented.
- Explain the pros and cons of traditional and newer approaches of organizing for marketing.
- Appreciate the critical role of systems, processes, and human resources in implementing market strategy.
- Realize the importance of other functions in contributing to marketing as a philosophy.
- Understand the importance of integrating many organizational functions.
- Take steps to ensure that your firm maintains an external orientation.
- Describe critical elements in the monitor-and-control process.
- Understand and recognize success factors.

## OPENING CASE: SONY ELECTRONICS

*Sony is the long-time leader in consumer electronics. Ron Boire, whose 17-year career at Sony culminated in the position of President, Sony Electronic Sales, talked about Sony's careful focus on well-chosen measures and how it uses them to secure the behavior it requires. "Sony is really driven by the concept of, 'If you can't measure it, you can't do it.' Sometimes that's straightforward; sometimes it's very complicated. Interactions that Sony's salespeople have with our retail trade channel customers are a good example.*

*"With national customers like Best Buy, Sears, Circuit City, Wal-Mart, and Target, or a strategically important regional chain, we used to do classic sales compensation. Each salesperson had a sales budget, and we measured salespeople's performance against budget. If you had a budget target of $1 million for a product category, and you sold at $1.1 million, you did a great job and you made a good bonus. Regardless of what was stuck in the barn at the end of the month or the end of the year. Regardless of whether or not they could pay for it. Regardless of whether you delivered it to them on time.*

*"Today, we base up to 70 percent of our inventory management/asset management group's compensation, and 50 percent of our salespeople's compensation, on customer scorecards. We agree on metrics individually with each national and strategic customer. Most focus on simple things like on-time delivery, percent in-stock, forecast accuracy, and gross margin return on inventory [GMROI] — the key retail performance metric. To set these metrics we ask each customer: 'What's important to you? What are your targets? What are your strategic concerns?' Best Buy's current target is 90 percent on-time delivery, plus or minus one day, and 95 percent in stock. We may or may not hit that metric due to a variety of reasons, but everybody has the same goal in mind. Depending on their size, we track retailers either monthly or weekly.*

*"And our salespeople are bonus compensated twice a year based on their customer scorecards. As the saying goes, 'People do what they're paid to do.' When you change the basis of people's paychecks, it really is remarkable how fast they change their behavior. We've seen a tremendous shift in the behavior of the organization, and a very positive reaction from the marketplace. No one else in the consumer electronics industry is doing this. And in most industries that our customers do business in — appliances, software, consumer electronics, or computers — all sales forces are compensated on sell-in. It's revolutionary in consumer electronics for a salesperson to say, 'No, I won't take your purchase order, because you have too much inventory.' Everybody talks about aligning with your customers, but if you're paying your salespeople to stuff the box you can't be aligned — it's impossible."*

Sony wants to know the profitability of its customers. Boire continued, *"We measure customer profitability from a contribution margin perspective. Once you get past that sell-in mentality, you can focus on simple measurements like contribution margin; incremental contribution margin is the best ongoing measure of a marketing relationship with our trade channel customers. Marketing holds the P&Ls on these major customer accounts, but the only thing we load in are direct costs attributable to that customer; we include the sales team and all its funding, but we take nothing from headquarters. We look at the contribution margin in dollars per customer; we project mid-range contributions some years ahead, and we calculate a net present value (NPV) with a conservative termination value.*

*"Outside the consumer electronics channel we have less influence. A major national multi-category retailer that's in difficulties, we're such a small percent of their total business that it wouldn't matter what we did. What we can do in those cases is manage our risk well, as we did with Kmart. We called the day Kmart would file for bankruptcy protection. We predicted it well in advance. We took some losses, but we managed our receivables with Kmart probably better than anyone in the trade."*[1]

**CASE QUESTION**

Compare and contrast Sony's old measurement-and-control system, and its new system. Suppose a firm with which you are familiar made this sort of change. What implementation problems would you anticipate, and how would you deal with them?

---

In previous chapters, we focused on gaining insight into markets, customers, competitors, the company, and complementers; developing market strategy; and designing implementation programs around product, promotion, distribution, service, and price. People with marketing titles tend to do much, but not all, of this work. In contrast, executing implementation programs involves many people throughout the firm, in a variety of functional areas.[2]

To execute well, the firm must align various implementation programs with its market thrust. All employees must recognize that customers are central to the firm's success and act accordingly. Vision, mission, and strategy form the superstructure within which they do their jobs; the firm's values underpin its culture. Much of the hard effort in implementation concerns organization structure, systems and processes, and HR practices. Unfortunately, these elements tend to evolve slowly and lag both environmental changes and the firm's market strategies.

We showed in Chapter 1 that getting appropriate alignment is much easier when the firm has customer-focused values leading to a true external orientation. In this chapter, we present a model for creating and maintaining an external orientation, including specific action steps and impediments, and lay out principles of monitor-and-control to keep the firm on track. We begin by showing how several externally oriented firms became successful by achieving excellence in particular functional areas. They are exemplars we all should try to emulate.

**Marketing Question**

When you place an order online, many organizational functions are involved in getting the product to you. Chart out the supplier's process.

## FUNCTIONAL EXCELLENCE IN EXTERNALLY ORIENTED FIRMS

What does it take to deliver customer value and secure differential advantage? As we have learned throughout this book, firms achieve these ends in different ways, deploying various resources, building core competencies, and using expertise. Expertise areas include operations and the supply chain, customer service, finance, research and development, sales, and even human resources. Table 19.1 shows firms that leveraged such expertise into success; we discuss one or more from each functional area.[3]

**TABLE 19.1**

**DELIVERING CUSTOMER VALUE AND SECURING DIFFERENTIAL ADVANTAGE VIA FUNCTIONAL EXCELLENCE**

| Functional Area | Company | Capability | Customer Benefit |
|---|---|---|---|
| Operations and the Supply Chain | Dell | Design/Build to order | Customization |
| | FedEx | System ownership | Reliability |
| | Wal-Mart | Logistics and inventory management | Low prices |
| Customer Service | Amazon | Collaborative filtering; one-click | Ease, enjoyment of purchasing |
| | Nordstrom | Values and reward system | Attentive personalized service |
| | Fidelity | 24/7/365 availability | Convenience |
| Finance | GE Capital | Sophisticated financial engineering | Innovative financing to leverage shareholder returns of clients |
| | Verizon (MCI) | Flexible billing software | Lower prices for calls to friends and family |
| | Praxair | Flexible billing system | Site-based bills to facilitate project management |
| Research and Development | DuPont | Research skills in chemistry | Synthetic fibers with new functionality |
| | 3M | Micro-replication technology | Even distribution of coatings |
| | Apple | Design skills | Aesthetically pleasing, functional, trendy products |
| Sales | Direct Line | Direct sales of insurance | Lower prices |
| | Saturn | Unique culture | Pleasurable (no negotiating) buying and owning experience |
| | Avon | *Avon Lady* sales force | Close personal relationships between buyer and seller |
| Human Resources | Ritz-Carlton | Selection and training | Superior/customized service |
| | Singapore Airlines | Selection and training | Superior service |
| | Virgin Airlines | Employees-first values | Superior service |

**Marketing Question**

Select three firms from Table 19.1. What investments in resources are they making to maintain their differential advantages?

## OPERATIONS AND THE SUPPLY CHAIN

Internal operations and the supply chain are important areas for the firm to improve its external focus, especially in services, where it touches the customer most often. All contemporary approaches to teaching operations systems design work back from the marketplace. The operations system is a great place for the firm to secure differential advantage.[4] Dell started out with a services model, modifying IBM and IBM-compatible PCs, then back-integrated into manufacturing. Michael Dell believed that the traditional model — forecast demand, build PCs to meet demand, then persuade customers to buy PCs the firm produced — was ineffective. He created an entirely new business model for building customized computers that users had already agreed to buy. Dell's demand-driven, direct-to-customer model is very successful. It minimizes costs and investment throughout the system.

## CUSTOMER SERVICE

We discussed aspects of customer service in Chapter 18 and revisit them here. Increased competition has made customer service very important for delivering value, securing differential advantage, and attracting, retaining, and growing customers. In many firms, customer service does not report to marketing. This may not matter when an external orientation is the firm's dominant philosophy. But poor customer service generates significant customer dissatisfaction, especially if expectations are high, and can destroy an otherwise effective market strategy.

Some externally oriented firms differentiate their offers from tough competitors via customer service excellence. U.S. department store Nordstrom's is famous for employees' customer service zeal. Careful employee selection, and supportive incentive systems, encourages the *right* behavior. Nordstrom's even accepts returned goods without question, sometimes from competitors!

Mutual fund giant, Fidelity, is a fine example of service excellence. Its key insight was that investors preferred to interact with brokers on their personal schedules, not just during arbitrary hours when the market was open. Fidelity's innovation was to be the first financial services firm open 24/7/365. Many other factors contributed to its leadership, but customers' confidence and trust in the brand and the convenience it offered were critical. Today, online brokerage competitors offer similar convenience and Fidelity has lost some ground. Recall our earlier message: Virtually all advantages are eventually competed away. The quest for differential advantage must be central and ongoing!

## FINANCE

Clearly, financial skills are a key success factor in financial services, but financial decisions and controls play a critical role in managing the operations of any successful firm. Financial engineering is central to marketing major capital goods and services, from aircraft and earthmoving equipment to business systems. Externally oriented firms galvanize their finance and accounting functions; they contribute to the firm's marketing efforts in many ways.

Financial software plays an increasing role in making complex systems work. Before being acquired by Verizon, MCI was reborn, phoenix-like, from the ashes of the WorldCom disaster. Software supporting its favored *Friends and Family (F&F)* numbers system for widely separated family members allowed MCI to gain significant market share.

Billing systems can be a major customer problem, but a good place to seek differential advantage. We know the bill is one supplier communication that customers always read! Construction customers of industrial gases firm Praxair work simultaneously on different projects and must account for costs by site and project. Praxair created a flexible billing system that offers this service to customers; they appreciate it.

*Marketing Question*

Think about your cell phone supplier. With what functions or departments have you had contact — mail, e-mail, retail store, or customer service rep? Did one area provide a good experience? Is this part of its differential advantage?

*Marketing Question*

Which firm has provided you personally with the best customer service? What did you think was so great about the customer service? How could the firm improve on its performance?

*Marketing Question*

Can you think of a firm whose finance operations made doing business with it easier? What specifically did you like? How could the firm improve?

## RESEARCH AND DEVELOPMENT

R&D breakthroughs have given birth to many great firms. 3M, DuPont, GlaxoSmithKline (GSK), Intel, and Medtronics are just a few that achieved and maintained pre-eminence based on their technological strengths. When the firm manages its R&D/Marketing interface well, the impact can be dramatic. 3M has a formidable record for innovation combined with successful, even ingenious, marketing. The elegant design and functionality of Apple's Macintosh computers, and more recently the iPod, reflect its flair for R&D. Apple also introduced iTunes, which became the leader in downloaded music.

## SALES

The sales function rarely reports to marketing yet, as with customer service, selling is critical for implementing the market strategy. Innovation in the sales process can be the key to success. In Chapter 16, we showed that many B2B firms are driving successful growth with Tier 1 customers by innovating strategic (key) account and global account programs.

In B2C, several firms have gained differential advantage through their selling efforts. Avon is a good example. Its Avon Ladies are independent businesswomen who have close personal relationships with their customers. They consult on cosmetics issues, help customers buy the most relevant products, and personally deliver orders.

## HUMAN RESOURCES

Human resources (HR) is a vital function for any business, but some firms create differential advantage by developing unique approaches to developing and motivating their work forces to achieve high levels of excellence. Many consultants claim HR advantages are the most sustainable, since they are difficult to copy. Indeed, *talent management* is becoming a key driver in many firms. GE is well known for developing successive generations of business leaders. Managing human resources is especially important in services firms, where employee/customer interaction is constant and ongoing. Major hotel chains like Marriott, Four Seasons, and Ritz-Carlton place particular emphasis in this area.

## INTEGRATED SYSTEMS

Specific functional areas bring success to externally oriented firms. They succeed, not just because of a single strong suit, but because they integrate efforts from many areas. Toyota is an outstanding example; it bases its performance on three integrated systems:

- **Research and development.** Toyota's process begins with extensive research into customer demographics and lifestyle trends. These feed into Toyota's four research and design studios in Japan (1), U.S. (2), and Europe (1). These studios compete for the best design in a target market.
- **Manufacturing.** Toyota's process is perhaps the world's best-known, most-discussed, and most-praised industrial operation. The Toyota system has spawned many books and is a model of Total Quality Management (TQM). Even Boeing and Airbus copied Toyota.
- **Dealer management and customer service.** Toyota invests heavily in its dealers and customer service. All Toyota's franchised dealers must adhere to a strong set of guidelines; if not, Toyota does not renew their agreements. When it introduced the Lexus, Toyota set up a completely independent dealer system. The first Lexus cars had a minor quality problem; Toyota fixed the problem on every car, then filled the gas tank and washed the car before returning it. For Lexus' first ten years, each management employee telephoned four customers per month to gain real-time data on the car and the dealer.

## KEY IDEA

➤ The most successful firms seek functional excellence in operations and the supply chain, customer service, finance, research and development, sales, and/or human resources. These efforts help implement the market strategy.

*Marketing Question*

In your experience, which firms do the best job of managing their human resources? How did this translate into marketplace success? Define key objectives and success for HR.

*Marketing Question*

Have you or a friend or colleague owned or leased a Toyota or Lexus? What was the experience? What are Toyota's differential advantages? How could it improve?

# A MODEL FOR DEVELOPING AN EXTERNAL ORIENTATION: THE VALUES STATEMENT

To achieve success in increasingly competitive markets, the firm must align its resources with the ever-changing environment to deliver customer value and secure differential advantage. In the final analysis, nothing else matters. Continual realignment is difficult, but some firms do it better than others. The most successful maintain an **external orientation**.

In Chapter 1, we introduced the idea of organizational orientations; we described the external orientation and various **internal orientations**. Firms with internal orientations focus inward on the needs of various functions. But the firm with an external orientation looks outward. It focuses on customers, competitors, and broader environmental variables. The externally oriented firm knows that its current products and processes are the key reasons for its past and present success. But it also knows the external environment is always changing and that it must make internal changes in its organization structure, systems and processes, and human resources to adjust to market realities. Rather than fearing change, the externally oriented firm knows that change is inevitable. It welcomes change as a challenge and understands that new opportunities are the firm's *lifeblood*.

It's one thing to recognize the value of an external orientation; it's quite another to instill it in an organization. Some successful corporate leaders believe that introducing an external orientation is a critical part of their job. Intel owes its success to addressing environmental discontinuities, like legal and regulatory issues, and competitive challenges. When asked about his most important achievement, former CEO Andy Grove said: "It's that I've played a significant part in developing the work environment and culture at the company and with the directors."[5]

Figure 19.1 shows the inverted pyramid framework used by externally oriented firms like SAS and Nordstrom's. This model places customers at the top of the pyramid and reinforces the critical role they play in the firm's success.

Many firms use a values statement emphasizing a customer-focused culture to reinforce placing customers at the top of the pyramid. **Values** are a common set of beliefs that guide the behavior of all organizational members. Some values are **hard**, like profitability and market share; other values are **soft**, like integrity, respect for others, trust, and customer pre-eminence.

## Marketing Question

Select two of your favorite firms. Identify their values statements. Are the firms living up to these values? If not, where are they falling short? What is the significance for marketing of communicating these values statements?

**Customers**
(needs, wants, priorities)

**Human Resource Management**
(recruit & select, train & develop, work processes & career paths, recognition & reward)

**Systems and Processes**

**Values**            **Values**

**Organization Structure**
(job design, reporting relationships)       Internal Architecture

**Strategy**

External Focus

**Vision, Mission**

**FIGURE 19.1**

**A FRAMEWORK FOR DEVELOPING AN EXTERNAL ORIENTATION**

KEY IDEA

➤ Organizational values are a common set of beliefs that guide the behavior of the firm's members. They are often integral to a firm's success.

➤ Values statements are worthwhile only if the entire firm embraces them.

# TRANSFORMING THE ORGANIZATION TO BECOME EXTERNALLY ORIENTED

Beginning with a values statement emphasizing the pre-eminence of customers, the remaining framework elements must reflect and reinforce the firm's commitment to an external orientation. Many organizational transformations start at the bottom of the pyramid, first developing (or reworking) external elements we discussed earlier in Chapter 7:

- **Vision.** A description of the firm's ideal future state or an impressionistic picture of what the future should be. Good vision statements set a broad direction — they should inspire employees for the long run. A good vision statement is not too broad, nor is it too specific or easily achievable.
- **Mission.** Guides the firm's search for market opportunities more directly. The firm with a well-developed mission stays focused in a limited arena where it is likely to be successful.
- **Strategy.** The firm's game plan for the market, pointing the way to the firm's actions. The market strategy specifies what the firm is trying to achieve, which segments it will target for effort, and how it will position itself in those market segments.

## ORGANIZING THE FIRM'S MARKETING EFFORTS

The firm must design the **internal architecture** of its marketing organization. Traditional ways of organization still have great value, but other approaches are breaking new ground.[6]

**TRADITIONAL: FUNCTIONAL MARKETING ORGANIZATION.** The firm places activities like marketing research, distribution, advertising and promotion, marketing administration, and new product development in a marketing department. This function is usually separate from the sales force and other functions like production, accounting, R&D, and human resources.

Reporting relationships vary across firms, particularly in today's diverse industries. Most commonly, the heads of sales and marketing departments report to a SVP of Marketing and Sales. One variant is separate sales and marketing VPs who then report to a more senior level. But this arrangement can produce conflict between a long-term marketing focus and a short-term sales focus that only a high organizational level — the C-Suite — can resolve. As one CEO commented: "The trouble with this company is that the functional elevators don't stop until they reach the 20th floor. I'm going to make sure that they stop much lower down!"

Functional organizations tend to work best when markets and products are homogeneous, as in many small firms. Sometimes, they linger too long in growing firms. As they become more complex, firms need specialized responsibility for either products or markets. Firms structured as product/brand management, and market segment, organizations try to solve this problem.

**TRADITIONAL: PRODUCT/BRAND MANAGEMENT ORGANIZATION.** P&G developed the original product management organization to provide a product/brand focus. Product and brand managers develop market plans for their products and brands. They are responsible for volume, share, and/or profit, but they do not control all the inputs. In many FMCG firms these managers compete for resources like promotional dollars and sales force time. Such brand-manager competition is sometimes viewed as healthy because it spurs extra effort, but it can undermine a coherent product-line strategy. This organization structure has two significant problems: internal brand manager competition (as noted) and brand manager turnover. Each can lead to long-term time incoherence and a disjointed long-run strategy.

**TRADITIONAL: CATEGORY MANAGEMENT ORGANIZATION.** This approach attempts to address problems with the product/brand management organization, and leverage success from strong brands to weaker brands. Firms with **category management** direct multiple brands in a complementary manner. P&G's category manager for laundry products is responsible for Tide, Downy, Gain, Cheer, Bounce, Febreze, Dryel, and Ivory.

**New Meaning to Category Management**

Retailers' increasing power in FMCG has given a new meaning to the term *category management*. Many retailers now manage operations on a category-by-category basis. Sophisticated data analysis helps them to determine individual product profitability, broken down by region, state, city, and even individual store. Retailers add new products and brands only if they help achieve category goals.

In the U.S., some retailers outsource product category management to suppliers. Retailers charge the chosen supplier with increasing its revenues and profits in that category. Mostly, but not always, the retailer appoints the market-leading supplier as *category captain*. The supplier gets privileged access to retail sales data for all suppliers in the category, including its competitors. This position typically lasts for several years.

**TRADITIONAL: MARKET SEGMENT ORGANIZATION.** This organization is more externally focused; managers are responsible for individual market segments. IBM organizes by industry: Business sector managers are responsible for broad industry categories like manufacturing, banking and financial services, transportation, and retailing. The market segment organization may overlie other marketing and sales functions. Typically, the rest of the firm is functionally organized.

**TRADITIONAL: COMBINED PRODUCT/BRAND MANAGEMENT/MARKET SEGMENT ORGANIZATION.** Product/brand and market segment organizations each omit a crucial dimension. In product/brand organizations, no one is specifically responsible for market segments. In the market segment organization, no one is specifically responsible for individual products or brands. Figure 19.2 shows how a synthetic fibers firm incorporated both dimensions. Segment managers were responsible for end-use markets like household textiles, apparel, and industrial products. Product managers were responsible for individual product lines like nylon, polyester, and new fibers.

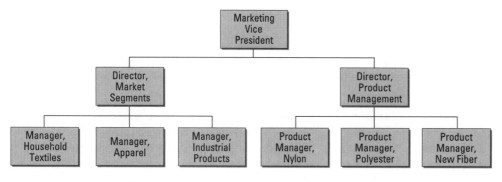

**FIGURE 19.2**

**THE COMBINED PRODUCT/BRAND MANAGEMENT-MARKET SEGMENT ORGANIZATION**

**NEWER: INCLUSION ORGANIZATION.** In the newer **inclusion organization**, the firm groups many activities under marketing — Figure 19.3. British Airways (BA) adopted this approach; it recognized that Operations controlled two critical customer requirements, safety and schedule reliability. BA restructured so that Operations, and 80 percent of employees, reported through Marketing. The inclusion organization can work well in service businesses, where marketing and operations are difficult to distinguish, but is not appropriate for all firms.

FIGURE 19.3

THE INCLUSION
ORGANIZATION

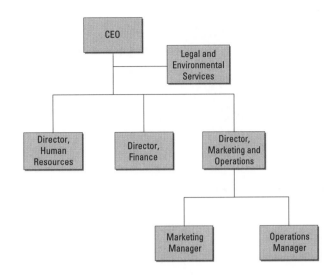

**NEWER: BUSINESS PROCESS ORGANIZATION.** One outgrowth of the early 1990s re-engineering movement is some firms' attempts to organize around **business processes**[7] — Figure 19.4. The firm retains a classic functional structure, but much organizational output results from cross-functional teams. Marketing's major responsibilities are innovation, brand development, and related strategic tasks. The sales force conducts operational marketing tasks like trade promotions.

FIGURE 19.4

THE BUSINESS
PROCESS-BASED
ORGANIZATION —
EXAMPLE FROM A
UNILEVER SUBSIDIARY

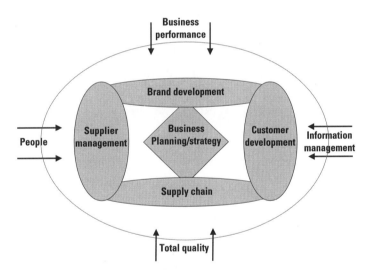

**NEWER: CUSTOMER-MANAGEMENT ORGANIZATION.** This organization focuses specifically on customers. We expect it to become more popular as firms become increasingly aware of the lifetime customer value concept and the importance of customer retention (Chapter 2). CRM systems that allow firms to identify customers by name, buying patterns, and history support this organization form.[8]

As Figure 19.5 shows, the **customer management organization** (CMO) turns the product/brand management organization (PBMO) on its side. In the PBMO, the brands (B1... B4...Bn) are the firm's pillars; all other functional activities serve the brands. In the CMO, customer portfolios (CP1...CP4...CPn) are the pillars; the brands and other functions serve the customer portfolios. Customer managers have responsibility and authority for customer portfolios, and brand management is almost a staff function.[9] Product/brand managers continue to manage the firm's brand assets, but support customer portfolio managers by developing products/brands to increase customer lifetime value.

A specific advantage of the CMO is that customer contact increases, and customer portfolio managers gain significant customer insight. The blinders that can occur in PBMOs diminish, but implementing the CMO typically requires significant organizational change:

> Microsoft faced problems of slow decision-making, defection of talented individuals, and increasingly tough competition. It redeveloped its vision and shifted to a customer-focused organization. Individual organizational units are now responsible for groups of customers — corporate customers, knowledge workers, home PC buyers, game players, software developers, web surfers, and cybershoppers. Said founder Bill Gates, "... the new structure puts the customer at the center of everything we do by reorganizing our business divisions by customer segment rather than along product lines."[10]

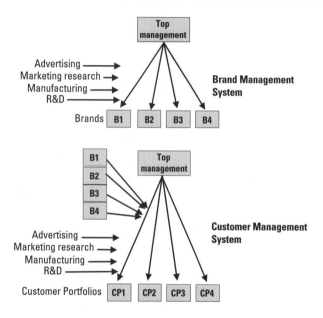

**FIGURE 19.5**

**THE TRANSITION FROM BRAND MANAGEMENT TO CUSTOMER MANAGEMENT**

More B2C firms will adopt the CMO as they become able to identify and understand individual customers. Most B2B firms can already identify their customers; hence, this organization is becoming more widespread via strategic (or key) account management programs; those with global customers are developing global account programs.

The firm may implement a CMO at the corporate level or in individual business units, but there are trade-offs. At corporate, customer management may be ineffective because the account manager does not have a deep understanding across the firm's many businesses. Focus at the business level only, and the firm may be unable to develop an integrated corporate-wide offer:

> Lucent used a business-unit organization to push authority and responsibility deep in the firm. But getting business units to cooperate was difficult. Several businesses developed a variation of the *softswitch* telecommunications product.[11] One customer said that he was "... confused on what Lucent is actually offering, because I've heard different descriptions of the same solution from different Lucent teams."[12]

**THE GLOBAL MARKETING ORGANIZATION.** An important debate concerns organizing for global markets. Some argue that customer needs are *homogenizing* worldwide, driven by greater information access like satellite TV, CNN, or Star TV (Asia), and the Internet.[13] Others believe that *heterogeneous* geographic segments remain, driven by cultural, nationalistic, and linguistic differences.[14] These different perspectives lead to separate recommendations for **global organizational structure** in general, and global marketing structure in particular. If *heterogeneity* is the norm, and national and regional differences are critical, the firm should consider a country-

KEY IDEA

➤ The firm's organizational structure should support an integrated marketing approach.

based organization, reporting into geographic regions: like North America; Latin America; Asia-Pacific; and Europe, Middle East, and Africa. Each region should have significant autonomy to make a broad range of marketing decisions at the regional and individual country level. McDonald's earns 70 percent of profits from its international divisions. Observers attribute its success to the flexibility it gives individual country franchises to tailor offerings to local tastes. In Vienna, McCafes offer blended coffee; Indonesian customers can have French fries or rice; and a South Korean option is roast pork on a bun, with a garlicky soy sauce.

If customer needs are *homogeneous*, global product management may be better. The global product manager controls most positioning, product, and pricing decisions. This organization usually overlies a geographic structure where regional and/or country organizations have sales and distribution responsibility. Headquarters provides regions with standardized advertising programs for adaptation to local markets. P&G transformed four business units based on geographic regions into seven global product groups, like Baby Care and Food and Beverage. To improve new product success, and reduce time-to-market, P&G flattened the organization, streamlined reporting, and aligned executive compensation with the new global product groups.

The homogeneity/heterogeneity debate continues in B2C firms, but homogenization is an increasing B2B trend. Many large multinationals demand both equal treatment from suppliers across geographies, and global contracts. The country-based organization compromises the firm's ability to treat customers comparably in multiple countries. Hence, many firms are shifting to new organizational forms where geography plays a reduced role. Previously, IBM had strong country managers reporting to powerful regional executives. In the mid-1990s, it adopted an industry-based structure where senior executives head up customer industries like manufacturing, financial services, and retail. In each industry organization, global account managers (GAMs) manage IBM's relationships with major global customers. Domestic salespeople report through the industry organization. Geographic organizational structures remain intact for government relations, corporate advertising, and the *care and feeding* of locally employed personnel, but IBM's country heads no longer have budget responsibility.[15]

"L'Oreal is the most amazing global company. It's really global in the truest sense of the word. Inherent in our structure for the past 15 years has been a desire to truly integrate global development and have global brands. We have a system called the Affair d'Marc, according to the brand's origin. So, L'Oreal and Lancôme are Parisian brands; Redken and Maybelline are U.S. brands. In those countries, each Affair d'Marc has a development team for the basic brand strategy, brand image, and brand health, globally.

"Now L'Oreal is a Paris brand, so it has an Affair d'Marc in Paris, a 60-person group responsible for the L'Oreal brand. But because the U.S. is the largest and most competitive country for L'Oreal business, in spite of that structure, we must be 100 percent integrated into L'Oreal development. So we are considered co-developers; we have video-conferences every week, meetings once a month, and we debate a lot.

"We're the lead on several projects. We have a lot of ownership on practically all hair color projects. For the latest hair color launch we were the lead country. We had many meetings with the international team in France, working on brand international expansion. If we took a U.S. brand to Latin America, we would work with that team.[16]

## KEY IDEA

➤ Systems and processes help produce organizational outputs and provide consistency to customers.

## SYSTEMS AND PROCESSES

All organizations use systems and processes to produce organizational outputs; we can array them along a continuum. One pole embraces **hard systems**. These typically require capital equipment and are often computer-based, like automatic teller machines and Internet portals and auction sites. At the other pole are human-resource-intensive **soft systems**, like retail customer service desks. Many customer interactions involve a combination of hard and soft systems. All systems can be improved.

**HARD SYSTEMS.** Hard systems improve operational efficiency and reduce costs. But they can also contribute to creating an external orientation, improve marketing effectiveness, optimize sales force efforts, and help secure differential advantage. Perhaps the most popular type of hard system in major firms is enterprise resource planning (ERP). ERP software contains customer-focused modules and attempts to integrate all departments and functions across the firm. It uses a single computer platform serving each department's needs and makes information available to others. Hard systems are also the core of supply-chain management, leading to better supply/demand matching, reduced inventories, fewer stockouts, and reduced customer disappointment. Benefits from hard systems are:

- **Customer information.** Customer information is more readily available and widely distributed; hence, employees better understand customer needs. At insurance firms like USAA, hard systems are essential to success. USAA's service associates have access to full client records at their desks, and the system prompts them to ask customers about other financial services. A customer telephone call about homeowners' insurance for a new home triggers a change of address for their auto insurance bill and a profile update.

- **Customer effort.** User-friendly computer systems are not just for employees. Many firms use externally facing systems for customers to access information and order online and to save time, effort, and risk in making purchases. These systems help the firm get closer to its customers and reinforce the brand. FedEx's package tracking and customer portals and customer-managed check-in kiosks at many major airlines are good examples.

> At Dell's website, customers design computers to meet their needs, place orders, and pay for purchases. Dell builds the product to order and delivers it promptly. Apple, HP, and IBM have emulated Dell for their production and ordering systems.

- **Customer intimacy.** Customer relationship management systems provide significant information about customers, including purchase histories, buying patterns, and other firm interactions. These data can address the soul-less anonymity of transaction-based markets. Large firms can emulate the high-touch personal service that small firms offer, like the local grocer who knew customers by name and built his business on that basis.

**SOFT SYSTEMS.** People-based soft systems can also help the firm become more externally oriented. Consider the planning process. Good planning is externally driven: It commences with a full environmental analysis, emphasizing insight into the market, customers, competitors, and the environment in general. Well-developed situation analyses can force an external orientation. Firms that build their market strategies in the form we discussed earlier necessarily become more externally focused. Try it yourself by using *The Virgin Marketer* to develop a market strategy for an organization of your choice.

Good planning is collaborative-participative. It should involve all functional areas and several management levels, bringing people across the firm face-to-face with external realities. Outputs from the market planning process set the firm's direction. They also play a critical role in driving an external orientation through the measurement and control process. Good planning produces measures that encourage organizational members to look beyond their narrow silos.

**MAKING THE FIRM'S SYSTEMS THE BEST THEY CAN BE.** More important than any individual system are methodologies for evolving and integrating systems to make the firm more externally oriented:

- **Re-engineering.** The **re-engineering** approach examines fundamental assumptions and seeks alternative approaches for redesigning and improving the firm's processes. Many organizational processes have a long history or tradition, but changes in customers, competitors, technology, and other environmental factors make them obsolete. The critical question is: Can introduction of a new process reduce costs and/or increase value for customers? The Internet has driven change in many business processes, like supplier-customer relationships where online communication has superseded telephone calls and faxes for purchase orders, invoices, and shipping notices. Most successful firms have made major commitments to process-based re-engineering:

IBM Credit's process for financing major computer system sales traditionally involved several steps: A salesperson provided purchase and customer data to a *logger*; the logger created a file and sent it onward; a credit specialist conducted a credit check; the business practices person requested changes in the standard loan covenants; the pricer decided the appropriate interest rate; the administrator developed a formal quote. Finally, the quote was sent overnight to the salesperson for presentation to the client.

To deliver a quote averaged six days, but sometimes took as long as two weeks. Salespeople could not access the application's status, and anxious customers switched to competitors. IBM Credit researched the actual work time per application — average, 90 minutes! The file spent much time at in- and out-boxes. IBM Credit appointed *deal structurers*; they averaged four hours for 90 percent of requests; specialists did the rest. Today, customers input data via the Internet; credit scoring, agreeing on terms and conditions, setting the interest rate and payment terms, and sending out contracts takes a few minutes.[17]

- **Best practice transfer.** For any process, some business units, departments, or functions are probably more effective than others. Unfortunately lateral communication within firms is generally poor, and underperforming units may know little about their more effective cousins. A **best practice** system helps identify and transmit superior processes, knowledge, and expertise across the firm. Samsung's system generates hundreds of best practice examples companywide. An extensive annual evaluation process identifies the *best of the best*; the winners personally receive awards from Samsung's CEO.

Starbucks shares best practices among U.S. operations and its international partners. Founder and chairman Howard Schultz opines, "In some cases the international partners are better than we are, and they're teaching us some things. At our first global conference, 30 countries were represented. We had a mini controlled Starbucks trade show where each country set up a booth to show its best practice."[18]

Some firms assign specific employees as *thought leaders* to identify and promote best practices throughout the organization. At Intel, the *data czar* identifies best-known methods and places them in a knowledge repository. At Bain, employees write up each consultancy project as a *knowledge module*; these are stored electronically so employees don't *reinvent the wheel* if they encounter similar challenges. For any firm, each market success or failure is an opportunity to identify best practices and barriers to best practices. Some firms institutionalize this process by analyzing every *win* and *loss* at customers.

Disseminating best practices, knowledge, and expertise across the firm can be a major challenge. Newer methods include specially tagged databases for easy search and collaborative *communities of practice* where experts share information. Other options include regular e-mail communications, *virtual meeting technology* for spur-of-the-moment knowledge-sharing, and meetings designed to break down barriers and facilitate transfer. Other ways to encourage internal communications are physical organization of workspaces and frequent personnel transfer from one organizational unit to another.

- **Benchmarking.** Best practices frequently occur in other firms. **Benchmarking** suppliers, customers, competitors, and firms in other industries, like Xerox's *best-in-class* concept, can improve the firm's processes.[19] Target has implemented *Horizontal Councils* in each merchandising and functional area. They meet regularly to share best and worst practices, but senior managers always ask council members: "What did you find out from other firms about this?" They have to have answers to these questions! Third-party organizations like the Columbia Initiative in Global Account Management enabled 3M, Citibank, Milliken, Deloitte & Touche, HP, Lucent, Square D-Schneider, and Saatchi and Saatchi to benchmark one another's global account management programs.

## HUMAN RESOURCE MANAGEMENT

Many firms trying to become more externally oriented believe the simple mantra, "Happy employees make happy customers." **Human resource management (HRM)** tools like recruiting, selecting, training and development, talent management, and measurement and reward systems provide many opportunities to emphasize the importance of an organization-wide customer focus. An external orientation should follow from hiring the *right* people and developing and managing their career transitions effectively.

Measurement and reward systems are critical for aligning employees to the firm's external orientation. The firm cannot simply ask employees to be externally oriented; it must hold them accountable. Nordstrom's entered the Cleveland market and was immediately successful, mainly because it outshone competitors in customer service. But many employees had previously worked for competitors like Dillard's, Kaufman's, Penney's, and Sears! Nordstrom success was due, in part, to its HRM development model that inculcated values and set high standards for employee behavior.

Measurement systems should be tightly linked to reward systems. When customer-focused measures drive incentive compensation, the external orientation effort has real teeth. Managers are often skeptical about basing take-home pay on survey findings, but Xerox and Microsoft each report excellent results using customer satisfaction measures. Good survey design, rigorously tested items, and competent and independent data collectors reduce skepticism. At Bloomberg, every employee, including the janitor and the person who stocks the kitchen, receives incentive compensation based on terminal sales. *Equity equivalence certificates* get everyone's attention; they know that Bloomberg's core objective is to sell terminals.

**KEY IDEA**

➤ HRM gives the firm many opportunities to focus on the customer.

➤ If the firm hires the *right* people and develops and manages them appropriately, an external orientation should follow.

## SUSTAINING AN EXTERNAL ORIENTATION

Many industry leaders have stumbled badly and lost their pre-eminent positions. Why? The stories are strikingly similar: They originally gained industry leadership by delivering customer value and securing differential advantage. They developed and focused their resources, core competencies, and expertise. They were externally oriented ... but then things changed. Their success began to hold them back; they could not sustain an external orientation and adjust to a new reality. We can find old and new leaders in many industries: air freight (Emery, FedEx), automobiles (General Motors, Toyota), and home video (Blockbuster, Netflix). The original leader had technological leadership, scale economies, substantial buying power, and well-established brands. But the new leaders brought new business models, technologies, and product designs to the market.

Getting everything right is difficult, and a chain is only as strong as its weakest link. For perfect integration of the marketing offer, the firm should execute every *moment of truth* flawlessly. It should not merely satisfy customers, but should delight them. Poor performance on some dimensions can overwhelm world-class performance on others.

Sustaining an external orientation is a little easier if the firm understands its challenges:

- **A functional view of marketing.** The firm must distinguish between marketing as a *philosophy* and marketing as a *department*. If the firm delegates all marketing problems to a marketing department, it will not create or deliver fully integrated offers. Achieving integration demands coordination among many different functional departments.

- **Bureaucracy.** As firms grow, departmentalization and task specialization are efficient ways to complete repetitive tasks. But rules and behaviors, reinforced by day-to-day work pressures, become embedded. As customers, we have all dealt with employees who tell us, "That's not my department" or "You'll have to talk to XYZ about that." Firms must

**KEY IDEA**

➤ The firm must clearly understand the implications for developing and sustaining an external orientation.

*Marketing Question*

How do you assess your college, school, or university on its degree of external orientation? Are some parts more externally focused than others? If yes, what accounts for these differences?

**KEY IDEA**

➤ Today's success sows the seeds of tomorrow's defeat.

complete day-by-day tasks, but they must also build in the agility to serve customers well and sensing mechanisms to identify and address market opportunities.

- **Getting the centralization/decentralization balance right.** Centralizing and standardizing can have great value, but excessive centralization leads to standardized actions, rather than *responsiveness* to customers' needs. Executives making key decisions are distant from the customer, and those with detailed market, customer, and competitor insight tend to play less significant decision-making roles. But too much decentralization can leave the organization without a clear focus. Deciding which activities are better centralized and which are better decentralized (closer to the customer) is a critical firm challenge.

- **Functional divisions.** Firms develop specialized functions to increase their expertise in key areas. But specialization can lead to silo thinking and divisiveness among specialties. Functional heads must recognize the importance of cross-functional cooperation.

- **Misaligned incentives.** People in organizations do what is *inspected* of them, **not** what is *expected* of them! They behave in ways that earn rewards. Conflicting and function-specific performance objectives and rewards make it difficult to integrate across functions. The result is often internal conflict and division.

- **Social fabric of institutions.** The firm's employees know one another and interact daily. Customers, competitors, and suppliers are occasional intruders who interrupt daily life! How often have employees ignored you, the customer, as they chat together, seemingly oblivious of your presence?

- **Internal politics.** The CEO or business head must actively support institutionalizing an external orientation and communicate this support frequently. If not, some functions will be suspicious about customer-focused initiatives. Jockeying for power and position occurs in all firms; the firm's leaders must not allow political concerns to override the customer's central importance.

- **Accounting systems.** The firm must produce data in a form that supports an external perspective. Many firms report profit data by product, but not by customer.

- **Inward-oriented marketing departments.** Marketing departments are sometimes their own worst enemies. They implement a not-invented-here (NIH) syndrome that quashes *foreign* ideas and initiatives to *protect their turf*. This problem tends to be most serious in firms with good reputations for marketing expertise, where the marketing department has great political power.

For long-run success, the firm's organization must become responsive yet initiating, learning but not forgetting, understanding of human resources yet demanding of high performance, customer-sensitive yet competitive, and shareholder-value-creating but not short-sighted. Jack Welch lifted performance at an already highly regarded GE to an entirely new level. In one of his more famous exhortations, he stated, "I want managers who manage with their face to the customer and their backside to the CEO!" Jeff Bezos, founder of famed dotcom Amazon describes himself and his organization as "customer obsessed!" And at IBM, customer-focused Lou Gerstner restored the fallen computer giant to its former glory with a *services* vision. Leadership counts! It must spread an external orientation throughout the firm.

## KEY PRINCIPLES OF MONITOR-AND-CONTROL PROCESSES

A popular saying in management is, *"If you can't measure it, you can't manage it."* Because people in organizations tend to do what is *inspected* of them, not what is *expected* of them, good monitor-and-control processes are critical for ensuring that the *right* actions lead to the *right* results. *Monitoring* focuses on measuring how well the firm is doing in various aspects of its business: *Control* is concerned with making changes or adjustments so it does better. Monitor-and-control processes are the most powerful means of changing individual behavior and enhancing long-term results. We focus on two complementary areas: firm performance and firm functioning:

- **Firm performance.** *Is the firm achieving its planned results?* Planned results are the **standards** against which the firm measures actual results. All things equal, if actual results meet or exceed standards, performance is satisfactory and the firm continues to operate as planned. If actual results vary significantly from standards, the firm should change its actions.

- **Firm functioning.** To achieve its desired results, the firm allocates resources and takes actions. *Is the firm functioning well?* To get greater insight, we break this question into three sub-questions:
  - **Implementation.** Did the firm implement its planned actions?
  - **Strategy.** Is the firm's market strategy well conceived and on target?
  - **Managerial processes.** Are the firm's managerial processes the best they can be?

**Marketing Question**

Consider your personal objectives and strategy: Have you thought through these rigorously? Are you achieving your planned objectives? Are you functioning well in trying to achieve your objectives?"

Monitor and control should not occur as a managerial whim; the firm should build a monitor-and-control philosophy into its DNA. This is not a simple task; it may take considerable time and effort to assemble the infrastructure for an effective system. Measurement is crucial, but the best-designed measures have no impact unless the firm first implements a process for developing standards and assessing its results against those standards. It should build its monitor-and-control processes on four key principles:

- Focus on market levers and develop alternative plans.
- Implement steering control rather than post-action control.
- Use the right performance measures at the right organizational levels.
- Model the relationship between input, intermediate, and output measures.

## FOCUS ON MARKET LEVERS AND DEVELOP ALTERNATIVE PLANS

**Market levers** flow from the firm's market strategy and implementation plans; they include actions like adding salespeople, doing better training, introducing new products, and changing the advertising. The firm allocates resources and takes actions to achieve its performance standards. The firm's actual results versus standards tell if its resource allocations and actions were successful. Monitor-and-control efforts should focus on market levers. If actual results are below standards, the firm should be ready with alternative plans to improve performance.

> Pfizer has built experimentation with marketing levers into its DNA. It continually tests different advertising and promotion strategies and ways of allocating selling effort. Pfizer's experiments cost millions of dollar as it tries to figure out optimal actions. Said a senior Pfizer executive, "We're measurement-intense. So 'metrics are us.' We believe in it. We measure everything. That is the root of our business."[20]
>
> Historically, Samsung focused on low-price, high-volume products so that production managers could optimize capacity utilization. A new monitor-and-control system measured its market price position and encouraged the sale of higher-price products.

## IMPLEMENT STEERING CONTROL

**Steering control** and **post-action control** are different monitor-and-control approaches. Firms using post-action control wait for a pre-set amount of time, then compare actual results against standards. If results are unsatisfactory, they take corrective action. Firms exercising post-action control typically develop annual marketing plans, but usually set standards by quarter. By contrast, steering control is dynamic, continuous, and anticipatory. Firms using steering control set standards for measures like sales, market share, and profit, then calendarize them by month, by week, or even by day. They set control limits for performance and continually

**KEY IDEA**

➤ Monitor-and-control processes are the most powerful means of changing individual behavior in firms.

➤ Monitor-and-control processes focus on the firm's results: Is the firm achieving its planned results? And on firm functioning: Is the firm functioning well?

**KEY IDEA**

➤ Post-action control means waiting for a pre-set time before comparing actual results against performance standards.

**KEY IDEA**

➤ Steering control continually compares the firm's actual results to performance standards and allows it to be more market responsive.

compare actual results against standards. Because they also track leading indicators, they are more market responsive.

Until 2001, Gillette consolidated its sales every quarter; now these figures are available daily. Cisco can close its books in a single day by converting 50 different ledgers in a single global system. Its managers can view revenues, margins, backlog, expenses, and other data by region, business unit, channel, and account manager daily and take appropriate actions. Dell focuses heavily on short **feedback cycles**. Discussing its salespeople, a senior Dell executive opined, "We drive to develop a meritocratic environment where people have a profit-per-minute mentality."[21]

## USE THE RIGHT PERFORMANCE MEASURES AT THE RIGHT ORGANIZATIONAL LEVELS

If possible, the firm should use objective measures like sales, market share, and profits in its monitor-and-control processes. When other, less concrete, measures like customer satisfaction are appropriate, the firm should use validated scales. It should also make sure it has the *right* measures. Many life insurance firms compensate agents on the number and value of new policies. But agents often receive little or no compensation for maintaining existing policies. Hence, agents *roll over* existing policyholders into new policies. But new policies must be in force for several years before the firm profits. Failure to measure and reward agents for serving existing policyholders creates profit problems for these firms.

**KEY IDEA**

➤ The firm should use objective measures for monitor-and-control purposes; if scales are appropriate, these should be validated.

The firm should measure performance at multiple organizational levels, like corporate, geographic region, business unit, market segment, marketing function, customer, sales region, sales district, and/or sales territory. Alcoa measures profitability by market sector, business, and customer and, in its aerospace division, by airplane program. Organizational position should largely drive the data employees receive. CEOs do not usually need to know individual performance variances by salesperson. Salespeople do not need to know performance variances of their peers in other sales regions. But as the **iceberg principle** — Figure 19.6 suggests, many problems may lie beneath the surface. Good performance in a unit or sub-unit can *hide* poor performance elsewhere. To improve overall performance, the firm must isolate problem areas.

**FIGURE 19.6**

**THE ICEBERG PRINCIPLE**

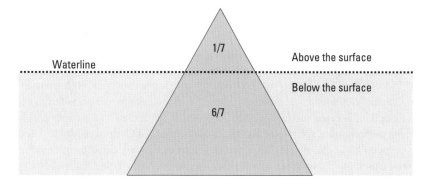

## MODEL THE RELATIONSHIP BETWEEN INPUT, INTERMEDIATE, AND OUTPUT MEASURES

Monitor-and-control systems must disentangle cause and effect. Suppose we observe that advertising spending increases and sales also increase. One interpretation is that advertising was effective: Increased advertising spending led to increased sales. The alternative interpretation is that increased sales led to increased advertising spending: the advertising budget is a fixed percentage of sales! To ensure it makes valid inferences, the firm must distinguish among:

- **Input measures.** Focus on actions the firm takes.

- **Intermediate measures.** Focus on customers' actions or changes in their state of mind.
- **Output measures.** Include performance variables like sales and profits.

Figure 19.7 shows that input measures lead to intermediate measures; in turn, intermediate measures lead to output measures, in a cause-and-effect relationship. Market levers provide the input measures; they affect the intermediate steps that must occur before customers purchase and provide the firm with outputs. Generally, collecting data on input and output measures is relatively easy; securing data on intermediate measures is often more resource-intensive. The firm must have confidence in the presumed relationships between inputs and intermediates and between intermediates and outputs. To illustrate, when the firm takes advertising and sales force actions, input, intermediate, and output measures might be:

- **Input measures.** Dollars spent on advertising, number of sales calls per day
- **Intermediate measures:**
  - **Customers' actions.** Number of customers who agree to a product trial, and/or place a deposit for future purchases
  - **Customers' mental states.** Degree of product awareness or product interest, and desire to purchase
- **Output measures.** Actual sales, market share, profits

Output measures are **lagging indicators** — *the rearview mirror*, or what has happened. Intermediate and input measures are **leading indicators** — the *dashboard*, or what should happen.[22]

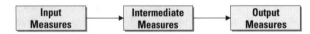

...........................

**FIGURE 19.7**

**RELATIONSHIPS AMONG CONTROL MEASURES**

# THE BALANCED SCORECARD

The **Balanced Scorecard** is an increasingly widespread approach for monitoring and controlling firm performance and firm functioning. It seeks a middle ground between using too few and too many measures. Each extreme leads to problems:

- **Too few measures.** One measure is too few. Managers may *game* the system to optimize performance on that measure, especially if it drives compensation, and cause unintended consequences. When short-term profit is the only standard, performing well can be very easy: Just cut back on advertising and R&D. Of course, this could hurt the firm in the long run. U.S. airlines used to compete by showing shorter flight times; when on-time performance data became publicized, they lengthened advertised flight times and improved *on-time* performance! When incoming Home Depot CEO Robert Nardelli focused on *inventory velocity*, the speed that inventory moves though the stores, some managers ordered fewer products. *Inventory velocity* improved, but customers couldn't find what they wanted.
- **Too many measures.** Multiple measures can be problematic if they are unclear or conflicting. Employees have difficulty discerning required behavior and may focus their efforts on actions that don't further the firm's goals.

Many firms address these problems via the **balanced scorecard**.[23] Well-balanced scorecards reflect a steering control philosophy; they *balance* output, intermediate, and input measures. PepsiCo's marketplace profit and loss system, used to decide managers' bonuses, includes:

- Quality
- Customer attitudes
- Market share
- Financial profit and loss
- Employee motivation

**KEY IDEA**

➤ The balanced scorecard reflects a steering control philosophy; it balances output, intermediate, and input marketing measures.

*Marketing Question*

In your educational institution, each instructor has his or her own way of measuring student performance. Can you suggest a balanced-scorecard framework that all instructors might use for measuring student performance?

Perhaps the most commonly used measures for balanced scorecards are:

- **Market share** — hard output measure
- **Customer satisfaction relative to competition** — soft output measure
- **Customer retention versus industry averages** — hard output measure
- **Investment as a percentage of sales (I/S ratio)** — hard input measure
- **Employee attitudes and retention** (especially customer-facing employees) — soft and hard input measures

**TABLE 19.2**

**CANDIDATE VARIABLES FOR A BALANCED SCORECARD APPROACH TO MEASURING THE GLOBAL ACCOUNT PROGRAM**

| Financial | Internal Business Process |
|---|---|
| • Year-on-year revenue and profit growth<br>• Sales expense as a percentage of revenues | • Percentage of customers with long-term contracts<br>• Percentage of customers with *solutions* contracts<br>• Process improvements from collaboration — summary billing, product development |
| **Customer** | **Learning and Growth** |
| • Customer satisfaction and loyalty<br>• Access to customer at the C-level — CIO, CEO, COO, and CFO | • Number of best practices adopters<br>• Improved management practices |

Many balanced scorecards focus on four measurement categories: financial, customer, internal business processes, and learning and growth. Table 19.2 shows candidate measures for a firm's global account management program — Chapter 16. Table 19.3 shows key elements in a balanced scorecard for gasoline marketing.[24] This scorecard is noteworthy for its *soft* measures; financial measures weight only 10 percent versus 90 percent for non-financial measures.

**TABLE 19.3**

**KEY ELEMENTS OF A BALANCED SCORECARD FOR MOBIL GASOLINE MARKETING**

| Perspective | Weighting | Objective | Measure |
|---|---|---|---|
| Financial | 10% | Service operating efficiency | Budget variance |
| Client | 30% | Evaluate organizational effectiveness | Client satisfaction service agreement feedback (5-point scale)<br>• gasoline marketing<br>• retail dealer operations<br>• franchise re-engineering<br>• training<br>• retail dealer operations<br>• fuels support<br>• leadership development<br>• real estate<br>• strategy implementation |
| Internal | 40% | Excel in channel management | Tracking versus channel strategy<br>• retail • wholesale • fuels support<br>• training • real estate |
| | | Optimize sales force management development | Area manager development index |
| | | Service integration/alignment | Quality service forums |
| Learning and Growth | 20% | Core competencies and skills | Personnel development<br>• 360 feedback on all employees<br>• competency plan on employees executed |
| | | Organizational involvement/ scorecard understanding | Idea generation index<br>Quarterly climate survey |

The firm should closely align scorecards for different functional areas and managerial levels, like category and brand managers and district, regional, and national sales managers. A carefully designed and aligned set of measures increases the likelihood that the firm will perform well. It should help avoid deviant behavior like channel loading and accounting manipulation; as noted, these put several firms in trouble.

....................................
## KEY MESSAGES

- For long-run success, the firm must develop and sustain an external orientation.

- Firms with an external orientation often build their success on functional excellence — operations and the supply chain, customer service, finance, research and development, sales, and human resources.

- The model for developing an external orientation contains external elements — vision, mission, and strategy — and internal architectural elements — organization structure, systems and processes, and HRM practices. Customer-focused values help achieve the necessary alignment.

- The firm can achieve an external orientation only if employees in various functional areas do their jobs with a keen understanding that customers are central to the firm's success.

- Sustaining an external orientation can be very difficult. The firm's current success contains the seeds of future failure. Inability to adapt leads to failure in many previously successful firms.

- The firm must beware of several impediments to sustaining an external orientation: a functional view of marketing, bureaucracy, failure to get the centralization/decentralization balance right, functional divisions, misaligned incentives, the social fabric of institutions, internal politics, accounting systems, and inward-oriented marketing departments.

The purpose of monitor-and-control systems is to improve firm performance. Four key principles are:

- Focus on market levers and develop alternative plans.

- In general, implement steering control rather than post-action control.

- Use the right performance measures at the right organizational levels.

- Model the relationship between input, intermediate, and output measures.

The firm should monitor and control three sorts of measures:

- Output measures — The final results the firm want to achieve, can be *hard* or *soft*.

- Intermediate measures — sit between input and output measures, affect other intermediate measures or output measures.

- Input measures — concerned with the firm's functioning, explicitly linked to intermediate measures.

- The balanced scorecard typically involves output, intermediate, and input measures.

# ENDNOTES

## CHAPTER 1

1 Based in part on an interview with the author. See N. Capon, *The Marketing Mavens*, New York: Crown Business, 2007, for a book based on this and other interviews.

2 In CFO magazine.

3 L.V. Gerstner, *Who Says Elephants Can't Dance?* New York, Harper Business, 2002.

4 P.F. Drucker, *The Practice of Management*, New York, Harper and Row, 1954, pp. 37-38. Innovation comes in many forms — disruptive, application, product, process, experiential, marketing, business model, and structural.

5 Other than new equity or debt.

6 P.F. Drucker, *Management: Tasks, Responsibilities, Practices*, New York, Harper & Row, 1973, p. 63.

7 Personal communication from David Haines, Director of Global Branding, Vodafone.

8 Gerstner, *op. cit.*, p. 72.

9 *Ibid*, p. 189.

10 This term is taken from military usage.

11 See J.C. Narver and S.F. Slater, "The Effect of a Market Orientation on Business Profitability," *Journal of Marketing*, 54 (October 1990), pp. 20-35. Kohli and Jaworski place more emphasis on using market intelligence and less on environmental understanding: A.K. Kohli and B.J. Jaworski, "Market Orientation: The Construct, Research Propositions and Management Implications," *Journal of Marketing*, 54 (April 1990), pp. 1-18; B.J. Jaworski and A.K. Kohli, "Market Orientation: Antecedents and Consequences," *Journal of Marketing*, 57 (July 1993), pp. 53-70. See also B. Shapiro, "What the Hell Is Market-Oriented," *Harvard Business Review*, 67 (November-December 1989), pp. 119-225, and R. Deshpandé, *Developing a Market Orientation*, Thousand Oaks, CA: Sage, 1999.

12 See A.J. Slywotsky and B.P. Shapiro, "Leveraging to Beat the Odds: The New Marketing Mind-Set," *Harvard Business Review*, 71 (September-October 1993), pp. 97-107.

13 "As Antidote to Slowdown, Intel Will Spend, Not Cut," *The New York Times*, February 28, 2001.

14 See "Wachovia Bank and Trust Company," in N. Capon, *The Marketing of Financial Services*, Englewood Cliffs, NJ: Prentice Hall, 1992.

15 Personal communication from Pat Kelly, Senior Vice President Worldwide Marketing, Pfizer Pharmaceuticals.

16 See K. Simmonds, "Removing the Chains from Product Strategy," *Journal of Management Studies*, 5 (1968), pp. 29-40.

17 Personal communication from Pat Kelly, *op. cit.*

18 "A Cheerleader, for a Company in a Midlife Funk," *The New York Times*, June 23, 2002.

19 H. Simon, *Hidden Champions: Lessons from 500 of the World's Best Unknown Companies*, Boston, MA: Harvard Business School Press, 1996. See also J.R. Williams, "How Sustainable is Your Competitive Advantage," *California Management Review*, 34 (Spring 1992), pp. 29-52; P. Ghemawat, "Sustainable Advantage," *Harvard Business Review*, 64 (September–October 1986), pp. 53-94.

20 Personal communication from Michael Francis, Senior Vice President of Marketing, Target Stores.

## CHAPTER 2

1 L. Selden and G. Colvin, *Angel Customers & Demon Customers*, New York: Portfolio, 2003; used by permission.

2 This chapter benefited considerably from discussions with our colleagues Sunil Gupta and Don Lehmann. See S. Gupta, D.R. Lehmann, and J. Ames Stuart, "Valuing Customers," *Journal of Marketing Research*,

41 (February 2004), pp. 7-19; S. Gupta and D.R. Lehmann, "Customers as Assets," *Journal of Interactive Marketing*, 17 (Winter 2003), pp. 9-24; and S. Gupta and D.R. Lehmann, *Managing Customers as Investments*, Philadelphia, PA: Wharton, 2004.

3 The sum of net margins across all customers is applied to the firm's fixed costs. The residual is overall firm profit.

4 In practice, deciding if a customer has defected is not a simple matter. Amazon, eBay, and L.L. Bean treat a customer who hasn't purchased within the prior year as having defected. This judgment varies with the purchase cycle.

5 Strictly speaking, this formula applies to a series of terms summed to infinity. We can then avoid arbitrary assumptions about actual customer lifetime. Further, with reasonable assumptions of the retention rate (r) and discount rate (d), after a few years, the impact of all terms is very small. You can check this out for yourself.

6 F.F. Reicheld, *The Loyalty Effect*, Boston, MA: Harvard Business School Press, 1996, p. 51.

7 Reicheld, *op. cit.*, p. 36. See also F.F. Reicheld, *Loyalty Rules*, Boston, MA: Harvard Business School Press, 2001; B.J. Pine II, D. Peppers, and M. Rogers, "Do You Want to Keep Your Customers Forever?" *Harvard Business Review*, 73 (March-April 1995), pp. 103–154; R.C. Blattberg and J. Deighton, "Manage Marketing by the Customer Equity Test," *Harvard Business Review*, 74 (July-August 1996), pp. 136–144; R.C. Blattberg, G. Getz, and J.S. Thomas, *Customer Equity*, Boston, MA: Harvard Business School Press, 2001; and R.T. Rust, V.A. Zeithaml, and K.N. Lemon, *Driving Customer Equity*, New York: Free Press, 2000.

8 Note that these results are independent of the starting positions. We selected 500 each for Jane and Joe, initially. You get the same result regardless of how Jane and Joe initially divide up the 1,000 customers.

9 Personal communication from Dave Goudge, senior vice president for marketing, Boise Office Solutions (now OfficeMax).

10 For this discussion, overhead comprises those costs not directly assigned to customers. It may include long-run R&D and corporate assessments for advertising, legal services, and government relations.

11 Lovelock and Wright term these five customer types and non-payers (deadbeats) as *jaycustomers*, C. Lovelock and L. Wright, *Principles of Service Marketing and Management*, Upper Saddle River, NJ: Prentice-Hall, 1999.

## CHAPTER 3

1 T. Levitt, "Marketing Myopia," *Harvard Business Review*, 53 (September-October 1975), p. 26 *et seq.*

2 R.K. Srivastava, M.I. Alpert, and A.D. Shocker, "A Customer Oriented Approach for Determining Market Structures," *Journal of Marketing*, 48 (Spring 1984), pp. 32–45.

3 Some use the term product category instead of product class, and product sub-category instead of product form.

4 Sometimes a product item is called a stock-keeping unit (sku).

5 Since demand in B2C markets drives demand in B2B markets, we focus on key indicators of B2C market size.

6 *International Migration Report 2002*, New York: United Nations, 2002.

7 World Population Prospects Population Database — *http://esa.un.org/unpp/p2k0data.asp*. Estimates of the percentage over 65 in 2050 are Italy and Spain — 70%, Germany — 57%, France — 53%, Sweden and Britain — 49%, and Ireland — 48%, *The Economist*, December 23, 2000.

8 See E.M. Rogers, *Diffusion of Innovations*, New York: Free Press, 1962. We address this topic in Chapter 12.

9 R.W. Olshavsky, "Time and the Rate of Adoption of Innovations," *Journal of Consumer Research*, 6 (March 1980), pp. 425-428; W. Qualls, R. W. Olshavsky, and R.E. Michaels, "Shortening of the PLC-An Empirical Test," *Journal of Marketing*, 45 (Fall 1981), pp. 76-80.

10 M. E. Porter, *Competitor Strategy: Techniques for Analyzing Industries and Competitors*, New York: Free Press, 1980. In B. Greenwald and J. Kahn, *Competition Demystified*, New York: Portfolio, 2005, the authors build on Porter's model but focus their attention on barriers to entry.

11 C. Zook with J. Allen, *Profit from the Core: Growth Strategy in an Era of Turbulence*, Boston, MA: Harvard Business School Press, 2001, pp. 26-28.

12 In pyramid sales forces, salespeople earn commissions from direct sales. They also earn overrides on sales of salespeople they recruit. They may also earn overrides on sales from their recruits' recruits, and so on.

13 R.M. Kanter, "Collaborative Advantage: The Art of Alliances," *Harvard Business Review*, 72 (July-August 1994), pp. 96-108.

14 K. Harrigan, *Strategies for Vertical Integration*, Lexington, MA: Lexington Books, 1983.

15 H. Simon, *Hidden Champions: Lessons from 500 of the World's Best Unknown Companies*, Boston, MA: Harvard Business School Press, 1996.

16 This section draws in part on P. Fitzroy and J.M. Hulbert, *Strategic Management: Creating Value In A Turbulent World*, New York: Wiley, 2004.

17 *The New Shorter Oxford English Dictionary*, Oxford: Clarendon, 1993.

18 *Baby Boomers* — 72 million people born in the U.S. between 1946 and 1964; *Generation X* — 17 million persons born between 1965 and 1978; *Generation Y* (echo boomers, the millennium generation) — 60 million persons born between 1979 and 1994.

19 C. M. Christensen, *The Innovator's Dilemma: When New Technologies Cause Great Firms to Fail*, Boston, MA: Harvard Business School Press, 1997.

20 L. Downes and C. Mui, *Unleashing the Killer App: Digital Strategies for Market Dominance*, Boston, MA: Harvard Business School Press, 1998.

21 D. A. Beck, J. N. Fraser, A. C. Reuter-Domenech, and P. Sidebottom, "Personal Financial Services Goes Global," *The McKinsey Quarterly*, 3 1999, pp. 39-47.

22 K. O'Neill Packard and F. Reinhardt, "What Every Executive Needs to Know About Global Warming," *Harvard Business Review*, 78 (July–August 2000), pp. 129-135.

## CHAPTER 4

1 T.V. Bonoma, "Major Sales: Who Really Does the Buying, *Harvard Business Review*, 60 (May–June 1982), pp. 111-120.

2 Personal communication from Dale Hayes, Vice President Brand Management and Customer Communications, UPS.

3 In addition to *communicating* value to customers, advertising may also *create* value.

4 A. Maslow, *Motivation and Personality*, New York: Harper, 1954. This framework raises the question, discussed extensively by Freud, whether all needs are fully conscious.

5 R. Friedmann, "Psychological Meaning of Products: Identification and Marketing Applications," *Psychology and Marketing*, 3 (Spring 1986), pp. 1-15.

6 J.L. Forbis and N.T. Mehta, "Value-Based Strategies for Industrial Products," *Business Horizons*, 24 (1981), pp. 32-42.

7  This calculation does not include savings from avoiding costs to repair cotton-based conveyor belts, or the downtime costs of more frequently replacing cotton conveyor belts.

8  B. Schmitt, *Experiential Marketing: How to Get Customers to SENSE, FEEL, THINK, ACT and RELATE to Your Company and Brands*: New York: The Free Press, 1999. See also B.J. Pine II and J.H. Gilmore, "Welcome to the Experience Economy," *Harvard Business Review*, 76 (July–August 1998), pp. 97–105.

9  H. Stern, "The Significance of Impulse Buying Today," *Journal of Marketing*, 26 (April 1962) pp. 59–62.

10  This section relies heavily on I. Simonson, "Get Closer to Your Customers by Understanding How They Make Choices," *California Management Review*, (Summer 1993), pp. 74–84.

11  I. Simonson and A. Tversky, "Choice in Context: Tradeoff Contrast and Extremeness Aversion," *Journal of Marketing Research*, 29 (1992), pp. 281–295. See also G.E. Smith and T.T. Nagle, "Frames of Reference and Buyers' Perception of Price and Value," *California Management Review*, 38 (1995), pp. 98–116.

12  R. Dhar and I. Simonson, "The Effect of the Focus of Comparison on Consumer Preferences," *Journal of Marketing Research*, 29 (November 1992), pp. 430–440.

13  See T. Levitt, "After the Sale is Over," *Harvard Business Review*, 61 (September–October 1983), pp. 87–93.

14  500 companies produce more than 2,000 Kretek brands.

15  W. Chan Kim and R. Mauborgne, *Blue Ocean Strategy*, Boston, MA: Harvard Business School Press, 2005, pp. 71-74.

16  See E. Hall, *The Silent Language*, Garden City, NY: Anchor, 1973.

17  Chapter 3 discussed broad environmental influences — globalization, industry concentration, and increased competition. We base this section on N. Capon, *Key Account Management and Planning*, New York: The Free Press, 2001.

## CHAPTER 5

1  The opening case is based on material from Boeing and Airbus websites and related material from *www.wikipedia.com.*

2  *Groupthink* refers to drawing conclusions based on the shared, and poorly examined, assumptions of group members.

3  L.M. Fuld, *The Secret Language of Competitive Intelligence*, New York: Crown Business, 2006, pp. 40-41. For a good example of gaining insight from a competitor's production process, see pp. 123-134.

4  Based on L. Fahey, *Outwitting, Outmaneuvering and Outperforming Competitors*, New York: Wiley, 1999, Table 5.3, p. 133, by permission.

5  For a good description of a war game, see Fuld 2006, *op. cit.*, pp. 69-118.

6  Based on a competitor analysis framework in Fahey, *op. cit.*, by permission.

7  The firm should conduct this analysis with a more general objective, systematic analysis of the firm versus competition such as SWOT — strengths, weaknesses, opportunities, and threats.

8  To reinforce this point, around 500 B.C., Chinese warrior Sun Tzu said, "All men see the tactics whereby I conquer, but none see the strategy out of which victory evolved."

9  Reproduced (and slightly modified) from Fahey, *op. cit.*, Table 4.1, p. 90, by permission.

10  This section is based on Fahey, *op. cit.*, Chapter 16, by permission.

11  For an excellent discussion of signaling, see Fahey, *op. cit.*, Chapter 4.

12  "AMD Sets a Course for 2008," ZDNet News, June 1, 2006.

13  H. Gatignon and D. Reibstein, "Formulating Competitive Strategies," *Wharton on Dynamic Competitive Strategies*, G. Day and D. Reibstein (eds.); New York: Wiley, 1997.

14  This section based in part on A. Brandenburger and B.J. Nalebuff, *Co-opetition*, New York: Doubleday, 1996. Broadly, complementarity includes relationships for the firm to secure needed resources. Formal agreements include joint ventures; R&D partnerships; agreements for supply; joint production, marketing, and distribution; and co-branding.

15  The firm can also be a complementer for its own products (see Chapter 12).

16  A complementer relationship may involve a formal partnership — but this is not necessary.

17  Disguised name.

18  A major exception is Southwest Airlines — it has no interline agreements.

## CHAPTER 6

1  One of the words you will see a lot in this chapter is "data." Many people think this is a singular word, but it is plural; the related singular word is "datum."

2  Based on material provided by Client Insight, LLC, Boston, MA, a marketing research and strategy firm whose principals have worked extensively with Thomson businesses.

3  Personal communication to the author.

4  Personal communication from Michael Francis, Executive Vice President of Marketing, Target Stores.

5  *http://www.geocities.com/hotofftheinternet/bbyquote.htm.* Attributed to Yogi Berra, player for, and manager of, the New York Yankees and New York Mets baseball teams.

6  Example provided by The Michael Allen Company.

7  F. Gouillart and F. Sturdivant, "Spend a Day in the Life of Your Customers, *Harvard Business Review*, 72 (January-February 1994), pp. 116-125.

8  Ordinal scales measure rank order; interval scales measure differences among scale points; ratio scales possess a non-arbitrary zero value.

9  Numbers of brands and comparisons are: 3 brands, 3 comparisons; 4 brands, 6 comparisons; 5 brands, 10 comparisons; 6 brands, 15 comparisons; 7 brands, 21 comparisons; etc.

10  For information on factor analysis, see any good marketing research textbook.

11  D.T. Campbell and J.C. Stanley, *Experimental and Quasi-Experimental Designs for Research*, New York: Houghton Mifflin, 1963.

12  Attributed (but not authenticated) to Yogi Berra, *op. cit.*

13  For information on regression analysis, see any good marketing research textbook.

## CHAPTER 7

1  See C. Zook with J. Allen, *Profit from the Core*, Boston, MA: Harvard Business School Press, 2001.

2  O. Gadiesh and J.M. Gilbert, "Profit Pools: A Fresh Look at Strategy," *Harvard Business Review*, 76 (May-June 1998), pp. 139-147.

3  An alternative term for *white space* is *blue ocean*. W.C. Kim and R. Mauborgne, *Blue Ocean Strategy: How to Create Uncontested Market*

*Space and Make the Competition Irrelevant*, Boston, MA: Harvard Business School Press, 2005.

4 In May 1961, President John Kennedy developed a vision statement for NASA. "Achieving the goal, before this decade is out, of landing a man on the moon and returning him safely to earth."

5 See J.C. Collins and J.I. Porras, "Building Your Company's Vision," *Harvard Business Review*, 74 (September-October 1996), pp. 65-77.

6 This was the key insight underlying Theodore Levitt's famous article: T. Levitt, "Marketing Myopia," *Harvard Business Review*, 53 (September–October 1975), p. 26 *et seq.*

7 J.B. Quinn, *The Intelligent Enterprise: A New Paradigm*, New York: Free Press, 1992.

8 Based in part on H.I. Ansoff and J.M. Stewart, "Strategies for a Technologically-Based Business," *Harvard Business Review*, 45 (November-December 1967), pp. 71–83.

9 T. Levitt, *Managing for Business Growth*, New York: McGraw-Hill, 1974.

10 G.J. Tellis and P.N. Golder, *Will and Vision: How Latecomers Grow to Dominate Markets*, New York: McGraw-Hill, 2002, introduce some of these requirements.

11 Tellis and Golder, *op. cit.*

12 See *We've Got Rhythm! Medtronic Corporation's Cardiac Pacemaker Business*, 9-698-004, Harvard Business School.

13 G.E. Blau, J.F. Pekny, V.A. Varma, and P.R. Bunch, "Managing a Portfolio of Interdependent New Product Candidates in the Pharmaceutical Industry," *Journal of Product Innovation Management*, 21 (2004), pp. 227-245.

14 See T. Kuczmarski, *Managing New Products*, Englewood Cliffs, NJ: Prentice Hall, 1988.

15 Chapter 12 describes systematic methods for incorporating such market factors into an evaluation scheme. For definitions of terms, also see the glossary and any good finance textbook.

16 The seminal article is C.K. Prahalad and G. Hamel, "Core Competence of the Corporation," *Harvard Business Review*, 68 (May–June 1990) pp. 79–91. K.P. Coyne, S.J.D. Hall, and P.G. Clifford, "Is Your Core Competence a Mirage," *The McKinsey Quarterly*, 1 (1997), pp. 40-54, propose a formal definition. "A core competence is a combination of complementary skills and knowledge bases embedded in a group or team that results in the ability to execute one or more critical processes to a world-class standard" (p. 43).

17 H.I. Ansoff, *Corporate Strategy*, New York: McGraw Hill, 1965; M. Goold and A. Campbell, "Desperately Seeking Synergy," *Harvard Business Review*, 76 (September–October 1998), pp. 131-143.

18 N. Capon and R. Glazer, "Marketing and Technology: A Strategic Co-Alignment," *Journal of Marketing*, 51 (July 1987), pp. 1–14.

19 N. Capon, J. U. Farley, and J. Hulbert, *Corporate Strategic Planning*, New York: Columbia University Press, 1988; and N. Capon, J.U. Farley, and S. Hoenig, *Toward an Integrative Explanation of Corporate Financial Performance*, Norwell, MA: Kluwer Academic Publishers, 1997.

20 L.V. Gerstner, Jr., *Who Says Elephants Can't Dance*, New York: HarperBusiness, 2003, p. 222. Gerstner adds that IBM often accelerated its technology development through highly focused acquisitions.

21 See M.A. Hayward and D.C. Hambrick, "Explaining the Premiums Paid for Large Acquisitions: Evidence of CEO Hubris," *Administrative Science Quarterly*, 42 (1997), pp. 103–127.

22 M. Bradley, A. Desai, and E.H. Kim, "Synergistic Gains from Acquisitions and Their Division between the Stockholders of Target and Acquiring Firms," *Journal of Financial Economics*, 21 (1988), pp. 3–40; E. Berkovitch and M.P. Narayanan, "Motives for Take-overs: An Empirical Investigation," *Journal of Financial and Quantitative Analysis*, 28 (1993), pp. 347–362; M.L. Sirower, *The Synergy Trap: How Companies Lose the Acquisition Game*, New York: Free Press, 1997.

23 Capon, Farley, and Hoenig, *op. cit.*

24 See W.H. Bergquist, *Building Strategic Relationships: How to Extend Your Organization's Reach through Partnerships, Alliances and Joint Ventures*, San Francisco, CA: Jossey-Bass, 1995.

## CHAPTER 8

1 We say that the segments are mutually exclusive and collectively exhaustive of all potential customers.

2 "Taxonomy at the Pump: Mobil's Five Types of Gasoline Buyers," *The Wall Street Journal*, January 30, 1995.

3 "Mirabella Told Summer Issue to Be its Last," *The New York Times*, April 28, 2000.

4 D.K. Rigby and V. Vishwanath, "Localization: The Revolution in Consumer Markets," *Harvard Business Review*, 84 (April 2006), pp. 82-92.

5 B.J. Pine II, B. Victor, and A.C. Boyton, "Making Mass Customization Work," *Harvard Business Review*, 71 (September–October 1993), pp. 108–119; B.J. Pine II, D. Peppers, and M. Rogers, "Do You Want to Keep Your Customers Forever?" *Harvard Business Review*, 73 (March–April 1995), pp. 103–114; and E. Feitzinger and H.L. Lee, "Mass Customization at Hewlett-Packard: The Power of Postponement," *Harvard Business Review*, 75 (January–February 1997), pp. 116-121.

6 A.J. Slywotzky, "The Age of the Choiceboard," *Harvard Business Review*, 78 (January–February 2000), pp. 40–41.

7 M.J.A. Berry and G. Linoff, *Data Mining Techniques for Marketing, Sales and Customer Support*, New York: Wiley, 1997.

8 *TESCO PLC: Getting to the Top ... Staying at the Top?* 599-037-1BW, European Case Clearing House. Tesco's loyalty card now comes in gold, silver, and bronze tiers, reflecting customer profitability.

9 H. Simon, *Hidden Champions: Lessons from 500 of the World's Best Unknown Companies*, Boston, MA: Harvard Business School Press, 1996.

10 "Wish I'd Thought of That!" *Fortune*, May 15, 2000.

## CHAPTER 9

1 Personal communication to the author.

2 We use *market* strategy rather than *marketing* strategy — many functional areas, not just marketing, should help develop and implement the strategy.

3 To ensure that the firm seriously considers competition, re-label *Market Strategy* as *Competitive Market Strategy*.

4 R.D. Buzzell, B.T. Gale, and R.G.M. Sultan, "Market Share — a Key to Profitability," *Harvard Business Review*, 53 (January-February 1975), pp. 97-106, was the first paper in a stream of research on the relationship between market share and profitability. In general, the relationship is positive, but it may break down at high market share levels.

5 The tree of alternatives in the strategic focus is related in spirit to the famous DuPont formula. See, for example, *www.12manage.com/methods_dupont_model.html*.

6 In this discussion, the end-user customer may be an individual, family, or formal organization.

7 H. Evans, *They Made America*, New York: Little Brown, 2004, pp. 391-392.

8   P. M. Nattermann, "Best Practice Does Not Equal Best Strategy," *The McKinsey Quarterly*, August 18, 2004.

9   Thanks to Mary Murphy for this acronym.

10  A. Ries and J. Trout, *Positioning: The Battle for Your Mind*, New York: McGraw-Hill, 1993.

11  Developed by Robert Christian, formerly of Impact Planning Group, Old Greenwich, CT.

12  Developed by the author from published data. Cemex saves on fuel, maintenance, and payroll and uses 35 percent fewer trucks. It secures higher prices by delivering a perishable item within minutes of receiving an order. Customers use the Internet to place orders, secure delivery information, and check payment records.

## CHAPTER 10

1   A separate but related issue is at what stage the firm should enter the market. We addressed this question in Chapter 7.

2   Refer to Chapter 3 for introductory material on product life-cycle stages.

3   Entry barriers retard a firm's entry *into* a market, whereas exit barriers retard a firm's exit *from* a market. The more general term for inhibiting a firm's movement is *mobility barriers*. For a framework on entry barriers, see T.S. Gruca and D. Sudharshan, "A Framework for Entry Deterrence Strategy: The Competitive Environment, Choices, and Consequences, *Journal of Marketing*, 59 (July 1995), pp. 44-55. See also B. Greenwald and J. Kahn, *Competition Demystified: A Radically Simplified Approach to Business Strategy*, New York: Portfolio Hardcover, 2005.

4   Many marketing textbooks address penetration and skim pricing in the pricing chapter. We believe the fundamental issues these strategies represent make it appropriate to address them in this chapter.

5   G.S. Carpenter and K. Nakamoto, "Consumer Preference Formation and Pioneering Advantage," *Journal of Marketing Research*, 26 (August 1989), pp. 285-298. Research that supports the success of pioneering firms includes G. Urban, T. Carter, S. Gaskin, and Z. Mucha, "Market Share Rewards to Pioneering Brands: An Empirical Analysis and Strategic Implications," *Management Science*, 32 (June 1986), pp. 645-659; and "Pioneering Advantages in Manufacturing and Service Industries: Empirical Evidence from Nine Countries," *Strategic Management Journal*, 20 (1999), pp. 811-836.

6   J. Dean, "Pricing Policies for New Products," *Harvard Business Review*, 28 (November-December 1950), pp. 28-36.

7   Personal communication from former senior marketing executive at Nokia, Richard Geruson. Later, Nokia lost market share when competitors switched to flip (clam-shell) phones.

8   R. Buaron, "New Game Strategies," *The McKinsey Quarterly*, (Spring 1981), pp. 24-30.

9   G. Stalk Jr., D.K. Pecaut, and B. Burnett, "Breaking Compromises, Breakaway Growth," *Harvard Business Review*, 74 (September-October 1996), pp. 131-139. See also Y. Moon, "Break Free from the Product Life Cycle," *Harvard Business Review*, 83 (May 2005), pp. 77-94.

10  Price elasticity = percentage change in quantity demanded divided by the percentage change in price $= dQ/Q \div dP/P$.

11  See W.C. Kim and R. Mauborgne, "Creating New Market Space," *Harvard Business Review*, 77 (January-February 1999), pp. 83–93, for interesting approaches to securing growth in mature markets. See also *Blue Ocean Strategy*, Boston, MA: Harvard Business School, 2005, by the same authors.

12  Sometimes managers confuse *milking* with *harvesting*. Milking focuses on securing resources for use elsewhere in the firm — *the cow must be fed so the milk continues to flow*. Harvesting implies a decision to exit the business, sooner or later.

13  K. Harrigan, "Strategies for Declining Industries," *Journal of Business Strategy*, 1 (Fall 1980), pp. 20-34. Of course, in the decline stage, the investment can be quite low if the firm has mostly depreciated its capital equipment.

## CHAPTER 11

1   J. Sampson, "Brand Valuation: Today and Tomorrow," Chapter 20 in *Brand Valuation*, London: Premier Books, 1997.

2   Adapted from B.H. Schmitt and D. Rogers, "SAP: Building a Leading Technology Brand," Center on Global Brand Leadership, Columbia Business School, and personal communication to the author.

3   Thanks to Dr. David James, Henley Management College, for this visual.

4   S. King, *Developing New Brands*, London: J. Walter Thompson Co. Ltd., 1984.

5   From the American Marketing Association, quoted in K.L. Keller, *Strategic Brand Management*, Upper Saddle River, NJ: Prentice-Hall, 2003, Chapter 1.

6   Adapted from J. M. Hulbert, N. Capon, and N. Piercy, *Total Integrated Marketing: Breaking the Bounds of the Function*, New York: Free Press, 2003.

7   B.H. Schmitt, *Experiential Marketing*, New York: Free Press, 1999; and B.H. Schmitt, *Customer Experience Management*, Hoboken, NJ: Wiley, 2003.

8   A. Muniz, Jr. and T.C. O'Guinn, "Brand Community," *Journal of Consumer Research*, 27 (March 2001), pp. 412-432.

9   Thanks to Dr. David James, Henley Management College, for this pedagogical device.

10  J. Aaker, "Dimensions of Brand Personality," *Journal of Marketing Research*, 34 (August 1997), pp. 334–356. Based on data from 1,000 U.S. respondents, 60 well-known brands, and 114 personality traits.

11  www.virgin.com

12  E. Joachimsthaler and D.A. Aaker, "Building Brands without Mass Media," *Harvard Business Review*, 75 (January-February 1997), pp. 3-10.

13  D.A. Aaker, *Managing Brand Equity*, New York: Free Press, 1991, p. 15. See also *Building Strong Brands*, New York: Free Press, 1995; and *Brand Leadership* (with E. Joachimsthaler), New York: Free Press, 2000.

14  Ohga-san, Chairman and CEO, Sony, quoted in *Fortune*, June 12, 1995. In the early 2000s, the Sony brand weakened; in 2006, it was no longer in the Top 25 global brands.

15  "Big Blue," *Fortune*, April 14, 1997.

16  P. Berthon, J.M. Hulbert, and L.F. Pitt, "Brand Management Prognostications," *Sloan Management Review*, 40 (Winter 1999), pp. 53-65.

17  M.E. Barth, M.B. Clement, G. Foster, and R. Kasznik, "Brand Values and Capital Market Valuation," *Review of Accounting Studies*, 3 (1998), pp. 41-68.

18  D.A. Ailawadi, D.R. Lehmann, and S.A. Neslin, "Revenue Premium as an Outcome Measure of Brand Equity," *Journal of Marketing*, 67 (October 2003), pp. 1-17.

19  The cost to create a successful mid-size brand is about $100 million. With a 15 percent success rate, brand value = $670 million (100/0.15).

20  Developed from G. Gordon, A. di Benedetto, and R. Calantone, "Brand equity as an evolutionary process," *The Journal of Brand Management*, 2 (1994), pp. 47-56.

21  "Bringing a Corporate Brand to Life Using the Principles of Experiential Marketing, Presentation by C.P. Lange and S. Tollefson" at *True Love or One-Night Stand?* Conference on Brand Relationships and Experiences." Columbia Business School, May 29-30, 2001.

22  See K.L. Keller, "Conceptualizing, Measuring, and Managing Customer-Based Brand Equity," *Journal of Marketing*, 57 (January 1993), pp. 1–22; and K.L. Keller, "The Brand Report Card," *Harvard Business Review*, 78 (January-February 2000), pp. 147–157.

23  D.A. Aaker, *Managing Brand Equity*, New York: Free Press, 1991.

24  S.P. Douglas, C.S. Craig, and E.J. Nijessen, "Integrating Brand Strategy Across Markets: Building International Brand Architecture," 9 (2001), pp. 97-114.

25  D.B. Holt, J.A. Quelch, and E.L. Taylor, "How Global Brands Compete," *Harvard Business Review*, 82 (September 2004), pp. 68-75.

26  J. Quelch, "Global Brands: Taking Stock," *Business Strategy Review*, 10 (1999), pp. 1–14.

27  A. McCormick, "The Delicate Balance Between Standardization and Localization in Global Branding," *Chazen Web Journal of International Business*, (Spring 2004), pp. 1-6.

28  A.J. Parsons, "Nestlé: The Visions of Local Managers," *The McKinsey Quarterly*, (1996-2), pp. 5–29.

29  Parsons, *op. cit.*

30  S. K. Reddy, S. L. Holak, and S. Bhat, "To Extend or Not to Extend: Success Determinants of Line Extensions," *Journal of Marketing Research*, 31 (May 1994), pp. 243-262.

31  D.A. Aaker and K.L. Keller, "Consumer Evaluation of Brand Extensions," *Journal of Marketing*, 54 (January 1990), pp. 27–41; S.J. Milberg, C.W. Park, and M.S. McCarthy, "Managing Negative Feedback Effects Associated With Brand Extensions: The Impact of Alternative Branding Strategies," *Journal of Consumer Psychology*, 6 (1997), pp. 119-140; D.R. John, B. Loken, and C. Joiner, "The Negative Impact of Extensions: Can Flagship Products Be Diluted?" *Journal of Marketing*, 62 (January 1998), pp. 19–32; V. Swaminathan, R.J. Fox, and S.K. Reddy, "The Impact of Brand Extension Introduction on Choice," *Journal of Marketing*, 65 (October 2001), pp. 1-15.

32  Personal communication from David Haines, Director of Global Branding, Vodafone.

# CHAPTER 12

1   We use the term *product* to include both physical products and intangible services. We also talk about *products* — of course, these may be grouped into product lines.

2   The firm can use the portfolio approach to allocate resources at both the business unit and corporate levels.

3   For a detailed treatment of financial analysis techniques, see J.C. Van Horne, *Financial Management and Policy*, 12th ed., Englewood Cliffs, NJ: Prentice Hall, 2001.

4   Typically, the firm seeks to maximize shareholder value by improving return on shareholder equity (ROE). Many firms use return-on-investment (ROI) as a proxy for ROE, N. Capon, J.U. Farley, and J. Hulbert, *Corporate Strategic Planning*, New York: Columbia University Press, 1988.

5   A simple principle underlies discounting — the future value of $1 is less than today's value of $1.

6   Stern Stewart trademarked EVA. See J. M. Stern, J. S. Shiely, and I. Ross, *The EVA Challenge*, New York: Wiley, 2001.

7   Portfolio analysis also helps set priorities among market segments — Chapter 8.

8   P. Haspeslagh, "Portfolio Planning: Uses and Limits," *Harvard Business Review*, 60 (January-February 1982), pp. 58–74.

9   The visual appearance of portfolio matrices — 2x2, 3x3 — is arbitrary. Regardless, by placing products in the matrix, the firm can assess potential return and risk and gain insight into strategic options.

10  See R. Vernon, "Gone Are the Cash Cows of Yesteryear," *Harvard Business Review*, 58 (November-December 1980), pp. 150–155.

11  Aka the stoplight matrix — three green (invest) cells, three red (don't invest) cells, and three amber (be careful) cells.

12  Note that we have defined the X-axis as low to high; as noted above, BCG's growth-share matrix is defined from high to low.

13  In 2006, GM sold 51% of GMAC to a group led by Cerberus Capital Management, an investment firm.

14  A.J. Slywotzky and D.J. Morrison, *The Profit Zone*, New York: Times Business, 1997.

15  C. Shapiro and H.R. Varian, *Information Rules*, Boston, MA: Harvard Business School Press, 1999.

16  R.F. Maruca, "Is Your Brand at Risk?" *Harvard Business Review*, 77 (November–December 1999), pp. 22, 25.

# CHAPTER 13

1   Based on material provided by Client Insight, LLC, Boston, MA, a marketing research and strategy firm whose principals have worked extensively with Thomson businesses.

2   P.F. Drucker, *The Practice of Management*, New York: Harper and Row, 1956, pp. 65–67.

3   R. Foster and S. Kaplan, *Creative Destruction: Why Companies That Are Built to Last Underperform the Market — and How to Successfully Transform Them*, New York: Currency/Doubleday, 2001.

4   C.M. Christensen, *The Innovator's Dilemma*, Boston, MA: Harvard Business School Press, 1997.

5   See G.S. Carpenter and K. Nakamoto, "Consumer Preference Formation and Pioneering Advantage," *Journal of Marketing Research*, 26 (August 1989), pp. 285–298; and G.S. Carpenter, R. Glazer, and K. Nakamoto, "Meaningful Brands from Meaningless Differentiation: The Dependence on Irrelevant Attributes," *Journal of Marketing Research*, 31 (August 1994), pp. 339–350.

6   F.J. Gouillart and F.D. Sturdivant, "Spend a Day in the Life of Your Customers," *Harvard Business Review*, 72 (January-February 1994), pp. 116–125; J. Johanson and I. Nonaka, "Market Research the Japanese Way," *Harvard Business Review*, 65 (May-June 1987), pp. 29–32.

7   R.T. Woodruff, "Customer Value: The Next Source for Competitive Advantage," *Journal of the Academy of Marketing Science*, 25 (1997), p. 139.

8   H. Courtney, "Making the most of uncertainty," *The McKinsey Quarterly*, 4 (2001), pp. 38-47; P. Berthon, J.M. Hulbert, and L. F. Pitt, "Innovation or Customer Orientation? An Empirical Investigation," *European Journal of Marketing*, 38 (2004), pp. 1065-1090.

9   Until recently, 3M scientists could spend 15% of time on non-official 3M projects — Art Fry developed Post-It notes in this system.

10  From Booz Allen and Hamilton — improvement is related to attention to core competence and focus to innovation efforts.

11  E. von Hippel, *The Sources of Innovation*, New York: Oxford University Press, 1988.

12  E. von Hippel, S. Thomke, and M. Sonnack, "Creating Breakthroughs at 3M," *Harvard Business Review*, 77 (September-October 1999), pp. 47-57, at p. 54. See also E. von Hippel, *Democratizing Innovation*, Cambridge, MA: MIT Press, 2005. Free download at *http://web.mit.edu/evhippel/www/*. The author was a lead user for gas phase chromatography.

13  Based in part on *www.mindtools.com*. See also J. Goldenberg, *Creativity in Product Innovation*, Cambridge, UK: Cambridge University Press, 2002.

14  E. De Bono, *Six Thinking Hats*, Boston, MA: Little Brown, 1985.

15  W.H. Davidow and B. Uttal, *Total Customer Service: The Ultimate Weapon*, New York: Harper & Row, 1989.

16  D.K. Sobek II, J.K. Liker, and A.C. Ward, "Another Look at How Toyota Integrates Product Development," *Harvard Business Review*, 76 (July-August 1998), pp. 36–49.

17  Personal communication from Ron Boire, President Consumer Sales Company, Sony Electronics. Boire is president of Toys "R" Us via a senior marketing position at Best Buy.

18  E.M. Rogers, *Diffusion of Innovations*, New York: Free Press, 1962.

19  These size percentages, based on standard deviations from the mean, have not been empirically validated.

20  G.A. Moore, *Crossing the Chasm — Marketing & Selling High-Tech Products to Mainstream Customers*, New York: HarperBusiness, 2002.

## CHAPTER 14

1  Personal communication from Lamar Muse. See also J.H. Gittell, *The Southwest Airlines Way*, New York: McGraw Hill, 2003; and *Southwest Airlines (A)*, 9-575-060, Harvard Business School.

2  Based on 2,463 companies in the Compustat database. M.V. Marn and R.L. Rosiello, "Managing Price, Gaining Profit," *Harvard Business Review*, 70 (September-October 1992), pp. 84–94. More recently, percentage reductions in operating profit from a 1% price decrease were — food and drug stores — 23.7%, airlines — 12.9%, computers and office equipment — 11%, tobacco — 4.9%, semiconductors — 3.9%, and diversified financial — 2.4%, *Fortune*, May 14, 2001.

3  P.C. Browne, N. Capon, T.S. Harris, H.N. Mantel, C.A. Newland, and A.H. Walsh, *The Ratemaking Process for the United States Postal Service*, New York: Institute of Public Administration, 1991. See also R. Cooper and R. Slagmulder, Develop Profitable New Products with Target Costing," *Sloan Management Review*, 40 (Summer 1999), pp. 23-33.

4  A third demand curve — **positive sloping** — is relatively rare. Volume increases as the price increases! This can occur with luxury products like perfumes and fragrances — price conveys information about product and/or service quality.

5  Over 80% of U.S. manufacturers use cost-plus pricing, E. Shim and E.F. Sudit, "How Manufacturers Price Products," *Management Accounting*, (February 1995), pp. 37–39.

6  Selling, general, and administrative costs.

7  The hurdle rate is the minimum return for a new investment. Typically hurdle rate is tied to the firm's cost of capital.

8  For example, if the firm adds fixed capacity or a new shift.

9  Of course, costs are important for cost-plus contracts.

10  N. Capon, J.U. Farley, and J. Hulbert, "Pricing and Forecasting in an Oligopoly Firm," *Journal of Management Studies*, 12 (1975), pp. 133–156.

11  A.K. Rao, M.E. Bergen, and S. Davis, "How to Fight a Price War," *Harvard Business Review*, 78 (March-April 2000), pp. 107–116.

12  We omit time value of money issues to simplify the example.

13  Traditional income statements partition costs into cost of goods sold (COGS) and all other costs — mostly marketing and SG&A. In Table 14.6, variable costs and fixed costs are gathered from these traditional categories:
   - *Variable costs*: raw materials, direct labor, electricity — for production, freight, and sales commissions.
   - *Fixed costs*: indirect labor, manufacturing overhead, and depreciation; also advertising, field sales (salary, expenses), and product and marketing management.
   We assume that variable costs per unit, and fixed costs, are constant over the volume range we consider.

14  VC per passenger is small on even the longest flights. VC elements include extra fuel, free snacks, and soft drinks.

15  For more detail on these and related terms, see *http://www.export911.com/e911/export/comTerm.htm*.

16  *Norton Company*, 9-581-046, Harvard Business School. The French firm Saint-Gobain acquired Norton.

17  Marn and Rosiello, *op. cit.*

18  An 18th-century economist quoted in R.B. Ekelund, "Price Discrimination and Product Differentiation in Economic Theory: An Early Analysis," *Quarterly Journal of Economics*, 84 (1970), pp. 268-278.

19  See E. Anderson and D. Simester, "Quick, What's a Good Price to Pay for ...," *Harvard Business Review*, 81 (September 2003), pp. 97-103.

20  J. Zale and Wise, "Pricing When Sales Slow," *The Professional Pricing Society Journal*, 10 (3rd Quarter 2001), pp.1-9).

21  S. Dutta, M. Bergen, D. Levy, M. Ritson, and M. Zbaracki, "Pricing as a Strategic Capability," *Sloan Management Review*, 43 (Spring 2002), pp. 61-66; and S. Dutta, M. Zbaracki, and M. Bergen, "Pricing Process as a Capability: A Resource-Based Perspective," *Strategic Management Journal*, 24 (2003), pp. 615-630. See also *Organizing for Pricing*, Perspectives, Boston Consulting Group, 2002.

22  For a fuller discussion and bibliography, see G.W. Ortmeyer, "Ethical Issues in Pricing," in N.C. Smith and J.A. Quelch, *Ethics in Marketing*, New York: McGraw Hill, 1993, Chapter 5.1. Before taking action on any subject discussed in this section, readers are advised to consult a knowledgeable attorney.

23  K. Eichenwald, *The Informant*, New York: Broadway, 2000.

## CHAPTER 15

1  G.E. Belch, M.A. Belch, and J. Pincus, *Advertising and Promotion: An Integrated Marketing and Communications Perspective*, 6th ed., Homewood, IL: McGraw-Hill/Irwin, 2003.

2  J. Hulbert and N. Capon, "Interpersonal Communication in Marketing: An Overview," *Journal of Marketing Research*, 9 (February 1972), pp. 27–34.

3  D. Peppers and M. Rogers, *The One-to-One Future: Building Relationships One Customer at a Time*, New York: Currency Doubleday, 1993.

4  The classic article on advertising effectiveness is H.E. Krugman, "What Makes Advertising Effective," *Harvard Business Review*, 53 (March-April 1975), pp. 96-103.

5  For a fine discussion of hierarchy-of-effects models, see G.E. Belch, M.A. Belch, and J. Pincus, *Advertising and Promotion: An Integrated Marketing and Communications Perspective*, 6th ed., Homewood, IL: McGraw-Hill/Irwin, 2003.

6   D. Vakratsas and T. Ambler, "How Advertising Works: What Do We Really Know?" *Journal of Marketing*, 63 (January 1999), pp. 26–43.

7   B.H. Schmitt, "Advertising and Mass Communications," in N. Capon (Ed.), Section 7, *Marketing*, in AMA Management Handbook (3rd ed.), J. Hampton (Ed.), AMACOM, 1994, 2-108 — 2-115, p. 2-112. Creativity is not the same as impact. Many advertising campaigns earn creativity prizes but do not achieve their objectives.

8   Comparative advertising is banned in some countries. B. Buchanan and D. Goldman, "Us vs. Them: The Minefield of Comparative Ads," *Harvard Business Review*, 67 (May-June 1989), pp. 38–50, reviews its legal status.

9   H.E. Krugman, "On Application of Learning Theory to TV Copy Testing," *Public Opinion Quarterly*, 26 (1962), pp. 626-639.

10  Insider's Report, McCann Worldgroup.

11  Sourced from McCann-Erickson Worldwide.

12  Cell phones are a new medium — because of their GPS capability, messages can be tailored to geographic location.

13  G.E. Belch and M.A. Belch, *Introduction to Advertising and Promotion Management*, Homewood, IL: Irwin, 1990, p. 311.

14  J.A. Simon and J. Arndt, "The Shape of the Advertising Response Function," *Journal of Advertising Research*, 20 (1980), pp. 11–28; P.B. Luchsinger, V.S. Mullen, and P.T. Jannuzzo, "How Many Advertising Dollars are Enough," *Media Decisions*, 12 (1977), p. 59. See also D.A. Aaker and J.M. Carman, "Are You Overadvertising?" *Journal of Advertising Research*, 22 (1982), pp. 57–70; and G. Assmus, J.U. Farley, and D.R. Lehmann, "How Advertising Affects Sales: Meta Analysis of Econometric Results," *Journal of Marketing Research*, 21 (1984), pp. 65–74.

15  For an excellent synopsis, see M. Kalter and E. Stearns, "Direct Marketing," in N. Capon (Ed.), Section 2, Marketing, in *AMA Management Handbook* (3rd ed.), J. Hampton (Ed.), New York: AMACOM, 1994, 2-116 — 2-121.

16  *College Savings Bank (A) and (B)* in N. Capon, *The Marketing of Financial Services: A Book of Cases*, Englewood Cliffs, NJ: Prentice Hall, 1992, pp. 93-121.

17  "Bad for you," *The Economist*, June 19, 1999. The problem was finally attributed to bottling system failures — use of "bad" carbon dioxide at one plant and fungicide contamination from wooden pallets moving Coke can packages.

18  *Spiffs* are direct cash payments from a firm to its customers' salespeople, contingent on their performance with the firm's products.

19  C.F. Mela, S. Gupta, and D.R. Lehmann, "The Long-Term Impact of Promotion and Advertising on Consumer Brand Choice," *Journal of Marketing Research*, 34 (May 1997), pp. 248–261.

20  "Blogs: Fad or Marketing Medium of the Future?" *Brandweek*, November 24, 2004.

## CHAPTER 16

1   Disguised name.

2   *2003 Strategic Sales Compensation Survey*, Deloitte & Touche, June 2003.

3   *Sales and Marketing Management* magazine, reported annually.

4   *Global* account managers have a single customer; *strategic* account managers, one to four; *corporate* account managers, 12 -18.

5   The following discussion is merely illustrative in assuming three tiers.

6   For critical factors driving key account management growth, see Chapter 2 and N. Capon, *Key Account Management*, New York: Free Press, 2001.

7   See N. Capon, D. Potter, and F. Schindler, *Managing Global Accounts*, Mason, OH: Thomson, 2005.

8   These breakdowns are especially important for firms with seasonal sales patterns.

9   Note that this task constitutes a key interface with the market strategy (Chapter 9).

10  "Steve Jobs: The graying prince of a shrinking kingdom," *Fortune*, May 14, 2001.

11  Disguised name.

12  Cleansing blood to compensate for failed kidneys.

13  For career salespeople, firms can develop alternative career tracks with increased responsibility, income, and recognition.

14  Personal communication to the author.

## CHAPTER 17

1   This system replaced an earlier classification based on revenues. Cisco has a level below Premier called Registered Partner; these firms account for a smaller portion of Cisco's revenues. Developed from interviews with Cisco executives and data from V.K. Rangan, *Transforming Your Go-To-Market Strategy*, Boston, MA: Harvard Business School Press, 2006.

2   In this chapter, an end-user customer is where the product loses its identity; consumers and firms can be end-user customers. Consumer advertising may push end-user customers down the channel. Previously, end-user customers for microprocessors were PC manufacturers. The *intel inside* campaign turned consumers into end-user customers. Sometimes we use the term end user instead of end-user customer.

3   The broad view includes concentration and dispersion. The inputs are concentrated in Korea, and prefabricated steel beams are dispersed to Argentina (and other customers).

4   C.B. Bucklin, S.P. DeFalco, J.R. DeVincentis, and J.P. Levis III, "Are You Tough Enough to Manage Your Channels," *The McKinsey Quarterly*, (1996), pp. 105–114.

5   The term *distribution* encompasses all of these functions — the **logistics** function is about getting the product from A to B.

6   Discussed in Chapter 18 under the rubric of customer relationship management.

7   J.A. Narus and J.C. Anderson, "Rethinking Distribution," *Harvard Business Review*, 74 (July-August 1996), pp. 112–120.

8   P.F. Nunes and F.V. Cespedes, "The Customer Has Escaped," *Harvard Business Review*, 81 (November 2003), pp. 96-105.

9   From Pegram, *Selecting and Evaluating Distributors*, reproduced in B. Rosenbloom, *Marketing Channels: A Managerial View*, 6th ed., Fort Worth, TX: Dryden, 1999, pp. 243-247.

10  L.W. Stern and F.D. Sturdivant, "Customer-Driven Distribution Systems," *Harvard Business Review*, 65 (July-August 1987), pp. 34–41; V.K. Rangan, A.J. Menzes, and E. Maier, "Channel Selection for New Industrial Products: A Framework, Method and Application," *Journal of Marketing*, 56 (July 1992), pp. 69–82; V.K. Rangan, *Designing Channels of Distribution*, Boston, MA: Harvard Business School, 1994, 9-594-116; J.M. Hulbert, *Marketing: A Strategic Perspective*, Katonah, NY: Impact Publishing, 1985; E. Anderson, G.S. Day, and V.K. Rangan, "Strategic Channel Design," *Sloan Management Review*, (Summer 1997), pp. 59-69.

11  Reproduced with permission from B. Rosenbloom, *Marketing Channels: A Management View*, 6th ed., Fort Worth, TX: Dryden 1999.

12  This section benefited from D. Ford, L.E. Gadde, H. Hakansson, A. Lundgren, I. Snehota, P. Turnbull, and D. Wilson, *Managing Business Relationships*, Chichester, UK: Wiley, 1988.

13  A.P. Chandler, Jr., *The Visible Hand: The Managerial Revolution in American Business*, Cambridge, MA: Harvard University Press, 1977.

14  A 2002 Financial Accounting Standards Board (FASB) rule required that manufacturers restate 2001 revenues by subtracting incentive payments from reported sales. This one-time event revealed the size of these payments.

15  C.B. Bucklin, P.A. Thomas-Graham, and E.A. Webster, "Channel Conflict: When Is It Dangerous," *The McKinsey Quarterly*, (1997), pp. 36–43.

16  G. Stalk, P. Evans, and L.E. Shulman, "Competing on Capabilities: The New Rules of Corporate Strategy," *Harvard Business Review*, 70 (March-April 1992), pp. 57–69.

# CHAPTER 18

1  From *The Economist*.

2  C.H. Lovelock and J. Wirtz, *Services Marketing*, 6th ed., Upper Saddle River, NJ: Prentice Hall, 2006; C.H. Lovelock, Product Plus: How Product + Service = Competitive Advantage, New York: McGraw-Hill, 1994. Government statistics typically count manufacturers' in-house activities as value-added manufacturing. The same outsourced activity is mostly counted as a service. This has helped fuel service growth in industry statistics.

3  B.G. Auguste, E.P. Hartmon, and V. Pandit, "The Right Service Strategies for Product Companies," *The McKinsey Quarterly*, 1 (2006) pp. 41-51.

4  J. Carlzon, *Moments of Truth*, Cambridge, MA: Ballinger, 1987.

5  C.W.L. Hart, "The Power of Unconditional Service Guarantees," *Harvard Business Review*, 66 (July-August 1988), pp. 54–62.

6  P. Kotler and S.J. Levy, "Demarketing, Yes, Demarketing," *Harvard Business Review* 49 (November-December 1971), pp. 74–80.

7  E.W. Anderson, C. Fornell, and S.K. Mazvancheryl, "Customer Satisfaction and Shareholder Value," *Journal of Marketing*, 68 (October 2004), pp. 172-186.

8  Not on perceived quality alone. A. Parasuraman, V.A. Zeithaml, and L.L Berry, "A Conceptual Model of Service Quality and Its Implications for Future Research," *Journal of Marketing*, (Fall 1985), pp. 41–50; and V.A. Zeithaml, A. Parasuraman, and L.L. Berry, *Delivering Quality Service: Balancing Customer Expectations and Perceptions*, Free Press, 1990.

9  V.A. Zeithaml, L.L. Berry, and A. Parasuraman, "The Behavioral Consequences of Service Quality," *Journal of Marketing*, 60 (April 1996), pp. 31-46.

10  Technical Assistance Research Program (TARP), Consumer Complaint Handling in America: An Update Study, Parts I and II, Washington, DC: TARP and U.S. Office of Consumer Affairs, April 1986.

11  Excerpted and abridged from M.J. Tucker, "Poppin' Fresh Dough," *Datamation*, (May 1997), pp. 50–58.

12  Lovelock, *op. cit.*

13  H. Takeuchi and J.A. Quelch, "Quality is More than Making a Good Product," *Harvard Business Review*, 61 (July-August 1983), pp. 139–145.

14  M.M. Lele and U.S. Karmarkar, "Good Product Support is smart marketing," *Harvard Business Review*, 61 (November-December 1983), pp. 124-132; I.C. MacMillan and R.G. McGrath, "Discovering New Points of Differentiation," *Harvard Business Review*, 75 (July-August 1997), pp. 133-145.

15  R.G. Bundschuh and T.M. Dezvane, "How to make after-sales services pay off," *The McKinsey Quarterly*, 4 (2003), pp. 116-127.

16  T. Baumgartner, R.H. John, and T. Nauclér, "Transforming Sales and Service," *The McKinsey Quarterly*, 4 (2005), pp. 81-91.

17  B. Donaldson and T. O'Toole, *Strategic Market Relationships: From Strategy to Implementation*, Chichester, UK: Wiley, 2002.

18  *Xerox Corporation: The Customer Satisfaction Program*, 9-591-055, Harvard Business School.

19  F.F. Reicheld and W.E Sasser Jr., "Zero Defections: Quality Comes to Services," *Harvard Business Review*, 68 (September-October 1990), pp. 105–111.

20  I. Gordon, I Relationship Marketing. *New Strategies, techniques and technologies to win the customers you want and keep them forever*, Ontario: Wiley, 1998, p. 9.

21  M. Ebner, A. Hu, D. Levitt, and J. McCrory, "How to Rescue CRM," *The McKinsey Quarterly*, 4 (2002), pp. 49-57. See also D.K. Rigby, F.F. Reicheld, and P. Schefter, "Avoid the Four Perils of CRM," *Harvard Business Review*, 80 (February 2002), pp. 101-109.

22  Peter Heffring, President CRM Division, Teradata, 2002.

23  R. Glazer, "Strategy and Structure in Information-Intensive Markets: the Relationship between Marketing and IT," *Journal of Market-Focused Management*, 2, (1997), pp. 65–81.

24  Personal communication from Lance Batchelor, Head Worldwide Marketing, Amazon.com.

# CHAPTER 19

1  Personal communication from Ron Boire, President Retail Sales, Sony Electronics. Boire is now president of Toys"R"Us, via a senior marketing position at Best Buy.

2  Some ideas are drawn from P. Berthon, J.M. Hulbert, and L.F. Pitt, "Brand Management Prognostications," *Sloan Management Review*, 40 (Winter 1999), pp. 53-65; and J.M. Hulbert and L.F. Pitt, "Exit Left Center Stage? The Future of Functional Marketing," *European Journal of Marketing*, 40 (February 1996), pp. 47–60.

3  For more, see J. M. Hulbert, N. Capon, and N. Piercy, *Total Integrated Marketing: Breaking the Bounds of the Function*, NY: Free Press, 2003.

4  B.F. Shapiro, "Can Marketing and Manufacturing Coexist," *Harvard Business Review*, 55 (September-October 1977), pp. 104-112.

5  J. Garten, "Andy Grove Made The Elephant Dance," *BusinessWeek*, April 11, 2005, p. 26.

6  J.P. Workman Jr., C. Homburg, and K. Gruner, "Marketing Organization: An Integrative Framework of Dimensions and Determinants," *Journal of Marketing*, 62 (July 1998), pp. 21-41; C. Homburg. J.P. Workman Jr. and O. Jensen, "Fundamental Changes in Marketing Organization: The Movement Toward a Customer-Focused Structure, *Journal of the Academy of Marketing Science*, 28 (2000), pp. 459-478; R.S. Achrol, "Evolution of the Marketing Organization," *Journal of Marketing*, 55 (October 1991), pp. 77-93.

7  M. Hammer and J. Champy, *Reengineering the Corporation: A Manifesto for Business Revolution*, New York: Nicholas Brealy, 1993.

8  R.C. Blattberg and J. Deighton, "Interactive Marketing: Exploiting the Age of Addressability," *Sloan Management Review*, 33 (Fall 1991), pp. 5–14; D. Peppers and M. Rogers, *The One-to-One Future: Building Relationships One Customer at a Time*, New York: Century Doubleday, 1993.

9  Wachovia Bank (a merger of First Union and Wachovia) has long managed retail customers like this. N. Capon, "Wachovia Bank and Trust

Company," *The Marketing of Financial Services*, Englewood Cliffs, NJ: Prentice Hall, 1992.

10 "Visionary-in-Chief," *BusinessWeek*, May 17, 1999.

11 A communications switch programmable by outsiders.

12 "The Genesis of a Giant's Stumble," *The New York Times*, January 21, 2001.

13 T. Levitt, "The Globalization of Markets," *Harvard Business Review*, 61 (May-June 1983), pp. 92–102. J.A. Quelch and E.J. Hoff, "Customizing Global Marketing," *Harvard Business Review*, 64 (May-June 1986), pp. 59–68, provides a more integrative view.

14 S. Douglas and Y. Wind, "The Myth of Globalization," *Columbia Journal of World Business*, (Winter 1987), pp. 19–29.

15 N. Capon, D. Potter, and F. Schnidler, *Managing Global Accounts*, Mason, OH: Thomson, 2006, N. Capon, *Key Account Management and Planning*, New York: Free Press, 2001.

16 Personal communication from Carol Hamilton, President of L'Oreal Paris USA.

17 M. Hammer and J. Champy, *Reengineering the Corporation: A Manifesto for Business Revolution*, New York: Harper Business, 1994.

18 Personal communication from Howard Schultz, Chairman of Starbucks.

19 R.C. Camp, *Benchmarking: The Search for Industry Best Practices that Lead to Superior Performance*, Milwaukee, WI: American Society for Quality, 1989.

20 Personal communication from Pat Kelly, Senior Vice President, Worldwide Marketing, Pfizer Pharmaceuticals.

21 Personal communication from Steve Larned, VP of Marketing, Dell Americas.

22 P. Lapoint, *Marketing By The Dashboard Light*, New York: Association of National Advertisers, 2005.

23 R.S. Kaplan and D.P. Norton, "Putting the Balanced Scorecard to Work," *Harvard Business Review*, 71 (September-October 1993), pp. 134-142.

24 Reproduced with permission from *Mobil USM&R (D): Gasoline Marketing*, N9-196-151, Harvard Business School.

# QUESTIONS FOR STUDY & DISCUSSION

Can you answer the questions implied by
each chapter's learning objectives? Check!

......................................
## CHAPTER 1

1. Select a well-known FMCG firm. From the firm's financial statements, identify the book value of its assets. Also identify the firm's market value based on its stock price. Is there a difference? What might account for this difference? Do these findings change the way you think about the role of marketing in delivering value?

2. Does your school approach the market for new students in a systematic way? How could it use the six marketing imperatives to improve its efforts?

3. How has the Internet affected the development of marketing practice?

......................................
## CHAPTER 2

1. A cable company spends an average of $600 to acquire a customer. Annual maintenance costs per customer are $45. Record-keeping and billing costs are $30 per customer per annum. The price of a basic service package is $30 per month. Typically, 40 percent of customers buy a premium package at $50 per month, and 10 percent buy the super-premium package at $80 per month. Over time, 80 percent of customers remain with the company from one year to the next.

   • What is the average lifetime value for all customers?

   • What is the lifetime value of a super-premium customer?

2. As we shall see in Chapter 11, marketers use the term *brand equity* to describe the value of a brand. What is the relationship between LTV and brand equity?

3. Which firms do a good job of retaining and growing current customers, while simultaneously acquiring new customers? What has made these firms successful?

## CHAPTER 3

1. For many years, Kodak has been a leading U.S. company. Use the five-forces model to assess the industry forces that Kodak faces.

2. American Airlines is the leading U.S. carrier. Use the five forces and PESTLE models to scope out the various external forces that American Airlines faces.

3. Identify and classify the environmental pressures that Wal-Mart faces. Why does Wal-Mart face these pressures? How do you assess Wal-Mart's performance in addressing them?

## CHAPTER 4

1. a. Airbus developed the A380, a new jet aircraft with more than 500 seats. Other than the airlines, what organizations should Airbus consider as its macro-customers? Why did you select them?

   b. Suppose you have the task of selling a fleet of A380s to Singapore Airlines. Whom would you target for effort? What issues would you focus on for each of these targets?

2. Many teenagers have cell phones. Use the feature/benefit/value ladder to identify the benefits and values that cell phones deliver to teenagers. Suppose you were advising Nokia on new products — what benefits and values could cell phones offer to teenagers that they are currently not offering? How would your strategy differ for adults?

3. a. Suppose that you are going to take a two-week vacation when you graduate. How will you decide on your destination? Use the five-stage purchase-decision process to structure your answer.

   b. Given your answer to 3a, what marketing program would you suggest for a vacation company that targets graduating students like you?

## CHAPTER 5

1. Some evidence suggests that large companies sometimes dismiss competitive threats as insubstantial. Do you believe this is true? Why or why not? How could you ensure that a successful large company retains a competitive outlook?

2. Many observers believe that competition between Microsoft and Google will increase. Identify one or two colleagues to act as Google's top managers; identify one or two colleagues to act as Microsoft's top managers. First, the Google team develops a market strategy for Google; the Microsoft team develops a market strategy for Microsoft. The two teams exchange strategies. Second, the Google team develops a market strategy to counteract Microsoft's strategy; the Microsoft team develops a market strategy to counteract Google's strategy. How did you define the competitive market? What did you learn from this competitive-gaming exercise?

3. In the hair-coloring market, L'Oreal competes with Clairol; in the men's shaving market, Gillette competes with Schick. Suppose you work for Clairol — use the competitive assessment analysis to evaluate L'Oreal and identify its strategic options. Or suppose you work for Gillette — use the competitive assessment analysis to evaluate Schick and identify its strategic options.

## CHAPTER 6

1. Suppose you are the product manager for a pharmaceutical firm that is hoping to launch a new drug to treat schizophrenia. Identify the types of people from whom you would secure marketing-research data.

2. As the marketing director for a hotel chain, you have implemented an observational technique to learn about customers' needs and to provide data to individual hotels. You get the following report from your San Francisco property. "Last night, one of our regular customers, Mr. Jackson, arrived to check in with a female companion. The desk clerk used the information system to greet the couple: 'Welcome back, Mr. and Mrs. Jackson, it's good to see you at the hotel again.' Apparently, the woman was not Mrs. Jackson, and Mr. Jackson had not told his companion he was married. She was furious with him; he was furious with us, and they both stormed out of the hotel." How would this incident affect your observational program?

3. You are consulting for a local eatery with strong brand recognition and loyalty that has many customers at weekends; yet from Monday through Thursday, business is slow. Design a questionnaire to help understand consumer behavior, lifestyle, and eating habits on weekdays. Your objective is to identify and address marketing opportunities during the week.

## CHAPTER 7

1. Google raised large sums of money by going public and making a secondary equity offering. From publicly available data — like Google's search feature — develop a *strategy for growth* for Google. What should be Google's vision, mission, growth path, and timing of entry? Identify growth options for Google. Assess this venture portfolio in terms of return and risk. Define and measure success.

2. From your knowledge of business, identify current-day examples of pioneer, follow-the-leader, segmenter, and me-too entry strategies.

3. Founded in 1998, by 2008 eBay had merchandising volume of about $70 billion and profits approaching $2 billion. What accounts for eBay's success? How should eBay ensure continued growth and profits?

## CHAPTER 8

1. Suppose your firm decides to address the human pain-relief market. How would you segment this market? What market segments can you identify? Can you identify both coarse- and fine-grained segments — market segments and customer segments?

2. Describe a segment of the higher education market that includes you. Appraise this segment in terms of the criteria for *good* segments — differentiated, identifiable, stable, measurable, appropriately sized, and accessible.

3. Visit retail outlets for Banana Republic, The Gap, and Old Navy. Observe the products and customers. What inferences can you make about owner Gap Inc.'s segmentation and targeting?

## CHAPTER 9

1. Apple's iPod is one of the 21st century's most successful consumer products. Using the framework in this chapter, describe Apple's market strategy for the iPod.

2. A few years ago, the National Basketball Association (NBA) was riding high. Now the NBA is in a slump and the National Football League (NFL) is very successful. Use the ideas in this chapter to diagnose the NBA's problems and offer a turnaround plan. Why is the NFL so successful?

3. In the history of U.S. enterprise, several competitive battles stand out: Sears vs. Montgomery Ward, GM vs. Ford, Coke vs. Pepsi, Adidas vs. Nike, Boeing vs. Airbus, Microsoft vs. Google, Intel vs. AMD, Reuters vs. Bloomberg. Compare and contrast two or more of these (or other) rivalries that interest you. What can you learn about market strategy?

## CHAPTER 10

1. Identify the product life-cycle stage for each of these products. Why did you choose the stages?

| Cell phones | Digital cameras | Movies on VHS tapes | Index mutual funds |
|---|---|---|---|
| Desktop PCs | Music on compact discs | Vacation travel | Books on tape |

2. Suppose you own several specialty coffee shops in a mid-sized U.S. urban center. Starbucks enters. What are your options? Be prepared to support your choices.

3. Installations of U.S. pay phones are decreasing by several percent each year — pay phone calls are also decreasing. ComChoice has an installed base of more than 1,000 payphones in Texas — it is profitable. A spokesperson for ComChoice's main competitor Southwestern Bell — which operates in Texas, Oklahoma, and three contiguous states — said, "We continue to view pay phones as a viable part of our business." How would you advise ComChoice?

## CHAPTER 11

1. The text quotes a leading advertising executive as saying "A successful brand is timeless." Do you agree or disagree with this statement? Should it be modified in the context of young consumers valuing innovation, unique choice, and change? Explain your answer with current examples.

2. Select a well-known brand and track its brand history over time. How have its brand identity and brand image evolved? Did the brand owner attempt to change the brand identity to keep the brand contemporary? Or was the brand owner trying to broaden its market?

3. Find an example of poor brand architecture and explain why you believe it is poor. The example could include multi-branding versus umbrella branding, global branding, unwise brand extensions or attempts at broadening (leveraging), brand migration, strategic alliances, and aging brands.

## CHAPTER 12

1. Review toothpaste products at your local drug store or supermarket. How do you assess P&G's and Colgate's product lines? What do you infer about their portfolio-management strategies? What recommendations do you have for P&G and Colgate?

2. The president of Sony Electronics put the problem this way: "If we're selling a $200 DVD player, we may want to give away Sony DVD software. But that's not in the best interest of Sony Pictures. And Sony Music may want to sell a Springsteen box set for $80 with a coupon that says, 'Get $20 off your Sony CD Player.' Why would Sony Electronics want to do that?" How would you advise the president of Sony Electronics? How would you advise the president of Sony Corporation?[1]

3. Some service providers bundle their services — amusement parks and ski hills provide unlimited use for a single price. Others are unbundled, like movie houses and restaurants with a la carte menus. Prepare guidelines for a service provider making the bundling/unbundling decision.

## CHAPTER 13

1. Customer dissatisfaction is an opportunity for firms to learn. When were you dissatisfied with a purchase experience? Why? What new product or service ideas would you suggest?

2. Suppose that, on graduation, you accept a position as new product director for a medium-size firm with a poor record for new product innovation. The CEO has set a three-year goal for 20 percent of sales to come from new products. What actions will you take in your first 100 days on the job?

---

1   Personal communication to the author from Ron Boire, then President, Sony Electronics Consumer Sales.

3. Apple has been successful with its G4 series of desktop and laptop computers and with the iPod and iTunes. But Apple withdrew the Newton and its G4 Cube computer — now in New York's Museum of Modern Art. How do you assess Apple's new product performance? How does your assessment reconcile with Apple's profit performance?

## CHAPTER 14

1. Develop a customer value map for soft drinks (or a product category of your choice). Interpret the map. What pricing options do the several competitors have?

2. A British entrepreneur is testing variable prices for movie-theater seating, similar to the approach that many airlines use. Do you think he will succeed? Why? Or why not?

3. Select a product in which you are interested. What price would you set? Why? Does your recommended price differ from the current price? Why?

## CHAPTER 15

1. Suppose you are the marketing VP at Rolls-Royce Aero Engines. Who are your communications targets? What are your communications objectives for each target?

2. Suppose that General Motors is about to launch a new car powered by fuel cells — suggested retail price about $20,000. Mileage for this car will be 80 mpg city, 100 mpg highway. Use the following table to develop a consumer advertising campaign.

| Advertising Element | Question |
|---|---|
| Target audience | Whom are we trying to influence? |
| Advertising objectives | What are we trying to achieve? |
| Messaging | What content should the target audience receive? |
| Execution | How shall we communicate the message? |
| Media selection and timing | Where and when shall we place our advertising? |
| Advertising budget | How much shall we spend on advertising? |
| Program evaluation | How shall we test our advertising and measure its effectiveness? |

3. Identify a direct marketing campaign to which you responded. Why did you respond to that campaign and ignore so many others?

## CHAPTER 16

1. Which of the six sales management tasks are the most important? Why? Interview a sales manager to develop your answer.

2. Aco sells adhesives for a high-end printing application. Printfirm is a major customer, but its specifications are difficult to meet. Historically, Aco was Printfirm's sole supplier, but Bco has started to supply Printfirm with similar adhesives. Aco believes Bco is a low-cost producer that sometimes cuts corners. Last year, Aco's plant flooded for one week. Aco halted all deliveries, and Printfirm is adamant that it wants a second supplier. Aco's top management has set a goal of retaining 80 percent of Printfirm's business. How would you advise Aco's sales and marketing managers?

3. PrdCo's recent sales growth has mirrored its industry — the incoming CEO is demanding improved performance. She wants to implement forced ranking evaluation like Jack Welch introduced at GE. In the sales force, 20 percent would be rated superior, 70 percent average, and 10 percent inferior. Inferior salespeople would be fired. PrdCo's salesforce comprises a national sales manager (NSM), three regional sales managers (RSM), 12 district managers (DSM), and 110 salespeople. Assume you are the NSM; how do you respond to the CEO's ideas?

## CHAPTER 17

1. Your friend operates a highly successful *loose-meat* sandwich restaurant — a regional specialty — in his hometown in Iowa. He wants to expand nationally. What are his options and the pros and cons? How would you advise him to proceed? Why? What pitfalls should he look out for?

2. Alasdair MacLean wanted a high-speed bicycle. He gathered information about several bicycles from a department store. He test-rode several models at a local bicycle store. But once he made his decision, he bought his favorite model from the manufacturer's website. Several major department stores and a trade association of local bicycle stores have complained about this kind of customer behavior to BikeCo, a leading bicycle manufacturer. How would you advise BikeCo?

3. U.S.-based Detha produces a wire harness to protect electric wires in automobiles. Detha sells to a distributor; the distributor sells to CarSup, a Tier I supplier to U.S. auto firms. Last year, Detha's sales to the distributor dropped by 20 percent. Detha discovered that the auto firms were demanding local supply in various geographic areas. CarSup was enforcing compliance; 40 percent of its requirements were now sourced in Asia, hence the drop in Detha's business. Detel, one of Detha's sister business units sells significant quantities of electric wire to CarSup. How should Detha proceed?

## CHAPTER 18

1. Use the SERVQUAL scale to assess service quality for some aspect of your school or college, like the admission process or a finance class. How does it rate on tangibles, reliability, responsiveness, assurance, and empathy?

2. Select a local restaurant. How could this institution improve customer service and enhance customer loyalty? What advice would you give its proprietor?

3. Many airlines are roundly criticized for poor customer service. Chart out your interactions with the airline on your last flight, from the time you decided to take the flight until you left your destination airport. Identify the various touch-points. At each touch-point where service was poor, develop a system to improve customer service.

## CHAPTER 19

1. Think about a time when you decided you would no longer be a customer of a business or other organization. Why did you quit? How could the organization have acted for you to have stayed? How would the organization have to change for you to become a customer again?

2. What markets does your school or college address? How does your school or college organize for addressing these markets? Do you think the organization is appropriate? How would you change it?

3. Use the input → intermediate → output framework to identify alternative measures for the market manager in charge of Apple's iPod. Using these alternative measures, develop a balanced scorecard to measure that executive's performance. Alternatively, complete this task for a product in which you are interested, or this book — *Capon's Marketing Framework*.

# GLOSSARY

**B2B — Business-to-business.** This acronym generally describes marketing products to another business—Business to (2) Business.

**B2C — Business-to-consumer.** This acronym generally describes marketing products to consumers.

**Branding.** The attachment of a symbol to a product, service, and/or organization that uniquely identifies the supplier and/or owner. The symbol may consist of words, a concept, or an auditory or visual signal.

**Cost of capital.** The financial return the firm must earn to recover its capital outlay. The cost of capital is a weighted average of the firm's cost of equity and debt. In evaluating investment opportunities, the firm discounts expected future cash flows at its cost of capital.

**Exchange.** The firm and its customers exchange value. Through its products and services, the firm offers value to customers. Customers typically offer value to the firm via their financial resources. If the firm and customer each accept the value offered by the other, an exchange occurs.

**Marketing.** There are several related meanings:

  **Philosophy.** Marketing as a guiding philosophy for the entire organization embraces an external orientation. It recognizes that revenues from customers are the critical source of cash flows.

  **Imperatives.** Marketing as six imperatives describes the specifics of the marketing job. These are the *must dos* of marketing.

  **Principles.** The firm must apply four marketing principles to do the marketing job well. They act as guidelines for making good marketing decisions based on the six imperatives.

**Marketing imperatives.** The six *must dos* of marketing.

  Imperative 1: Determine and recommend which markets to address.
  Imperative 2: Identify and target market segments.
  Imperative 3: Set strategic direction and positioning.
  Imperative 4: Design the marketing offer.
  Imperative 5: Secure support from other functions.
  Imperative 6: Monitor and control execution and performance.

**Marketing mix.** The traditional description of the tools marketers use to construct an offer. They are often called the 4Ps—**p**roduct, **p**lace (distribution), **p**romotion, and **p**rice. Today, **s**ervice is often treated separately to form 4Ps and an **S**.

**Marketing offer.** The package of benefits and values the firm offers to customers.

**Marketing principles.** Guidelines for making good marketing decisions:

    **Selectivity and concentration.** Because resources are scarce, the firm should be selective in its choice of market and market segment. It should concentrate its resources against its chosen targets.

    **Customer value.** Success in target market segments depends on the firm's ability to provide customers with value.

    **Differential advantage.** To be profitable, the firm must provide a net benefit, or cluster of benefits, to a sizable group of customers, that they value and are willing to pay for, but cannot get, or believe they cannot get, elsewhere. Competition eventually erodes away any differential advantage—the firm must continually renew its differential advantage.

    **Integration.** The firm must carefully integrate and coordinate all elements in the design and execution of its market strategy. Integration includes elements of the marketing mix and the activities of all functions that play a role in delivering promised benefits.

**Market segment.** A subset of a total market; a group of actual and potential customers with similar needs, seeking similar benefits and values, with similar levels of priority.

**Market segmentation.** A conceptual and analytic process for grouping actual and potential customers into market segments.

**Organizational orientations, types of:**

    **External.** A firm with this orientation focuses on customers, competitors, complementers, and factors in the external environment that could affect its future health.

    **Internal.** A firm with this orientation looks inward. It focuses on internal functions like finance, operations, sales, and technology (R&D), rather than external factors.

        **Finance.** This firm is *run by the numbers* with scant regard for strategic issues. It avoids expenses with long-term payoff like R&D and marketing, in favor of increasing short-term profits. It often minimizes capital investment.

        **Operations.** This firm's culture revolves around operational efficiency; there is typically a shared belief that cost reduction and volume maximization will ensure success. The firm does not have a deep understanding of customers' needs.

        **Sales.** Maximizing short-term sales volume is the over-arching goal. This firm often cuts prices to secure orders, but does little forward planning. As markets evolve, broadly acceptable new products are not available.

        **Technology (R&D).** "Have technology, will travel—our technology will sell itself." This firm is often technologically sophisticated but rarely understands marketing and makes new product decisions with little or no customer input.

**Shareholder value.** The total value to shareholders—market capitalization—is measured by the market price of the firm's shares times the number of shares outstanding. Increasing shareholder value has become a mantra for many firms.

**Shareholder-value perspective.** Management's job is to maximize returns for shareholders. The shareholder-value perspective is prevalent in many capitalist countries—particularly in the U.S.

..............................

# CHAPTER 2

**80:20 rule.** 80 percent of a firm's revenues come from 20 percent of its customers.

**20:80 rule.** This rule follows directly from the 80:20 rule: 20 percent of a firm's revenues come from 80 percent of its customers.

**Acquisition cost (AC).** The cost of attracting a new customer to the firm.

**Cost of capital.** The financial return the firm must earn to recover its capital outlay. The cost of capital is a weighted average of the firm's cost of equity and the cost of debt. The firm uses its cost of capital to discount expected future cash flows to their present value.

**Cross-selling.** Selling different products to a customer who has already purchased from the firm.

**Customer lifetime.** The estimated length of time a firm's customer will remain a customer.

**Customer lifetime value (LTV).** The economic value to the firm from a customer over the lifetime of its relationship. LTV is the discounted future stream of profits the customer generates.

**Customer profitability.** The profit the firm earns from an individual customer or group of customers.

**Defection rate (l-r).** The rate at which the firm loses customers from one time period to the next (also called *churn*). Sometimes calculated as a probability. The opposite of retention rate.

**Discount rate (d).** The rate at which the firm discounts future earnings so as to calculate customer lifetime value. The discount factor is typically set equal to the firm's cost of capital.

**Lock-in.** The situation when customers are committed to buying from the firm.

**Maintenance expenses.** Expenses specifically designed to enhance customer retention.

**Margin.** In this chapter, margin refers to customer margin — sales revenues less all attributable customer costs.

**Margin multiple.** A quick way to calculate LTV if customer margin, customer retention rate, and discount rate are constant from time period to time period. LTV equals customer margin multiplied by the margin multiple.

**Retention rate (r).** The rate at which the firm retains customers from one time period to the next. Sometimes calculated as a probability. The opposite of defection rate.

**Winback.** Securing sales from a customer that previously defected.

........................

# CHAPTER 3

**Acquisition.** A firm purchases another firm or business.

**Backward integration.** A customer undertakes activities currently performed by its suppliers.

**Five-forces model.** A set of forces impinging on the firm:
   **Current direct competitors.** Satisfy customer needs by offering similar benefits with similar products, technology, or business models.
   **New direct entrants.** Offer similar products, but were not previously competitors.
   **Indirect competitors.** Satisfy similar customer needs by offering alternative products, technologies, or business models.
   **Suppliers.** Provide the firm's inputs.
   **Buyers.** Purchase the firm's products.

**Forward integration.** A supplier undertakes activities currently performed by its customers.

**Leveraged buyout (LBO).** Formation of a new firm when an existing firm spins off a business to a group of investors and/or management — a management buyout (MBO).

**Life cycles.** A common means for describing the evolution of markets and products. Product class and product form life cycles are typically partitioned into several stages:
   **Introduction.** The period from product launch until sales take off and grow at an accelerating rate. Total sales during introduction are generally low.
   **Early growth.** The period from sales take-off until the growth rate begins to slow.
   **Late growth.** Sales are still growing, but the rate of growth is slowing.
   **Maturity.** The sales growth rate ranges from flat to growth in gross national product (GNP).
   **Decline.** Overall sales decrease year by year.

**Market.** Customers — people and organizations — who require goods and services to satisfy their needs. Customers must have sufficient purchasing power and a willingness to pay for the products that suppliers offer.

**Market insight.** The understanding firms secure about future market changes that lead to an appreciation of opportunities and threats.

**Market structure.** The market, products serving the market, and suppliers offering these products.

**Marketing myopia.** The tendency for firms to have such an overly narrow view of their market that they miss opportunities and/or fail to recognize threats.

**Merger.** Two firms join together to form a new entity.

**PESTLE model.** An acronym for identifying the environmental forces acting on an industry — **P**olitical, **E**conomic, **S**ociocultural, **T**echnological, **L**egal, and **E**nvironmental (Physical).

**Product, types of:**
   **Product class.** A set of products offered by competing suppliers that serve a set of customer needs in a roughly similar manner.

**Product form**. A group of products offered by competing suppliers that are more closely similar in the way they meet customer needs than products in a product class.

**Product item**. A uniquely identified product offered by the firm.

**Product line**. A group of related products offered by the firm.

**Strategic alliance**. A cooperative arrangement that pools the strengths of individual partner firms. Strategic alliances range in formality from a new joint-venture firm to temporary, informal arrangements.

**Technology, types of:**

**Disruptive technology**. A new technology offering new and very different value propositions, initially for new applications and a limited number of new-to-the-market customers.

**Sustaining technology**. A new technology that improves the performance of established products along dimensions valued by mainstream customers.

.................................

# CHAPTER 4

**Benefits and values, categories of:**

**Functional**. Follow from the product's design.

**Psychological.** Satisfy customer needs like status, affiliation, reassurance, risk, and security.

**Economic**. Result from financial considerations of purchasing a product or service.

**Search**. Customers can gain good information before they purchase.

**Use**. Customers do not know the value at the time of purchase.

**Credence**. Customers do not know the value until long after the purchase.

**Customer**. Any person or organization in the channel of distribution or decision (other than competitors) whose actions can affect the purchase of the firm's products and services. Categories of customers include:

**Current (today)**. The firm does business with these customers today.

**Potential (tomorrow)**. The firm hopes to do business with these customers in the future.

**Direct**. Exchange money or other resources with the firm for its products.

**Indirect**. Secure the firm's products from intermediaries like manufacturers or distributors.

**Macro-level**. Organizational units like manufacturers, wholesalers, retailers, government entities, and families.

**Micro-level**. Individuals with influence or decision-making authority within the macro-level customer.

**Customer experience**. A state, condition, or event that consciously affects a customer.

**Customer insight**. A deep and unique understanding of customers' needs and required benefits and values.

**Customer needs, types of:**

**Recognized**. The customer is consciously aware of these needs; they may be **expressed** to others, or **non-expressed**.

**Latent**. The customer is not consciously aware of these needs.

**Customer relationship management (CRM)**. The process of managing the supplier/customer interface so that the relationship endures over time.

**Customer value**. The utility a customer receives from purchasing the firm's product or service. Value is a higher-level construct embracing several benefits the product offers.

**Decision-making process (DMP)**. The individual stages that members of the decision-making unit complete in making a purchase.

**Decision-making unit (DMU)**. The individuals involved in a purchase decision.

**Economic value for the customer (EVC)**. The price the customer pays for a competitive product, plus the net additional value the firm's product provides. EVC is an upper bound for price.

**Environmental influences**. Factors external to the consumer that affect decision-making, embracing culture, social class, other people, family, and the situation.

**Feature or attribute**. A characteristic, function, or property of the seller's offer.

**Feature/benefit/value ladder**. A hierarchy that joins the product's features with the benefits and values those features deliver to customers.

**Hierarchy of needs**. Developed by psychologist Maslow; needs are in five groups, ordered low to high — physiological, safety and security, social, ego, and self-actualization.

**Reference groups.** Individuals and groups that influence customers in their decision-making:
>  **Primary.** Include family members and organizational work groups.
>  **Secondary.** Include club and church members and professional organizations.
>  **Aspirational.** Those to which the customer would like to belong.

**Strategic sourcing.** A discipline of specially designed systems and processes for reducing the costs of purchased materials and services.

..............................

# CHAPTER 5

**Alliances.** Formal economic relationships between the firm and other entities (partners) — suppliers, customers, and distributors.

**Complementer.** Any organization like independents and competitors whose actions can affect the firm's sales.

**Competitive assessment analysis.** A way of mapping customer needs, required benefits, and values, with the required resources, to assess the competitive position of various suppliers.

**Competitive Data:**
>  **Level of.** The organizational level for collecting data — corporate, business unit, market, and market segment.
>  **Type of.** The sorts of quantitative and qualitative data the firm can collect.
>  **Secondary.** Data that have been collected for another purpose.
>  **Primary.** Data that require a focused acquisition effort.

**Competitive intelligence department.** An organizational unit that collects, analyzes, and distributes competitive information.

**Competitive intelligence system.** A process to collect, analyze, and distribute competitive information.

**Competitor.** Any organization whose products and services provide similar or superior benefits and values to the same customers that the firm seeks to attract and retain. They may be:
>  **Current.** Competitors that the firm faces *today*.
>  **Potential.** Competitors that the firm may face *tomorrow*.
>  **Direct.** Offer similar benefits with similar products, technologies, or business models.
>  **Indirect.** Offer similar benefits with alternative products, technologies, or business models.

**Cooperation with Competitors:**
>  **Back-office.** Competitors work together in non-customer-facing activities to reduce costs and improve efficiency for all firms.
>  **Marketplace or front-office.** Competitors work together to better satisfy customer needs like developing a new technology standard.

**Insight.** Securing understanding of strengths and weaknesses in order to gain strategic perspectives. There are three types.
>  **Competitive insight** is the ability to describe, evaluate, project, and manage competitors.
>  **Company insight** is the firm's understanding of itself — its advantages and disadvantages compared to the competition.
>  **Complementer insight** is insight into any organization whose actions affect the firm's sales.

**Intra-firm competition.** A type of competition where different firm units compete with each other.

**Non-compete agreement.** An employee agrees not to work for a direct competitor for a specified period of time after he or she leaves the company.

**Non-disclosure agreement (NDA).** Aka a confidentiality agreement; a contract promising to protect confidential data disclosed during employment or other business transaction.[1]

**Scenario.** A descriptive narrative of how the future may evolve for a plausible option.

**Shadow system.** Securing competitive information by having executives *shadow* specific competitors.

**Signal.** Information the firm sends to competitors, hoping they will process the information and act accordingly. A special type of signal designed to mislead competitors is **misinformation.**

**Special relationships.** Informal economic relationships between the firm and other entities such as government agencies, political parties, and public interest groups, as well as suppliers and customers.

---

[1]  Definitions of non-compete and non-disclosure definitions from *Everyday law for everyday people,"* <www.nolo.com>.

## CHAPTER 6

**Ethnographic research.** An observational research technique derived from anthropology.

**Experiment.** A research approach where the researcher manipulates one or more independent variables to assess the impact on a dependent variable.

**Focus group.** A small number of people, typically eight to 12, assembled by a marketing researcher to discuss a topic of interest.

**Forecasts, types of:**
> **Market.** The predicted market-level sales in a future time period.
> **Sales.** The firm's predicted sales in a future time period:
>> **Bottom-up.** A forecast that starts with customer-by-customer forecasts.
>> **Top-down.** A forecast that starts with a market-size forecast.
>> **Synthetic.** A forecast that combines top-down and bottom-up forecasts.

**Marketing research, types of:**
> **Primary.** The firm collects data for the specific purpose of the study.
> **Secondary.** Based on data that has already been collected for another purpose.
> **Qualitative.** A flexible and versatile approach comprising several techniques that is not concerned with numbers. Often used for exploratory studies.
> **Quantitative.** A research approach that uses numerical data to test hypotheses.

**Marketing research process.** A rigorous methodology for improving the probability that investments in marketing research will produce actionable insights.

**Multiple regression analysis.** A research technique for assessing the relationship between one or more independent variables and a dependent variable.

**One-on-one interviews.** A marketing research approach conducted by interviewing respondents individually.

**Panel.** A group of respondents who agree to provide data over time.

**Potentials, types of:**
> **Market.** The maximum market-level sales that the firm expects in a future time period.
> **Sales.** The maximum sales that the firm could achieve in a future time period.

**Survey.** A common technique for securing data by asking respondents questions.

**Tracking study.** A method of securing research data. In a tracking study, aka a longitudinal study, a panel of individuals agrees to provide responses periodically over time.

## CHAPTER 7

**Growth path.** Describes the route the firm or business unit takes to achieve its growth objectives. Nine individual approaches reduce to four basic options:
> **Market penetration.** Focus on existing products in existing markets.
> **Product growth.** Bring related and new products to existing customers.
> **Market growth.** Engage related and new customers with existing products.
> **Product and market diversification.** Bring new products to new customers.

**Implementation (of growth strategy).** Alternative approaches for the firm to achieve its objectives:
> **Internal development.** The firm develops the opportunity in-house.
> **Insourcing.** The firm undertakes activities currently done by others.
> **Outsourcing.** The firm secures other firms to undertake activities it previously conducted in-house so it can focus on higher return opportunities.
> **Acquisition.** The firm acquires another firm or a business unit.
> **Strategic alliance.** Two firms join together to develop a stronger combined entity.
> **Licensing and technology purchase.** The firm secures access to technology developed by others. License — the original firm maintains ownership. Technology purchase — the firm gains ownership.
> **Equity investment.** The firm takes an ownership position.

**Mission.** Guides the firm's search for opportunity so it can focus on a limited number of areas where it is likely to be successful.

**Screening criteria.** Aids for evaluating and selecting opportunities. Important screening criteria are:
> **Objectives.** What does the firm seek to achieve by investing in the opportunity?

    **Compatibility (or fit).** Can the firm successfully address the opportunity?

    **Core competence.** Can the firm use its core competencies or gain new core competencies?

    **Synergy.** Can the firm use existing resources and earn greater returns than a standalone entry?

**Strategy for growth.** A set of frameworks that helps the firm decide which businesses to be in and which businesses not to be in. Includes vision, mission, growth path, and timing of entry.

**Timing of entry.** Denotes alternative entry stages in the product form life cycle:

    **Pioneer.** Creates new markets.

    **Follow-the-leader.** Enters markets when they are growing rapidly.

    **Segmenter.** Enters in the late-growth stage by matching offers to emerging customer needs.

    **Me-too.** Enters mature markets.

**Venture portfolio.** The set of opportunities the firm decides to pursue.

**Vision.** A description of an ideal future state; an impressionistic picture of what the future should be:

    **Corporate vision.** Focuses on the firm

    **Business-unit vision.** Focuses on the business.

# CHAPTER 8

**Business strengths.** Capabilities, competences, and resources the firm needs to be successful.

**Candidate descriptor variables — segmentation variables.** Used to identify segments; typically fall into one of four categories: geography, demography, behavioral, and socio-psychological.

**Customer needs.** A basis for identifying market segments.

**Customer segment.** A finer-grained group of customers than a market segment. Within a market segment, the firm might identify several customer segments.

**Data warehouse.** A place to store data on an individual customer's characteristics and purchase transactions.

**Data mining.** A quantitative approach to gain insight into customers' purchasing behavior as the basis for making specialized offers.

***Good* market segments.** Segments that satisfy six criteria: differentiated, identifiable, stable, measurable, appropriate size, and accessible.

**Market segment.** A group of actual and potential customers with similar needs, seeking similar benefits and values, with similar levels of priority. Customers' need profiles differ from segment to segment.

**Market segment attractiveness.** How attractive a segment is to the firm. An individual segment may be differentially attractive to different firms.

**Market segmentation.** A conceptual and analytic process for grouping actual and potential customers into market segments.

**Mass customization.** Related to segments-of-one. The firm customizes its products to individual requirements on a large scale.

**Modularity.** A design approach in which the firm uses common components (modules) to produce a broad product line.

**Multifactor matrix.** Helps the firm decide which segments to target by assessing the attractiveness of market segments and the extent to which the firm possesses the business strengths to succeed.

**Segment-of-one.** The firm addresses customers individually by developing customized offers.

**Targeting.** Deciding the market segments against which the firm should concentrate its resources.

# CHAPTER 9

**Competitor target.** The organizational entity against which the firm decides to compete.

**Customer target.** Individuals and/organizations that the firm tries to make its customers.

**Implementation programs.** Alternative approaches for the firm to achieve its objectives. In the context of market strategy, these include the marketing mix and other functional programs.

**Market strategy.** The firm's game plan for addressing the market.

**Means/ends tree.** A diagrammatic method for outlining, assessing, and choosing among various alternatives.

**Performance objectives.** Describe the business results the firm hopes to achieve. A performance objective has two components:

    **Strategic.** The qualitative and directional results the firm wants to achieve. Strategic objectives typically fall into three categories: growth and market share, profitability, and cash flow.

    **Operational.** Quantitative statements of business results the firm hopes to achieve that relate directly to the strategic objectives. How much is required and by when.

**Positioning.** The heart of the market strategy that should create a unique and favorable image in the minds of target customers. Positioning requires four key decisions: select customer targets, frame competitor targets, design the value proposition, and articulate the reasons to believe.

**Reasons to believe.** Support the firm's value proposition. Provide compelling facts to make the firm's claims believable.

**SMART goals.** Goals that are **s**pecific, **m**easurable, **a**chievable, **r**ealistic, and **t**imely.

**Strategic focus.** Selected from a tree of alternatives and states broadly how the firm will achieve its performance objectives.

**Synergy.** Occurs when the combined effect of two or more elements is greater than the sum of their separate effects — **positive synergy**. If the combined effect is less than the sum of the separate effects, there is **negative synergy**.

**Value proposition.** The heart of positioning that provides a convincing answer to a deceptively simple question: Why should target customers prefer the firm's offer to competitors' offers?

....................................

# CHAPTER 10

**Angel investors.** Wealthy individuals who provide funding for new business ventures at a very early stage. Angel investors typically invest before venture capitalists.

**Concentrated market.** A market with few substantial competitors.

**Divest.** Selling a business to another firm.

**Entry barrier.** Something that forestalls or slows a firm's entry into a market.

**Experience curve.** An empirical relationship between unit product cost and the firm's experience in making and distributing the product.

**First-mover advantage.** An advantage gained simply by being first. The firm may earn a leading reputation for quality and/or gain superior market knowledge.

**Follower.** A firm that enters after the pioneer has created a new market.

**Fragmented market.** A market with many competitors.

**Harvest.** The firm seeks short-term cash flow at the expense of sales and market share.

**Hospitable market.** A market that is attractive to the firm.

**Inhospitable market.** A market that is unattractive to the firm.

**IPO.** An initial public offering of stock. Venture capitalists often sell equity stakes in an IPO.

**Imitation.** Copying a competitor's strategy; often used in early-growth markets to surpass leaders.

**Kenneling.** The practice of purchasing low-share businesses in low growth markets and placing them together. The acquirer typically makes profits by rationalizing operations to achieve lower costs.

**Leapfrog.** A way of surpassing the market leader by developing innovative and superior products, and/or entering emerging market segments; often used in early growth markets.

**Life-cycle framework.** See Chapter 3, Life cycles.

**Liquidate.** Closing down a business and selling its assets.

**Opportunity costs.** Costs incurred by not taking a course of action. They are not out-of-pocket costs but represent forgone profits due to inaction.

**Penetration pricing.** A long-run low-price strategy to grow a market and secure high market share.

**Pioneer.** A firm that creates new markets and is the first, or among the first, with a new product form.

**Pre-emptive.** Acting before competitors.

**Price skimming.** A strategy of setting high prices even though costs are falling. Often used in the early stages of the product life cycle.

**Strategic options.** A variety of alternatives, each requiring significant investment, among which the firm must choose.

**Venture capitalists.** Individuals and firms that provide funds for new early-stage businesses.

..............................

# CHAPTER 11

**Brand.** The traditional definition is: *a name, term, sign, symbol, or design (or letter, number, or character), or a combination of them intended to identify the goods and services of one seller or group of sellers and to differentiate them from competition.* A more customer-focused definition is: *a collection of perceptions and associations that customers hold about a product, a service, or a company. This collection embodies values that create meaning for customers that represent a promise of the experience customers expect when they have contact with the brand.*

**Brand architecture.** The organizing structure for the firm's brand portfolio.

**Brand associations.** The meanings the brand has for customers.

**Brand awareness.** The extent to which customers know that the brand exists.

**Brand broadening/leveraging.** A branding approach for extending an existing brand into a new product form/class.

**Brand equity.** The classic definition is: *a set of brand assets and liabilities linked to a brand, its name, and symbol that add to (or subtract from) the value provided by a product or service to a firm and/or that firm's customers.* There are two types of brand equity:

  **Customer brand equity** is the value customers receive from a brand, less the value they receive from a generic product. Customer brand equity comprises value received before purchase — **pre-purchase equity**, and value received after purchase — **post-purchase equity**.

  **Firm brand equity** derives directly from customer brand equity when the firm secures in its customers brand awareness, positive attitudes, high perceived quality, positive word-of-mouth, intentions to purchase, purchase, brand loyalty, positive brand image and associations (or brand personality), and satisfaction.

**Brand health check.** A way of measuring the overall health of the brand.

**Brand identity.** What the firm wants the brand to mean to customers, including brand personality and the brand promise.

**Brand image.** The overall meaning that the brand has to customers.

**Brand loyalty.** The extent to which customers are predisposed to make repeat purchases of the brand.

**Brand migration.** The process of transferring the equity in a brand being retired to a surviving brand.

**Brand personality.** A set of enduring and distinct human characteristics associated with a brand.

**Brand revitalization.** An approach designed to rejuvenate under-performing brands.

**Co-branding.** An approach to branding typically involving cooperation between two brands from different firms.

**Dollarmetric method.** A method for estimating the monetary value of customer brand equity.

**Endorsed brand.** The firm uses one firm brand to support — endorse — another.

**Family or masterbrand.** The brand for a group of closely related products serving a similar function.

**Global branding.** A branding approach that uses a common brand around the world.

**Monolithic brand.** The brand for a group of products fulfilling many different functions. A **corporate brand** — for the firm as a whole — is a special case of a monolithic brand.

**Multi-branding.** A brand architecture approach in which the firm uses multiple brands for its entries in various product classes.

**Strategic alliance.** A cooperative arrangement that pools the strengths of individual partner firms. Strategic alliances range in formality from a new joint-venture firm to temporary, informal arrangements.

**Standalone brand.** An individual brand with no apparent relationship to any other firm brand.

**Umbrella branding.** A brand architecture approach in which the firm uses a monolithic brand for several products, like a corporate brand.

## CHAPTER 12

**Bundling.** The firm sells a product and sets a price only in combination with other products and/or services. **Unbundling.** The firm sells products and sets prices for each item individually. **Mixed bundling.** The firm offers its products as part of a bundle, but also individually.

**Counterfeiting.** Illegal copying of a firm's products.

**Financial analysis approaches.** Methods for making resource decisions.

    **Economic profit or economic value added (EVA).** The firm's annual profit less an explicit charge for capital.

    **Internal rate of return (IRR).** A method of evaluating investment opportunities using future cash flows. IRR is the discount rate that equalizes cash inflows and cash outflows.

    **Net present value (NPV).** A method of evaluating investment opportunities using future cash flows. NPV is the dollar value from discounting cash flows at a predetermined rate, typically the firm's cost of capital.

    **Payback.** Payback is the forecast time to pay back the investment. In general, shorter paybacks are better than longer paybacks.

    **Return on investment (ROI).** ROI calculations project future accounting data. They compare the product's forecast rate of return with a target (or *hurdle*) rate.

**Financial analysis perspective.** Making resource allocations based on financial analysis.

**Firewalls.** Brands or products that defend the firm's profitable products, sometimes termed *fighting brands*.

**Growth-share matrix.** BCG's portfolio analysis system; dimensions are forecast long-run market growth rate and relative market share. Product types in the growth-share matrix are:

    **Cash cows.** High market shares in low growth markets; should generate cash.

    **Dogs.** Low market shares in low growth markets; many *dog* products have poor financial performance, but some are respectable.

    **Stars.** High market shares in high growth markets; comparatively rare. Many *stars* consume significant cash, but should create generous returns later.

    **Problem children, question marks, lottery tickets, or wildcats.** Low market shares in high growth markets. Need a lot of investment and are high risk.

**Hurdle rate.** A minimum return that any investment opportunity must exceed.

**Multifactor matrix.** A portfolio analysis system using several variables to define each of two key dimensions.

**Negative complementarity.** The negative effect on sales of one product caused by customer dissatisfaction with another product.

**Portfolio analysis.** A method of evaluating investment opportunities that arrays the firm's products in two dimensions.

**Portfolio approach.** Individual products play different roles in the firm's portfolio. Some products generate growth and market share, some products earn profits, and some deliver cash flow.

**Product cannibalization.** Sales of the firm's lower margin product decrease sales of a higher margin product.

**Product complementarity.** Relationships among the firm's products. *Positive* complementarity occurs when one product helps another; negative complementarity when one product hurts another.

**Product portfolio.** Describes the set of products that the firm or business unit offers.

**Product portfolio imbalance.** The firm's products are misbalanced between resource generating and resource consuming. In the growth/share matrix, this imbalance refers to cash flows.

**Product proliferation.** The firm offers a large number of products. Often viewed as undesirable, but can act as a barrier against competitive entry. Sometimes confused with market segmentation.

**Secondary market.** Resale of a product or service. Most financial markets are secondary markets.

## CHAPTER 13

**ACCORD.** An acronym for factors that affect the speed of new product adoption: **A**dvantage, **C**ompatibility, **C**omplexity, **O**bservability, **R**isk, and **D**ivisibility.

**Adoption categories.** Describe consumer behavior in adopting innovations — innovators, early adopters, early majority, late majority, and laggards.

**Alpha test.** A new product test within the firm by company employees.

**Beta test.** A new product test by cooperating customers.

**Business-case analysis.** Assesses the financial viability of a project, including various risk factors.

**Chasm.** The transition between making sales to innovating and early-adopting customers, and to the mainstream market. Products failing to **cross the chasm** do not realize their potential.

**Commercialization.** The final step in bringing a new product to market.

**Concept definition.** See product concept.

**Development.** The process of turning a product concept into an actual product.

**Idea library.** A storage medium for ideas that were suggested and/or discussed but not used.

**Independent inventors.** Innovators working independently outside any corporate umbrella.

**Innovation.** Endowing human and material resources with new and greater wealth-producing capacity.

**Innovation, types of:**
    **Disruptive innovations.** Developed from a new technology offering new and very different value propositions, initially for new applications and a limited number of new-to-the-market customers.
    **Sustaining innovations.** An innovation that improves the performance of established products along dimensions valued by mainstream customers.

**Innovation, firm types.** Four types based on their orientations toward technology and customers:
    **Isolates.** Low customer orientation, low technology orientation.
    **Followers.** High customer orientation, low technology orientation.
    **Shapers.** Low customer orientation, high technology orientation.
    **Interactors.** High customer orientation, high technology orientation.

**Kill point.** A point where the firm must decide to proceed or drop the project.

**Lead users.** Organizations and individuals who think up, and may even prototype, new products.

**Market-factor testing.** A process for exploring the effect of one or more marketing-mix elements on expected sales. Typically performed in a simulated environment.

**New idea processes.** Methods for generating new ideas:
    **Structured thinking.** Logical ways to create new product ideas.
    **Unstructured thinking.** A family of approaches that attempt to *break the mold* and develop totally new ideas by thinking *outside the box.*

**Preliminary screening.** The first stage for eliminating new product ideas.

**Product concept.** A description of a product idea that details the benefits and values the product should deliver to customers.

**Stage-gate process.** A systematic approach for condensing a large number of ideas to a few products the firm can successfully launch. After each **stage**, the idea or project must pass through a **gate** (meet or exceed a standard) to continue. Each gate is a **kill point** where the firm must decide whether to proceed or drop the project.

**Test marketing.** Tests a full-scale product launch on a limited basis.

# CHAPTER 14

**Auction pricing.** A product's price resulting from competition among potential buyers:
    **English auction.** Prices start low and potential buyers bid up the price.
    **Vickery auction.** A form of **sealed-bid** English auction where the winning bidder pays the price of the second-highest bid.
    **Dutch auction.** Prices start high; the seller reduces price until a buyer bids.
    **Reverse auction.** The buyer states product requirements; suppliers bid to provide the product, and prices go down.

**Bait and switch.** Retailers advertise a low price for a product with limited availability. The *bait* sells quickly. Retailers offer most customers a higher-priced product — the *switch.*

**Bundling.** The firm sells a product and sets a price only in combination with other products and/or services. **Unbundling.** The firm sells products and sets prices for each item individually. **Mixed bundling.** The firm offers its products as part of a bundle, but also individually.

**Contribution margin (CM).** Sales revenues less variable costs, and:

   **Contribution margin per unit (CMU).** Contribution margin stated on a per-unit basis.

   **Contribution margin rate (CMR).** Contribution stated per dollar of sales revenues.

**Costs, types of:**

   **Fixed.** Do not vary with the volume of sales or production over a reasonable range. Usually comprise overhead items like managerial salaries, depreciation, and selling, general, and administrative expenses (SG&A).

   **Variable.** Vary directly with the volume of sales and production. Increase as volume increases and decrease as volume decreases.

   **Marginal.** The cost to make and sell one additional unit. Includes all variable costs and some incremental fixed costs, but *excludes* overhead charges.

   **Fully loaded.** Incremental costs plus overhead charges.

**Customer value, methods of assessing:**

   **Dollarmetric method.** A method for assessing customer value. For several pairs of alternatives, the customer states which alternative she prefers and how much extra she would pay.

   **Direct value assessment.** The firm simply asks customers what they would pay for various products.

   **Economic value for the customer (EVC).** The price the customer pays for a competitive product, plus the net additional value the firm's product provides. EVC is an upper bound for price.

   **Perceived value analysis.** The firm secures data directly from customers, but sometimes experienced managers provide *best-guess* data that can be validated later by marketing research.

   **Price experiment.** The firm offers the test product at different prices in different market areas, like geographic locations.

**Demand curve.** A graph of the relationship between price and volume showing price sensitivity.

**Dumping.** Selling products in foreign markets below home market prices at "less than fair market value" and often below average costs.

**Dynamic pricing.** A special case of price discrimination where the price varies over time.

**Economic value for the customer (EVC).** The price the customer pays for a competitive product, plus the net additional value the firm's product provides. EVC is an upper bound for price.

**Floor price.** The price below which a firm should never sell a product, typically the marginal cost.

**Perceived customer value.** The value the customer believes the firm is delivering.

**Pocket price.** The amount of money the firm actually receives — in its pocket.

**Predatory pricing.** Pricing below cost with the intent to eliminate a competitor.

**Price discrimination.** Setting different prices for the same product to different segments or customers.

**Price sensitivity.** Degree of change in volume related to change in price:

   **Price-elastic market.** Volume *increases/decreases* significantly as price *decreases/increases*.

   **Price-inelastic market.** Volume is *relatively insensitive* to price changes.

**Price setting, types of:**

   **Cost-plus pricing.** Setting price by identifying costs and adding a *satisfactory* profit margin.

   **Competitive-driven pricing.** Pricing based on competitors' prices.

   **Customer-driven pricing.** Customers name the prices they are prepared to pay. If the product is available, they must complete the purchase.

   **Deceptive.** False prices and prices that might confuse or mislead customers.

   **Flat rate pricing.** Pricing for a fixed time period. **Variable rate pricing.** Pricing by use.

   **Loss-leader pricing.** Retailers deliberately take losses to build customer traffic.

   **Psychological.** A common retail practice of pricing just below a *benchmark* number, like $9.95 or $9.99 versus $10.00.

   **Variable pricing.** Setting different prices for different customers or segments.

**Price strategies.** The firm's overall approach to setting prices; should be based on four considerations — perceived customer value, costs, competition, and strategic objectives:

   **Penetration pricing.** The firm sets prices close to costs as it seeks growth and market share.

   **Skim pricing.** The firm keeps prices high to secure high margins.

**Price waterfall.** The reduction, by discounts and allowances, from list price to pocket price.

**Pricing, and transportation:**
CIF (carriage, insurance, freight). The supplier pays the cost, insurance, and freight.
FOB (free on board). The customer pays freight, insurance, and other charges.

**Pricing toolkit.** A set of pricing tactics for the firm to change a product's price.

**Resale price maintenance (RPM).** A distribution practice where suppliers set the prices at which retailers can sell their products. RPM is now illegal in the U.S. and many other countries.

**Tactical pricing.** The ongoing stream of pricing decisions the firm makes on a daily basis.

**Yield management.** Continuous price adjustments based on demand and available capacity.

## CHAPTER 15

**Advertising.** Paid communications directed at a mass audience.

**Advertising agency.** A third-party organization to which many firms outsource the development and execution of their advertising.

**Advertising budget.** The dollar amount to be spent on advertising. Approaches to budget setting are:
Objective and task. A *bottom-up* approach focusing on advertising objectives and the tasks to be accomplished.
Percentage of sales. A rule-of-thumb approach that sets the budget as a percentage of sales: current sales, anticipated next-year sales, or some combination.
Competitive parity. An approach that bases the budget on competitors' spending.

**Advertising effectiveness measures.** Used to test advertising effectiveness. Options include:
Recognition. Advertising that respondents recognize.
Aided recall. Advertising that respondents remember with prompting.
Unaided recall. Advertising that respondents remember without prompting.

**Advertising objectives.** What the firm is trying to achieve with its advertising:
Output objectives. What the firm ultimately wants to achieve, like sales, repeat purchase, market share, and brand loyalty.
Intermediate objectives relate to the hierarchy-of-effects models and include awareness, knowledge, liking or preference, trial, and emotional commitment (to a brand).

**Advertising response function (ARF).** Relates advertising spending to an objective like sales.

**Advertising strategy.** Specifies how the firm will spend resources to achieve advertising objectives and includes decisions about target audience, advertising objectives, messaging, execution, media selections and timing, advertising budget, and program evaluation.

**Blog.** An Internet vehicle for individuals to offer opinions and receive feedback from others.

**Communication process.** The activities involved in sending and receiving information.

**Cost per 1000 (CPM).** A measure of the advertising cost. CPM = Absolute Cost of Advertising Space × 1000/Circulation.

**Creative brief.** A *contract* between the firm and its advertising agency that provides parameters and information for translating the firm's market strategy into an advertising message.

**Direct marketing (DM).** Paid and sponsored communications directed at individuals.

**Executional style.** The way the firm turns the core message into effective advertising:
Rational-style advertising appeals to people's sense of logic.
Emotional-style advertising appeals to the emotions.

**Frequency.** The average number of times a targeted individual is exposed to the advertising.

**Gross rating points (GRPs)** Combines reach and frequency. GRP = Reach x Frequency.

**Hierarchy-of-effects models.** Describes how advertising works for different types of products:
High-involvement products. The purchase involves financial and/or psychosocial risks.
Low-involvement products. The purchase involves little risk.

**Integrated marketing communications.** The integration of the firm's various communications efforts, using various tools, for various communications targets.

**Internet communications.** Information available electronically on websites, blogs, and other methods.

**Media class.** A group of closely related media — newspapers, TV, and billboards are each media classes.

**Media objectives.** What the firm wants to accomplish with its media strategy:

 **Reach.** The number of targeted individuals exposed to the advertising message at least once.

 **Duplicated reach.** The portion of the target audience exposed to the advertising message from multiple media sources.

 **Unduplicated reach.** The portion of the target audience exposed to the advertising message from a single source.

**Media schedule.** The placement and timing of advertisements for the advertising program.

**Media vehicle.** A specific exemplar of a media class — *The New York Times* and *60 Minutes* are each media vehicles.

**Miscommunication.** Misperception and/or misunderstanding by a *receiver* of a message the *sender* intended to send. Problems may occur in:

 **Encoding.** Translating and interpreting the intended message into the actual sent message.

 **Distortion.** Receiving a different message from the message that was sent.

 **Decoding.** Misperceiving and/or misunderstanding the received message because of selective attention, distortion, and/or retention.

**Non-personal communication.** Communications without interpersonal contact between sender and receiver.

**Packaging communication.** Communication delivered by the package containing the product.

**Paid search.** Online advertisers pay to appear next to and be associated with search results based on keywords. For example, an electronics retailer might pay to appear next to searches for HDTVs.

**Personal communication.** Face-to-face communications with targeted individuals or groups.

**Publicity.** Communication for which the firm does not pay, typically via the press.

**Public relations (PR).** Communication that embraces publicity but is broader — includes other ways of managing the firm's image to gain favorable responses.

**Pull.** A communications approach that focuses on indirect customers.

**Push.** A communications approach that focuses on direct customers.

**Quasi-personal communication (QPC).** Interaction and feedback without human involvement, usually via artificial intelligence software.

**Sales promotion (SP).** Activities providing extra customer value, often for immediate sales. Includes:

 **Trade shows.** Products displayed to large numbers of customers at one time.

 **Product placement.** Products placed in movies and TV shows.

**Search Engine Optimization.** Optimizing the firm's website and choosing significant key words to attract search engines, with the goal of appearing high in the rankings for search results.

**Target audience.** Who the firm is trying to reach with its advertising.

**Telemarketing.** Communication by telephone, usually viewed as a subset of personal communication.

**Timing pattern.** When the advertising will appear. The major options are:

 **Continuous.** A regular periodic advertising pattern.

 **Flighting.** Repeated high advertising levels followed by low (or no) advertising.

 **Pulsing.** Continuous and flighting advertising combined, within a single media vehicle or class or across multiple media vehicles and classes.

**Tracking study.** A way of evaluating an advertising program by taking measurements at different times.

**Word-of-mouth (WOM) communication.** Communication between and among current and potential customers.

## CHAPTER 16

**80:20 rule.** 80 percent of the firm's revenues come from 20 percent of its customers.

**20:80 rule.** 20 percent of the firm's revenues come from 80 percent of its customers.

**Calendarize.** Partitioning sales objectives by time period like quarter, month, or week.

**Control unit.** An element of the sales force for monitoring and controlling sales activities and performance, like a sales region, sales district, or sales territory.

**Customer tiers.** A term for classifying customers in terms of importance to the firm. For example:
　　**Tier I (platinum).** The firm's most important current and potential customers.
　　**Tier II (gold).** Important current and potential customers but less so than Tier 1.
　　**Tier III (bronze).** Important current and potential customers but less so than Tiers 1 and 2.

**Face time.** The time a salesperson spends face-to-face with customers.

**Global account manager (GAM).** A person responsible for the firm's most important global customers.

**Pipeline analysis.** A method for tracking the firm's performance at different selling process stages.

**Reward system.** The way to compensate salespeople for their efforts and performance. Includes elements like financial compensation, recognition, and promotions and work assignments.

**Sales approach.** The essential message that the salesperson delivers to customers.

**Sales force management tasks.** Six related jobs that sales managers must complete to be effective.

**Sales objectives.** The firm's desired results — typically stated in terms of sales revenues, sales units, or profit contribution.

**Sales potential.** The maximum sales that the firm could achieve in a future time period.

**Salesperson workload.** The effort a salesperson must expend to complete assigned activities; a key variable for designing sales territories.

**Sales quotas.** Sales objectives stated in terms of specific performance requirements.

**Sales response function.** The relationship between selling effort and sales results.

**Sales territory.** A set of customers or geographic area assigned to an individual salesperson.

**Selling effort.** The demands of the sales job. Methods to estimate required selling effort include:
　　**Single-factor model.** Uses a simple classification of customer importance.
　　**Portfolio model.** A more complex approach for estimating required selling effort.

**Span of control.** The ratio of subordinates to supervisors. For example, a sales manager supervising 10 salespeople would be a span of 10-to-1.

**Strategic account manager (SAM).** A person responsible for the firm's most important customers.

**Strategic (or key) accounts.** Customers that provide the highest levels of current and/or potential sales and profits.

## CHAPTER 17

**Antitrust.** U.S. laws that prohibit actions to reduce competition.

**Direct marketing (DM).** Paid and sponsored communications directed at individuals. Customers buying products receive them by direct delivery from remote locations, typically via third-party freight companies.

**Disintermediation.** The removal of a layer in a distribution system.

**Distribution approaches:**
　　**Exclusive.** A distribution strategy that focuses on a few well-chosen outlets.
　　**Intensive.** A distribution strategy that maximizes the number of outlets.
　　**Selective.** A sort of compromise between intensive and exclusive distribution.

**Distribution channel or Distribution.** Encompasses the entities, interrelationships, and functions they perform, so that the supplier's products reach customers.

**Distribution channel breadth.** The number of members at a particular level in the channel system.

**Distribution conflict:**
　　**Operational.** Focuses on day-to-day issues like late shipments, invoicing errors, unfulfilled salesperson promises, unacceptable product quality, supplier attempts to load channels, and price and margin disputes.
　　**Strategic.** May change the relationships among distribution channel members.

**Distribution exclusivity:**
　　**Geographic.** The supplier gives the distributor a monopoly on selling products in its territory.
　　**Product.** The supplier gives the distributor exclusivity to sell a group of products.
　　**Supplier.** The intermediary agrees to distribute only the supplier's products.

**Distribution functions.** The activities that the distribution channel must perform. Concerned with the physical product, information, and/or ownership.

**Distribution, method:**
    **Direct.** The supplier supplies products directly to consumers and end users.
    **Indirect.** Intermediaries like distributors, wholesalers, and retailers play a major role in transferring products to consumers and end users.

**Distribution, view of:**
    **Broad view.** Encompasses changes in *state, physical location,* and *time.*
    **Narrow view.** Encompasses mainly changes in *physical location* and *time.*

**Downstream.** The firm's customers and its customers' customers, etc.

**Franchising.** A distribution strategy in which the franchisor develops a business model. Franchisees agree to implement the franchisor's model and typically pay an initiation fee and ongoing fees.

**Full-line forcing.** See tying agreements.

**Just-in-time (JIT).** An approach to reducing inventory by making raw materials and parts deliveries shortly before use in the production line.

**Logistics.** The process of moving a product from point A to point B:
    **Outbound.** Getting the product from the supplier to the customer.
    **Inbound (reverse).** Getting the product from the customer back to the producer.

**Partnership model.** An approach to distribution channel members that involves building cooperation and trust.

**Power.** The ability of one channel member to get another to do what it wants it to do.

**Reintermediation.** The re-introduction of a layer in a distribution system.

**Retail price maintenance (RPM).** A distribution practice where suppliers set the prices at which retailers can sell their products. RPM is now illegal in the U.S. and many other countries.

**Slotting fees.** Payments that suppliers make to retailers for providing shelf space for their products.

**Systems integrators.** Firms that install, service, and integrate software from many vendors.

**Supply chain.** A coordinated system of organizations, people, activities, information, and resources that move a product or service, physically or virtually, from supplier to customer.

**Telemarketing.** Communication by telephone, usually viewed as a subset of personal communication:
    **Inbound.** Initiated by the customer.
    **Outbound.** Initiated by the firm.

**Tying agreements.** Strong suppliers *force* resellers to sell their entire product line. This practice is illegal in the U.S. if it reduces competition.

**Upstream.** The firm's suppliers and its suppliers' suppliers, etc.

**Value-added resellers (VARs).** Firms that build additional software modules onto other firms' platforms and modify hardware for niche markets.

# CHAPTER 18

**Communications tipping point.** The level above which communications generate customer resentment.

**Core product.** The central element in the firm's offer of a physical product, like an automobile.

**Core service.** The central element in the firm's service offer, like overnight package delivery.

**Customer relationship management (CRM).** The ongoing process of identifying and creating new value with individual customers and sharing these benefits over a lifetime of association with them.

**Customer service.** Any act, performance, or information that enhances the firm's core product or service.

**Customer service strategy.** An approach to delivering customer service based on understanding customers' needs for customer service.

**Data-mining.** A quantitative approach to gain insight into customers' purchasing behavior as the basis for making specialized offers.

**Expectations disconfirmation.** A key feature of the SERVQUAL model. Customer satisfaction is the *difference* between expected quality and perceived quality.

**Features of Services:**
    **Divisibility.** A feature of services emphasizing that they often comprise a sequence of activities.

**Inseparability.** A feature of services emphasizing that production and consumption occur simultaneously.

**Intangibility.** A feature of services emphasizing that they have no physical presence. They cannot be touched, driven, flown, worn, kicked, batted, squashed, or sat upon.

**Perishability.** A feature of services relating to *inseparability*. Services cannot be inventoried.

**Variability.** A feature of services emphasizing a lack of consistency because of human involvement in service delivery.

**Flower of customer service.** Eight elements of customer service.

**Franchising.** A distribution strategy in which the franchisor develops a business model. Franchisees agree to implement the franchisor's model and typically pay an initiation fee and ongoing fees.

**Loyalty programs.** Methods that firms use to enhance customer retention.

**Moment of truth.** An interaction between a service customer and service personnel.

**Outsourcing.** When the firm engages a supplier to conduct an activity previously done inhouse.

**Product.** Sometimes *product* refers to the core offer, both *physical products* and *services*. We use this shorthand in much of the book. But tangible physical products can be touched, worn, kicked, or sat upon; a service cannot.

**Service.** Any act or performance that one party can offer another that is essentially intangible and does not result in the ownership of anything. Anything that cannot be dropped on your foot.

**Service equipment.** Physical products needed to perform the service.

**Service facilities.** Where the firm produces the service. These facilities can be:
    **Offstage.** Out of the customers' sight.
    **Onstage.** Where customers experience deeds, performances, or efforts.

**Service guarantee.** A promise about the service experience that includes elements of value if the firm does not keep its promise.

**Service personnel.** People who provide the service.

**Service quality.** The extent to which the firm's service performance exceeds customers' expectations.

**SERVQUAL.** A popular model and measurement device for service quality based on several *gaps*.

**Six sigma.** A data-driven methodology for eliminating defects in any process.

## CHAPTER 19

**Balanced scorecard.** A performance measurement system that balances input, intermediary, and output variables.

**Benchmarking.** The practice of securing best practices from outside the firm at other organizations.

**Best practice transfer.** An approach to identifying and transmitting superior processes across the firm.

**Control, types of:**
    **Firm functioning.** Asks the question, "Is the firm functioning well?" Three sub-areas are:
        **Implementation.** Did the firm implement its planned actions?
        **Strategy.** Is the firm's market strategy well conceived and on target?
        **Managerial control.** Are the firm's managerial processes the best they can be?
    **Post-action.** The firm waits until a pre-set time, then compares actual results against standards.
    **Steering.** A dynamic, continuous, and anticipatory system. The firm sets control limits for performance standards and compares results against standards on an ongoing basis.

**External orientation.** A firm with this orientation focuses on customers, competitors, complementers, and factors in the external environment that could affect its future health.

**Feedback cycle.** The time period between the firm's actions and its measured results.

**Human resource management (HRM).** Processes for managing people including recruiting, selecting, training and development, work processes, talent management and career paths, and recognition and reward.

**Iceberg principle.** An analogy to the iceberg whereby good aggregate performance in a unit or subunit can *hide* poor performance elsewhere in the same unit.

**Indicators, types of:**
> **Leading.** Help managers assess if they are on track to achieve planned results.
> **Lagging.** Measure what has already occurred.

**Internal architecture.** The firm's organizational structure, systems and processes, and HRM practices.

**Internal orientation.** A firm with this orientation looks inward. It focuses on internal functions like finance, operations, sales, and technology (R&D), rather than external factors.

**Market levers.** The actions the firm takes to achieve its performance standards.

**Measures, types of:**
> **Input.** Focus on actions taken by the firm — leading indicators.
> **Intermediate.** Focus on actions that customers take — leading indicators.
> **Output.** Focus on performance variables like sales and profits — lagging indicators.
> **Hard.** Objectively measured like sales volume, profit, and market performance.
> **Soft.** Rating scale measures like customer satisfaction or attitudes.

**Organization structures, types of:**
> **Business process.** An outgrowth of re-engineering movement, the firm organizes around business processes.
> **Category management.** An evolutionary development of a product/brand management structure in which the firm manages multiple brands in a complementary manner.
> **Combined product/brand management/market segment.** Combines a product/brand focus with a market segment focus.
> **Customer management.** An organization focused specifically on customers.
> **Functional marketing.** The firm places activities like marketing research, distribution, advertising and promotion, marketing administration, and new product development in a marketing department. Other major functional areas are likewise in separate departments.
> **Global.** May be country-based if the market segments are heterogeneous, and national or regional differences are critical; or product-management based if customer needs are homogeneous.
> **Inclusion.** The firm groups many activities together under marketing.
> **Market segment.** Managers are responsible for individual market segments.
> **Traditional product/brand management.** Product and brand managers develop market plans for their products and brands. They are responsible for volume, share, and/or profit — they compete for resources like advertising dollars and sales force time.

**Re-engineering.** Examines fundamental assumptions about the way the firm conducts its activities. Seeks alternative approaches for redesigning and improving the firm's processes.

**Standards.** The firm's planned results; criteria against which the firm measures its performance.

**Systems, types of:**
> **Hard.** Based on information technology.
> **Soft.** Based on employees.

**Values, types of.** A common set of beliefs that guide the behavior of the firm's employees. Values can be:
> **Hard.** Like profitability and market share.
> **Soft.** Like integrity, respect for others, trust, and customer pre-eminence.

# IMAGE CREDITS

# INDEX

## SUBJECT INDEX

*Locators beginning with "G" indicate
terms defined in the glossary.*